交通能源融合发展战略

中国陆路交通能源融合的形态、模式与解决方案

Scenarios, Patterns and Solutions of Ground Transportation and Energy Convergence in China

贾利民 马 静 吉 莉 程 鹏 师瑞峰 著

科 学 出 版 社

北 京

内 容 简 介

本书在全面评估我国陆路交通系统的资产能源化潜力的基础上，展开深入挖掘与延伸。结合我国可再生能源出力的地域分布特性、骨干电网的布局特性及交通网络的建设特性，根据基础支撑技术的发展规律，研究了陆路交通与可再生能源融合发展的形态与模式，提出了能源交通融合网建设创新模式集，并为未来15年我国交通与可再生能源的融合创新发展进程指出了明确的发展方向和演进步骤；希望有助于更深刻地理解交通对能源的需求以及交通能源利用模式的转型，并期望为社会经济的可持续发展找到切实可行的路径。

本书可作为能源、交通领域的高等院校、科研机构的专家学者、教师、研究生，政府部门的研究、管理和决策人员，以及相关企事业单位人员掌握能源与交通融合发展方向的参考资料。

图书在版编目（CIP）数据

中国陆路交通能源融合的形态、模式与解决方案=Scenarios, Patterns and Solutions of Ground Transportation and Energy Convergence in China / 贾利民等著. —北京：科学出版社，2020.11

（交通能源融合发展战略）

ISBN 978-7-03-057457-2

Ⅰ. ①交… Ⅱ. ①贾… Ⅲ. ①陆路运输－节能－研究报告－中国 Ⅳ. ①F542 ②TK01

中国版本图书馆CIP数据核字（2020）第184576号

责任编辑：范运年 霍明亮 / 责任校对：王萌萌

责任印制：吴兆东 / 封面设计：蓝正设计

科学出版社 出版

北京东黄城根北街16号

邮政编码：100717

http://www.sciencep.com

北京中科印刷有限公司 印刷

科学出版社发行 各地新华书店经销

*

2020年11月第 一 版 开本：720×1000 1/16

2021年11月第二次印刷 印张：27 1/4

字数：549 000

定价：368.00元

（如有印装质量问题，我社负责调换）

【研 究 团 队】

【顾　　问】

杨勇平　教授　校长
华北电力大学
严新平　教授　中国工程院院士
武汉理工大学
綦树立　党组成员　副主任
海南省发展和改革委员会
黎　津　处长
国家发展和改革委员会基础司能源处
檀勤良　教授　副校长
华北电力大学

【研究负责人】

贾利民　教授　院长　工学博士
华北电力大学国家能源交通融合发展研究院
北京交通大学轨道交通控制与安全国家重点实验室
马　静　教授　执行院长　工学博士
华北电力大学国家能源交通融合发展研究院

【主要研究成员】

师瑞峰　副教授　工学博士
华北电力大学控制与计算机工程学院
吉　莉　副研究员　工学博士
华北电力大学国家能源交通融合发展研究院
程　鹏　助理研究员　工学博士
华北电力大学国家能源交通融合发展研究院
张　充　副院长　工学博士
华北电力大学科学技术研究院
金成日　总经理　工学硕士
北京能高自动化技术股份有限公司

前　言

在习近平新时代中国特色社会主义思想指引下，党中央国务院立足国情、着眼全局、面向未来，于 2019 年 9 月提出了《交通强国建设纲要》（以下简称“纲要”），要提高交通领域的智能化、绿色化和共享化；构筑多层级、一体化的能源交通融合的综合交通枢纽体系；优化交通能源结构，推进可再生能源、清洁能源应用；促进公路货运节能减排，推动城市公共交通工具和城市物流配送车辆全部实现电动化、可再生能源化和清洁化。在这一目标的指引下，交通与可再生能源的一体化发展成为不可逆转的时代潮流，是关系到国家未来发展的战略布局，构建绿色、弹性、自洽和可持续发展的交通能源一体化系统已成为新时代建设美丽中国的必然路径！

作为两大战略性、全局性和基础性行业，交通与能源是经济社会发展的基础保障，直接决定经济发展质量、效率和可持续性；新时代背景下，为了有效地推进“四个革命、一个合作”能源安全新战略与交通强国战略，构建清洁低碳、安全高效的现代化交通能源体系，交通和能源行业将担当重大的历史使命，且其融合发展也对实现“两个一百年”奋斗目标和中华民族的伟大复兴具有重要意义。

面对资源紧缺、气候变化、环境污染带来的严峻挑战，推动能源与交通供给革命，促进产业转型与升级是应对各项挑战的根本途径。通过交通和能源行业的统一战略部署，推动能源消费革命，加强国际合作，对保障能源安全、维护经济稳定发展具有重要意义。加快能源与交通领域的技术革命和体制革命，优化能源与交通运营管理体系，实现能源与交通领域的追赶和创新，可以为我国经济发展注入全新的驱动力。

为探索交通能源融合发展之路，为我国交通能源绿色化发展提供根本依据、指明发展方向、规划发展路径，本书试图全景式地回答如下问题：

(1) 我国陆路交通系统能源化的自然禀赋布局与利用潜力。

(2) 我国陆路交通可再生能源利用的模式、形态与路径。

(3) 我国陆路交通网络与电力能源网的互动方式与模式。

(4) 我国陆路交通系统全局弹性导向的能源自洽效率与效能。

本书深入全面地分析与评估了我国交通系统通过深入开发自身潜力，最大限度地实现用能自洽的潜力与可行性；而后，针对道路交通和轨道交通两种规模最大、最典型的陆地交通方式，在明确交通运载体、交通基础设施和交通服务设施的能源化潜力基础上，结合我国可再生能源出力的地域分布特性、骨干电网的布局特性及交通网络自身特性，根据基础支撑技术的发展规律，提出了交通能源融合网建设创新模式集；并对采用新模式的交通可再生能源融合系统给出了目前和未来15年的用电自洽率、用能自洽率、可再生能源渗透率以及交通运输全过程的碳减排量等关键参数进行了详细的测算，试图为规划未来15年交通与可再生能源的融合创新发展进程指出明确方向和演进路径；着重探讨如何利用可再生能源，尤其是太阳能，实现陆路交通与可再生能源融合发展，从而探索构建绿色、弹性、自洽和可持续的交通能源系统的未来道路。持续的研究将覆盖水路交通、航空运输和其他各类交通方式。

作为国内外首次系统分析研究交通能源融合发展的首批研究成果，本书由统一但各有侧重的两卷组成，第一卷是对我国陆路交通系统资产能源化潜力的全面评估；第二卷通过对陆路交通系统的能源需求特性、电网系统的布局特点、可再生能源的出力特性进行时间和空间的融合研究，提出了陆路交通与可再生能源融合发展的形态、模式与解决方案集。

希望本书能帮助读者更深刻地理解能源转型、交通对能源的需求以及能源利用模式的转型，为绿色交通能源系统的构建提供具有丰富场景的交通能源系统解决方案参考集，为交通系统绿色可持续发展并支撑经济社会可持续发展找到切实可行、符合国情并具有普适意义的路径提供有益的帮助。本书数据来源主要是国家权威机构的统计数据、网络公开的权威数据以及国内外知名机构发表的学术论文等。本书相关研究得到了国家发展和改革委员会和中国工程院咨询项目支持。

由于本书涉及面广，交通能源融合发展研究尚处于发展初期，可以借鉴的系统性研究稀少，再加上研究者水平有限，不足之处在所难免，恳请广大读者斧正。

贾利民

2020年8月于北京

Preface

Guided by Xi Jinping's socialism with Chinese characteristics in new era and based on the national context, the overall landscape, and the Chinese Dream of national rejuvenation, the Outline on Building China's Strength in Transportation (hereinafter referred to as the Outline) was proposed by the Communist Party of China Central Committee and the state Council in September 2019. The Outline indicates that it is necessary to deeply improve the intelligence, green and cooperation of the transportation sector; build an architecture of comprehensive transportation hub with multi-level and integrated development of energy and transportation sectors; optimize the structure of transportation energy system by permeating more renewable energy and clean energy; boost the energy conservation and emission reduction of road freight; and promote the whole symphysis with electrification, renewable energy and clean energy of urban electric vehicles and urban logistics distribution vehicles. Therefore, it is clearly that the integrated development of transportation and renewable energy is an anti-reversion tide according to this blueprint, and is a strategic reform which related to the future development of China. Constructing a green, resilient, self-contained and sustainable integrated system of transportation and energy has been an inevitable process for building a Beautiful China in the new era.

Transportation and energy, as two strategic, comprehensive and fundamental sectors, are the basic guarantee of socio-economic development and determine the quality, efficiency and sustainability of economic development. In the context of the new era, the transportation and energy sectors are undertaking the historical mission for promoting "the four-evolution and one-cooperation" energy development new strategy and the Outline on Building China's Strength in Transportation strategy and further constructing modern energy system and transportation system featuring clean, low-carbon, safe and efficiency characteristics. The integrated development in these two sectors is of great importance in realizing the two centenary goals and the great rejuvenation of the Chinese nation.

Promoting the supply-side revolution in both energy and transportation fields and enhancing industrial transformation and upgradation have been already become the essential approach to solve severe challenges such as resource shortage, climate change and environmental pollution. The unified strategic deployment of transportation and energy sectors could not only promote the energy consumption revolution and strengthen the international cooperation, but also play a significant role in ensuring energy security and maintaining stable economic development. Accelerating the technological and structural reform, optimizing the operating management system and achieving progress and innovation in the field of energy and transportation can inject a new driving force into national economic development.

In order to explore integrated development path of transportation and energy, and further provide the fundamental basis, point out the development direction and lay out the development path for the green development of these two sectors, this book strives to answer the following questions comprehensively:

(1) The natural endowment distribution and utilization potential of the energization in Chinese ground transportation system;

(2) The utilization patterns, scenarios and paths of renewable energy in Chinese ground transportation system;

(3) The interaction modes and patterns of the national ground transportation network and power energy grid;

(4) The energy self-containment rate and efficiency of the resilience orientation in Chinese ground transportation system.

This book analyzes and assesses the feasibility and possibility of realizing the energy consumption self-containment maximally in Chinese ground transportation system through the deep-going development of its endowment. Furthermore, focusing on land and rail transport, which are the two largest and most typical ground transportation modes, clarifying the energization potential in-depth on transport carriers, transport infrastructure and transport service facilities, and considering the regional distribution characteristics of China's renewable energy output, distribution characteristics of backbone grid and construction characteristics of transport network, this book puts forward a set of innovation patterns for constructing the trans-energy network, and points out development directions and evolution paths clearly for innovated integration process in the next 15 years by using new patterns and calculating key parameters, including electricity consumption self-containment rate, energy consumption self-containment rate, renewable energy permeability and carbon emission reduction in a whole lifecycle of transportation in details at present and in the next 15 years; this book focuses on the integrated development of ground transportation and renewable energy through the utilization of renewable energy (mainly about photovoltaic resources), thus constructs the novel trans-energy system featuring green, resilient, self-contained and sustainable characteristics. Continuous research will cover other types of transport modes, containing water and air transport.

As the first batch of systematic analysis and research on transportation and energy integration development at home and abroad, this book is composed of two volumes which are unified but maintained different emphases. The first volume is a comprehensive assessment of energization potential of ground transportation infrastructure assets in China; the second volume puts forward the scenarios, patterns and solutions of the integrated development on ground transportation and renewable energy through the temporal-spatial research on energy demand characteristics of ground transportation system, distribution characteristics of power grid system and the output characteristics of renewable energy.

We sincerely hope that this book can contribute to understanding the energy transition, the energy demand on transportation sector and the energy utilization transition, thus provide references of the trans-energy system solution with various scenarios for constructing the green trans-energy system and be beneficial for figuring out practical, suitable and meaningful patterns by which the green and sustainable development of transportation system can support the socio-economic sustainable development. The data of this book are mainly from state authorities, authoritative data published on the Internet and academic papers published by well-known institutions at home and abroad. The studies concerned with this book were also supported by consulting projects from The National Development and Reform Commission of China and Chinese Academy of Engineering.

The research on the integrated development of transportation and energy is still in the early stage, there are few systematic studies that can be used for reference. Coupled with extensive research range, although this book has been revised in several times, careless omissions and errors are still inevitable. We earnestly request the experts' criticisms and pointing out our mistakes.

Jia Limin

Beijing, 2020.8.20

摘　要

交通，纵横而交错，往来而通达，承载着人类历史的繁衍轨迹；能源，自然之造粹，动力之根本，维系着人类的生存与发展。交通与能源是人类各文明共同关注的两大永恒主题！

回顾历史，能源作为交通的基础使能领域，交通作为能源的最大负荷领域，能源与交通的融合发展一直是保障人类社会合理、有效和可持续演进的重要客观条件。能源与交通的每一次协同创新，都极大地提高了社会生产率，促进了科技进步，进而塑造了不同时期的人类文明特征。生物质能源与畜力交通的融合成就了农业文明，蒸汽机与第一代化石能源-煤炭的融合拉开了工业文明的序幕，机车及铁路与第一代二次能源-电力的融合促成了第二次工业革命，大力推动了工业文明的发展。与此同时，借由历次工业革命，在能源与交通相辅相成、互相促进和融合发展的作用下，世界各国的经济地位和战略格局在不断发生着变化与革新。

然而，自工业革命以来，交通对于能源的大量消耗以及能源使用中所带来的负面效应，使二者产生了不可调和的矛盾，尤其是自从电气化交通的普及以来，城市、交通、能源、环境之间的矛盾日渐凸显。遏制气候危机，拯救地球家园是人类面临的最复杂挑战之一。随着《巴黎协定》的签订，世界各国均提出温室气体减排目标，都把发展可再生能源和低碳交通作为竞相争占的新的战略制高点，成为争取可持续发展主动权的关键因素。

滚滚的历史车轮正驱动着人类文明迈向新的阶段，即遵循人、自然、社会和谐发展这一客观规律的生态文明。党的十八大、十九大明确将习近平同志生态文明理念和建设思想纳入了中国特色社会主义“五位一体”的总体布局和“四个全面”的战略布局。在绿色、低碳、清洁、可持续等生态文明共同目标的引领下，交通能源融合发展是能源系统和交通系统转变发展模式并协同共进的新阶段；是尊重自然、顺应自然和保护自然的有力举措；是建设美丽中国、实现中华民族伟大复兴“中国梦”及实现习近平总书记“一带一路”倡议的创新实践；是绿色发展支撑构建人类命运共同体的必然路径。在中国特色社会主义发展新时代下，交通能源融合发展必将贯穿和影响我国的政治、经济、社会与文化建设的全过程，成为建设中国特色社会主义并惠及全人类生态文明的重要物质基础！

从发展路径角度来看，我国现阶段及未来 15 年将面临资源紧缺、气候变化、环境污染带来的严峻挑战，因此粗排放非协同增长的方式将难以为继。面向绿色发展的战略规划和产业转型升级已成为我国应对这些挑战的主要政策取向和根本途径。应运而生的能源转型与供给侧改革，以及交通绿色化与智能化发展，需要协同能源与交通进行顶层规划。在全世界倡导节能减排，国家大力推行可持续发展，建设“安全、绿色、便捷、高效、经济”交通的背景下，重新审视新时代交通和能源系统的内涵和外延，厘清交通与能源的相互关系与协同演进路径，并从中汲取能源交通融合促进社会经济高质量发展的有效政治措施和政策取向极为必要和迫切。

从经济建设的角度来看，我国经济发展步入新常态，高质量发展成为新时代经济建设与社会发展的主旋律。能源与交通作为经济发展和社会运行的主要基础保障，直接决定经济发展的模式、形态与质量。能源交通融合将形成具有产业生成、聚集、引领和带动作用的新技术、新业态、新产业和新模式；创造一批新的经济增长点，形成相关产业群新的共生、互动、协同与演进的新范式；引领和带动新时代经济的低碳化、绿色化、协同化和可持续高质量发展；全面提升我国经济的总体安全水平和经济运行的弹性；是能源和交通系统变革保障国民经济高质量发展和高效运行的重大措施和有效途径。

从社会与文化建设的角度来看，能源与交通协同创新发展，必将在有力推进包括生产、生活在内的人类活动保障体系的低碳、智能、高效、便捷发展的同时，促进绿色发展和生态文明理念的广泛传播，对形成和强化绿色、低碳和可持续社会共识及其对人和社会行为的良性影响具有重大的意义。交通能源融合发展而成的能源交通融合网将在网络形态、业务功能、资源利用、共性支撑技术等方面产生前所未有的新需求，能极大地促进具有生态文明理念的各层次人才的培养和使用，造就大批适应高质量发展需求的社会成员，并通过他们影响和提升整个社会的生态文明建设水平。

近年来，能源领域在“四个革命、一个合作”能源战略的指引下，加快建设科技创新体系，树立了“创新、协调、绿色、开放、共享”的能源发展理念，从较为粗放、低效、污染、欠安全的能源体系，转变为精细、高效、洁净、多元、安全的现代化能源体系。我国可再生能源领域的科技与产业化水平有了长足的进步和显著的提高。然而，一方面我国能源电力系统的布局与负荷布局严重不匹配，另一方面交通系统是具有空间布局特征的最大负荷，且其自然禀赋充足。因此如何因地制宜地为交通可再生能源资源利用与交通负荷的全面匹配建立适用的机制和成套的解决方案关乎交通系统的能源转型，更关乎人类赖以生存的碧水蓝天。

交通运输是我国国民经济的命脉。随着我国人口的不断增加、经济的持续发展，道路交通和轨道交通的客运和货运运输需求量不断提升，交通运输对社会经济发展的支撑和保障作用更加凸显。然而，随着交通运输需求的快速增长，我国交通运输业的能源消耗总量和其占全社会总量的比重均呈现逐年递增的趋势，且增速也在逐年迅速上升。据统计，交通运输业已成为我国第三大能源消耗行业，仅次于工业和生活消费业。

因此，探讨可再生能源与交通融合发展的新形态、新模式与关键技术，不仅可以促进可再生能源产业的健康、有序发展，同时对于提高交通运输的能源效率、优化交通运输的能源结构、推动交通运输的转型发展也大有裨益。可再生能源形态多样，主要包括太阳能、风能、生物质能、海洋能、地热能等，鉴于太阳能自然禀赋独特的空间分布特征和可利用途径的灵活性，本报告所指的可再生能源以太阳能为主。

交通系统由于其完成位移使命的方式不同，主要包括陆路交通、空中交通和水路交通等方式。其中，陆路交通是各种交通运输方式中规模最大、空间布局最广、社会经济活动渗透性最强、可独立完成运输服务全过程、涉及产业门类最多、能源消耗最多、资产能源化潜力最大的交通运输方式。对中国这样的大陆型国家，其在综合交通运输体系中的作用尤为重要。本报告主要涉及陆路交通运输方式。陆路交通系统包括以公路为主的道路交通和以铁路为主的轨道交通。

本报告所涉及的基础技术包括光伏、储能及能源互联网等。在光伏技术方面，我国在晶体硅太阳电池产业化技术方面已处于世界先进水平，掌握了从多晶硅提纯技术、单晶/多晶生长技术到高效电池和组件制备技术的全产业链核心技术，我国太阳电池和组件产量占据全球的70%以上，光伏产品具有成本和质量优势，光伏产业已成为我国具有国际竞争力的优势产业之一。但是，我国在薄膜太阳电池规模化生产和实验室效率方面与国际差距较大，薄膜电池制备的核心设备部分依赖国外进口，国内缺乏具备大规模生产能力和成本优势的薄膜电池企业，产、学、研结合不够紧密，相关科研成果没能够有效转化为产业化技术。因此，亟须深入研究和突破光伏相关基础理论、关键技术、高端装备等方面存在的一系列重大科技问题。在储能技术方面，我国已开始形成规模化产业格局，产品开始在世界范围内形成影响，并逐渐参与国际标准制定。但是，储能电池在效率、成本、寿命与安全性等方面存在瓶颈技术问题，亟须解决储能相关材料的设计与高效制备问题；储能技术应用还存在投资成本过高、能量密度低、系统可靠性差、能量损耗等问题，亟须储能系统状态评估、残值评估、峰值功率评估和能量配置管理等相关理论和技术突破。在能源互联网技术方面，我国充分地将能源科技与互联网思维和先进信息通信技术相融合，横向实现多种能源形式的互补协同和高效运行，纵向实现源-网-荷-储整个能源链条各个环节的互动，并通过对等共享的新型市场机制与商业模式营造全新的能源生态。在对能源互联网领域的概念思考和学术探索方面，国内比欧美更加全面和深入。但是，受前期发展侧重点的影响，我国在配用电侧相关技术、市场模式与商业模式等领域仍处于跟跑阶段，在一些关键的材料、器件和装备方面与国外最高水平差距较大，甚至受制于人。此外，尽管国内开展了较多的工程示范应用，但在一些关键基础理论方面尚未完全突破，例如，综合多种能流形式的分析仿真与优化协同理论、含高比例电力电子装置的复杂电力系统安全与稳定理论等。预计到2035年，通过对以上三大技术方向的重点科技任务和重大技术问题的有效实施与部署，我国能源领域的自主创新能力将大幅提升，一批关键技术将取得重大突破，能源技术装备、关键部件及材料对外依存度将显著降低，我国将在储能基础科学问题、可再生型储能技术、储能全产业链升级、储能新技术的放大化、应用化、示范化与产业化、光伏电池新型结构、材料与规模化制备技术、能源互联网基础理论与关键技术、复杂互联电网运行与控制、多能流综合能源系统分析、规划与运行、信息-能量融合理论与技术、市场机制与商业模式设计等方面建成与国情相适应的完善的能源技术创新体系，将全面地支撑我国能源交通融合产业的布局与战略规划。

本卷由三个部分构成，第一部分为总启，主要概述了中国陆路交通系统资产能源化的潜力；第二部分为上篇，主要涉及公路交通与可再生能源融合发展的形态、模式与解决方案；第三部分为下篇，主要涉及铁路交通与可再生能源融合发展的形态、模式与解决方案。

总启　中国陆路交通系统资产能源化的潜力

为进一步地分析我国现阶段能源交通系统存在的内在矛盾与宏观趋势等诸因素的共同影响，为能源清洁化、交通电动化及二者融合发展提供依据，本报告在交通载运工具电动化、交通用能清洁化的新形势下，对我国现有交通基础设施所拥有的光资源发电潜力进行评估，旨在分析和预测我国交通系统通过发掘自身潜力、最大限度地实现用能自洽的可能性，为后续相关经济政策、产业政策的制定者，以及产业规划、科技布局的决策者提供决策依据；为相关企业与个体参与产业示范、应用示范、产业配套等提供商业预判的依据；同时，还可为相关学者提供学术与产业研究交流的主题与素材。

对于陆路交通系统中的公路系统，本报告分别按照高速公路、国道、省道三大体系对其可开发潜力进行评估；对于陆路交通系统中的铁路系统，本报告分别按照电气化和非电气化铁路两大分类进行潜力评估。

对于高速公路，按照保守测算、一般测算和乐观测算三种利用方式(不限于)对其可利用潜力进行评估。根据一般场景测算，我国高速公路的日可发电量最高可达 143GW·h，年发电量约为 25178GW·h。根据乐观场景测算，我国高速公路的日可发电量最高可达 1076GW·h，年发电量为 193674GW·h。

对于国道及省道道路系统，本报告分别按照保守测算、一般测算 1、一般测算 2 和乐观测算四种利用方式对其可开发潜力进行评估。根据保守场景测算，我国国道及省道道路系统，年发电量约为 31783GW·h。根据乐观场景测算，我国国道及省道道路系统，年发电量约为 531514GW·h。

对于电气化铁路，本报告分别按照保守测算、一般测算和乐观测算三种利用方式对其可开发潜力进行评估。根据一般场景测算，我国高速铁路系统的日可发电量最高达 792GW·h，年可发电量约为 170316.3GW·h。根据乐观场景测算，我国高速铁路系统的日可发电量最高达 871.2GW·h，年可发电量约为 274746.5GW·h。

对于非电气化铁路，本报告分别按照保守测算 1(双线)、保守测算 2(单线)、乐观测算 1(双线)、乐观测算 2(单线)四种利用方式对其可开发潜力进行评估。根据保守场景测算，我国非电气化铁路系统的日可发电量最高达 159.6GW·h，年可发电量约为 13587GW·h。根据乐观场景测算，我国非电气化铁路系统的日可发电量最高达 344.9GW·h，年可发电量约为 30385GW·h。

上篇　公路交通与可再生能源融合发展的形态、模式与解决方案

高速公路作为便捷、高效的交通基础设施，在工业化和城镇化的进程中发挥着重要作用，我国的高速公路交通基础设施建设规模持续扩大。2018 年底，我国累计建成并通车的高速公路里程达到 14.3 万 km，高速公路服务区约有 2850 对。与 2011 年的 8.5 万 km 的高速公路通车里程相比，增加了 68%，2011～2018 年间的平均增速为 6.7%。

本报告首先梳理了公路交通能源系统用能形态和模式，预测了未来公路交通系统中电能、化石能源、氢能燃料的应用前景，并展望了我国公路交通能源系统的高质量发展趋势：一是能源供给从高碳向低碳的减排趋势，通过能源结构的持续调整，持续提升公路交通能源系统中清洁能源渗透率，不仅可降低公路交通能源系统的直接/间接碳排放，也是实现能源可持续发展的关键举措；二是能源配用从低效到高效的增效趋势，通过能源配置的大范围优化，稳步拓展公路交通能源系统覆盖范围，不仅可提高能源利用效率，也是解决能源产销不平衡的重要方式。

其次，顺应公路交通能源系统的发展趋势，本报告以智能电网为纽带，通过太阳能光伏发电与公路交通系统的集成，秉承就近开发、就近消纳的建设理念，构建清洁化、高效化的新型公路交通能源系统。通过对新型公路交通系统的源属性、网属性、荷属性的进一步挖掘，本报告提出多属性、多层次、多角度的新型能源交通系统演化新模式。

在“源属性”层面，通过在交通基础设施、交通服务设施可利用空间资源加装分布式光伏发电，从而使公路交通能源系统从“荷”向“源-荷”共存状态转变，使公路交通能源系统具有发电能力。

在“网属性”层面，通过多端、多点公路交通能源系统的协作化运行，可实

现公路交通能源系统的多点互联、资源互补，就地满足了负荷需求，实现从“局部平衡”到“大范围优化配置”的转变，有效地提高了能源利用率。

在“荷属性”层面，通过对公路交通能源系统负荷侧的控制，实现负荷的可调节、可转移，使其具有可控功能，实现交通能源系统负荷从“随机”到“可控”的转变，有助于交通能源系统的电力平衡。

然后，在“源-网-荷”三重属性驱动下，本报告梳理了新型公路交通能源系统的差异化应用场景，并构建了交通专用能源系统、交通特有能源系统、交通适配能源系统和能源支撑交通系统 4 类典型解决方案，而后提出能源交通融合网作为新型公路交通能源系统的系统技术解决方案。

新型公路交通能源系统可充分地利用交通系统的自然禀赋，协同能源与交通的共同发展，并融合了交通、电网、环境等多元需求。在交通侧，通过新型交通能源系统的建设，促进了交通再电气化的发展进程，推进可再生能源、清洁能源在交通系统中应用；在电网侧，可再生能源公路交通能源系统可推动交通能源系统由单纯消费者向产销者的转型，缓解区域电网供电压力，并可作为新一代电力系统在交通领域中的基本应用；在环境侧，充分地利用交通系统自然禀赋，优化交通系统能源结构，降低交通系统用能碳排放。

本报告充分地考虑了各地区自然资源禀赋、用电负荷等差异，秉承就近开发、就近消纳的建设理念，充分地利用公路服务区、隧道隔离带以及公路沿线等易开发空间，优先在光资源Ⅰ类地区启动新型公路交通能源系统开发建设工作，而后再持续提升光资源Ⅰ类地区的开发强度，并依次启动光资源Ⅱ类、Ⅲ类地区的开发建设工作。

预计 2025 年，优先启动光资源Ⅰ类地区的开发建设。在保守开发场景下，全国高速公路分布式光伏年发电量为 400GW·h，全国高速公路用电自洽率为 2.1%，可再生能源电力渗透率为 17.8%，年减少碳排放 39.8 万 t；在基本开发场景下，全国高速公路分布式光伏年发电量为 780GW·h，全国高速公路用电自洽率为 4.2%，可再生能源电力渗透率为 19.2%，年减少碳排放 77.8 万 t；在积极开发场景下，全国高速公路分布式光伏年发电量为 1180GW·h，全国高速公路用电自洽率为 6.3%，可再生能源电力渗透率为 21.3%，年减少碳排放 117.6 万 t。

预计 2030 年，深入推进光资源Ⅰ类、Ⅱ类地区的开发建设。在保守开发场景下，全国高速公路分布式光伏年发电量为 7260GW·h，全国高速公路用电自洽率为 16.0%，可再生能源电力渗透率为 36.2%，年减少碳排放 723.8 万 t；在基本开发场景下，全国高速公路分布式光伏年发电量为 8990GW·h，全国高速公路用电自洽率为 19.9%，可再生能源电力渗透率为 39.1%，年减少碳排放 896.3 万 t；在积极开发场景下，全国高速公路分布式光伏年发电量为 10840GW·h，全国高速公路用电自洽率为 28.4%，可再生能源电力渗透率为 45.6%，年减少碳排放

1080.7 万 t。

预计 2035 年，逐步向光资源III类地区推进，持续提高光资源Ⅰ类、Ⅱ类地区的开发规模。在保守开发场景下，全国高速公路分布式光伏年发电量为 31380GW·h，全国高速公路用电自洽率为 26.7%，可再生能源电力渗透率为 48.7%，年减少碳排放 3128.6 万 t；在基本开发场景下，全国高速公路分布式光伏年发电量为 52460GW·h，全国高速公路用电自洽率为 44.6%，可再生能源电力渗透率为 61.2%，年减少碳排放 5230.0 万 t；在积极开发场景下，全国高速公路分布式光伏年发电量为 73300GW·h，全国高速公路用电自洽率为 62.4%，可再生能源电力渗透率为 73.7%，年减少碳排放 7308.2 万 t。

最后，以全国高速公路用电预期为导向，本报告按照从易开发到难开发、从易消纳到难消纳的方式，阐述了新型公路交通能源系统的演化发展路径，助推公路交通能源系统的节能减排与提质增效发展。

下篇　铁路交通与可再生能源融合发展的形态、模式与解决方案

铁路是一个国家得以运行和发展的基础之一。特别是对于有着 960 万 km^2 陆地领土的中国来说，铁路更是在我国人口流动、资源输运和区域经济协同等方面发挥着不可或缺的作用。

根据《2019 年铁道统计公报》，全国铁路营业里程达到 13.9 万 km，其中，高速铁路营业里程达到 3.5 万 km；电气化里程 10.0 万 km，电化率 71.9%；西部地区铁路营业里程 5.6 万 km。全国铁路路网密度 145.5km/万 km^2。从我国铁路路网的位置分布来看，我国电气化铁路的分布主要集中在中部和东部等强电网但太阳能资源禀赋丰度较低区域；而在西北、西南、东北等太阳能资源较为丰富地区但处于弱电网或无电网地带，依然有大量的非电气化铁路在运营，承担着改善当地人民生产、生活的重要任务。

本报告在细致梳理了我国铁路系统目前的用能形态和用能模式、分析了我国电气化铁路与非电气化铁路与四类光照幅度区域及骨干电网(包括强电网、弱电网和无网)的联合分布特性的基础上，针对我国铁路与可再生能源融合的 SWOT 特性(优势、劣势、机遇及挑战)进行了战略态势分析，指出铁路与可再生能源的融合发展将在高效能、高弹性和绿色化三大历史使命的指引下，呈现三大创新方向：①铁路资产向绿色能源化方向发展；②铁路能源供给向自洽多元化方向发展；③铁路用能管理向协同弹性化方向发展。

在三大创新方向的指引下，当前的铁路系统、能源系统需要从三个调整角度分别或同时做适应性调整向新型智能化、绿色化、高效化、弹性化与高度环境友好化的铁路能源融合网发展。铁路做适应性调整将使得铁路能源系统呈现“源、网、荷”三重属性：“源属性”即充分地利用铁路系统的运载体、基础设施和服务

设施的外在空间铺设太阳能光伏板，作为新型的分布式铁路可再生能源；“网属性”即铁路能源系统逐渐向小型分布式微网群方向发展；“荷属性”即铁路能源系统荷属性在源属性和网属性的作用下，逐渐从原来的高能量密集性及间歇冲击性逐渐演化为明显的季节耦合性、空间分布性及时间空间不平稳性。能源做适应性调整将使得铁路能源系统从原有的单一的架空电网铁路供电模式，通过配置超级电容器和锂离子电池等储能设施作蓄水池和缓冲池，构建基于变电站、储能站和信息站三合一牵引变储能站，并通过“先就地，再就近，后上网”的调度原则构建基于能源互联网的新型铁路能源供给系统。铁路与能源共同做适应性调整将根据我国光伏出力分布特性、骨干电网分布特性及铁路地域的分布特性，以铁路能源融合网为总目标，从交通与能源互动联系和占不同主导地位两个视角，从交通专用的能源系统、交通特用的能源系统、交通适用的能源系统以及能源支持的交通系统四个维度，提出了八种因地制宜、因网制宜、因荷制宜的“源-网-荷-储”协同化、智能化、高效化铁路可再生能源系统演化新模式和相应的解决方案。

采用新模式，本报告针对我国铁路能源融合网的演进目标，以从局部到整体、从现在到未来两个视角，进行了当前及未来 15 年铁路可再生能源的用电自洽率、用能自洽率、可再生能源渗透率、可再生能源利用率以及节能减排等数据测算。根据测算结果，结合电网的部署规划、中长期铁路网的发展预期以及铁路系统的光伏出力特性，按照 5 年为一阶段共三个演进步骤，针对不同的开发强度(保守场景、基本场景和积极场景)分别描绘了未来 15 年我国铁路可再生能源系统的演进目标和演进步骤。

预计 2021～2025 年，将优先开发强电且多光区域，如陕西、甘肃等地。我国铁路可再生能源用能自洽率为 15.6%，用电自洽率为 19.5%，可再生能源渗透率为 29.33%，铁路减排量达 2384.57 万 t。

预计 2026～2030 年，将深入推进少负荷但多光区域，如西藏、新疆等地。我国铁路可再生能源用能自洽率为 31.0%，用电自洽率为 34.5%，可再生能源渗透率为 41.14%，铁路减排量达 4947.11 万 t。

预计 2031～2035 年，将在全国范围内逐步推动其他区域，如山东、江苏等地。我国铁路可再生能源用能自洽率可达到 44.2%，用电自洽率达到 46.5%，可再生能源渗透率为 50.16%，铁路减排量达 6969.46 万 t。

Executive Summery

Transportation, as the crisscross pattern and the accessible path, carries the migrating track of human society. Energy, as the nature essence and the power foundation, sustains the survival and development of mankind. Transportation and energy are the two eternal themes which concerned by all civilizations.

Looking back on history, the integration of energy, which is the enabler of transportation, and transportation, which is the largest load of energy, constitutes the important objective conditions for ensuring the rational, effective and sustainable evolution of human society. Every collaborative innovation of energy and transportation has greatly improved the productivity of society, promoted scientific and technological progress, and further shaped the characteristics of human civilization in different historical period. The integration of biomass energy and livestock transport contributed to the agricultural civilization; the integration of steam engine and the first generation of fossil fuel energy-coal inaugurated the first Industrial Revolution; the inclusion of the first generation of secondary energy-electric power and the rail sector promoted the second Industrial Revolution and thus push-forwarded greatly the industrial civilization. Meanwhile, the economics-centric economic status and power distribution globally have been in constant change and reformation through those energy-transportation-integration driven industrial revolutions.

However, since the Industrial Revolution, the energy consumption of transportation and resulted negative external effects caused irreconcilable contradictions in these two sectors. It's particularly worth noticing that conflicts among urbanization, transportation, energy and environment have been gradually getting prominent since the popularization of the electrified transportation. How to contain the climate crisis and further save the earth is the most complicated and difficult challenge faced by all humankind. Under the Paris Agreement, countries all over the world have established ambitious goals for greenhouse gas emissions reduction and competed for strategic high ground through the development of renewable energy and low-carbon transportation and take it as the key initiative for sustainable development.

The history is now driving the civilization to a new era, during which the objective law of human, nature and society orchestration harmonious is primarily respected. The 18th and 19th National Congresses of the Communist Party of China (CPC) explicitly incorporated the concept of ecological civilization and construction of Xi Jinping into the Five-sphere Integrated Plan and the Four-pronged Comprehensive Strategy on socialism with Chinese characteristics. Under the guidance of the common goal on ecological civilization featuring green, low-carbon, clean and sustainable, the integration of transportation and energy is the new phase of pattern shift on these two sectors respectively, and their collaborative development; it is a powerful initiative for respecting, protecting and orchestrating with nature, and the innovative practice for constructing a Beautiful China, realizing the Chinese Dream of national rejuvenation, and supporting the Belt and Road initiative sketched by General Secretary Xi Jinping, and an destined roadmap supporting the construction of a community with a shared future for mankind. Under socialism with Chinese characteristics in the new era, the integration of transportation and energy will definitely permeate and influence the whole process of Chinese political, economic, social and cultural construction, and become the momentous material foundation of the ecological civilization of socialism with Chinese characteristics and benefiting all mankind.

From development paradigm perspective, severe challenges such as resource shortage, climate change and environmental pollution enhanced by the existing emission and non-synergism featured development modes will jeopardize the sustainability of social development and economic growth of China in the period from now on up to the next 15 years. Green development oriented strategic planning and industrial transformation and upgradation have been already become the essential approach and the major policy priority. As the natural consequence of policy choice, and the response to the requirement posed by green and intelligent transportation development, the energy related scheme shifting and supply-side reform need urgently the top design with the collaboration of transportation and energy sectors. In the global context of energy saving and emission reduction, and domestic determination to promote sustainable development and construct a safe, green, convenient, efficient and economical transportation system, based on reassessment of the intension and stretch of the modern transportation and energy systems, it is extremely crucial to clarify the interaction and the synergistic evolution path, and thus take effective political measures and policy orientation for high-quality socio-economic development through the integration of transportation and energy sectors.

From economic construction perspective, the high-quality development in both economic construction and social development is the mainstream theme of China's economy under the new normal. As fundamentals of economic development and social operation, energy and transportation directly determine patterns, forms and qualities of economic growth. The integration of transportation and energy will create new technologies, business types, industries and schemes with the ability of generating, gathering, leading and promoting industries; it will also create a batch of new economic growth pole and shape new paradigms through which the relevant industrial clusters could be of symbiosis, interaction, coordination and evolution; it can lead and drive the economy's high-quality development into a new stage, thus make the economic growth low-carbon, green, coordinated and sustainable, and fully be a lever among the economy security and resilience level; and is eventually the significant step and efficient path to ensure the high-quality and high-efficient development of national economy through revolutionary change in energy and transportation systems.

From social and cultural construction perspective, the synergistic innovation development of transportation and energy will certainly boost the wide spread of green development and the concept of ecological civilization while vigorously promoting the low-carbon, intelligent, efficient and convenient development of the human activity protection system including productions and lifestyles. At the same time, in forming and strengthening the green, low-carbon and sustainable social consensus and its impact on human and social behaviors, it is of tremendous importance. The integration network of transportation and energy is going to create unprecedented requirements in terms of network form, business function, resource utilization and generic technology, greatly promote the cultivation and employment of talents at all levels with the concept of ecological civilization, and train a large number of social members who meet the needs of high-quality development and could influence and upgrade the ecological civilization construction level of the whole society.

In recent years, the energy sector has accelerated the technological innovation system construction and firmed up the concept of innovative, coordinated, green and open development under the guidance of four-revolution and one-cooperation energy strategy. Energy system upgrades from an extensive, ineffective, polluted and unsafe pattern to a modern energy system with fine, efficient, clean, pluralistic and safe features. It's worth mentioning that the science, technology and industrialization levels of the renewable energy sector in China are making great progress and significant improvement. However, on one hand, the temporal-spatial distribution productivity of energy and power system in China is in serious mismatch with the temporal-spatial distribution of energy requirement. On the other hand, transportation system with sufficient natural endowment is the maximum load with spatial distribution characteristics. Therefore, how to establish suitable mechanisms and corresponding technological solutions to promote the shift of transportation dedicated energy systems to the new paradigm through comprehensive matching of sufficient utilization of renewable energy resources and the transportation energy requirement, and thus to keep the blue sky and lucid water on which human beings can survive.

Transportation is the lifeline of national economy. As population growth, demographic change, the continuous economic development and the consequently increasing requirement on passenger and freight transportation in road and rail sectors, the supporting and securing role of ground transportation system to social-economic development is increasingly essential. However, with the demand of traffic activity accelerated rapidly, the total energy consumption in the transportation sector and its proportion in the national total amount are increasing year by year, besides, its growth rate is also rising rapidly year by year. According to statistics, the transportation sector has become the third-highest volume of the total national energy consumption, after industry and living consumption sectors.

Hence, the discussion of new scenarios, new patterns and solutions of renewable energy and transportation integration could not only promote the sound and orderly development of the renewable energy sector, but also be significant beneficial to improve the energy efficiency, strengthen the energy structure and support the transformation of transportation sector. There are various types of renewable energy, chiefly containing solar energy, wind energy, biomass energy, ocean energy, geothermal energy, etc. The renewable energy in this book is mainly refers to the solar energy in view of its natural endowment with unique spatial distribution characteristic and flexible utilization ways. For different migration mission, the transportation system falls into three major categories: ground, air and water transport. Of which, ground transportation is a transport mode with the largest scale, the widest spatial distribution, the strongest permeability of socio-economic activities, the ability to independently complete the whole process of transportation services, the most industry related categories, the most energy consumption, and the greatest energization potential of assets. The ground transportation in such a continental country as China is crucial in its comprehensive transportation system. This book deals with the ground transportation principally. The ground transportation system mainly includes road transportation based on roadway and rail transportation based on railway.

The supporting technologies involved in this book include photovoltaic cells, energy storage, energy internet, etc. In terms of photovoltaic generation, China has already been in the world advanced level in crystalline silicon photovoltaic cells industrialization technology, and mastered the core technologies of the whole industry chain from polysilicon purification technology, single crystal/ poly crystal growth technology to high-efficiency cells and component preparation technology, the production of solar cells and components in China is over 70% of the global products. Cost and quality advantages of photovoltaic products made the photovoltaic industry became one of the most competitive industries in China. However, there is a big gap between China and the world on large-scale production and laboratory efficiency of thin film solar cells-some, and the core equipment still relies on import, the number of domestic enterprise with large-scale production capacity and cost advantages is not sizable, the combination of production, learning and research is not related enough and thus the research cannot convert into industrialization production effectively. Therefore, a series of major scientific and technological problems in photovoltaic fields including basic theory, key technology and high-value equipment is the priority which needed urgently to be studied and broke though. In terms of energy storage, China has already formed a scaled industrial layout, and gradually participate in international standards setting with its products impacted the world. However, on one hand, energy storage battery has bottleneck technical problems in efficiency, cost, life cycle and safety aspects which need to be solved in the design and efficient preparation of energy storage related materials. On the other hand, high investment cost, low energy density, poor system reliability and large energy loss are also exist in the application of energy storage, it is urgent to make relevant theoretical and technical breakthroughs such as the evaluation of state, residual value and peak power of the energy storage system and energy configuration management. In terms of energy Internet, China fully integrates energy technology with advanced information and communication technology, so that the complementary coordination and efficient operation of various energy forms can be achieved widely, all segments of the whole energy chain with source-network-load-storage attributes can interact with each other deeply, and a novel energy ecology through the peer to peer new market and business model can be created. China did more comprehensive and deeper research in the concept and exploration of energy Internet than any other European and American countries, we are in the following stage in the fields of power distribution and consumption related technology, market mode and business type under the influence of the previous development focus, but there is a huge gap between China and world highest level in key materials, devices and equipment fields. What's more, even though more and more engineering demonstration applications have been carried out, some key basic theories have not been completely broken though yet, including Synthesizing Analysis Simulation and Optimization Synergy Theory of Multiple Energy Flow Forms, and the Theory of Safety and Stability of Complex Power Systems with High Proportional Power Electronic Devices. It is predicted that by 2035, through the effective implementation and deployment of the major technological tasks and key technical issues of the above three technical fields, the independent innovation capacity in energy sector will be greatly enhanced in China, a large number of key technologies will make significant breakthroughs and the dependence on imports of energy technology equipment, components and materials will decrease apparently. Furthermore, China will constructs the energy technology innovation system which adapted to the national conditions in basic energy storage scientific issues, energy storage technology, the upgrading of energy storage industry chain, the amplification, application, demonstration and industrialization of renewable energy technology, the new structure of photovoltaic cells, materials and scaled preparation technology, basic theory and key technology of energy Internet, operation and controlling of complex interconnected power grid, analysis, planning and operation of integrated energy system, integrated theory and technology of information and energy, and design of market mechanism and business model.

This book contains three sections. The first section is a general introduction of the energization potential of ground transportation infrastructure assets in China; the second section is greatly discussing scenarios, patterns and solutions of the integrated utilization on road and renewable power; the third section is mainly researching scenarios, patterns and solutions of the integrated utilization on railway and renewable power.

Section One—Energization Potential of Ground Transportation Infrastructure Assets in China

In order to analyze the influence of internal contradictions and macro-tendency of China's energy and transportation systems, and provide opportunities for the development on clean energy, electrified transportation and the integration in these two sectors, this book assess the solar energy generation potential of the existing transport infrastructure in China on the basis of new tendencies in electrified transportation and clean energy consumption, so as to analyze and forecast the feasibility and possibility of maximum self-containment potential in transportation system through the deep-going development of its endowment. This book can provide basis for policy makers of economic and industrial policy, as well as for decision makers of industry planning and technology layout. Meanwhile, it can afford business discrimination and prediction basis of industry demonstration, application demonstration and industry matching for relevant enterprises and individuals. Furthermore, it can provide scholars with exchange themes and materials of academic and industrial research.

For the road system in ground transportation system, this book assesses its development potential in three sections, that are, highway, national highway and provincial highway; as for the railway system in ground transportation system, electrified and non-electrified railway are two categories that have been assessed in this book to get its development potential.

Three utilization patterns (not limited to), including Conservative, Basic and Positive Scenario, have been investigated in this book to estimate the utilization potential of China's highway. The daily power generation potential of China's highway can hit 143GW·h, and the annual power generation potential is about 25178GW·h in Basic Scenario. The daily power generation potential of China's highway can up to 1076GW·h, and the annual power generation potential is about 193674GW·h in Positive Scenario.

As for national highway and provincial highway, this book gives four utilization patterns, namely, Conservative Scenario, Basic Scenario 1, Basic Scenario 2 and Positive Scenario, to estimate their development potential. The annual power generation potential of national highway and provincial highway is about 31783GW·h in Conservative Scenario; the corresponding volume approaches 531514GW·h in Positive Scenario.

Three utilization patterns are applied in this book to assess the development potential of the electrified railway, including Conservative, Basic and Positive Scenario. The daily power generation potential of China's high-speed railway system can hit 792GW·h, and the annual power generation potential is about 170316.3GW·h in Basic Scenario. The daily power generation potential of China's high-speed railway system approaches 871.2GW·h, and the annual power generation potential reaches 274746.5GW·h in Positive Scenario.

This book assesses the development potential of the non-electrified railway in four utilization patterns, that are, Conservative Scenario 1 (double-track), Conservative Scenario 2 (single-track), Positive Scenario 1 (double-track), Positive Scenario 2 (single-track). The daily power generation potential of China's non-electrified railway system will hit 159.6GW · h, and the annual power generation potential approaches 13587GW · h in Conservative Scenario. In Positive Scenario, the daily power generation potential of China's non-electrified railway system can up to 344.9GW · h, and the annual power generation potential is about 30385GW · h.

Section Two-Scenarios, Patterns and Solutions of the Integrated Development on Road Transportation and Renewable Energy

Highway, as a convenient and efficient transport infrastructure, plays an important role in the process of industrialization and urbanization. The scale of China's highway transport infrastructure has been accelerating rapidly. By the end of 2018, the total highway length reached 143 000 kilometers with about 5 700 highway service areas. Compared to 85000 kilometers in 2011, 68% increases in 7 years, with an average annual growth rate of 6.7%.

This book points out the energy consumption scenarios and patterns of the road transport energy system, prospects the future application and development of electricity, fossil fuel and hydrogen in road transportation, and further looks forward to the high-quality development tendency of road transport energy system in China. That is, firstly, the emission reduction from high carbon to low carbon with the continuous adjustment of the energy structure. This can greatly increase the penetration of renewable energy in the road transport energy system and thereby results in the reduction of carbon emissions and the realization of sustainable energy development. Secondly, it is the synergism tendency of energy utilization from an inefficient path to an efficient path with a large-scale optimization of energy delivery. This can expand the range of the road transport energy system and then address the imbalance between energy production and consumptions with higher energy efficiency.

Following the aforementioned tendency, the road transport energy system is reconstructed with of smart grid. In the new road transport energy system, the photovoltaic generation and road transportation are integrated with the concept of local generation and local consumption. Through further research of the source, network and load attributes, the evolution of the road transport energy system is presented with multi-attribute, multi-level and multi-viewpoint features in this section.

In the source attribute aspect, the photovoltaic generation can be widely installed in the available space resources of road transportation. By this means, the road transport energy system is transferred from the pure load state to the coexistence state of supply and load with the generation capacity.

In the network attribute aspect, the road transport energy system can achieve the multi-energy complement for source-load balance with the interconnection and coordination of multiple energy systems of road transportation. The transition from local equilibrium to wide range optimized dispatching can greatly increase the energy efficiency.

In the load attribute aspect, the orderly power utilization is realized with the demand side management, where the load is adjustable and transferable. The load transformation from random to controllable is useful to balance the power supply and the demand for road transportation.

Driven by the source-network-load triple attributes, this book clarifies different application scenarios on the novel trans-energy system in road transportation with four typical solutions, i.e., the transport dedicated energy system, the transport specific energy system, the transport adaptive energy system and the energy system supported transport system. The novel trans-energy network is put forward as the systematic technological solutions for energy and transportation integration.

The novel trans-energy system in road transportation can make full use of the natural endowment of the transportation system, coordinate the common development of energy and transportation sectors and integrate the multiple demands of transportation, power grid, environment, etc. On the traffic side, the construction of the novel trans-energy system promote the development of transportation re-electrification and further enhance the application of renewable energy and clean energy in transportation system; on the grid side, the novel trans-energy system in road transportation can be used as the basic application of the novel generation power system in the transportation sector to push forward the transformation of the novel trans-energy system from the consumer to the producer, and alleviate the power supply pressure in the regional grid; on environment side, the novel trans-energy system can take full advantage of the transportation natural endowment, optimize the energy structure of transportation system and reduce the carbon emission in energy consumption.

On enough consideration of natural resource endowment and power consumption in different regions, this book aims at the easily developed area such as highway service area, tunnel isolation strip and highway line with the construction concept of nearby development and nearby consumption, makes the development and construction of the novel trans-energy system in area 1 (with the rich solar resource) as a top priority, continuously enhances the development intensity in area 1, and starts the development and construction of area 2(with the general solar resource) and area 3 (with the less solar resource).

It can be predicted that by 2025, the development and construction of area 1 is the top priority. Under Conservative Scenario, the annual photovoltaic generation in highways is 400GW·h, the electricity self-containment rate is 2.10%, the penetration of renewable power utilization is 17.80%, and the annual carbon emission reduction is 398 000 tons; under Basic Scenario, the annual photovoltaic generation in highways is 780GW·h, the electricity self-containment rate is 4.20%, the penetration of renewable power utilization is 19.20%, and the annual carbon emission reduction is 778 000 tons; under Positive Scenario, the annual photovoltaic generation of national highway is 1180GW·h, the electricity self-containment rate is 6.30%, the penetration of renewable power utilization is 21.30%, and the annual carbon emission reduction is 1.17 million tons.

The development and construction of area 1 and area 2 will be further advanced in 2030. Under Conservative Scenario, the annual photovoltaic generation in highways is 7260GW·h, the electricity self-containment rate is 16.00%, the penetration of renewable power utilization is 36.20%, and the annual carbon emission reduction is 7.23 million tons; under Basic Scenario, the annual photovoltaic generation in highways is 8990GW·h, the electricity self-containment rate is 19.90%, the penetration of renewable power utilization is 39.10%, and the annual carbon emission reduction is 8.96 million tons; under Positive Scenario, the annual photovoltaic generation of national highway is 10840GW·h, the electricity self-containment rate is 28.40%, the penetration of renewable power utilization is 45.60%, and the annual carbon emission reduction is 10.80 million tons.

It is expected that in 2035, when continuously increasing the development scale of area 1 and area 2, the development and construction of area 3 will gradually be promoted. Under Conservative Scenario, the annual photovoltaic generation in highways is 31380GW·h, the electricity self-containment rate is 26.70%, the penetration of renewable power utilization is 48.70%, and the annual carbon emission reduction is 31.28 million tons; under Basic Scenario, the annual photovoltaic generation in highways is 52460GW·h, the electricity self-containment rate is 44.60%, the penetration of renewable power utilization is 61.20%, and the annual carbon emission reduction is 52.3 million tons; under Positive Scenario, the annual photovoltaic generation of national highway is 73300, the electricity self-containment rate is 62.40%, the penetration of renewable power utilization is 73.70%, and the annual carbon emission reduction is 73.08 million tons.

In the end, with the intended power consumption of China's highways, this book elaborates the evolutionary path of the novel trans-energy system in the way from easy development to difficult development and from easy consumption to difficult consumption and then promotes the further development of the energy conservation and emission reduction and better quality and efficiency of the road transport energy systems.

Section Three-Scenarios, Patterns and Solutions of the Integrated Development on Railway Transportation and Renewable Energy

As the operation and development pillars, railway plays an essential role in a country's history. Especially for China, which is a great country with 9.6 million square kilometers, railway is of tremendous importance for its passenger and freight traffic activities, and coordination on regional economic development.

According to the National Railway Statistical Communique in 2019, the total operating mileage of national railway activities has reached 139 000 kilometers, including 10 000 kilometers for electrified railway, and the electrification rate ups to 71.9%. The total mileage of high-speed railway approaches 35 000 kilometers. The total operating mileage of western China reaches 56 000 kilometers. Up to now, the density of national railway network is 145.5 km/ 10 000 square kilometer. According to the distribution characteristics of national railway network, most of the electrified railways are concentrated in central and eastern China with strong power grid but low solar energy resources; on the contrary, a large number of the non-electrified railways are operating in northwest, southwest and northeast China, and undertaking the critical task of enhancing the production and livelihood of local people.

Based on carefully study of the current scenarios and patterns of railway-energy system in China, and the joint distribution characteristics of railway (including electrified and non-electrified railway), four levels of solar photovoltaic areas and backbone power grid (including strong, weak and no network), this book applies SWOT to analyze the strengths, weaknesses, opportunities and threats for integration of railway and renewable energy. The orchestrated development of railway and renewable energy will present three innovative directions follow the three historical missions which are high efficiency, high resilience and green construction:

(1) Railway assets energization develops in a green direction;

(2) Energy supply of railway develops in a self-contained and diverse direction;

(3) Energy consumption management of railway develops in a synergetic and resilient direction.

Under the guidance of these three innovative directions, the current railway system and energy system need to make adaptive adjustment from three angles, respectively or at the same time, to meet a new intelligent, green, efficient, resilient and highly environment-friendly railway-energy system. The railway-energy system will represent the source-network-load triple attributes through adaptive adjustment: Source attribute, that is, making full use of the external space of railway system carriers, infrastructure and service facilities to lay solar photovoltaic panels as a new type of distributed railway renewable energy. Network attribute, namely, the railway-energy system is gradually developing towards small distributed micro-grid group. Load attribute, what is to say, the railway-energy system gradually evolves from the original high energy density and interim surge characteristics to the obvious characteristics of seasonal migration, local distribution and surge transfer. By using energy storage facilities such as super-capacitors and lithium-ion batteries as cisterns and buffer pools, and constructing energy storage station combined transformer station, energy storage station and information station, the energy adaptive adjustment will transform the railway-energy system from the original and single overhead power grid railway power supply model with to a new railway renewable energy supply network by adopting the local-nearby-grid scheduling principle.

The adaptive adjustment of railway and energy takes the railway-energy system into four dimensions according to the distribution characteristics of solar photovoltaic, backbone grid and railway system, which including transport dedicated energy system, transport specific energy system, transport adaptive energy system and energy system supported transport system from the perspective of the interaction and dominant position between transportation and renewable energy. 8 types of future-proofing railway energy system evolution models featuring coordination, intelligence and efficiency of source-network-load-storage are promoted in this section by orchestrating the grid, transportation load and PV resources.

From part to overall, and from present to future, this book calculates the electricity consumption self-containment rate of renewable energy, the energy consumption self-containment rate of renewable energy, the renewable energy penetration rate, the new renewable utilization rate and the carbon emission reduction at present and in the next 15 years by taking the promoted new evolution models. While taking 5 years as one stage, the whole evolution process can be separated into three evolution stages. Three scenarios, Conservative, Basic and Positive Scenario, are used for calculating according to different development intensities. After analyzing the calculation results, this book portrays the evolution goals and steps of the national railway energy-system in the next 15 years.

Regions with strong power grid and rich solar resource such as Shaanxi and Gansu will give the priority to development and construction in 2021-2025. The energy consumption self-containment rate of renewable energy for national railway is 15.60%, the electricity consumption self-containment rate of renewable energy is 19.50%, the renewable energy penetration rate is 29.33%, rail carbon emission reduction is 23.84 million tons.

Regions with less load but rich solar resource such as Tibet and Xinjiang will get further promoted in 2026-2030. The energy consumption self-containment rate of renewable energy for national railway is 31.00%, the electricity consumption self-containment rate of renewable energy is 34.50%, the renewable energy penetration rate is 41.14%, rail carbon emission reduction is 49.47 million tons.

Other regions such as Shandong and Jiangsu will be gradually developed in 2031-2035. The energy consumption self-containment rate of renewable energy for national railway is for national railway is 44.20%, the electricity consumption self-containment rate of renewable energy is 46.50%, the renewable energy penetration rate is 50.16%, rail carbon emission reduction is 69.69 million tons.

目　录

下篇　铁路交通与可再生能源融合发展的形态、模式与解决方案

符号说明

总启部分	
符号	含义
L	隧道长度
N	设计交通流量
V	设计车速
QA	明路面的年能耗
QB	暗路面的年能耗
Q	高速公路沿线设备的日耗能
$q_{1,\mathrm{wind}}$	隧道通风的一天总耗电
$w_{d,i}$	第 i 个风机的功率
t_i	第 i 个风机工作的时间
n	高速公路的车辆检测器数量
$w_{c,i}$	第 i 个车辆检测器功率
m	高速公路的紧急电话数量
$w_{t,j}$	第 j 个紧急电话功率
P_E	实际装机容量
S_E	实际可利用面积
S	建设 10MW 光伏发电站的用地面积
P_d	日可发电量
P	年发电量

续表

总启部分	
符号	含义
p_t	发电功率
η	自洽率
μ	产用比
Q_1	可实现完全自主、即发即用、自给供电的电量
Q_2	该线路典型日的总耗电量
Q_3	该线路在典型日利用光伏设备可提供的最大发电量
γ	电能时移率
γ_{max}	最大电能时移率
$Q'_{3,used}$	通过储能设备或并网外送等方式实现电能时空转移的实际 Q_3 部分电量
上篇部分	
Q_a	到达地面的太阳总辐射
Q_b	地外太阳辐射
δ	月日照百分率
L	光伏电池板理论年发电量
Q	区域年平均太阳辐射量
S_{PV}	光伏组件面积
η	光伏电站系统转换效率
L_T	太阳能电池板实际发电量
η_1	实际发电效率
β	光伏系统的可利用率
P_V	光伏系统的日平均出力

续表

T_v	光伏系统的出力时间
上篇部分	
符号	含义
T_1、T_2	一天中光伏出力的始末时刻
T_0	一天中光伏出力时间
C_g	市电供电容量
C_0	储能配置容量
P_i	交通分布式光伏系统发电量
E_i	交通能源系统用电量
S_i	交通能源系统总能耗(折算为电能)
γ	可再生能源电力渗透率
SCR_E	用电自洽率
SCR_S	用能自洽率
NEPR	交通系统可再生能源电力渗透率
下篇部分	
P_{pv}	铁路系统年光伏出力
E_{need}	铁路系统的负荷年总耗能量
P_{need}	铁路系统的负荷年总耗电量
$\mathrm{SOC}(i)$	蓄电池组在 i 时刻的荷电状态
$P_{\mathrm{pv}}(i)$	i 时刻的光伏出力
$p_{\mathrm{need}}(i)$	i 时刻的负荷需求
E_B	蓄电池组的总容量
$e_{\mathrm{sold}}(i)$	i 时刻的售电量
$e_{\mathrm{bought}}(i)$	i 时刻的购电量
E_{sold}	全年售电量

续表

E_{bought}	全年购电量
下篇部分	
符号	含义
E_{save}	节省购电量
I_{PV}	光伏组件投资额
S_{PV}	光伏组件面积
U_{PV}	光伏组件单价
I_B	蓄电池储能投资
U_B	蓄电池储能单价
I_C	超级电容器投资
E_C	超级电容器容量
U_C	超级电容器单价
I_{sum}	总投资
R_{sum}	总收益
R_{pv}	光伏补贴收入
R_{sold}	上网售电收入
R_{save}	节省购电量收益
U_{PVS}	光伏补贴单价
U_{sold}	上网售电单价
U_{save}	节省购电单价
ROI	投资收益比
PBY	回收年限
$P_{train}(i)$	第 i 辆列车的额定功率
n	本级牵引变区段上的列车数

续表

k	可靠系数
下篇部分	
符号	含义
$P_{B\min}$	储能系统的最大可输出功率
ΔP_i	i 时刻储能系统出力需求
Δt	时间间隔
$1\sim m_1$、$m_2\sim m_3$、$m_j\sim m_n$	需要连续充放电的时段
i_{pv}	光伏组件电流
n_p	并联单元数
n_s	串联单元数
I_{ph}	光电流
I_{sat}	模块反向饱和电流
q	电子电荷
A	理想系数
k	玻尔兹曼常量
T	光伏组件面温度
V_{pv}	光伏组件电压
R_s	光伏电池的串联电阻
I_{sso}	短路电流
k_i	短路电流温度系数
T_r	参考温度
S	太阳辐射水平
I_{rr}	T_r 温度下的反向饱和电流
E_{gap}	硅的带隙能

续表

V_b	终端电压
下篇部分	
符号	含义
V_o	蓄电池的开路电压
R_b	蓄电池的内阻抗
i_b	电池的充电电流
K	极化电压
Q_{BE}	蓄电池容量
A	电压常数
B	容量常数
S_{train}	列车车厢光伏板面积
l_{train}	单节列车长度
C_{train}	列车宽度
n_{train}	列车编组数量
C_{rad}	弧线转化系数
S_{rail}	光伏篷的面积
c_{rail}	光伏篷的等效宽度
L_{rail}	排除桥隧线路全长
p_n	铺设比例
$\mathrm{GHI}(i)$	i 时刻辐射量
V_d	节油量
C_D	柴油发电机的油耗
ρ_D	柴油密度
E_{re}	二氧化碳减排量
C_C	柴油的排放因子

续表

R_D	节省的燃油量收益
下篇部分	
符号	含义
U_d	柴油单价
P_{need}	列车所需电量
m_{train}	该区间的日班次数
t_{run}	运营时间
P_{train}	每辆列车的牵引功率
c_{PV}	光伏组件的等效宽度
L_{PV}	光伏组件的等效长度
S_B	蓄电池储能总占地面积
S_b	单个蓄电池占地面积
E_b	单个蓄电池容量
C_{CE}	减排量换算常数
P_{train}	铁路运载体光伏出力
GHI_{avg}	全国平均年辐射量
ρ	光伏组件转化效率
P_{rail}	铁路线路光伏出力
l_{I}、l_{II}、l_{III}、l_{IV}	四类辐照地区铁路线路长度
GHI_{I}、GHI_{II}、GHI_{III}、GHI_{IV}	四类辐照地区平均年辐射量
P_{trac}	铁路牵引变电所光伏出力
$n_{\text{trac I}}$、$n_{\text{trac II}}$、$n_{\text{trac III}}$、$n_{\text{trac IV}}$	四类辐照地区铁路牵引变电所数量
s_{tracavg}	铁路牵引变电所平均面积

续表

$P_{station}$	铁路服务设施光伏出力
下篇部分	
符号	含义
$n_{sta\,I}$、$n_{sta\,II}$、$n_{sta\,III}$、$n_{sta\,IV}$	四类辐照地区车站数量
SCR_E	用电自洽率
SCR_S	用能自洽率
NEPR	交通系统可再生能源渗透率
γ	电力系统中可再生能源在电力一次侧能源中所占比重

单 位 说 明

中文习惯表述	英文习惯表述
千瓦	kW
万千瓦	10MW
亿千瓦	100GW
千瓦时	kW·h
万千瓦时	10MW·h
亿千瓦时	100GW·h
米	m
公里	km
百公里	100km
万公里	10000km
万平方米	$10000m^2$
公顷	$10000m^2$
万公顷	$100km^2$
千伏	kV
兆焦每平方米	MJ/m^2
坎德拉每平方米	cd/m^2
公里每小时	km/h
万升	10000L
万吨	10000t
瓦特每平方米	W/m^2
立方米每小时	m^3/h

总启 中国陆路交通系统资产能源化的潜力

当前，世界面临百年未有之大变局，中国特色社会主义进入新时代，能源与交通行业处于深刻的变革之中。实现能源与交通的可持续发展，交通与能源的一体化战略规划与融合发展是大势所趋！面对纷繁复杂和急剧变化的内外部环境，能源与交通的融合发展既面临难得机遇，也面临不少困难和挑战。

首先，能源与交通的供需呈现新特征。无论是能源还是交通行业，我国由高速增长阶段转向高质量发展阶段，交通能源需求增长旺盛，分布式能源、储能等交互式能源设施快速发展，多能供给、综合服务、智能用能等各种新型能源形式不断涌现，交通发展的电气化水平不断提升的需求和资源环境更加苛刻的约束共同作用，为加快交通资产的能源化利用提出了新的要求，创造了前所未有的机遇。

其次，能源与交通的安全运行面临新挑战。可再生能源的大规模建设和高比例接入电网，以及网络安全等新的风险因素与自然灾害、外力破坏等传统因素交织叠加，给能源网络，尤其是交通系统的总体安全运行带来了前所未有的压力和挑战。

要把握历史机遇，破解发展难题，贯彻落实党的十九大部署，必须要有科学的理论指导和战略指引，必须要以高度的战略自信和战略定位，更加全面系统深入地贯彻执行“四个革命、一个合作”能源安全战略与“交通强国”战略部署，持久发力，久久为功。能源与交通的融合发展必须从国情和实际需求出发，深入落实各项改革部署，加快构建交通能源一体化发展体系，进一步丰富交通系统与能源(尤其是可再生能源)系统的融合模式，显著地提升交通系统能源自洽水平，从而持续构建具有绿色、经济和高弹性特征的交通系统技术与装备体系。瞄准交通能源交叉前沿关键技术的集中攻关，提高能源与交通融合发展的规模和水平，抢占颠覆性技术国际制高点。交通与能源的融合发展必将增强我国能源供给和交通系统的总体安全水平，提升国民经济整体发展的质量和效益，确保交通强国建设的扎实有序推进，行稳致远。

第 1 章　我国陆路交通系统资产能源化总体潜力评估与应用潜力分析

1.1　我国陆路交通系统资产能源化潜力评估

1.1.1　我国现有陆路交通系统的基础设施布局状况

本报告涉及的陆路交通系统主要包括公路系统和铁路系统。

1. 公路交通网络的基础设施布局状况

本报告涉及的公路交通系统由高速公路、国道和省道三类道路交通网络组成。

由《国家公路网规划(2013～2030 年)》可知，国家高速公路网由 7 条首都放射线、11 条北南纵线、18 条东西横线，以及地区环线、并行线、联络线等组成，截至 2018 年底，我国高速公路总里程为 14.3 万 km。

国道是指具有全国性政治、经济意义的主要干线公路，包括重要的国际公路，国防公路，连接首都与各省(区、市)的公路，连接各大经济中心、港站枢纽、商品生产基地和战略要地的公路。截至 2018 年末，我国国道总里程为 36.3 万 km。

省道又称省级干线公路。在省公路网中，具有全省性的政治、经济、国防意义，并经省(区、市)统一规划确定为省级干线公路。截至 2018 年末，我国省道总里程为 37.22 万 km。

2. 铁路交通网络的基础设施布局状况

我国大陆铁路系统可划分为电气化铁路和非电气化铁路，闻名世界的高速铁路(以下简称高铁)便属于电气化铁路。中国高铁属高铁级，而国铁 I 级只用于快速铁路和骨干线普通铁路。中国通过引进加创新，研制“和谐号”动车组列车以及“复兴号”中国标准动车组列车。

四纵四横是《中长期铁路网规划(2008 年调整)》规划建设的客运专线，客车速度目标值达到 200km/h 以上。

四纵为京沪客运专线(京沪高铁)、京港客运专线(京港高铁)、京哈客运专线、杭福深客运专线(东南沿海客运专线)；四横为沪汉蓉客运专线、徐兰客运专线、沪昆客运专线、青太客运专线。

八纵八横是中国高速铁路网络的短期规划。2016 年 7 月，国家发展和改革委员会、交通运输部、中国铁路总公司联合发布了《中长期铁路网规划》，勾画了新时期“八纵八横”高速铁路网的宏大蓝图。

八纵通道包括沿海通道、京沪通道、京港(台)通道、京哈—京港澳通道、呼南通道、京昆通道、包(银)海通道、兰(西)广通道；“八横”通道包括绥满通道、京兰通道、青银通道、陆桥通道、沿江通道、沪昆通道、厦渝通道、广昆通道。

2018年底中国高铁运营里程超过2.9万km，占全球高铁运营里程的2/3以上，超过其他国家总和。2019年完成投产高铁新线3200km。截至2019年4月，中国高铁桥梁长度突破1.6万km。

1.1.2 我国陆路交通系统基础设施所在地区的太阳能资源状况

根据文件《2017年度光伏发电市场环境监测评价结果》中对我国各个地区的资源等级划分，得出我国全境整体光资源分布如表1-1所示。表1-2为京沪高速沿途省份月均辐射总量。

表1-1 我国光伏资源区域划分(根据标杆上网电价划分)

资源区	地区
Ⅰ类	宁夏、青海(海西)、甘肃(嘉峪关、武威、张掖、酒泉、敦煌、金昌)、新疆(哈密、塔城、阿勒泰、克拉玛依)、内蒙古(除赤峰、通辽、兴安盟、呼伦贝尔以外地区)
Ⅱ类	北京、天津、黑龙江、吉林、辽宁、四川、云南、内蒙古(赤峰、通辽、兴安盟、呼伦贝尔)、河北(承德、张家口、唐山、秦皇岛)、山西(大同、朔州、忻州、阳泉)、陕西(榆林、延安)、青海(除Ⅰ类外其他地区)、甘肃(除Ⅰ类外其他地区)、新疆(除Ⅰ类外其他地区)
Ⅲ类	河北(除Ⅱ类外其他地区)、山西(除Ⅱ类外其他地区)、陕西(除Ⅱ类外其他地区)、上海、江苏、浙江、安徽、福建、江西、山东、河南、湖北、湖南、广东、广西、海南、重庆、贵州、西藏

表1-2 京沪高速沿途省份月均辐射总量

省(区、市)	观测站区站号	月均总辐射量/(MJ/m^2)											
		一月	二月	三月	四月	五月	六月	七月	八月	九月	十月	十一月	十二月
北京	54511	248.2	306.7	470.8	489.6	631.7	443.7	565.4	518.8	428.6	366.9	282.7	151.7
天津	54527	302.5	355.3	502.6	509.6	633.4	528.4	586.2	546.4	454.2	370.5	268.6	152.6
河北	54539	243.2	315.1	459.7	525.3	657.1	557.7	600.5	568.7	466.7	366.6	266.5	191.8
上海	58362	260.2	294.0	279.0	282.5	335.5	460.0	463.9	404.9	414.7	313.1	254.1	144.8
江苏	58144	265.6	316.7	375.6	414.7	441.7	562.8	553.2	562.1	458.3	365.1	289.6	195.0
	58238	256.8	282.0	330.0	364.1	384.9	501.0	596.8	477.3	445.3	368.6	266.5	148.0
	58265	309.5	290.7	326.3	337.3	394.8	512.9	539.1	478.2	468.7	373.1	307.3	193.4
安徽	58321	256.0	267.6	352.0	367.1	368.9	493.4	492.1	501.8	426.6	368.4	263.9	142.7
	58531	258.3	259.8	293.1	285.1	365.6	501.1	562.4	449.8	437.4	363.2	265.2	140.6
山东	54764	273.7	344.4	488.7	579.1	614.7	650.6	543.5	549.5	507.9	333.3	268.7	206.2
	54823	233.1	262.7	398.6	514.8	541.3	539.8	598.0	532.2	436.3	350.4	279.5	163.2
	54936	279.2	328.8	452.6	508.0	527.5	558.4	585.4	554.1	466.1	360.2	282.4	196.4
平均		265.5	302.0	394.1	431.4	491.4	525.8	557.2	512.0	450.9	358.3	274.6	168.9

1. 公路交通基础设施所在地区的太阳能资源状况

按照我国光资源区的划分，概算公路系统交通基础设施对应的可利用资源分布情况。由于高速公路整体数据较为庞大，本报告此处采用京沪高速公路(G2)为典型案例开展定量分析研究，测算光伏资源的分布情况，并以此为依据测算其他线路情况。

按照我国光资源区的划分，首都辐射线大多数位于光资源Ⅱ、Ⅲ区，北南纵线和东西横线大部分位于光资源Ⅰ区，部分位于Ⅲ区。具体分布情况见表1-3。

表1-3　我国国道的光资源区域分布

光资源区域	首都辐射线	北南纵线	东西横线
Ⅰ	G109～G111	G207～G219、G227	G301～G307、G309～G310、G312～G318
Ⅱ	G101～G112	G201～G203、G220～G222	G301～G310、G316～G318
Ⅲ	G103～G108	G204～G207、G223～G225	G318～G343

2. 铁路交通基础设施所在地区的太阳能资源状况

按照我国风、光资源区的划分，概算铁路系统交通基础设施对应的可利用资源分布情况。由于电气化铁路整体数据较为庞大，本报告此处以京沪高铁为典型案例开展定量分析研究，测算光伏资源的分布情况，并以此为依据测算其他线路情况。表1-4为京沪高速铁路线路月均总辐射量的平均值[①]。

表1-4　京沪高速铁路线路月均总辐射量

省(区、市)	观测站区站号	月均总辐射量/(MJ/m^2)											
		一月	二月	三月	四月	五月	六月	七月	八月	九月	十月	十一月	十二月
北京	54511	248.2	306.7	470.8	489.6	631.7	443.7	565.4	518.8	428.6	366.9	282.7	151.7
河北	54539	243.2	315.1	459.7	525.3	657.1	557.7	600.5	568.7	466.7	366.6	266.5	191.8
天津	54527	302.5	355.3	502.6	509.6	633.4	528.4	586.2	546.4	4542	370.5	268.6	152.6
山东	54764	273.7	344.4	488.7	579.1	614.7	650.6	543.5	549.5	507.9	333.3	268.7	206.2
江苏	58144	265.6	316.7	375.6	414.7	441.7	562.8	553.2	562.1	458.3	365.1	289.6	195.0
上海	58362	260.2	294.0	279.0	282.5	335.5	460.0	463.9	404.9	414.7	313.1	254.1	144.8
平均		265.5	302.0	394.01	431.4	491.4	525.8	557.2	512.0	450.9	358.3	274.6	168.9

1.2　我国陆路交通系统资产能源化应用潜力分析

1.2.1　我国陆路交通基础设施拥有的光伏资源量分析

对于陆路交通系统中的公路系统，本报告分别按照高速公路、国道、省道三

① 本书中表格中数据稍有出入是因为在计算过程中不同的步骤有四舍五入。

类道路类型测算其太阳能可利用潜力；对于铁路系统，分别按照电气化铁路、非电气化铁路类型测算其太阳能可利用潜力。

1）公路系统

（1）对于高速公路，按下述三种利用方式进行评估。

方式一：保守测算，即在道路两侧边坡、边沟上铺设光伏设备。

方式二：一般测算，即在道路两侧边坡、边沟上及服务区70%的面积铺设光伏设备。

方式三：乐观测算，即在高速公路两侧边坡、边沟上及服务区的所有面积都铺设光伏设备；道路上方全部铺设光伏隧道。

（2）对于国道，按下述四种利用方式进行评估。

方式一：保守测算，即在道路两侧各铺设0.5m的光伏设备。

方式二：一般测算1，即在道路两侧各铺设0.75m的光伏设备。

方式三：一般测算2，即在道路两侧各铺设1m的光伏设备。

方式四：乐观测算，即在道路两侧各铺设1m的光伏设备，道路上方全部铺设光伏隧道。

（3）对于省道，按下述四种利用方式进行评估。

方式一：保守测算，即在道路两侧各铺设0.25m的光伏设备。

方式二：一般测算1，即在道路两侧各铺设0.5m的光伏设备。

方式三：一般测算2，即在道路两侧各铺设0.75m的光伏设备。

方式四：乐观测算，即在道路两侧各铺设0.75m的光伏设备，道路上方全部铺设光伏隧道。

2）铁路系统

（1）对于电气化铁路，按下述三种利用方式进行评估。

方式一：保守测算，即在电气化铁路沿线两侧6m范围内铺设光伏设备、高铁站70%的面积铺设光伏设备。

方式二：一般测算，即在电气化铁路沿线两侧10m范围内铺设光伏设备、高铁站的全部面积都铺设光伏设备。

方式三：乐观测算，即在电气化铁路沿线两侧10m范围内铺设光伏设备、高铁站的全部建筑面积铺设光伏设备；铁路上方铺设光伏隧道。

（2）对于非电气化铁路，按下述四种利用方式进行评估。

方式一：一般测算1（双线），即在非电气化铁路沿线两侧共铺设10m光伏设备。

方式二：一般测算2（单线），即在非电气化铁路沿线两侧共铺设10m光伏设备。

方式三：乐观测算 1(双线)，即在非电气化铁路沿线两侧共铺设 10m 的光伏设备，同时轨道上方铺设宽度为 13m 的光伏隧道。

方式四：乐观测算 2(单线)，即在非电气化铁路沿线两侧共铺设 10m 的光伏设备，同时轨道上方铺设宽度为 7m 的光伏隧道。

基于以上各种利用方式，本报告装机容量采用国土资源部 2015 年发布的《光伏发电站工程项目用地控制指标》文件为依据进行测算，其中，“安装方式”指不同的光伏设备安装排列方式/工作模式；“并网电压等级”指光伏输出电能升压并网外送的电压等级。

1. 公路交通基础设施拥有的光伏资源量分析

在效率选取 30%，安装方式采取斜单轴跟踪式，电压等级采取 110kV 的情况下，京沪高速公路、京哈高速公路、京藏高速公路、京新高速公路及全国高速公路的典型日可发电量如表 1-5 所示。

表 1-5　我国高速公路系统在利用方式二下典型日可发电量　（单位：10MW · h）

高速公路线	1 月	4 月	7 月	10 月
京沪高速公路	73	144	183	117
京哈高速公路	31	83	102	54
京藏高速公路	85	193	223	142
京新高速公路	58	153	195	112
全国高速公路	4774	11310	14276	8376

由表 1-5 可知，若采用利用方式二，则全国高速公路的日可发电量最高达 142.76GW · h，年可发电量约为 25178GW · h。

当采用利用方式三时，京沪高速公路、京哈高速公路、京藏高速公路、京新高速公路及全国高速公路的典型日可发电量如表 1-6 所示。

表 1-6　我国高速公路系统在利用方式三下典型日可发电量　（单位：10MW · h）

高速公路线	1 月	4 月	7 月	10 月
京沪高速公路	486	960	1222	781
京哈高速公路	257	700	857	455
京藏高速公路	601	1365	1575	1007
京新高速公路	441	1157	1474	842
全国高速公路	37925	87685	107635	64715

由表 1-6 可知：若采用利用方式三，则全国高速公路的日可发电量最高可达 1076.35GW · h，年可发电量约为 193674GW · h。

2. 铁路交通基础设施拥有的光伏资源量分析

我国高速铁路在利用方式二下的典型日可发电量如表 1-7 所示。

表 1-7　我国高速铁路在利用方式二下的典型日可发电量　（单位：100GW·h）

铁路线	1 月	4 月	7 月	10 月
京沪客运专线	0.0599	0.0874	0.1200	0.0815
京港客运专线	0.1182	0.1725	0.2369	0.1609
京哈客运专线	0.0635	0.0926	0.1272	0.0864
杭福深客运专线	0.0749	0.1093	0.1501	0.1019
徐兰客运专线	0.0720	0.1050	0.1442	0.0979
沪昆客运专线	0.1096	0.1599	0.2196	0.1491
青太客运专线	0.0414	0.0604	0.0830	0.0563
沪汉蓉客运专线	0.0966	0.1409	0.1935	0.1314
全国电气化铁路可发电总量	3.9534	5.7684	7.9200	5.3790

由表 1-7 可知：若采用利用方式二，则我国高速铁路的日可发电量最高达 792GW·h，年可发电量约为 170316.3GW·h。

我国高速铁路在利用方式三下的典型日可发电量如表 1-8 所示。

表 1-8　我国高速铁路在利用方式三下的典型日可发电量　（单位：100GW·h）

铁路线	1 月	4 月	7 月	10 月
京沪客运专线	0.0659	0.0961	0.1320	0.0897
京港客运专线	0.2216	0.3233	0.4439	0.3015
京哈客运专线	0.0610	0.0889	0.1221	0.0829
杭福深客运专线	0.0862	0.1258	0.1727	0.1173
徐兰客运专线	0.0793	0.1156	0.1588	0.1078
沪昆客运专线	0.1896	0.2766	0.3798	0.2579
青太客运专线	0.0245	0.0357	0.0491	0.0333
沪汉蓉客运专线	0.1461	0.2131	0.2926	0.1987
全国电气化铁路可发电总量	4.3494	6.3426	8.7120	5.9202

由表 1-8 可知，若采用利用方式三，则我国高速铁路的日可发电量最高达 871.2GW·h，年可发电量约为 274746.5GW·h。

采用利用方式一对我国非电气化铁路的典型日可发电量进行测算，结果如表 1-9 所示。

表 1-9　我国非电气化铁路在利用方式一下的典型日可发电量　　（单位：100GW·h）

铁路线	1 月	4 月	7 月	10 月
全国非电气化铁路	0.520	0.737	1.301	1.042

由表 1-9 可知：若采用利用方式一对全国非电气化铁路系统的太阳能潜力进行开发，则其日可发电量最高达 130.1GW·h，年可发电量约为 12820GW·h。

同理，当采用利用方式三时，全国非电气化铁路的典型日可发电量结果如表 1-10 所示。

表 1-10　我国非电气化铁路在利用方式三下的典型日可发电量　　（单位：100GW·h）

铁路线	1 月	4 月	7 月	10 月
全国非电气化铁路	1.180	1.672	2.951	2.364

由表 1-10 可知：若采用利用方式三对全国非电气化铁路系统的太阳能潜力进行开发，则其日可发电量最高达 295.1GW·h，年可发电量约为 29087GW·h。

对青藏铁路格拉段进行基础设施发电潜力测算。由于青藏铁路格拉段非电气化铁路的轨道铺设方式为单轨，因此本报告分别选用利用方式二和利用方式四进行测算，结果如表 1-11 和表 1-12 所示。

表 1-11　青藏铁路格拉段在利用方式二效率为 20%下典型日可发电量

月份	1 月	4 月	7 月	10 月
日可发电量/(10MW·h)	156.0	249.0	295.1	273.4

表 1-12　青藏铁路格拉段在利用方式四效率为 20%下典型日可发电量

月份	1 月	4 月	7 月	10 月
日可发电量/(10MW·h)	263.9	421.2	499.2	462.5

由表 1-11 可知：若采用利用方式二对青藏铁路格拉段的太阳能潜力进行开发，则其日可发电量最高达 2951MW·h，年可发电量约为 767.3GW·h。

由表 1-12 可知：若采用利用方式四对青藏铁路格拉段的太阳能潜力进行开发，则其日可发电量最高达 4992MW·h，年可发电量约为 1297.9GW·h。

1.2.2　我国陆路交通系统年运行耗电总量分析

1. 公路交通系统年运行耗电总量分析

在当前情况下，我国高速公路的典型日耗电量如表 1-13 所示。

表 1-13 我国高速公路的典型日耗电量 (单位：10MW·h)

高速公路线	1月	4月	7月	10月
京沪高速公路	29.63	23.77	32.07	25.52
京哈高速公路	25.14	19.29	27.59	21.04
京藏高速公路	29.54	22.37	32.45	24.49
京新高速公路	30.03	23.61	32.63	25.52
全国总耗能	2504.95	1953.04	2732.98	2117.52

2. 铁路交通系统年运行耗电总量分析

在当前情况下，我国高速铁路的典型日耗电量如表 1-14 所示。

表 1-14 我国高速铁路的典型日耗电量 (单位：100GW·h)

铁路线	1月	4月	7月	10月
京沪客运专线	0.0425	0.0284	0.0498	0.0325
京港客运专线	0.0655	0.0438	0.0768	0.0501
京哈客运专线	0.0567	0.0379	0.0664	0.0433
杭福深客运专线	0.1133	0.0757	0.1328	0.0867
徐兰客运专线	0.0514	0.0343	0.0602	0.0393
沪昆客运专线	0.0939	0.0627	0.1100	0.0718
青太客运专线	0.0460	0.0308	0.0540	0.0352
沪汉蓉客运专线	0.0478	0.0320	0.0560	0.0366
全国总耗能	2.5500	1.7040	2.9880	1.9500

1.2.3 我国陆路交通系统资产能源化潜力分析

1. 公路交通系统资产能源化潜力分析

当采用利用方式二时，京沪高速公路、京哈高速公路、京藏高速公路、京新高速公路及全国高速公路的典型日经时自洽率、总自洽率和最大电能时移率结果分别如表 1-15～表 1-17 所示。

表 1-15 我国高速公路系统在利用方式二下的典型日经时自洽率 (单位：%)

高速公路线	1月	4月	7月	10月
京沪高速公路	48.57	62.16	62.86	54.75
京哈高速公路	46.90	61.63	61.55	54.15
京藏高速公路	48.79	62.65	63.48	54.79
京新高速公路	48.04	62.25	63.01	54.74
全国高速公路	48.08	62.17	62.73	54.61

表 1-16　我国高速公路系统在利用方式二下的典型日总自洽率　（单位：%）

高速公路线	1 月	4 月	7 月	10 月
京沪高速公路	246.09	605.46	571.39	458.74
京哈高速公路	121.74	432.59	369.84	257.23
京藏高速公路	287.42	862.11	685.77	580.55
京新高速公路	194.63	650.03	599.03	437.71
全国高速公路	212.47	637.55	556.51	433.56

表 1-17　我国高速公路系统在利用方式二下的典型日最大电能时移率　（单位：%）

高速公路线	1 月	4 月	7 月	10 月
京沪高速公路	80.82	89.58	89.07	88.03
京哈高速公路	61.48	85.75	83.36	78.95
京藏高速公路	83.02	92.73	90.74	90.56
京新高速公路	75.32	90.42	89.48	87.49
全国高速公路	77.37	90.25	88.73	87.40

同理，采用利用方式三时，京沪高速公路、京哈高速公路、京藏高速公路、京新高速公路及全国高速公路在当前条件下的典型日经时自洽率、总自洽率和最大电能时移率结果分别如表 1-18～表 1-20 所示。

表 1-18　我国高速公路系统在利用方式三下的典型日经时自洽率　（单位：%）

高速公路线	1 月	4 月	7 月	10 月
京沪高速公路	50.08	64.52	66.80	55.94
京哈高速公路	49.94	64.48	66.78	55.31
京藏高速公路	50.18	64.71	66.84	55.95
京新高速公路	50.04	64.60	66.83	55.94
全国高速公路	50.06	64.58	66.81	55.79

表 1-19　我国高速公路系统在利用方式三下的典型日总自洽率　（单位：%）

高速公路线	1 月	4 月	7 月	10 月
京沪高速公路	1640.92	4037.18	3810.02	3058.82
京哈高速公路	1021.97	3631.35	3104.64	2164.07
京藏高速公路	2034.44	6102.19	4853.99	4109.27
京新高速公路	1467.17	4900.32	4515.84	3299.75
全国高速公路	1541.13	4667.76	4071.12	3157.98

表 1-20　我国高速公路系统在利用方式三下的典型日最大电能时移率　（单位：%）

高速公路线	1 月	4 月	7 月	10 月
京沪高速公路	96.91	98.44	98.28	98.20
京哈高速公路	95.11	98.22	97.85	97.44
京藏高速公路	97.53	98.94	98.62	98.64
京新高速公路	96.59	98.68	98.52	98.30
全国高速公路	96.75	98.62	98.36	98.23

2. 铁路交通系统资产能源化潜力分析

若我国四纵四横高速铁路系统采取利用方式二，整个高速铁路系统的经时自洽率、总自洽率和最大电能时移率，结果如表 1-21～表 1-23 所示。

表 1-21　我国主要高速铁路及全国电气化铁路在利用方式二下的经时自洽率　（单位：%）

铁路线	1 月	4 月	7 月	10 月
京沪客运专线	45.88	63.50	64.00	63.07
京港客运专线	55.77	72.76	78.84	70.32
京哈客运专线	33.04	43.10	46.70	41.65
杭福深客运专线	19.80	25.83	27.98	24.96
徐兰客运专线	41.82	54.56	59.12	52.73
沪昆客运专线	35.94	46.88	50.80	45.31
青太客运专线	25.05	32.68	35.41	31.58
沪汉蓉客运专线	61.68	80.47	87.19	77.76
全国电气化铁路	41.20	52.23	56.00	50.40

表 1-22　我国主要高速铁路及全国电气化铁路在利用方式二下的总自洽率　（单位：%）

铁路线	1 月	4 月	7 月	10 月
京沪客运专线	141.17	318.99	281.12	250.00
京港客运专线	180.47	394.06	308.54	321.10
京哈客运专线	112.05	244.67	191.58	199.37
杭福深客运专线	66.09	144.32	113.00	117.60
徐兰客运专线	140.13	305.98	239.58	249.33
沪昆客运专线	116.77	254.97	199.64	207.77
青太客运专线	89.95	196.41	153.79	160.04
沪汉蓉客运专线	201.99	441.05	345.34	359.39
全国电气化铁路	131.08	284.84	229.00	233.08

表 1-23　我国主要高速铁路及全国电气化铁路在利用方式二下的最大电能时移率

（单位：%）

铁路线	1 月	4 月	7 月	10 月
京沪客运专线	67.44	80.09	73.50	74.84
京港客运专线	69.09	81.53	74.45	78.10
京哈客运专线	70.52	82.38	75.62	79.11
杭福深客运专线	70.05	82.10	75.24	78.78
徐兰客运专线	70.16	82.17	75.32	78.85
沪昆客运专线	69.23	81.61	74.55	78.19
青太客运专线	72.15	83.36	76.98	80.27
沪汉蓉客运专线	69.46	81.76	74.75	78.36
全国电气化铁路	68.83	81.78	76.00	78.51

当采用利用方式三时，我国主要高速铁路系统的经时自洽率、总自洽率和最大电能时移率计算结果如表 1-24～表 1-26 所示。

表 1-24　我国主要高速铁路及全国电气化铁路在利用方式三下的经时自洽率　（单位：%）

铁路线	1 月	4 月	7 月	10 月
京沪客运专线	55.06	71.53	77.71	69.23
京港客运专线	66.93	87.32	94.61	84.38
京哈客运专线	39.64	51.72	56.04	49.98
杭福深客运专线	23.76	30.99	33.58	29.95
徐兰客运专线	50.19	65.47	70.94	63.27
沪昆客运专线	43.12	56.26	60.96	54.37
青太客运专线	30.06	39.21	42.49	37.89
沪汉蓉客运专线	74.01	93.56	96.63	90.31
全国电气化铁路	47.85	62.42	68.00	60.32

表 1-25　我国主要高速铁路及全国电气化铁路在利用方式三下的总自洽率　（单位：%）

铁路线	1 月	4 月	7 月	10 月
京沪客运专线	155.04	350.72	265.06	276.00
京港客运专线	338.21	738.48	578.22	601.75
京哈客运专线	132.58	264.90	205.93	231.41
杭福深客运专线	76.04	166.04	130.01	135.30
徐兰客运专线	154.34	337.00	263.87	274.60
沪昆客运专线	201.98	441.01	345.31	359.36
青太客运专线	112.20	210.16	180.95	200.65
沪汉蓉客运专线	305.47	666.99	522.25	543.50
全国电气化铁路	173.98	379.89	297.00	309.55

表 1-26 我国主要高速铁路及全国电气化铁路在利用方式三下的最大电能时移率

（单位：%）

铁路线	1月	4月	7月	10月
京沪客运专线	64.49	79.60	70.68	74.91
京港客运专线	80.21	88.18	83.64	85.98
京哈客运专线	63.15	77.98	69.53	73.89
杭福深客运专线	68.76	81.34	74.17	77.86
徐兰客运专线	67.48	80.57	73.11	76.96
沪昆客运专线	78.65	87.24	82.35	84.87
青太客运专线	43.50	66.24	53.28	59.96
沪汉蓉客运专线	75.77	85.52	79.97	82.83
全国电气化铁路	67.75	80.73	73.00	77.15

若采用利用方式一，我国非电气化铁路的经时自洽率、总自洽率和最大电能时移率如表 1-27 所示。

表 1-27 我国非电气化铁路在利用方式一下的经时自洽率、总自洽率、最大电能时移率

月份	1月	4月	7月	10月
经时自洽率 η/%	59.09	60.13	70.71	54.33
总自洽率 μ/%	474.7	807.3	678.5	620.3
最大电能时移率 γ_{max} /%	86.39	92.50	89.28	91.33

若采用利用方式三，我国非电气化铁路的经时自洽率、总自洽率和最大电能时移率如表 1-28 所示。

表 1-28 我国非电气化铁路在利用方式三下的经时自洽率、总自洽率、最大电能时移率

月份	1月	4月	7月	10月
经时自洽率 η/%	73.61	62.47	75.52	55.92
总自洽率 μ/%	1077	1832	1539	1407
最大电能时移率 γ_{max} /%	92.57	96.54	94.80	96.12

同理，若采用利用方式二，青藏铁路格拉段的经时自洽率、总自洽率和最大电能时移率如表 1-29 所示。

表 1-29 我国非电气化铁路在利用方式二下的经时自洽率、总自洽率、最大电能时移率

月份	1月	4月	7月	10月
经时自洽率 η/%	68.59	62.12	66.02	55.04
总自洽率 μ/%	836.9	1603	594.5	956.5
最大电能时移率 γ_{max} /%	91.04	96.08	88.60	94.34

同理，若采用利用方式四，青藏铁路格拉段的经时自洽率、总自洽率和最大电能时移率如表 1-30 所示。

表 1-30　我国非电气化铁路在利用方式四下的经时自洽率、总自洽率、最大电能时移率

月份	1 月	4 月	7 月	10 月
经时自洽率 η/%	79.77	63.76	75.49	56.20
总自洽率 μ/%	1416	2712	1531	1618
最大电能时移率 γ_{max} /%	93.92	97.60	94.77	96.62

第2章　能源网布局

2.1　我国电网布局

2.1.1　骨干输电网

我国的骨干输电网是全国性的统一网络。我国国土面积广，资源的分布极其不平衡，火电容量集中在山西、内蒙古、陕西、宁夏、黑龙江、贵州和安徽等省(区)，并且能源和负荷中心的分布并不统一。未来较长时间内，我国的电力需求将持续较快增长，2030年、2050年全国全社会用电量将分别达到10^7GW·h和1.2×10^7GW·h左右，但负荷中心仍在东中部，全国电力需求格局基本不变。基于我国一次资源构成和分布特点，西部能源和电力基地的重要性将日益突出，西电东送的基本格局也将长期不变。

从电力流向看，中国的电力负荷和能源资源不平衡特点决定了在本地平衡的基础上西电东送、南北互济的长期格局，远距离输电的电力潮流主要来自西部、西北部和北部地区的水电、煤电、风电及太阳能发电基地。东北电网覆盖的蒙东地区有丰富的煤炭资源，可以借助本网资源优势以及核电和可再生能源建设满足本地需要，并有外送的电力流。而骨干输电网可以实现跨区域输电，即将发电富余地区的电能输送到电力匮乏的地区，提高能源利用效率。

高压直流输电能够更好地实现长距离、大容量的输电，因此我国各地区的骨干电网大量地采用高压输电技术。我国高压输电布局的主要要求是“西电东送，南北互供”，目前已建成“八交十直”特高压工程，例如，平顶山—武汉，青海官亭—甘肃兰州，晋东南—南阳—荆门，淮南—皖南—浙北—沪西等，而“四交一直”工程正在建设。预计将建成“五纵五横”特高压交流骨干网架和特高压输电工程，华北、华中、华东地区内将形成更大规模的大区特高压电网，大区电网之间联系进一步加强；蒙西、陕北、晋东南、内蒙古锡林郭勒盟、宁夏、关中煤电基地通过特高压电网和特高压直流输电系统实现“北电南送”；西部水电通过特高压交流电网和特高压直流输电系统实现“西电东送”。

我国骨干电网的总体布局表现为东部地区的骨干输电网结构比较坚强，电网末端主要分布在西北部，四川西部、青海西部、新疆南部和西藏等地区基本没有骨干输电网网架。西北部电网末端的电网结构十分薄弱，难以适应大规模可再生能源并网、远距离传输的要求，随机的、不稳定的可再生能源所造成的电压、频率波动会对电网电压的质量造成不良影响，严重时会危害电网的安全稳定运行。

2.1.2 区域电网

在我国，目前主要有西北电网、西南电网、华北电网、华东电网、华中电网、东北电网以及南方电网七大区域电网(图2-1)。区域电网分布在城市和乡村的广大地区，将各个发电厂联系在一起，有各种形式的网络结构和较长的输电线路。西北电网覆盖地域广阔，东西、南北跨度大，电网输送距离远，而华北地区、华东地区用电需求较大，电网也相对较为密集，而西藏地区基本无电网覆盖。

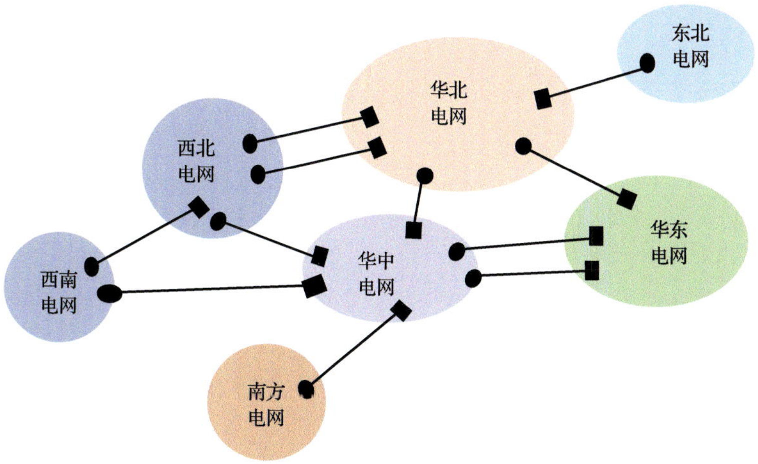

图2-1 我国七大区域电网

华北电网覆盖地区是主要负荷中心之一，在主要依靠本地煤电的同时，可接受东北电网和西北电网东部地区部分电力。西北电网覆盖区域的煤炭、水能、风能和太阳能资源丰富，而负荷相对较轻，需要外送电力。华中电网主要依靠西部水电提供新增发电容量，网内电力流主要是承接西部、输送东部水电和其他电力。华东电网是主要负荷中心，具有接受西部水电、煤电、风电、太阳能发电的需求和潜力。南方电网主要从西部向东部输送西南地区的水电，远期可能接受西藏及周边国家水电。

(1)西北电网：2017年末，西北五省区调度口径装机7144台(座)，容量为238657.14MW，其中火电为125649.7MW，占总装机容量的52.64%；水电为30974.77MW，占总装机容量的12.98%；风电为45593.2MW，占总装机容量的19.10%；光伏为34987.24MW，占总装机容量的14.66%；其他为1441.2MW，占总装机容量的0.6%。

西北电网600MW及以上大容量机组共计60台(含国调直调)，容量为40700MW，占总装机容量的17.05%。

直接接入750kV及以上输电网络的机组为23800MW(含国调直调)，占总装机容量的 9.97%；直接接入 330(500)kV 输电网络的机组为 65215MW，占总装机容量的 27.33%；直接接入 220kV 网络的机组为 55394.6MW，占总装机容量的 23.21%；直接接入 110kV 及以下网络的机组为 94248.45MW，占总装机容量的 39.49%。

各省(区)装机容量分别为陕西 43765.8MW，占总装机容量的 18.34%；甘肃 46906MW，占总装机容量的 19.65%；青海 25565.1MW，占总装机容量的 10.71%；宁夏 40221.4MW，占总装机容量的 16.85%；新疆 82198.9MW，占总装机容量的 34.45%。(其中西北网调直调 28760MW，占总装机容量的 12.05%)。

截至 2017 年底，西北五省区系统 220kV 及以上降压变压器变电容量为 361001MV·A，其中 750kV 变压器容量为 149600MV·A(49 站 84 变压器，其中含有 3 个 750kV 直流换流站)，330kV 降压变压器变电容量为 136485MV·A。西北电网 220kV 及以上交流输电线路长度为 73815.377km(1554 条)，其中 750kV 线路长度为 18669.097km(126 条)，330kV 线路长度为 30960.91km (731 条)。

(2) 西南电网：西南电网区域包括四川省、重庆市和西藏自治区，区域面积约为 177 万 km^2，覆盖人口 1.15 亿人。西南电网是中国最大的清洁能源送端电网，东联华东电网和华中电网、北接西北电网，其中：与华东电网通过±800kV 复奉、锦苏、宾金三大特高压直流输电线路相联，总输电容量为 21600MW；与西北电网通过±500kV 德宝直流、±4002 柴拉直流相联，输电容量为 3600MW；与华中电网通过盘龙Ⅰ、Ⅱ线，张恩Ⅰ、Ⅱ线共四回 500kV 交流线路相联，断面最大外送能力为 2600MW；西藏电网分为藏中电网、昌都电网和阿里电网不相联的三个部分，昌都电网通过川藏联络线与四川电网相联。

截至 2017 年底，西南电网调度口径装机容量为 116GW。其中，水电为 82470MW(含国调直调机组)，占 71.3%；火电为 28360MW，占 24.5%；风电光伏等为 4860MW，占 4.2%。网内 500kV 变电站为 60 座，总变电容量为 1.08×10^8kV·A；500kV 线路 219 条，总长为 1.76 万 km。国网西南分部直调 500kV 线路 36 条，电厂 1 座(装机容量为 3300MW)。

2017 年，西南电网调度口径总发电量为 382270GW·h，较 2016 年增加 21930GW·h，同比增长 6.09%；西南电网调度口径用电量为 269490GW·h，较 2016 年增加 15460GW·h，同比增长 6.09%。

(3) 华北电网：截至 2017 年底，华北电网装机容量为 347350MW，最大负荷为 217090MW。华北及区域内各省(区、市)电网负荷均创历史新高。1000kV 变电站 13 座，变压器 23 台，变电容量为 69000MV·A；500kV 变电站 154 座，变压器 340 台，变电容量为 294807MV·A，1000kV 输电线路 26 条共 5431km；500kV 输电线路 500 条共 38792km。京津唐电网装机容量为 81240MW，最大负荷为 62840MW，500kV 变电站 40 座，变压器 91 台，变电容量为 89309MV·A；500kV 输电线路 149 条共 13939km。华北电网风电装机容量为 48030MW，占总装机容量 14.9%，最大风电电力为 28550MW，全年风电电量为 95100GW·h；京津唐电网风电装机容量为 11630MW，占总装机容量的 14.6%，最大风电电力为 7500MW，全年风电电量为 25900GW·h。

(4)华东电网：华东区域电网供电范围包括上海、江苏、浙江、安徽和福建，土地面积为 47.19 万 km^2，经济总量为 20.34 万亿元，供电人口为 2.61 亿人。

截至 2017 年底，华东电网装机容量为 348210MW，其中，火电装机容量为 259610MW，占 74.56%；水电装机容量为 30420MW，占 8.74%；核电装机容量为 17290MW，占 4.96%；风电及其他装机容量为 40890MW，占 11.74%。华东电网全社会用电量为 1556449GW·h，同比增长 6.72%；全网最高用电负荷为 275230MW，同比增长 8.38%，发生在 2017 年 7 月 25 日。华东电网累计发电量为 1375400GW·h，同比增长 5.53%。华东电网 1000kV 线路共 19 条，长度为 3289km，500kV 线路共 596 条，长度为 33087.8km。500kV 厂站共 232 座，其中变电站 157 座，开关站 3 座，电厂 72 座。500kV 变压器共 370 台，变电容量为 332950MV·A。

(5)华中电网：截至 2017 年底，华中电网调度口径装机容量为 216660MW，同比增加 15350MW，其中火电占 57%，水电占 29%，可再生能源及其他占 14%。调度口径机组发电量为 728000GW·h，同比增长 6.11%，其中火电发电量为 494600GW·h(占比 67.94%，同比增长 6.14%)，水电发电量为 209100GW·h(占比 28.72%，同比增长 1.59%)。

截至 2017 年底，华中电网 1000kV 交流输电线路 1 条，总长 359km；1000kV 变电站 2 座，变压器 4 台，变电容量为 12000MV·A；500kV 交流输电线路 363 条，总长为 26794km；500kV 变电站 112 座，变压器 188 台，变电容量为 162951MV·A。

(6)东北电网：截至 2017 年底，东北电网总装机容量为 139085.8MW。火电装机容量为 92511.8MW，约占总装机容量的 66.51%；水电装机容量为 8122.7MW，约占总装机容量的 5.84%；风电装机容量为 27621.7MW，约占总装机容量的 19.86%；核电装机容量为 4475.2MW，约占总装机容量的 3.22%；太阳能装机容量为 6354.4MW，约占总装机容量的 4.57%。2017 年东北电网总发电量为 463606GW·h，同比增加 5.10%；全社会用电量完成 435117GW·h，同比增加 4.59%；最大发电电力为 64560MW，同比增长 7.05%；500kV 线路长度为 19867.36km，500kV 变电容量为 106749000kV·A。

(7)南方电网：南方电网覆盖五省(区)，并与香港、澳门地区以及东南亚国家的电网相联，供电面积为 100 万 km^2。供电人口为 2.54 亿人，供电客户为 8741 万户。2018 年全网统调最高负荷为 169GW，增长 3.4%；全社会用电量为 1162800GW·h，增长 8.3%。南方电网东西跨度近 2000km，网内拥有水、煤、核、抽水蓄能、油、气、风力等多种电源，截至 2018 年底，全网总装机容量为 320GW(其中火电 160GW、水电 120GW、核电 16770MW、风电 18380MW，分别占 48.2%、

37.4%、5.1%、5.6%）；110kV 及以上变电容量为 9.8×10^{8}kV·A，输电线路总长度为 22.2 万 km。2018 年底全网非化石能源装机容量、发电量占比为 52.6%、51.5%。

图 2-2 为我国各地区电力概览。

(a) 各地区发电装机容量(单位：10MW)

(b) 各地区发电量(单位：100GW·h)

(c) 各地区新能源发电量(单位：100GW·h)

(d) 各地区用电量(单位：100GW·h)

图 2-2　我国各地区电力概览

不含港澳台地区，部分地区由于数值较小未显示数据标签

2.2　光伏资源网

在众多可再生能源中，我国太阳能储能丰富，作为一种环保清洁的可再生能源，太阳能还具有光照充足、长寿、分布广泛、安全、清洁等优点，使得太阳能光伏发电越来越广泛地应用于各行各业，它和风力发电已一并成为今后重点开发的可再生能源。据估算，我国每年平均获得的太阳能约为 1×10^{16}kW·h，相当于 1.2×10^{12}t 标准煤所具有的能量。且我国陆地每年接受太阳能辐射量约有 5×10^{16}MJ，全国太阳能年辐射量为 930.56～2325kW·h/m^2。根据各地区经纬度及气候差异，我国太阳能资源可分为四类地区，其中Ⅰ类区域年辐射量在 1750kW·h/m^2 以上，Ⅱ类区域年辐射量为 1400～1750kW·h/m^2，Ⅲ类区域年辐射量为 1050～1400kW·h/m^2，Ⅳ类区域年辐射量在 1050kW·h/m^2 以下。

由上述数据可知，我国太阳能资源分布的主要特点是西部地区年总辐射量高于东部地区，除西藏和新疆两个自治区外，基本呈现南部低于北部，辐射量以青藏高原为中心达到最高值，而以四川盆地为中心达到最低值。且由于南方多数地区云雾雨天较多，在北纬 30°～40°地区，太阳能的分布情况与一般的太阳能随纬度而变化的规律相反，而是随着纬度的增加而增加。

第3章　交通网布局

3.1　公路网布局

3.1.1　高速公路网

我国高速公路建设起步于1984年，最早开工的是沈大高速公路，最早通车的是1988年10月31日的上海至嘉定高速公路，至2017年，中华人民共和国高速公路的通车里程已超过14万km，是世界上规模最大的高速公路系统。20世纪90年代后期，中华人民共和国政府实施积极的经济政策引导基础设施建设，对高速公路的资金投入执行倾斜政策，每年建成高速公路达到3000km以上。

中国地域辽阔，地形地貌差别极大，给高速公路的建设带来很大的挑战性。在初期，高速公路的建设从经济发达同时修建难度比较小的地区开始建设，而后随着国家经济社会的快速发展，我国高速公路规划共经历了四次制定和调整。

1992年制定的《国道主干线系统规划》计划建设省级高速公路体系，并指出我国高速公路网由5条纵向和7条横向共12条路线组成，简称“五纵七横”公路网，总规划里程约3.5万km，全部由二级公路以上的高等级公路组成，其中高速公路2.5万km。按规划，我国将在2010年前建成“五纵七横”高速公路网，其中纵向线分别为G010同三高速公路(黑龙江同江—海南三亚)、G020京福高速公路(北京—福建福州)、G030京珠高速公路(北京—广东珠海)、G040二河高速公路(内蒙古二连浩特—云南河口)、G050渝湛高速公路(重庆—广东湛江)，横向线分别为G015绥满高速公路(黑龙江绥芬河—内蒙古满洲里)、G025丹拉高速公路(辽宁丹东—西藏拉萨)、G035青银高速公路(山东青岛—宁夏银川)、G045连霍高速公路(江苏连云港—新疆霍尔果斯)、G055沪蓉高速公路(上海—四川成都)、G065沪瑞高速公路(上海—云南瑞丽)、G075衡昆高速公路(湖南衡阳—云南昆明)。五横七纵公路网建成后，将贯通首都北京和直辖市及各省(自治区)省会城市，将人口在100万以上的所有特大城市和人口在50万以上大城市中的93%连接起来，使贯通和连接的城市总数超过200个，覆盖的人口约为6亿人，占全国总人口的50%左右。

2001年制定的《国家重点干线公路规划》，是对《国道主干线系统规划》的补充，其规划方案由13条纵向线路和15条横向线路组成，总规模约为7.3万km，同时“五纵七横”高速公路线路的编号即告废止。在国家重点干线公路规划中，高速公路为 4.2 万 km，一级公路为 1.2 万 km，二级公路为 1.1 万 km，三级公路为 0.8 万 km，其中纵向具体线路为嘉荫至南平(含支线南通至嘉兴)、黑河至通化(含支线伊春至大庆)、加格达奇至锦州(含支线齐齐哈尔至白城)、天津至汕尾(含支线盐城至徐州)、东营至香港(含支线铜陵至九江)、阿荣旗至广州(含支线赤峰至承德)、太原至澳门(含支线新乡至晋城)、临汾至三亚(含支线海口经通什至三亚)、包头至友谊关、兰州至磨憨、张掖至打洛、阿勒泰至若羌、阿勒泰至拉孜，横向具体线路为长白山至阿尔山、集安至锡林浩特(含支线通化至阜新)、丹东至伊尔克斯坦、威海至乌海(含支线黄骅至石家庄)、青岛至红其拉甫(含支线西安至茫崖)、日照至南阳、上海至洛阳、上海至武威(含支线合肥至铜陵、六安至武汉)、杭州至兰州(含支线武汉至汉中)、成都至那曲、宁波至樟木(含支线金华至温州、广元至重庆、拉萨至错那)、泉州至毕节(含支线常德至永顺、泰和至邵阳)、厦门至昆明、汕头至昆明、汕尾至清水河(含支线玉林至山口)。国家重点干线公路将与国道主干线一起，共同构成一个总规模约 10.8 万 km 骨架公路网，其中东部地区为 2.7 万 km，中部地区为 3.0 万 km，西部地区为 5.1 万 km；骨架公路的平均间距缩小至 190km，其中东部地区为 90km，中部地区为 120km，西部地区为 300km。全国骨架公路网将覆盖全国所有的省会城市(直辖市、自治区首府)、人口在 50 万以上的大城市、地级市以及 95%的人口在 20 万～50 万的中等城市，覆盖人口约为 9 亿人，形成省际畅通、连接城市的快速公路网络。

2005 年制定的《国家高速公路网规划》采用放射线与纵横网格相结合的布局方案，形成由中心城市向外放射以及横贯东西、纵贯南北的大通道，布局方案由 7 条首都放射线、9 条南北纵线、18 条东西横线等组成，简称“7918”网，总规模约为 8.5 万 km，其中主线为 6.8 万 km，地区环线、联络线等其他路线约为 1.7 万 km。在本规划中，首都放射线包括北京—上海、北京—台北、北京—港澳、北京—昆明、北京—拉萨、北京—乌鲁木齐、北京—哈尔滨，南北纵向线包括鹤岗—大连、沈阳—海口、长春—深圳、济南—广州、大庆—广州、二连浩特—广州、包头—茂名、兰州—海口、银川—昆明，东西横向线包括绥芬河—满洲里、珲春—乌兰浩特、丹东—锡林浩特、荣成—乌海、青岛—银川、青岛—兰州、连云港—霍尔果斯、南京—洛阳、上海—西安、上海—成都、上海—重庆、杭州—瑞丽、上海—昆明、福州—银川、泉州—南宁、厦门—成都、汕头—昆明、广州—昆明。此外，规划方案还包括：辽中环线、成渝环线、海南环线、珠三角环线、杭州湾环线共 5 条地区性环线、2 段并行线和 30 余段联络线。本规划强化高速公路对于国土开发、区域协调以及社会经济发展的促进作用，贯彻国家经济发展战略，并覆盖地区的 GDP 占到全国总量的 85%以上，规划的实施将对促进经济增长、带动相关产业发展、扩大就业等做出重要贡献。

2013 年出台的《国家公路网规划(2013～2030 年)》为最近的一次调整。根据这份规划，国家高速公路网按照“实现有效连接、提升通道能力、强化区际联系、优化路网衔接”的思路，保持原国家高速公路网规划总体框架基本不变，补充连接新增 20 万以上城镇人口城市、地级行政中心、重要港口和重要国际运输通道，在运输繁忙的通道上布设平行路线，增设区际、省际通道和重要城际通道，适当增加有效提高路网运输效率的联络线。调整后的国家高速公路由 7 条首都放射线、11 条北南纵线、18 条东西横线以及地区环线、并行线、联络线等组成，简称“71118”网，约 11.8 万 km。此外，规划方案还有辽中环线、成渝环线、海南环线、珠三角环线、杭州湾环线、首都环线，共 6 条地区性环线，广澳高速、常台高速 2 段并行线以及 30 余段联络线。

中国各省(区、市)根据自身的需要，都分别制定了庞大的高速公路规划，其中包含地方高速公路和其境内的国家高速公路。地方高速公路的编号一般以 S 开头，以区别以 G 开头的国家高速公路。

随着《国家公路网规划(2013～2030 年)》的逐步实施，2018 年底我国累计建成高速公路里程达到 14.3 万 km，与 2011 年的 8.49 万 km 相比，增加了 68%，2011～2018 年的年平均增速为 6.7%。图 3-1 为 2011～2018 年高速公路里程。

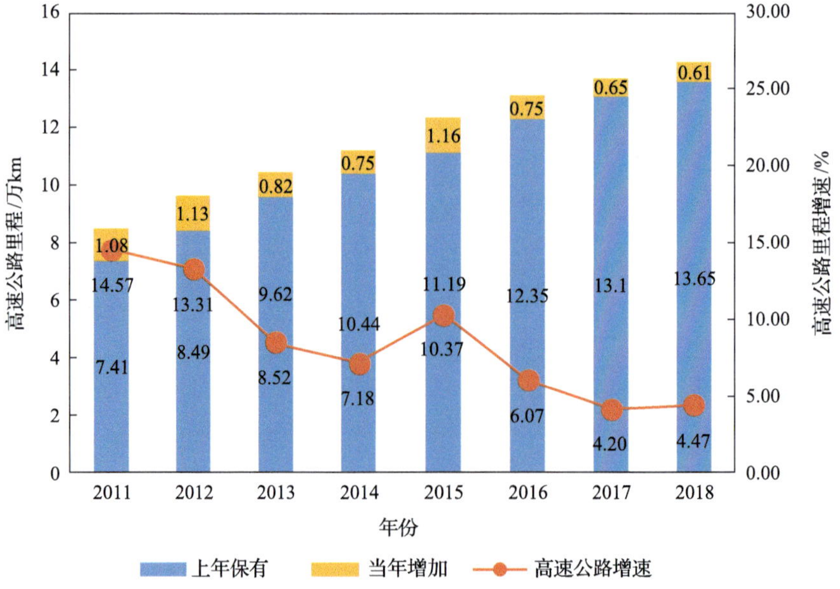

图 3-1 2011～2018 年高速公路里程

数据来源：《2011～2018 年交通运输行业发展统计公报》

广东省作为我国高速公路里程最多的省份，2009 年全省高速公路通车里程为 4100km，2010 年达到 5000km，2012 年通车里程达到 5500km，2013 年通车里程达到 5700km，2014 年、2015 年、2017 年分别突破 6000km、7000km、8000km。根据《广东省高速公路 2015 年至 2017 年建设计划及中远期规划》，预计到 2020 年，广东全省高速公路通车里程要达到 1.1 万 km，建成出省通道 30 条。

四川省 2017 年高速公路通车里程达到 6821km，位居全国第二位。《国家公路网规划(2013～2030 年)》颁布之后，国家高速公路在四川省境内规划路线由 8 条增至 22 条，规模由 3300km 涨到 8000km，格局巨变。《四川省高速公路网规划(2014～2030 年)》于 2014 年颁布，未来四川省形成了包括省境内国家高速公路在内的 16 条成都放射线、8 条纵线、8 条横线、4 条环线、19 条联络线的格局。规划线总里程 12000km，远期展望线 2200km，进出川高速公路通道增至 39 个，其中连接重庆 15 个、云南 11 个、陕西 4 个、贵州 3 个、甘肃 3 个、西藏 2 个、青海 1 个。表 3-1 为 2018 年我国各省(区、市)高速公路通车里程。

表 3-1 2018 年我国各省(区、市)高速公路通车里程

省(区、市)	里程/km	省(区、市)	里程/km	省(区、市)	里程/km
广东	8347	陕西	5279	青海	3223
四川	6821	广西	5259	吉林	3119
河北	6531	福建	5039	重庆	3023
河南	6523	云南	5022	宁夏	1609
湖南	6419	江苏	4688	天津	1248
内蒙古	6320	安徽	4673	北京	1013
湖北	6252	新疆	4578	上海	829
江西	5916	黑龙江	4512	海南	795
贵州	5835	辽宁	4212	西藏	38
山东	5821	浙江	4154	—	—
山西	5335	甘肃	4016	—	—

数据来源：《中国统计年鉴 2018》.

目前为止，除大都市的绕城高速公路与海南省外，我国的高速公路均为收费公路，小型车费率为 0.4～0.6 元/km，大车再乘上规定倍率。在 2017 年底，收费高速公路里程达 13.26 万 km，占当时通车里程的 97.14%。

3.1.2 普通国道网

国道是指具有全国政治、经济意义并由交通运输部规划的公路干线。国道按技术等级分为国家高速公路与普通国道两个系统，编号均以 G 开头。由于早期只有普通国道系统，而后来出现的国家高速公路的名称中也不含“国道”，因此本报告若无特别强调，国道通常指三位数字编号的普通国道。

1981 年 11 月经国务院授权，国家计划委员会、国家经济委员会和交通部联合发布《国家干线公路网(试行方案)》。方案规定国家干线公路(简称国道)由“12 射、28 纵、30 横”共 70 条路线组成。规划总里程约为 10.92 万 km，其中待建里程约为 5019km。可见，尽管高速公路承担了较大的通行流量，但国道并未废弃，仍是我国公路交通中的重要组成部分，并呈现一定的地区差异。在东部地区，国道大部分是一级公路和二级公路。在中西部地区，国道大部分是二级公路和二级以下公路。

2013 年，《国家公路网规划(2013～2030 年)》获国务院批准实施。新的普通国道网在 1981 年规划的“12 射、28 纵、30 横”基础上扩至“12 射、47 纵、60 横”共 119 条路线，另增加 81 条联络线。规划总里程增至 26.5 万 km，其中利用原国道 10.4 万 km、原省道 12.4 万 km、原县乡道 2.9 万 km，另需新建约 0.8 万 km。扩展重点在西部地区和欠发达地区。《国家公路网规划(2013～2030 年)》在原有国道基础上，将改扩建、新建北南纵线国道 27 条、20 条，改扩建、新建东西横线国道 29 条、31 条，新建联络线 81 条。

随着《国家公路网规划(2013～2030 年)》的逐步实施，2018 年底我国累计建成国道 36.30 万 km，与 2011 年的 16.94 万 km 相比，增加了 114.3%，2011～2018 年间的年平均增速为 11.5%。图 3-2 为 2011～2015 年普通国道里程。

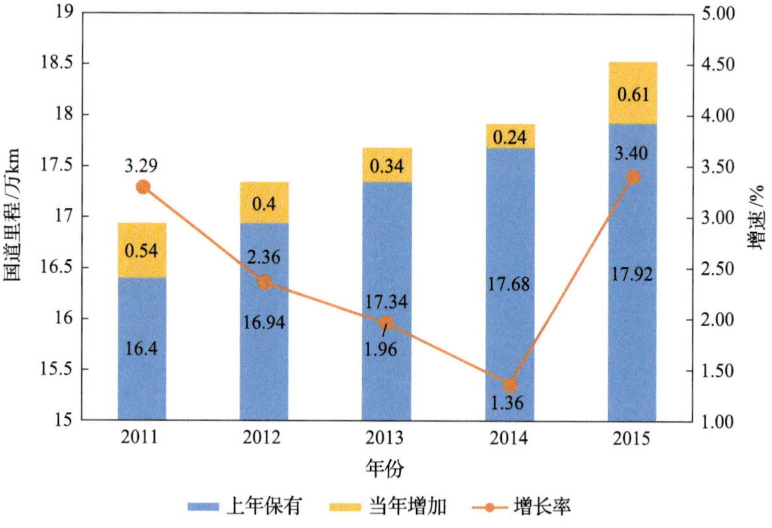

图 3-2　2011～2015 年普通国道里程

数据来源：《2011～2015 年交通运输行业发展统计公报》

我国是一个地形崎岖的国家，山地、高原和丘陵约占陆地面积的 67%，山脉、河流众多，海域辽阔。复杂多样的地形给交通运输的发展造成了巨大阻碍。在初期，高速公路的建设从经济发达同时修建难度比较小的地区开始建设，为实现成网的要求，建设重点也向地形复杂的地区转移，长大隧道及高跨、长跨桥梁占的比例也越来越大。表 3-2 为我国隧道数量和里程。

表 3-2 我国隧道数量和里程

年份	公路隧道		特长隧道		长隧道	
	数量/处	长度/万 m	数量/处	长度/万 m	数量/处	长度/万 m
2011	8522	625.34	326	143.32	1504	251.84
2012	10022	805.27	441	198.48	1944	330.44
2013	11359	960.56	562	250.69	2303	393.62
2014	12404	1075.67	626	276.62	2623	447.54
2015	14006	1268.39	744	329.98	3138	537.68
2016	15181	1403.97	815	362.27	3520	604.55
2017	16229	1528.51	902	401.32	3841	659.93
2018	17738	1723.61	1058	470.66	4315	742.18

数据来源：交通运输部。

随着隧道技术的不断发展，现代公路建设中，已广泛采用挖掘隧道的方式穿越山岭、河流和海底，以缩短线路里程，提高道路技术标准，公路隧道已成为一种重要的交通基础设施。中国的公路隧道按长度分为四类：特长隧道（$L>3000\text{m}$）、长隧道（$1000\text{m}\leqslant L\leqslant 3000\text{m}$）、中隧道（$250\text{m}<L<1000\text{m}$）、短隧道（$L\leqslant 250\text{m}$）。我国公路隧道数量从 2011 年的 8522 处增加到 2018 年的 17738 处，而公路隧道总长度从 2011 年的 625.34 万 m 增加到 2018 年的 1723.61 万 m，年平均增速约为 15.6%。截至 2018 年，我国现有公路隧道 17738 处、1723.61 万 m，其中特长隧道 1058 处、470.66 万 m，长隧道 4315 处、742.18 万 m。

图 3-3 给出了我国已建成和在建的长度在 5km 以上特长隧道分布情况，其中四川省、云南省、陕西省分居前三位。四川省作为拥有超过 5km 的特长隧道条数最多和里程最长的省份，共拥有长度超过 5km 的特长隧道 33 条，隧道总长度为 240.99km；云南省拥有长度超过 5km 的特长隧道 21 条，隧道总长度为 156.29km，居全国第二位，仅为四川省特长隧道总长度的 65.0%；陕西省拥有长度超过 5km 的特长隧道 17 条，隧道总长度为 142.35km，居全国第三位。

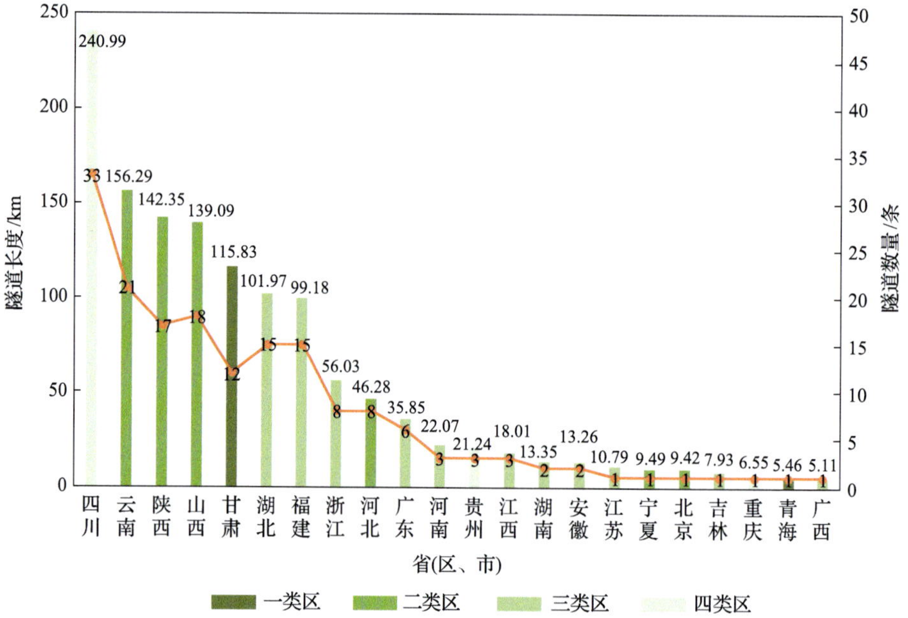

图 3-3　我国已建成和在建 5km 以上特长隧道

表 3-3 给出了长度排名前十的公路隧道，主要集中在太行山、秦岭、横断山脉地区，分别为位于陕西省的秦岭终南山隧道、位于四川省的锦屏山隧道、位于陕西省的米仓山隧道、位于山西省的西山隧道、位于四川省的二郎山隧道、位于山西省的虹梯关隧道、位于甘肃省的麦积山隧道、位于山西省的云山隧道、位于陕西省的包家山隧道、位于山西省的宝塔山隧道。其中，秦岭终南山隧道是我国第一长双洞公路隧道，也是亚洲第二长公路隧道、世界第三长公路隧道，位于包茂高速 G65 包头至北海段在陕西境内的西康高速公路北段，隧道穿越秦岭山脉的终南山，隧道长 18.020km。锦屏山隧道由两条长约 17.5km 的平行单车道隧道组成，并且也是国内第一、世界第二的深埋隧道，该隧道最大埋深为 2375m，埋深大于 1500m 的隧道段占总长的 73.1%。图 3-4 为我国构建 5km 以上的特长隧道。

表 3-3　我国十大公路隧道

隧道	长度/m	位置	隧道	长度/m	位置
终南山隧道	18020	G65 包茂高速	虹梯关隧道	13122	S76 平长高速
锦屏山隧道	17504	锦屏水电站内	麦积山隧道	12290	G30 连霍高速
米仓山隧道	13833	G85 银昆高速	云山隧道	11408	G2516 东吕高速
西山隧道	13654	S56 太古高速	包家山隧道	11200	G65 包茂高速
二郎山隧道	13469	G4218 雅叶高速	宝塔山隧道	10480	G2516 东吕高速

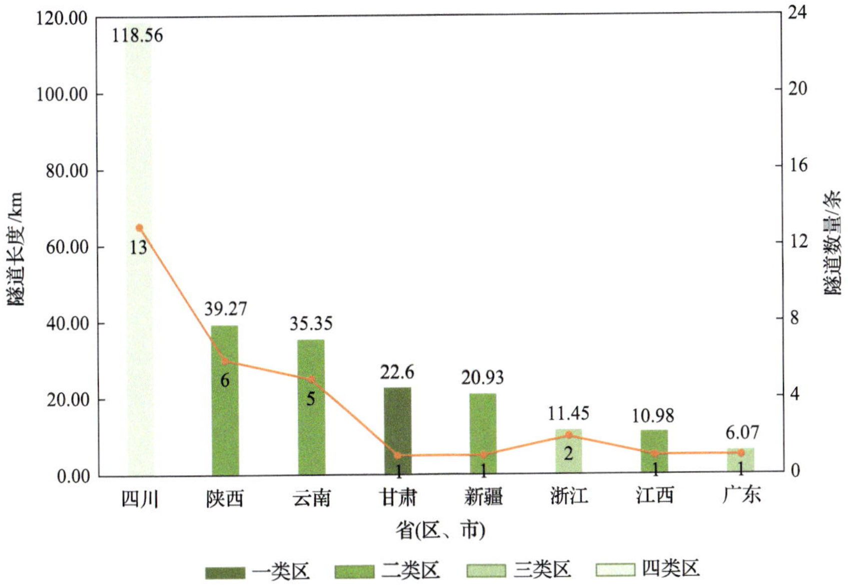

图 3-4 我国拟建 5km 以上的特长隧道

随着《国家公路网规划(2013～2030 年)》的逐步实施，我国公路联网规模持续扩大。现阶段，我国规划拟建设的长度在 5km 以上特长隧道共计 30 条，里程为 265.21km，超过 2018 年我国现有长度在 5km 以上的特长隧道总里程。我国拟建设的长度在 5km 以上特长隧道主要集中在陕川滇地区，三地区拟建设长度在 5km 以上特长隧道有 24 条，总里程达到 193.18km，约占总建设里程的 72.8%。四川省拟建设长度在 5km 以上特长隧道有 13 条，里程达到 118.56km，约占全国拟建设长度在 5km 以上特长隧道总里程的一半。陕西省、云南省拟建设长度在 5km 以上特长隧道分别为 6 条、5 条，里程分别达到 39.27km、35.35km。

3.2 铁路网布局

铁路网规模、结构和质量，不仅直接反映出一个国家轨道交通的发展水平，也深刻地影响着一个国家整个国民经济的发展速度。

自 2004 年颁布和 2008 年修编《中长期铁路网规划规划》以来，我国铁路发展成效显著，基础网络初步形成、服务水平明显提升、创新能力显著增强、铁路改革实现突破，对促进经济社会发展、保障和改善民生、支撑国家重大战略实施、增强我国综合实力和国际影响力发挥了重要作用。

截至 2018 年底，我国铁路营业里程达 13.2 万 km，全国各省(区、市)的铁路营业里程和路网密度如图 3-5 所示，其中，华北 5 省(区、市)铁路网规模为 2.7

万 km，路网密度为 174km/万 km^2，东北 3 省(区、市)为 1.7 万 km，路网密度为 210km/万 km^2，华东 6 省(区、市)为 1.9 万 km，路网密度为 298km/万 km^2，中南 7 省(区、市)为 2.9 万 km，路网密度为 243km/万 km^2，西北、西南 10 省(区、市)为 3.3 万 km，路网密度为 61km/万 km^2。从整体来看，我国东部地区的铁路网络结构逐步优化，中部地区铁路网络规模逐渐增加，西部地区铁路网络覆盖水平逐步提高。

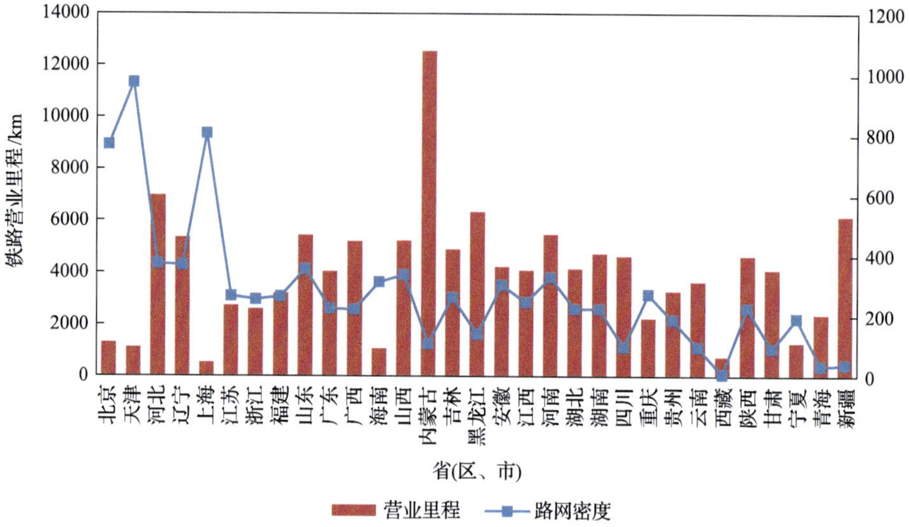

图 3-5 截至 2018 年底我国各省(区、市)铁路营业里程和路网密度

从路网密度角度来看，天津的路网密度最高，达到 970km/万 km^2，西藏地区最低，为 6km/万 km^2；从营业里程角度来看，内蒙古自治区的营业里程最长，为 1.25 万 km，上海地区最低，为 505.3km。

我国铁路网覆盖全国且十分密集，全国路网密度达到 136.9km/万 km^2。但从图 3-6 可以看出，我国铁路网主要分布于兰州—成都—昆明连线以东地区，西部地区的路网密度与东部地区相比相去甚远。

截至 2011 年，中国铁路已基本形成以北京为中心，以四纵、三横、三网和关内外三线为骨架，联结着众多的支线、辅助线、专用线，可通达全国各省(区、市)的铁路网。四纵指京广线、京九线、京沪线、北同蒲—太焦—湘渝—川黔—焦柳线；三横是指京秦—京包—包兰—兰青—青藏线、陇海—兰新线、沪杭—浙赣—湘黔—成渝—贵昆线；三网是指东北铁路网、西南铁路网和台湾铁路网；关内外三线是指京沈线、京通线和京承—锦承线。

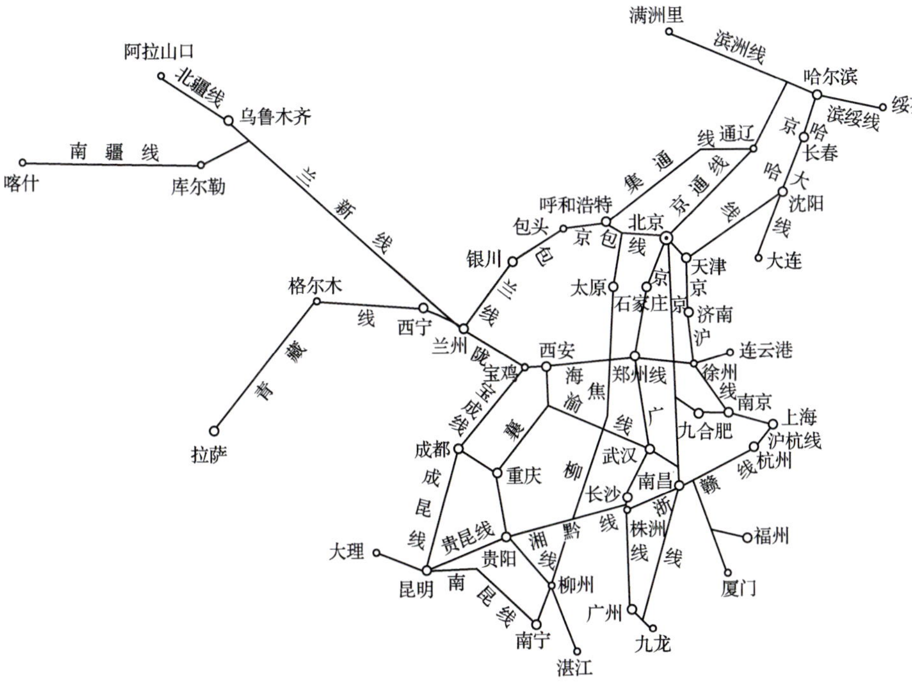

图 3-6 我国铁路干线分布图

3.2.1 按照归属特性的铁路网布局

我国铁路按照其归属可分为国家铁路、地方铁路、合资铁路、专用铁路和铁路专用线等。

1) 国家铁路

国家铁路简称国铁，是由中央政府主管部门管理的铁路，在国民经济中占有特别重要的地位，是国家重点发展的基础设施。

国铁有多种铁路等级，分为国铁Ⅰ级、国铁Ⅱ级、国铁Ⅲ级。由于国家铁路的性质十分重要，因此对国家铁路的管理不仅仅是行政管理，而且对国家铁路实行高度集中、统一指挥的运输管理体制。

本报告所统计和研究的铁路主要是国家铁路。

2) 地方铁路

地方铁路主要是由地方自行投资修建或者与其他铁路联合投资修建，担负地方公共旅客、货物短途运输任务的铁路。地方铁路与国家铁路相比，所不同的是管理主体的变化，一个是国务院铁路主管部门，一个是地方人民政府；前者是代表国家，代表的是中央人民政府的总体经济利益，后者虽然也是国家的一个部分，但代表的是地方本地区的经济利益。

2016年，全国地方铁路运输完成客运量790万人次，旅客周转量70702万人公里；货运量19660万t，货物周转量1266081万吨公里，换算周转量1336783万吨公里；运输收入462177万元，实现利润58971万元，上缴税金23218万元。至2016年底，全国地方铁路从业人员有1.89万人，延展里程5974.4km，正线里程4443.4km，其中窄轨铁路597.8km；拥有机车299台，其中内燃机车274台，蒸汽机车6台，电力机车19台。

3)合资铁路

一般指中国铁路总公司与地方政府、企业或其他投资者合资建设和经营的铁路，包括规范改制的铁路支线有限责任公司或股份有限公司。合资铁路打破了多年来我国铁路建设投资主体单一的局面，调动了中央和地方两个积极性，拓宽了筹资渠道，铁路建设初步形成了投资主体多元化的格局。

截至2016年底，国铁出资的合资铁路公司共219个(不含上市公司)，其中控股公司181家(运营144家，在建37家)，参股公司38家。控股合资公司投资规模为60224亿元，建设和运营里程69767km。144家国铁控股运营合资公司中有112家于2015年前投入运营，全年营业收入为2015亿元，同比增加214亿元，增长11.9%。

4)专用铁路

专用铁路是指由企业或者其他单位管理，专为本企业或者本单位内部提供运输服务的铁路。一般来说，专用铁路大都是大中型企业自己投资修建的，自备机车车辆，用来完成自己企业自身的运输任务的铁路。也有一些军工企业、森林管理部门为运输生产需要修建了一些专用铁路。

5)铁路专用线

铁路专用线是指由企业或者其他单位管理的与国家铁路或者其他铁路线路接轨的岔线。铁路专用线与专用铁路都是企业或者其他单位修建的主要为本企业内部运输服务的，两者所不同的是，专用铁路一般都自备动力，自备运输工具，在内部形成运输生产的一套系统的运输组织，而铁路专用线则仅仅是一条线，其运输动力使用的是与其相接轨的铁路的动力。

3.2.2 按照建设类型的铁路网布局

按照建设类型来分，我国铁路网可分为传统铁路网和高速铁路网。目前，在全部的铁路营业里程中，高速铁路营业里程为2.9万km，传统铁路营业里程为10.2万km。

我国的高速铁路建设主要围绕省会城市展开，兼顾全国各地的连接。从连接上来看，我国高速铁路的建设主要布局在东部沿海地区，以京广、京沪两条线路作为主要纵线，以北京、郑州、武汉、长沙、西安、兰州等城市作为枢纽向西延伸，形成一张覆盖我国中东部大部分地区的高速铁路网络。从路网密度方面来看，布局最为密集的地区位于京津冀地区和长三角地区，华中、华南地区次之，西北、西南地区路网密度稍显稀疏，新疆地区仅有一条高速铁路线路，而西藏地区尚无高速铁路。

1. 传统铁路网与光照资源网的联合布局

根据北京大学地理数据平台交通数据和大贤·风格气象数据可计算得出，我国传统铁路在Ⅰ类光辐射地区的长度为2511km，在Ⅱ类、Ⅲ类、Ⅳ类地区的长度分别为39665km、61337km和10874km(图3-7)。

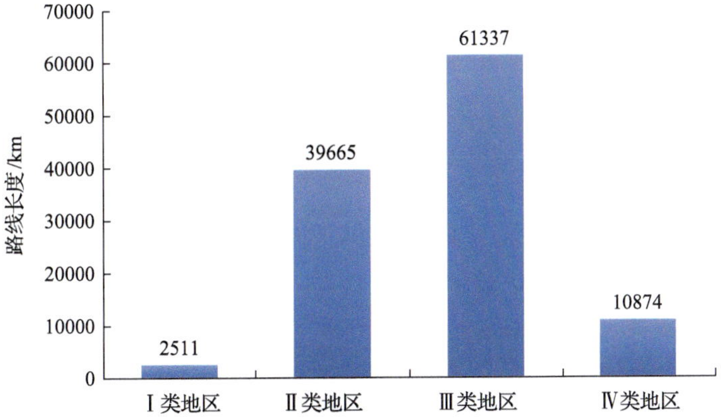

图3-7　传统铁路在四类光辐射地区的路线长度

2. 高速铁路网与光照资源网的联合布局

中国高速铁路是目前世界上最大规模的高速铁路网，1999年8月16日中国第一条客运专线秦沈客专正式开工，2003年10月12日秦沈客专正式建成通车。截至2018年12月中国高速铁路总里程达2.9万km，其中运营时速可达300km的线路总里程超1万km，占世界2/3以上，包括香港特别行政区的30个省级行政区开通高铁；中国的高铁路线仍持续兴建中，预计在2025年将建成约3.8万km的高速铁路网。

根据北京大学地理数据平台交通数据和大贤·风格气象的数据可以计算得出，我国高速铁路在Ⅰ类光辐射地区的长度为458km，在Ⅱ类、Ⅲ类、Ⅳ类地区的长度分别为4638km、16024km和3317km(图3-8)。

到2020年，全国铁路网规模预计达到15万km，其中高速铁路超过3万km，覆盖80%以上的大城市。可以说，我国的铁路建设正在以中国速度领跑全世界。

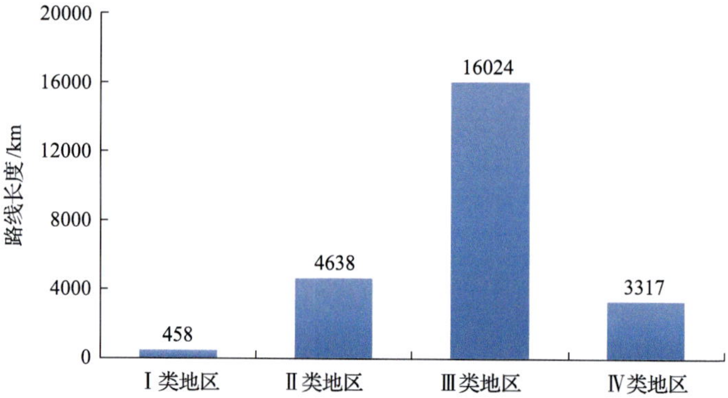

图 3-8　我国高速铁路分布在四类光照地区的路线长度

为满足快速增长的客运需求，优化拓展区域发展空间，我国高速铁路网络在“四纵四横”高速铁路的基础上，增加客流支撑、标准适宜、发展需要的高速铁路，部分利用时速 200km 铁路，形成以“八纵八横”主通道为骨架、区域连接线衔接、城际铁路补充的高速铁路网，实现省会城市高速铁路通达、区际之间高效便捷相连。

高速铁路主通道规划新增项目原则采用时速 250km 及以上标准(地形地质及气候条件复杂困难地区可以适当降低)，其中沿线人口城镇稠密、经济比较发达、贯通特大城市的铁路可采用时速 350km 标准。区域铁路连接线原则采用时速 250km 及以下标准。城际铁路原则采用时速 200km 及以下标准。构筑“八纵八横”高速铁路主通道。

1)“八纵”通道

(1)沿海通道：大连(丹东)—秦皇岛—天津—东营—潍坊—青岛(烟台)—连云港—盐城—南通—上海—宁波—福州—厦门—深圳—湛江—北海(防城港)高速铁路(其中青岛至盐城段利用青连、连盐铁路，南通至上海段利用沪通铁路)，连接东部沿海地区，贯通京津冀、辽中南、山东半岛、东陇海、长三角、海峡西岸、珠三角、北部湾等城市群。

(2)京沪通道：北京—天津—济南—南京—上海(杭州)高速铁路，包括南京—杭州、蚌埠—合肥—杭州高速铁路，同时通过北京—天津—东营—潍坊—临沂—淮安—扬州—南通—上海高速铁路，连接华北、华东地区，贯通京津冀、长三角等城市群。

(3)京港(台)通道：北京—衡水—菏泽—商丘—阜阳—合肥(黄冈)—九江—南昌—赣州—深圳—香港(九龙)高速铁路；另一支线为合肥—福州—台北高速铁路，包括南昌—福州(莆田)铁路。连接华北、华中、华东、华南地区，贯通京津冀、长江中游、海峡西岸、珠三角等城市群。

(4) 京哈—京港澳通道：哈尔滨—长春—沈阳—北京—石家庄—郑州—武汉—长沙—广州—深圳—香港高速铁路，包括广州—珠海—澳门高速铁路。连接东北、华北、华中、华南、港澳地区，贯通哈长、辽中南、京津冀、中原、长江中游、珠三角等城市群。

(5) 呼南通道：呼和浩特—大同—太原—郑州—襄阳—常德—益阳—邵阳—永州—桂林—南宁高速铁路。连接华北、中原、华中、华南地区，贯通呼包鄂榆、山西中部、中原、长江中游、北部湾等城市群。

(6) 京昆通道：北京—石家庄—太原—西安—成都(重庆)—昆明高速铁路，包括北京—张家口—大同—太原高速铁路。连接华北、西北、西南地区，贯通京津冀、太原、关中平原、成渝、滇中等城市群。

(7) 包(银)海通道：包头—延安—西安—重庆—贵阳—南宁—湛江—海口(三亚)高速铁路，包括银川—西安以及海南环岛高速铁路。连接西北、西南、华南地区，贯通呼包鄂、宁夏沿黄、关中平原、成渝、黔中、北部湾等城市群。

(8) 兰(西)广通道：兰州(西宁)—成都(重庆)—贵阳—广州高速铁路。连接西北、西南、华南地区，贯通兰西、成渝、黔中、珠三角等城市群。

2) “八横”通道

(1) 绥满通道：绥芬河—牡丹江—哈尔滨—齐齐哈尔—海拉尔—满洲里高速铁路。连接黑龙江及蒙东地区。

(2) 京兰通道：北京—呼和浩特—银川—兰州高速铁路。连接华北、西北地区，贯通京津冀、呼包鄂、宁夏沿黄、兰西等城市群。

(3) 青银通道：青岛—济南—石家庄—太原—银川高速铁路(其中绥德至银川段利用太中银铁路)。连接华东、华北、西北地区，贯通山东半岛、京津冀、太原、宁夏沿黄等城市群。

(4) 陆桥通道：连云港—徐州—郑州—西安—兰州—西宁—乌鲁木齐高速铁路。连接华东、华中、西北地区，贯通东陇海、中原、关中平原、兰西、天山北坡等城市群。

(5) 沿江通道：上海—南京—合肥—武汉—重庆—成都高速铁路，包括南京—安庆—九江—武汉—宜昌—重庆、万州—达州—遂宁—成都高速铁路(其中成都至遂宁段利用达成铁路)，连接华东、华中、西南地区，贯通长三角、长江中游、成渝等城市群。

(6) 沪昆通道：上海—杭州—南昌—长沙—贵阳—昆明高速铁路。连接华东、华中、西南地区，贯通长三角、长江中游、黔中、滇中等城市群。

(7) 厦渝通道：厦门—龙岩—赣州—长沙—常德—张家界—黔江—重庆高速铁路(其中厦门至赣州段利用龙厦铁路、赣龙铁路，常德至黔江段利用黔张常铁路)。连接海峡西岸、中南、西南地区，贯通海峡西岸、长江中游、成渝等城市群。

(8)广昆通道：广州—南宁—昆明高速铁路。连接华南、西南地区，贯通珠三角、北部湾、滇中等城市群。

3.2.3 按照牵引类型的铁路网布局

我国铁路运输规模增长迅速。如图 3-9 所示，1995 年，我国的铁路营业里程为 6.24 万 km，2018 年达到 13.1 万 km，电气化铁路从 2013 年的 5.6 万 km 增长至 2018 年的 9.2 万 km，电气化率从 54.37%增长至 70.23%。

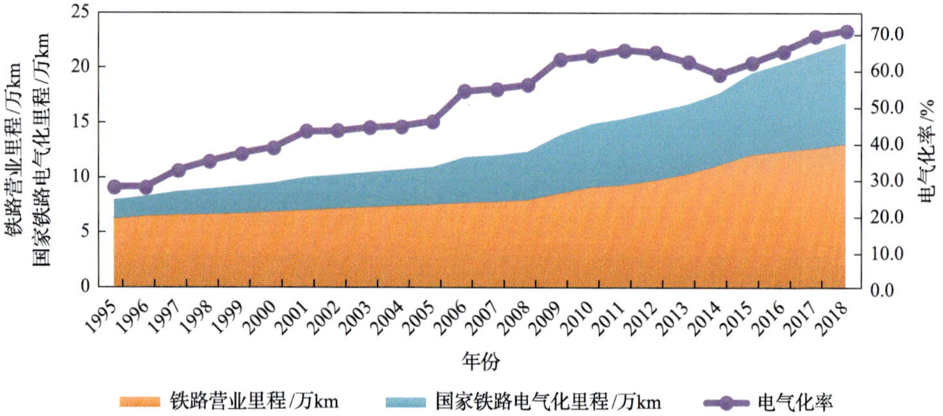

图 3-9 我国铁路营业里程、电气化里程及电气化率变化趋势图

2018 年，在全部的铁路营业里程中电气化铁路营业里程达 9.2 万 km，非电气化铁路营业里程为 3.9 万 km。我国电气化铁路的分布主要集中在中部和东部等强电网区域；而在西北、西南、内蒙古及东北等太阳能资源丰富地带依然有大量的非电气化铁路在运营，承担着改善当地人民生产、生活的重要任务，而这些地区往往是电网的末端或者无电区域，使得这些铁路的用电设备，如空调、照明等往往得不到应有的保证，严重降低了当地的铁路服务水平，影响了当地人民的出行便捷性，同时降低了当地人民的幸福感。

1. 电气化铁路网与光照资源网的联合布局

电力机车本身不自带能源，需要铁路沿途的供电系统源源不断地为其输送电能来驱动车辆。由于电力机车相比内燃机车有更强的运力优势，所以相同规模下电气化铁路的运输能力远超过非电气化铁路，成为现代化铁路的主流类型。电气化铁路广泛地运用于高快速铁路和城市轨道交通的建设中，很多非电气化铁路也相继实现电气化升级改造。

根据统计北京大学地理数据平台交通数据和大贤·风格气象数据可以计算得出，我国电气化铁路在 I 类、II 类、III类、IV类光辐射地区的长度分别为 1075km、

31489km、57182km 和 12331km，如图 3-10 所示。

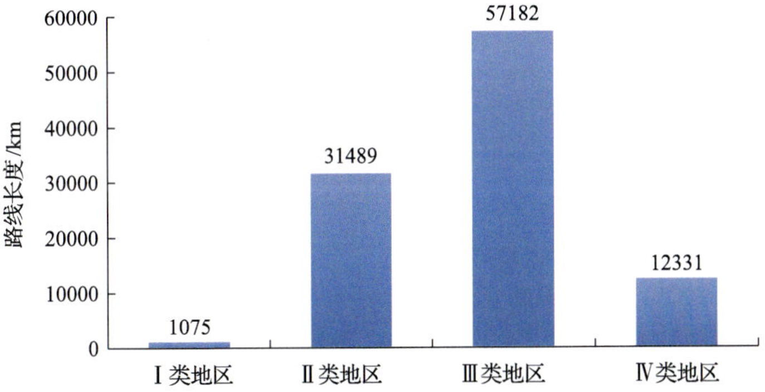

图 3-10　我国电气化铁路在四类光照地区的路线长度

电气化铁路的建设使全国各省(区、市)的电气化铁路用电量不断攀高，2016年，仅河北省的电气化铁路用电量就超过了 5600GW·h，河南省电气化铁路的用电量也在 5000GW·h 以上，但是由于建设成本和区域负荷的不平衡，西藏自治区电气化铁路用电量最低，仅为 10MW·h，图 3-11 是我国各省(区、市)电气化铁路的用电量分布图。

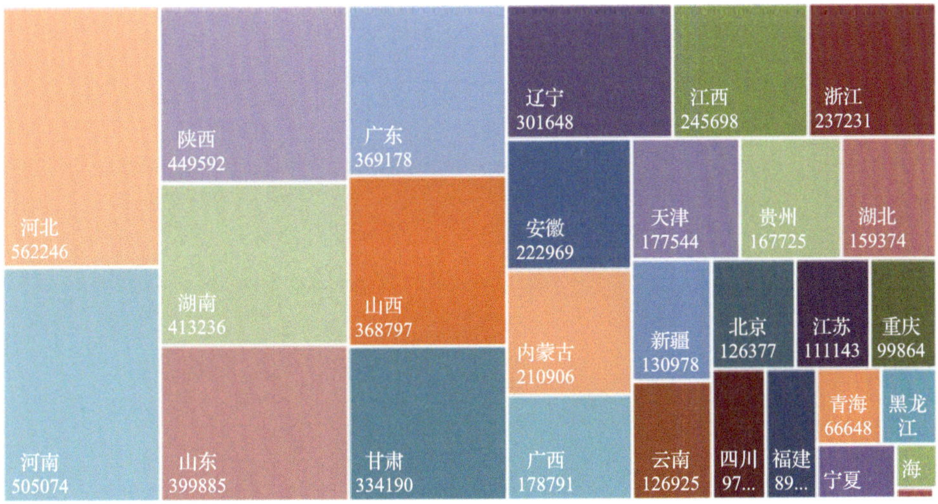

图 3-11　全国各省(区、市)电气化铁路用电量分布图(单位：100GW·h)

不含港澳台地区，部分地区由于数值较小未显示数据标签

2. 非电气化铁路网与光照资源网的联合布局

非电气化铁路的牵引动力主要是蒸汽机车和内燃机车，小部分铁路会出现燃气涡轮机车。由于非电气化铁路不行驶电力机车或动车组，因此运输能力比电气

化铁路要低，在运输成本方面也较电气化铁路高。

根据北京大学地理数据平台交通数据和大贤·风格气象数据可以计算得出，我国非电气化铁路在Ⅰ类、Ⅱ类、Ⅲ类、Ⅳ类光辐射地区的长度分别为 1894km、12814km、20179km 和 1860km，如图 3-12 所示。

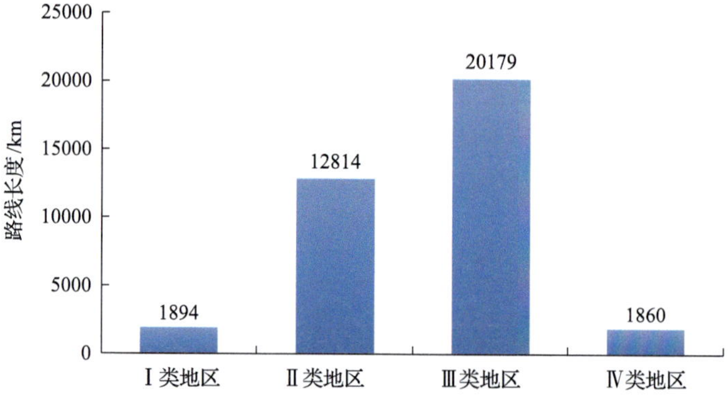

图 3-12　我国非电气化铁路在四类光照地区的路线长度

根据北京大学地理数据平台交通数据和大贤·风格气象数据可以计算得出，全国各省(区、市)的非电气化铁路占比情况如图 3-13 所示。

图 3-13　我国各省(区、市)非电气化铁路占比情况

不含港澳台地区，部分地区由于数值较小未显示数据标签

从图 3-13 可以看出，我国非电气化铁路主要集中于边疆地区，如东三省、内蒙古北部、贵州南部、云南南部以及青海、西藏等地区。从各省(区、市)的非电气化线路比例而言，西藏完全没有电气化铁路，非电气化率为 100%；其次为黑龙

江、青海、吉林三省，非电气化率超过 50%；北京、天津、上海、海南则基本全部为电气化铁路。图 3-14 为我国各省(区、市)非电气化铁路占比排序情况。

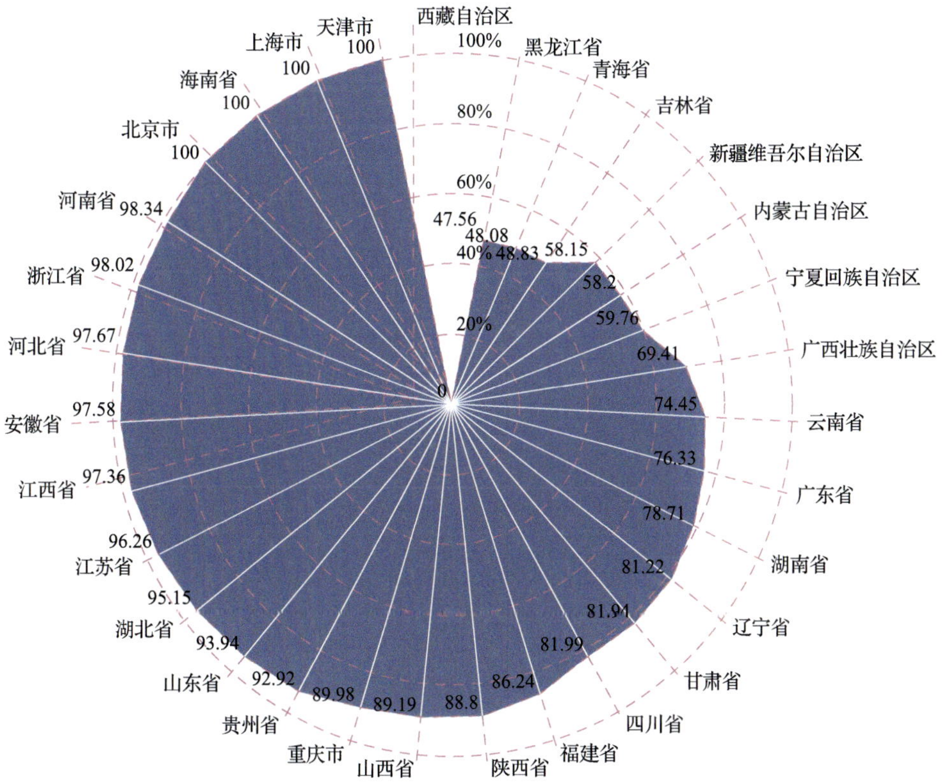

图 3-14　我国各省(区、市)非电气化铁路占比排序情况

根据我国铁路的中长期发展规划，我国铁路网络发展的目标是扩大规模、完善结构、提高质量、快速扩充运输能力及迅速提高装备水平，运输能力满足国民经济和社会发展需要，主要技术装备达到或接近国际先进水平。

从图 3-15 可知，我国的铁路网营业规划是到 2025 年，铁路网络规模将达到 17.5 万 km 左右，其中高速铁路达 3.8 万 km 左右，全国铁路网络覆盖进一步扩大且路网结构更加优化，骨干作用更加显著，将更好地发挥铁路对经济社会发展的保障作用；到 2030 年，铁路网络规模将达到 20 万 km，其中高速铁路将达到 4.5 万 km，铁路网络将全面实现内外互联互通、区际多路畅通、省会高铁联通、地市快速通达、县域基本覆盖。

总体来说，目前我国铁路网络规模、供给水平基本可以适应区域经济社会发展。但是，实现我国铁路网络的宏伟目标，仍然存在一些不足之处，亟须寻找解决途径，主要包括：

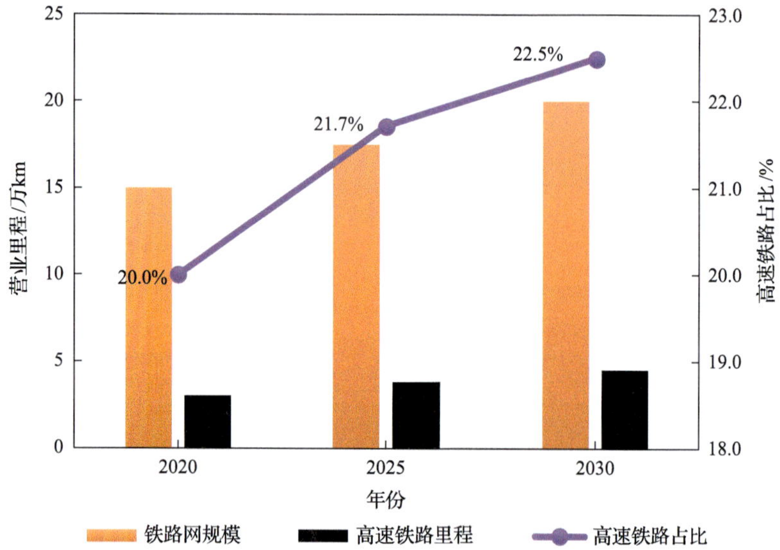

图 3-15　我国铁路网营业里程规划

数据来源：《中长期铁路网规划》

(1)路网结构布局仍不完善，路网在各大区域布局很不均衡，东部地区路网规模相对饱和，中西部地区路网规模相对欠缺，覆盖度仍需提高，但是中西部的电网较弱，大多处于末端或无电区域，因此，如何因地制宜地为这些地区的铁路建设寻找能源供给方案是实现我国铁路网络宏伟规划的关键之处。

(2)供能来源较为单一，严重依赖电网进行电气化铁路的建设，导致电气化铁路的投资占比居高不下，因此，电气化铁路的电能来源亟须寻找新的供能方式。

(3)非电气铁路的用能严重依赖于非清洁能源，导致碳排放居高不下，因此，为非电气化铁路的用能寻求清洁绿色的能源供给十分必要。

上篇　公路交通与可再生能源融合发展的形态、模式与解决方案

第 1 章　交通能源需求的形态和模式

经济持续发展带来社会对交通运输需求的快速增长，我国交通运输行业的能源消耗也在不断增加，占全社会总能耗的比重也在逐年提升，按照近几年国家统计数据分析，交通运输行业能耗已成为第三大能源消耗行业，仅次于工业和生活消费业。

图 1-1 和图 1-2 分别给出了 2006～2016 年交通运输业的能源和电力消耗。

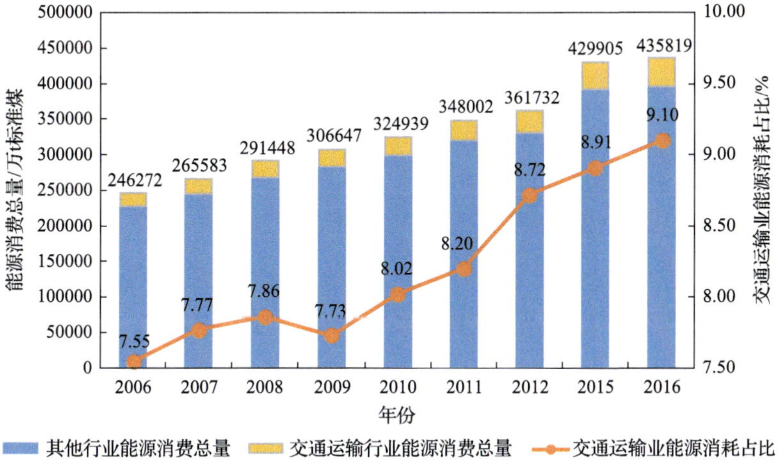

图 1-1　交通运输业能源消耗状况图

数据来源：《中国统计年鉴 2018》

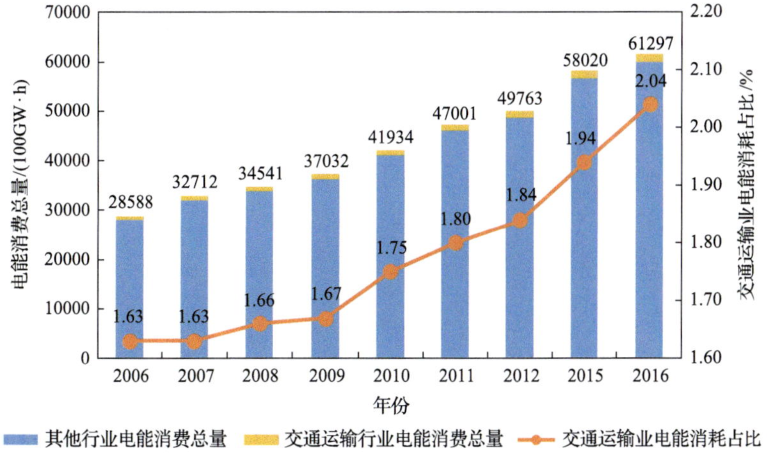

图 1-2　交通运输业电力消耗状况图

数据来源：《中国统计年鉴 2018》

可见，交通运输行业能源消耗和全社会能源消耗均呈现递增趋势，并且占全社会总量的比重从 7.55%提高到 9.10%，交通运输行业能源消耗总量和其占全社会总量的比重基本呈现逐年递增的趋势，且递增的速度呈现缓慢上升的趋势。与此同时，交通运输行业的电能消耗呈现出逐年递增的趋势，其占全社会电能消耗的比重达到约 2.04%。

1.1 公路交通的用能形态

1.1.1 公路交通基础设施的用能形态

公路交通基础设施的用能主要指提供基本交通运输条件过程中产生的能源消耗，如提供公路交通安全、维持公路设施运行能力的辅助设施。交通基础设施用能主体主要包括隧道设施、沿线设施两类，其中隧道设施主要包括隧道照明设施、隧道通风设施、隧道消防管理设施等；沿线设施包括线路监控设施、可变信息指示设施、连接线照明等。表 1-1 为公路基础设施主要用能设备。

表 1-1 公路基础设施主要用能设备

用能设备	耗能项目	耗能设备	能耗种类
隧道设施	隧道照明系统	照明灯具	电
	隧道通风系统	风机	电
	隧道监控系统	监控设备	电
	隧道消防系统	消防设备	电、水
	隧道供电系统	供配电设备	电
	隧道交通安全设施	交通信号灯	电
沿线设施	主线监控系统	监控设备	电
	主线通信系统	通信设备	电
	交通信号系统	可变信息标志	电

为保障车辆在隧道中的行车安全，根据隧道的实际情况，应选择性地设置隧道照明设备、隧道通风设备、隧道监控设备、隧道安全警示及相应的消防设备等。根据我国《公路隧道照明设计细则》(JTG/T D70/2-01-2014)规定：在长度大于 100m 的公路隧道中都应设置白天的照明设备，照明灯具通常选择隧道专用无极灯和隧道专用 LED 灯，隧道洞口引道灯常选择高压钠灯；在长度大于 300m 的隧道中都应装设机械通风设施，以利用新鲜空气来稀释和排除隧道中的污染空气从而提高行车时能见度，且可以在火灾发生时疏散排出烟雾；除此之外，隧道监控设置是通过监控设备实时监控隧道运行情况，并上传至监控中心由工作人员及时地将隧道内实际情况反馈司乘人员，以起到警报、报警的作用。

与此同时，为了确保隧道内行车的安全，需加装额外的监控设施，主要包括隧道监控摄像机、隧道可变信息标志和隧道控制器这些电能消耗较多的机电设备，且隧道监控设施的设置规模由隧道监控等级决定，在众多的监控设施中，隧道监控摄像机、隧道可变信息标志和隧道控制器属于电能消耗较多的机电设备。图 1-3 为公路隧道用能设施示例，图 1-4 为公路沿线用能设施及形态。

图 1-3　公路隧道用能设施示例

图 1-4　公路沿线用能设施及形态

公路沿线需加装监控设施，以监测公路断面交通量、车辆速度信息和气象环境数据，其中典型的监控设施包括监控摄像机、车辆检测器、气象检测器、可变信息标志等，这些设施根据运营管理的需求分别设置在沿线道路两侧的重要地点和方位。同时，高速公路连接线是高速公路正线与城市街道、省干道或距离较远的另一条高速公路连接起来的专用公路，为引起人们注意常需设置路灯等设备，也可认为是沿线设施用能的一部分。高速公路沿线基础设施用能主体主要为监控设施，其主要包括高速监视系统以及车辆检测器、气象检测器、可变信息标志等。按照运营管理要求，沿线监控设施应 24h 正常工作。

根据公开资料整理[1,2]，云南大丽高速 196km 沿线设施日用电量为 1075kW·h，年用电量为 392MW·h。由于公路沿线监控、指示等设施布局安装基本类似，则可推算，单位公里公路沿线监控、指示等设施平均功率为 0.22kW，日用电量约为 5.3kW·h，年用电量约为 2MW·h。云南省昆龙高速四角田隧道双向洞长 3.0km，照明灯具采用高压钠灯，在入口段、入口过渡 1 段、入口过渡 2 段、入口过渡 3

段、基本段、出口过渡段、出口段共需加装400W高压钠灯54盏、250W高压钠灯36盏、150W高压钠灯64盏、100W高压钠灯380盏。按常规控制策略，7:30～19:30隧道照明灯具全部开启、19:30至次日7:30开启基本段照明，则四角田隧道照明日用电量约为1400kW·h。为稀释隧道内汽车尾气浓度，隧道左右洞共加装额定功率为22kW的风机24台，平均使用时间为6h，则隧道通风风机日用电量为3168kW·h。同时，为保证公路隧道正常运行，隧道内监控摄像机、可变信息标志、本地控制器全天开启，日用电量约为150kW·h。因此，四角田隧道日用电量约为4718kW·h，年平均用电量为1720MW·h，则单位公里隧道年平均用电量约为573MW·h。

据公路交通安全技术交通行业重点实验室公布数据，秦岭终南山隧道双向洞长36.04km，引线双洞长2.75km，共38.79km[3]。建有13个10kV箱式变压器用于射流风机和隧道照明供电，共配置22kW射流风机144台，隧道照明设施共有208组照明回路，高压钠灯8700盏，疏散指示灯7488盏，LED诱导灯10346盏，功率为100W、250W和400W，总用电功率达到12652kW，其中，照明1278kW，风机11274kW，其他弱电设备100kW，建成初期日用电量约为80MW·h，单位公里隧道年平均用电量约为752MW·h。这主要是隧道较长而通风设施配置较多，导致其单位公里年平均用电量偏高。

综上所述，以云南四角田公路隧道和陕西秦岭终南山公路隧道为例，对公路隧道用能情况进行了分析。为综合表征公路基础设施能耗，本报告假定公路隧道单位公里年平均用电量为650MW·h，单位公里公路沿线机电设施年平均用电量为2MW·h。

在过去几年间，我国公路交通基础设施建设规模持续扩大。截至2018年，我国现有公路隧道17738处、17236.1km，其中特长隧道1058处、4706.6km，长隧道4315处、7421.8km，公路隧道数量和长度均居世界前列。按单位公里隧道年平均用电量650MW·h、公路沿线机电设施年平均用电量2MW·h计算，并根据工业和信息化部公布的各种能源折算标准煤参考系数进行折算[4]，截至2018年，我国已建成通车的公路隧道总里程达到17236.1km，每年耗电量约为11200GW·h，折算为标准煤约为137.6万t；我国已建成通车的高速公路总里程达到14.2万km，每年耗电量约为280GW·h，折算为标准煤约为3.4t万t。

综上所述，我国公路基础设施年耗电量为11480GW·h，折算为标准煤为140.9万t，其中公路隧道负荷占主要地位，约占全部电力消耗的97.6%，而公路沿线负荷仅占全部电力消耗的2.4%。

1.1.2 公路交通载运工具的用能形态

汽车是指本身具有动力能够驱动，不需依赖轨道或电缆即可行驶的车辆。在广义范畴上来说，具有两轮或以上以原动机行驶的车辆，即可称为汽车；在狭义范畴上来说，仅四轮以上以原动机行驶的车辆为汽车，这也是广为大众接受的汽车。因此本报告若无特别强调，汽车通常仅指四轮以上以原动机行驶的车辆。

汽车作为最常见的公路交通载运工具，汽车的分类方式并无定论。若依使用性质区分，一般分为客车、货车、客货两用车（或称厢形车）及特种车，若依所用燃料分类，则分为燃油汽车、混合动力汽车、纯电动汽车、氢动力汽车等。

燃油汽车是指采用汽油引擎或柴油引擎作为动力来源的一类汽车，包括汽油车和柴油车。这一类汽车通过汽、柴油燃料在引擎中燃烧，而产生的高温高压气体，推动发动机运转，从而为汽车提供动力。柴油和汽油的燃烧会产生大量氮氧化物、非甲烷挥发性有机化合物和微粒等污染排放，这是造成空气污染、全球变暖及酸雨的原因之一。

为了解决这些问题，发展新能源汽车，已成为热门方向，已吸引许多汽车制造商的投入研发。在本报告中，新能源汽车是指采用非常规的车用燃料作为动力来源，综合车辆的动力控制和驱动方面的先进技术，形成的技术原理先进、具有新技术、新结构的汽车。按动力源不同，新能源汽车可分为混合动力电动汽车（hybrid electric vehicle，HEV）、纯电动汽车（battery electric vehicle，BEV）、燃料电池电动汽车（fuel cell electric vehicle，FCEV）三大类：第一，混合动力电动汽车是使用两种或两种以上能量来源驱动的车辆，而驱动系统可以有一套或多套；第二，纯电动汽车通过蓄电池给电动机供电，而蓄电池的电量由外部电源补充；第三，燃料电池电动汽车是使氢或含氢物质及空气中的氧通过燃料电池以产生电力，推动车辆运转。

根据中国汽车工程学会发布的《汽车生命周期温室气体及大气污染物排放评价报告 2018》，以汽车全生命周期的行驶里程（按 15 万 km 计算）及其累计产量为衡量标准，在现有技术储备、采用应用、研发设计及报废回收环节上，混合动力、传统燃油动力与可再生能源平分秋色，但宏观来看，纯电动汽车的全生命周期碳减排要普遍优于同级别燃油汽车。表 1-2 为燃油汽车与纯电动汽车的碳排放量估算。

表 1-2　燃油汽车与纯电动汽车的碳排放量估算

类型	生产过程中碳排放量/t	万公里碳排放量/t	全生命周期碳排放量/t	总碳排放量/t
燃油汽车	5.6	2.16	32.4	38.0
纯电动车	8.8	1.39	20.8	29.6

数据来源：《汽车生命周期温室气体及大气污染物排放评价报告 2018》.

中国汽车技术研究中心数据资源中心公布了 2016 年我国车用能源测算结果，其中，乘用车成品油消耗量占车用成品油总消耗量的比重升至 47.5%，商用车成品油消耗量占车用成品油总消耗量的比重下降至 52.5%。2016 年，我国车用汽、柴油总油耗达 2.32 亿 t，占社会汽、柴油消费总量的 81.4%。表 1-3 为 2016 年中国汽车分车种汽油、柴油消费情况。

表 1-3　2016 年中国汽车分车种汽油、柴油消费情况　　（单位：万 t）

燃油	乘用车	载客汽车			载货汽车			
		大型	中型	轻型	重型	中型	轻型	微型
汽油	10870.3	11.1	26.5	251.9	0.0	12.8	674.9	62.5
柴油	133.9	504.5	387.3	428.7	7283.8	657.9	1863.7	4.5
合计	11004.2	515.6	413.8	680.6	7283.8	670.7	2538.6	67.0
					12170.1			
比例	47.5%				52.5%			

数据来源：《中国节能与新能源汽车发展研究报告(2017)》。

根据公安部统计数据，截至 2018 年底，全国汽车保有量达 2.4 亿辆，比 2017 年增长 10.51%[5]。从车辆类型看，小型载客汽车保有量达 2.01 亿辆，比 2017 年增加 2085 万辆，增长 11.56%；私家车(私人微型载客汽车)持续快速增长，2018 年保有量达 1.89 亿辆，近五年年均增长 1952 万辆；载货汽车保有量达 2570 万辆。

假定不同车型燃油消耗量与 2016 年基本相同，则 2018 年，我国乘用车消耗汽柴油 13777.2 万 t，载客汽车消耗汽柴油 1516.6 万 t，载货汽车消耗汽柴油 10465.1 万 t。因此，我国汽车消耗汽柴油量为 2.6 亿 t，折算为标准煤约为 3.8 亿 t。根据国家电网有限公司和中国南方电网有限公司统计数据，2018 年我国电动汽车充换电量为 4320GW·h，折算为汽柴油约为 35.9 万 t，折算为标准煤约为 52.8 万 t。

综上所述，我国公路交通载运工具年消耗汽柴油 2.6 亿 t，其中电动汽车能源消耗量仅占 0.1%，而燃油汽车能源消耗量占绝对主要地位，约为 99.9%。同时，根据《中国统计年鉴 2018》公布的各类汽车保有量，经过加权平均计算后，平均每车百公里消耗汽柴油 8.27L，按汽柴油密度为 0.73kg/L 计算，折算为电力约为 71.8kW·h。

1.1.3　公路交通服务设施的用能形态

根据行业标准《高速公路交通工程及沿线设施设计通用规范》(JTG D80—2006)规定，高速公路上设置的服务区平均间距不宜大于 50km、最大间距不宜大于 60km。同时，行业标准《高速公路交通工程及沿线设施设计通用规范》(JTG D80—2006)给出服务区域的用地面积和建筑面积，详见表 1-4。

表 1-4　服务区域的用地面积和建筑面积

用地面积/万 m^2	建筑面积/m^2
4.0～5.3	5500～6500

按中位数计算，服务区域用地面积为 4.7 万 m^2。通常，高速公路服务区包括服务区域与停车区域，因此本报告若无特别强调，服务区通常由服务区域与停车区域共同构成。

2018 年，我国高速公路总里程达到 14.3 万 km，考虑高速公路服务区多采用同区域对向分布的特点，我国正在运营的服务区约为 2850 对。假定每对服务区平均用地面积为 4.7 万 m^2，全国 2850 对对向分布的服务区总用地面积约为 134.0km^2。

在服务区用电量方面，根据嘉通集团公布数据，嘉兴市南湖服务区日平均负荷为 3000kW·h。公路服务区内用电设施基本相同，主要包括照明、取暖、生活用电，由于全国公路服务区用地面积基本相同，因此，可假定全国公路服务区平均用电量为 3000kW·h/d，年用电量为 1095MW·h。

综上所述，我国高速公路服务区总用地面积为 134.0km^2，年耗电量约为 2990GW·h，相当于燃烧掉 36.7 万 t 标准煤。

1.2　公路交通的用能模式

1.2.1　公路交通基础设施的用能模式

隧道交通的正常运行需要以隧道监控系统、通风系统、照明系统、消防系统等各机电设备正常运行为基础，若供配电系统不稳定，将会导致整个交通管理系统失调，甚至使整个系统陷于瘫痪，严重造成交通安全。根据高速公路隧道自身特点，根据高速功率自身存在的供电距离长、线性分布相对集中造成总长度增加等问题，相应的配电设备数量也会增多。因此，对于隧道的供电有别于一般的工业和居民供配电系统。有两种方式，一种是就近取电的分散供电模式，另一种是自建专用供配电系统的集中供电模式。

早期山区公路建设由于隧道数量少，用电相对集中，通常采用就近取电的供电方式。由于低压供电距离有限，按设计要求通常在短隧道一侧设配电房，在长隧道的两侧各设一个配电房，就近取电于地方 10kV 配电网，经过 10kV 配电变压器降压后使用。为了达到对一级负荷的供电标准，在配电房内设置备用发电机组，除在隧道口配电房配备备用发电机组外，还配备 2h 的储能以备电网突然停电时隧道应急灯、监控等一级负荷的不间断供电。对于可以正常取电的隧道尽量选用就近取电的方式，以减少工程总体投资，而有些隧道附近无法正常取电，再考虑其他供电方式。

目前国内对于呈长距离、负荷分散布置的供电系统通常采用相对集中的供电方式，在中心变电所引入稳定可靠的外部电源，在高速公路沿线铺设 10kV 高压电缆送至各用电点，建立起一个相对独立的高速公路专用 10kV 内部供电系统，以保证供电的可靠性和质量。

供配电方式采取就近修建 10kV 变电所，若隧道长度小于 1.3km，只需在隧道的一端进行电源布置；若隧道长度为 1.3～3km，则需在隧道两端均进行电源布置，而中间一般无须设置高压供电点(不含单口掘进隧道工程)。若隧道长度超过 3km 且进出口同时掘进施工，那么在两端进行电源布设的同时，应考虑在隧道中间增设变配电站，以便高压进洞。而后对于隧道内的机电设备采用放射式低压配电，在修建的 10kV 变电站分出若干个 0.4kV 回路线进行配电，对于超出供电半径的情况，常通过增大 0.4kV 电缆截面，而延长其输送距离。图 1-5 为公路隧道供配电系统。

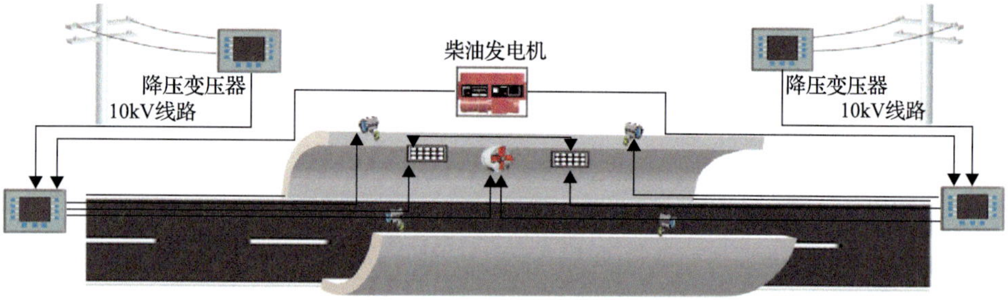

图 1-5　公路隧道供配电系统

为保证隧道的安全稳定运行，隧道内的道路及应急照明设备、监控设备等均需配备齐全，对于长隧道而言，还需要额外加装通风设备，且不同的用电设备根据其行使的功能不同，各负荷等级的供电设备所采用的供电方式也会不同。隧道监控、照明等一级负荷设备通常由两个电源供电，当一个电源发生故障时，另一个电源不致同时受到损坏，从而保证隧道一级负荷的不间断供电。隧道系统中，两个电源可一备一用，也可以同时工作，各供一部分负荷。一般在实际应用中，接线方式有以下两种。

第一种，直接从隧址区附近电力网引接两回路电源进线加备用自投的供电方式(图 1-6)。

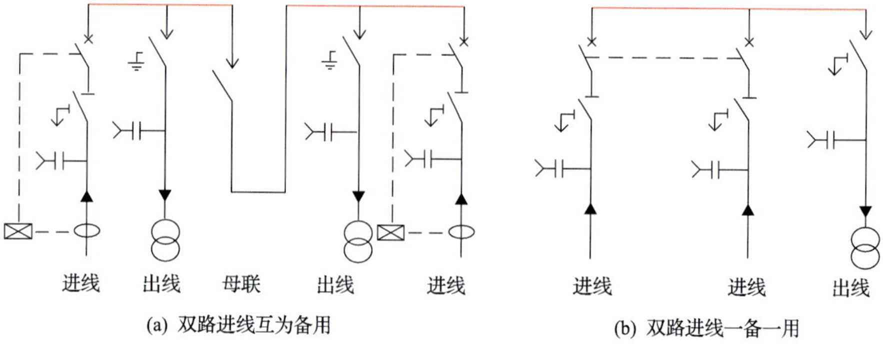

图 1-6　公路隧道供电方式 1

第二种，直接从隧址区附近电力网引接 1 回路电源进线供电，另外增加应急柴油发电机组作为备用电源的供电方式。此外，对于隧道中特别重要的一级负荷，采用与电网相对独立的应急电源供电，常用的有不间断电源(图 1-7)。

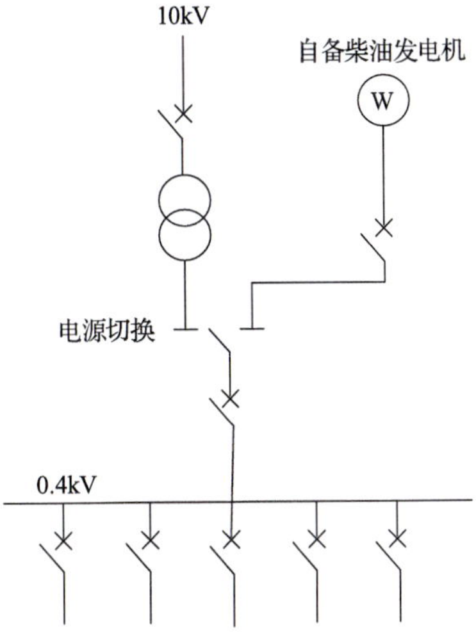

图 1-7　公路隧道供电方式 2

隧道部分的能耗设备主要包括照明灯具、通风设备、监控设备等，另外在营运中对能耗有较大影响的因素还包括隧道长度和路面等。其中，影响隧道能耗大小的因素主要包括：照明灯具的安装规格与数量、通风设备的规格与数量、监控设备的安装规格与数量，隧道的长度也对其造成的损耗大小有着重要影响。图 1-8 为公路隧道主要用能设备。

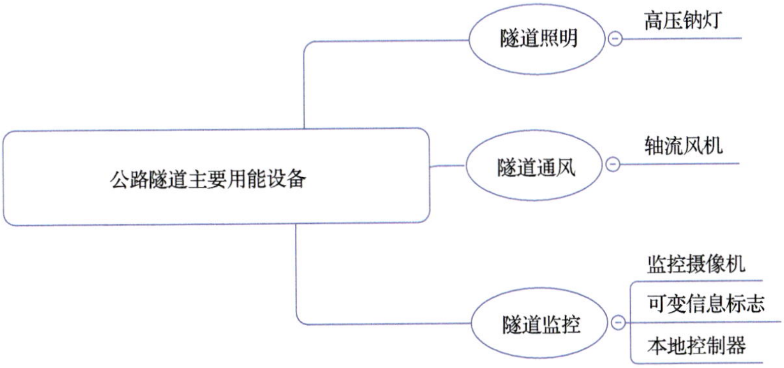

图 1-8　公路隧道主要用能设备

公路沿线的用电设施主要以外场监控设备、交通信号指示牌以及气象监控设备为主，布置方式主要是在高速公路沿线分布，其主要功能是采集高速公路道路状况、交通流状况、视频图像信息、沿线气象信息、设备运行状况与事故告警等信息；全天候监测公路断面交通量、车辆速度信息和气象环境数据；并上传采集的原始或按要求处理后的监控数据至管理中心，且接受管理中心的控制；当出现交通异常事件时，能及时地发布相关交通信息，可向司乘人员发布显示各种警告、禁止、诱导、行驶时间等信息。

目前，我国传统的监控系统供电方式主要有两种。一是从服务区或收费站的变电所引出三相低压电源沿线铺设，在各监控设备处采用调压器进行调压，使设备正常工作，然后为监控设备供电。二是从服务区或收费站站区引来一路架空10kV 电源，电源引入后，以高压电缆的形式向两侧配出支线供电，线路沿高速公路路边铺设，在每个用电点设置一台地下式电缆分支箱为变电所或箱变配出支线供电，同时在配电所低压侧设置柴油发电机作为备用电源以保证供电的可靠性。图 1-9 为高速公路沿线主要监控设备。

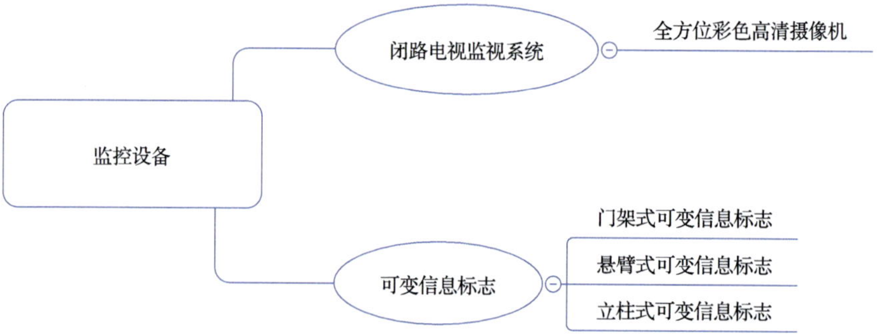

图 1-9　高速公路沿线主要监控设备

1.2.2　公路交通载运工具的用能模式

燃油汽车通过汽柴油燃料在内燃机中燃烧，而产生的高温高压气体推动发动机运转，为燃油汽车提供动力。一般情况下，汽柴油燃料与空气混合燃烧产生热能，内燃机中气体受热膨胀，通过机械装置转化为机械能对外做功，其最常见的例子为车用汽油机与柴油机。

纯电动车以蓄电池为车辆提供电力给电动机，电动机把电能转化为动能，推动车辆运转。近年电池技术在充电速度上有突破性进展，一般充电需 3～4h，某些种类的电池使用专用充电设施的话可以在半小时内充完 80%，理论上未来的电池可在 8min 内充满。针对电动汽车的不同需求，提供不同类型的电动汽车充电模式也十分重要。目前使用的电动汽车充电模式主要有三种：常规充电模式、快速充电模式和换电模式。表 1-5 比较了不同充电方式在充电参数、充电速度、充电成本、适用对象、所需设施以及对电网的影响方面的性能。

表 1-5　电动汽车常规充电模式、快速充电模式和换电模式的比较

充电模式	充电参数	充电速度	充电成本	适用对象	所需设施	对电网的影响
常规充电	220～250V 16～32A 3～10kW 单相交流电	慢，一般需6～10h	充电设施建设、充电费用低	具有较长停车时间，充电成本低	车载充电桩 小型充电桩 220V 用电	充电负荷高峰与电网负荷晚高峰部分重合，但可以转移至夜间电网负荷低谷时段
快速充电	250～750V 80～250A 50～150kW 直流电	较快，10～30min 可充 80%	充电设施建设、充电费用高	行驶中但电量不足的车	快速充电站的大功率直流电桩	瞬间的大电流高功率会对电网产生瞬时的冲击
换电模式	—	极快，3～8min 可达100%	换电站设施建设、足够的电池储备	行驶中电量不足又急需使用	电量为 80%以上的备用电池	无影响

1.2.3　公路交通服务设施的用能模式

高速公路是实现客运和货运的重要动脉，而高速公路服务区作为长途运输中的基础设施有着不可或缺的作用。高速公路服务区作为公共服务设施，休息区全年昼夜无休运转，照明、空调等能耗巨大。由于高速公路一般远离城区修建，其服务区所用电源常采用就近取电的方式，从四周地区的 10kV 高压电网引到配电房中，经变压器变压后供给 380V/220V 电压，然后，再由低压配电柜及输配电路送到相关的用电设备。为保证在外部农业或民用电因故中断后，高速公路治理系统的重要设备能够正常工作，高速公路的供配电系统常采用双电源供电。一般采用柴油发电机组发电作为市电的备用电源，能够在停电后的 10～15s 内自启动柴油发电机组发电并经双电源开关自动切换，确保向重要负荷的持续供电。图 1-10 为公路服务区供配电系统示意图。

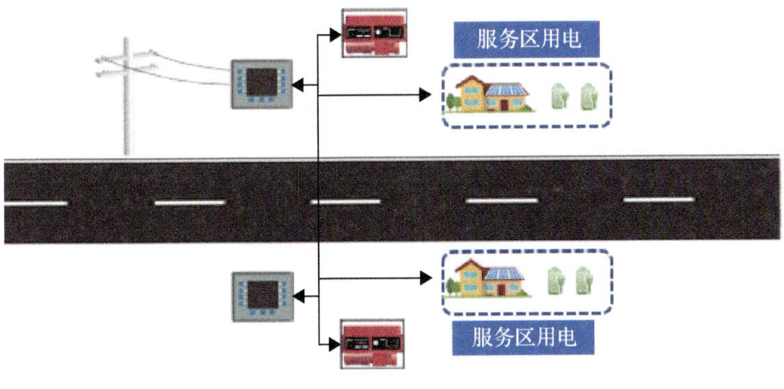

图 1-10　公路服务区供配电系统示意图

高速公路服务区的主要用电负荷为办公照明、空调、厨房和停车场照明(高杆灯照明)等，其中服务区的空调用电容量较大，消耗的电能较多，而且空调的使用以夏季和冬季为主。

第2章 公路交通能源需求的演化趋势

当前全球能源结构正处于逐步转型阶段。在科技进步、环保需求和政策支持的共同推动下，能源结构正在向更加清洁和低碳的能源转型。根据国际能源机构发布的2017年可再生能源发展报告，2016年可再生能源占初级能源供应总量份额的15%，达到1990年以来的最高份额。而从更长的时间维度来看，可再生能源对于传统化石能源的替代，使石油产业受到长期转型所带来的持续压力。预计到2030年，全球能源消耗中煤炭消耗量将从2016年的28%下降到24%，原油消耗量将从2016年的33%下降到2030年的28%，而可再生能源和其他能源将从2016年的15%上升为2030年的22%。图2-1为2030年全球能源消耗预测。

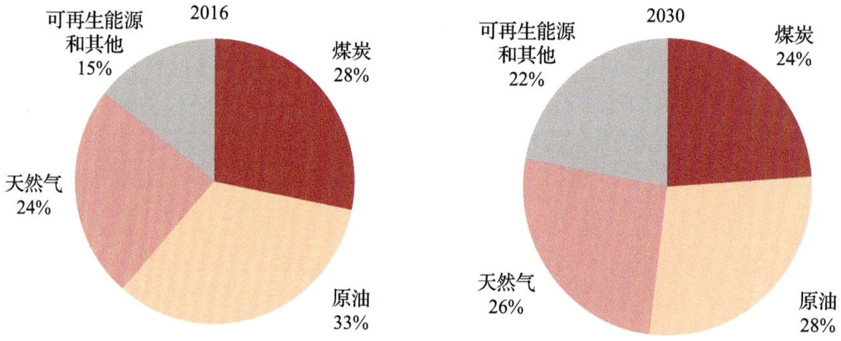

图2-1 2030年全球能源消耗预测

数据来源：《2030年能源结构主要区域趋势》

2.1 电能用能形态的发展模式

能源是经济与社会可持续发展的基础，是人类生产与生活不可缺少的动力保障。2017年，全球一次能源消费增长2.2%，增速高于2016年的1.2%，也是自2013年以来的最快增速，而过去十年的平均增速仅为1.7%。我国能源消费增长3.1%，连续17年成为全球能源消费增量最大的国家。同时，碳排放在2014～2016年间几乎没有增长后，2017年能源消费产生的碳排放在2017年增长了1.6%。为应对全球气候变化，降低碳排放，2015年12月，包括我国在内的170多个国家联合签署了《巴黎协定》，争取到2050年，全球温度升温要保持在1.5℃以下。图2-2为2050年交通运输业的能源消耗量预测。

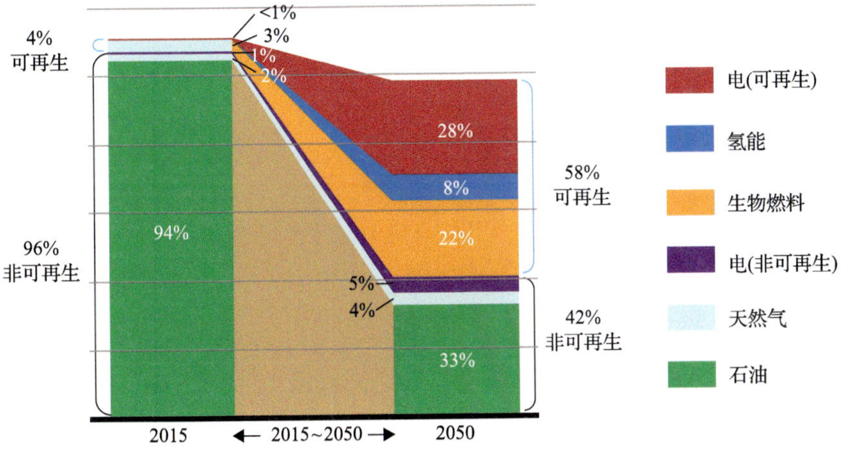

图 2-2　2050 年交通运输业的能源消耗量预测

数据来源：*Global Energy Transformation 2018*

为实现《巴黎协定》的预期目标，交通运输业作为我国能源最大的消耗行业，节能减排任务艰巨。根据国际可再生能源署的总计和预测[6]，交通运输业利用的可再生能源仅占全部能源消耗的 4%，而由可再生能源产生的电力仅占 1%不到，到 2050 年可再生能源消耗占比将提升到 58%，同时电能消耗量将提升到 33%，其中可再生能源产生的电量占比为 28%，增长迅速。

表 2-1 给出了我国部分省(区、市)电动汽车保有量，其中截至 2019 年 6 月底，广东省、北京市、浙江省分别以 38.2 万辆、21.7 万辆和 18.9 万辆居全国前三位(此处数据引用保留小数点后一位小数)。可见，华南、华东、华北地区是我国电动汽车集中地区，华中地区各省电动汽车保有量也在 5 万～7 万辆间。

表 2-1　我国部分省(区、市)电动汽车保有量

省(区、市)	数量/辆	省(区、市)	数量/辆
广东省	382421	湖北省	76003
北京市	217153	河北省	75752
浙江省	189559	福建省	72412
上海市	159677	四川省	69000
山东省	156586	湖南省	61159
安徽省	150500	山西省	54193
河南省	126916	重庆市	46000
江苏省	111631	甘肃省	40329
天津市	93984	江西省	37135

数据来源：新能源汽车国家监测与管理中心。

自 2018 年以来，广东省深圳市、东莞市、佛山市相继实现了电动化公交的全面覆盖，同时也大力推进电动汽车在环卫、物流、市政等公共服务领域的应用，更新或新增公共服务领域车辆全部为电动汽车，力争 2020 年在公共服务领域电动汽车保有量占比超过 90%。

图 2-3 给出了全球新能源汽车保有量及发展趋势，其中新能源汽车包括纯电动汽车（BEV）和插电式混合动力电动汽车（PHEV）。可见，2017 年，全球新能源汽车保有量超过 300 万辆，与 2016 年相比，新能源汽车保有量增加 56%，发展势头迅猛。中国是新能源汽车保有量最多的国家。2017 年中国拥有 153 万辆新能源汽车，约占全球新能源汽车保有量的 40%。

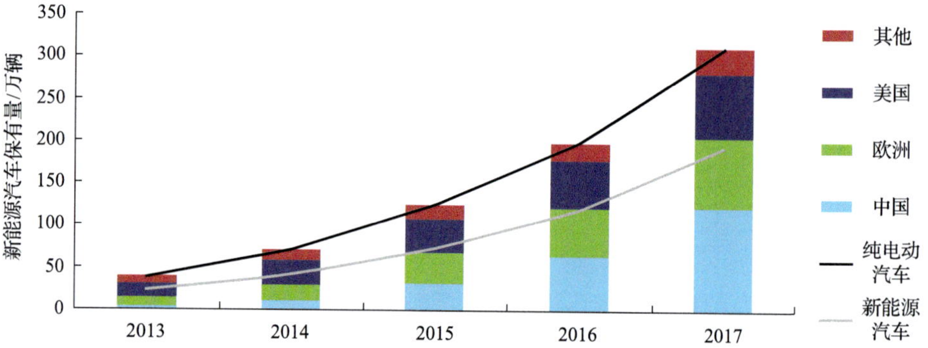

图 2-3　全球新能源汽车保有量及发展趋势

数据来源：*Global EV Outlook 2018*

在国务院印发的《节能与新能源汽车产业发展规划（2012～2020 年）》中[7]，明确提出了“到 2020 年，纯电动汽车和插电式混合动力电动汽车生产能力达到 200 万辆、累计产销量超过 500 万辆”的电动汽车产业发展目标。2018 年，我国新能源汽车产销量继续保持全球第一，全年产销分别为 127 万辆和 125.6 万辆，截至 2018 年底，全球新能源汽车总销量突破 550 万辆，其中我国占比超过 53%。根据国际能源署预计，到 2030 年，全球电动汽车的总保有量有望达到 2.2 亿辆，其中包括 1.3 亿辆纯电动汽车和 9000 万辆插电式混合动力汽车，而电动汽车充电设施也有望达到 1:1 的车桩比。表 2-2 为世界主要国家和地区电动汽车发展目标。

美国、欧盟、日本和中国等高电动汽车保有量国家和地区相继公布了“EV30@30”计划[8]，承诺到 2030 年实现电动车销量达到 30%的目标。美国政府计划到 2025 年在八个州实现 3300 万辆的电动汽车保有量、在 2040 年美国电动汽车总保有量达到 2.5 亿辆，美国能源部还在 2013 年拨 1.2 亿美元用于建设 1.4 万个电动汽车充电桩。欧盟计划到 2025 年电动汽车销量占比达到 15%、到 2040 年达到 30%。日本政府更是计划到 2030 年电动汽车的销售占比达到 50%，并在 2020 年拥有 200 万个常规充电站和 5000 个快速充电站。

表 2-2　世界主要国家和地区电动汽车发展目标

国家和地区	电动汽车发展目标
中国	①2020 年，拥有 500 万辆电动汽车，其中包括 460 万辆轻型电动汽车、20 万辆电动公共汽车和 20 万辆电动卡车 ②2020 年，电动汽车市场占比为 7%～10%；2025 年，电动汽车市场占比为 15%～20%；2030 年，电动汽车市场占比为 40%～50%
美国	2025 年，预计拥有 330 万辆电动汽车
欧盟	①2020 年，电动汽车市场占比为 15% ②2025 年，电动汽车市场占比为 30%
芬兰	2030 年，预计拥有 25 万辆电动汽车
新西兰	2021 年，预计拥有 6.4 万辆电动汽车
印度	①2030 年，电动汽车占比为 30% ②2030 年，公共汽车全部为电动汽车
爱尔兰	2030 年，预计拥有 50 万辆电动汽车
日本	2030 年，电动汽车占比达到 20%～30%
荷兰	①2020 年，电动汽车占比达到 10% ②2030 年，轻型汽车全部实现电动化 ③2025 年，只销售公共电动汽车 ④2030 年，公共汽车全部实现电动化
挪威	①2025 年，100%轻型汽车和城市公共汽车实现电动化 ②2030 年，75%长距离公共汽车和 50%重型卡车实现电动化
韩国	2020 年，拥有 20 万辆电动汽车
斯洛文尼亚	2030 年，100%电动汽车销售
英国	2020 年，拥有 39.6 万～43.1 万辆电动汽车

此外，一些国家也采取了相关的措施来应对电动汽车的飞速发展。挪威政府宣布在 2025 年将停售和停运所有内燃机汽车，全部替换为电动汽车；英国政府计划到 2020 年电动汽车保有量超过 40 万辆，并在 2040 年停售和停运内燃机汽车；韩国政府计划到 2020 年电动汽车保有量达到 20 万辆。

图 2-4 对比了 2030 年世界主要国家和地区在 EV30@30 场景预期下的电动汽

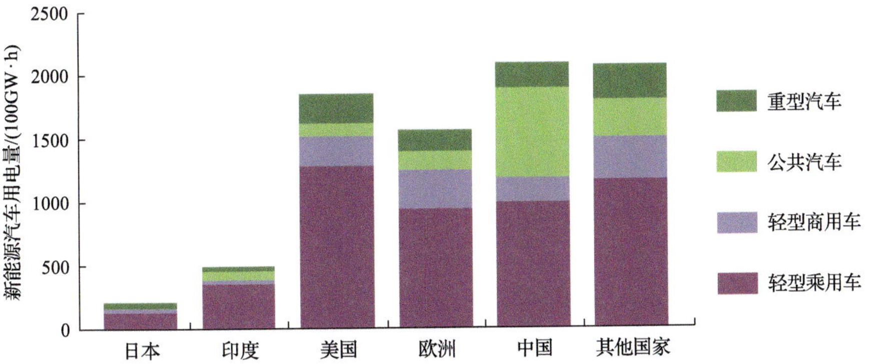

图 2-4　2030 年世界主要国家和地区未来电力需求展望

数据来源：*Global EV Outlook 2018*

车用能情况，其中 EV30@30 是指符合“巴黎协定”碳强度降低的电动汽车发展规划，预计电动汽车将占全球汽车保有量的 30%。

在电动汽车的快速发展大潮中，未来世界各国、各地区的电力需求将会显著增加。预计到 2030 年，电动汽车的全球电力消耗在 EV30@30 情景中达到 928000GW·h，与 2017 年电动车消耗的电量相比增加了 17 倍。面向居民的轻型乘用车消耗电量将占全球电动汽车用电量的 64%，公共汽车、两轮/三轮电动车和重型卡车分别消耗 14%、11%和 11%的用电量。从电力消耗的空间来看，2030 年中国仍然是电动汽车用电量最大的国家，约为全球电动汽车用电量的 29%，而美国将成为第二大电量消耗国，约占全球用电总量的 20%。同时，电动汽车用电量在欧洲、印度也将显著增加，到 2030 年约占全球用电总量的 17%、7%。

中国作为电动汽车发展和普及规模最大的国家，预计到 2030 年电动汽车电力消耗量将是 2017 年电动汽车电力消耗量的 5 倍，美国作为全球电动汽车用电量第二大国，其电力需求约为中国的 70%。在 EV30@30 场景下，预计 2030 年，电动汽车将节约 2.2 亿 t 油当量(9.2EJ①)的汽、柴油消耗。

综上，随着电动汽车保有量的持续增加，未来交通用能中电能将占据相当的比例。根据国际可再生能源署预计，在 2050 年，交通所用电能将占交通用能总量的 33%，其中 28%来自可再生能源，5%来自非可再生能源，相比 2015 年的 1%，提高了 27 个百分点。

2.2 非电能用能形态的发展模式

2.2.1 化石燃料用能形态的发展模式

在可再生能源的发展中尤其突出的是太阳能光伏市场和新能源汽车的发展。太阳能成本的大幅下降和政策支持，推动了太阳能光伏市场的蓬勃发展。2016 年可再生能源占全球净新增电力容量的 2/3，其中太阳能光伏发电增长了 50%，首次超过了煤炭的净增长。同时，可再生能源电力协议价格低至 3 美分/(kW·h)，接近或低于新建天然气和煤炭发电厂的发电成本。

2017 年 G20 峰会上一些国家已经拟定对燃油汽车销售和使用的限制措施，新能源汽车的发展前景备受瞩目。事实上，得益于产业产能、新能源汽车性能的提高以及补贴政策的影响，新能源汽车全球销售在 2014～2016 年期间已实现了 48%的年复合增长率，2017 年全球可再生能源乘用车增长 58%。尽管电动汽车是影响石油需求的一个重要因素，但根据国际能源机构估计，到 2022 年

① $1EJ=10^{18}J$.

电动汽车也只能取代有限数量的运输燃料，还有占公路交通汽油消耗比例 43%的货运车尚未得到有效渗透。虽然目前可再生能源的发展仍是一个相对缓慢的过程，但石油产业应当警惕能源转型所带来的长期压力。图 2-5 为全球石油需求的来源。

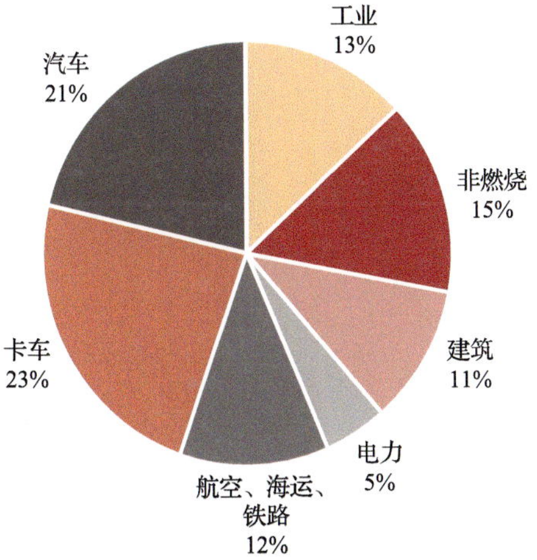

图 2-5　全球石油需求的来源

数据来源：《2030 年能源结构主要区域趋势》

虽然全球石油需求在过去 15 年中以 1.4%的年均复合增长率上升，但汽车的需求增长速度更快，年均复合增长率分别为 2.5%和 2.0%，因此，它们的份额一直在增加。到 2030 年，电动汽车将导致石油需求量下降大约 2.85 亿 t 石油当量或约 530 万桶/天，相当于当年石油需求总量的 6%(假设电动汽车不存在)。图 2-6 为电动汽车对石油需求的影响。

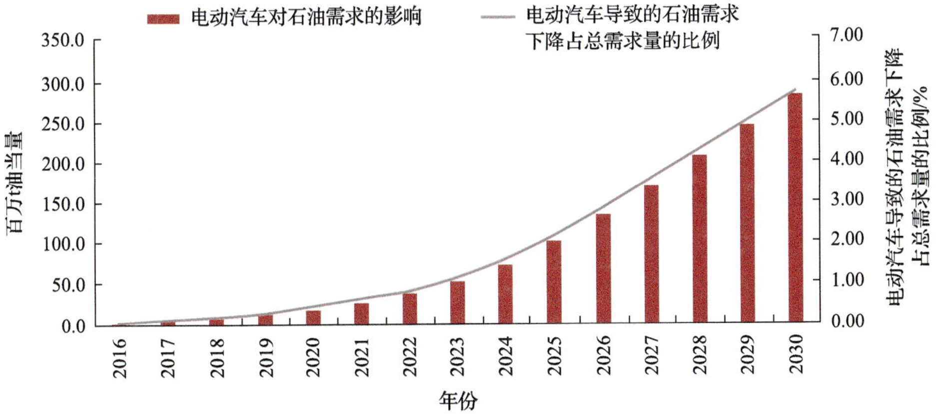

图 2-6　电动汽车对石油需求的影响

数据来源：《2030 年能源结构主要区域趋势》

2.2.2 氢燃料用能形态的发展模式

氢能被视为21世纪最具发展潜力的清洁能源，世界许多国家都将氢能作为战略性能源来发展，由于其具有零污染、高效率、来源丰富、用途广泛等优势，备受环境污染困扰的诸多国家都将氢能视为“未来能源”[9-13]。相对于其他燃料，氢能具有较高的能量密度，且具有可再生性和零碳含量，是清洁的二次能源，这些特性就使得氢能可以长期储存由间歇性能源所产生的电量，而且这种类型的储存技术灵活，便于分散操作。

然而，在交通运输行业，要想实现交通的低碳化发展，仅靠电动化可能难以做到。这一挑战可通过产自可再生能源的氢能加以解决，这将使大量可再生能源从电力部门引向终端使用部门。因此，氢能可能是能源转型过程中缺失的一环：可再生能源电力可用来制氢，而氢能反过来又可为难以通过电气化实现低碳化的部门提供能源。

图2-7给出了以氢能为桥梁的电力系统与交通运输系统的关联图。可见，氢能有助于实现电力系统与交通运输之间的“产业互连”，同时能够促进可再生能源与电力系统的整合。电解制氢可为电力系统提供足够的灵活性，可为电力系统提供低成本的平衡服务，同时所生产的氢气，可通过管网输送给交通运输业用能装备。在氢气传输官网中，可内置存储装置，以便根据电力系统的需求，实时调节氢气产量，并可长时间消纳可再生能源，从而实现季节性存储。

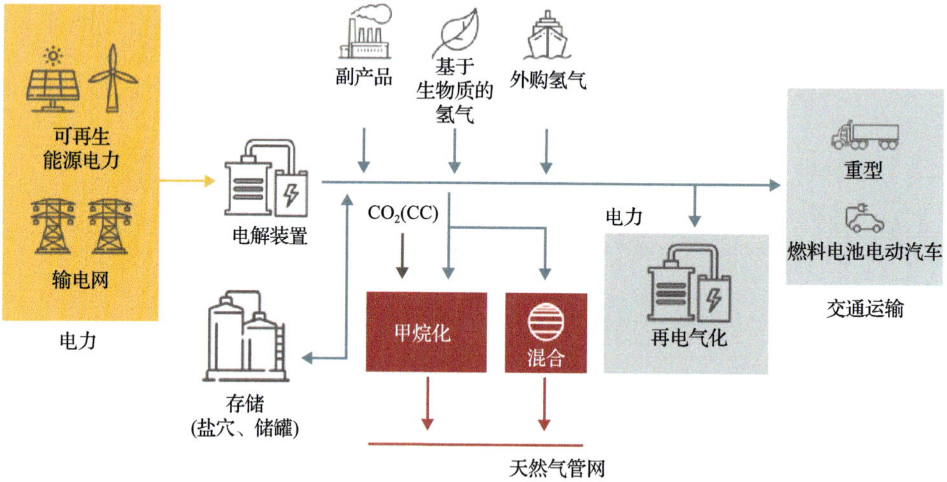

图2-7 电力系统与交通运输业的整合关联

从技术角度来看，氢能是能源生产和消费中的缺失环节，凭借可再生能源制氢，大量可再生能源从电力转移到难以实现电气化、低碳化的交通运输业，发挥关键作用并有助于产生积极成果。通过氢能的制备与运输，可将可再生能源的生产过程与消费过程分离，并有助于交通运输业的低碳化发展。

在交通运输行业中，燃料电池电动汽车作为以氢气作为驱动能源的电动化载运工具，可为用户提供低碳出行的新工具，同时 FCEV 燃料电池电动汽车的驾驶性能可与传统燃油汽车相媲美。针对电动汽车在中高负载循环过程中存在的重量、可行驶里程和燃料加注时间等限制，FCEV 燃料电池电动汽车能够克服这些问题，也是对电动汽车的补充。燃料电池电动汽车的可行驶里程和燃料加注时间的性能类似于传统车辆。从这个角度来看，它们将电动化交通方式的范围扩展到高负载循环部分，如长途或高利用率的卡车、公共汽车，这些车辆当前使用的电池存在不足。因此，在更广泛的能源转型背景下，氢气应该被视为纯电池电动汽车的补充。

图 2-8 给出了 2017 年和 2018 年全球燃料电池电动汽车保有量[14]。2018 年，全球累计销售燃料电池电动汽车约为 4000 辆，总保有量达到 11200 辆，同比增长 56%。然而，全球汽车保有量约为 10 亿辆，与二者相比较，燃料电池电动汽车占比仍然较小。美国燃料电池电动汽车约占全球燃料电池电动汽车保有量的 50%，约为 5600 辆，日本、德国、法国和韩国以 25%、11%、11%、8%的燃料电池电动汽车占比紧随其后。

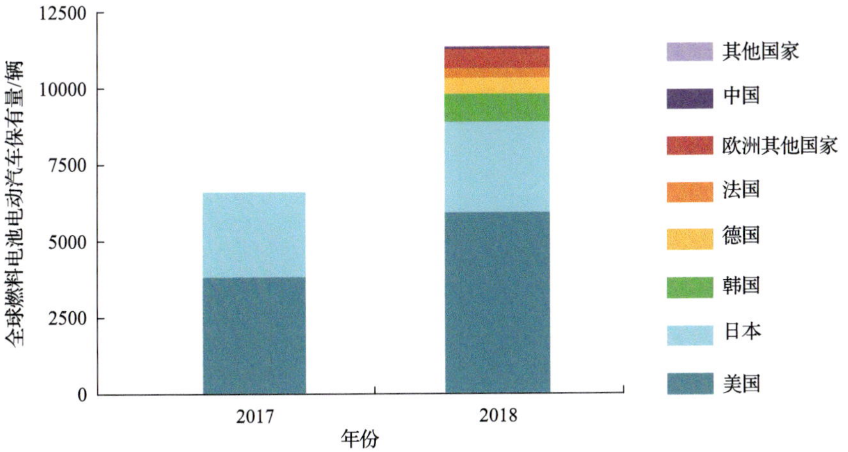

图 2-8　2017 年和 2018 年全球燃料电池电动汽车保有量

数据来源：*The Future of Hydrogen*

2018 年，我国以商用车为主的 FCEV 燃料电池电动汽车已突破千辆，数据显示，2017 年我国 FCEV 燃料电池电动汽车销售 1098 辆，运营区域从东北辽宁一直到广东佛山。在氢能示范城市江苏如皋，现已开通全国首条 FCEV 燃料电池电动汽车公交线。图 2-9 为全球加氢站发展情况。

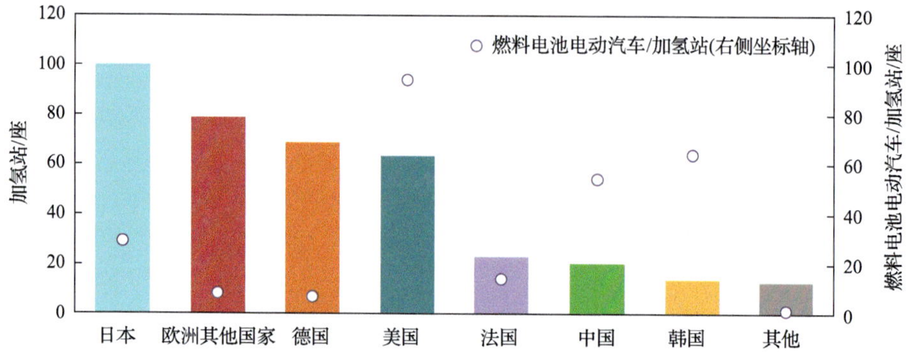

图 2-9　全球加氢站发展情况

数据来源：*The Future of Hydrogen*

作为燃料电池电动汽车的重要能源加注站，加氢站在过去几年已经有所增强，日本、德国和美国是建成公路交通加氢站最多的三个国家，其中日本拥有 100 座加氢站，德国拥有 69 座加氢站，美国拥有 63 座加氢站。但与纯电动汽车相比，每座加氢站服务的燃料电池电动汽车仍然偏多。因此，加快加氢站的建设，是推动燃料电池电动汽车发展的关键环节，也是提升氢能在交通运输终端能耗中占比的重要举措。

从中长期来看，氢气可成为远距离运输和分配可再生能源的一种方式，特别是在电网容量不足或者电网建设难度大成本高的情况下。海上风力发电可能就是如此，氢气可以在海上生产，然后通过天然气管道运输到岸上，管道无论是通过现有的海上管道改造而成还是进行重新安装，其成本均低于海底电缆的铺设成本。拥有丰富且廉价可再生能源的地区可生产氢气，运输到可再生能源发电潜力有限或发电成本较高的地区。以氢气为载体运输可再生能源，可以发展不同的规模，从本地到国际均可。到目前为止，管道输送仍是大规模氢气运输的最经济方式，因此“绿化天然气管网”能迅速地增加输送量，并可提供降低氢气成本所需的规模经济。

综上，通过氢能将电力生产与交通运输二者联系起来，可以显著地驱动交通运输业的低碳化发展，同时提高电力系统的灵活性，以更经济的方式整合高比例可再生能源并网，推动能源交通的协同前进与融合发展。预计到 2030 年，我国燃料电池电动汽车保有量将达到 100 万辆，并建成 1000 座以上的加氢站，氢能占整个交通运输业能源消耗总量的 1.0%，整个燃料电池电动汽车产业产值有望突破万亿元大关。

2.3　现有常用模式的未来发展方向

2.3.1　能源供给从高碳向低碳的发展方向

能源发展过程中，人类不断地寻找更多种类的能源，保障能源供应，满足交通发展对能源的需求，但不同的发展阶段主导的能源不同。技术的发展与社会的需求主导能源不断升级，总体是朝着更加低碳的方向发展。从薪柴到煤炭、石油，再到太阳能、风能等清洁能源的发展过程，就是逐步减少碳排放的过程[15,16]。表 2-3 给出了各类能源的碳排放强度。

表 2-3　各类能源的碳排放强度

类型	煤炭	石油	太阳能	风能
排放强度 （t 二氧化碳/t 标准煤）	2.77	2.15	0	0

数据来源：《全球能源互联网》.

化石能源碳排放强度高，持续上百年的开发利用已经排放了大量二氧化碳，对全球气候的影响已经开始显现，最近 100 年全球平均气温上升了 0.74℃。1979 年以来，北极海冰面积每年较少超过 7 万 km^2。要减缓气候变化、实现人类可持续发展，必须降低能源结构中化石能源比重、提高清洁能源比重。图 2-10 为中国发电能源结构预测。

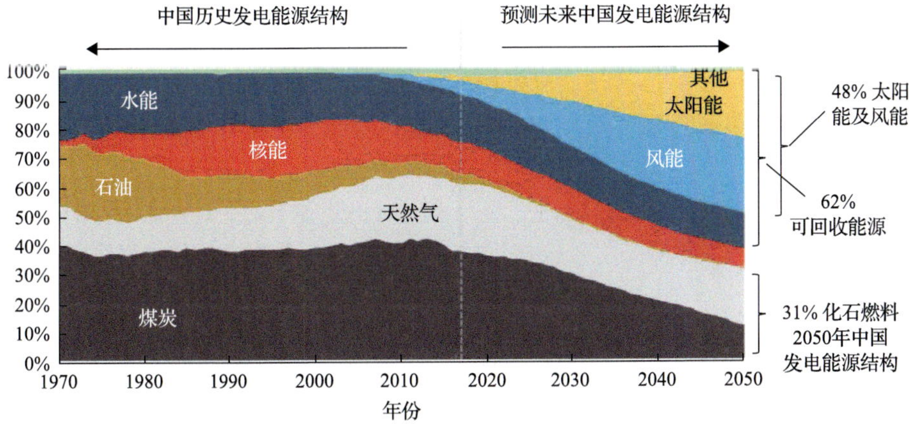

图 2-10　中国发电能源结构预测

根据 BloombergNEF 出版的 *New Energy* 2000 *Outlook* 预测，我国电力能源结构中煤炭发电量占比将逐步降低，天然气发电量占比将逐渐升高，石油发电量占比将逐步衰减为零，预计到 2050 年，化石燃料在我国发电能源占比降为 31%。然而，可再生能源发电量快速增加，预计到 2050 年，可再生能源发电量占比增加到 62%，其中，太阳能与风能发电量占比为 48%。根据彭博能源财经预测，我国 2020 年太阳能及风能在发电能源结构中占比为 9%，2025 年升高到 16%，2030 年升高到 24%，2035 年升高到 30%，电力的低碳化、清洁化发展为交通用能的清洁替代提供了有力的支持。表 2-4 为 2050 年交通用能预测表。

表 2-4　2050 年交通用能预测表

形态	类型	2018 年占比/%	2050 年占比/%	增幅/%
电能	可再生能源	<1	28	+27
	非可再生能源	1	5	+4
氢能	可再生能源	≈0	8	+8
生物燃料	可再生能源	3	22	+19
天然气	非可再生能源	2	4	+2
石油	非可再生能源	94	33	−61

数据来源：*Global Energy Transformation 2018*.

全球具有丰富的太阳能和风能资源，大规模开发利用的潜力巨大，将成为未来最重要的清洁能源。在现有和未来预期的技术、交通空间资源条件下，太阳能转换为电能是最便捷的利用方式。在交通用能中，提高太阳能利用率，不仅可为交通用能提供充足的清洁电力，也可促进交通用能的低碳化发展。

根据国际可再生能源署的预测，2050 年交通用能中非可再生能源从 96%下降为 42%，降幅显著。石油作为消耗量最大的非化石能源，2018 年占全球交通用能总量的 94%，预计到 2050 年，降低到全球交通用能总量的 33%。

因此，为进一步降低碳排放，实现节能减排，可大规模开发清洁能源并转换为电能，全面提升可再生能源发电量在交通用电量中的占比，并且化石能源的消耗量将逐渐降低，有助于交通系统的节能减排与提质增效。

大规模开发清洁能源并转化为电力，同时采用电能利用终端替代传统燃油、燃气终端，交通用能的效率将获得极大的提升。在未来，随着高效率电能利用终端的逐渐普及，化石能源的消耗量将逐渐降低，有助于交通系统的节能减排与提质增效。

2.3.2　能源配用从低效向高效的发展方向

提高交通用能的效率关键在于基础创新[17-19]。18 世纪后期，煤炭与蒸汽机的结合，形成了第一次工业革命，蒸汽机车应运而生，这不仅提高了交通运输的效率，也促使交通驱动力从畜力到机器的转变，极大地提高了交通用能效率和社会生产力。19 世纪后期，蒸汽机技术提升的空间潜力越来越小，对煤炭和蒸汽机主导的交通用能模式发展的驱动作用开始逐渐减缓。随着内燃机的出现和广泛的应用，以石油为代表的交通用能新模式登上了历史舞台，推动交通用能效率和劳动生产力的进一步提升。时至今日，化石能源效率的提升空间已遇到瓶颈。汽油内燃机直接燃油效率在 30%左右，而燃煤发电机的效率最高可达 50%左右，电动机效率可以超过 90%。图 2-11 为交通用能从低效向高效的发展趋势。

考虑到未来清洁可再生能源将在交通用能结构中占主导地位，能源利用效率将主要取决于一次能源的太阳能、风能转换效率，而电能的终端利用效率远高于化石能源直接利用的效率，要高于蒸汽机、汽油内燃机、煤炭直接燃烧等。采用电能终端替代传统燃油、燃气终端，交通用能的效率将获得极大的提升。因此，交通载运工具作为化石能源消耗的主要设备，将面临电动化、高效化的重要变革。图 2-12 为交通用能的大范围优化配置。

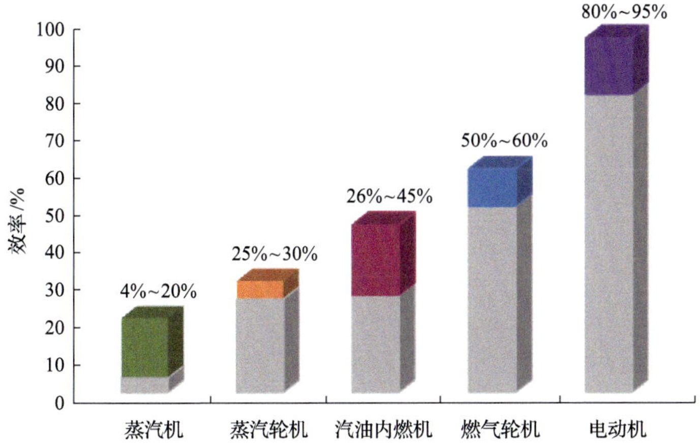

图 2-11　交通用能从低效向高效的发展趋势

数据来源：《全球能源互联网》

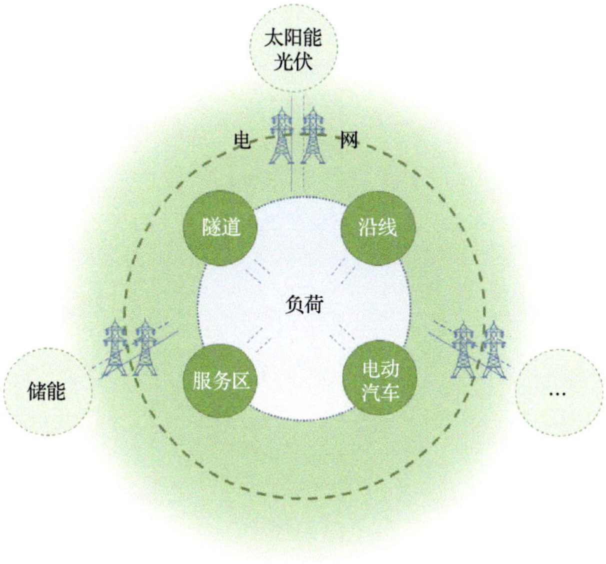

图 2-12　交通用能的大范围优化配置

网络作为现代社会发展的产物，可通过网络把各个点、面、体联系到一起。交通侧作为一个包含负荷点、传输网且具有发电能力的整体，能够利用自身潜力进行可再生能源的生产，在满足自身负荷用电需求前提下，还可向距离较远的负荷点进行供电，能实现资源的传输、接收和共享，形成特有的交通能源网。未来，在以清洁能源为主导、以电为中心的能源发展格局下，电网将成为能源配置的主要载体。在交通能源网中，隧道、沿线及服务区的设施用电作为其特有的交通负荷，同时也是开发可再生能源的有利场所，使得交通能源网实现就近发电、就近使用，减少了能源上网及远距离传输产生的费用，是最经济便捷的能源配置方式。随着交通清洁能源的大规模开发，用能自洽率逐步提高，交通能源网也将实现与地区电力网泛在互联的能源网络。

第 3 章　公路交通能源系统的新模式

顺应公路交通能源系统的发展趋势，本章以智能电网为纽带，通过太阳能光伏发电与公路交通系统的集成，秉承就近开发、就近消纳的建设理念，构建清洁化、高效化的新型公路交通能源系统。然后，通过对新型公路交通系统的“源属性”、“网属性”、“荷属性”的进一步挖掘，本章提出多属性、多层次、多角度的新型能源交通系统演化新模式。最后，结合我国光资源属性、负荷属性、电网属性的特点，梳理归纳了新型公路交通能源系统应用的潜在场景，面对差异化需求，从交通与能源间主导、互动关系，给出了公路交通能源系统演化新模式。

3.1　考虑交通做适应性调整的交通能源系统演化新模式

3.1.1　考虑交通“源属性”的公路交通能源系统演化新模式

我国煤炭储量丰富，逐渐形成了以火电为主、水电、核电与可再生能源发电为辅的电力结构，2018 年我国发电装机容量达到 1900GW，火电机组突破 1000GW，约为 1140GW，占总装机容量的 60.2%，而火电发电量为 4.9×10^6GW·h，约占全国总发电量的 70.4%，风、光发电量为 543500GW·h，约占全国总发电量的 7.8%[20]。

现阶段，随着节能减排需求的日益增加，公路交通用能应向更清洁、更低碳的方向发展。《巴黎协定》预计到 2050 年全球气温升高控制在 2℃以内，国际可再生能源署预计交通用能中有 33%为电能，其中 85%来自可再生能源发电。因此，顺应交通用能清洁化、低碳化发展趋势，需从交通资源入手，充分开发交通“源属性”构建清洁低碳电源，构建公路交通能源系统新模式，以提高风、光资源发电量在交通用电量占比，降低交通用能的间接碳排放量，具有重要的意义。

公路交通主要由道路、隧道、桥梁、匝道等交通基础设施，燃油车、电动车等交通载运工具以及服务区、集散中心等交通服务设施组成。由于交通载运工具用能形态主要为汽柴油，用电量较小，则忽略其潜在电源属性，因此本节重点关注公路交通基础设施和交通服务设施的“源属性”交通能源系统演化新模式。

在交通基础设施方面，利用双洞公路隧道间隔、公路边坡、匝道等空间资源，为分布式光伏发电提供布局空间，同时公路隧道、沿线负荷又为可再生能源提供了消纳空间，从而形成自发自用的分布式光伏发电开发新模式，可间接降低公路交通系统的外购电力与碳排放量。同时，对于无网地区小负荷供配电需求，也可建立分布式光伏发电与储能相结合的供电系统，从而避免新建 10kV 配电线路，降低隧道建设成本。通过对隧道周围装设环境的调查，隧道的出现常因山体阻碍，要对隧道处装设太阳能光伏组件，最佳光伏组件安装点可选择在隧道的进出口的左右两门洞之间的绿化地。在高速公路沿线，互联匝道、路肩、边坡等开发较为容易，路面架空光伏由于支架复杂、安装高度高等原因，开发难度较大。因此，在交通基础设施“源属性”开发中，应首先关注隧道隔离带、互联匝道、路肩、边坡等易开发交通资源，并随着光伏高架、光伏路面的技术进步与成本降低，交通资源开发重心将逐步转向开发面积广阔、潜力巨大的道路上方、路面等难开发交通资源。

2017 年 6 月，全国首例高速公路匝道圈分布式光伏发电项目——齐鲁交通发展集团山东交通可再生能源科技有限公司孟疃收费站 1700kW 分布式光伏发电项目正式并网发电。按照山东高速集团的测算，以 2017 年的山东青兰高速为例，每对服务区的屋顶、停车场及周围匝道护栏可建成 1000kW 的分布式光伏电站；每百公里的互通立交匝道圈可建两座 2000kW 的发电站；每百公里的边坡至少可建 50MW 的发电站。统筹考虑，如果每百公里能够建成 55MW 分布式光伏发电，按照当时山东省高速公路 5000km 的里程，以可利用 1/2 计算，光伏安装量可达 1375MW。图 3-1 为分布式光伏发电在交通基础设施中的应用。

图 3-1　分布式光伏发电在交通基础设施中的应用

在交通服务设施方面，由于服务区、停车区、集散中心等建筑集中，存在较为容易开发的屋顶、停车棚等空间资源，十分便于建设分布式光伏发电系统。交通服务设施“源属性”开发模式，充分地利用交通服务设施的空间资源，倡导就近发电、就近并网、就近使用的原则，通过分布式光伏发电与屋顶、停车棚的结合，实现交通服务设施从消费者向生产者的转变，替代和减少非可再生能源电力的用量，这也是一种新型、具有广阔前景的交通电源潜力开发方式。光伏屋顶安装高性能的太阳能电池组件，由光伏组件将太阳能转换为直流电能，通过逆变器将直流电转换为供家庭使用和并网的交流电。运行方式以用户自发自用余电上网，也可全额上网，且在配电系统平衡调节为特征的光伏发电设施，包括光伏组件、光伏逆变器、并网箱、支架、线缆及其他辅材。浙江嘉兴南湖服务区屋顶光伏铺装面积为 5000m^2，年发电量可达到 250MW，同时按商业电价计算，每年仅节约电费就有 20 多万元，经济效益明显。

光伏车棚主要由支架系统、电池组件阵列、照明及控制逆变系统、充电装置系统和防雷及接地系统组成。光伏车棚支架型式多样，支架系统主要包括支撑立柱、固接在支撑立柱之间的斜梁、接在斜梁上用于支撑太阳电池组件阵列的支架及固定电池组件阵列的紧固件等。光伏车棚建设规模可大可小，大到如宁波杭州湾项目，总装机容量为 55MW·h，相当于 20 个足球场大小，可停放车辆 2 万多辆，是世界上最大的光伏建筑一体化项目。图 3-2 为分布式光伏发电在交通服务设施中的应用。

图 3-2 分布式光伏发电在交通服务设施中的应用

在公路交通能源系统“源属性”层面，通过在交通基础设施、交通服务设施可利用空间上加装分布式光伏发电，从而使公路交通能源系统从“荷”向“源-荷”共存状态转变，使公路交通能源系统具有发电能力。

3.1.2 考虑交通“网属性”的公路交通能源系统演化新模式

随着公路交通“源属性”的持续开发，借助分布式光伏发电，公路交通资源已逐渐由能源消费者转变为能源生产者，潜力与后劲十足。由于分布式可再生能源并网单元靠近负荷末端，省却了大规模远距离传输过程，因此我国可再生能源并网方式逐渐向分散式接入倾斜。然后，由于分布式光伏发电具有经时波动性、间歇性的不稳定电源，则如何更好地将这些不可控的可再生能源接入配电网，就显得更为重要。

为应对分布式电源接入的问题，需要升级现有公路交通能源系统的组织架构和运行方式，加强对本地资源的自我管理，从被动消纳模式演进为主动控制模式。微电网作为一种特殊的分布式发电系统，是集成了多种可再生能源、储能、本地负荷、监视保护和控制单元的局部供电系统。因此，对于公路交通能源系统而言，通过对多端、多点能源系统的融合集成，借助先进电力电子和信息电子技术，能够智能地调控本地资源，弥合分布式光伏发电与电网、负荷之间的矛盾，这正是公路交通能源系统“网属性”的集中体现。

通过对公路交通能源系统“网属性”的开发，一方面，可将分布式光伏、用电负荷和储能系统等一次设备及其控制系统有机地结合起来，形成一个有序的局部供电系统，这是具有“物理实体属性”的网；另一方面，随着先进信息电子技术，将智能化交通基础设施、载运工具互联，形成融合装备信息、出行信息的信息网，这是具有“数字虚体属性”的网。在公路交通能源系统“网属性”开发驱动下，可实现公路交通能源系统的源荷共存、多点互联、资源互补，为用户和公共电网提供优质的电力供给和智能的信息交互。图 3-3 为“网属性”视角下公路交通能源系统。

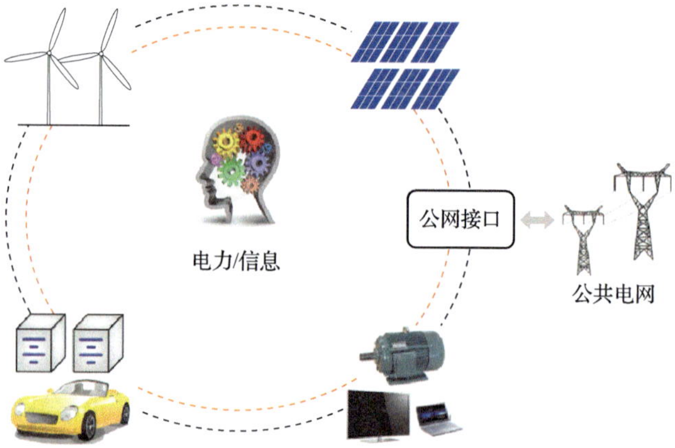

图 3-3 “网属性”视角下公路交通能源系统

在“网属性”视角下，公路交通能源系统既可以与大电网并网运行，也可以脱离大电网独立运行。通过分布式电源、储能装置和需求侧管理的协调控制和综合管理，使公路交通能源系统成为一个可控单元，向大电网提供安全、稳定、高效、清洁的能源，提高电力系统运行灵活性和可靠性。公路交通能源系统可以满足用户多样化的需求，降低大电网电力传输压力，并向大电网提供辅助服务。在大电网故障时，公路交通能源系统还可以离网运行，保证重要负荷供电，提高系统可靠性。同时，公路交通能源系统也是一种极具潜力的偏远地区供电模式，在传统资源枯竭和负荷增长的双重压力下，公路交通能源系统通过资源互补利用，就地满足了负荷需求，有效地提高了能源利用率，并节省了电网延伸费用。图 3-4 为公路交通能源系统群。

随着公路交通能源系统“网属性”的深入以及逐步工程化，多端、多点公路交通能源系统群运行成为可能。公路交通能源子网是一种特殊的智能化的大规模公路交通能源系统运行模式，是由局部地区相邻较近的多个公路交通能源系统组成的，各子公路交通能源系统既可独立自治运行，也可部分子公路交通能源系统

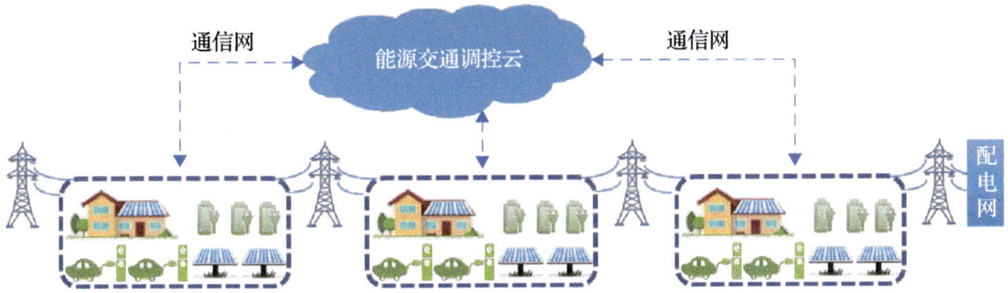

图 3-4　公路交通能源系统群

或全部子公路交通能源系统互联运行并完成某一特定的运行目标，如经济性、可靠性、稳定性等。公路交通能源系统群还需要在其子公路交通能源系统出现暂态过程的情况下起到相互支撑的作用。与单一公路交通能源系统相类似，公路交通能源系统群还可并入大电网运行。与单一的公路交通能源系统相比，公路交通能源系统群能够实现分布式可再生能源的合理调配和充分利用，与多个公路交通能源系统运行相比，公路交通能源系统群基于共同目标的协作化运行更强，同时暂态过程中能够在某公路交通能源系统出现功率缺额、负荷突增等“危急”情况时，通过其他公路交通能源系统与其实现“拉手”对该子公路交通能源系统进行频率和电压支撑，从而保证负荷的正常运行。

在公路交通能源系统“网属性”层面，通过多端、多点公路交通能源系统的协作化运行，可实现公路交通能源系统的可控制、可调度，就地满足了负荷需求，实现从“局部平衡”到“大范围优化配置”的转变，有效地提高了能源利用率。

3.1.3　考虑交通“荷属性”的公路交通能源系统演化新模式

公路交通能源系统是由分布式光伏发电、储能装置和本地负荷有机融合而成的，借助先进电力电子和信息电子技术，能够智能调控本地资源，实现本地电力平衡。在“荷属性”层面，公路交通能源系统最重要的负荷就是电动汽车充电负荷，这种新兴负荷具有典型的移动特性，集中体现在时空不确定性，这将极大地增加公路交通能源系统源-网-荷-储的平衡难度。同时，大量电动汽车的接入充电，将会带来新一轮负荷增长，充电负荷引发的集聚效应对电力系统的影响是不确定的，这种无序充电可能导致充电负荷集中在某一区域、某一配电变压器、某一配电线路上，造成一些配变和线路过载甚至堵塞，进而导致配电系统负荷曲线出现峰峰叠加的情况，进一步增大峰谷差和降低负荷率，影响系统运行的经济性和供电的可靠性。因此，必须重点关注公路交通能源系统的“荷属性”，通过对公路交通能源系统“荷属性”有序主动调控，合理引导和利用负荷，实现充电负荷在空间和时间的合理分布。

北京地区的一项调研发现，大部分用户回家后立即对电动汽车进行充电，充电时间集中在18时和次日11时，充电高峰在22时至次日0时，与现有的居民负荷重合率高达85%。如果2030年电动汽车的年销量达到120万辆，居民区的充电负荷将达到210kW，现有配网很难承载，配网改造的投资将高达64亿元。如果实现智慧有序充电，就可以大大提高充电桩的使用效率，减少充电桩的重复建设。

在公路交通能源系统“荷属性”层面，通过对交通能源系统负荷侧的控制，实现负荷的可调节、可转移，使其具有可控功能，并可根据交通能源系统的源特性、网特性做出响应，实现交通能源系统负荷从“随机”到“可控”的转变，有助于交通能源系统的电力平衡。

3.2 考虑能源做适应性调整的公路交通能源系统演化新模式

2018年，中国能源消费总量为46.4亿t标准煤，同比增长3.3%。从消费结构看，虽然近年来随着能源转型的提速和电力体制改革的不断深入，清洁能源所占比重稳步提高，化石能源所占比重逐步降低，但化石能源的核心地位依然没变。2018年，中国清洁能源占比为22.1%。近十年来，中国化石能源平均占比为83.4%，煤炭占比逐步下降，石油占比稳中有升。煤炭作为中国的重要能源，2018年消费量同比下降1.4%，但其仍占能源消费总量的59.0%。BP 2019年预测，2040年中国仍是全球最大能源消费国，将占全球能源消费总量的22%，煤炭所占比重降至35%，同时可再生能源占比将增至18%。图3-5为2009～2018年中国能源消费量及煤炭、清洁能源所占比重情况。

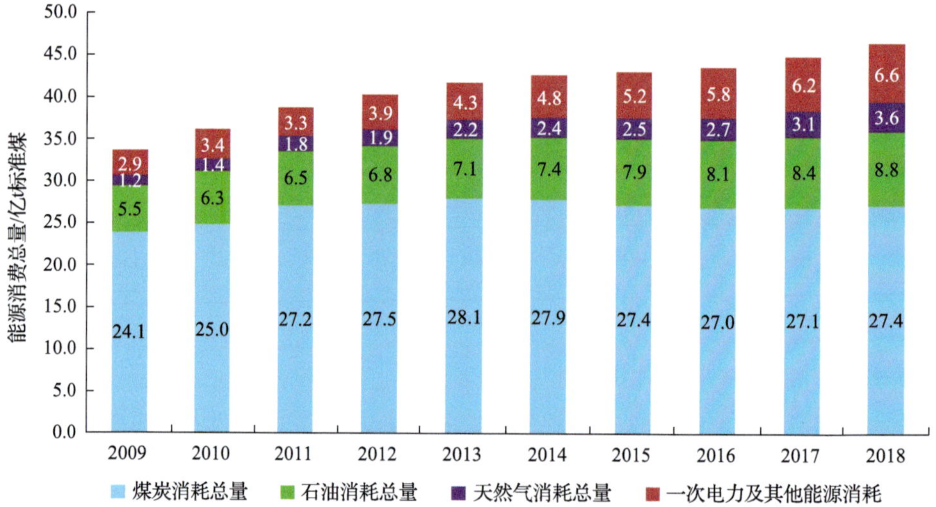

图3-5 2009～2018年中国能源消费量及煤炭、清洁能源所占比重情况

数据来源：《中国统计年鉴2018》《2018年国民经济和社会发展统计公报》

现阶段，石油依然是我国交通行业的主导能源，约占总体的94%。但随着绿色低碳的观念深入人心同时国家大力支持新能源汽车的发展，可替代能源尤其是天然气和电力在交通行业的使用逐年增长。根据国际可再生能源署预测，石油在交通用能终端占比将从2018年的94%下降到2050年的33%，下降近70%。电力在交通用能终端占比快速提升，从2018年的1%上升到2050年的33%，其中85%是可再生能源产生的电力。

为进一步加快公路交通能源系统的低碳化、清洁化进程，可采用“分散接入”的可再生能源开发模式。然而，可再生能源的接入，特别是分散式风电、分布式光伏，不可避免地存在间歇性、波动性的特点，是典型的不可控源。如何更好地将这些间歇性、波动性电源接入电网，对于提供区域电网低碳化程度，就显得十分关键。

微电网作为一种特殊的分布式发电系统，是集成了多种可再生能源、储能、本地负荷、监视保护和控制单元的局部供电系统。微电网的开发和工程示范已经被提升到国家战略意义上来。在2006年国务院发布的《国家中长期科学和技术发展规划纲要(2006～2020年)》中，已将包含微电网的分布式供能技术列为先进能源技术方面的前沿技术。在2016年国家能源局发布的《可再生能源“十三五”规划》中，提出建立容纳高比例波动性可再生能源电力的配用储一体化的局域电力系统，按照“因地制宜、多能互补、技术先进、创新机制”的原则，推进以可再生能源为主、分布式电源多元互补的可再生能源微电网应用示范工程建设。图3-6为能源做调整视角下交通能源系统演化新模式。

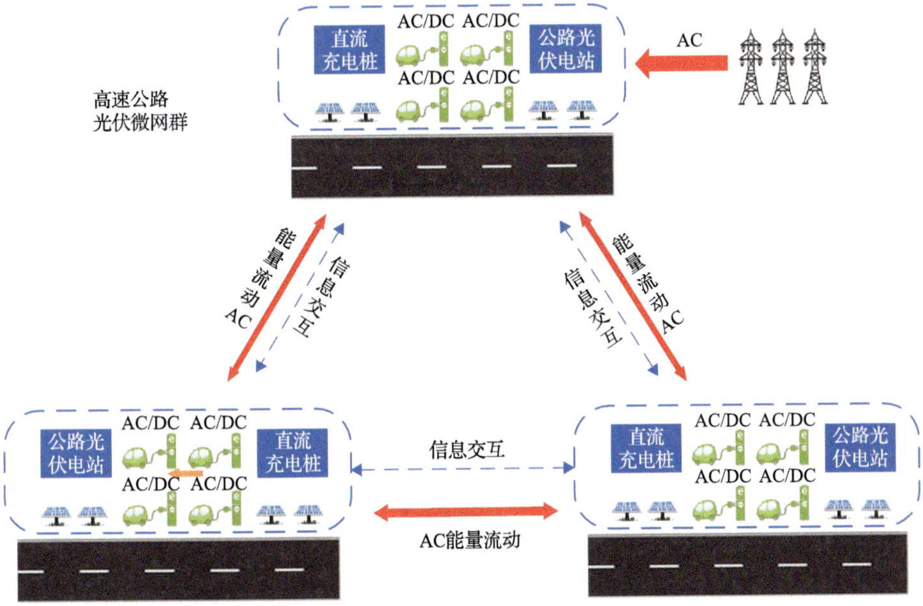

图3-6　能源做调整视角下交通能源系统演化新模式

对于交通能源系统而言，采用微电网供电模式，通过将一定地理范围内的分布式光伏、储能装置、可控负荷、稳定的主电源进行统一整合，形成一个既可以与大电网并联运行，又可以独立于大电网的、孤岛运行的微型电力网络，通过对多可控资源的分类调控，可实现分布式光伏的高效利用，提高区域交通能源系统的低碳化、清洁化水平，具有重要的意义。

采用微电网供电的交通能源系统应以需求为导向，由于其分布式光伏发电、交通负荷分散化特征要求交通能源系统边界开发，并能够实施重构网络架构。同时，电动汽车充电负荷、公路隧道照明负荷、服务区负荷根据气象、用户需求等复杂工况灵活加入或退出交通能源系统，而且不能影响交通能源系统的正常运行，这就要求交通能源系统更具有即插即用功能。交通能源系统作为电力信息复合网络除信息共享外，还需实现网络各个节点的静态和动态功率平衡，确保电压和频率稳定，保证功率/能量在电力网络上稳定、平衡、高效传输。

相对于由单一微电网构成的交通能源系统的能量管理与控制，由多微电网构成的交通能源系统网的运行相对复杂，需要采用分层的能量管理和控制模式，除了需要考虑单个分布式电源的发电控制和负荷控制以及微电网内部多个分布式电源的协调控制，还要考虑多微电网构成的交通能源系统网与大电网之间的功率调配，而对于多微电网构成的交通能源系统来说，其还需要考虑各子微电电网之间的互联状态以及群级协作下各子微电网之间的功率优化调配和协调控制。

在考虑能源做调整的交通能源系统中，通过采用微电网替代大电网的供电模式，可对本地资源进行智能调控，充分地发挥多可控资源的互补性优势，实现交通能源系统分节点、分区域的能量/功率平衡，从而化解间歇性、波动性可再生能源发电接入所带来的问题，有助于交通能源系统的低碳化、清洁化发展，并可为用户和大电网提供可靠、稳定、优质的电力供给。

3.3 考虑交通能源共同做适应性调整的公路交通能源系统演化新模式

图 3-7 为能源交通共同调整的交通能源系统。

随着我国高速公路网络的日趋发达，高速公路对于能源的消耗量越来越大，对高效、经济、安全和高容量运输的能源交通需求更加迫切。但是就能源与交通的体系而言，我国仍然是以石油-内燃机为主要动力的能源系统。考虑到不可再生能源的发展约束、环境承载力及经济的可持续发展能力，目前的能源交通体系并不能长期维持与发展。因此，在限制气候变化和促进可持续增长的双重要求的推动下，全球能源体系正在转型。在传统能源供应基础上，一方面，借助先进电力电子技术，依托可再生能源进行发电，首先从发电端改变能源供应形式，并逐步

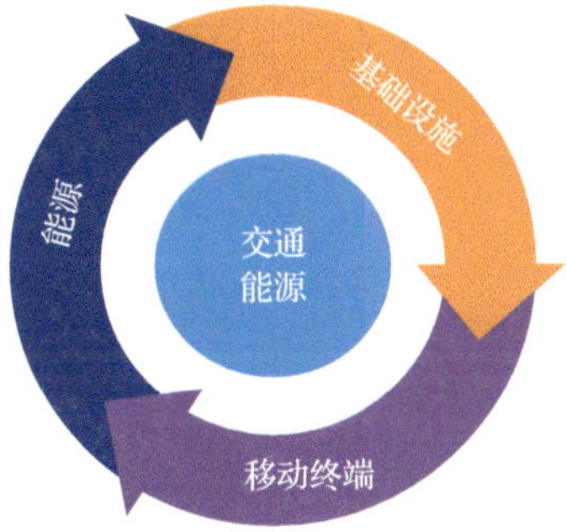

图 3-7　能源交通共同调整的交通能源系统

调整交通侧终端设备以及交通载体的用能模式以适应能源转变，从而在“源-网-荷-储”四端均形成以可再生能源为主要的用能主体的能源交通系统新结构；另一方面，借助先进信息电子技术，实现能源信息的发、储、配、用各方面的互联互通，逐步实现新型公路交通系统的弹性化运行。

在能源与交通共同做调整的交通能源系统(图 3-8)中，充分地利用公路交通的空间资源和光伏发电安装布置的灵活性，最大化开发可再生能源的发电潜力，为交通能源系统提供充足的能源电力供给；在公路服务区，加速推广大功率快速充电的布局，为电动汽车长距离出行提供充足的电力供给，同时也为光伏发电提供广阔的电力消纳空间；由于用电负荷和发电量在时间上的不平衡，可通过储能对能量的时间平移，实现负荷与发电量的匹配。

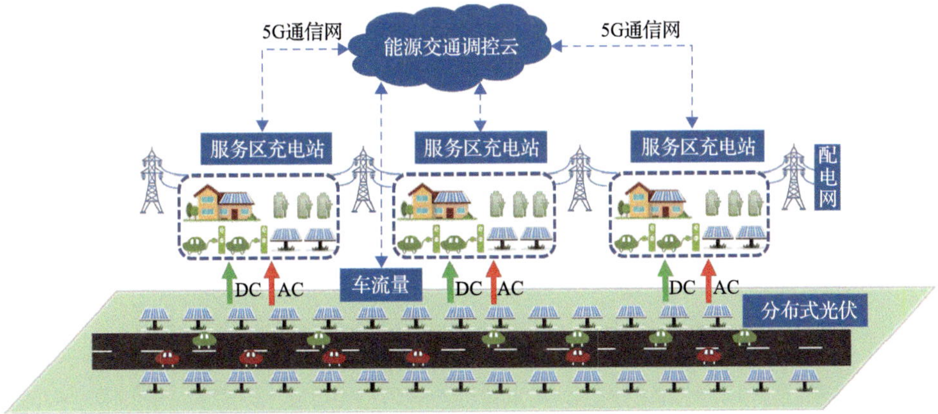

图 3-8　能源与交通共同做调整的交通能源系统

综上所述，由可再生能源发电、交通用电及储能组网而成的交通能源系统，最大限度地开发利用交通资源的发电潜力，为公路交通运载工具和服务设施提供清洁的电力供应，借助储能系统实现能量/功率的平移，形成“源-网-荷-储”协同联动的交通能源系统新模式。因此，根据源特性、网特性、荷特性，归纳出交通能源系统应用的 12 种场景。图 3-9 为交通能源系统应用场景。

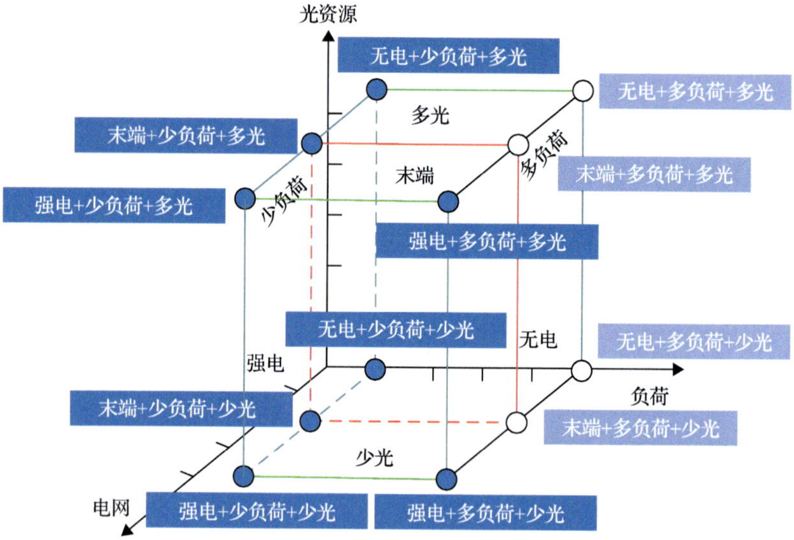

图 3-9 交通能源系统应用场景

可见，根据源特性，即可供开发的资源潜力，可划分为资源丰富区、资源一般区[21-23]，其中资源丰富区是指光资源 I 类和 II 类地区，包括甘肃、青海、北京、河北、陕西、山西、云南、新疆、宁夏，资源一般区是指光资源III类和IV类地区，包括湖北、福建、浙江、广东、河南、江西、湖南、安徽、江苏、吉林、广西、四川、贵州、重庆；根据网特性，即电网形态和架构，可划分为强电网、弱电网、无电网地区；根据荷特性，即用电量，可划分为大负荷区、小负荷区。表 3-1 为不同场景下交通能源系统运行方式。

表 3-1 不同场景下交通能源系统运行方式

源属性	网属性	荷属性	运行方式	解决方案
资源丰富区	强电网	大负荷	全额自用、网电补缺	交通专用能源系统
		小负荷	上网为主、自用为辅	交通特有能源系统
	弱电网	小负荷	提升外送、降低弃光	交通适配能源系统
	无电网	小负荷	光储协同、发用平衡	能源支撑交通系统
资源一般区	强电网	大负荷	全额自用、网电补缺	交通专用能源系统
		小负荷	上网为主、自用为辅	交通特有能源系统
	弱电网	小负荷	提升外送、降低弃光	交通适配能源系统
	无电网	小负荷	光储协同、发用平衡	能源支撑交通系统

考虑到交通能源需求与电力网络铺设的实际，大负荷地区一定处于强电网地

区，并结合图 3-9 给出的预期场景，因此交通能源系统将在资源丰富区与一般区共同面对强电网大负荷、强电网小负荷、弱电网小负荷、无电网小负荷的功能需求。然而，在光资源丰富区与一般区，交通能源系统运行方式基本相同，仅存在发电量的差异。因此，本节将针对强电网大负荷、强电网小负荷、弱电网小负荷、无电网小负荷的应用场景，给出交通能源系统的工作模式。图 3-10 为能源交通融合网的源-网-荷-储示意图。

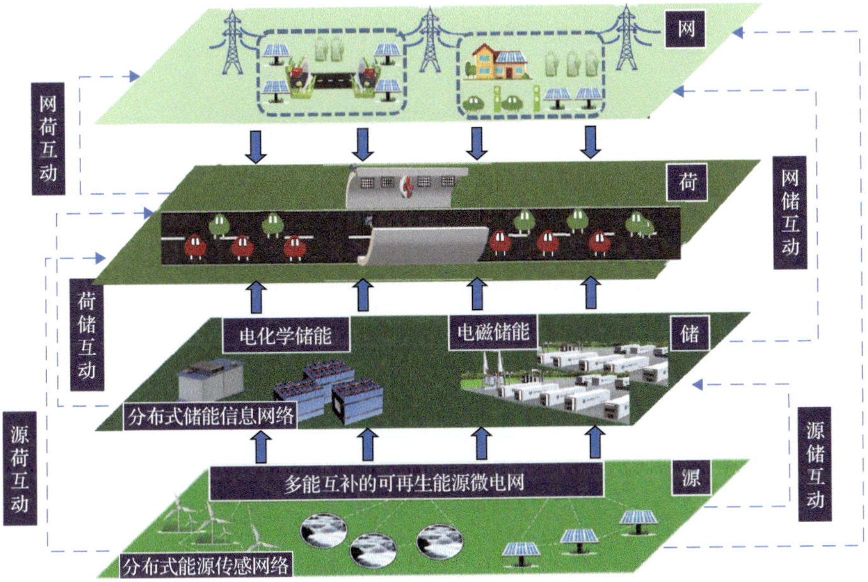

图 3-10　能源交通融合网的源-网-荷-储示意图

综上所述，由可再生能源发电、交通用电以及储能混合组网而成的交通能源系统，最大限度地开发利用交通资源的发电潜力，为公路交通运载工具和服务设施提供清洁的电力供应，借助储能系统实现能量/功率的平移，形成“源-网-荷-储”协同联动的交通能源系统新模式。

3.3.1　基于交通与能源间互动联系的交通能源系统演化新模式

1. 光资源丰富区的强电网、大负荷应用场景

强电网环境为光伏发电提供了良好的并网与传输通道，同时本地大负荷也为分布式光伏发电提供了充足消纳空间，主要消纳场所有光资源丰富区近枢纽变电站的特长隧道供配电、集中式电动汽车充电站等。图 3-11 为光资源丰富区强电网、大负荷场景下交通能源系统演化新模式。

因此，交通能源系统以辅助自用电源形态运行，其发电量全部为本地负荷消纳，并且与强电网共同为本地大负荷供电，降低本地大负荷对电网供电容量的要

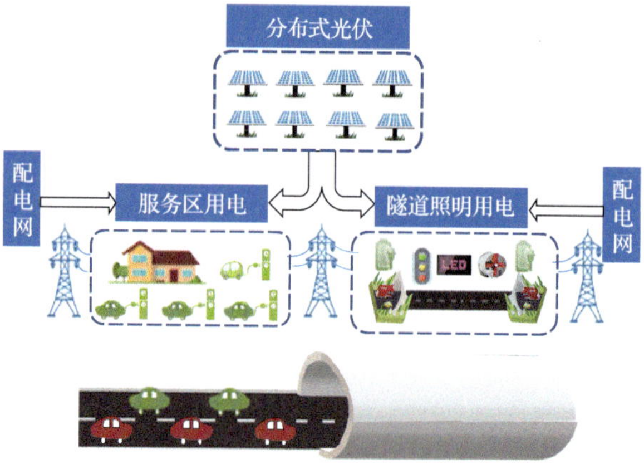

图 3-11　光资源丰富区强电网、大负荷场景下交通能源系统演化新模式

求，从而形成双电源互动的供电模式。由于本地负荷较大，可再生能源仅能满足部分负荷需求，这就必须要接入强电网作为支撑，以实现电力/电量的平衡，从而形成“全额自用、网电补缺”的运行方式。

在这种场景下，充分地利用建筑屋顶、匝道空地等空间资源加装分布式光伏，同时分布式光伏以向电网注入最大的有功功率为目标运行，最大限度地将可再生能源转化为电能，供给本地负荷。

2. 光资源丰富区的强电网、小负荷应用场景

光资源丰富区有大量的可再生能源可供利用，为分布式光伏发电的开发提供足够的资源潜力，并且强电网环境为光伏发电提供了良好的并网与传输通道，但由于本地负荷较小，决定了这种场景下光伏发电以自用优先、余量上网的方式运行，主要有光资源丰富区近枢纽变电站的公路沿线、匝道等，详见图 3-12。

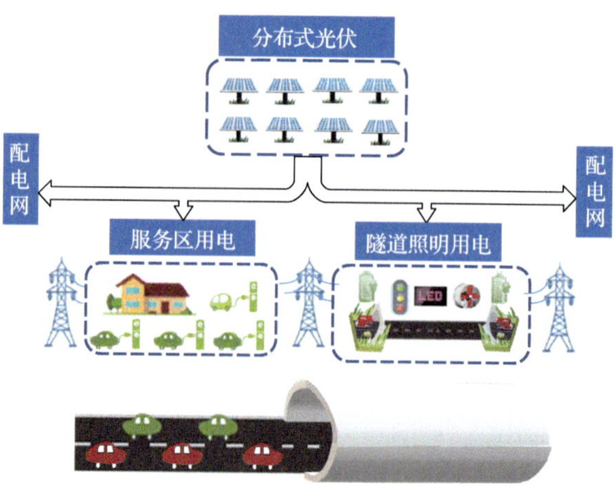

图 3-12　光资源丰富区强电网、小负荷场景下交通能源系统演化新模式

因此，交通能源系统主要以外送电源形态运行，发电量在供给本地负荷消纳后，剩余电量通过强电网接入电力系统，通过产能与交通用能的互动调整，形成“上网为主、自用为辅”的运行方式。通过这种模式的开发利用，不仅实现了交通用能的自我供给，也实现了交通资源由“荷”向“源”的转变，可为电力系统提供大量清洁电力。

在这种场景下，充分地利用公路沿线、匝道可供开发的交通资源，在强电网输电断面限定值范围下最大限度地建设分布式光伏，分布式光伏以向电网注入最大的有功功率为目标运行，最大限度地将可再生能源转化为电能，通过强电网并入电力系统。

3. 光资源丰富区的弱电网、小负荷应用场景

光资源丰富区有大量的可再生能源可供利用，为分布式光伏发电的开发提供足够的资源潜力，但受限于弱电网接入环境的限制，无法输送大容量的可再生能源，同时考虑本地用电负荷较小的因素，本地并不具备充足的可再生能源消纳空间，主要有远离枢纽变电站的公路沿线、匝道等。图 3-13 为光资源丰富区弱电网、小负荷场景下交通能源系统演化新模式。

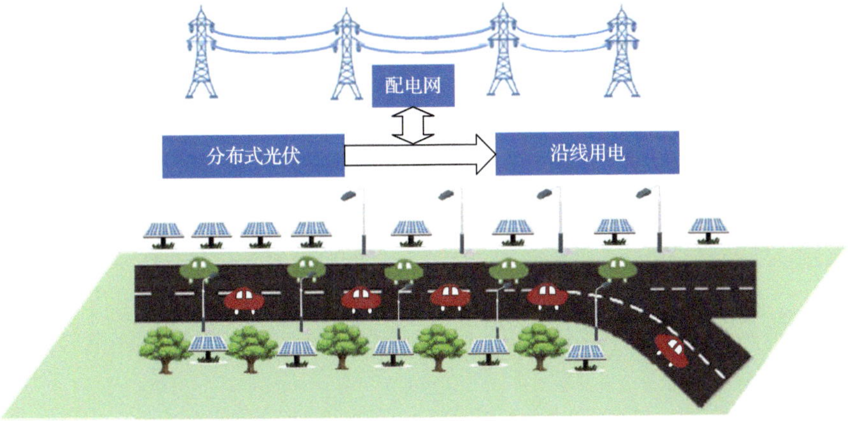

图 3-13　光资源丰富区弱电网、小负荷场景下交通能源系统演化新模式

因此，交通能源系统中分布式光伏与外部配电网分时互动、协同供电，确保沿线机电设施的正常运转。在该场景下，交通能源系统应重点从提升分布式光伏接入系统的灵活性着手，通过对分布式光伏发电控制的技术改造，使分布式光伏发电响应电力系统频率、电压调节，提高电源侧灵活性的改造提升，提升弱电网可外送的可再生能源发电量，从而形成“提升外送、降低弃光”的运行方式。

在这种场景下，应通过技术改造与升级，提高分布式光伏发电的灵活性，而后以弱电网断面外送电量为约束，利用公路沿线、立交匝道等空间，合理地开发

分布式光伏发电，避免由于过度开发造成的大量弃光。

4. 光资源丰富区的无电网、小负荷应用场景

图 3-14 为光资源丰富区无电网、小负荷场景下交通能源系统演化新模式。

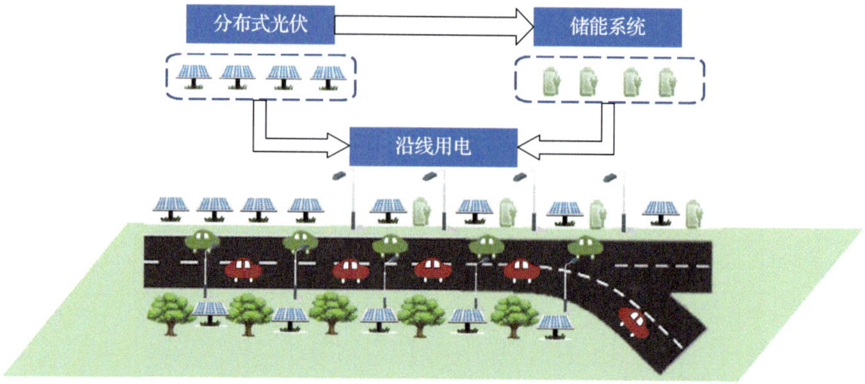

图 3-14　光资源丰富区无电网、小负荷场景下交通能源系统演化新模式

光资源丰富区有大量的可再生能源可供利用，为分布式光伏发电的开发提供足够的资源潜力，但在无电网环境下，为满足本地小负荷配用电需求，分布式光伏需要具备稳定频率、电压的能力，同时由于发电量与用电量在时间尺度上的不平衡，而需加装储能装置以实现能量的时间位移与功率的再平衡，主要有偏远地区的短隧道、小型服务区、收费站等。

因此，交通能源系统应以建立频率、电压稳定的电力生产为目标，并结合储能的灵活调节作用，通过光储能源系统与交通用电系统的灵活互动，实现本地小负荷的稳定可靠供电，从而形成“光储协同、发用平衡”的运行方式。通过储能的嵌入，可在分布式光伏发电出力高于负荷用电需求时储存富余能量，并在分布式光伏发电出力低于负荷用电需求时释放储存的能量，从而实现能量的时间位移与功率的平衡。

在这种场景下，以满足本地负荷用电需求为目标，按需开发分布式光伏发电，同时建设小容量储能装置，通过对能量的时间位移，平衡分布式光伏发电与本地负荷用电的需求，分布式光伏发电以控制供电电压和频率为目标，因荷制宜、因储制宜调节其有功、无功功率。

3.3.2　考虑交通与能源不同主导地位的交通能源系统演化新模式

1. 光资源一般区的强电网、大负荷应用场景

光资源一般区强电网、大负荷场景下交通能源系统演化新模式与图 3-11 仅存

在光伏资源多少上的差异，其余均相同。此处分布式光伏发电系统的安装量只需满足该场景下电量的平衡即可。

强电网环境为光伏发电提供了良好的并网与传输通道，同时本地大负荷也为分布式光伏发电提供了充足消纳空间，主要有光资源一般区近枢纽变电站的特长隧道供配电、集中式电动汽车充电站等。

因此，交通能源系统以强电网为主导，分布式光伏以辅助自用电源形态运行，其发电量全部为本地负荷消纳，并且与强电网共同为本地大负荷供电，降低本地大负荷对电网供电容量的要求。由于本地负荷较大，可再生能源仅能满足部分负荷需求，这就必须要接入强电网作为支撑，以实现电力/电量的平衡，从而形成“全额自用、网电补缺”的运行方式。

在这种场景下，充分地利用建筑屋顶、匝道空地等空间资源加装分布式光伏，同时分布式光伏以向电网注入最大的有功功率为目标运行，最大限度地将可再生能源转化为电能，供给本地负荷。

2. 光资源一般区的强电网、小负荷应用场景

图 3-15 为光资源一般区强电网、小负荷场景下交通能源系统演化新模式。

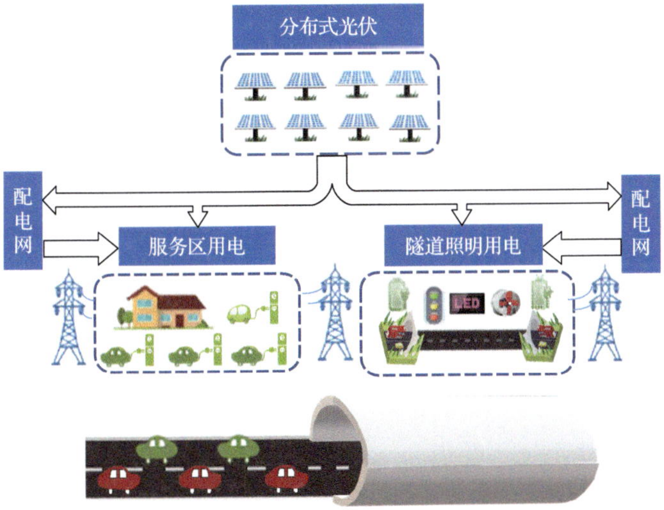

图 3-15 光资源一般区强电网、小负荷场景下交通能源系统演化新模式

光资源一般区有较多的可再生能源可供利用，为分布式光伏发电的开发提供相对充足的资源潜力，并且强电网环境为光伏发电提供了良好的并网与传输通道，但由于本地负荷较小，决定了这种场景下光伏发电以自用优先、余量上网的方式运行，主要有光资源一般区近枢纽变电站的公路沿线、匝道等，详见图 3-16。

因此，交通能源系统应以分布式光伏为主导电源，发电量在供给本地负荷消

纳后，剩余电量通过强电网接入电力系统，从而形成“上网为主、自用为辅”的运行方式。通过这种模式的开发利用，不仅实现了交通用能的自我供给，也实现了交通资源由“荷”向“源”的转变，可为电力系统提供大量清洁电力。

在这种场景下，充分地利用公路沿线、匝道可供开发的交通资源，在强电网输电断面限定值范围下最大限度地建设分布式光伏，分布式光伏以向电网注入最大的有功功率为目标运行，最大限度地将可再生能源转化为电能，通过强电网并入电力系统。

3. 光资源一般区的弱电网、小负荷应用场景

光资源一般区弱电网、小负荷场景下交通能源系统演化新模式与图 3-13 仅存在光伏资源多少上的差异，其余均相同。此处分布式光伏发电系统的安装量只需满足该场景下电量的平衡即可。

光资源一般区有较多的可再生能源可供利用，为分布式光伏发电的开发提供相对充足的资源潜力，但受限于弱电网接入环境的限制，无法输送大容量的可再生能源，同时考虑本地用电负荷较小的因素，本地并不具备充足的可再生能源消纳空间，主要有远离枢纽变电站的公路沿线、匝道等。

因此，交通能源系统应以分布式光伏发电为主导，以配电网供电为辅，重点从提升分布式光伏接入系统的灵活性着手，通过对分布式光伏发电控制的技术改造，使分布式光伏发电响应电力系统频率、电压调节，提高电源侧灵活性的改造提升，提升弱电网可外送的可再生能源发电量，从而形成“提升外送、降低弃光”的运行方式。

在这种场景下，应通过技术改造与升级，提高分布式光伏发电的灵活性，而后以弱电网断面外送电量为约束，利用公路沿线、立交匝道等空间，合理地开发分布式光伏发电，避免由于过度开发造成的大量弃光。

4. 光资源一般区的无电网、小负荷应用场景

光资源一般区有较多的可再生能源可供利用，为分布式光伏发电的开发提供相对充足的资源潜力，但在无电网环境下，为满足本地小负荷配用电需求，分布式光伏需要具备稳定频率、电压的能力，同时由于发电量与用电量在时间尺度上的不平衡，而需加装储能装置以实现能量的时间位移与功率的再平衡，主要有偏远地区的短隧道、小型服务区/收费站等。光资源一般区无电网、小负荷场景下交通能源系统演化新模式也与图 3-13 相同，差异也只在于光伏资源的多少。

因此，交通能源系统应以建立频率、电压稳定的电力生产为目标，并结合储能的灵活调节作用，形成光储主导的供电模式，实现本地小负荷的稳定可靠供电，从而形成“光储协同、发用平衡”的运行方式。通过储能的嵌入，可在分布式光

伏发电出力高于负荷用电需求时储存富余能量，并在分布式光伏发电出力低于负荷用电需求时释放储存的能量，从而实现能量的时间位移与功率的平衡。

在这种场景下，以满足本地负荷用电需求为目标，按需开发分布式光伏发电，同时建设小容量储能装置，通过对能量的时间位移，平衡分布式光伏发电与本地负荷用电的需求，分布式光伏发电以控制供电电压和频率为目标，因荷制宜、因储制宜调节其有功、无功功率。

第 4 章　新模式的技术解决方案

在“源-网-荷”三重属性驱动下，以新型公路交通能源系统的差异化应用为需求，本章首先构建了交通专用能源系统、交通特有能源系统、交通适配能源系统和能源支撑交通系统 4 类典型解决方案，并提出能源交通融合网作为新型公路交通能源系统的技术解决方案。最后，对未来 15 年公路交通能源系统的用电自洽率、用能自洽率和可再生能源电力渗透率等指标进行了推算，并按照从易开发到难开发、从易消纳到难消纳的方式，提出了新型公路交通能源系统的演化发展路径。

4.1　不同新模式的共性技术提炼

4.1.1　因地制宜的太阳能资源利用

在太阳能资源开发中，太阳能资源开发利用过程中，要尽量地避免占用耕地、林地和生态湿地，水域地区因不适宜进行设备安装也可排除在外，其考虑到在城镇用地上进行太阳能开发也十分有限，城镇用地本身所占比例很小，也不重点考虑。因此，在太阳能开发利用中应首先考虑未利用的裸地和森林生态价值较低的灌木、草地等。我国高速公路的建设正是充分地利用了远离城镇地区的裸地，这正与太阳能资源开发下的地理要求不谋而合，因此在高速公路沿途进行太阳能资源的开发具有得天独厚的优势。

由于太阳能是对自然能量的转化和利用，因此太阳能铺设受太阳日照条件及地理环境的影响最为明显。高速公路作为基本交通运输方式，是连接两个城市之间的快速通道，因此，高速公路建设一般远离城市中心向四周发展，其主要组成单元还包括隧道和服务区等。

由于我国现有太阳辐射观测站点较少，要了解太阳辐射的分布情况，主要是利用太阳总辐射与日照百分率的关系，采用经验公式计算的方法获得。参照国家标准《太阳能资源等级总辐射》(GB/T 31155—2014) 中的经验计算方法，有

$$Q = Q_0 + (a + bS) = Q_0 + \left(a + b\frac{n}{N}\right)$$

式中，Q 为到达地表的太阳总辐射，$kW \cdot h/m^2$；Q_0 为地外太阳辐射；S 为实际日

照小时数与可照时数的比值，即每月日照百分率；a，b 为各月的经验系数。通过有太阳辐射和日照时数观测的站点建立统计关系，并采用统计方法推广到无太阳辐射观测的地区。

根据《太阳能资源等级总辐射》中的等级划分[24]，可判定某地区的太阳能资源丰富程度。$Q \geqslant 1750\text{kW} \cdot \text{h/m}^2$ 为极丰富等级（Ⅰ类地区）；$1400\text{kW} \cdot \text{h/m}^2 \leqslant Q \leqslant 1750\text{kW} \cdot \text{h/m}^2$ 为较丰富等级（Ⅱ类地区）；$1050\text{kW} \cdot \text{h/m}^2 \leqslant Q \leqslant 1400\text{kW} \cdot \text{h/m}^2$ 为丰富等级（Ⅲ类地区）；$Q \leqslant 1050\text{kW} \cdot \text{h/m}^2$ 为一般等级（Ⅳ类地区）。

太阳能光伏组件的发电量的影响因素主要受到安装面积及区域太阳能辐射的影响[25-28]。安装面积越大则发电量越大，而在相同安装面积下，地区太阳能辐射量越高则发电效率越高，根据上述四类地区的辐射量结论可知，在光伏组件相同安装面积下，一类资源地的发电量将远高于四类资源地，则光伏组件的理论年发电量计算公式为

$$L = Q_a \times S_{\text{PV}} \times \eta$$

式中，L 为光伏电池板理论年发电量，MJ；Q_a 为区域年平均太阳辐射量；S_{PV} 为光伏组件面积；η 为光伏电站系统的转换效率，一般取 17.5%。

在光伏组件的实际发电中，光伏组件发电量还会受到诸多因素的影响，如灰尘、雨水遮挡引起的效率降低与组件串联不匹配产生的效率降低以及逆变器的功率损耗、直流交流部分线缆功率损耗、变压器功率损耗等。

光伏电池的效率会随着其工作时的温度变化而变化。随着光伏组件温度的升高，不同类型电池的输出功率呈现降低的趋势。光伏温度因子为−0.36%/℃，根据统计光伏组件平均工作气温高于 25℃，折减因子取 96%。

组件上有灰尘或积雪造成的污染，会减弱辐射到电池板表面的太阳能辐射强度，从而影响太阳电池板的输出功率。经统计经常受雨水冲洗的光伏组件其影响平均为 2%～4%，无雨水冲洗较脏的光伏组件其影响平均为 8%～10%。因此，综合考虑折减系数取 6%，即污染的折减因子取 94%。

除光伏温度、光伏灰尘损耗等，光伏逆变器效率、可利用率等因素仍会对实际发电量造成影响，具体为并网光伏逆变器的平均效率取 96%；站内用电、输电线路等，约占总发电量的 5%，其配电综合损耗系数为 95%；虽然太阳能电池的故障率极低，但定期检修及电网故障依然会造成损失，其损失系数取 1%，光伏发电系统的可利用率为 99%；太阳能电池板差异性损耗为 3%，则利用率为 97%；早晚不可利用辐射损失为 3%，则利用率为 97%。

综上所述，太阳电池板的实际发电量 L_T 计算公式为

$$L_T = L \times \eta_1 \times 0.28$$

式中，L_T 为太阳能电池板实际发电量，kW·h；L 为太阳能电池板理论发电量，kW·h;0.28 表示 MJ 与 kW·h 之间的折算系数；η_1 为实际发电效率，η_1=0.96×0.94×0.96×0.95×0.99×0.97×0.97≈0.77。

上述分析是从各地区太阳能资源分配对资源的利用，除此之外，不同地形条件(坡度、坡向)对太阳能辐射的接受总量也有较大影响，当基于地形进行区域划分时，结合水土保持规定中对坡度的划分标准，综合考虑地形对太阳能资源被动分配的影响，主动开发的难易程度主要遵循以下两个原则：

第一，阳坡优先原则。安装太阳能光伏组件时，最佳倾角总是向阳的，阴坡将会对太阳直接辐射的获取时长产生一定影响，因此，开发选址时南坡要优先于北坡。

第二，平坡优先原则。无论从资源获取、水土保持和开发成本等角度来考虑，在地势平坦地区开发利用太阳能相对容易，在考虑坡度因素影响时，结合《水土保持综合治理规划通则》(GB/T 15772—2008)中坡度等级界定划分。该通则将坡度划分为以下 6 个等级：微坡[0°, 5°)、较缓坡[5°, 8°)、缓坡[8°, 15°)、较陡坡[15°, 25°)、陡坡[25°, 35°)、急陡坡[35°, 90°)。

根据上述原则，可将各地区太阳能资源的可利用程度划分为 4 个等级，划分依据如表 4-1 所示。其中，Ⅰ类为最适宜开发利用地区；Ⅱ类为较适宜开发利用地区；Ⅲ类为可开发利用地区；Ⅳ类为不适宜开发利用地区。

表 4-1　依据坡度、坡向划分的太阳能开发适宜性划分标准

坡向	角度	坡度				
		[0°, 5°)	[5°, 8°)	[8°, 15°)	[15°, 25°)	[35°, 90°)
偏南	[135°, 225°]	Ⅰ	Ⅰ	Ⅱ	Ⅲ	Ⅳ
偏东南/偏西南	[90°, 135°]或[225°, 270°]	Ⅰ	Ⅱ	Ⅱ	Ⅲ	Ⅳ
偏东北/偏西北	[45°, 90°]或[270°, 315°]	Ⅱ	Ⅲ	Ⅲ	Ⅳ	Ⅳ
偏北	[0°, 45°]或[315°, 360°]	Ⅱ	Ⅲ	Ⅲ	Ⅳ	Ⅳ

注：0°为正北方向，90°为正东方向，180°为正南方向，270°为正西方向。

由于地理位置不同，各省(区、市)分布式光伏铺设的最佳倾角存在差异，如表 4-2 所示，给出了我国各省(区、市)分布式光伏铺设最佳倾角[29]。可见，分布式光伏铺设的最佳倾角与铺设地点的纬度密切相关，全国各省(区、市)分布式光伏铺设最佳倾角详见表 4-2。

表 4-2　我国各省(区、市)分布式光伏铺设最佳倾角

区域	省(区、市)	纬度ϕ/(°)	日辐射量/(kJ/m^2)	最佳倾角β/(°)	斜面日辐射量/(kJ/m^2)
直辖市	北京	39.8	15261	φ+4	18035
	天津	39.7	14356	φ+5	16722
	上海	31.17	12760	φ+3	13691
	重庆	29.35	12670	φ+3	12460
东北地区	黑龙江省	43.25～53.33	12703	φ+3	15838
	吉林省	40.52～46.18	13572	φ+1	17127
	辽宁省	38.43～43.26	13793	φ+1	16563
华北地区	内蒙古自治区	37.24～53.23	16574	φ+3	20075
	山西省	34.34～40.43	15061	φ+5	17394
	河北省	36.01～42.37	14707	φ+4	18734
华中地区	河南省	31.23～36.22	13332	φ+7	14558
	湖北省	29.05～33.2	13201	φ+7	13707
	湖南省	24.38～30.8	11377	φ+6	11589
西南地区	四川省	26.03～34.19	10392	φ+2	10304
	贵州省	24.37～29.13	10327	φ+8	10235
	云南省	21.13～29.25	14194	φ−8	15333
	西藏自治区	26.73～36.53	21301	φ−8	24151
西北地区	新疆维吾尔自治区	34.22～49.1	14464	φ+12	16594
	青海省	31.42～39.07	16777	φ+1	19617
	甘肃省	32.11～42.57	14966	φ+8	15842
	宁夏回族自治区	35.14～39.23	16553	φ+2	19615
	陕西省	31.42～39.35	12781	φ+14	12852
华南地区	广东省	20.12～25.31	12110	φ−7	12702
	海南省	18.1～20.1	13835	φ+12	13510
	广西壮族自治区	20.54～26.23	12515	φ+5	12734
华东地区	江苏省	30.45～35.2	13099	φ+5	14207
	安徽省	29.41～34.38	12525	φ+9	13299
	浙江省	27.12～31.31	1668	φ+3	12372
	江西省	24.39～30.04	13094	φ+2	13714
	福建省	23.3～28.22	12001	φ+4	12451
	山东省	34.22～38.23	14043	φ+6	15994

除了地面可利用面积，高速公路光伏顶棚也具有较大开发潜力。针对公路南北走向与东西走向的差异，为获取最大量的太阳辐射，其铺设方式也不同。

如图 4-1 所示，其中β为最佳倾角。在东西走向公路，光伏顶棚呈现南低北高的结构，光伏组件直接平铺在顶棚支架上，顶棚支架的倾斜角度为光伏铺设的最佳倾角。在南北走向公路，光伏顶棚为东西同高的结构，光伏支架与地面平行，光伏组件在顶棚支架上呈现南向、锯齿状分布，锯齿排列的光伏组件与地面夹角为最佳倾角。

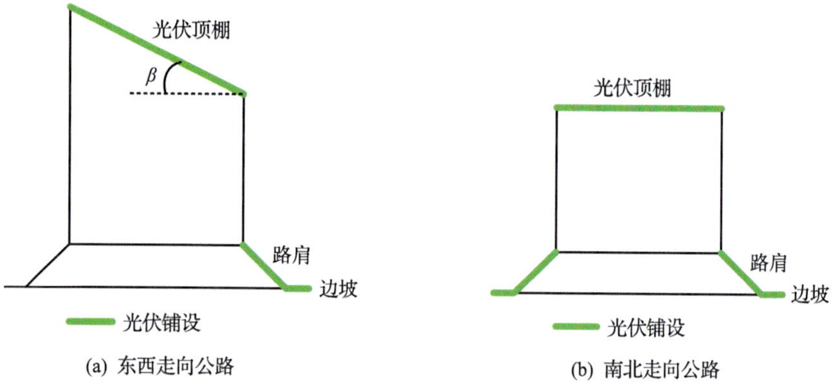

图 4-1　公路交通光伏顶棚

在光伏系统固定安装面积下，假设光伏发电量为 P_i、公路交通能源系统的用电量为 E_i，则用电自洽率为

$$\mathrm{SCR}_E = \frac{P_i}{E_i}$$

在此基础上，将交通能源系统全部能源消耗折算为电力消耗，假设交通能源系统总能耗(折算为电能)为 S_i，则用能自洽率为

$$\mathrm{SCR}_S = \frac{P_i}{S_i}$$

为进一步明晰交通能源系统可用可再生能源电力，在交通能源系统总用电量小于光伏系统总发电量前提下，引入交通系统中的可再生能源电力渗透率 NEPR，表征交通用能中可再生能源电力占比，具体计算为

$$\mathrm{NEPR} = \frac{(E_i - P_i)\times\gamma + P_i}{E_i}$$

式中，γ 为电力系统中可再生能源电力的渗透率。

4.1.2　高效可靠的储能系统配置

由于光伏发电的随机性、波动性和间歇性，为满足对隧道负荷的持续性供电，加装储能装置对平滑分布式电源出力，减小其发电随机性对电网的冲击，对提高分布式电源的渗透率等有着重要的作用[30-33]。且储能装置的容量配置问题十分关键，储能容量配置太小则无法有效地消纳光伏电力，储能容量配置太大则电池投资成本升高。

假设光伏系统的可利用率为β，该值定义为光伏系统平均出力P_V与光伏系统的装机容量S_V的比值，满足以下关系式

$$\beta = P_V / S_V$$

式中

$$P_V = M_V / T_V$$

式中，M_V为光伏系统出力曲线与时间轴之间的面积；T_V为光伏系统出力总时间。

光伏系统在一天内的出力曲线近似正态分布，根据历史数据对光伏出力曲线进行拟合，在光伏系统装机容量为S_0时，令光伏出力曲线的正态分布函数为

$$P_0 = f_0(t)$$

则光伏出力曲线的面积为

$$M_0 = \int_{T_1}^{T_2} f_0(t)\mathrm{d}t$$

式中，T_1和T_2分别为一天中光伏出力的始末时刻，若一天中光伏出力时间为T_0，则$T_0 = T_2 - T_1$。

当光伏系统装机容量为S_1时，光伏出力曲线的拟合预测如下式所示。根据隧道的用能特点，在同一地区的光伏系统可利用率β不变，则

$$\beta = M_0 / (T_0 S_0)$$

假设同一地区的光伏系统在一天中的出力时间不变，则光伏系统出力曲线的面积为

$$M_1 = S_1 \beta T_0 = M_0 S_1 / S_0$$

令光伏系统装机容量为S_1时的光伏系统出力曲线为$P_1 = f_1(t)$，则满足

$$\frac{M_1}{M_0} = \frac{S_1}{S_0} = \frac{\int_{T_1}^{T_2} f_1(t)\mathrm{d}t}{\int_{T_1}^{T_2} f_0(t)\mathrm{d}t} = \frac{f_1(t)}{f_0(t)}$$

由此可推出，光伏系统装机容量为 S_1 时的光伏出力曲线为

$$f_1(t) = \frac{S_1}{S_0} f_0(t)$$

假设地区日总负荷与光伏出力的差值为净负荷，则当净负荷超过配电容量达到峰荷时，释放储能容量，对净负荷曲线起到削峰作用；当净负荷低于配电容量时，可通过电网对储能进行充电，等下一个峰荷到来时释放能量。含光储系统出力的电力电量平衡示意图如图 4-2 所示。

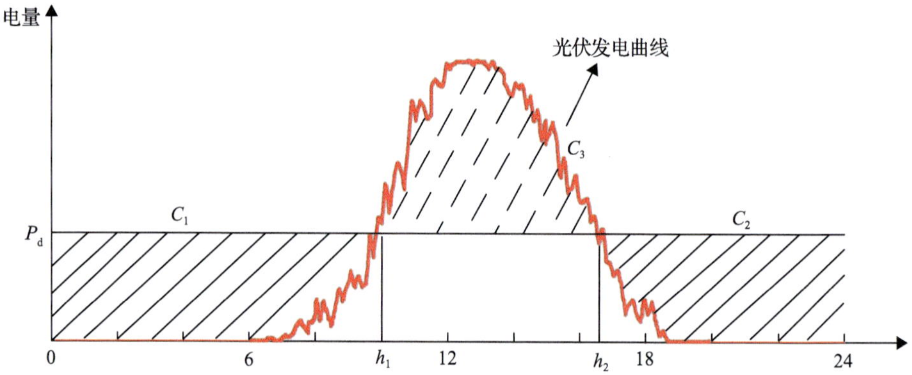

图 4-2　含光储系统出力的电力电量平衡示意图

如图 4-2 所示，低谷 1 的用电量 C_1 和低谷 2 的用电量 C_2 均为用电负荷在夜间的总用电量，而 C_3 为分布式光伏组件日发电剩余电量。令配置的储能容量为 C_0，且考虑到市电供电容量为 C_g，低谷 C_1 和 C_2 的总用电量满足

$$C_0 + C_g \geqslant C_1 + C_2$$

在 h_1 时刻，分布式光伏用电量在满足地区用电量前提下，开始对储能进行充电，在最大化利用分布式光伏发电和减少储能配置成本的前提下，根据工程实际需求，一般以 2h 负荷总量配置储能，则到达 h_2 时刻储能 C_0 所具有的能量需满足

$$\begin{cases} C_3 \geqslant C_0 \\ C_0 \geqslant \dfrac{C_1 + C_2}{6} \end{cases}$$

当不能满足上式时，证明分布式光伏组件日发电剩余电量不能满足 2h 储能容量前提下，发电量效率较低。则应提高市电供电容量 C_g，或提升储能容量的配置，假设提升的容量为 ΔC，则提升后的储能容量 $C_0 + \Delta C$ 应满足

$$C_0 + \Delta C + C_g \geqslant C_1 + C_2$$

由于储能的充电过程是在分布式光伏发电量高于配电容量时优先考虑分布式光伏发电，而在分布式光伏发电量较低且储能容量不足2h负荷用电时使用市电供电，因此，市电供电的容量有一定的限制，需满足

$$C_g \leqslant C_1 + C_2 - C_0$$

因此，在考虑锂电池的放电深度(90%放电容量)情况下，提升后的储能容量 $C_0 + \Delta C$ 应满足

$$(C_0 + \Delta C + C_g) \times 90\% \geqslant C_1 + C_2$$

根据上式分析，在考虑到锂电池的放电深度情况下，则储能系统的配置容量 C 至少为

$$C = \max\left\{C_0, (C_1 + C_2 - 0.9C_g)/0.9\right\}$$

4.1.3　多态资源的功率协同管理

图4-3为能量管理系统控制示意图。

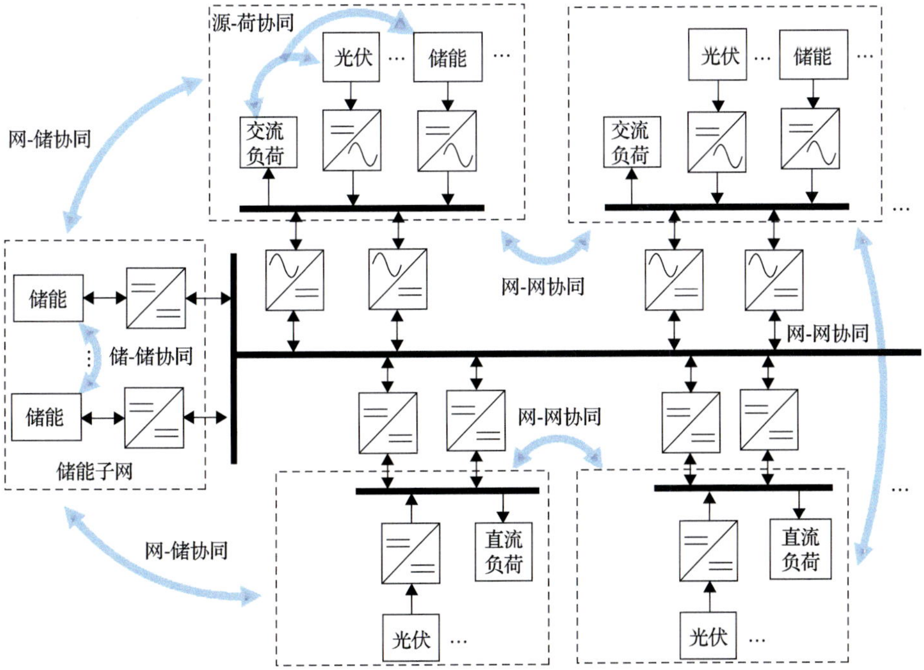

图4-3　能量管理系统控制示意图

能量管理系统借助信息与通信技术，对直流微电网内的资源进行更为智能的

调度，以优化潮流分布和电能质量，其目标是围绕源、储、荷展开，即保证可再生能源的最大化利用，维持储能的正常工作区间，保障负荷的连续可靠供电[34-38]。

能量管理系统按照区域大小和时间尺度长短可分为网内协同和网间协同控制，其中网内的协同控制时间尺度相对较短，主要包括源-荷协同控制、储-储协同控制等；网间的协同控制时间尺度相对较长，主要是网-网协同控制、网-储协同控制等。不同的协同控制有不同的控制目标，如网内的储-储协同控制主要实现各储能设备之间的功率均分及 SOC 均衡，网间的网-储协同控制主要是通过协调整个混合微电网的功率产出和消耗，尽可能地维持储能子网整体的 SOC 处于正常区间。不同类型的协同控制之间的划分以及控制目标可能会有重叠，网-储协同也可以划归为网-网协同等，但是由于想强调对于储能的控制，则可称为网-储协同。

互联电力系统通常需要覆盖较大的地理区域，完全集中式控制无法满足大量的数据实时交换的需求，而完全分散式控制仅仅使用了本地变量信息，难以实现对系统中多种单元的协调管理。分层控制方式综合了集中控制和分散控制的优势，将系统的控制功能分解为不同的层次，各层相对独立地承担管理职责，能够在不同的控制层次上满足不同时间尺度的多种需求，在电力系统中得到了广泛应用。微电网系统同样能够从分层控制中获益，其电量控制、电能调节和经济运行等各类需求在不同的控制层上实现，共同完成微电网优化运行的整体目标，有利于微电网系统的标准化。

微电网的分层控制包括三个控制层次，分别是一次控制、二次控制和三次控制，各层功能如图 4-4 所示。

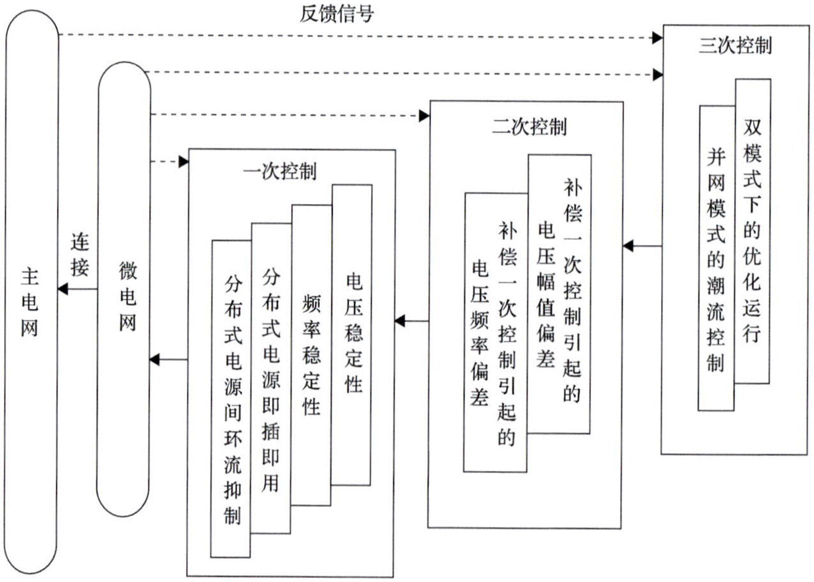

图 4-4　微电网的分层控制

1. 一次控制

一次控制又称为本地控制，在分布式电压的本地控制器中执行，用作分布式电源的本地变量控制，如频率、电压和入网电流的控制，具有较快的响应速度。

一次控制主要有以下需求：第一，保持电压和频率的稳定。在进入孤岛模式之后，微电网内部电源产能和负荷耗能之间的不匹配可能会引起电压和频率的不稳定；第二，分布式电源间有功和无功功率的合理分配；第三，分布式电源具有即插即用的能力。

下垂型逆变器的一次控制一般包括功率控制外环和逆变器的电压电流控制内环。功率控制环采用下式所示下垂方程，使逆变器模拟同步发电机的下垂特性调节有功和无功出力，并根据下垂系数共同承担系统负荷。一次控制的响应曲线如图 4-5 所示。

$$\begin{cases} f - f^* = -k_p(P - P^*) \\ E - E^* = -k_q(Q - Q^*) \end{cases}$$

式中，f、E 分别为逆变器的输出的电压频率和电压幅值；P、Q 分别为有功功率和无功功率的输出值；f^*、E^* 分别为额定的电压频率和额定电压幅值；P^*、Q^* 分别为有功功率和额定无功功率的额定值；k_p、k_q 分别为有功功率和无功功率下垂系数。

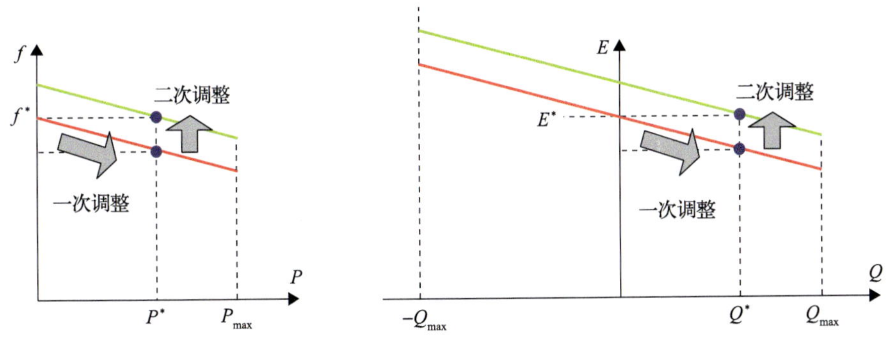

图 4-5　P-f 和 Q-E 的一次控制、二次控制响应曲线

一次控制中，通常还会加入虚拟输出阻抗环。虚拟阻抗可以调节阻抗相角，削弱有功、无功功率的耦合。当设计虚拟阻抗在总阻抗中起主导作用时，能够提高功率的分配精度。时变虚拟阻抗还能够为逆变器的热插拔提供软启动功能。在逆变器连接至 AC 母线的瞬间，虚拟阻抗具有较大的初值 Z_i，避免了电流尖冲，之后按照下式以时间常数 T 减小至终值 Z_f，作为正常运行时的虚拟阻抗值。

$$Z_D(t) = Z_f - (Z_f - Z_i)e^{-t/T}$$

式中，Z_i 为虚拟阻抗的初始值；Z_f 为虚拟阻抗的终值；Z_D 为正常运行时的虚拟阻抗值。

逆变器的电压电流环以功率环的输出作为参考，调节逆变器的输出电压和电流，一般采用电压外环和电流内环的双环控制方法。控制器的选择和坐标系相关：在同步旋转坐标系(dq)中，基波成为直流分量，基于比例-积分(PI)控制器可以实现无静差控制；在静止坐标系(αβ)中，采用比例-谐振(PR)控制器实现正弦量的无静差控制，还能够附加低次谐波补偿器；PI、PR、滞环和无差拍控制在自然坐标系(ABC)中都有应用，PR 控制器的传递函数和低次谐波补偿器的传递函数可分别表示为。

$$G_{\mathrm{PR}}(s) = K_{\mathrm{P}} + K_{\mathrm{i}}\frac{s}{s^2+\omega^2}$$

$$G_{\mathrm{HC}}(s) = \sum_{h=3,5,7,\cdots} K_{\mathrm{i}h}\frac{s}{s^2+(\omega h)^2}$$

式中，K_{P} 为比例系数；K_{i} 为谐振系数，ω 为角频率；h 为谐波次数；$K_{\mathrm{i}h}$ 为 h 次低次谐波下的谐振系数

2. 二次控制

二次控制通过向一次控制提供参考或补偿信号，对微电网的工作点作二次调整。二次控制能够恢复微电网的电压幅值和频率，补偿在微电网中负荷或产能发生变化时一次控制引起的偏差。二次控制的动态响应速度一般比一次控制要缓慢，以实现一次控制和二次控制的动态解耦，有助于二者的独立设计。

图 4-5 表示了二次控制的工作过程。以输出功率增加为例，一次控制的下垂特性使电压频率和幅值沿下垂曲线降低，偏离参考值。在二次控制提供的补偿信号下，下垂曲线平行上移，使电压频率和幅值恢复到参考值。

二次控制一般有集中式和分布式两种结构，如图 4-6 所示。在集中式的控制方案中，二次控制环在微电网中心控制器中执行。中心控制器通过远程传感器采集微电网母线信号，经二次控制得到补偿信号，再由低带宽的通信将补偿信号传递至各个分布式电源，改变分布式电源内部一次控制的参考值。而在分布式的控制方法中，二次控制和一次控制都在分布式电源的本地控制器中实现，不需要中心控制器。

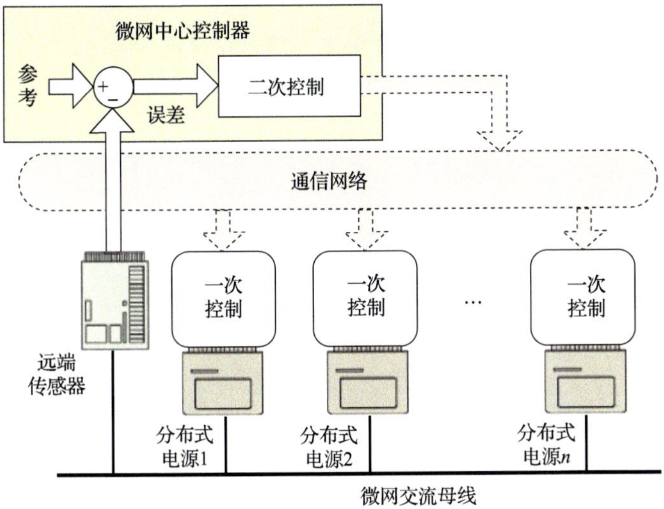

(a) 集中式控制

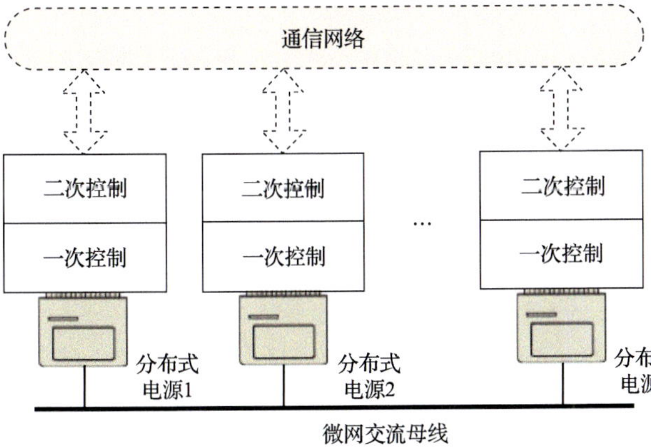

(b) 分布式控制

图 4-6 二次控制的结构

3. 三次控制

三次控制作为微电网系统级层面的控制，考虑微电网运行的经济优化问题，管理微电网和主电网之间的潮流，负责微电网与大电网之间的协调运行。它是分层控制中响应速度最慢的控制层。

在并网模式下，三次控制通过调整分布式电源的电压幅值和频率，实现微电网和主电网之间功率流动的调节功能。起初微电网工作在离网状态，ω_{MG}^* 和 E_{MG}^* 由二次控制内部所确定。并网前首先启动同步过程，此时设置 ω_{MG}^* 和 E_{MG}^* 与电网相同。同步过程结束后，旁路开关闭合，微电网连接大电网运行，ω_{MG}^* 和 E_{MG}^* 由三次控制给出，一般采用下式所示的控制方程。其中 P_G 和 Q_G 分别是有功和无功功率的测量值。ω_{MG}^* 和 E_{MG}^* 进行限幅后，作为二次控制中微电网的频率和幅值参考。

$$\begin{cases} \omega_{MG}^* = K_{PP}(P_G^* - P_G) + K_{IP}\int(P_G^* - P_G)\,dt \\ E_{MG}^* = K_{PQ}(Q_G^* - Q_G) + K_{IQ}\int(Q_G^* - Q_G)\,dt \end{cases}$$

式中，ω_{MG}^*、E_{MG}^* 分别为二次控制中微电网的频率和幅值参考值；P_G^*、Q_G^* 分别为有功和无功功率的额定值；K_{PP}、K_{IP} 分别为微电网有功功率和无功功率的比例系数和谐振系数；K_{PQ}、K_{IQ} 分别为微电网无功功率和无功功率的比例系数和谐振系数。

根据 P_G^* 和 Q_G^* 的符号，功率可以在微电网和主电网之间双向流动。图 4-7 描述了三次控制的行为。以有功功率为例，在一定时间内，电网具有稳定的频率，即 $f_G=f^*$ 为常数，用水平线表示。微电网和主电网所交换的有功功率由微电网的 P-f 下垂特性曲线和电网频率的水平线唯一确定，通过调整微电网下垂曲线的频率参考值，就能够控制有功功率。当 $P_G=P_G^*>0$，下垂曲线平行上移，使频率参考值 $f_{MG}^*>f_G$，反之亦然。无功功率的控制具有类似的分析方法。

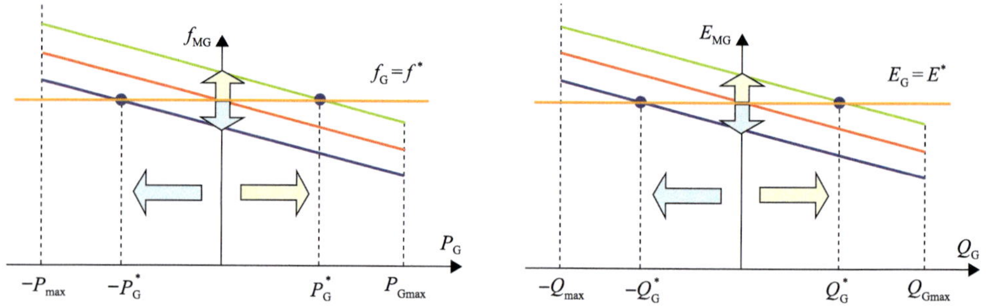

图 4-7　P-f 和 Q-E 的三次控制功能

当 $K_{IP}=K_{IQ}=0$ 时，上式类似于分布式电源的一次控制。因此，将一个微电网系统视为一个分布式电源，三次控制能够实现多个微电网互联形成微电网集群。另外，三次控制能够为微电网提供低电压穿越能力。当并网点电压跌落时，微电网自动向并网点注入无功功率；相反，电压骤升时，微电网吸收无功功率，从而使并网点处的电能质量得到提高。

三次控制能够为微电网提供最优经济运行方案。通常需要考虑发电量和负荷变化的预估值，储能单元的容量，输配电的特殊要求，电力市场提供的电价等因素及限制条件。一般来说，最优经济运行发生在所有分布式电源具有相同边际成本的情况下。根据边际成本曲线和其中一对分布式电源的总功率设定值，确定这两个分布式电源各自的局部最优输出功率点，而后对于系统中所有的分布式电源对，重复相同的过程，最终实现全局最优运行。

4.2　特定模式的专门技术解决方案

4.2.1　强电网大负荷场景下交通专用的能源系统

1. 系统架构

交通专用的能源系统针对强电网、大负荷应用场景，面向隧道供配电需求，通过分布式光伏与原有供配电专线、专网相结合而形成多电源供电模式，主要指隧道照明与通风的供配电系统。图 4-8 为公路隧道光伏板安装示意图。

图 4-8　公路隧道光伏板安装示意图

根据前面分析，我国公路基础设施年耗电量为 11480GW·h，折算为标准煤为 140.9 万 t，其中公路隧道负荷占主要地位，约占全部电力消耗的 97.6%，则提升公路隧道耗能的低碳化程度，可有效地降低公路基础设施用能的间接碳排放量，从而实现公路交通的节能减排发展。因此，建设分布式光伏发电与公路隧道专用供配电网络相结合的交通专用能源系统，不仅可降低公路隧道用能的间接碳排放量，也可减少公路隧道的外购电量。

通过对隧道周围装设环境的调查，隧道的出现常因山体阻碍，要对隧道处装设太阳能光伏组件，根据隧道的宽度与绿化带面积，最佳光伏组件安装点可选择在隧道的进出口的左右两门洞之间的绿化地。为使发电效率达到最高，需根据各地区的纬度不同而适当地调整光伏组件的倾斜角度，以实现最大面积吸收太阳辐射。

图 4-9 给出了交通专用的能源系统组网结构图。可见，在原有隧道两段 400V 母线分别接入分布式光伏发电和储能装置。通过分布式光伏发电，为公路隧道内部照明设施、通风风机和监控设施提供电力：在分布式光伏发电量超过公路隧道负荷用电量时，分布式光伏发电先满足公路隧道负荷的本地用电需求，剩余电量通过配电网向电网传输，实现余量上网；在分布式光伏发电量不满足公路隧道负荷用电量时，公路隧道负荷优先使用分布式光伏发电量，缺额电量由电网提供，形成双电源的供电架构。

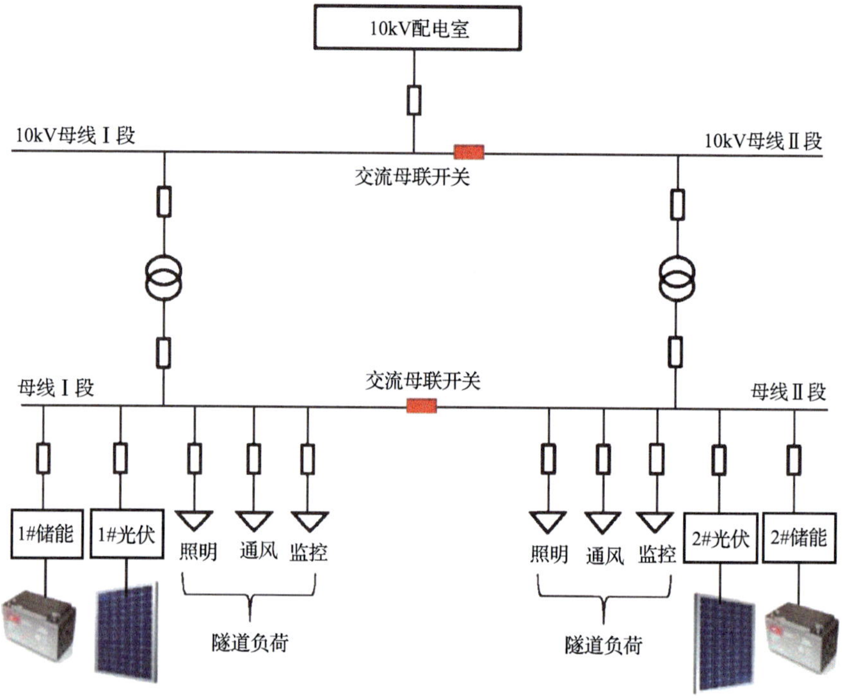

图 4-9 交通专用的能源系统组网结构图

2. 用电自洽率

针对公路隧道用能情况，按单位公里隧道年平均用电量 650MW·h 计算，500m 短隧道、1km 中长隧道、2km 长隧道和 4km 特长隧道的年用电量为 325MW·h、650MW·h、1300MW·h 和 2600MW·h。按前面分析，短隧道和中长隧道双洞隔离带间可供开发的面积均为 2000m^2，分布式光伏发电装机潜力为 320kW，而长隧道和特长隧道双洞隔离带间可供开发的面积分别为 4000m^2、6000m^2，分布式光伏发电装机潜力分别为 640kW、960kW。图 4-10 为交通专用的能源系统发用电量。

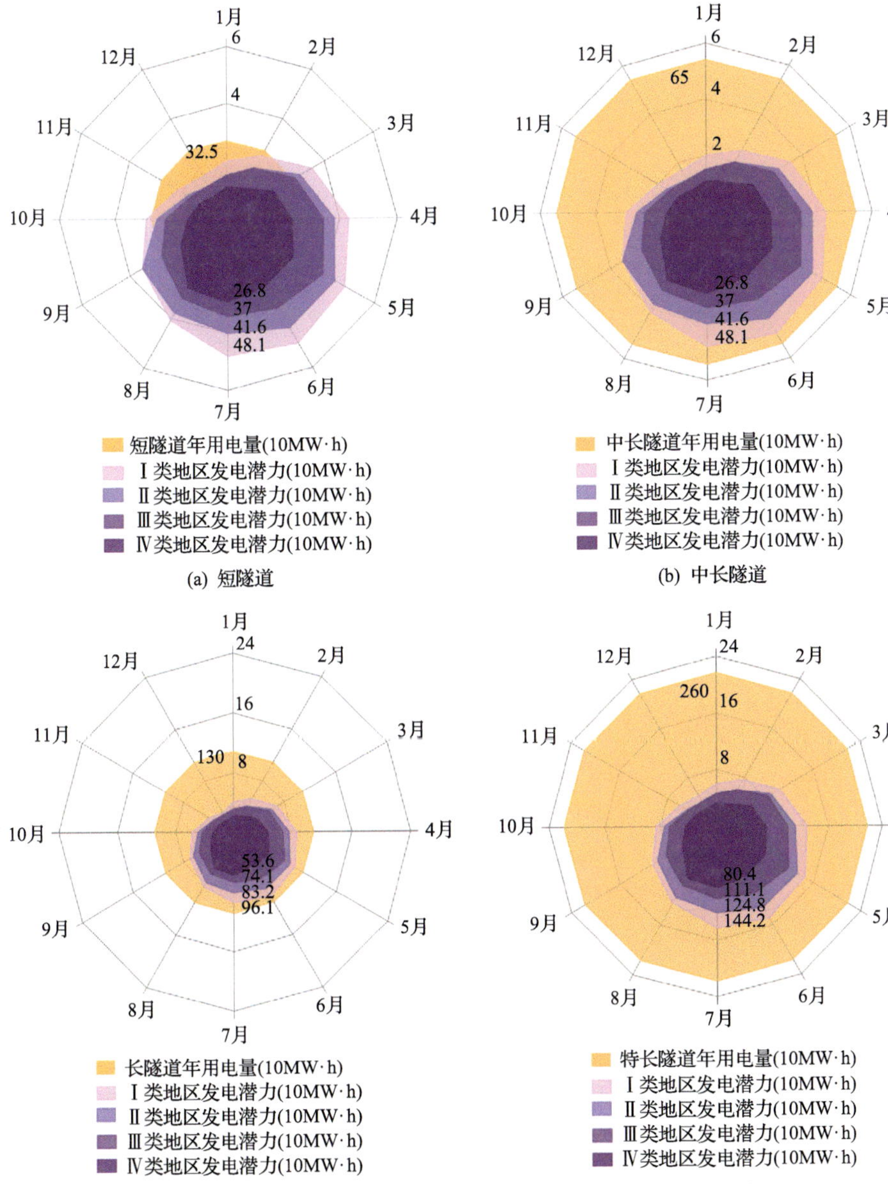

(a) 短隧道 (b) 中长隧道 (c) 长隧道 (d) 特长隧道

图 4-10 交通专用的能源系统发用电量

针对 500m 短隧道而言，在太阳能Ⅰ类、Ⅱ类、Ⅲ类和Ⅳ类地区，加装在短隧道隔离带间的分布式光伏发电年发电潜力分别为 481MW·h、416MW·h、370MW·h 和 268MW·h，具体月均发电量详见表 4-3。按 500m 短隧道年均用电量 325MW·h 计算，短隧道交通专用能源系统在太阳能Ⅰ类、Ⅱ类、Ⅲ类、Ⅳ类地区的自洽率分别为 148.4%、128.4%、114.2%和 82.7%。

表 4-3 短隧道交通专用能源系统

月份	月用电量/(10MW·h)	I类地区		II类地区		III类地区		IV类地区	
		发电量/(10MW·h)	自洽率/%	发电量/(10MW·h)	自洽率/%	发电量/(10MW·h)	自洽率/%	发电量/(10MW·h)	自洽率/%
1	2.7	2.3	85.2	1.8	66.7	1.8	66.7	1.3	48.1
2	2.7	3	111.1	2.3	85.2	2.3	85.2	1.4	51.9
3	2.7	4.1	151.9	3.5	129.6	3.3	122.2	2.2	81.5
4	2.7	5.1	188.9	4.4	163.0	4	148.1	2.7	100.0
5	2.7	5.7	211.1	5.2	192.6	4.6	170.4	3.1	114.8
6	2.7	5.8	214.8	5.1	188.9	4.2	155.6	3.2	118.5
7	2.7	5.6	207.4	4.7	174.1	3.9	144.4	3.4	125.9
8	2.7	4.8	177.8	4.5	166.7	3.7	137.0	3.2	118.5
9	2.7	4.1	151.9	3.8	140.7	3.2	118.5	2.2	81.5
10	2.7	3.4	125.9	2.9	107.4	2.6	96.3	1.7	63.0
11	2.7	2.3	85.2	1.9	70.4	1.8	66.7	1.3	48.1
12	2.7	1.9	70.4	1.5	55.6	1.6	59.3	1.1	40.7
总计	32.4	48.1	148.4	41.6	128.4	37	114.2	26.8	82.7

针对 1km 中长隧道而言，在太阳能 I 类、II 类、III类和IV类地区，加装在中长隧道隔离带间的分布式光伏发电年发电潜力分别为 481MW·h、416MW·h、370MW·h 和 268MW·h，具体月均发电量详见表 4-4。按 1km 中长隧道年均用电量 650MW·h 计算，中长隧道交通专用能源系统在太阳能 I 类、II 类、III类、IV类地区的自洽率分别为 74.2%、64.2%、57.1%和 41.4%。

表 4-4 中长隧道交通专用能源系统

月份	月用电量/(10MW·h)	I类地区		II类地区		III类地区		IV类地区	
		发电量/(10MW·h)	自洽率/%	发电量/(10MW·h)	自洽率/%	发电量/(10MW·h)	自洽率/%	发电量/(10MW·h)	自洽率/%
1	5.4	2.3	42.6	1.8	33.3	1.8	33.3	1.3	24.1
2	5.4	3	55.6	2.3	42.6	2.3	42.6	1.4	25.9
3	5.4	4.1	75.9	3.5	64.8	3.3	61.1	2.2	40.7
4	5.4	5.1	94.4	4.4	81.5	4.0	74.1	2.7	50.0
5	5.4	5.7	105.6	5.2	96.3	4.6	85.2	3.1	57.4
6	5.4	5.8	107.4	5.1	94.4	4.2	77.8	3.2	59.3
7	5.4	5.6	103.7	4.7	87.0	3.9	72.2	3.4	63.0
8	5.4	4.8	88.9	4.5	83.3	3.7	68.5	3.2	59.3
9	5.4	4.1	75.9	3.8	70.4	3.2	59.3	2.2	40.7
10	5.4	3.4	63.0	2.9	53.7	2.6	48.1	1.7	31.5
11	5.4	2.3	42.6	1.9	35.2	1.8	33.3	1.3	24.1
12	5.4	1.9	35.2	1.5	27.8	1.6	29.6	1.1	20.4
总计	64.8	48.1	74.2	41.6	64.2	37.0	57.1	26.8	41.4

针对 2km 长隧道而言，在太阳能Ⅰ类、Ⅱ类、Ⅲ类和Ⅳ类地区，加装在中长隧道隔离带间的分布式光伏发电年发电潜力分别为 961MW、832MW、741MW 和 536MW，具体月均发电量详见表 4-5。按 2km 长隧道年均用电量 1300MW 计算，中长隧道交通专用能源系统在太阳能Ⅰ类、Ⅱ类、Ⅲ类、Ⅳ类地区的自洽率分别为 74.2%、64.2%、57.2%和 41.4%。

表 4-5　长隧道交通专用能源系统

月份	月用电量/(10MW·h)	Ⅰ类地区		Ⅱ类地区		Ⅲ类地区		Ⅳ类地区	
		发电量/(10MW·h)	自洽率/%	发电量/(10MW·h)	自洽率/%	发电量/(10MW·h)	自洽率/%	发电量/(10MW·h)	自洽率/%
1	10.8	4.7	43.5	3.6	33.3	3.6	33.3	2.5	23.1
2	10.8	6.0	55.6	4.6	42.6	4.6	42.6	2.8	25.9
3	10.8	8.1	75.0	7.0	64.8	6.7	61.1	4.4	40.7
4	10.8	10.1	93.5	8.8	81.5	7.9	73.1	5.5	50.9
5	10.8	11.2	103.7	10.3	95.4	9.2	85.2	6.4	59.3
6	10.8	11.6	107.4	10.3	95.4	8.4	77.8	6.4	59.3
7	10.8	11.2	103.7	9.5	88.0	7.9	73.1	6.7	62.0
8	10.8	9.7	89.8	9.0	83.3	7.4	68.5	6.5	60.2
9	10.8	8.2	75.9	7.5	69.4	6.5	60.2	4.3	39.8
10	10.8	6.8	63.0	5.8	53.7	5.2	48.1	3.3	30.6
11	10.8	4.6	42.6	3.7	34.3	3.6	33.3	2.6	24.1
12	10.8	3.9	36.1	3.1	28.7	3.1	28.7	2.2	20.4
总计	129.6	96.1	74.2	83.2	64.2	74.1	57.2	53.6	41.4

针对 4km 特长隧道而言，在太阳能Ⅰ类、Ⅱ类、Ⅲ类和Ⅳ类地区，加装在中长隧道隔离带间的分布式光伏发电年发电潜力分别为 1442MW、1248MW、1111MW 和 804MW，具体月均发电量详见表 4-6。按 4km 特长隧道年均用电量 2600MW 计算，中长隧道交通专用能源系统在太阳能Ⅰ类、Ⅱ类、Ⅲ类、Ⅳ类地区的自洽率分别为 55.4%、47.9%、42.7%和 30.9%。

表 4-6　特长隧道交通专用能源系统

月份	月用电量/(10MW·h)	Ⅰ类地区		Ⅱ类地区		Ⅲ类地区		Ⅳ类地区	
		发电量/(10MW·h)	自洽率/%	发电量/(10MW·h)	自洽率/%	发电量/(10MW·h)	自洽率/%	发电量/(10MW·h)	自洽率/%
1	21.7	7	32.3	5.3	24.4	5.4	24.9	3.8	17.5
2	21.7	9	41.5	6.9	31.8	6.9	31.8	4.2	19.4
3	21.7	12.2	56.2	10.6	48.8	9.9	45.6	6.5	30.0
4	21.7	15.2	70.0	13.2	60.8	11.9	54.8	8.2	37.8
5	21.7	17	78.3	15.5	71.4	13.8	63.6	9.6	44.2
6	21.7	17.4	80.2	15.4	71.0	12.7	58.5	9.6	44.2
7	21.7	16.8	77.4	14.2	65.4	11.8	54.4	10.1	46.5
8	21.7	14.5	66.8	13.5	62.2	11.2	51.6	9.7	44.7
9	21.7	12.3	56.7	11.3	52.1	9.6	44.2	6.5	30.0

续表

月份	月用电量/(10MW·h)	Ⅰ类地区		Ⅱ类地区		Ⅲ类地区		Ⅳ类地区	
		发电量/(10MW·h)	自洽率/%	发电量/(10MW·h)	自洽率/%	发电量/(10MW·h)	自洽率/%	发电量/(10MW·h)	自洽率/%
10	21.7	10.1	46.5	8.7	40.1	7.8	35.9	5	23.0
11	21.7	6.9	31.8	5.6	25.8	5.4	24.9	3.9	18.0
12	21.7	5.8	26.7	4.6	21.2	4.7	21.7	3.3	15.2
总计	260.4	144.2	55.4	124.8	47.9	111.1	42.7	80.4	30.9

因此，充分地利用公路隧道双洞间空间资源，构建交通专用的能源系统可为公路隧道负荷提供部分电量，缺额电量仍由配电网提供。图 4-11～图 4-14 总结了在太阳能Ⅰ类、Ⅱ类、Ⅲ类和Ⅳ类地区的交通专用能源系统自洽率情况。可见，

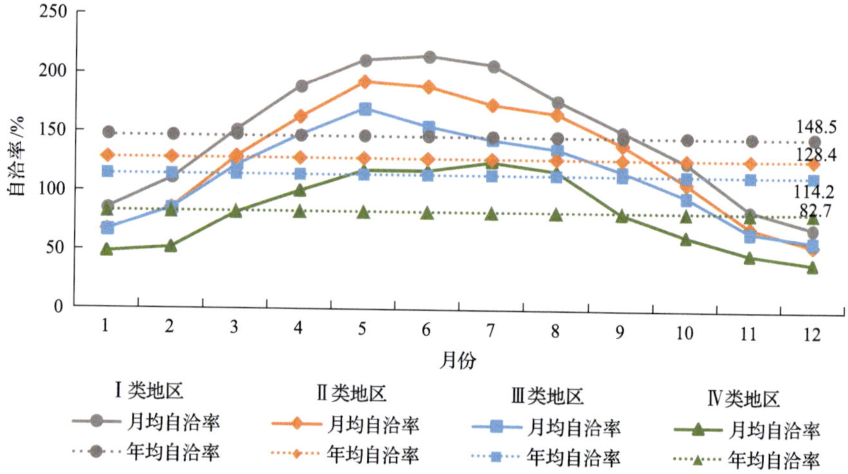

图 4-11　短隧道交通专用能源系统用电自洽率

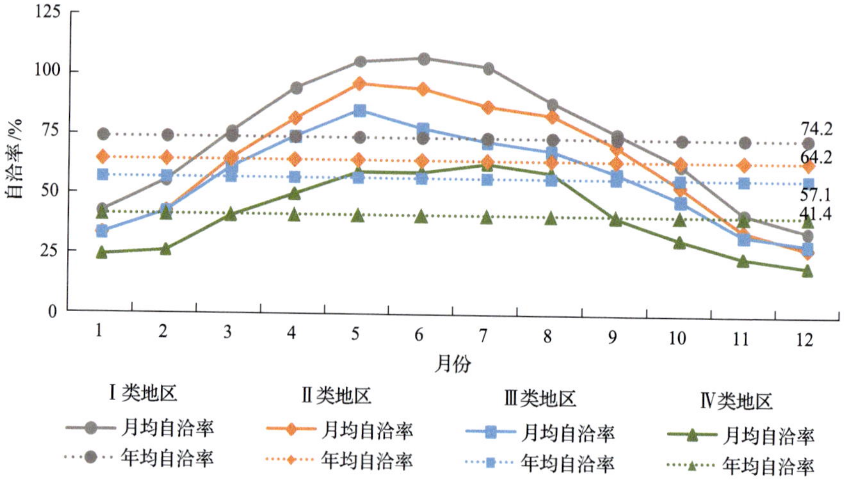

图 4-12　中长隧道交通专用能源系统用电自洽率

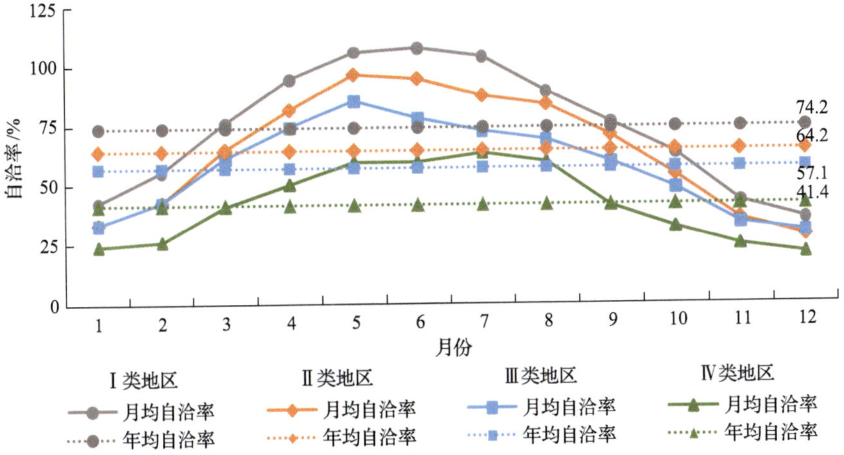

图 4-13　长隧道交通专用能源系统用电自洽率

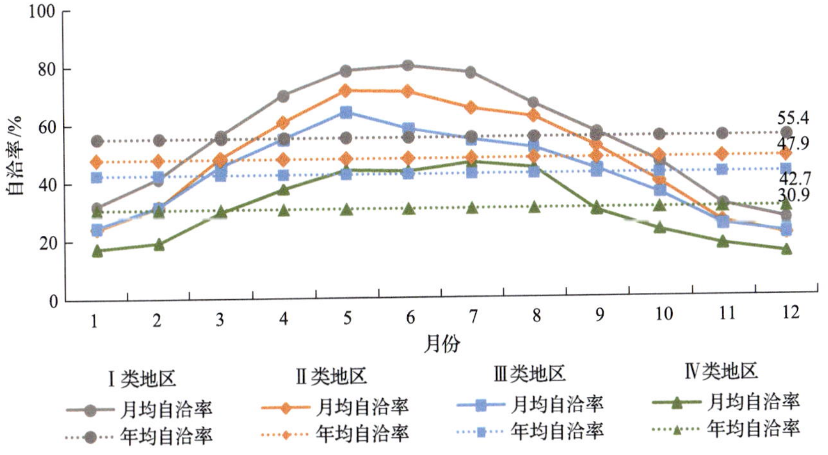

图 4-14　特长隧道交通专用能源系统自洽率

在太阳能资源丰富地区，交通专用能源系统自洽率相对较高，而在太阳能资源匮乏地区，交通专用能源系统自洽率相对较低。因此，在交通专用能源系统开发进程中，应首先开发太阳能资源丰富区的资源和潜力，利用交通专用能源系统可实现较高比例的能源自洽，同时分布式光伏发电的使用也可间接地降低公路隧道负荷的碳排放量，有助于公路隧道用电的节能减排发展。

3. 建设投资收益预测

根据国家能源局公布数据[39]，2018 年光伏发电成本已降至 7 元/W 左右。同时，根据彭博能源财经数据显示[40]，2018 年全球范围内锂电池组的平均成本为 176 美元/(kW·h)。因此，在后续对公路交通能源系统进行投资收益预测时，以每千瓦光伏需投资 0.7 万元、每千瓦时储能需投资 0.15 万元计算。同时，根据国家发展和改革委员会公布的《关于 2018 年光伏发电项目价格政策的通知》(发改价格规〔2017〕2196 号)[41]，对分布式光伏发电项目给予 0.37 元/(kW·h) 的补贴，按一般工商业平峰电价计算，公路交通能源系统用电费用为 0.87 元/(kW·h)。表 4-7 为短隧道交通专用能源系统投资收益表。

表 4-7　短隧道交通专用能源系统投资收益表　（单位：万元）

类型	费用	Ⅰ类地区	Ⅱ类地区	Ⅲ类地区	Ⅳ类地区
年收益	节省电费	41.8	36.2	32.2	23.3
	发电补贴	4.8	4.2	3.7	2.7
	年收益	46.6	40.4	35.9	26.0
总投资	储能一次性投资	12.0			
	光伏一次性投资	224.0			
	合计	236.0			

针对 500m 短隧道而言，其隔离带可供开发的面积为 $2000m^2$，按每平方米可加装光伏组件 160W 计算，短隧道隔离带可加装光伏 320kW，光伏系统建设一次性投资为 224 万元。该短隧道年用电量为 325MW，平均用电功率为 37.1kW，以储能装置可满足短隧道两小时用电量并向上取整计算，需配置储能装置为 40kW/80kW·h，储能系统建设一次性投资为 12 万元。因此，构建面向短隧道的交通专用能源系统需一次性投资 236 万元。

在太阳能资源Ⅰ类、Ⅱ类、Ⅲ类和Ⅳ类地区，安装在短隧道隔离带的分布式光伏发电年发电量分别为 481MW、416MW、370MW 和 268MW，年节约电费为 41.8 万元、36.2 万元、32.2 万元和 23.3 万元，年发电补贴为 4.8 万元、4.2 万元、3.7 万元和 2.7 万元，则安装在短隧道隔离带的分布式光伏发电年总收益分别为 46.6 万元、40.4 万元、35.9 万元和 26.0 万元。图 4-15 为短隧道交通专用能源系统投资回收年限与年收益。

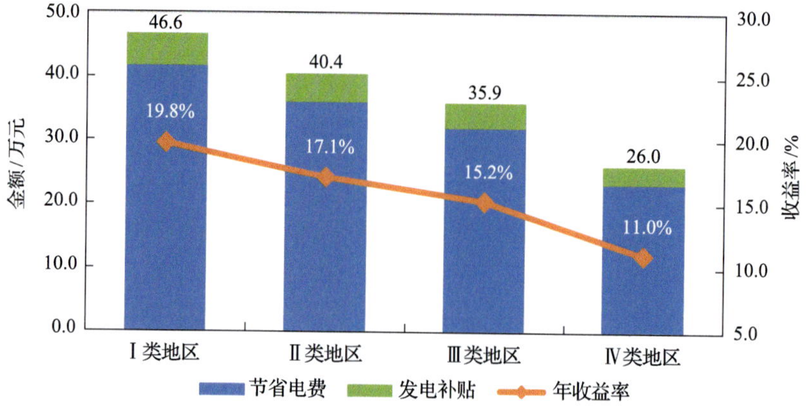

图 4-15　短隧道交通专用能源系统投资回收年限与年收益

短隧道交通专用能源系统中，在太阳能资源Ⅰ类、Ⅱ类、Ⅲ类和Ⅳ类地区，光伏投资占一次性投资的大部分，分布式光伏发电替代市电提供短隧道用电带来的替代收益占年收益的大部分。年收益率在四类地区分别为19.8%、17.1%、15.2%、11.0%，在太阳能Ⅰ类地区最高，约5年可收回一次性投资成本；在太阳能Ⅳ类地区最低，约9年才可收回一次性投资成本。表4-8为中长隧道交通专用能源系统投资收益表。

表4-8　中长隧道交通专用能源系统投资收益表　（单位：万元）

类型	费用	Ⅰ类地区	Ⅱ类地区	Ⅲ类地区	Ⅳ类地区
年收益	节省电费	41.8	36.2	32.2	23.3
	发电补贴	4.8	4.2	3.7	2.7
	年收益	46.6	40.4	35.9	26.0
总投资	储能一次性投资	22.5			
	光伏一次性投资	224.0			
	合计	246.5			

针对1km中长隧道而言，其隔离带可供开发的面积为$2000m^2$，按每平方米可加装光伏组件160W计算，中长隧道隔离带可加装光伏320kW，光伏系统一次性建设投资为224万元。该中长隧道年用电量为650MW·h，平均用电功率为74.2kW，以储能装置可满足中长隧道两小时用电量并向上取整计算，需配置储能装置为75kW/150kW·h，储能系统建设一次性投资为22.5万元。因此，构建面向中长隧道的交通专用能源系统需一次性投资246.5万元。在太阳能Ⅰ类、Ⅱ类、Ⅲ类和Ⅳ类地区，安装在中长隧道隔离带的分布式光伏发电年发电量分别为481MW·h、416MW·h、370MW·h和268MW·h，年节约电费为41.8万元、36.2万元、32.2万元和23.3万元，年发电补贴为4.8万元、4.2万元、3.7万元和2.7万元，则安装在中长隧道隔离带的分布式光伏发电年总收益分别为46.6万元、40.4万元、35.9万元和26.0万元。图4-16为中长隧道交通专用能源系统投资回收年限与年收益。

中长隧道交通专用能源系统中，在太阳能四类地区，光伏投资占一次性投资的大部分，分布式光伏发电替代市电提供中长隧道用电带来的替代收益占年收益的大部分。年收益率在四类地区分别为18.9%、16.4%、14.6%、10.5%，在太阳能Ⅰ类地区最高，约6年可收回一次性投资成本；在太阳能Ⅳ类地区最低，约10年才可收回一次性投资成本。表4-9为长隧道交通专用能源系统投资收益表。

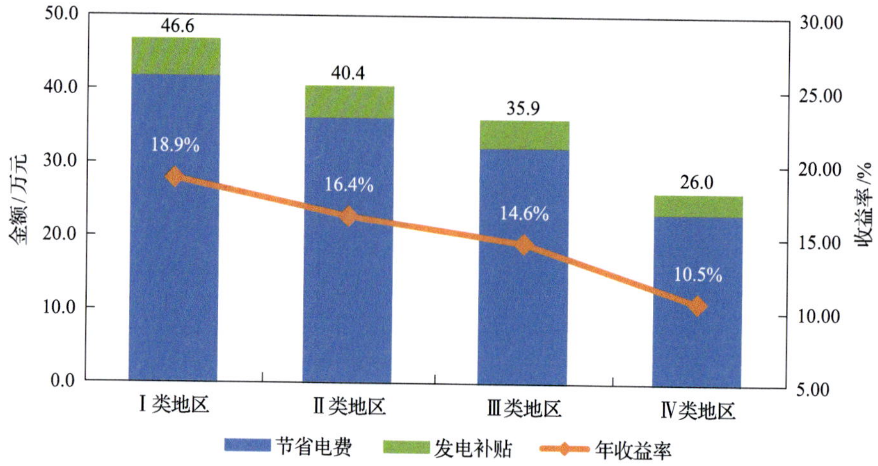

图 4-16　中长隧道交通专用能源系统投资回收年限与年收益

表 4-9　长隧道交通专用能源系统投资收益表　（单位：万元）

类型	费用	Ⅰ类地区	Ⅱ类地区	Ⅲ类地区	Ⅳ类地区
年收益	节省电费	83.6	72.4	64.5	46.6
	发电补贴	9.6	8.3	7.4	5.4
	年收益	93.2	80.7	71.9	52.0
总投资	储能一次性投资	45.0			
	光伏一次性投资	448.0			
	合计	493.0			

针对 2km 长隧道而言，其隔离带可供开发的面积为 4000m^2，按每平方米可加装光伏组件 160W 计算，长隧道隔离带可加装光伏 640kW，光伏系统建设一次性投资为 448 万元。该长隧道年用电量为 1300MW·h，平均用电功率为 148.4kW，以储能装置可满足长隧道两小时用电量并向上取整计算，需配置储能装置为 150kW/300kW·h，储能系统建设一次性投资为 45 万元。因此，构建面向长隧道的交通专用能源系统需一次性投资 493 万元。在太阳能Ⅰ类、Ⅱ类、Ⅲ类和Ⅳ类地区，安装在长隧道隔离带的分布式光伏发电年发电量分别为 961MW、832MW、741MW、536MW，年节约电费为 83.6 万元、72.4 万元、64.5 万元和 46.6 万元，年发电补贴为 9.6 万元、8.3 万元、7.4 万元和 5.4 万元，则安装在长隧道隔离带的分布式光伏发电年总收益分别为 93.2 万元、80.7 万元、71.9 万元和 52.0 万元。图 4-17 为长隧道交通专用能源系统投资回收年限与年收益。

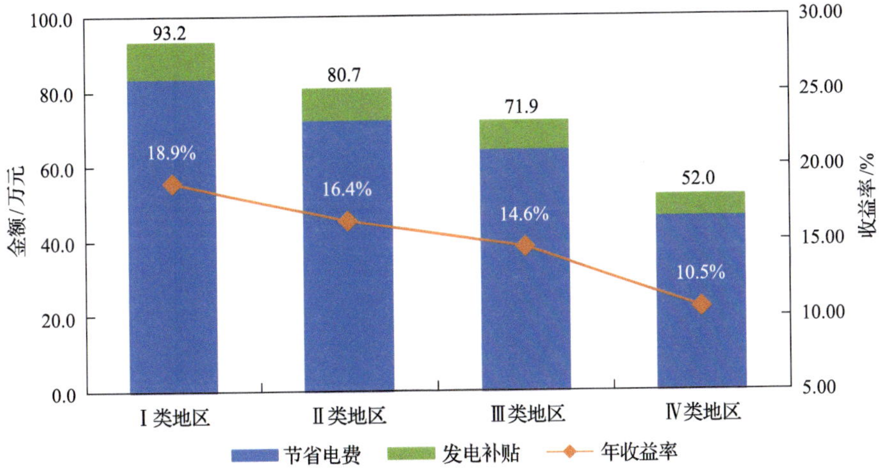

图 4-17　长隧道交通专用能源系统投资回收年限与年收益

长隧道交通专用能源系统中，在太阳能四类地区，光伏投资占一次性投资的大部分，分布式光伏发电替代市电提供长隧道用电带来的替代收益占年收益的大部分。年收益率在四类地区分别为 18.9%、16.4%、14.6%、10.5%，在太阳能Ⅰ类地区最高，约 6 年可收回一次性投资成本；在太阳能Ⅳ类地区最低，约 10 年才可收回一次性投资成本。表 4-10 为长隧道交通专用能源系统投资收益表。

表 4-10　长隧道交通专用能源系统投资收益表　　（单位：万元）

类型	费用	Ⅰ类地区	Ⅱ类地区	Ⅲ类地区	Ⅳ类地区
年收益	节省电费	125.5	108.6	96.7	69.9
	发电补贴	14.4	12.5	11.1	8.0
	年收益	139.9	121.1	107.8	77.9
总投资	储能一次性投资	90.0			
	光伏一次性投资	896.0			
	合计	986.0			

针对 4km 特长隧道而言，其隔离带可供开发的面积为 8000m^2，按每平方米可加装光伏组件 160W 计算，特长隧道隔离带可加装光伏 1280kW，光伏系统建设一次性投资为 896 万元。该特长隧道年用电量为 2600MW·h，平均用电功率为 296.8kW，以储能装置可满足特长隧道两小时用电量并向上取整计算，需配置储能装置为 300kW/600kW·h，储能系统建设一次性投资为 90 万元。因此，构建面向特长隧道的交通专用能源系统需一次性投资 986 万元。在太阳能Ⅰ类、Ⅱ类、

Ⅲ类和Ⅳ类地区，安装在特长隧道隔离带的分布式光伏发电年发电量分别为1442MW·h、1248MW·h、1111MW·h和804MW·h，年节约电费为125.5万元、108.6万元、96.7万元和69.9万元，年发电补贴为14.4万元、12.5万元、11.1万元和8.0万元，则安装在特长隧道隔离带的分布式光伏发电年总收益分别为139.9万元、121.1万元、107.8万元和77.9万元。图4-18为特长隧道交通专用能源系统投资回收年限与年收益。

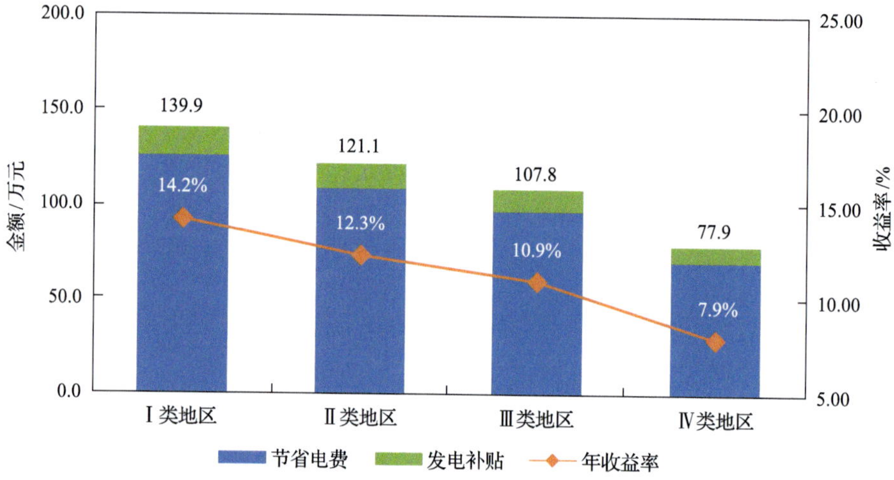

图4-18　特长隧道交通专用能源系统投资回收年限与年收益

特长隧道交通专用能源系统中，在太阳能四类地区，光伏投资占一次性投资的大部分，分布式光伏发电替代市电提供特长隧道用电带来的替代收益占年收益的大部分。年收益率在四类地区分别为14.2%、12.3%、10.9%、7.9%，在太阳能Ⅰ类地区最高，约7年可收回一次性投资成本；在太阳能Ⅳ类地区最低，约13年才可收回一次性投资成本。

按每千瓦时分布式光伏发电即可减少0.997kg CO_2排放计算[42]，对于短隧道交通专用能源系统，在太阳能Ⅰ类、Ⅱ类、Ⅲ类和Ⅳ类地区，分别可以减少479.6t、414.8t、368.9t和267.2t CO_2排放。对于中长隧道交通专用能源系统，在太阳能资源Ⅰ类、Ⅱ类、Ⅲ类和Ⅳ类地区，分别可以减少479.6t、414.8t、368.9t和267.2t CO_2排放。对于长隧道交通专用能源系统，在太阳能Ⅰ类、Ⅱ类、Ⅲ类和Ⅳ类地区，分别可以减少958.1t、829.5t、738.8t和534.4t CO_2排放。对于特长隧道交通专用能源系统，在太阳能Ⅰ类、Ⅱ类、Ⅲ类和Ⅳ类地区，分别可以减少1437.7t、1244.3t、1107.7t和801.6t CO_2排放。图4-19为交通专用能源系统CO_2减排量。

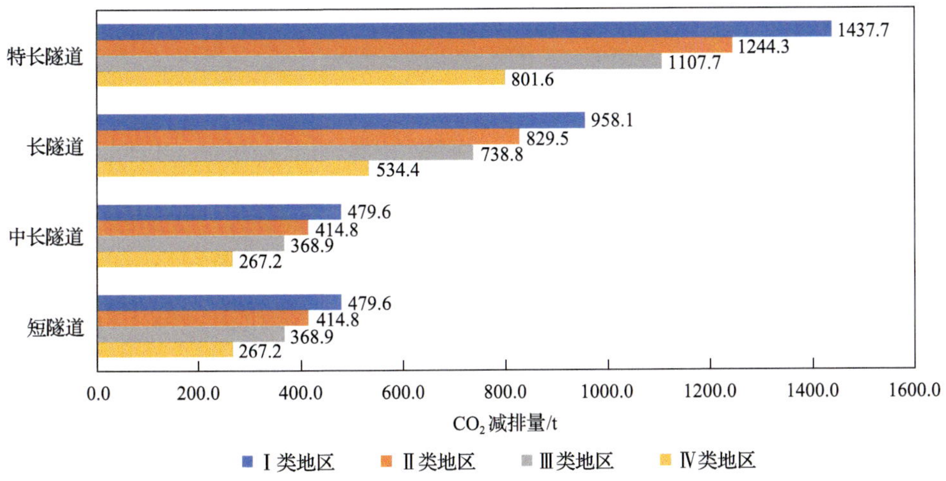

图 4-19　交通专用能源系统 CO_2 减排量

4.2.2　强电网小负荷场景下交通特有的能源系统

1. 系统架构

交通特有的能源系统针对强电网、小负荷应用场景，面向交通运输业特定需求，利用分布式光伏发电作为辅助电源，降低对电力系统供电容量的要求，主要包括为电动汽车充电网。

随着新能源汽车销量的快速增长，为有力地支撑电动汽车的跨区域、远距离出行，消除用户的里程焦虑并提升用户体验，在高速公路服务区建设电动汽车快速充电站已成为典型的解决方案。同时，充分地利用我国高速公路服务区既有空间资源，建设分布式光伏发电，不仅可为电动汽车充电提供清洁电力，减少电动汽车出行的间接碳排放，并可降低电动汽车充电站对电网扩容的要求。因此，建设分布式光伏发电与电动汽车快速充电集成的交通特有能源系统，不仅可降低电动汽车出行的间接碳排放，也可为服务区原有负荷提供清洁电力供给。

图 4-20 给出了交通特有的能源系统组网结构图。可见，在服务站原本 10kV 母线的基础上，装设一路与原负荷并行的线路连结至充电站母线，在充电站母线上分别接入分布式光伏发电和充电装置。通过分布式光伏发电，为服务站中原负荷以及充电桩提供能量。在光照充足且分布式光伏发电量超过服务站原负荷及充电桩所需电量的条件下，分布式光伏发电先满足服务站原负荷及充电桩的本地用电需求，剩余电量通过配电网向电网传输，实现余量上网；在光照充足且分布式光伏发电量不足支撑服务站原负荷及充电桩所需电量的条件下，服务站原负荷及充电桩的本地用电需求优先由分布式光伏发电提供，剩余电量通过配电网提供，

实现光伏优先供能；在光照不足的条件下，服务站原负荷及充电桩的用电需求完全由电网提供。

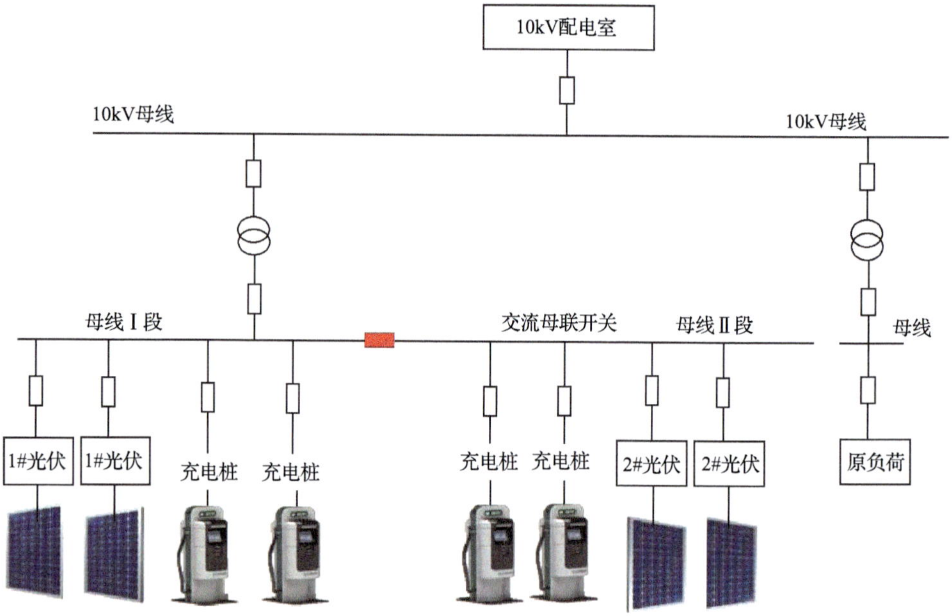

图 4-20　交通特有的能源系统组网结构图

2. 用电自洽率

根据公安部交通管理局公布的数据[5]，截至 2018 年，我国汽车保有量达 2.4 亿辆，其中小型载客汽车保有量达 2.01 亿辆，约占 83.3%，纯电动汽车保有量为 211 万辆，渗透率约为 0.9%。根据交通运输部统计数据[43]，2018 年全国高速公路年平均日交通量为 26435 辆，按 2018 年小型载客汽车占比为 83.3%和小客车驶入率为 10%计算，高速公路服务区驶入小客车日平均为 2202 辆。

现阶段，60kW 直流快速充电桩作为主流桩型，可在 30min 内，使电动汽车 SOC 状态超过 80%，而在 SOC 状态超过 80%后，为保护电池安全，直流快速充电桩由恒流充电模式转变为恒压充电模式[44,45]，充电电流明显减小，则在综合考虑出行时间需求、充电时间等因素后，可预估平均每台电动汽车充电电量为 30kW·h。对于高速公路服务而言，渗透率为 1%、5%和 10%时高速公路服务区，充电站年平均用电量分别为 238MW·h、1189MW·h 和 2378MW·h，在考虑高速功率服务区原有负荷年用电量，高速公路服务区年平均用电量分别为 1354MW·h、2284MW·h 和 3473MW·h。

在太阳能Ⅰ类、Ⅱ类、Ⅲ类和Ⅳ类地区，由高速公路分布式光伏发电构成的交通特有的能源系统年发电潜力为 11295MW·h、9772MW·h、8705MW·h 和 6296MW·h，具体月发电潜力详见表 4-11。图 4-21 为交通特有的能源系统发电潜力与用电量。

表 4-11　交通特有能源系统易开发与难开发潜力　（单位：10MW·h）

月份	Ⅰ类地区		Ⅱ类地区		Ⅲ类地区		Ⅳ类地区	
	易开发	难开发	易开发	难开发	易开发	难开发	易开发	难开发
1	11.7	43.4	8.9	33.0	9.1	33.6	6.3	23.2
2	14.9	55.5	11.6	42.7	11.6	42.8	6.9	25.6
3	20.3	75.0	17.5	64.9	16.5	61.2	11.0	40.0
4	25.3	93.5	22.1	81.6	19.7	73.1	13.7	50.7
5	28.3	104.5	25.9	95.6	23.1	85.6	16.0	59.3
6	29.0	107.5	25.6	94.9	21.1	78.1	15.9	58.9
7	28.0	103.5	23.7	87.9	19.7	72.8	16.8	62.3
8	24.2	89.5	22.5	83.4	18.6	68.9	16.1	59.8
9	20.5	75.8	18.8	69.6	16.0	59.2	10.9	40.2
10	16.9	62.4	14.4	53.2	13.0	47.9	8.3	30.9
11	11.5	42.6	9.3	34.2	9.0	33.4	6.5	24.2
12	9.7	36.0	7.6	28.3	7.8	28.7	5.6	20.5
总计	240.3	889.2	207.9	769.3	185.2	685.3	134.0	495.6

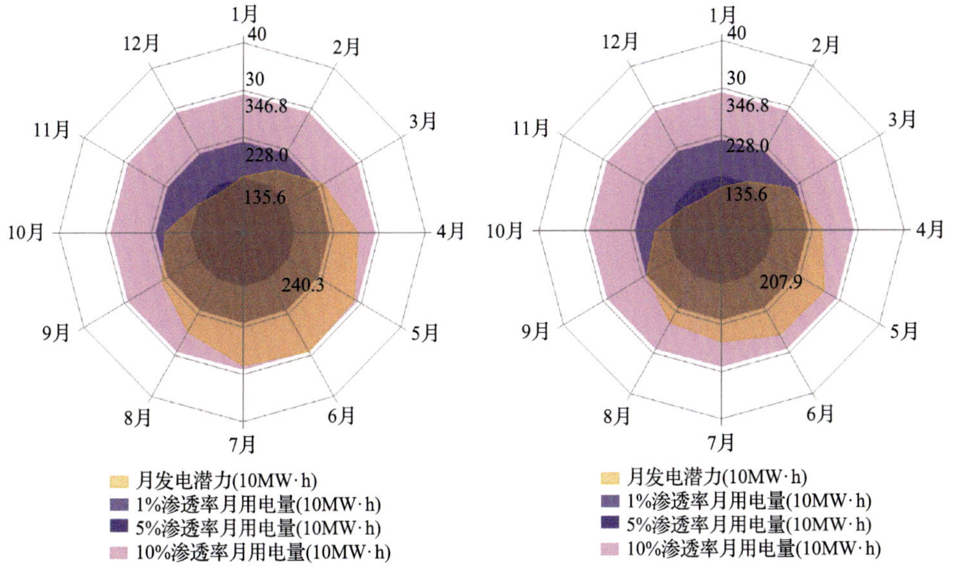

(a)　Ⅰ类地区　　(b)　Ⅱ类地区

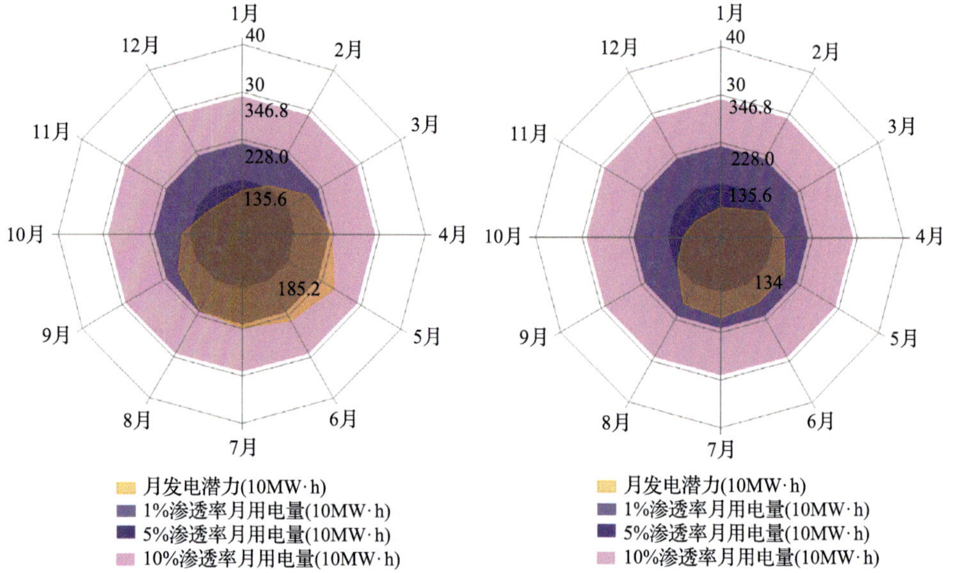

(c) Ⅲ类地区　　(d) Ⅳ类地区

图 4-21　交通特有的能源系统发电潜力与用电量

交通特有能源系统开发的难易程度主要是考虑光伏电站建设过程中施工的程度，主要包含光伏技术和产品的成熟度以及建设成本等因素。因此，对于面向服务区/停车区的交通特有能源系统，应优先开发服务区屋顶、停车棚等空余面积的分布式发电项目，为服务区负荷提供清洁能源。服务区作为交通服务设施，其屋顶和车棚面积充足，且周围无建筑阻挡、无人流量、便于管理，对于开发屋顶光伏项目创造了条件。服务区基本负荷稳定，迎合了光伏屋顶就近发电、就近并网、就近转换、就近使用的理念，对于充分地利用太阳能资源，替代和减少化石能源消费提供了便利。按对向分布的每对服务区屋顶、车棚面积约 1 万 m^2 计算，则每对服务区易开发面积约占服务区总面积的 21.3%，而包括路面在内的剩余 3.7 万 m^2 属于难开发资源，约占总资源的 78.7%。因此，本节将以服务区易开发空间资源为基础开发交通特有能源系统，对整个系统的发电潜力与自洽率进行测算。

在太阳能Ⅰ类地区，面向高速公路服务区的交通特有的能源系统年发电量为 2403MW·h，在电动汽车 1%渗透率下，交通特有能源系统的自洽率为 177.2%。在太阳能Ⅱ类地区，面向高速公路服务区的交通特有的能源系统年发电量为 2079MW·h，在电动汽车 1%渗透率下，交通特有能源系统的自洽率为 153.3%。在太阳能Ⅲ类地区，面向高速公路服务区的交通特有的能源系统年发电量为 1852MW·h，在电动汽车 1%渗透率下，交通特有能源系统的自洽率为 136.6%。在太阳能Ⅳ类地区，面向高速公路服务区的交通特有的能源系统年发电量为

1340MW·h，在电动汽车 1%渗透率下，交通特有能源系统的自洽率为 98.8%。表 4-12 为高速公路服务区交通特有能源系统自洽率(1%渗透率)。

表 4-12　高速公路服务区交通特有能源系统自洽率(1%渗透率)

月份	月用电量/(10MW·h)	Ⅰ类地区		Ⅱ类地区		Ⅲ类地区		Ⅳ类地区	
		发电量/(10MW·h)	自洽率/%	发电量/(10MW·h)	自洽率/%	发电量/(10MW·h)	自洽率/%	发电量/(10MW·h)	自洽率/%
1	11.3	11.7	103.5	8.9	78.8	9.1	80.5	6.3	55.8
2	11.3	14.9	131.9	11.6	102.7	11.6	102.7	6.9	61.1
3	11.3	20.3	179.6	17.5	154.9	16.5	146.0	11.0	97.4
4	11.3	25.3	223.9	22.1	195.6	19.7	174.3	13.7	121.2
5	11.3	28.3	250.4	25.9	229.2	23.1	204.4	16	141.6
6	11.3	29.0	256.6	25.6	226.5	21.1	186.7	15.9	140.7
7	11.3	28.0	247.8	23.7	209.7	19.7	174.3	16.8	148.7
8	11.3	24.2	214.2	22.5	199.1	18.6	164.6	16.1	142.5
9	11.3	20.5	181.4	18.8	166.4	16	141.6	10.9	96.5
10	11.3	16.9	149.6	14.4	127.4	13	115.0	8.3	73.5
11	11.3	11.5	101.8	9.3	82.3	9	79.6	6.5	57.5
12	11.3	9.7	85.8	7.6	67.3	7.8	69.0	5.6	49.6
总计	135.6	240.3	177.2	207.9	153.3	185.2	136.6	134	98.8

在太阳能Ⅰ类地区，面向高速公路服务区的交通特有的能源系统年发电量为2403MW·h，在电动汽车 5%渗透率下，交通特有能源系统的自洽率为 105.4%。在太阳能Ⅱ类地区，面向高速公路服务区的交通特有的能源系统年发电量为2079MW·h，在电动汽车 5%渗透率下，交通特有能源系统的自洽率为 91.2%。在太阳能Ⅲ类地区，面向高速公路服务区的交通特有的能源系统年发电量为1852MW·h，在电动汽车 5%渗透率下，交通特有能源系统的自洽率为 81.2%。在太阳能Ⅳ类地区，面向高速公路服务区的交通特有的能源系统年发电量为1340MW·h，在电动汽车 5%渗透率下，交通特有能源系统的自洽率为 58.8%。表 4-13 为高速公路服务区交通特有能源系统自洽率(5%渗透率)。

表 4-13　高速公路服务区交通特有能源系统自洽率(5%渗透率)

月份	月用电量/(10MW·h)	Ⅰ类地区		Ⅱ类地区		Ⅲ类地区		Ⅳ类地区	
		发电量/(10MW·h)	自洽率/%	发电量/(10MW·h)	自洽率/%	发电量/(10MW·h)	自洽率/%	发电量/(10MW·h)	自洽率/%
1	19.0	11.7	61.6	8.9	46.8	9.1	47.9	6.3	33.2
2	19.0	14.9	78.4	11.6	61.1	11.6	61.1	6.9	36.3
3	19.0	20.3	106.8	17.5	92.1	16.5	86.8	11.0	57.9

续表

月份	月用电量/(10MW·h)	I类地区		II类地区		III类地区		IV类地区	
		发电量/(10MW·h)	自洽率/%	发电量/(10MW·h)	自洽率/%	发电量/(10MW·h)	自洽率/%	发电量/(10MW·h)	自洽率/%
4	19.0	25.3	133.2	22.1	116.3	19.7	103.7	13.7	72.1
5	19.0	28.3	148.9	25.9	136.3	23.1	121.6	16.0	84.2
6	19.0	29.0	152.6	25.6	134.7	21.1	111.1	15.9	83.7
7	19.0	28.0	147.4	23.7	124.7	19.7	103.7	16.8	88.4
8	19.0	24.2	127.4	22.5	118.4	18.6	97.9	16.1	84.7
9	19.0	20.5	107.9	18.8	98.9	16.0	84.2	10.9	57.4
10	19.0	16.9	88.9	14.4	75.8	13.0	68.4	8.3	43.7
11	19.0	11.5	60.5	9.3	48.9	9.0	47.4	6.5	34.2
12	19.0	9.7	51.1	7.6	40.0	7.8	41.1	5.6	29.5
总计	228.0	240.3	105.4	207.9	91.2	185.2	81.2	134	58.8

在太阳能Ⅰ类地区，面向高速公路服务区的交通特有的能源系统年发电量为2403MW·h，在电动汽车10%渗透率下，交通特有能源系统的自洽率为69.3%。在太阳能Ⅱ类地区，面向高速公路服务区的交通特有的能源系统年发电量为2079MW·h，在电动汽车10%渗透率下，交通特有能源系统的自洽率为59.9%。在太阳能Ⅲ类地区，面向高速公路服务区的交通特有的能源系统年发电量为1852MW·h，在电动汽车10%渗透率下，交通特有能源系统的自洽率为53.4%。在太阳能Ⅳ类地区，面向高速公路服务区的交通特有的能源系统年发电量为1340MW·h，在电动汽车10%渗透率下，交通特有能源系统的自洽率为38.6%。表4-14为高速公路服务区交通特有能源系统自洽率(10%渗透率)。

表4-14 高速公路服务区交通特有能源系统自洽率(10%渗透率)

月份	月用电量/(10MW·h)	I类地区		II类地区		III类地区		IV类地区	
		发电量/(10MW·h)	自洽率/%	发电量/(10MW·h)	自洽率/%	发电量/(10MW·h)	自洽率/%	发电量/(10MW·h)	自洽率/%
1	28.9	11.7	40.5	8.9	30.8	9.1	31.5	6.3	21.8
2	28.9	14.9	51.6	11.6	40.1	11.6	40.1	6.9	23.9
3	28.9	20.3	70.2	17.5	60.6	16.5	57.1	11.0	38.1
4	28.9	25.3	87.5	22.1	76.5	19.7	68.2	13.7	47.4
5	28.9	28.3	97.9	25.9	89.6	23.1	79.9	16.0	55.4
6	28.9	29.0	100.3	25.6	88.6	21.1	73.0	15.9	55.0
7	28.9	28.0	96.9	23.7	82.0	19.7	68.2	16.8	58.1
8	28.9	24.2	83.7	22.5	77.9	18.6	64.4	16.1	55.7
9	28.9	20.5	70.9	18.8	65.1	16.0	55.4	10.9	37.7

续表

月份	月用电量/(10MW·h)	Ⅰ类地区		Ⅱ类地区		Ⅲ类地区		Ⅳ类地区	
		发电量/(10MW·h)	自洽率/%	发电量/(10MW·h)	自洽率/%	发电量/(10MW·h)	自洽率/%	发电量/(10MW·h)	自洽率/%
10	28.9	16.9	58.5	14.4	49.8	13.0	45.0	8.3	28.7
11	28.9	11.5	39.8	9.3	32.2	9.0	31.1	6.5	22.5
12	28.9	9.7	33.6	7.6	26.3	7.8	27.0	5.6	19.4
总计	346.8	240.3	69.3	207.9	59.9	185.2	53.4	134	38.6

因此，充分地利用高速公路服务区易开发空间资源，构建交通特有的能源系统可为高速公路服务负荷提供部分电量，缺额电量仍由配电网提供。图 4-22 总结了在太阳能Ⅰ类、Ⅱ类、Ⅲ类和Ⅳ类地区的交通特有能源系统用电自洽率情况。

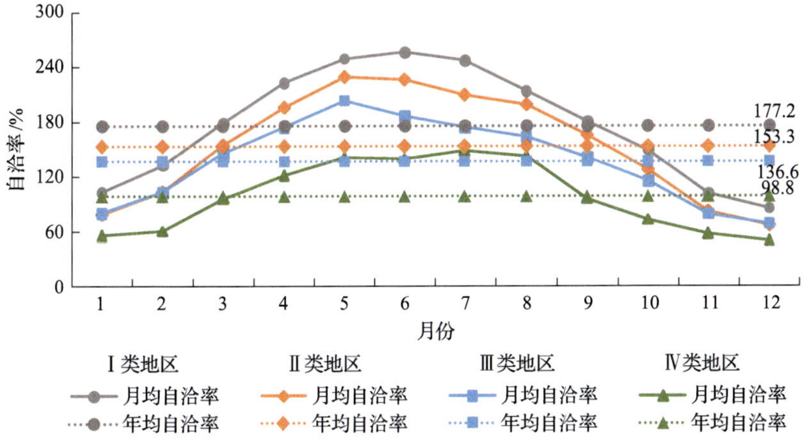

(a) 电动汽车渗透率为1%

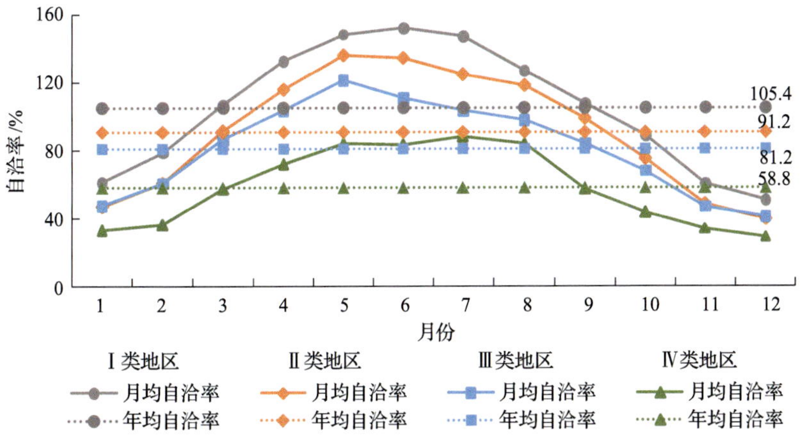

(b) 电动汽车渗透率为5%

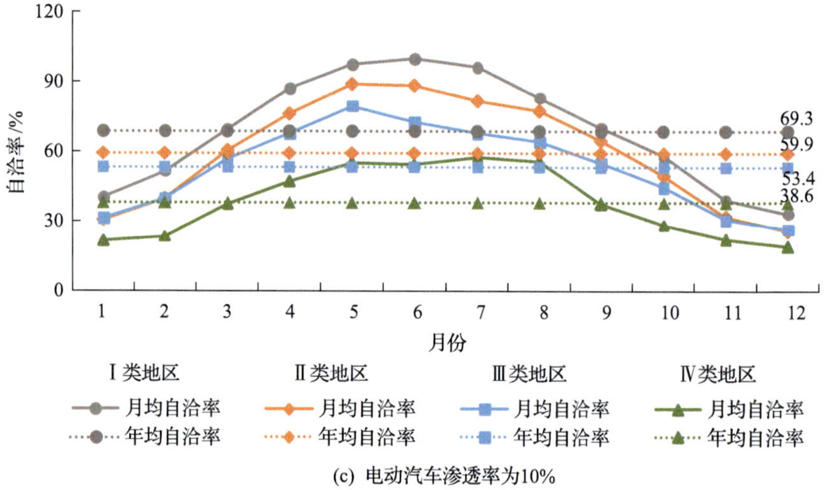

图 4-22　交通特有能源系统用电自洽率

可见，在有限的高速公路服务区易开发资源下，应先开发太阳能资源丰富区的交通特有能源系统，交通专用能源系统不仅可为高速公路纯电动汽车出行提供电力保障，也可为高速公路服务区原有负荷供电，可实现高速公路服务区从用电负荷向供电电源的转变。

3. 建设投资收益预测

根据国家能源局公布数据[39]，2018 年光伏发电成本已降至 7 元/W 左右。同时，根据《海南省电动汽车充电基础设施规划(2019～2030)》的数据显示[46]，60kW 直流双枪快速充电桩价格为 11 万元。因此，在后续对公路交通能源系统进行投资收益预测时，以每千瓦光伏需投资 0.7 万元、充电桩以 11 万元计算。同时，根据国家发展和改革委员会公布的《关于完善光伏发电上网电价机制有关问题的通知》(发改价格〔2019〕761 号)[47]，对分布式光伏发电项目给予 0.10 元/(kW·h)的补贴，按一般工商业平峰电价计算，公路交通能源系统用电费用为 0.87 元/(kW·h)。根据《关于电动汽车用电实行扶持性电价政策有关问题的通知》(琼价价管〔2017〕668 号)的数据显示[48]，充电服务费按充电电度数收取(不包含电费)，上限标准为 0.80 元/(kW·h)，本报告以市面上较常见的每千瓦时 0.6 元计算。表 4-15 为电动汽车渗透率为 1%交通特有能源系统投资收益表。

假设进入服务区的新能源汽车渗透率为 1%，假设一对服务站易开发的面积为 1 万 m^2，按每平方米可加装光伏组件 160W 计算，服务区屋顶以及充电车棚顶棚可加装光伏 1600kW，光伏系统建设一次性投资为 1120 万元。日均驶入高速公路服务区小客车为 2202 辆，以新能源汽车 1%的渗透率，日均驶入高速公路服务区新能源汽车为 22 辆，根据充电分布规律，最高峰一小时内有 3 辆新

表 4-15　电动汽车渗透率为 1%交通特有能源系统投资收益表　（单位：万元）

类型	费用	Ⅰ类地区	Ⅱ类地区	Ⅲ类地区	Ⅳ类地区
年收益	节省电费	209.1	180.9	161.1	116.6
	发电补贴	24.0	20.8	18.5	13.4
	服务收益	28.9	28.9	28.9	28.9
	年收益	262.0	230.6	208.5	158.9
总投资	充电桩一次性投资	22.0			
	光伏一次性投资	1120.0			
	合计	1142.0			

能源汽车同时充电，需配置充电桩为 2 台，充电设备建设一次性投资为 22 万元。因此，满足新能源汽车渗透率为 1%充电需求的交通特有能源系统需一次性投资 1142 万元。在太阳能Ⅰ类、Ⅱ类、Ⅲ类和Ⅳ类地区，安装在服务区易开发面积的分布式光伏发电年发电量分别为 2403MW·h、2079MW·h、1852MW·h、1340MW·h，年节约电费为 209.1 万元、180.9 万元、161.1 万元和 116.6 万元，年发电补贴为 24.0 万元、20.8 万元、18.5 万元和 13.4 万元，充电站的服务收益为 28.9 万元，则安装在服务站的分布式光伏发电及充电站年总收益分别为 262.0 万元、230.6 万元、208.5 万元和 158.9 万元。图 4-23 为电动汽车渗透率为 1%交通特有能源系统年收益与年收益率。

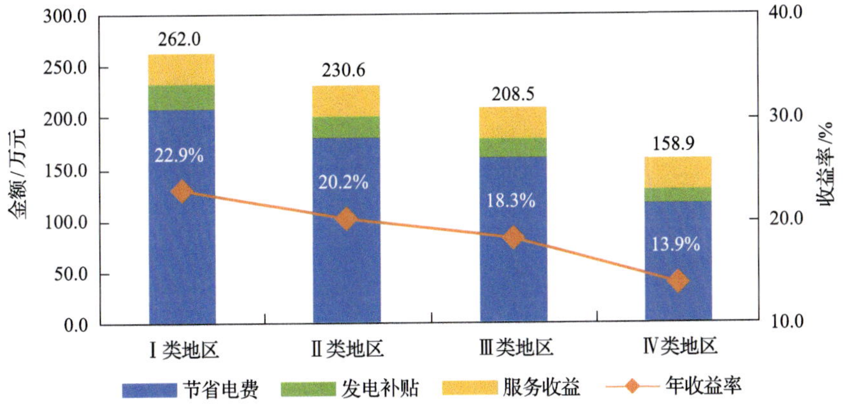

图 4-23　电动汽车渗透率为 1%交通特有能源系统年收益与年收益率

新能源汽车渗透率为 1%交通特有能源系统中，在太阳能四类地区，光伏投资占一次性投资的大部分，分布式光伏发电替代市电提供服务区用电带来的替代收益占年收益的大部分。年收益率在Ⅳ类地区分别为 22.9%、20.2%、18.3%、13.9%，在太阳能Ⅰ类地区最高，约 5 年可收回一次性投资成本；在太阳能Ⅳ类地区最低，约 7 年可收回一次性投资成本。表 4-16 为电动汽车渗透率为 5%交通特有能源系统投资收益表。

表 4-16　电动汽车渗透率为 5%交通特有能源系统投资收益表　（单位：万元）

类型	费用	Ⅰ类地区	Ⅱ类地区	Ⅲ类地区	Ⅳ类地区
年收益	节省电费	209.1	180.9	161.1	116.6
	发电补贴	24.0	20.8	18.5	13.4
	服务收益	144.5	144.5	144.5	144.5
	年收益	377.6	346.2	324.1	274.5
总投资	充电桩一次性投资	77.0			
	光伏一次性投资	1120.0			
	合计	1197.0			

假设进入服务区的新能源汽车渗透率为 5%，一对服务站易开发的面积为 1 万 m^2，按每平方米可加装光伏组件 160W 计算，服务区屋顶以及充电车棚顶棚可加装光伏 1600kW，光伏系统建设一次性投资为 1120 万元。日均驶入高速公路服务区小客车为 2202 辆，以新能源汽车 5%的渗透率，日均驶入高速公路服务区新能源汽车为 110 辆，根据充电分布规律，最高峰时有 3 辆新能源汽车同时充电，需配置充电桩为 7 台，充电设备建设一次性投资为 77 万元。因此，满足新能源汽车渗透率为 5%充电需求的交通特有能源系统需一次性投资 1197 万元。在太阳能Ⅰ类、Ⅱ类、Ⅲ类和Ⅳ类地区，安装在服务区易开发面积的分布式光伏发电年发电量分别为 2403MW·h、2079MW·h、1852MW·h、1340MW·h，年节约电费为 209.1 万元、180.9 万元、161.1 万元和 116.6 万元，年发电补贴为 24.0 万元、20.8 万元、18.5 万元和 13.4 万元，充电站的服务收益为 144.5 万元，则安装在服务站的分布式光伏发电及充电站年总收益分别为 377.6 万元、346.2 万元、324.1 万元和 274.5 万元。图 4-24 为电动汽车渗透率为 5%交通特有能源系统年收益与年收益率。

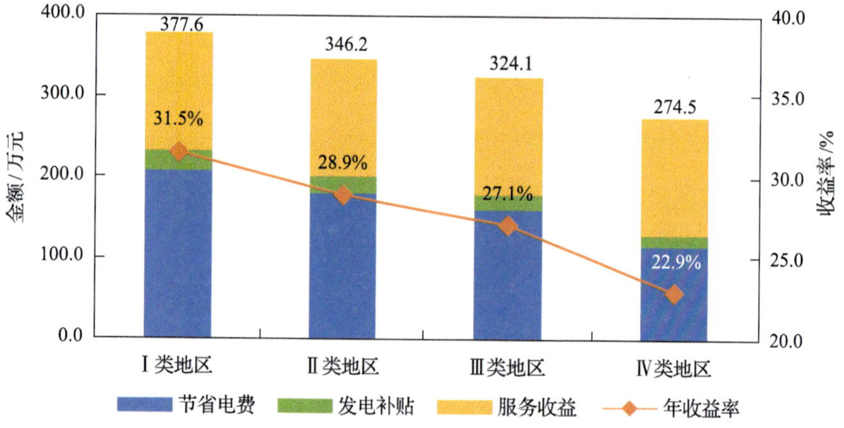

图 4-24　电动汽车渗透率为 5%交通特有能源系统年收益与年收益率

新能源汽车渗透率为5%交通特有能源系统中，在太阳能四类地区，光伏投资占一次性投资的大部分，分布式光伏发电替代市电提供服务区用电带来的收益与充电站提供充电服务收益大致相当。年收益率在四类地区分别为31.5%、28.9%、27.1%、22.9%，在太阳能Ⅰ类地区最高，约3年可收回一次性投资成本；在太阳能Ⅳ类地区最低，约5年可收回一次性投资成本。表4-17为电动汽车渗透率为10%交通特有能源系统投资收益表。

表4-17　电动汽车渗透率为10%交通特有能源系统投资收益表　（单位：万元）

类型	费用	Ⅰ类地区	Ⅱ类地区	Ⅲ类地区	Ⅳ类地区
年收益	节省电费	209.1	180.9	161.1	116.6
	发电补贴	24.0	20.8	18.5	13.4
	服务收益	289.1	289.1	289.1	289.1
	年收益	522.2	490.8	468.7	419.1
总投资	充电桩一次性投资	143.0			
	光伏一次性投资	1120.0			
	合计	1263.0			

假设进入服务区的新能源汽车渗透率为10%，一对服务站易开发的面积为1万m^2，按每平方米可加装光伏组件160W计算，服务区屋顶以及充电车棚顶棚可加装光伏1600kW，光伏系统建设一次性投资为1120万元。日均驶入高速公路服务区小客车为2202辆，以新能源汽车10%的渗透率，日均驶入高速公路服务区新能源汽车为220辆，根据充电分布规律，最高峰一小时内有22辆新能源汽车同时充电，需配置充电桩为13台，充电设备建设一次性投资为143万元。因此，满足新能源汽车渗透率为10%充电需求的交通特有能源系统需一次性投资1263万元。

在太阳能Ⅰ类、Ⅱ类、Ⅲ类和Ⅳ类地区，安装在服务区易开发面积的分布式光伏发电年发电量分别为2403MW·h、2079MW·h、1852MW·h、1340MW·h，年节约电费为209.1万元、180.9万元、161.1万元和116.6万元，年发电补贴为24.0万元、20.8万元、18.5万元和13.4万元，充电站的服务收益为289.1万元，则安装在服务站的分布式光伏发电及充电站年总收益分别为522.2万元、490.8万元、468.7万元和419.1万元。图4-25为电动汽车渗透率为10%交通特有能源系统年收益与年收益率。

新能源汽车渗透率为10%交通特有能源系统中，在太阳能四类地区，光伏投资占一次性投资的大部分，充电站提供充电服务收益占年收益的大部分。年收益率在四类地区分别为41.3%、38.9%、37.1%、33.2%，在太阳能Ⅰ类地区最高，约

2 年可收回一次性投资成本；在太阳能Ⅳ类地区最低，约 3 年可收回一次性投资成本。图 4-26 为交通特有能源系统 CO_2 减排量。

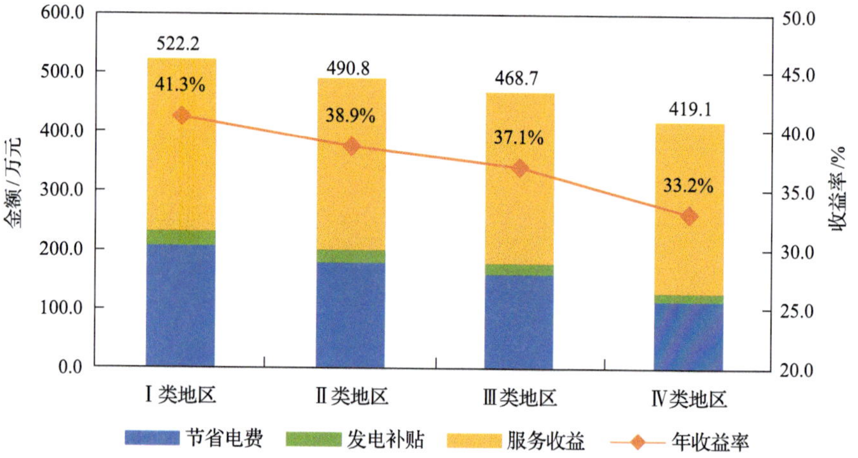

图 4-25　电动汽车渗透率为 10%交通特有能源系统年收益与年收益率

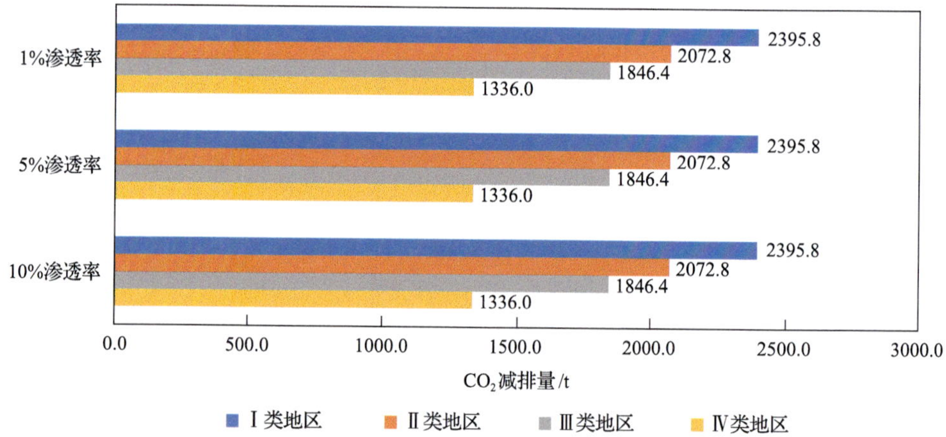

图 4-26　交通特有能源系统 CO_2 减排量

按每千瓦时分布式光伏发电即可减少 0.997kg CO_2 排放计算，对于新能源汽车渗透率为 1%交通特有能源系统，在太阳能Ⅰ类、Ⅱ类、Ⅲ类和Ⅳ类地区，分别可以减少 2395.8t、2072.8t、1846.4t 和 1336.0t CO_2 排放。对于新能源汽车渗透率为 5%交通特有能源系统，在太阳能Ⅰ类、Ⅱ类、Ⅲ类和Ⅳ类地区，分别可以减少 2395.8t、2072.8t、1846.4t 和 1336.0t CO_2 排放。对于新能源汽车渗透率为 10%交通特有能源系统，在太阳能Ⅰ类、Ⅱ类、Ⅲ类和Ⅳ类地区，分别可以减少 2395.8t、2072.8t、1846.4t 和 1336.0t CO_2 排放。

4.2.3　弱电网小负荷场景下交通适配的能源系统

1. 系统架构

交通适配的能源系统针对弱电网、小负荷应用场景，面向公路交通资源空间，通过分布式光伏发电向交通领域大规模集成，而构建交通供配电系统的新电源，主要指分布式公路交通光伏发电。

目前，高速公路沿线设施用能主要来自于附近收费站电源或者是从临近市电供电，需建设新的供配电网络，同时由于引出线路过长造成线路损耗也会较大。因此，充分地利用高速沿线空间资源，开发分布式光伏发电，不仅可满足对公路沿线机电设备的用能需求，同时也可以作为交通电源，为公路沿线其他用能设施提供清洁电力供给。

图 4-27 给出了交通适配的能源系统组网结构图。可见，在高速公路沿线原本 10kV 母线的基础上，接入分布式光伏发电装置。通过分布式光伏发电，为高速公路沿线原负荷提供能量。在光照充足的条件下，分布式光伏发电量远远超过高速

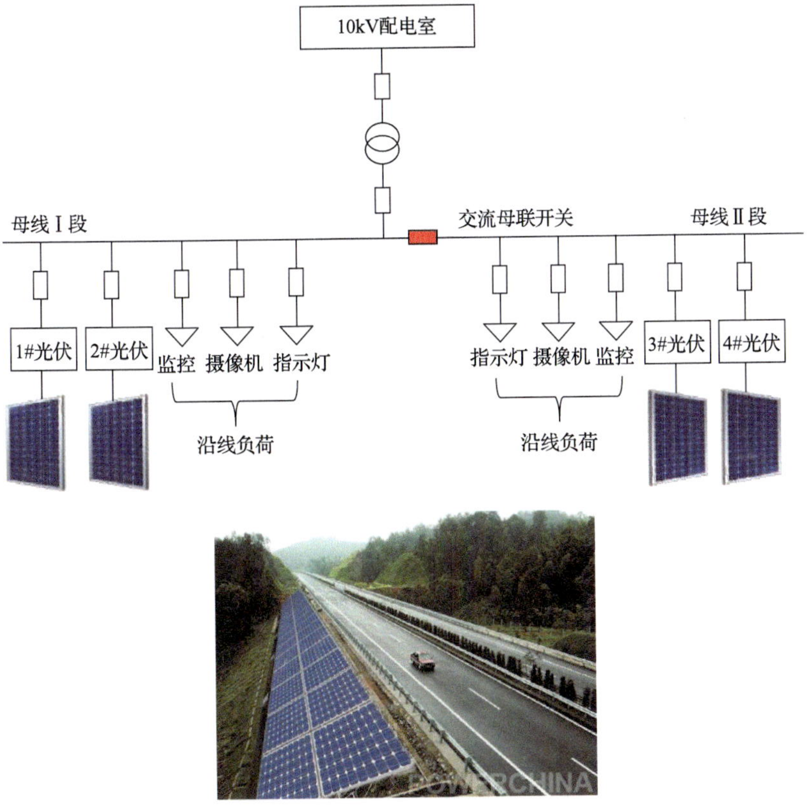

图 4-27　交通适配的能源系统组网结构图

公路沿线原负荷所需电量，分布式光伏发电在满足高速公路沿线原负荷的本地用电需求的基础上，大部分剩余电量通过配电网向电网传输，实现余电上网；在光照不足的条件下，高速公路沿线原负荷用电量由电网提供。

2. 用电自洽率

分布式光伏发电在公路沿线的铺设，将会使公路沿线设施具有发电潜力，具体结构详见图 4-27，并且由于公路沿线负荷相对较小，则公路交通沿线设施将实现由荷向源的转变。考虑到公路沿线可供开发空间资源潜力巨大，通过分布式光伏发电的安装，公路沿线设施将成为公路交通系统中的电源。根据附表 A5，全国高速公路分布式光伏发电装机潜力为 910GW，年发电潜力为 1029770GW·h，远超高速公路沿线年平均用电量 270GW·h 。

对于面向公路沿线的交通适配能源系统，由于高速公路路面车流量较大，无法直接利用高速公路路面面积，而需要对行车路面进行改建，包括建设光伏顶棚支架、承载式光伏路面等，这些空间资源开发难度较大。而高速公路两旁的边坡和隔离带内空间，无车辆行驶，便于直接利用建设分布式光伏发电，这些空间资源开发难度相对较小，并结合线路走向，选择合适的光伏组件铺设方式，如东西走向公路可在两侧平铺、南北走向工作可在两侧锯齿状铺设。

按高速公路沿线两侧易开发边坡与隔离栅内土地宽度为 10m、难开发路面宽度为 30m 计算，则单位公里高速公路易开发空间资源为 1 万 m^2，而难开发空间资源为 3 万 m^2。因此，本节将以高速公路沿线易开发空间资源为基础开发交通适配的能源系统，对整个系统的发电潜力与自洽率进行测算。图 4-28 为交通适配的能源系统发用电情况。表 4-18 为单位公里高速公路沿线发电量潜力及用电量。

对于单位公里沿线而言，交通机电设施年均用电量为 2MW·h；在太阳能 Ⅰ类、Ⅱ类、Ⅲ类和Ⅳ类地区，交通适配的能源系统年发电量为 2401MW·h、2078MW·h、1851MW·h 和 1338MW·h，均远超高速公路交通沿线机电设备负荷 2MW·h 用电量，可供开发潜力是负荷用电量的上百倍。因此，构建交通适配的能源系统，不仅可为高速公路沿线机电设施用电服务，也可作为电源为其他行业、其他设备提供电力供给。

3. 建设投资收益预测

根据国家能源局公布数据，2018 年光伏发电成本已降至 7 元/W 左右。因此，在后续对公路交通能源系统进行投资收益预测时，每千瓦光伏需投资 0.7 万元。同时，根据国家发展和改革委员会公布的《关于完善光伏发电上网电价机制有关问题的通知》(发改价格〔2019〕761 号)，对分布式光伏发电项目给予 0.10 元/(kW·h)的补贴，按一般工商业平峰电价计算，公路交通能源系统用电费用为 0.87 元/(kW·h)。表 4-19 为易开发沿线交通适配能源系统投资表。

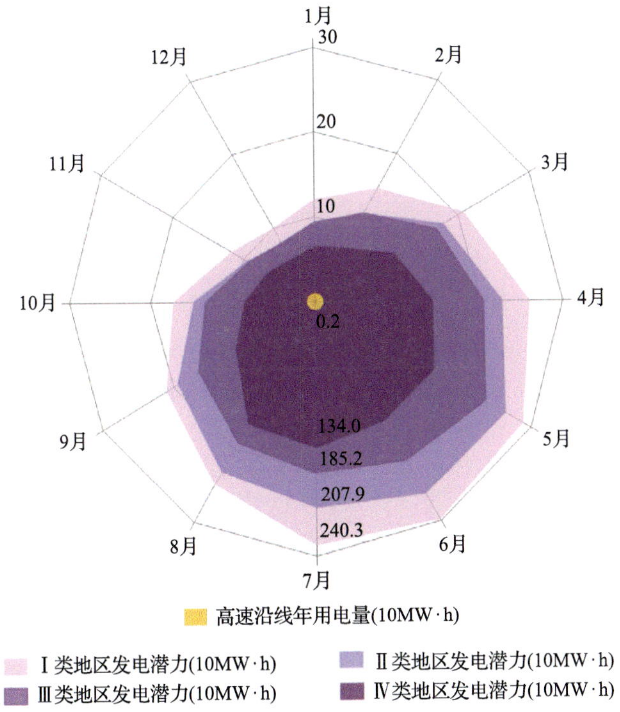

图 4-28　交通适配的能源系统发电潜力与用电量

表 4-18　单位公里高速公路沿线发电量潜力及用电量　（单位：10MW·h）

月份	Ⅰ类地区		Ⅱ类地区		Ⅲ类地区		Ⅳ类地区	
	易开发	难开发	易开发	难开发	易开发	难开发	易开发	难开发
1	11.7	35.1	8.9	26.7	9.1	27.2	6.3	18.8
2	14.9	44.8	11.6	34.7	11.6	34.7	6.9	20.8
3	20.3	60.8	17.5	52.6	16.5	49.6	11.0	32.6
4	25.3	75.9	22.1	66.2	19.7	59.3	13.7	41.1
5	28.3	84.8	25.9	77.7	23.1	69.4	16.0	48.1
6	29.0	87.2	25.6	76.9	21.1	63.3	15.9	47.7
7	28.0	83.9	23.7	71.2	19.7	59.1	16.8	50.4
8	24.2	72.6	22.5	67.5	18.6	55.8	16.1	48.4
9	20.5	61.4	18.8	56.4	16.0	48.0	10.9	32.6
10	16.9	50.7	14.4	43.1	13.0	38.9	8.3	25.1
11	11.5	34.5	9.3	27.9	9.0	27.1	6.5	19.6
12	9.7	29.2	7.6	22.9	7.8	23.3	5.6	16.7
总计	240.3	720.9	207.9	623.8	185.2	555.7	134	401.9

表 4-19　易开发沿线交通适配能源系统投资表　（单位：万元）

类型	费用	Ⅰ类地区	Ⅱ类地区	Ⅲ类地区	Ⅳ类地区
年收益	节省电费	208.9	180.8	161.0	116.4
	发电补贴	24.0	20.8	18.5	13.4
	年收益	232.9	201.6	179.5	129.8
总投资	光伏投资	1120.0			

针对易开发公路沿线而言，每公里高速公路沿线可供开发的面积为 1 万 m^2，按每平方米可加装光伏组件 160W 计算，光伏系统建设一次性投资为 1120 万元。因此，公路沿线易开发光伏资源完全开发的交通适配能源系统需一次性投资 1120 万元。在太阳能Ⅰ类、Ⅱ类、Ⅲ类和Ⅳ类地区，安装在服务区的分布式光伏发电年发电量分别为 2403MW·h、2079MW·h、1851MW·h、1338MW·h，年节约电费为 208.9 万元、180.8 万元、161.0 万元和 116.4 万元，年发电补贴为 24.0 万元、20.8 万元、18.5 万元和 13.4 万元，则安装在公路沿线的分布式光伏发电装置年收益分别为 232.9 万元、201.6 万元、179.5 万元和 129.8 万元。图 4-29 为易开发沿线交通适配能源系统投资回收年限与年收益。

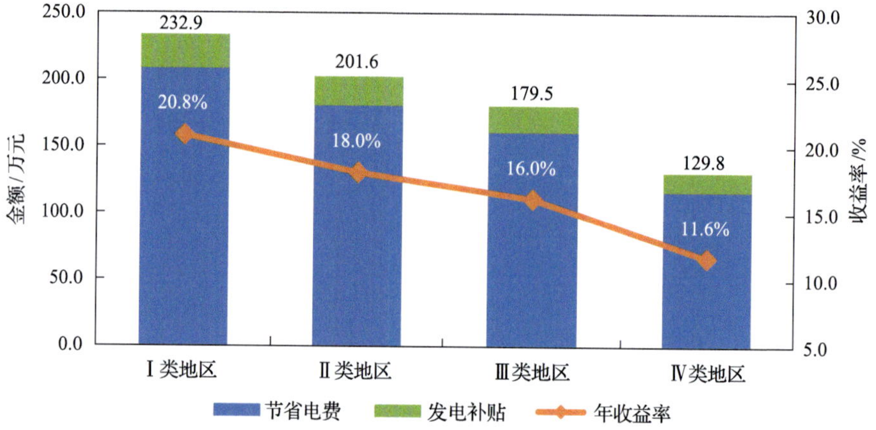

图 4-29　易开发沿线交通适配能源系统投资回收年限与年收益

易开发沿线交通适配能源系统中，在太阳能四类地区，光伏投资占一次性投资的大部分，分布式光伏发电替代市电提供高速公路沿线用电带来的替代收益占年收益的大部分。年收益率在四类地区分别为 20.8%、18.0%、16.0%、11.6%，在太阳能Ⅰ类地区最高，约 5 年可收回一次性投资成本；在太阳能Ⅳ类地区最低，约 9 年才可收回一次性投资成本。表 4-20 为难开发沿线交通适配能源系统投资表。

表 4-20　难开发沿线交通适配能源系统投资表　　（单位：万元）

类型	费用	Ⅰ类地区	Ⅱ类地区	Ⅲ类地区	Ⅳ类地区
年收益	节省电费	627.2	542.7	483.5	349.7
	发电补贴	72.1	62.4	55.6	40.2
	年收益	699.3	605.1	539.1	389.9
总投资	光伏投资	65300.0			

根据法国可再生能源行业联合会公布数据，法国投资 500 万欧元在诺曼底小镇建设了一条约 2m 宽、1000m 长的光伏公路，其每平方米造价折合 1.4 万元，每生产 1W 电力的成本折合为 136 元，而传统光伏系统成本约为 7 元，成本高昂。

针对难开发公路沿线而言，每公里高速公路沿线可供开发的面积为 3 万 m^2，按每平方米可加装光伏组件 160W 计算，光伏系统建设一次性投资为 65300 万元。因此，公路沿线难开发光伏资源完全开发的交通适配能源系统需一次性投资 65300 万元。在太阳能Ⅰ类、Ⅱ类、Ⅲ类和Ⅳ类地区，安装在服务区的分布式光伏发电年发电量分别为 7209MW·h、6238MW·h、5557MW·h、4019MW·h，年节约电费为 627.2 万元、542.7 万元、483.5 万元和 349.7 万元，年发电补贴为 72.1 万元、62.4 万元、55.6 万元和 40.2 万元，则安装在公路沿线的分布式光伏发电装置年收益分别为 699.3 万元、605.1 万元、539.1 万元和 389.9 万元。图 4-30 为难开发沿线交通适配能源系统投资回收年限与年收益。

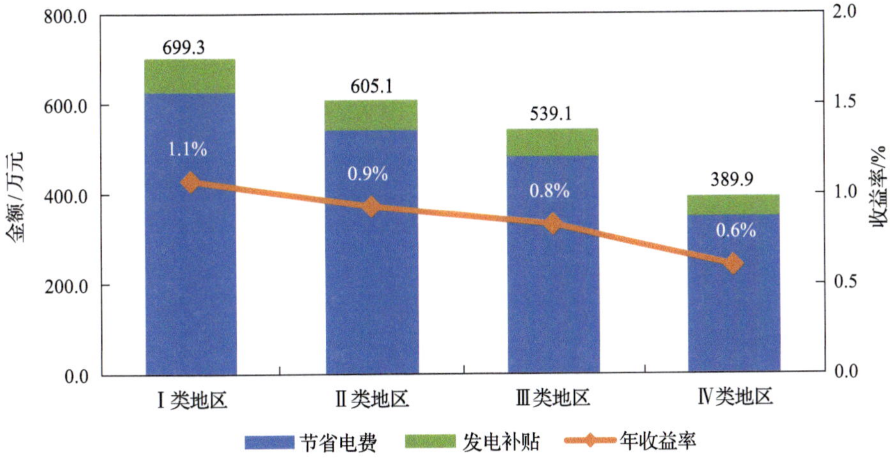

图 4-30　难开发沿线交通适配能源系统投资回收年限与年收益

难开发沿线交通适配能源系统中，在太阳能Ⅰ类、Ⅱ类、Ⅲ类和Ⅳ类地区，年收益率分别为 1.1%、0.9%、0.8%、0.6%。可见，由于高架光伏、承载式路面光伏开发建设成本较高，交通适配能源系统投资收益率相对较低。图 4-31 为交通适配能源系统 CO_2 减排量。

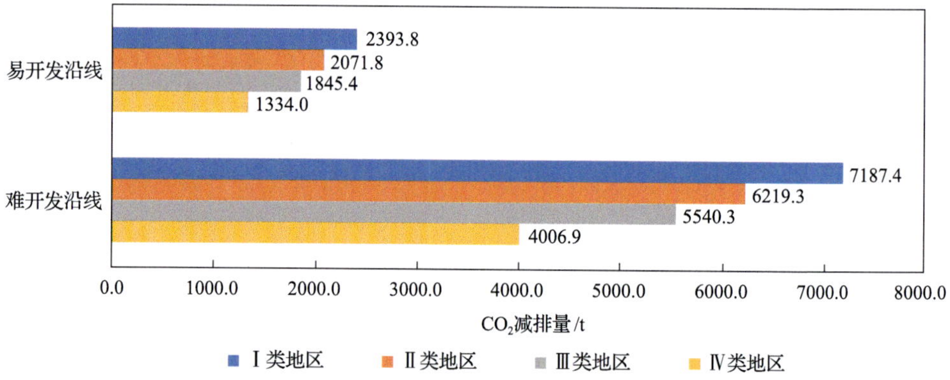

图 4-31　交通适配能源系统 CO_2 减排量

按每千瓦时分布式光伏发电即可减少 0.997kg CO_2 排放计算，对于易开发沿线交通适配能源系统，在太阳能Ⅰ类、Ⅱ类、Ⅲ区和Ⅳ类地区，分别可以减少 2393.8t、2071.8t、1845.4t 和 1334.0t CO_2 排放。对于难开发的沿线交通适配能源系统，在太阳能Ⅰ类、Ⅱ类、Ⅲ类和Ⅳ类地区，分别可以减少 7187.4t、6219.3t、5540.3t 和 4006.9t CO_2 排放。

4.2.4　无电网小负荷场景下能源支撑的交通系统

1. 系统架构

能源支撑的交通系统面向无电地区、交通小负荷供配电场景，借助分布式能源供给方式，通过源-储-荷互动支撑无电地区交通用电设施正常运行与工作，主要指分布式光伏交通机电设施供电等。

在我国中西部偏远地区，供电网络密度低，存在大量无配电网地区，这给公路沿线机电设施供配电带来了极大的困难。采用分布式光伏发电对无配电网地区的公路沿线机电设施进行供电，无须建设与附近 10kV 配电网相连的供电线路，减少配电线路和电源建设费用，同时分布式光伏发电具有无燃料消耗、无运动磨损、无污染、无噪声、运行费用低、系统维护简单等优势，可广泛地用于弯道警示、限速、连续急转弯、视频监控、测速设施、指示信息等机电设备供电。

分布式光伏交通沿线机电设施采用一体化独立供电方式，施工安装简单，无须另外接线，特别适用于偏远无电地区公路监控与指示设施，利用分布式光伏发电作为沿线机电设施的电源系统，扩大了交通机电设施的覆盖范围，节省了配电系统建设投资。图 4-32 为公路沿线太阳能光伏板安装示意图。

图 4-32 公路沿线太阳能光伏板安装示意图

分布式光伏发电是充分地利用高速公路沿线监控设施及信号设备的安装支架或门型架构，随同监控或信号设备同时安装光伏组件。由于此类安装方式不需要考虑公路可开发土地资源，所以适用范围广，但由于支架本身安装面积及承重力有限，因此安装组件面积有限，发电量一般只能够维持该支架用电设备的用能。同时，由于光伏发电在阴天、夜晚等无光环境下无法使用，则这种分布式光伏交通机电设施必须配置储能装置，在光伏发电量超过交通机电设施用电量时，将多余能量储存起来，在光伏发电量不足以供给交通机电设施用电时，释放储能装置内部能量，借助储能装置对功率/能量的时间位移，从而实现光储协同、发用平衡。

因此，通过构建由分布式光伏发电和储能系统组成的能源支撑的交通系统，可为偏远、无电地区的公路交通机电设施提供灵活供电，避免了配电网建设与供电线路投资，拓展了公路交通机电设施的覆盖范围。

2. 用电自洽率

本节以公路交通沿线的门架式信息指示牌为对象，阐述能源支撑的交通系统配置方案与用电自洽率。通常，门架式信息指示牌用于指示前方道路、车辆、天气信息等，一般功率在 1.5kW 左右。

对于无网场景下，门架式信息指示牌用电量完全由分布式光伏发电提供，则要求分布式光伏日均最小发电量应大于门架式信息指示牌用电量，考虑每月内光辐射量基本不变，则可用能源支撑的交通系统月均发电量和门架式信息指示牌月均负荷来表征开发面积、装机规模和自洽率。

因此，在太阳能Ⅰ类、Ⅱ类、Ⅲ类和Ⅳ类地区，最小发电量均为 12 月份，则需开发面积分别为 $112m^2$、$138m^2$、$154m^2$ 和 $182m^2$，装机潜力分别为 1.8kW、2.2kW、

2.5kW 和 2.9kW，具体月发电量和自洽率详见表 4-21。

表 4-21　能源支撑的交通系统自洽率统计表

月份	月用电量/(10MW·h)	Ⅰ类地区		Ⅱ类地区		Ⅲ类地区		Ⅳ类地区	
		发电量/(10MW·h)	自洽率/%	发电量/(10MW·h)	自洽率/%	发电量/(10MW·h)	自洽率/%	发电量/(10MW·h)	自洽率/%
1	1080	1300.4	120.4	1259.9	116.7	1261.4	116.8	1214	112.4
2	1080	1658.9	153.6	1633.5	151.3	1606.9	148.8	1345.7	124.6
3	1080	2293.6	212.4	2481.4	229.8	2297.4	212.7	2106.5	195.0
4	1080	2808.1	260.0	3123.1	289.2	2744.6	254.1	2661.5	246.4
5	1080	3138.3	290.6	3665.4	339.4	3213.5	297.6	3111	288.1
6	1080	3225.7	298.7	3627.1	335.8	2932.8	271.6	3087.6	285.9
7	1080	3106.7	287.7	3357.9	310.9	2736.2	253.4	3262.6	302.1
8	1080	2728	252.6	3185.6	295.0	2585.7	239.4	3130.1	289.8
9	1080	2272.6	210.4	2660.7	246.4	2221.9	205.7	2108.7	195.3
10	1080	1914.6	177.3	2035.1	188.4	1803	166.9	1621.1	150.1
11	1080	1277.7	118.3	1309.6	121.3	1255.2	116.2	1266	117.2
12	1080	1080	100.0	1080	100.0	1080	100.0	1080	100.0
总计	12960	26804.5	206.8	29419.3	227.0	25738.6	198.6	25994.8	200.6

在储能装置配置时，门架式信息指示牌用电功率为 1.5kW，预留一定的功率裕量，储能装置的功率可配置为 2.0kW，同时以储能装置一天独立运行的容量为目标，储能装置的容量可配置为 48kW·h。因此，在能源支撑的交通系统中，需配置 2kW/48kW·h 的锂电池储能装置。

3. 建设投资收益预测

根据国家能源局公布数据，2018 年光伏发电成本已降至 7 元/W 左右。同时，根据彭博能源财经数据显示，全球范围内锂电池组的平均成本为 176 美元/(kW·h)。因此，在后续对公路交通能源系统进行投资收益预测时，以每千瓦光伏需投资 0.7 万元、每千瓦时储能需投资 0.15 万元进行投资计算。同时，根据国家发展和改革委员会公布的《关于完善光伏发电上网电价机制有关问题的通知》(发改价格〔2019〕761 号)，对分布式光伏发电项目给予 0.10 元/(kW·h)的补贴，按一般工商业平峰电价计算，公路交通能源系统用电费用为 0.87 元/(kW·h)。表 4-22 为能源支撑交通系统投资收益表。

表 4-22　能源支撑交通系统投资收益表　（单位：万元）

类型	费用	Ⅰ类地区	Ⅱ类地区	Ⅲ类地区	Ⅳ类地区
年收益	节省电费	1.2	1.2	1.2	1.2
	发电补贴	0.1	0.1	0.1	0.1
	年收益	1.3	1.3	1.3	1.3
总投资	储能一次性投资	7.2	7.2	7.2	7.2
	光伏一次性投资	12.5	15.5	17.2	20.4
	合计	19.7	22.7	24.4	27.6

针对无电地区能源支撑的交通系统而言，在太阳能Ⅰ类、Ⅱ类、Ⅲ类和Ⅳ类地区，其需要在高速公路沿线开发的面积分别为 $112m^2$、$138m^2$、$154m^2$ 和 $182m^2$，按每平方米可加装光伏组件 160W 计算，高速公路沿线可加装光伏分别为 17.92kW、22.08kW、24.64kW 和 29.12kW，光伏系统建设一次性投资分别为 12.5 万元、15.5 万元、17.2 万元和 20.4 万元。门架式信息指示牌一般功率在 1.5kW 左右，所用电量完全由分布式光伏发电提供。储能装置的功率可配置为 2.0kW，同时以储能装置两天独立运行的容量为目标，储能装置的容量可配置为 48kW·h，储能系统建设一次性投资为 7.2 万元。因此，构建面向无电地区能源支撑的交通系统分别需要一次性投资 19.7 万元、22.7 万元、24.4 万元和 27.6 万元。门架式信息指示牌年用电量为 1080kW·h，可节省电费 1.2 万元，年发电补贴 0.1 万元，则安装在高速公路沿线的分布式光伏发电年收益为 1.3 万元。图 4-33 为无电地区能源支撑的交通系统投资回收年限与年收益。

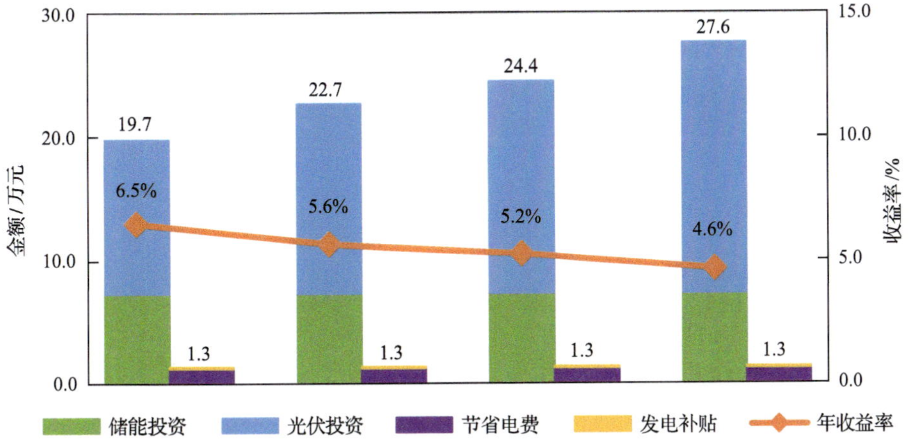

图 4-33　无电地区能源支撑的交通系统投资回收年限与年收益

无电地区能源支撑的交通系统中，在太阳能四类地区，光伏投资和储能投资占比大致相当，分布式光伏发电替代市电提供门架式信息指示牌的替代收益占年收益的大部分。年收益率在四类地区分别为6.5%、5.6%、5.2%、4.6%。一般情况下，架设380/220V线路每公里线路成本为15万～20万元，由于地形差异、负荷差异而略有不同。在后续测算中，以每公里线路架设成本15万元计，假定门架式信息指示牌需额外架设线路 1km，则在原有供电模式下门架式信息指示牌供电成本为15万元。图4-34为无电地区能源支撑的交通系统与新建电力线路投资对比。

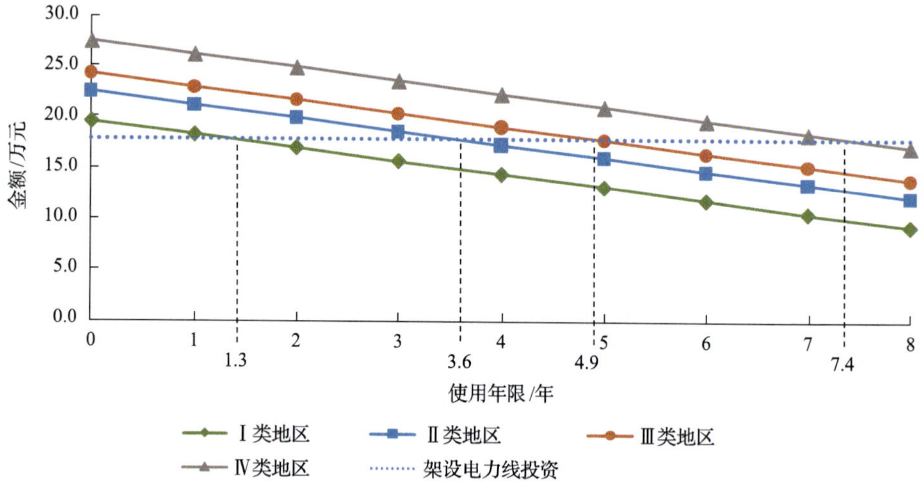

图4-34　无电地区能源支撑的交通系统与新建电力线路投资对比

在太阳能资源Ⅰ类、Ⅱ类、Ⅲ类和Ⅳ类地区中，无电地区能源支撑的交通系统分别在1.3年、3.6年、4.9年和7.4年后与电力线路架设一次性投资成本相当。与电力线路架设一次性投资成本相比，在太阳能Ⅰ类地区投资持平时间最短，在太阳能Ⅳ类地区最低投资持平时间最长。

4.3　系统技术解决方案：能源交通融合网

4.3.1　能源交通融合网

在智能化、低碳化、高效化、综合一体化的共同目标引领下，能源与交通将呈现相互交叉、相互支撑、相互协同的发展态势，二者共性驱动、融合发展。能源的变革将改变交通的形态，而交通的转型也将对能源的发展产生深刻影响，则能源与交通两大领域的融合发展与协同演进已成为未来发展的大趋势。从长远来看，能源与交通的协同创新、融合发展，必将推动能源供给体系与交通保障体系的智能、清洁、高效、便捷发展，并形成能源与交通领域协同开发、统筹配置、综合利用的能源交通融合网（图 4-35）。

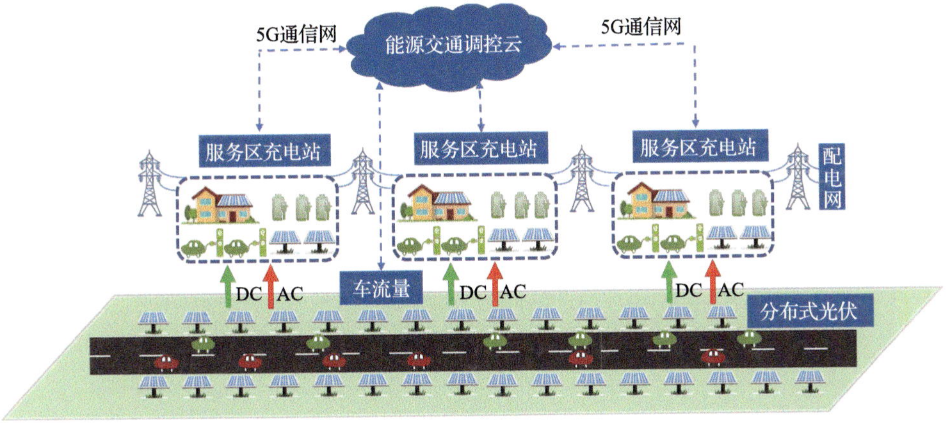

图 4-35　能源交通融合网

能源交通融合网以泛在能源互联网为纽带，通过光伏发电、风力发电等方式将可再生能源转化为清洁、高效、便捷的电能，并与铁路、公路等交通系统互联互通、分工协作，共同构成高度智能化、低碳化、高效化、综合一体化的现代能源与交通融合体系。通过能源交通融合网，能源系统可将各类清洁能源与用户相互联系，实现各类清洁能源的集约开发，而交通系统则可最大限度优化配置、提高效率，实现多种交通资源的统筹配置。同时，能源交通融合网是新一代电力系统在交通领域的集中体现，以充分利用交通侧的地理优势开展可再生能源发电技术为核心、以交通独有的用电设备为基本用户、以交通侧资源为主要载体，最终形成新型交通能源系统。

新型公路交通能源系统可充分利用交通系统的自然禀赋，协同能源与交通的共同发展，并融合了交通、电网、环境等多元需求。在交通侧，通过新型交通能源系统的建设，促进了交通再电气化的发展进程，推进可再生能源、清洁能源在交通系统中应用；在电网侧，由于交通能源系统由单纯消费者向产销者的转型，实现部分能源电力的自主供给，缓解区域电网供电压力；在环境侧，充分利用交通系统自然禀赋，优化交通系统能源结构，降低交通系统用能碳排放。

因此，能源交通融合网将是未来重要的能源和交通公共服务枢纽，并以此为基础，实现能量网和交通网的深度融合发展。能源交通融合网是技术创新的重要领域，也是新技术应用的重要载体，对可再生能源、新材料、智能装备、信息技术等新兴产业具有很强的带动作用，能够提升能源和交通产业的整体发展水平和发展速度。

4.3.2 公路交通能源系统发电潜力与负荷预测

1. 发电潜力预测

公路作为便捷、高效的交通基础设施，在工业化和城镇化的进程中发挥着重要作用，我国的高速公路网覆盖了经济最发达、最活跃的区域。高速公路的可利用土地资源包括公路路面、边坡、隔离带、服务区、匝道等。

2018 年，我国等级公路总里程达到 433.8 万 km，其中高速公路 14.3 万 km、一级公路 10.5 万 km、二级公路 38.0 万 km、三级及以下公路 371.7 万 km。按目前公路设计与实际建设情况，高速公路按双向六车道计算，每条车道宽度为 3.75m，则高速公路路面宽度为 22.5m，考虑应急车道、隔离带后，可按高速公路宽 30m 计算，同时假定一级公路、二级公路、三级及以下公路路面宽度分别为 20m、10m、6m，并且高速公路、一级公路两侧隔离带、边坡等可利用宽度分别为 10m、5m，则高速公路、一级公路、二级公路、三级及以下公路可供开发的路面宽度分别为 40m、25m、10m 和 6m，单位面积装机容量为 160W。因此，全国高速公路分布式光伏发电装机潜力为 910GW，年发电潜力为 1029770GW·h；一级公路分布式光伏发电装机潜力为 420GW，年发电潜力为 467160GW·h，二级公路分布式光伏发电装机潜力为 640GW，年发电潜力为 687630GW·h；其他等级公路分布式光伏发电装机潜力为 3570GW，年发电潜力为 4×10^6GW·h，分布式光伏发电装机潜力与年发电量详见附录。表 4-23 为全国公路分布式光伏装机潜力。

表 4-23　全国公路分布式光伏装机潜力

类型	高速公路	一级公路	二级公路	三级及以下公路
总里程/万 km	14.3	10.5	38.0	371.7
可用面积/亿 m^2	57.0	26.3	38.0	223.0
装机潜力/(100GW)	9.1	4.2	6.1	35.7
年发电量/(100GW·h)	10297.7	4671.6	6876.3	40041.3
总可用面积/亿 m^2	344.3			
总装机潜力/(100GW)	55.1			
总发电量/(100GW·h)	61886.9			

截至 2018 年，我国共有隧道 17738 处，其中特长隧道 1058 处、长隧道 4315 处、中长隧道和短隧道 12365 处。按目前公路设计与实际建设情况，假定每处双洞公路特长隧道、长隧道以及中长和短隧道出入口可供开发的面积分别为 6000m^2、4000m^2、4000m^2、2000m^2，平均辐射量为 5040MJ/m^2，单位面积装机容量为 160W。

我国公路隧道周围分布式光伏发电装机潜力约为 7735MW，年发电量潜力为 7840GW·h。表 4-24 为全国隧道分布式光伏装机潜力。

表 4-24　全国隧道分布式光伏装机潜力

类型	特长隧道	长隧道	中长及短隧道
特长隧道数量/处	1058.0	4315.0	12365.0
可利用面积/万 m^2	634.8	1726.0	2473.0
装机潜力/(10MW)	101.6	276.2	395.7
年发电量/(100GW·h)	12.1	32.8	47.0
总可用面积/万 m^2	4833.8		
总装机潜力/(10MW)	773.4		
总发电量/(100GW·h)	91.9		

2018 年，我国高速公路总里程达到 14.3 万 km，考虑高速公路服务区多采用同区域对向分布的特点，我国正在运营服务区约为 2850 对。假定服务区平均用地面积为 4.7 万 m^2、平均辐射量为 5040MJ/m^2，全国 2850 对对向分布的服务区总用地面积约为 13395 万 m^2，按单位面积装机容量为 160W，全国高速公路服务区中分布式光伏发电装机潜力约为 21431MW，年发电量潜力为 21740GW·h。

综上所述，依托公路交通基础设施，可供开发的分布式光伏发电总潜力将高达 554MW，是我国目前光伏装机容量的 30.8 倍，开发前景巨大。因此，分布式光伏发电作为未来可再生能源发展背景下的重要发电单元，将在公路交通能源低碳化发展中起到积极的助推作用。通过分布式光伏发电与公路交通的结合，实现公路交通能源供给方式由集中式向分布式的转变，可为公路交通提供清洁电力，直接或间接地降低公路交通用能设施的碳排放量。

根据我国 2018 年公路隧道与高速公路的统计数据，百公里高速公路路面里程为 88km，隧道里程为 12km，其中特长隧道 1 处、长隧道 3 处、中长及短隧道 8 处。同时，按高速公路服务区平均间距为 50km，百公里高速公路共配置 2 对对向分布的服务区。因此，百公里高速公路分布式光伏发电总可用面积为 364.8 万 m^2，其中，沿线可用面积为 352 万 m^2，隧道隔离带可用面积为 3.4 万 m^2，服务区可用面积为 9.4 万 m^2。按单位面积装机潜力为 160W 计算，百公里高速公路分布式光伏发电装机总潜力为 584MW。表 4-25 为高速公路分布式光伏建设难易指数与就近消纳指数。

在分布式光伏建设过程中，常使用建设难易指数和就近消纳指数来表征分布式光伏开发的制约因素。建设难易指数主要是考虑光伏电站建设过程中施工的程度，主要包含光伏技术和产品的成熟度以及建设成本等因素，建设难易指数越高

表 4-25　高速公路分布式光伏建设难易指数与就近消纳指数

光伏类别		建设难易指数	就近消纳指数
服务区	屋顶	★	★★★★★
	路面	★★★★★	★★★
隧道	隔离	★	★★★★★
公路	路侧	★★	★★
	路面	★★★★★	★★

则更不易建设。而就近消纳指数主要是考虑光伏电站附近是否有足够的负载，接入电网的方式及成本等因素，就近消纳指数越高则越容易消纳。通过对高速公路服务区、隧道、公路等基本设施周围环境的调查，可得不同地区分布式光伏建设难易指数与就近消纳指数。

根据高速公路分布特点，地域覆盖范围广，而负荷密度相对较低，因此在高速公路周围的分布式光伏建设可采用局部有序开发。综合考虑建设难易指数和就近消纳指数，其较易开发场景主要有服务区屋顶和车棚、隧道周围、高速公路沿线路边等，具体如下所示。

优先开发服务区屋顶、停车棚等空余面积的分布式发电项目，为服务区负荷提供清洁能源。服务区作为交通服务设施，其屋顶和车棚面积充足，且周围无建筑阻挡、无人流量、便于管理，对于开发屋顶光伏项目创造了条件。服务区基本负荷稳定，迎合了光伏屋顶就近发电、就近并网、就近转换、就近使用的理念，对于充分地利用太阳能资源，替代和减少化石能源消费提供了便利。按每对服务区屋顶、车棚总占地面积约 1 万 m^2 计算，则百公里高速公路服务区易开发面积为 2 万 m^2。

其次开发高速公路隧道周围空余面积的分布式发电项目，为隧道负荷提供清洁能源。隧道作为交通基础设施，在进、出口位置均存在大量空余面积，为建设分布式光伏项目提供了便利，且因隧道负荷稳定，分布式光伏出力也可就近提供给隧道负荷，节省了长距离并网带来的损耗增加。由于隧道隔离带面积均较易开发，则百公里隧道可供开发面积为 3.4 万 m^2，装机潜力约为 5MW。

然后开发高速公路沿线路边空余面积的分布式发电项目。由于高速公路沿线负荷较小，无法消纳分布式光伏出力，因此分布式光伏出力选择提供给临近服务区或隧道等负荷用电，相较于在服务区屋顶和隧道开发分布式发电项目，公路沿线因距离较远，造成线路成本增加的同时会带来出力损耗。按高速公路沿线两侧路面宽度共 10m，则百公里高速公路总开发面积为 88 万 m^2，装机潜力约为 141MW。

除上述场景之外，高速公路中较难开发场景主要有服务区路面、高速公路沿线天棚等地。从建设难易程度来看，由于服务区路面和高速公路路面车流量较大，因此此类开发方式无法直接利用已有路面，需先对已有路面进行改造，如在路面上方建设天棚、打造光伏路面等。其次再进行分布式发电项目的铺设。此类型开发方式大大提高了分布式光伏建设难度，同时也使得经济成本增加。从消纳情况来看，由于高速公路沿线负荷较小，无法消纳光伏路面出力，其出力多提供给临近服务区或村庄等大型负荷用户，因输送距离较远在增加经济成本的同时，还会带来出力的损耗。表 4-26 为百公里高速公路分布式光伏可开发面积与发电潜力。

表 4-26　百公里高速公路分布式光伏可开发面积与发电潜力

类型	可开发面积/万 m^2	装机潜力/(10MW)	发电潜力/(100GW·h)			
			Ⅰ类地区	Ⅱ类地区	Ⅲ类地区	Ⅳ类地区
易开发资源	93.4	14.8	2.2	2.0	1.4	1.3
难开发资源	271.4	43.6	6.5	5.8	4.2	3.9
合计	364.8	58.4	8.7	7.8	5.6	5.2

因此，在考虑服务区屋顶和车棚、隧道隔离带空间、高速公路沿线空间这些易开发空间时，百公里高速公路较易开发场景总面积约为 93.4 万 m^2，总装机潜力约为 149MW。在考虑服务行车道、高速公路路面等难开发空间时，百公里高速公路较难开发面积共计 271.4 万 m^2，总装机潜力为 434MW。表 4-27 为全国高速公路可开发面积与装机潜力。

表 4-27　全国高速公路可开发面积与装机潜力

类型	易开发场景		难开发场景		合计	
	可开发面积/万 m^2	装机潜力/(10MW)	可开发面积/万 m^2	装机潜力/(10MW)	可开发面积/万 m^2	装机潜力/(10MW)
服务区空间	2850	456.0	10545	1687.2	13395.0	2143.2
隧道隔离带	4833.8	773.4	0	0	4833.8	773.4
公路沿线	142600	23000	427800	68000	570400	91000
合计	150263.8	24226.2	438271	69675.4	588534.8	93901.6

2018 年，我国高速公路总里程达到 14.3 万 km，服务区 2850 对，且我国共有隧道 17738 处，其中特长隧道 1058 处、长隧道 4315 处、中长隧道和短隧道 12365 处，可供开发面积为 58.9 万亿 m^2，总装机潜力为 9.4×10^6GW。

针对每对服务区屋顶、车棚，高速公路沿线、隧道隔离带等易开发资源，我国高速公路较易开发总面积为 15.0 亿 m^2，装机潜力约为 240GW，其中，服务区较易开发面积为 2830 万 m^2，装机潜力约为 4528MW；隧道较易开发面积为 4833.8

万 m^2，装机潜力约为 7734MW；高速公路沿线较易开发面积为 14.3 亿 m^2，装机潜力约为 230GW。

针对高速公路路面、服务区路面等难开发资源，我国高速公路较难开发总面积为 43.8 亿 m^2，装机潜力约为 696GW，其中，服务区较难开发面积为 10101 万 m^2，装机潜力约为 16162MW；高速公路沿线较难开发面积为 42.8 亿 m^2，装机潜力约为 680GW·h。

2. 负荷预测

截至 2019 年 6 月，国内汽车保有量已达到 2.5 亿辆，按 13.95 亿人口计算，我国千人汽车保有量达到 179 辆，超过世界千人汽车保有量平均 170 辆的水平。根据汽车工业协会预测，在基本发展场景下，2035 年我国汽车产销量将达到峰值，汽车保有量达到 4.5 亿辆，按 14.5 亿人口计算，2035 年我国千人汽车保有量约为 310 辆，年平均增长率为 3.3%。因此，根据预测，我国 2025 年、2030 年、2035 年汽车保有量分别为 3.1 亿辆、3.7 亿辆、4.5 亿辆。

根据《电动汽车充电基础设施发展指南(2015～2020 年)》[49]，在 2020 年，我国电动汽车保有量将达到 500 万辆。根据中国电动汽车百人会预测，2030 年，我国电动汽车保有量将达 8000 万辆，渗透率为 21.6%，年销量超 1500 万辆。假定维持电动汽车 28.6%的增速不变，2025 年、2035 年我国电动汽车保有量预计为 1758 万辆、2.8 亿辆，渗透率约为 5.7%、62.2%。

根据《国家公路网规划(2013～2030 年)》[50,51]预测，2030 年，我国主要公路通道平均交通量将超过 10 万辆/日，达到 2018 年高速公路平均日交通量 26435 辆的 4 倍以上，年平均增速在 12%左右。因此，假定 2020～2035 年高速公路平均日交通量维持 12%不变，则 2025 年、2035 年我国高速公路平均日交通量约为 35.8 万辆、16.7 万辆。

1)2020 年公路交通负荷预测

针对高速公路载运工具用能情况，根据前面分析，2020 年我国汽车保有量将达 2.6 亿辆，其中电动汽车保有量将超 500 万辆，渗透率约为 1.9%。高速公路平均日交通量约为 3.3 万辆，其中燃油汽车 3.2 万辆，电动汽车约为 630 辆。按燃油汽车百公里消耗汽柴油 8.27L(72.3kW·h)、电动汽车百公里消耗电力 16.1kW·h 计算，在百公里高速公路区间内燃油汽车、电动汽车年平均行驶总能耗分别为 7.2 万 t 汽柴油(850GW·h)、3702MW·h。

针对高速公路服务设施用能情况，按平均驶入率为 10%计算，高速公路服务区驶入小客车日平均为 3300 辆，其中电动汽车约为 63 辆。由于电动汽车续航里程多在 300km 上下，考虑到行驶续航、SOC 状态等因素，可假定每百公里电动汽车进入高速公路服务区充电，并且根据前面分析，平均每台电动汽车充电电量为

30kW·h，则高速公路服务区日均充电负荷为 1890kW·h，年均负荷约为 690MW·h，同时考虑到既有负荷，则高速公路服务区年均用电量为 2880MW·h。表 4-28 为 2020 年百公里高速公路电力消耗与综合能耗。

表 4-28　2020 年百公里高速公路电力消耗与综合能耗

类型	电力消耗/(10MW·h)	车辆行驶消耗/(10MW·h)	综合能耗/(10MW·h)
公路交通基础设施	797.6	—	797.6
公路交通载运工具	0	85793	85793
公路交通服务设施	288.0	—	288.0
总计	1085.6	85793	86878.6

注：按 1L 汽柴油可发电 8.74kW·h 计算；表中数据在文内引用时进行了四舍五入。

综上所述，在考虑公路交通基础设施、载运工具和服务设施用能情况后，2020 年百公里高速公路电力消耗为 10856MW·h，综合能耗则高达 869GW·h。

2）2025 年公路交通负荷预测

针对高速公路载运工具用能情况，根据前面的分析，2025 年我国汽车保有量将达 3.1 亿辆，其中电动汽车保有量将超 1758 万辆，渗透率约为 5.7%。高速公路平均日交通量约为 5.8 万辆，其中燃油汽车为 5.5 万辆，电动汽车约为 3300 辆。按燃油汽车百公里消耗汽柴油 8.27L（72.3kW·h）、电动汽车百公里消耗电力 16.1kW·h 计算，在百公里高速公路区间内燃油汽车、电动汽车年平均行驶总能耗分别为 13.9 万 t 汽柴油（1450GW·h）、19392MW·h。

针对高速公路服务设施用能情况，按平均驶入率为 10%计算，高速公路服务区驶入小客车日平均为 5800 辆，其中电动汽车约为 330 辆。假定每百公里电动汽车进入高速公路服务区充电 1 次，并且根据前面分析，平均每台电动汽车充电电量为 30kW·h，则高速公路服务区日均充电负荷为 9900kW·h，年均负荷约为 3614MW·h，同时考虑到既有负荷，则高速公路服务区年均用电量为 5804MW·h。表 4-29 为 2025 年百公里高速公路电力消耗与综合能耗。

表 4-29　2025 年百公里高速公路电力消耗与综合能耗

类型	电力消耗/(10MW·h)	车辆行驶消耗/(10MW·h)	综合能耗/(10MW·h)
公路交通基础设施	797.6	—	797.6
公路交通载运工具	0	147081.5	147081.4
公路交通服务设施	580.4	—	580.4
总计	1378	147081.5	148459.4

综上所述，在考虑公路交通基础设施、载运工具和服务设施用能情况后，2025年百公里高速公路电力消耗为13780MW·h时，综合能耗则高达1485GW·h。

3)2030年公路交通负荷预测

针对高速公路载运工具用能情况，根据前面分析，2030年我国汽车保有量将达3.7亿辆，其中电动汽车保有量将达到8000万辆，渗透率约为21.6%。高速公路平均日交通量约为10万辆，其中燃油汽车7.9万辆，电动汽车约为2.1万辆。按燃油汽车百公里消耗汽柴油 8.27L(72.3kW·h)、电动汽车百公里消耗电力16.1kW·h计算，在百公里高速公路区间内燃油汽车、电动汽车年平均行驶总能耗分别为17.4万t汽柴油(2080GW·h)、120GW·h。

针对高速公路服务设施用能情况，按平均驶入率为10%计算，高速公路服务区驶入小客车日平均为10000辆，其中电动汽车约为2100辆。由于电动汽车续航里程多在300km上下，考虑到行驶续航、SOC状态等因素，可假定每百公里电动汽车进入高速公路服务区充电，并且根据前面分析，平均每台电动汽车充电电量为 30kW·h，则高速公路服务区日均充电负荷为 63MW·h，年均负荷约为22995MW·h，同时考虑到既有负荷，则高速公路服务区年均用电量为25185MW·h。表4-30为2030年百公里高速公路电力消耗与综合能耗。

表4-30　2030年百公里高速公路电力消耗与综合能耗

类型	电力消耗/(10MW·h)	车辆行驶消耗/(10MW·h)	综合能耗/(10MW·h)
公路交通基础设施	797.6	—	797.6
公路交通载运工具	0	220817.7	220817.7
公路交通服务设施	2518.5	—	2518.5
总计	3316.1	220817.7	224133.8

综上所述，在考虑公路交通基础设施、载运工具和服务设施用能情况后，2030年百公里高速公路电力消耗为33161MW·h，综合能耗则高达2241GW·h。

4)2035年公路交通负荷预测

针对高速公路载运工具用能情况，根据前面分析，2035年我国汽车保有量将达4.5亿辆，其中电动汽车保有量将超2.8亿辆，渗透率约为62.2%。高速公路平均日交通量约为16.7万辆，其中燃油汽车为6.3万辆，电动汽车约为10.4万辆。按燃油汽车百公里消耗汽柴油 8.27L(72.3kW·h)、电动汽车百公里消耗电力16.1kW·h计算，在百公里高速公路区间内燃油汽车、电动汽车年平均行驶总能耗分别为16.0万t汽柴油(1660GW·h)、610GW·h。

针对高速公路服务设施用能情况，按平均驶入率为10%计算，高速公路服务区驶入小客车日平均为1.7万辆，其中电动汽车约为1.0万辆。由于电池储能技术、电动机技术的发展，预计到2035年，电动汽车续航里程为400～500km，则可假定每两百公里电动汽车进入高速公路服务区充电1次，并且根据前面分析，平均每台电动汽车充电电量为40kW·h，则高速公路服务区日均充电负荷为200MW·h，年均负荷约为75390MW·h，同时考虑到既有负荷，则高速公路服务区年均用电量为78110MW·h。表4-31为2035年百公里高速公路电力消耗与综合能耗。

表4-31　2035年百公里高速公路电力消耗与综合能耗

类型	电力消耗/(10MW·h)	车辆行驶消耗/(10MW·h)	综合能耗/(10MW·h)
公路交通基础设施	797.6	—	797.6
公路交通载运工具	0	227369.5	227369.5
公路交通服务设施	7811.0	—	7811.0
总计	8608.6	227369.5	235978.1

综上所述，在考虑公路交通基础设施、载运工具和服务设施用能情况后，2035年百公里高速公路电力消耗为86086MW·h，综合能耗则高达2360GW·h。

4.3.3　近期2020年公路交通用能展望

1. 用电自洽率

根据我国2018年公路隧道与高速公路的统计数据，我国百公里高速公路分布式光伏发电总面积为364.8万m^2。其中，高速公路路面里程为88km，隧道里程为12km，其中特长隧道1处、长隧道3处、中长及短隧道8处。同时，按高速公路服务区平均间距为50km，百公里高速公路共配置2对对向分布的服务区。

在考虑高速公路交通基础设施、载运工具和服务设施用能情况后，2020年百公里高速公路电力消耗为10856MW·h，因此每月电力消耗为905MW·h。2025年百公里高速公路电力消耗为13780MW·h，因此每月电力消耗为1148MW·h。2035年百公里高速公路电力消耗为86086MW·h，因此每月电力消耗为7174MW·h。

1)保守开发场景

高速公路分布式光伏发电总可用面积为364.8万m^2，其中，较易开发面积为93.4万m^2。根据各年份高速公路分布式光伏开发强度不同，在保守开发场景下，按百公里高速公路较易开发面积的1%开发计算，则开发面积为9000m^2，分布式光伏发电装机规模约为1440kW。图4-36为2020年保守开发场景下百公里高速公路交通能源系统电力产用图。则在太阳能Ⅰ类、Ⅱ类、Ⅲ类和Ⅳ类地区，年发电潜力分别为2149MW·h、1925MW·h、1498MW·h和1284MW·h，详见表4-32。

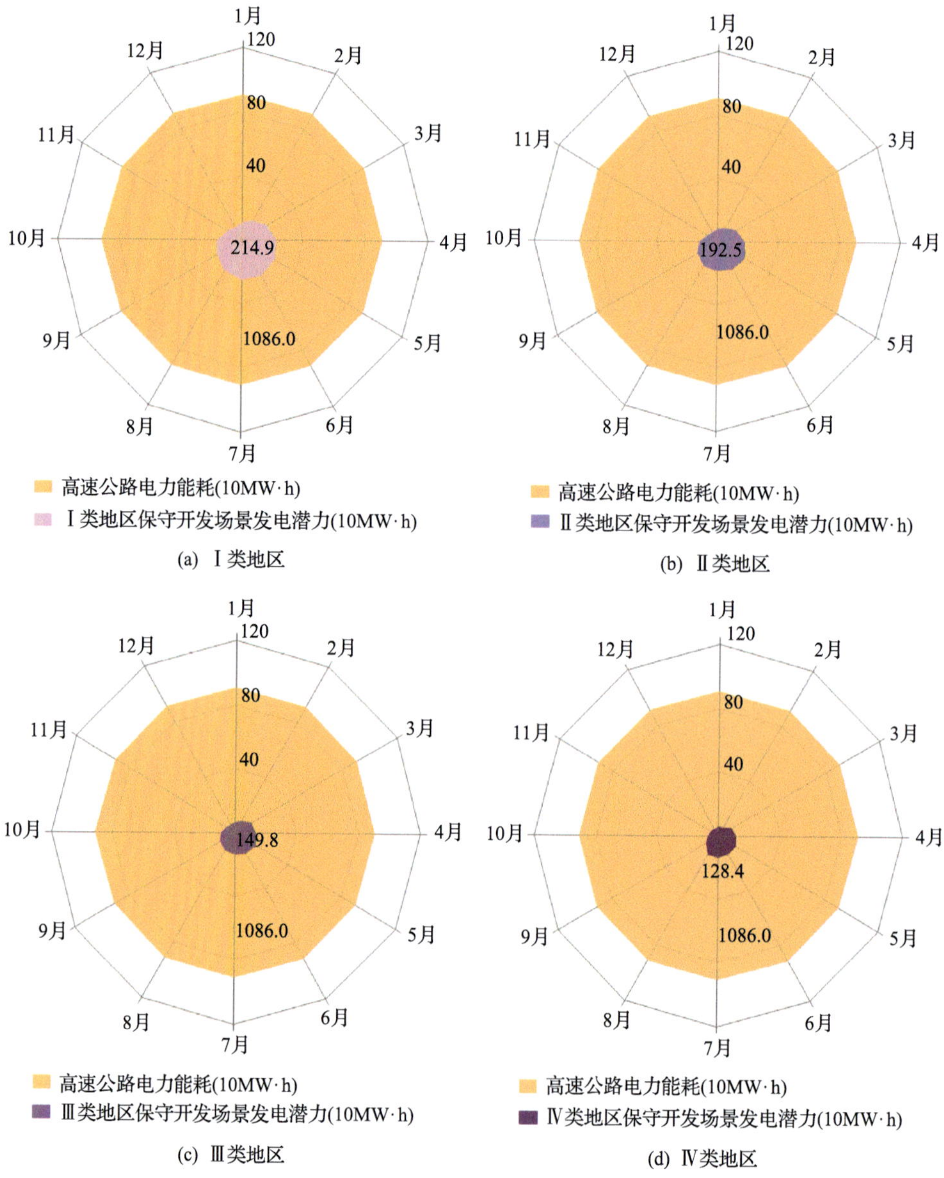

图4-36 2020年保守开发场景下百公里高速公路交通能源系统电力产用图

表 4-32　2020 年保守开发场景下百公里高速公路交通能源系统电力生产表

月份	月用电量/(10MW·h)	Ⅰ类地区		Ⅱ类地区		Ⅲ类地区		Ⅳ类地区	
		发电量/(10MW·h)	自洽率/%	发电量/(10MW·h)	自洽率/%	发电量/(10MW·h)	自洽率/%	发电量/(10MW·h)	自洽率/%
1	90.5	10.4	11.5	8.2	9.1	7.3	8.1	6.0	6.6
2	90.5	13.2	14.6	10.8	11.9	9.3	10.3	6.6	7.3
3	90.5	18.4	20.3	16.2	17.9	13.4	14.8	10.4	11.5
4	90.5	22.5	24.9	20.4	22.6	16.0	17.6	13.1	14.5
5	90.5	25.2	27.8	24.0	26.5	18.7	20.7	15.4	17.0
6	90.5	25.9	28.6	23.7	26.2	17.1	18.9	15.2	16.8
7	90.5	24.9	27.5	22.0	24.3	15.9	17.6	16.1	17.8
8	90.5	21.9	24.2	20.8	23.0	15.0	16.6	15.5	17.1
9	90.5	18.2	20.1	17.4	19.2	12.9	14.3	10.4	11.5
10	90.5	15.4	17.0	13.3	14.7	10.5	11.6	8.0	8.8
11	90.5	10.2	11.3	8.6	9.5	7.4	8.2	6.4	7.1
12	90.5	8.7	9.6	7.1	7.8	6.3	6.9	5.3	5.9
合计	1086.0	214.9	19.8	192.5	17.7	149.8	13.8	128.4	11.8

从月用电自洽率来看，在太阳能Ⅰ类地区，6 月交通能源系统发电量最大，为 259MW·h，用电自洽率最大为 28.6%，而 12 月交通能源系统发电量最小，仅为 87MW·h，用电自洽率最小为 9.6%；在太阳能Ⅱ类地区，5 月交通能源系统发电量最大，为 240MW·h，用电自洽率最大为 26.5%，而 12 月交通能源系统发电量最小，仅为 71MW·h，用电自洽率最小为 7.8%；在太阳能Ⅲ类地区，5 月交通能源系统发电量最大，为 187MW·h，用电自洽率最大为 20.7%，而 12 月交通能源系统发电量最小，仅为 63MW·h，用电自洽率最小为 6.9%；在太阳能Ⅳ类地区，7 月交通能源系统发电量最大，为 161MW·h，用电自洽率最大为 17.8%，而 12 月交通能源系统发电量最小，仅为 53MW·h，用电自洽率最小为 5.9%。

由图 4-37 可见，百公里高速公路交通能源系统自洽率盈缺情况随太阳辐射变化而变化，但可发现在太阳能辐射量较高的 3 月到 9 月间月用电自洽率高出年平均用电自洽率，在 10 月到次年 2 月间月用电自洽率低于年平均用电自洽率。在 1%的保守开发场景下，百公里高速公路交通能源系统在Ⅰ类、Ⅱ类、Ⅲ类和Ⅳ类地区的平均自洽率分别为 19.8%、17.7%、13.8%和 11.8%。

2) 基本开发场景

高速公路分布式光伏发电总可用面积为 364.8 万 m^2，其中，较易开发面积为 93.4 万 m^2。根据各年份高速公路分布式光伏开发强度不同，在基本开发场景下，

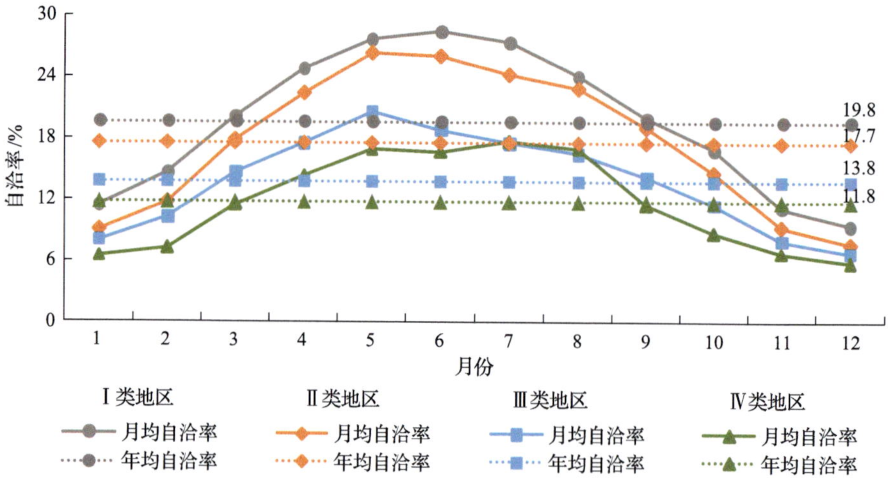

图 4-37　2020 年保守开发场景下百公里高速公路交通能源系统用电自洽率

按百公里高速公路较易开发面积的 3%开发计算，则开发面积为 2.8 万 m^2，分布式光伏发电装机规模约为 4480kW。则在太阳能Ⅰ类、Ⅱ类、Ⅲ类和Ⅳ类地区，年发电潜力分别为 6687MW·h、5990MW·h、4659MW·h 和 3993MW·h，详见表 4-33。图 4-38 为 2020 年基本开发场景下百公里高速公路交通能源系统电力产用图。

表 4-33　2020 年基本开发场景下百公里高速公路交通能源系统电力生产表

月份	月用电量/(10MW·h)	Ⅰ类地区		Ⅱ类地区		Ⅲ类地区		Ⅳ类地区	
		发电量/(10MW·h)	自洽率/%	发电量/(10MW·h)	自洽率/%	发电量/(10MW·h)	自洽率/%	发电量/(10MW·h)	自洽率/%
1	90.5	32.4	35.8	25.7	28.4	22.8	25.2	18.6	20.6
2	90.5	41.4	45.7	33.3	36.8	29.1	32.2	20.7	22.9
3	90.5	57.2	63.2	50.5	55.8	41.7	46.7	32.4	35.8
4	90.5	70.0	77.3	63.6	70.3	49.7	54.9	40.9	45.2
5	90.5	78.3	86.5	74.6	82.4	58.2	64.3	47.8	52.8
6	90.5	80.5	89.0	73.8	81.5	53.1	58.7	47.4	52.4
7	90.5	77.5	85.6	68.4	75.6	49.5	54.7	50.1	55.4
8	90.5	68.1	75.2	64.9	71.7	46.8	51.7	48.1	53.1
9	90.5	56.7	62.7	54.2	59.9	40.2	44.4	32.4	35.8
10	90.5	47.8	52.8	41.4	45.7	32.6	36.0	24.9	27.5
11	90.5	31.9	35.2	26.7	29.5	22.7	25.1	19.4	21.4
12	90.5	26.9	29.7	22.0	24.3	19.5	21.5	16.6	18.3
合计	1086.0	668.7	61.6	599.0	55.2	465.9	42.9	399.3	36.8

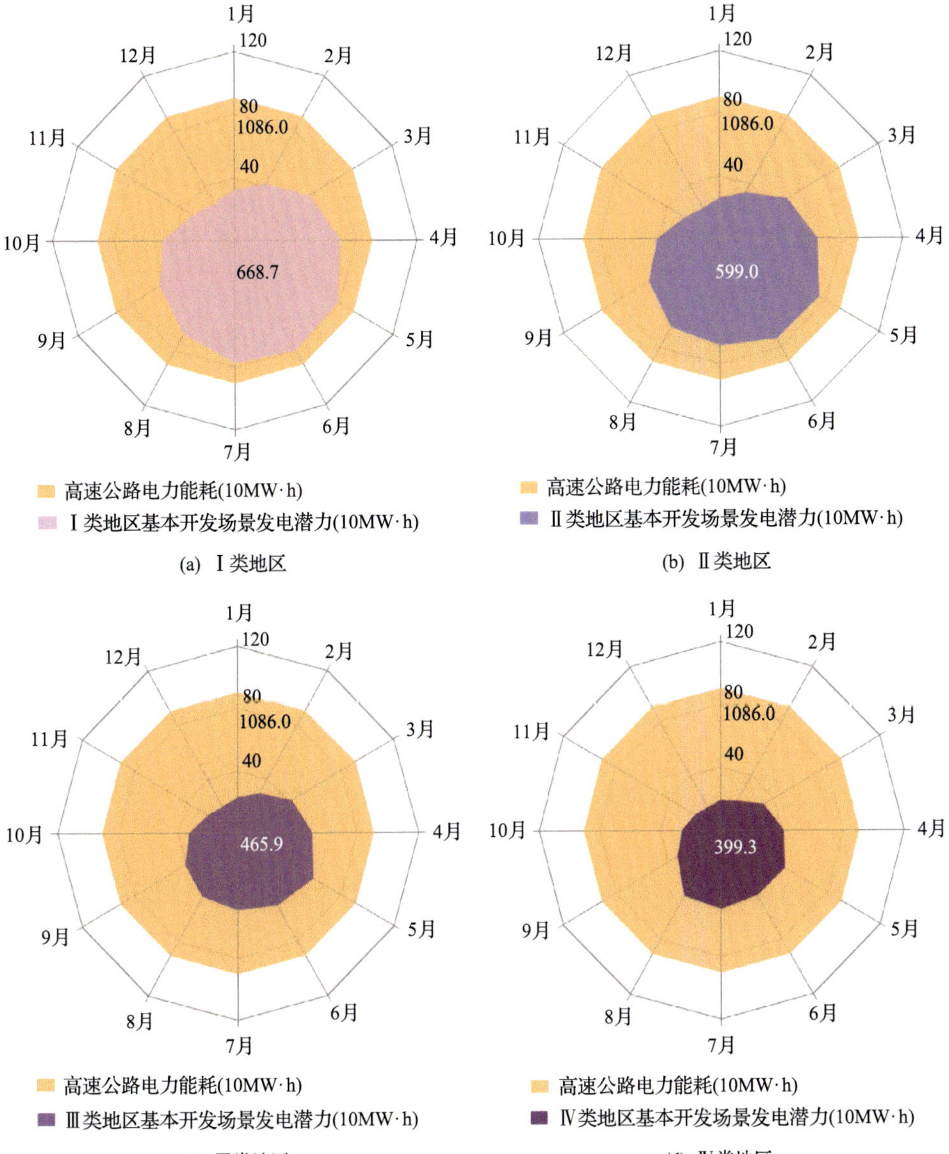

(a) Ⅰ类地区　(b) Ⅱ类地区　(c) Ⅲ类地区　(d) Ⅳ类地区

图 4-38　2020 年基本开发场景下百公里高速公路交通能源系统电力产用图

从月用电自洽率来看，在太阳能Ⅰ类地区，6 月交通能源系统发电量最大，为 805MW·h，用电自洽率最大为 89.0%，而 12 月交通能源系统发电量最小，仅为 269MW·h，用电自洽率最小为 29.7%；在太阳能Ⅱ类地区，5 月交通能源系统发电量最大，为 746MW·h，用电自洽率最大为 82.4%，而 12 月交通能源系统发电量最小，仅为 220MW·h，用电自洽率最小为 24.3%；在太阳能Ⅲ类地区，5 月交通能源系统发电量最大，为 582MW·h，用电自洽率最大为 64.3%，而 12 月交通能源系统发电量最小，仅为 195MW·h，用电自洽率最小为 21.5%；在太阳能Ⅳ类地区，7 月交通能源系统发电量最大，为 501MW·h，用电自洽率最大为 55.4%，而 12 月交通能源系统发电量最小，仅为 166MW·h，用电自洽率最小为 18.3%。

由图 4-39 可见，百公里高速公路交通能源系统自洽率盈缺情况随太阳辐射变化而变化，但可发现在太阳能辐射量较高的 3 月到 9 月间月用电自洽率高出年平均用电自洽率，在 10 月到次年 2 月间月用电自洽率低于年平均用电自洽率。在 3%的基本开发场景下，百公里高速公路交通能源系统在Ⅰ类、Ⅱ类、Ⅲ类和Ⅳ类地区的平均自洽率分别为 61.6%、55.2%、42.9%和 36.8%。

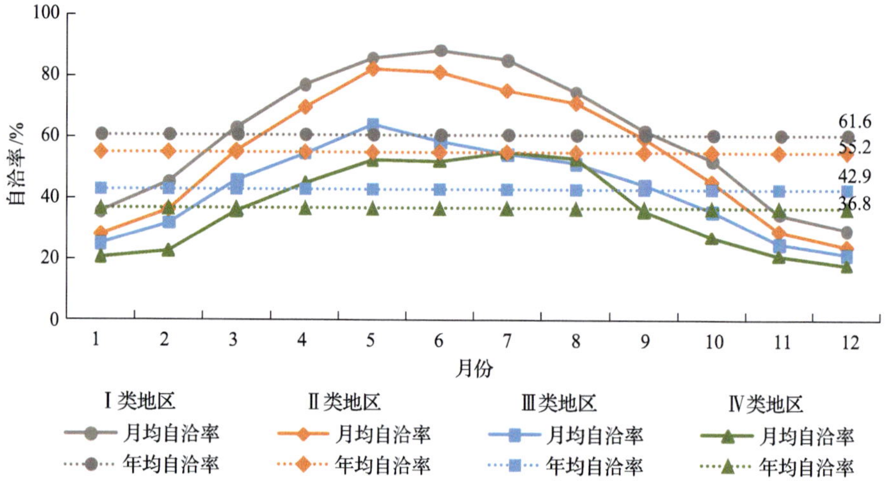

图 4-39 2020 年基本开发场景下百公里高速公路交通能源系统用电自洽率

3）积极开发场景

高速公路分布式光伏发电总可用面积为 364.8 万 m^2，其中，较易开发面积为 93.4 万 m^2。在保守开发场景下，按百公里高速公路较易开发面积的 5%开发计算，则开发面积为 4.7 万 m^2，分布式光伏发电装机规模约为 7520kW。在太阳能Ⅰ类、Ⅱ类、Ⅲ类和Ⅳ类地区，年发电潜力分别为 11224MW·h、10055MW·h、7820MW·h 和 6703MW·h，详见表 4-34。图 4-40 为 2020 年积极开发场景下百公里高速公路交通能源系统电力产用图。

从月用电自洽率来看，在太阳能Ⅰ类地区，6 月交通能源系统发电量最大，为 1351MW·h，用电自洽率最大为 149.3%，而 12 月交通能源系统发电量最小，仅为 452MW·h，用电自洽率最小为 49.9%；在太阳能Ⅱ类地区，5 月交通能源系统发电量最大，为 1253MW·h，用电自洽率最大为 138.5%，而 12 月交通能源系统发电量最小，仅为 369MW·h，用电自洽率最小为 40.8%；在太阳能Ⅲ类地区，

表 4-34 2020 年积极开发场景下百公里高速公路交通能源系统电力生产表

月份	月用电量/(10MW·h)	Ⅰ类地区		Ⅱ类地区		Ⅲ类地区		Ⅳ类地区	
		发电量/(10MW·h)	自洽率/%	发电量/(10MW·h)	自洽率/%	发电量/(10MW·h)	自洽率/%	发电量/(10MW·h)	自洽率/%
1	90.5	54.4	60.2	43.1	47.6	38.3	42.3	31.3	34.6
2	90.5	69.5	76.8	55.7	61.6	48.8	53.9	34.9	38.6
3	90.5	96	106.1	84.8	93.7	69.8	77.1	54.3	60.0
4	90.5	117.6	129.9	106.7	117.9	83.4	92.2	68.6	75.8
5	90.5	131.4	145.2	125.3	138.5	97.6	107.8	80.2	88.6
6	90.5	135.1	149.3	124	137.0	89.1	98.5	79.6	88.0
7	90.5	130.1	143.7	114.8	126.8	83.1	91.8	84.1	92.9
8	90.5	114.2	126.2	108.9	120.3	78.6	86.9	80.7	89.2
9	90.5	95.2	105.2	90.9	100.5	67.5	74.6	54.4	60.1
10	90.5	80.2	88.6	69.6	76.9	54.8	60.6	41.8	46.2
11	90.5	53.5	59.1	44.8	49.5	38.2	42.2	32.6	36.0
12	90.5	45.2	49.9	36.9	40.8	32.8	36.2	27.8	30.7
合计	1086.0	1122.4	103.4	1005.5	92.6	782	72.0	670.3	61.7

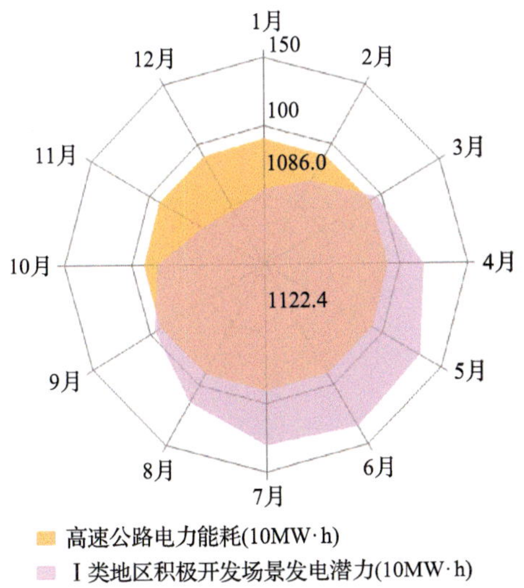

(a) Ⅰ类地区

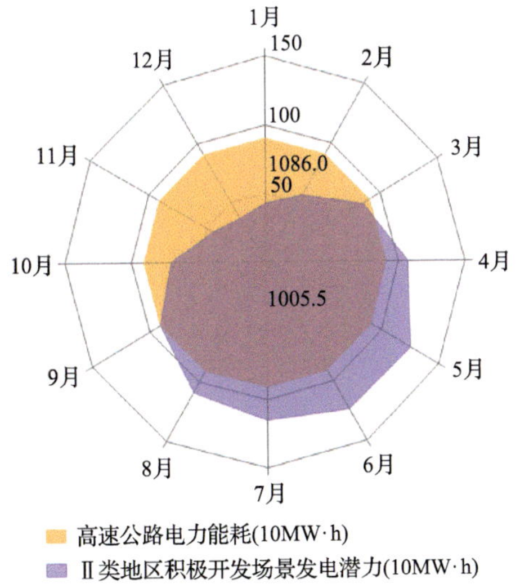

(b) Ⅱ类地区

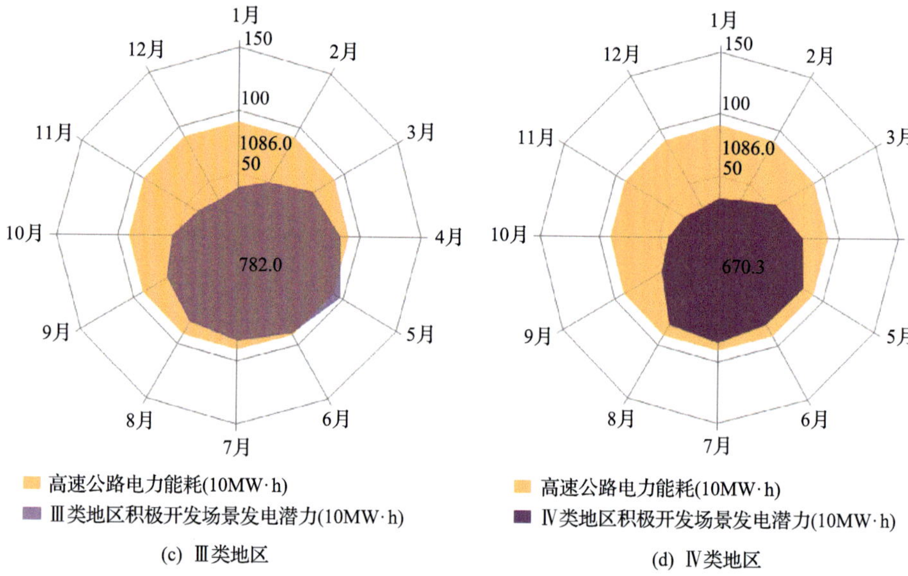

图 4-40　2020 年积极开发场景下百公里高速公路交通能源系统电力产用图

5 月交通能源系统发电量最大，为 976MW·h，用电自洽率最大为 107.8%，而 12 月交通能源系统发电量最小，仅为 328MW·h，用电自洽率最小为 36.2%；在太阳能Ⅳ类地区，7 月交通能源系统发电量最大，为 841MW·h，用电自洽率最大为 92.9%，而 12 月交通能源系统发电量最小，仅为 278MW·h，用电自洽率最小为 30.7%。

由图 4-41 可见，百公里高速公路交通能源系统自洽率盈缺情况随太阳辐射变化而变化，但可发现在太阳能辐射量较高的 3 月到 9 月间月用电自洽率高出年平均用电自洽率，在 10 月到次年 2 月间月用电自洽率低于年平均用电自洽率。在

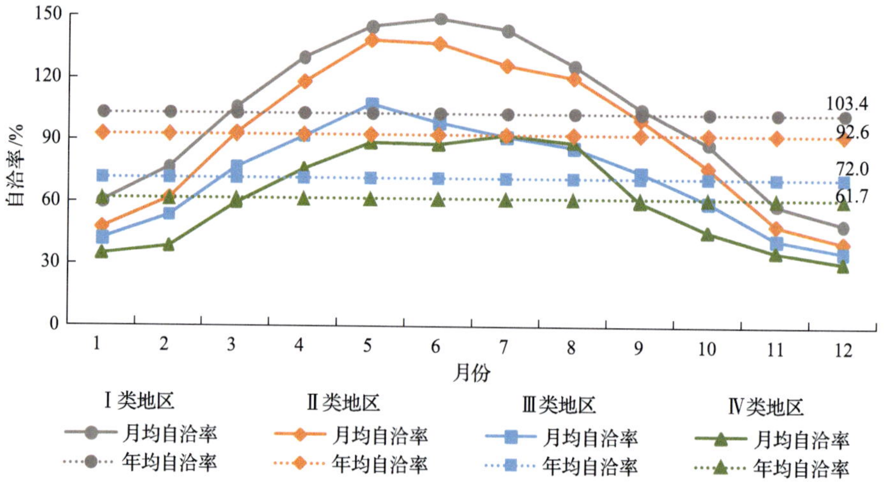

图 4-41　2020 年积极开发场景下百公里高速公路交通能源系统用电自洽率

5%的积极开发场景下，百公里高速公路交通能源系统在Ⅰ类、Ⅱ类、Ⅲ类和Ⅳ类地区的平均自洽率分别为103.4%、92.6%、72.0%和61.7%。

2. 可再生能源电力渗透率

表4-35为2020年百公里高速公路交通能源系统用电自洽率与可再生能源电力渗透率。

表4-35　2020年百公里高速公路交通能源系统用电自洽率与可再生能源电力渗透率

地区	保守开发场景		基本开发场景		积极开发场景	
	自洽率/%	渗透率/%	自洽率/%	渗透率/%	自洽率/%	渗透率/%
Ⅰ类地区	19.8	27.0	61.6	65.1	103.4	100
Ⅱ类地区	17.7	25.1	55.2	59.2	92.6	93.3
Ⅲ类地区	13.8	21.6	42.9	48.1	72.0	74.6
Ⅳ类地区	11.8	19.8	36.8	42.5	61.7	65.2

注：渗透率为用电量中可再生能源发电量与总用电量的比值。

可见，在太阳能Ⅰ类地区，保守开发场景、基本开发场景、积极开发场景下，百公里高速公路交通能源系统的用电自洽率分别为19.8%、61.6%和103.4%，并且可再生能源电力渗透率分别为27.0%、65.1%和100%；在太阳能Ⅱ类地区，保守开发场景、基本开发场景、积极开发场景下，百公里高速公路交通能源系统的用电自洽率分别为17.7%、55.2%和92.6%，并且可再生能源电力渗透率分别为25.1%、59.2%和93.3%；在太阳能Ⅲ类地区，保守开发场景、基本开发场景、积极开发场景下，百公里高速公路交通能源系统的用电自洽率分别为13.8%、42.9%和72.0%，并且可再生能源电力渗透率分别为21.6%、48.1%和74.6%；在太阳能Ⅰ类地区，保守开发场景、基本开发场景、积极开发场景下，百公里高速公路交通能源系统的用电自洽率分别为11.8%、36.8%和61.7%，并且可再生能源电力渗透率分别为19.8%、42.5%和65.2%。图4-42为2020年百公里高速公路交通能源系统的用电自洽率与可再生能源电力渗透率。

3. 用能自洽率

根据上述分析，在考虑公路交通基础设施、载运工具和服务设施电力用能情况后，2020年百公里高速公路能源消耗预计为868788MW·h，其中，较易开发总面积约为93.4万m^2，分布式光伏发电量分别在保守开发场景、基本开发场景、积极开发场景下，开发强度分别为较易开发面积的1%、3%、5%时，开发面积分别为9000m^2、2.8万m^2、4.7万m^2。此时，高速公路分布式光伏发电产能潜力在太阳能Ⅰ类、Ⅱ类、Ⅲ类和Ⅳ类地区保守开发场景、基本开发场景、积极开发场景下的用能自洽率如表4-36所示。

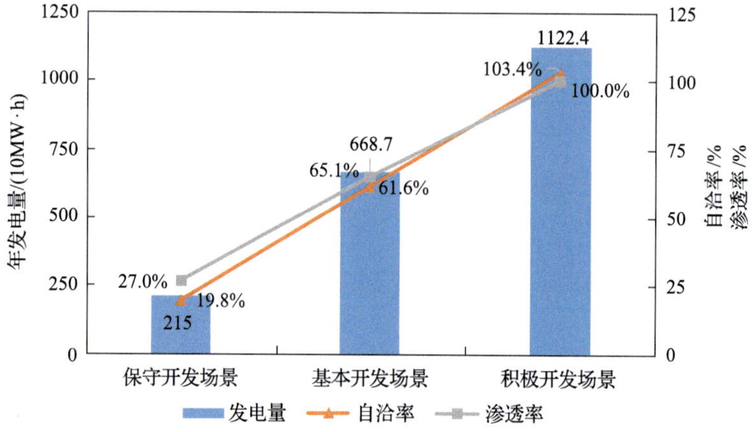

(a) Ⅰ类地区

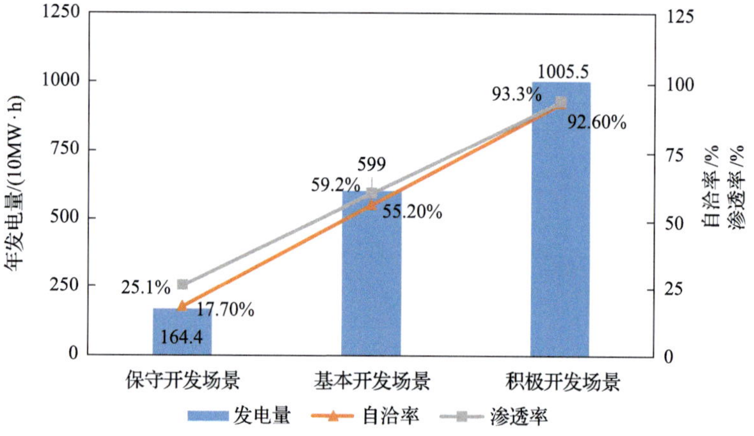

(b) Ⅱ类地区

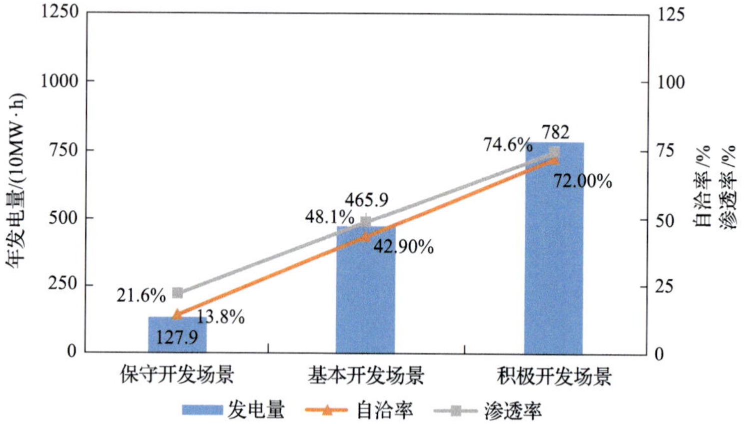

(c) Ⅲ类地区

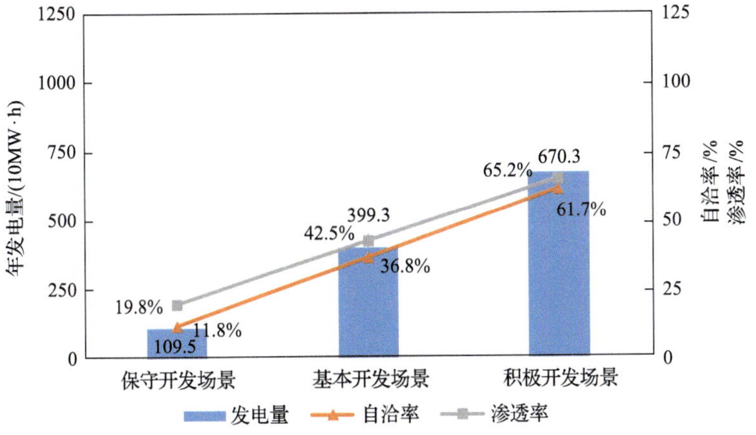

(d) Ⅳ类地区

图 4-42　2020 年百公里高速公路交通能源系统的用电自洽率与可再生能源电力渗透率

表 4-36　2020 年百公里高速公路交通能源系统用能自洽率

月份	Ⅰ类地区			Ⅱ类地区			Ⅲ类地区			Ⅳ类地区		
	保守开发场景/%	基本开发场景/%	积极开发场景/%	保守开发场景/%	基本开发场景/%	积极开发场景/%	保守开发场景/%	基本开发场景/%	积极开发场景/%	保守开发场景/%	基本开发场景/%	积极开发场景/%
1	0.14	0.45	0.75	0.11	0.35	0.59	0.10	0.32	0.53	0.08	0.26	0.43
2	0.18	0.57	0.96	0.15	0.46	0.77	0.13	0.40	0.67	0.09	0.29	0.48
3	0.25	0.79	1.33	0.22	0.70	1.17	0.18	0.57	0.96	0.14	0.45	0.75
4	0.31	0.97	1.62	0.28	0.88	1.47	0.22	0.69	1.15	0.18	0.56	0.95
5	0.35	1.08	1.81	0.33	1.03	1.73	0.26	0.80	1.35	0.21	0.66	1.11
6	0.36	1.11	1.87	0.33	1.02	1.71	0.24	0.73	1.23	0.21	0.66	1.10
7	0.34	1.07	1.80	0.30	0.94	1.59	0.22	0.68	1.15	0.22	0.69	1.16
8	0.30	0.94	1.58	0.29	0.90	1.50	0.21	0.65	1.09	0.21	0.66	1.11
9	0.25	0.78	1.31	0.24	0.75	1.26	0.18	0.56	0.93	0.14	0.45	0.75
10	0.21	0.66	1.11	0.18	0.57	0.96	0.14	0.45	0.76	0.11	0.34	0.58
11	0.14	0.44	0.74	0.12	0.37	0.62	0.10	0.31	0.53	0.09	0.27	0.45
12	0.12	0.37	0.62	0.10	0.30	0.51	0.09	0.27	0.45	0.07	0.23	0.38
年均	0.25	0.77	1.29	0.22	0.69	1.16	0.17	0.54	0.90	0.15	0.46	0.77

从月用能自洽率来看，在太阳能Ⅰ类地区，6 月分布式光伏发电量最大，能源自洽率在保守开发场景、基本开发场景、积极开发场景下最大分别为 0.36%、1.11%、1.87%；而 12 月分布式光伏发电量最小，能源自洽率在保守开发场景、基本开发场景、积极开发场景下最小分别为 0.12%、0.37%、0.62%；在太阳能Ⅱ类地区，5 月分布式光伏发电量最大，能源自洽率在保守开发场景、基本开发场

景、积极开发场景下最大分别为 0.33%、1.03%、1.73%；而 12 月分布式光伏发电量最小，能源自洽率在保守开发场景、基本开发场景、积极开发场景下最小分别为 0.1%、0.30%、0.51%；在太阳能Ⅲ类地区，5 月分布式光伏发电量最大，能源自洽率在保守开发场景、基本开发场景、积极开发场景下最大分别为 0.26%、0.80%、1.35%；而 12 月分布式光伏发电量最小，能源自洽率在保守开发场景、基本开发场景、积极开发场景下最小分别为 0.09%、0.27%、0.45%；在太阳能Ⅳ类地区，7 月分布式光伏发电量最大，能源自洽率在保守开发场景、基本开发场景、积极开发场景下最大分别为 0.22%、0.69%、1.16%；而 12 月分布式光伏发电量最小，能源自洽率在保守开发场景、基本开发场景、积极开发场景下最小分别为 0.07%、0.23%、0.38%。

可知，在太阳能Ⅰ类地区，公路交通能源系统在保守开发场景、基本开发场景、积极开发场景下年平均能源自洽率分别为 0.25%、0.77%、1.29%。在太阳能Ⅱ类地区，公路交通能源系统在保守开发场景、基本开发场景、积极开发场景下年平均能源自洽率分别为 0.22%、0.69%、1.16%。在太阳能Ⅲ类地区，公路交通能源系统在保守开发场景、基本开发场景、积极开发场景下年平均能源自洽率分别为 0.17%、0.54%、0.90%。在太阳能Ⅳ类地区，公路交通能源系统在保守开发场景、基本开发场景、积极开发场景下年平均能源自洽率分别为 0.15%、0.46%、0.77%。

4.3.4 中期 2025 年公路交通用能展望

1. 用电自洽率

1)保守开发场景

根据上述分析，考虑高速公路交通基础设施、载运工具和服务设施用能情况后，2025 年百公里高速公路电力消耗为 13776MW·h，因此每月电力消耗为 1148MW·h。

高速公路分布式光伏发电总可用面积为 364.8 万 m^2，其中，较易开发面积为 93.4 万 m^2。2025 年高速公路在保守开发场景下，按百公里高速公路较易开发面积的 2%开发计算，则开发面积为 1.9 万 m^2，分布式光伏发电装机规模约为 3040kW。则在太阳能Ⅰ类、Ⅱ类、Ⅲ类和Ⅳ类地区，年发电潜力分别约为 4537MW·h、4065MW·h、3161MW·h 和 2710MW·h。图 4-43 为 2025 年保守开发场景下百公里高速公路交通能源系统电力产用图。

从月用电自洽率来看，在太阳能Ⅰ类地区，6 月交通能源系统发电量最大，为 546MW·h，用电自洽率最大为 47.6%，而 12 月交通能源系统发电量最小，仅为 183MW·h，用电自洽率最小为 15.9%；在太阳能Ⅱ类地区，5 月交通能源系统发电量最大，为 506MW·h，用电自洽率最大为 44.1%，而 12 月交通能源系统

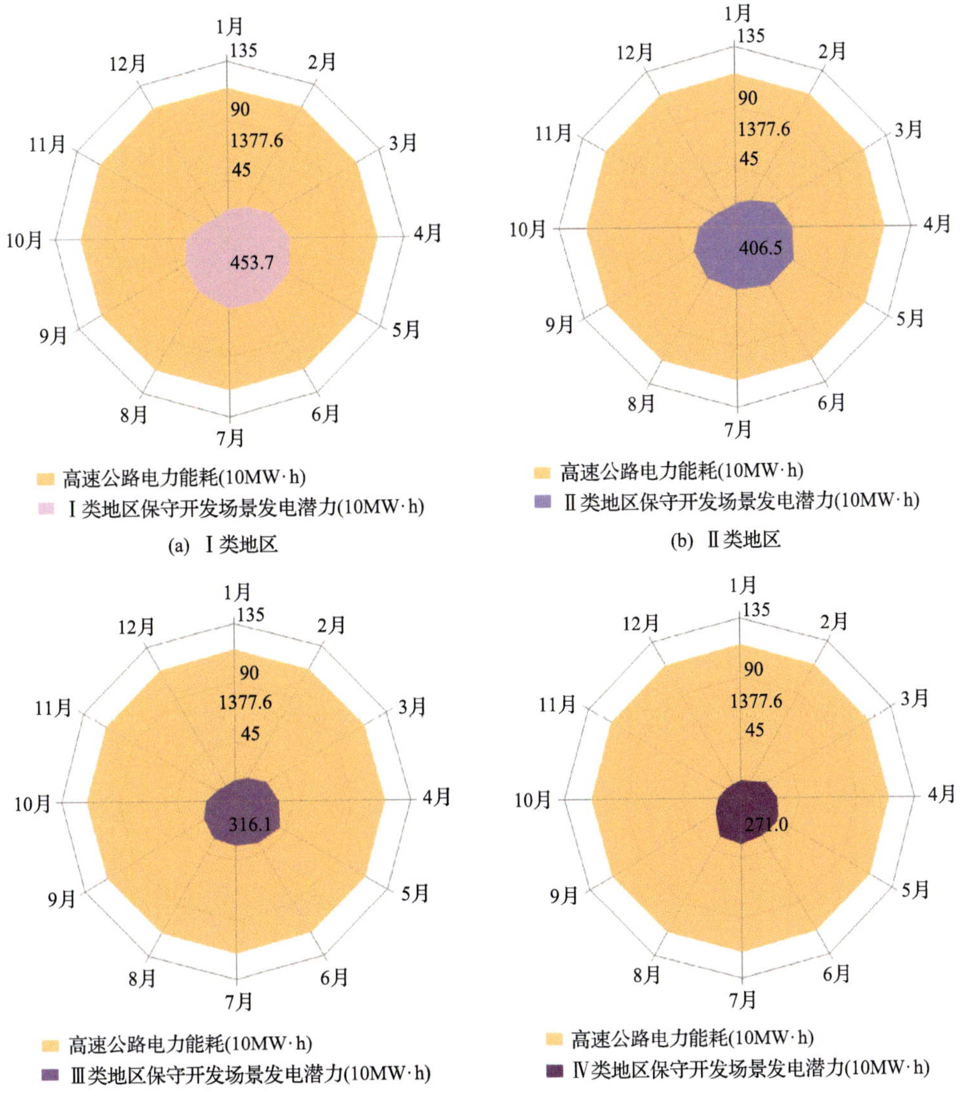

(a) Ⅰ类地区　(b) Ⅱ类地区　(c) Ⅲ类地区　(d) Ⅳ类地区

图 4-43　2025 年保守开发场景下百公里高速公路交通能源系统电力产用图

发电量最小，仅为 149MW·h，用电自洽率最小为 13.0%；在太阳能Ⅲ类地区，5 月交通能源系统发电量最大，为 395MW·h，用电自洽率最大为 34.4%，而 12 月交通能源系统发电量最小，仅为 133MW·h，用电自洽率最小为 11.6%；在太阳能Ⅳ类地区，7 月交通能源系统发电量最大，为 340MW·h，用电自洽率最大为 29.6%，而 12 月交通能源系统发电量最小，仅为 113MW·h，用电自洽率最小为 9.8%。表 4-37 为 2025 年保守开发场景下百公里高速公路交通能源系统电力生产表。

表 4-37　2025 年保守开发场景下百公里高速公路交通能源系统电力生产表

月份	月用电量/(10MW·h)	保守开发场景(2%)							
		Ⅰ类地区		Ⅱ类地区		Ⅲ类地区		Ⅳ类地区	
		发电量/(10MW·h)	自洽率/%	发电量/(10MW·h)	自洽率/%	发电量/(10MW·h)	自洽率/%	发电量/(10MW·h)	自洽率/%
1	114.8	22.0	19.2	17.4	15.2	15.5	13.5	12.7	11.1
2	114.8	28.1	24.5	22.6	19.7	19.7	17.2	14.0	12.2
3	114.8	38.8	33.8	34.3	29.9	28.2	24.6	22.0	19.2
4	114.8	47.5	41.4	43.1	37.5	33.7	29.4	27.7	24.1
5	114.8	53.1	46.3	50.6	44.1	39.5	34.4	32.4	28.2
6	114.8	54.6	47.6	50.1	43.6	36.0	31.4	32.2	28.0
7	114.8	52.6	45.8	46.4	40.4	33.6	29.3	34.0	29.6
8	114.8	46.2	40.2	44.0	38.3	31.8	27.7	32.6	28.4
9	114.8	38.5	33.5	36.8	32.1	27.3	23.8	22.0	19.2
10	114.8	32.4	28.2	28.1	24.5	22.1	19.3	16.9	14.7
11	114.8	21.6	18.8	18.2	15.9	15.4	13.4	13.2	11.5
12	114.8	18.3	15.9	14.9	13.0	13.3	11.6	11.3	9.8
合计	1377.6	453.7	32.9	406.5	29.5	316.1	22.9	271	19.7

由图 4-44 可见，百公里高速公路交通能源系统自洽率盈缺情况随太阳辐射变化而变化，但可发现在太阳能辐射量较高的 3 月到 9 月间月用电自洽率高出年平均用电自洽率，在 10 月到次年 2 月间月用电自洽率低于年平均用电自洽率。在 2%的保守开发场景下，百公里高速公路交通能源系统在Ⅰ类、Ⅱ类、Ⅲ类和Ⅳ类地区的平均自洽率分别为 32.9%、29.5%、22.9%和 19.7%。

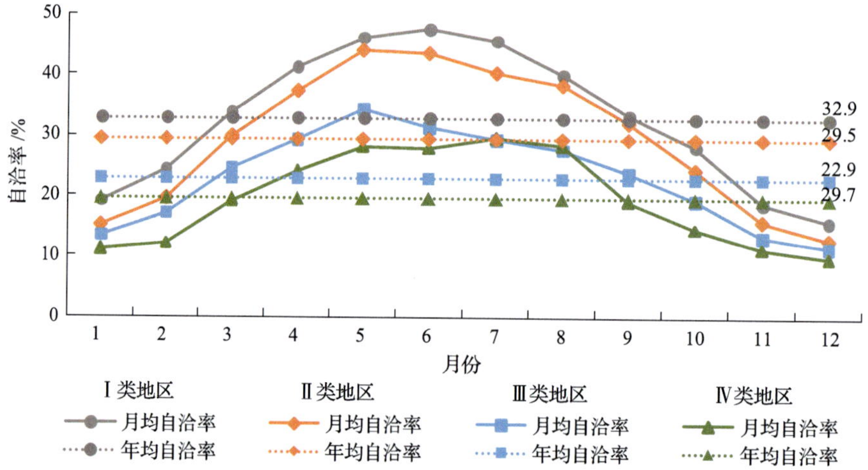

图 4-44　2025 年保守开发场景下百公里高速公路交通能源系统用电自洽率

2）基本开发场景

2025 年高速公路在基本开发场景下，按百公里高速公路较易开发面积的 4%开发计算，则开发面积为 3.7 万 m^2，分布式光伏发电装机规模约为 59200MW。则在太阳能Ⅰ类、Ⅱ类、Ⅲ类和Ⅳ类地区，年发电潜力分别约为 8836MW·h、7915MW·h、6156MW·h 和 5277MW·h。图 4-45 为 2025 年基本开发场景下百公里高速公路交通能源系统电力产用图。

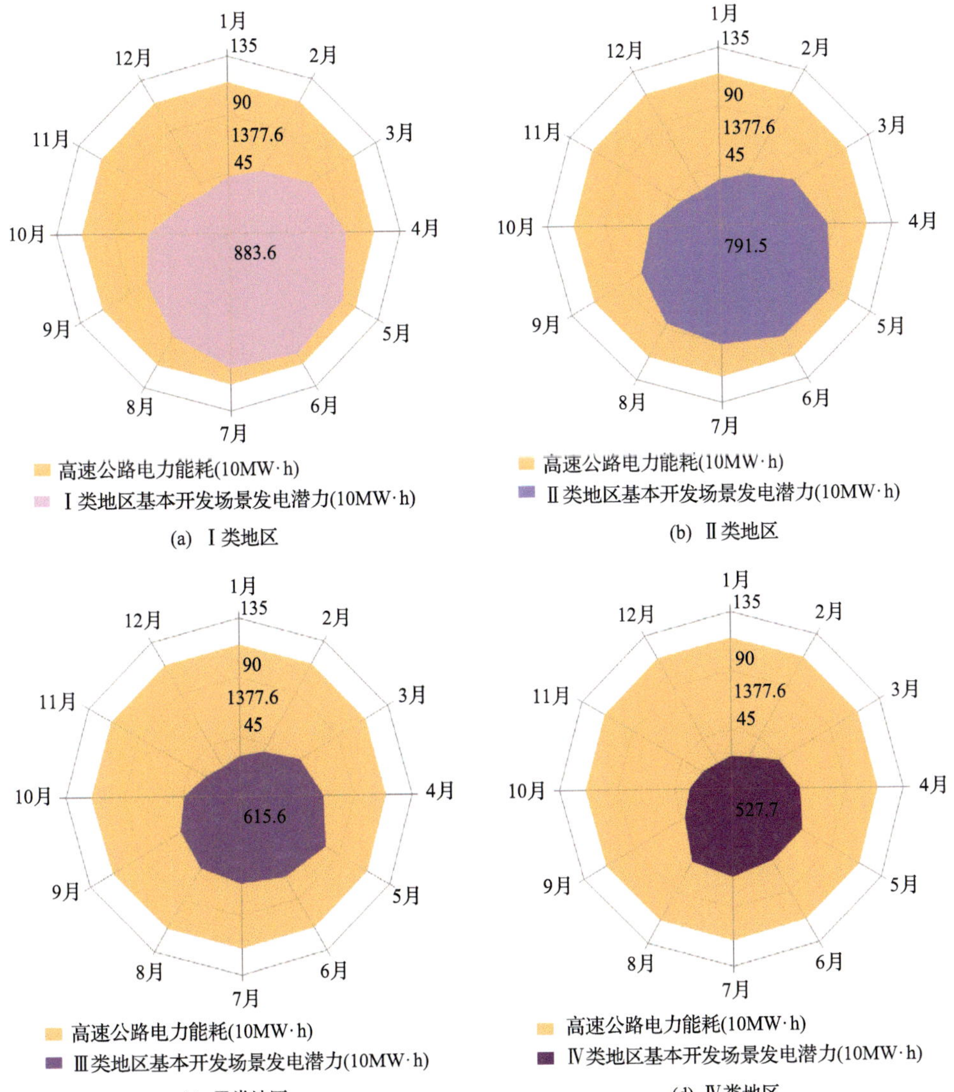

(a) Ⅰ类地区　(b) Ⅱ类地区　(c) Ⅲ类地区　(d) Ⅳ类地区

图 4-45　2025 年基本开发场景下百公里高速公路交通能源系统电力产用图

从月用电自洽率来看，在太阳能Ⅰ类地区，6 月交通能源系统发电量最大，为 1063MW·h，用电自洽率最大为 92.6%，而 12 月交通能源系统发电量最小，仅为 356MW·h，用电自洽率最小为 31.0%；在太阳能Ⅱ类地区，5 月交通能源系统发电量最大，为 986MW·h，用电自洽率最大为 85.9%，而 12 月交通能源系统发电量最小，仅为 291MW·h，用电自洽率最小为 25.3%；在太阳能Ⅲ类地区，5 月交通能源系统发电量最大，为 769MW·h，用电自洽率最大为 67.0%，而 12 月交通能源系统发电量最小，仅为 258MW·h，用电自洽率最小为 22.5%；在太阳能Ⅳ类地区，7 月交通能源系统发电量最大，为 662MW·h，用电自洽率最大为 57.7%，而 12 月交通能源系统发电量最小，仅为 219MW·h，用电自洽率最小为 19.1%。表 4-38 为 2025 年基本开发场景下百公里高速公路交通能源系统电力生产表。

表 4-38　2025 年基本开发场景下百公里高速公路交通能源系统电力生产表

月份	月用电量/(10MW·h)	基本开发场景(4%)							
		Ⅰ类地区		Ⅱ类地区		Ⅲ类地区		Ⅳ类地区	
		发电量/(10MW·h)	自洽率/%	发电量/(10MW·h)	自洽率/%	发电量/(10MW·h)	自洽率/%	发电量/(10MW·h)	自洽率/%
1	114.8	42.9	37.4	33.9	29.5	30.2	26.3	24.6	21.4
2	114.8	54.7	47.6	43.9	38.2	38.4	33.4	27.3	23.8
3	114.8	75.6	65.9	66.8	58.2	55	47.9	42.8	37.3
4	114.8	92.6	80.7	84	73.2	65.6	57.1	54	47.0
5	114.8	103.4	90.1	98.6	85.9	76.9	67.0	63.2	55.1
6	114.8	106.3	92.6	97.6	85.0	70.2	61.1	62.7	54.6
7	114.8	102.4	89.2	90.3	78.7	65.4	57.0	66.2	57.7
8	114.8	89.9	78.3	85.7	74.7	61.8	53.8	63.5	55.3
9	114.8	74.9	65.2	71.6	62.4	53.1	46.3	42.8	37.3
10	114.8	63.1	55.0	54.8	47.7	43.1	37.5	32.9	28.7
11	114.8	42.2	36.8	35.2	30.7	30.1	26.2	25.8	22.5
12	114.8	35.6	31.0	29.1	25.3	25.8	22.5	21.9	19.1
合计	1377.6	883.6	64.1	791.5	57.4	615.6	44.7	527.7	38.3

由图 4-46 可见，百公里高速公路交通能源系统自洽率盈缺情况随太阳辐射变化而变化，但可发现在太阳能辐射量较高的 3 月到 9 月间月用电自洽率高出年平均用电自洽率，在 10 月到次年 2 月间月用电自洽率低于年平均用电自洽率。在 4%的基本开发场景下，百公里高速公路交通能源系统在Ⅰ类、Ⅱ类、Ⅲ类和Ⅳ类

地区的年均自洽率分别为64.1%、57.4%、44.7%和38.3%。

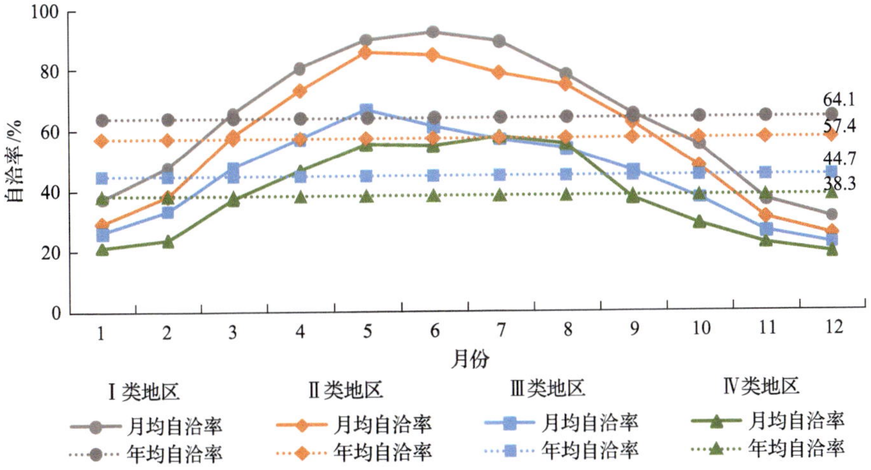

图4-46　2025年基本开发场景下百公里高速公路交通能源系统用电自洽率

3）积极开发场景

2025年高速公路在积极开发场景下，按百公里高速公路较易开发面积的6%开发计算，则开发面积为5.6万m^2，分布式光伏发电装机规模约为8960kW。则在太阳能Ⅰ类、Ⅱ类、Ⅲ类和Ⅳ类地区，年发电潜力分别约为13373MW·h、11980MW·h、9318MW·h和7987MW·h。图4-47为2025年积极开发场景下百公里高速公路交通能源系统电力产用图。

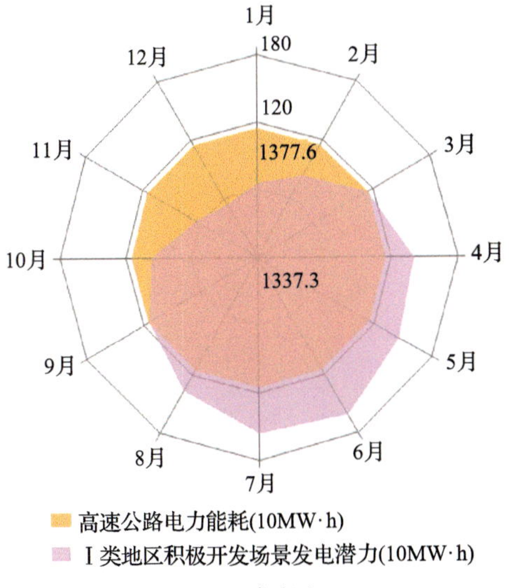

(a)　Ⅰ类地区

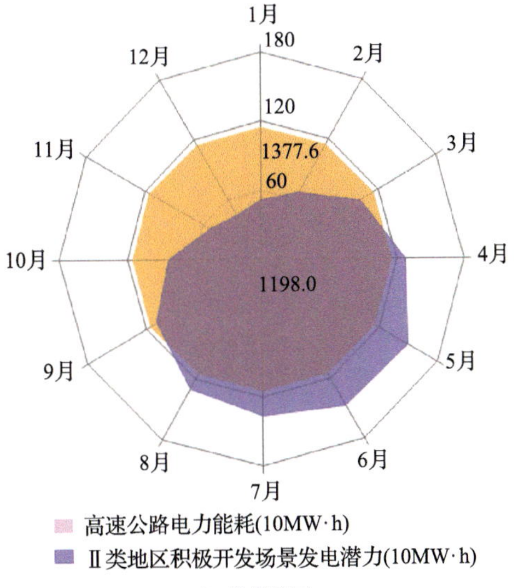

(b)　Ⅱ类地区

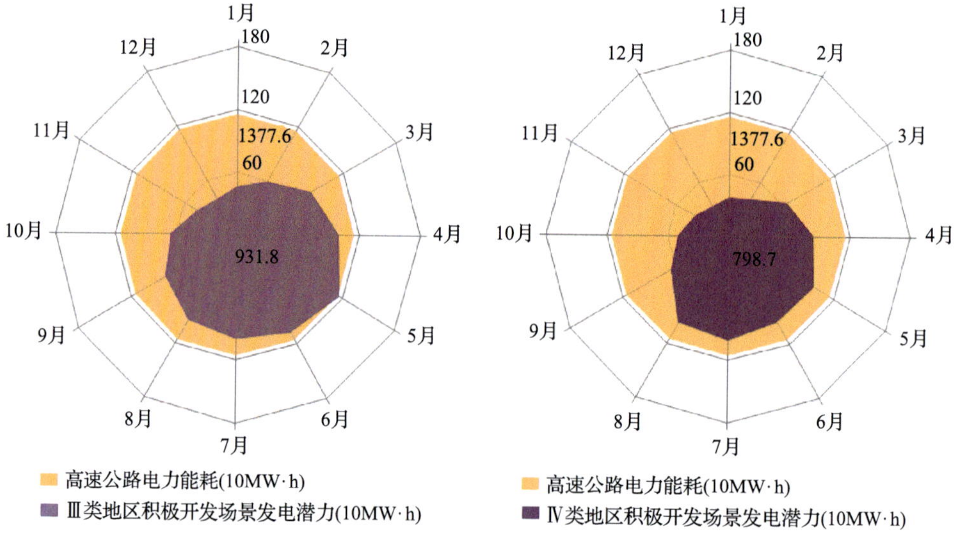

(c) Ⅲ类地区　　(d) Ⅳ类地区

图 4-47　2025 年积极开发场景下百公里高速公路交通能源系统电力产用图

从月用电自洽率来看，在太阳能Ⅰ类地区，6 月交通能源系统发电量最大，为 1609MW·h，用电自洽率最大为 140.2%，而 12 月交通能源系统发电量最小，仅为 539MW·h，用电自洽率最小为 47.0%；在太阳能Ⅱ类地区，5 月交通能源系统发电量最大，为 1493MW·h，用电自洽率最大为 130.1%，而 12 月交通能源系统发电量最小，仅为 440MW·h，用电自洽率最小为 38.3%；在太阳能Ⅲ类地区，5 月交通能源系统发电量最大，为 1163MW·h，用电自洽率最大为 101.3%，而 12 月交通能源系统发电量最小，仅为 391MW·h，用电自洽率最小为 34.1%；在太阳能Ⅳ类地区，7 月交通能源系统发电量最大，为 1002MW·h，用电自洽率最大为 87.3%，而 12 月交通能源系统发电量最小，仅为 332MW·h，用电自洽率最小为 28.9%。表 4-39 为 2025 年积极开发场景下百公里高速公路交通能源系统电力生产表。

表 4-39　2025 年积极开发场景下百公里高速公路交通能源系统电力生产表

月份	月用电量/(10MW·h)	积极开发场景(6%)							
		Ⅰ类地区		Ⅱ类地区		Ⅲ类地区		Ⅳ类地区	
		发电量/(10MW·h)	自洽率/%	发电量/(10MW·h)	自洽率/%	发电量/(10MW·h)	自洽率/%	发电量/(10MW·h)	自洽率/%
1	114.8	64.9	56.5	51.3	44.7	45.7	39.8	37.3	32.5
2	114.8	82.8	72.1	66.5	57.9	58.1	50.6	41.3	36.0
3	114.8	114.4	99.7	101.0	88.0	83.2	72.5	64.7	56.4

续表

月份	月用电量/(10MW·h)	积极开发场景(6%)							
		Ⅰ类地区		Ⅱ类地区		Ⅲ类地区		Ⅳ类地区	
		发电量/(10MW·h)	自洽率/%	发电量/(10MW·h)	自洽率/%	发电量/(10MW·h)	自洽率/%	发电量/(10MW·h)	自洽率/%
4	114.8	140.1	122.0	127.2	110.8	99.4	86.6	81.8	71.3
5	114.8	156.6	136.4	149.3	130.1	116.3	101.3	95.6	83.3
6	114.8	160.9	140.2	147.7	128.7	106.2	92.5	94.9	82.7
7	114.8	155.0	135.0	136.7	119.1	99.1	86.3	100.2	87.3
8	114.8	136.1	118.6	129.7	113.0	93.6	81.5	96.2	83.8
9	114.8	113.4	98.8	108.4	94.4	80.4	70.0	64.8	56.4
10	114.8	95.5	83.2	82.9	72.2	65.3	56.9	49.8	43.4
11	114.8	63.7	55.5	53.3	46.4	45.4	39.5	38.9	33.9
12	114.8	53.9	47.0	44.0	38.3	39.1	34.1	33.2	28.9
合计	1377.6	1337.3	97.0	1198.0	86.9	931.8	67.6	798.7	58.0

由图 4-48 可见，百公里高速公路交通能源系统自洽率盈缺情况随太阳辐射变化而变化，但可发现在太阳能辐射量较高的 3 月到 9 月间月用电自洽率高出年平均用电自洽率，在 10 月到次年 2 月间月用电自洽率低于年平均用电自洽率。在 6%的积极开发场景下，百公里高速公路交通能源系统在Ⅰ类、Ⅱ类、Ⅲ类和Ⅳ类地区的平均自洽率分别为 97.0%、86.9%、67.6%和 58.0%。

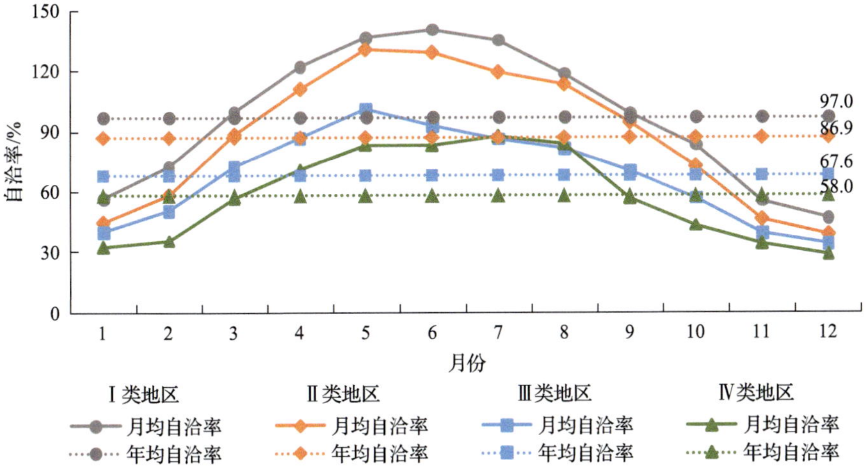

图 4-48　2025 年积极开发场景下百公里高速公路交通能源系统用电自洽率

2. 可再生能源电力渗透率

表 4-40 给出了 2025 年在保守开发场景、基本开发场景、积极开发场景下百公里高速公路交通能源系统的用电自洽率与渗透率统计表。可见，在太阳能Ⅰ类地区，保守开发场景、基本开发场景、积极开发场景下，百公里高速公路交通能源系统的用电自洽率分别为 32.9%、64.1%和 97.0%，并且可再生能源电力渗透率分别为 43.7%、69.9%和 97.5%；在太阳能Ⅱ类地区，保守开发场景、基本开发场景、积极开发场景下，百公里高速公路交通能源系统的用电自洽率分别为 29.5%、57.4%和 86.9%，并且可再生能源电力渗透率分别为 40.8%、64.2%和 89.0%；在太阳能Ⅲ类地区，保守开发场景、基本开发场景、积极开发场景下，百公里高速公路交通能源系统的用电自洽率分别为 22.9%、44.7%和 67.6%，并且可再生能源电力渗透率分别为 35.3%、53.5%和 72.8%；在太阳能Ⅳ类地区，保守开发场景、基本开发场景、积极开发场景下，百公里高速公路交通能源系统的用电自洽率分别为 19.7%、38.3%和 58.0%，并且可再生能源电力渗透率分别为 32.5%、48.2%和 64.7%。图 4-49 为 2025 年百公里高速公路交通能源系统用电自洽率与可再生能源电力渗透率。

表 4-40　2025 年百公里高速公路交通能源系统用电自洽率与可再生能源电力渗透率

地区	保守开发场景		基本开发场景		积极开发场景	
	自洽率/%	渗透率/%	自洽率/%	渗透率/%	自洽率/%	渗透率/%
Ⅰ类地区	32.9	43.7	64.1	69.9	97.0	97.5
Ⅱ类地区	29.5	40.8	57.4	64.2	86.9	89.0
Ⅲ类地区	22.9	35.3	44.7	53.5	67.6	72.8
Ⅳ类地区	19.7	32.5	38.3	48.2	58.0	64.7

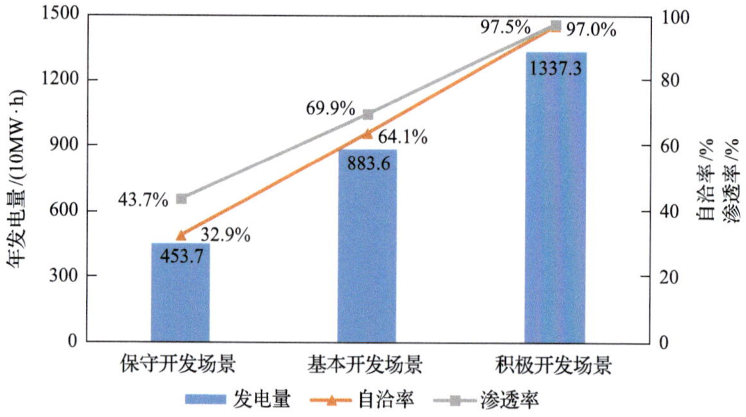

(a) Ⅰ类地区

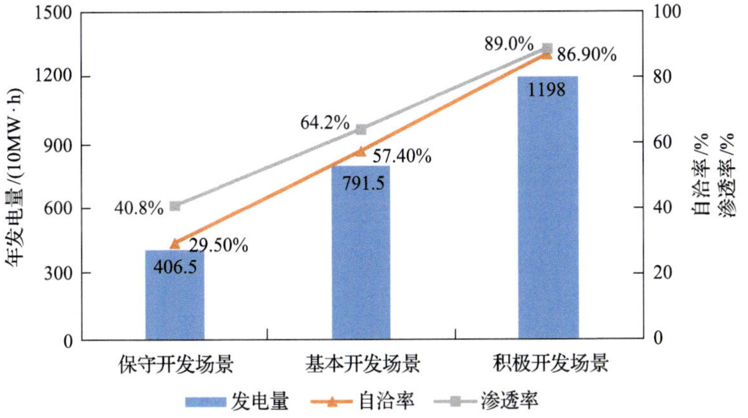

(b) Ⅱ类地区

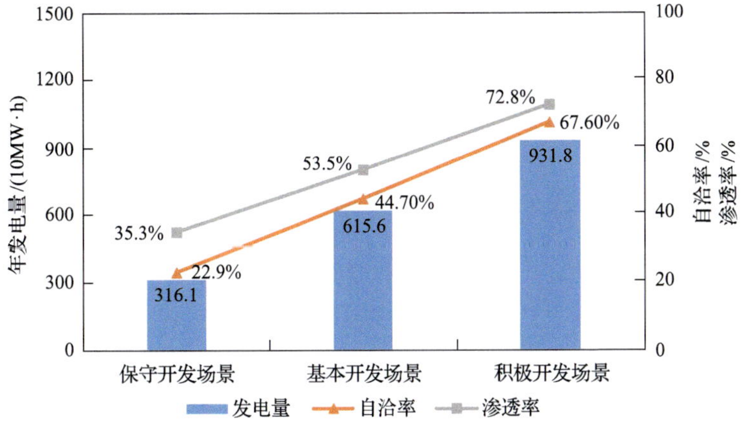

(c) Ⅲ类地区

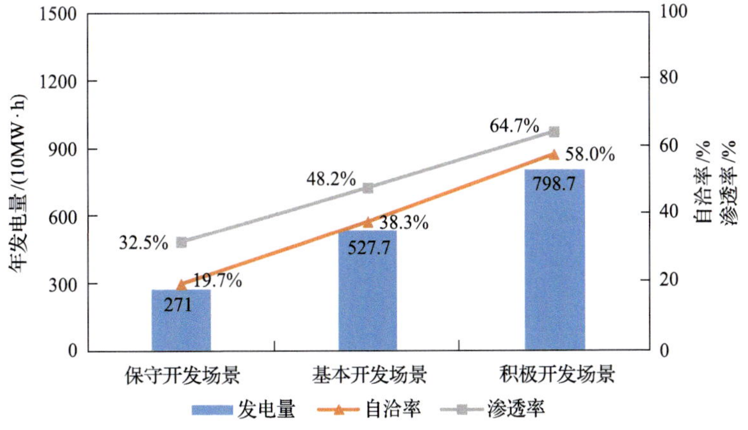

(d) Ⅳ类地区

图 4-49　2025 年百公里高速公路交通能源系统的用电自洽率与可再生能源电力渗透率

3. 用能自洽率

根据上述分析，在考虑公路交通基础设施、载运工具和服务设施电力用能情况后，2025 年百公里高速公路能源消耗预计为 1484594MW·h，其中，较易开发总面积约为 93.4 万 m^2，分布式光伏发电量分别在保守开发场景、基本开发场景、积极开发场景下，开发强度分别为较易开发面积的2%（1.9 万 m^2）、4%（3.7 万 m^2）、6%（5.6 万 m^2）时。高速公路分布式光伏发电产能潜力在太阳能Ⅰ类、Ⅱ类、Ⅲ类和Ⅳ类地区保守开发场景、基本开发场景、积极开发场景下的能源自洽率如表 4-41 所示。

表 4-41　2025 年百公里高速公路交通能源系统用能自洽率

月份	Ⅰ类地区			Ⅱ类地区			Ⅲ类地区			Ⅳ类地区		
	保守开发场景/%	基本开发场景/%	积极开发场景/%	保守开发场景/%	基本开发场景/%	积极开发场景/%	保守开发场景/%	基本开发场景/%	积极开发场景/%	保守开发场景/%	基本开发场景/%	积极开发场景/%
1	0.18	0.35	0.52	0.14	0.27	0.41	0.13	0.24	0.37	0.10	0.20	0.30
2	0.23	0.44	0.67	0.18	0.36	0.54	0.16	0.31	0.47	0.11	0.22	0.33
3	0.31	0.61	0.92	0.28	0.54	0.82	0.23	0.44	0.67	0.18	0.35	0.52
4	0.38	0.75	1.13	0.35	0.68	1.03	0.27	0.53	0.80	0.22	0.44	0.66
5	0.43	0.84	1.27	0.41	0.80	1.21	0.32	0.62	0.94	0.26	0.51	0.77
6	0.44	0.86	1.30	0.41	0.79	1.19	0.29	0.57	0.86	0.26	0.51	0.77
7	0.43	0.83	1.25	0.38	0.73	1.11	0.27	0.53	0.80	0.27	0.54	0.81
8	0.37	0.73	1.10	0.36	0.69	1.05	0.26	0.50	0.76	0.26	0.51	0.78
9	0.31	0.61	0.92	0.30	0.58	0.88	0.22	0.43	0.65	0.18	0.35	0.52
10	0.26	0.51	0.77	0.23	0.44	0.67	0.18	0.35	0.53	0.14	0.27	0.40
11	0.17	0.34	0.52	0.15	0.28	0.43	0.12	0.24	0.37	0.11	0.21	0.31
12	0.15	0.29	0.44	0.12	0.23	0.36	0.11	0.21	0.32	0.09	0.18	0.27
年均	0.31	0.60	0.90	0.27	0.53	0.81	0.21	0.41	0.63	0.18	0.36	0.54

从月能源自洽率来看，在太阳能Ⅰ类地区，6 月分布式光伏发电量最大，能源自洽率在保守开发场景、基本开发场景、积极开发场景下最大分别为 0.44%、0.86%、1.30%；而 12 月分布式光伏发电量最小，能源自洽率在保守开发场景、基本开发场景、积极开发场景下最小分别为 0.15%、0.29%、0.44%；在太阳能Ⅱ类地区，5 月分布式光伏发电量最大，能源自洽率在保守开发场景、基本开发场景、积极开发场景下最大分别为 0.41%、0.80%、1.21%；而 12 月分布式光伏发电量最小，能源自洽率在保守开发场景、基本开发场景、积极开发场景下最小分别为 0.12%、0.23%、0.36%；在太阳能Ⅲ类地区，5 月分布式光伏发电量最大，能

源自洽率在保守开发场景、基本开发场景、积极开发场景下最大分别为 0.32%、0.62%、0.94%；而 12 月分布式光伏发电量最小，能源自洽率在保守开发场景、基本开发场景、积极开发场景下最小分别为 0.11%、0.21%、0.32%；在太阳能Ⅳ类地区，7 月分布式光伏发电量最大，能源自洽率在保守开发场景、基本开发场景、积极开发场景下最大分别为 0.27%、0.54%、0.81%；而 12 月分布式光伏发电量最小，能源自洽率在保守开发场景、基本开发场景、积极开发场景下最小分别为 0.09%、0.18%、0.27%。

可知，在太阳能Ⅰ类地区，公路交通能源系统在保守开发场景、基本开发场景、积极开发场景下年平均能源自洽率分别为 0.31%、0.60%、0.90%。在太阳能Ⅱ类地区，公路交通能源系统在保守开发场景、基本开发场景、积极开发场景下年平均能源自洽率分别为 0.27%、0.53%、0.81%。在太阳能Ⅲ类地区，公路交通能源系统在保守开发场景、基本开发场景、积极开发场景下年平均能源自洽率分别为 0.21%、0.41%、0.63%。在太阳能Ⅳ类地区，公路交通能源系统在保守开发场景、基本开发场景、积极开发场景下年平均能源自洽率分别为 0.18%、0.36%、0.54%。

4.3.5 中远期 2030 年公路交通用能展望

1. 用电自洽率

1）保守开发场景

根据上述分析，考虑高速公路交通基础设施、载运工具和服务设施用能情况后，2030 年百公里高速公路电力消耗为 33156MW·h，因此每月电力消耗为 2763MW·h。

高速公路分布式光伏发电总可用面积为 364.8 万 m^2，其中，较易开发面积为 93.4 万 m^2。2030 年高速公路在保守开发场景下，按百公里高速公路较易开发面积的 8%开发计算，则开发面积为 7.5 万 m^2，分布式光伏发电装机规模约为 1.2×10^4kW。则在太阳能Ⅰ类、Ⅱ类、Ⅲ类和Ⅳ类地区，年发电潜力分别约为 17909MW·h、16042MW·h、12478MW·h 和 10697MW·h。图 4-50 为 2030 年保守开发场景下百公里高速公路交通能源系统电力产用图。

从月用电自洽率来看，在太阳能Ⅰ类地区，6 月交通能源系统发电量最大，为 2155MW·h，用电自洽率最大为 78.0%，而 12 月交通能源系统发电量最小，仅为 722MW·h，用电自洽率最小为 26.1%；在太阳能Ⅱ类地区，5 月交通能源系统发电量最大，为 1997MW·h，用电自洽率最大为 72.3%，而 12 月交通能源系统发电量最小，仅为 588MW·h，用电自洽率最小为 21.3%；在太阳能Ⅲ类地区，5 月交通能源系统发电量最大，为 1559MW·h，用电自洽率最大为 56.4%，而 12

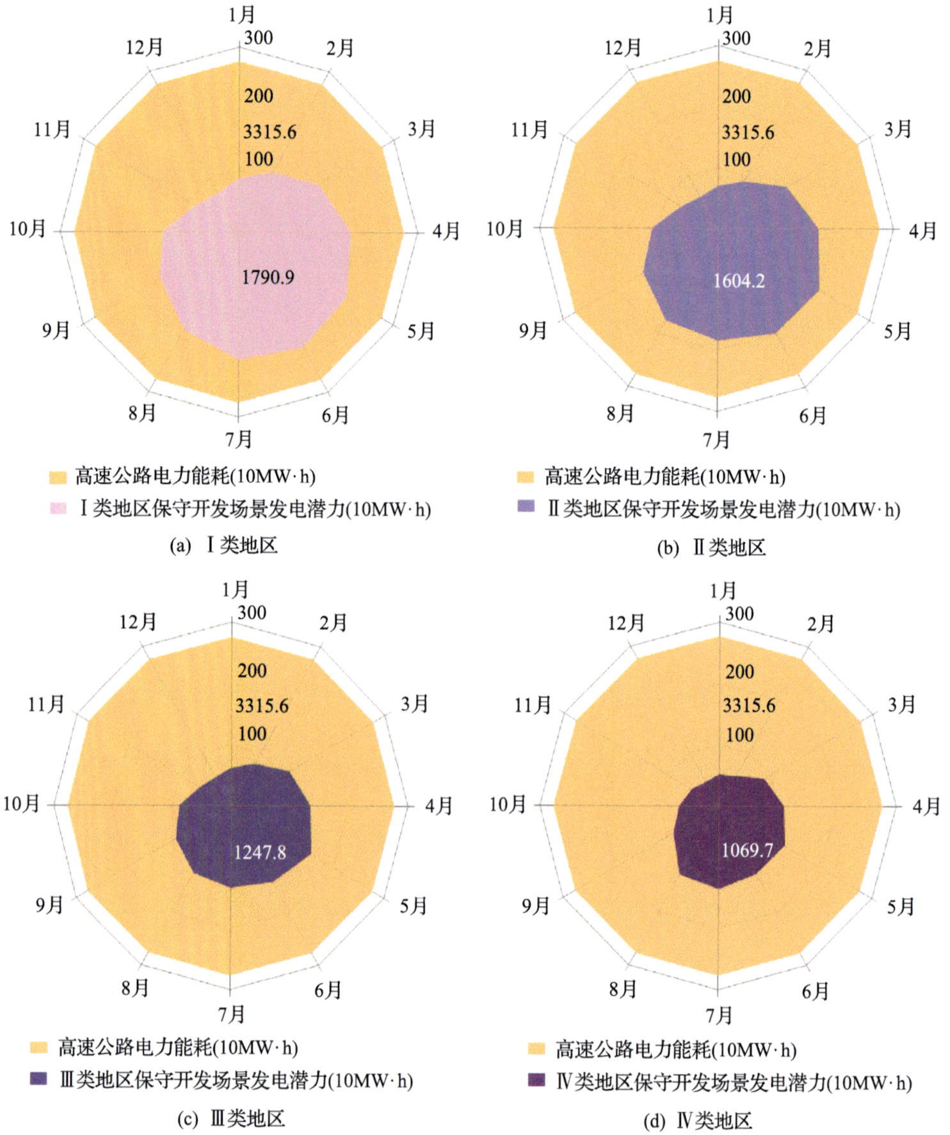

(a) Ⅰ类地区　(b) Ⅱ类地区　(c) Ⅲ类地区　(d) Ⅳ类地区

图 4-50　2030 年保守开发场景下百公里高速公路交通能源系统电力产用图

月交通能源系统发电量最小，仅为 525MW·h，用电自洽率最小为 19.0%；在太阳能Ⅳ类地区，7 月交通能源系统发电量最大，为 1342MW·h，用电自洽率最大为 48.6%，而 12 月交通能源系统发电量最小，仅为 446MW·h，用电自洽率最小为 16.1%。表 4-42 为 2030 年保守开发场景下百公里高速公路交通能源系统电力生产表。

表 4-42 2030 年保守开发场景下百公里高速公路交通能源系统电力生产表

月份	月用电量/(10MW·h)	保守开发场景(8%)							
		Ⅰ类地区		Ⅱ类地区		Ⅲ类地区		Ⅳ类地区	
		发电量/(10MW·h)	自洽率/%	发电量/(10MW·h)	自洽率/%	发电量/(10MW·h)	自洽率/%	发电量/(10MW·h)	自洽率/%
1	276.3	86.8	31.4	68.7	24.9	61.2	22.1	50.1	18.1
2	276.3	110.9	40.1	89.2	32.3	77.8	28.1	55.3	20.0
3	276.3	153.2	55.4	135.4	49.0	111.3	40.3	86.8	31.4
4	276.3	187.5	67.9	170.1	61.6	133.0	48.1	109.3	39.6
5	276.3	209.6	75.9	199.7	72.3	155.9	56.4	127.9	46.3
6	276.3	215.5	78.0	197.8	71.6	142.1	51.4	127.1	46.0
7	276.3	207.6	75.1	183.2	66.3	132.6	48.0	134.2	48.6
8	276.3	182.4	66.0	173.7	62.9	125.5	45.4	128.7	46.6
9	276.3	152.0	55.0	145.3	52.6	107.8	39.0	86.8	31.4
10	276.3	127.9	46.3	110.9	40.1	87.2	31.6	66.7	24.1
11	276.3	85.3	30.9	71.4	25.9	60.9	22.0	52.2	18.9
12	276.3	72.2	26.1	58.8	21.3	52.5	19.0	44.6	16.1
合计	3315.6	1790.9	54.0	1604.2	48.4	1247.8	37.6	1069.7	32.3

由图 4-51 可见，百公里高速公路交通能源系统自洽率盈缺情况随太阳辐射变化而变化，但可发现在太阳能辐射量较高的 3 月到 9 月间月用电自洽率高出年平均用电自洽率，在 10 月到次年 2 月间月用电自洽率低于年平均用电自洽率。在 8%的保守开发场景下，百公里高速公路交通能源系统在Ⅰ类、Ⅱ类、Ⅲ类和Ⅳ类地区的平均用电自洽率分别为 54.0%、48.4%、37.6%和 32.3%。

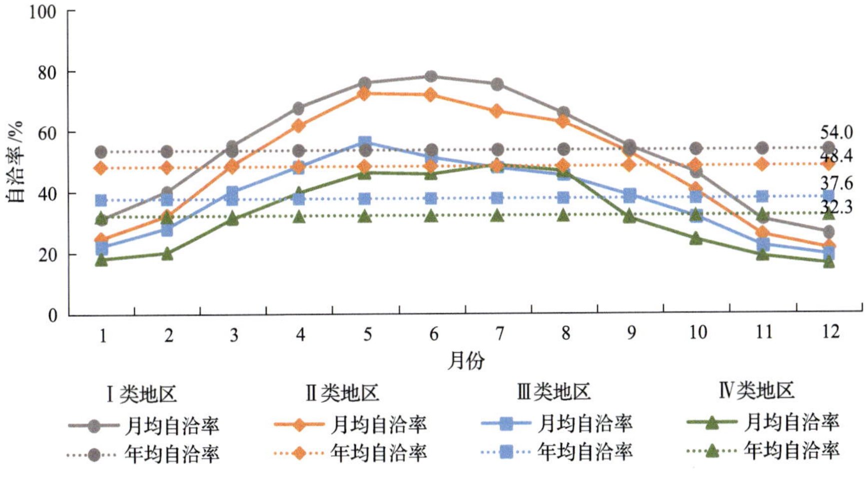

图 4-51 2030 年保守开发场景下百公里高速公路交通能源系统用电自洽率

2)基本开发场景

2030 年高速公路在基本开发场景下，按百公里高速公路较易开发面积的10%开发计算，则开发面积为 9.3 万 m^2，分布式光伏发电装机规模约为 15MW。则在太阳能Ⅰ类、Ⅱ类、Ⅲ类和Ⅳ类地区，年发电潜力分别约为 22207MW·h、19892MW·h、15472MW·h 和 13265MW·h。图 4-52 为 2030 年基本开发场景下百公里高速公路交通能源系统电力产用图。

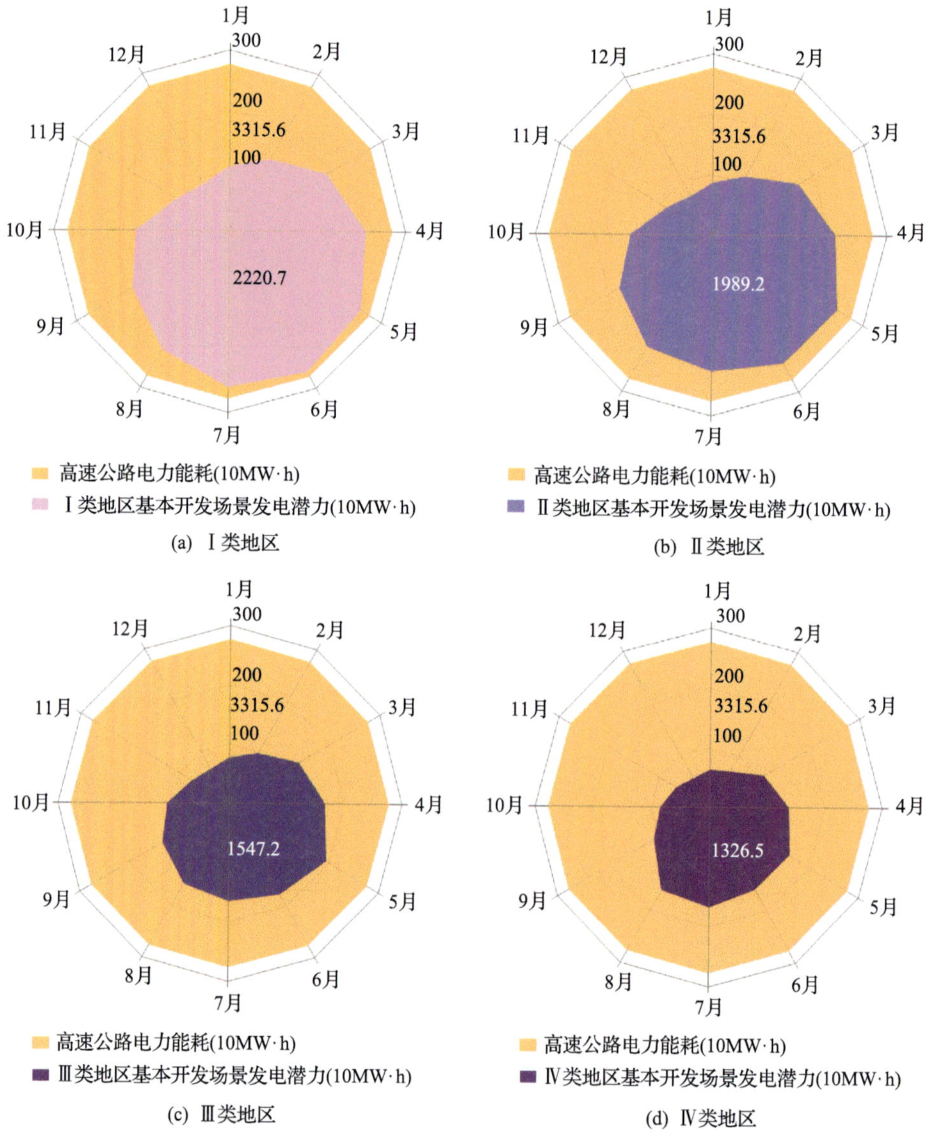

(a) Ⅰ类地区

(b) Ⅱ类地区

(c) Ⅲ类地区

(d) Ⅳ类地区

图 4-52 2030 年基本开发场景下百公里高速公路交通能源系统电力产用图

从月用电自洽率来看，在太阳能Ⅰ类地区，6 月交通能源系统发电量最大，为 2673MW·h，用电自洽率最大为 96.7%，而 12 月交通能源系统发电量最小，仅为 896MW·h，用电自洽率最小为 32.4%；在太阳能Ⅱ类地区，5 月交通能源系统发电量最大，为 2477MW·h，用电自洽率最大为 89.6%，而 12 月交通能源系统发电量最小，仅为 729MW·h，用电自洽率最小为 26.4%；在太阳能Ⅲ类地区，5 月交通能源系统发电量最大，为 1933MW·h，用电自洽率最大为 70.0%，而 12 月交通能源系统发电量最小，仅为 651MW·h，用电自洽率最小为 23.6%；在太阳能Ⅳ类地区，7 月交通能源系统发电量最大，为 1664MW·h，用电自洽率最大为 60.2%，而 12 月交通能源系统发电量最小，仅为 553MW·h，用电自洽率最小为 20.0%。表 4-43 为 2030 年基本开发场景下百公里高速公路交通能源系统电力生产表。

表 4-43 2030 年基本开发场景下百公里高速公路交通能源系统电力生产表

月份	月用电量/(10MW·h)	基本开发场景(10%)							
		Ⅰ类地区		Ⅱ类地区		Ⅲ类地区		Ⅳ类地区	
		发电量/(10MW·h)	自洽率/%	发电量/(10MW·h)	自洽率/%	发电量/(10MW·h)	自洽率/%	发电量/(10MW·h)	自洽率/%
1	276.3	107.7	39.0	85.2	30.8	75.9	27.5	62.2	22.5
2	276.3	137.5	49.8	110.6	40.0	96.3	34.9	68.5	24.8
3	276.3	189.9	68.7	167.9	60.8	138.0	50.0	107.7	39.0
4	276.3	232.5	84.1	211.0	76.4	165.0	59.7	135.6	49.1
5	276.3	259.9	94.1	247.7	89.6	193.3	70.0	158.6	57.4
6	276.3	267.3	96.7	245.2	88.8	176.2	63.8	157.6	57.0
7	276.3	257.5	93.2	227.1	82.2	164.5	59.5	166.4	60.2
8	276.3	226.1	81.8	215.4	77.9	155.7	56.3	159.6	57.8
9	276.3	188.4	68.2	180.1	65.2	133.6	48.4	107.7	39.0
10	276.3	158.6	57.4	137.5	49.8	108.2	39.2	82.7	29.9
11	276.3	105.7	38.3	88.6	32.1	75.4	27.3	64.6	23.4
12	276.3	89.6	32.4	72.9	26.4	65.1	23.6	55.3	20.0
合计	3315.6	2220.7	67.0	1989.2	60.0	1547.2	46.7	1326.5	40.0

由图 4-53 可见，百公里高速公路交通能源系统自洽率盈缺情况随太阳辐射变化而变化，但可发现在太阳能辐射量较高的 3 月到 9 月间月用电自洽率高出年平均用电自洽率，在 10 月到次年 2 月间月用电自洽率低于年平均用电自洽率。在 4%的基本开发场景下，百公里高速公路交通能源系统在Ⅰ类、Ⅱ类、Ⅲ类和Ⅳ类

地区的平均自洽率分别为 67.0%、60.0%、46.7%和 40.0%。

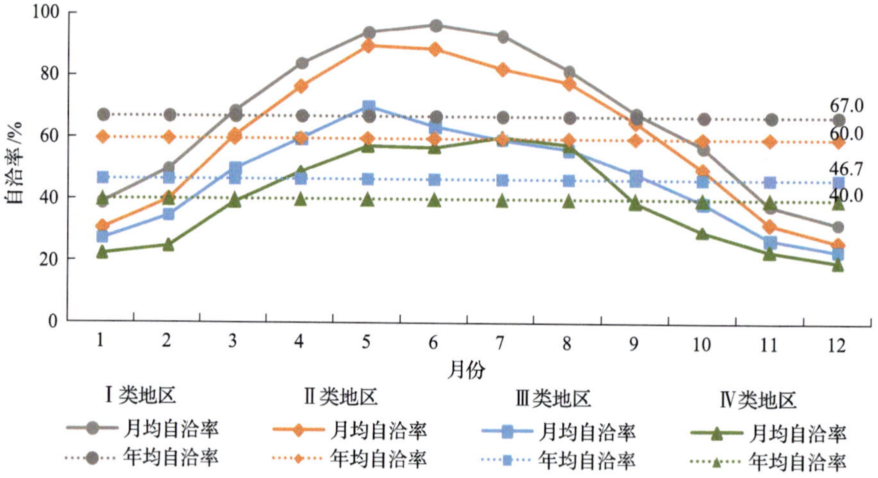

图 4-53　2030 年基本开发场景下百公里高速公路交通能源系统用电自洽率

3）积极开发场景

2030 年高速公路在积极开发场景下，按百公里高速公路较易开发面积的 12% 开发计算，则开发面积为 11.2 万 m^2，分布式光伏发电装机规模约为 18MW。则在太阳能Ⅰ类、Ⅱ类、Ⅲ类和Ⅳ类地区，年发电潜力分别约为 26744MW·h、23956MW·h、18633MW·h 和 15975MW·h。图 4-54 为 2030 年积极开发场景下百公里高速公路交通能源系统电力产用图。

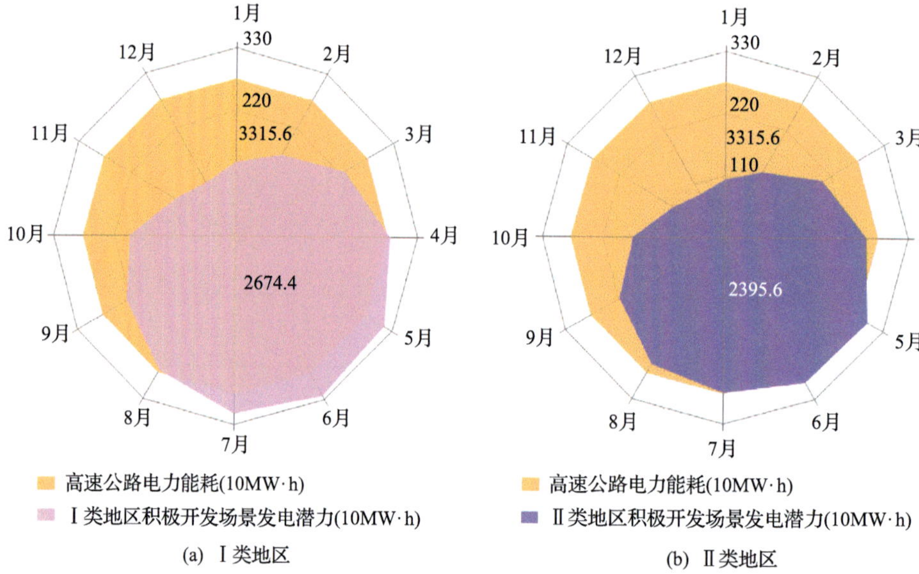

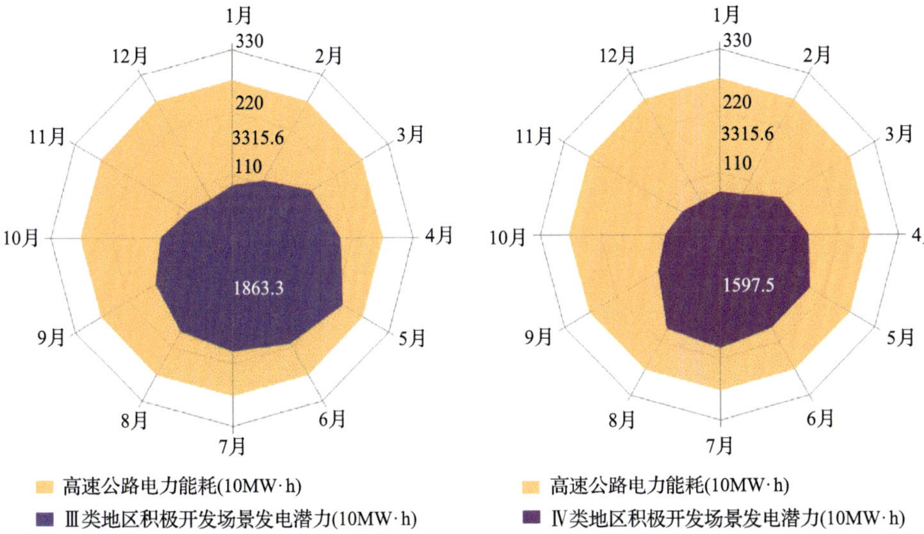

(c) Ⅲ类地区　　　　(d) Ⅳ类地区

图 4-54　2030 年积极开发场景下百公里高速公路交通能源系统电力产用图

从月用电自洽率来看，在太阳能Ⅰ类地区，6 月交通能源系统发电量最大，为 3219MW·h，用电自洽率最大为 116.5%，而 12 月交通能源系统发电量最小，仅为 1079MW·h，用电自洽率最小为 39.0%；在太阳能Ⅱ类地区，5 月交通能源系统发电量最大，为 2983MW·h，用电自洽率最大为 108.0%，而 12 月交通能源系统发电量最小，仅为 878MW·h，用电自洽率最小为 31.8%；在太阳能Ⅲ类地区，5 月交通能源系统发电量最大，为 2328MW·h，用电自洽率最大为 84.3%，而 12 月交通能源系统发电量最小，仅为 784MW·h，用电自洽率最小为 28.4%；在太阳能Ⅳ类地区，7 月交通能源系统发电量最大，为 2004MW·h，用电自洽率最大为 72.5%，而 12 月交通能源系统发电量最小，仅为 666MW·h，用电自洽率最小为 24.1%。表 4-44 为 2030 年积极开发场景下百公里高速公路交通能源系统电力生产表。

表 4-44　2030 年积极开发场景下百公里高速公路交通能源系统电力生产表

月份	月用电量 /(10MW·h)	积极开发场景(12%)							
		Ⅰ类地区		Ⅱ类地区		Ⅲ类地区		Ⅳ类地区	
		发电量 /(10MW·h)	自洽率/%	发电量 /(10MW·h)	自洽率/%	发电量 /(10MW·h)	自洽率/%	发电量 /(10MW·h)	自洽率/%
1	276.3	129.7	46.9	102.6	37.1	91.4	33.1	74.9	27.1
2	276.3	165.6	60.0	133.2	48.2	116.0	42.0	82.5	29.9

续表

月份	月用电量/(10MW·h)	积极开发场景(12%)							
		Ⅰ类地区		Ⅱ类地区		Ⅲ类地区		Ⅳ类地区	
		发电量/(10MW·h)	自洽率/%	发电量/(10MW·h)	自洽率/%	发电量/(10MW·h)	自洽率/%	发电量/(10MW·h)	自洽率/%
3	276.3	228.7	82.8	202.2	73.2	166.2	60.2	129.7	46.9
4	276.3	280.0	101.3	254.1	92.0	198.7	71.9	163.3	59.1
5	276.3	313.0	113.3	298.3	108.0	232.8	84.3	191.0	69.1
6	276.3	321.9	116.5	295.3	106.9	212.2	76.8	189.8	68.7
7	276.3	310.1	112.2	273.5	99.0	198.1	71.7	200.4	72.5
8	276.3	272.3	98.6	259.4	93.9	187.5	67.8	192.2	69.6
9	276.3	226.9	82.1	216.9	78.5	160.9	58.2	129.7	46.9
10	276.3	191.0	69.1	165.6	60.0	130.3	47.1	99.6	36.1
11	276.3	127.3	46.1	106.7	38.6	90.8	32.9	77.8	28.2
12	276.3	107.9	39.0	87.8	31.8	78.4	28.4	66.6	24.1
合计	3315.6	2674.4	80.7	2395.6	72.3	1863.3	56.2	1597.5	48.2

由图 4-55 可见，百公里高速公路交通能源系统自洽率盈缺情况随太阳辐射变化而变化，但可发现在太阳能辐射量较高的 3 月到 9 月间月用电自洽率高出年平均用电自洽率，在 10 月到次年 2 月间月用电自洽率低于年平均用电自洽率。在 12%的积极开发场景下，百公里高速公路交通能源系统在Ⅰ类、Ⅱ类、Ⅲ类和Ⅳ类地区的平均自洽率分别为 80.7%、72.3%、56.2%和 48.2%。

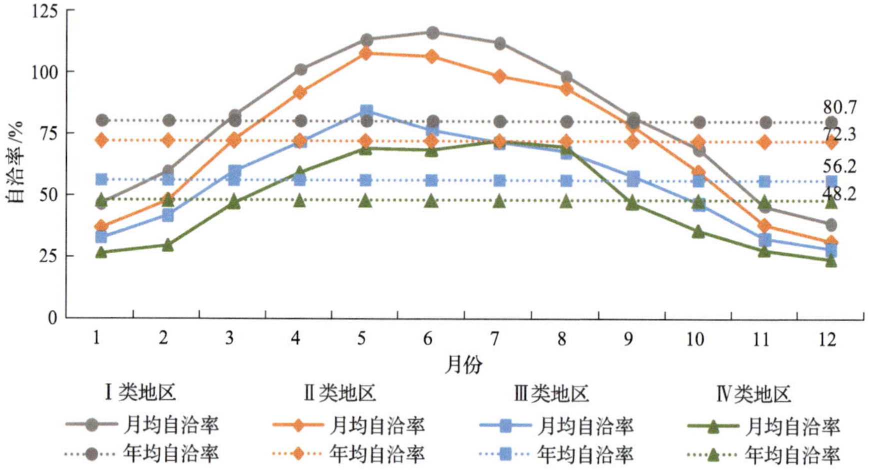

图 4-55　2030 年积极开发场景下百公里高速公路交通能源系统用电自洽率

2. 可再生能源电力渗透率

表 4-45 给出了 2030 年在保守开发场景、基本开发场景、积极开发场景下百公里高速公路交通能源系统的用电自洽率与渗透率统计表。可见，在太阳能Ⅰ类地区，保守开发场景、基本开发场景、积极开发场景下，百公里高速公路交通能源系统的用电自洽率分别为 54.0%、67.0%、80.7%，并且可再生能源电力渗透率分别为 65.0%、74.9%、85.3%；在太阳能Ⅱ类地区，保守开发场景、基本开发场景、积极开发场景下，百公里高速公路交通能源系统的用电自洽率分别为 48.4%、60.0%、72.3%，并且可再生能源电力渗透率分别为 60.8%、69.6%和 78.9%；在太阳能Ⅲ类地区，保守开发场景、基本开发场景、积极开发场景下，百公里高速公路交通能源系统的用电自洽率分别为 37.6%、46.7%、56.2%，并且可再生能源电力渗透率分别为 52.6%、59.5%和 66.7%；在太阳能Ⅳ类地区，保守开发场景、基本开发场景、积极开发场景下，百公里高速公路交通能源系统的用电自洽率分别为 32.3%、40.0%、48.2%，并且可再生能源电力渗透率分别为 48.5%、54.4%和 60.6%。图 4-56 为 2030 年百公里高速公路交通能源系统的用电自洽率与可再生能源电力渗透率。

表 4-45　2030 年百公里高速公路交通能源系统的用电自洽率与可再生能源电力渗透率

地区	保守开发场景		基本开发场景		积极开发场景	
	自洽率/%	渗透率/%	自洽率/%	渗透率/%	自洽率/%	渗透率/%
Ⅰ类地区	54.0	65.0	67.0	74.9	80.7	85.3
Ⅱ类地区	48.4	60.8	60.0	69.6	72.3	78.9
Ⅲ类地区	37.6	52.6	46.7	59.5	56.2	66.7
Ⅳ类地区	32.3	48.5	40.0	54.4	48.2	60.6

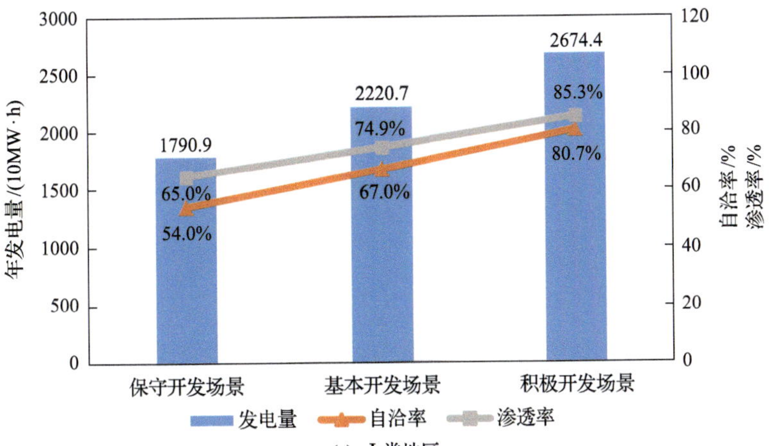

(a) Ⅰ类地区

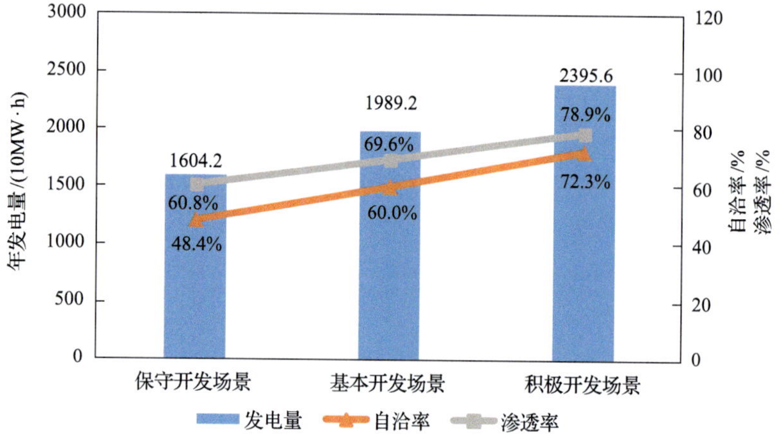

(b) Ⅱ类地区

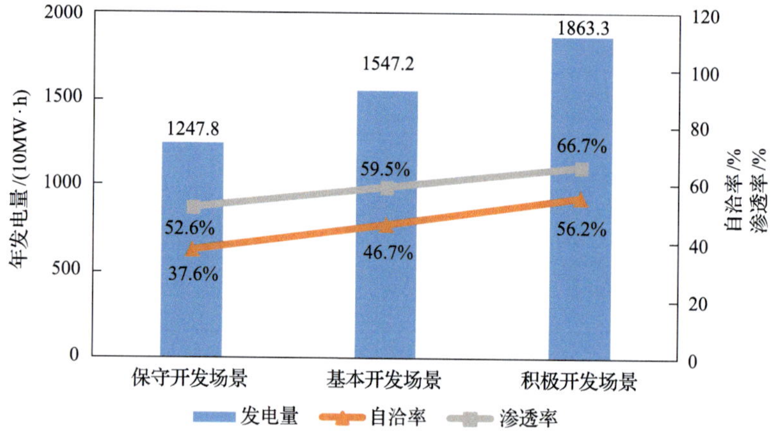

(c) Ⅲ类地区

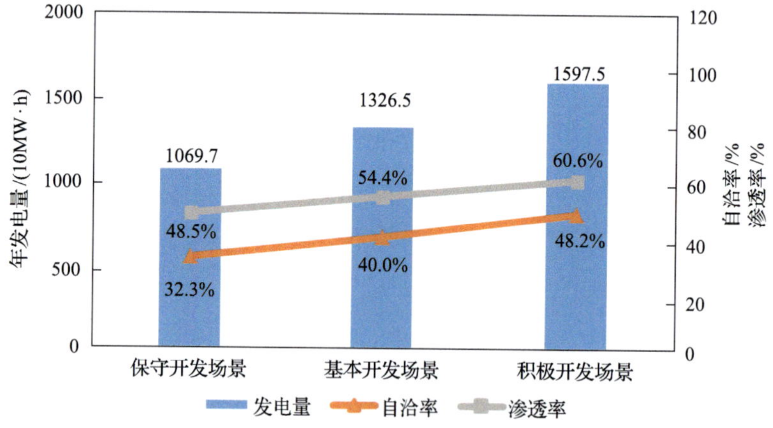

(d) Ⅳ类地区

图 4-56　2030 年百公里高速公路交通能源系统的用电自洽率与可再生能源电力渗透率

3. 用能自洽率

根据上述分析，在考虑公路交通基础设施、载运工具和服务设施电力用能情况后，2025 年百公里高速公路能源消耗预计为 2241338MW·h，其中，较易开发总面积约为 93.4 万 m^2，分布式光伏发电量分别在保守开发场景、基本开发场景、积极开发场景下，开发强度分别为较易开发面积的 8%、10%、12%时，开发面积分别为 7.5 万 m^2、9.3 万 m^2、11.2 万 m^2。此时，高速公路分布式光伏发电产能潜力在太阳能Ⅰ类、Ⅱ类、Ⅲ类和Ⅳ类地区保守开发场景、基本开发场景、积极开发场景下的能源自洽率如表 4-46 所示。

表 4-46　2030 年百公里高速公路交通能源系统用能自洽率

月份	Ⅰ类地区			Ⅱ类地区			Ⅲ类地区			Ⅳ类地区		
	保守开发场景/%	基本开发场景/%	积极开发场景/%	保守开发场景/%	基本开发场景/%	积极开发场景/%	保守开发场景/%	基本开发场景/%	积极开发场景/%	保守开发场景/%	基本开发场景/%	积极开发场景/%
1	0.47	0.58	0.70	0.37	0.46	0.55	0.33	0.41	0.49	0.27	0.33	0.40
2	0.59	0.74	0.89	0.48	0.59	0.71	0.42	0.52	0.62	0.30	0.37	0.44
3	0.82	1.02	1.23	0.72	0.90	1.08	0.60	0.74	0.89	0.46	0.58	0.69
4	1.01	1.25	1.50	0.91	1.13	1.36	0.71	0.88	1.06	0.59	0.73	0.88
5	1.12	1.39	1.68	1.07	1.33	1.60	0.83	1.03	1.25	0.69	0.85	1.02
6	1.15	1.43	1.72	1.06	1.31	1.58	0.76	0.94	1.14	0.68	0.84	1.02
7	1.11	1.38	1.66	0.98	1.22	1.47	0.71	0.88	1.06	0.72	0.89	1.07
8	0.98	1.21	1.46	0.93	1.15	1.39	0.67	0.83	1.00	0.69	0.86	1.03
9	0.81	1.01	1.21	0.78	0.96	1.16	0.58	0.72	0.86	0.46	0.58	0.69
10	0.69	0.85	1.02	0.59	0.74	0.89	0.47	0.58	0.70	0.36	0.44	0.53
11	0.46	0.57	0.68	0.38	0.47	0.57	0.33	0.40	0.49	0.28	0.35	0.42
12	0.39	0.48	0.58	0.32	0.39	0.47	0.28	0.35	0.42	0.24	0.30	0.36
年均	0.80	0.99	1.19	0.72	0.89	1.07	0.56	0.69	0.83	0.48	0.59	0.71

从月能源自洽率来看，在太阳能Ⅰ类地区，6 月分布式光伏发电量最大，能源自洽率在保守开发场景、基本开发场景、积极开发场景下最大分别为 1.15%、1.43%、1.72%；而 12 月分布式光伏发电量最小，能源自洽率在保守开发场景、基本开发场景、积极开发场景下最小分别为 0.39%、0.48%、0.58%；在太阳能Ⅱ类地区，5 月分布式光伏发电量最大，能源自洽率在保守开发场景、基本开发场景、积极开发场景下最大分别为 1.07%、1.33%、1.60%；而 12 月分布式光伏发电量最小，能源自洽率在保守开发场景、基本开发场景、积极开发场景下最小分别为 0.32%、0.39%、0.47%；在太阳能Ⅲ类地区，5 月分布式光伏发电量最大，能

源自洽率在保守开发场景、基本开发场景、积极开发场景下最大分别为 0.83%、1.03%、1.25%；而 12 月分布式光伏发电量最小，能源自洽率在保守开发场景、基本开发场景、积极开发场景下最小分别为 0.28%、0.35%、0.42%；在太阳能Ⅳ类地区，7 月分布式光伏发电量最大，能源自洽率在保守开发场景、基本开发场景、积极开发场景下最大分别为 0.72%、0.89%、1.07%；而 12 月分布式光伏发电量最小，能源自洽率在保守开发场景、基本开发场景、积极开发场景下最小分别为 0.24%、0.30%、0.36%。

可知，在太阳能Ⅰ类地区，公路交通能源系统在保守开发场景、基本开发场景、积极开发场景下年平均能源自洽率分别为 0.8%、0.99%、1.19%。在太阳能Ⅱ类地区，公路交通能源系统在保守开发场景、基本开发场景、积极开发场景下年平均能源自洽率分别为 0.72%、0.89%、1.07%。在太阳能Ⅲ类地区，公路交通能源系统在保守开发场景、基本开发场景、积极开发场景下年平均能源自洽率分别为 0.56%、0.69%、0.83%。在太阳能Ⅳ类地区，公路交通能源系统在保守开发场景、基本开发场景、积极开发场景下年平均能源自洽率分别为 0.48%、0.59%、0.71%。

4.3.6 远期 2035 年公路交通用能展望

1. 用电自洽率

1)保守开发场景

2035 年高速公路在保守开发场景下，按百公里高速公路较易开发面积的 15% 开发计算，则开发面积为 14 万 m^2，分布式光伏发电装机规模约为 22MW。则在太阳能Ⅰ类、Ⅱ类、Ⅲ类和Ⅳ类地区，年发电潜力分别约为 33433MW·h、29950MW·h、23295MW·h 和 19967MW·h。图 4-57 为 2035 年保守开发场景下百公里高速公路交通能源系统电力产用图。

从月用电自洽率来看，在太阳能Ⅰ类地区，6 月交通能源系统发电量最大，为 4023MW·h，用电自洽率最大为 56.1%，而 12 月交通能源系统发电量最小，仅为 1347MW·h，用电自洽率最小为 18.8%；在太阳能Ⅱ类地区，5 月交通能源系统发电量最大，为 3732MW·h，用电自洽率最大为 52.0%，而 12 月交通能源系统发电量最小，仅为 1099MW·h，用电自洽率最小为 15.3%；在太阳能Ⅲ类地区，5 月交通能源系统发电量最大，为 2908MW·h，用电自洽率最大为 40.5%，而 12 月交通能源系统发电量最小，仅为 977MW·h，用电自洽率最小为 13.6%；在太阳能Ⅳ类地区，7 月交通能源系统发电量最大，为 2506MW·h，用电自洽率最大为 34.9%，而 12 月交通能源系统发电量最小，仅为 830MW·h，用电自洽率最小为 11.6%。

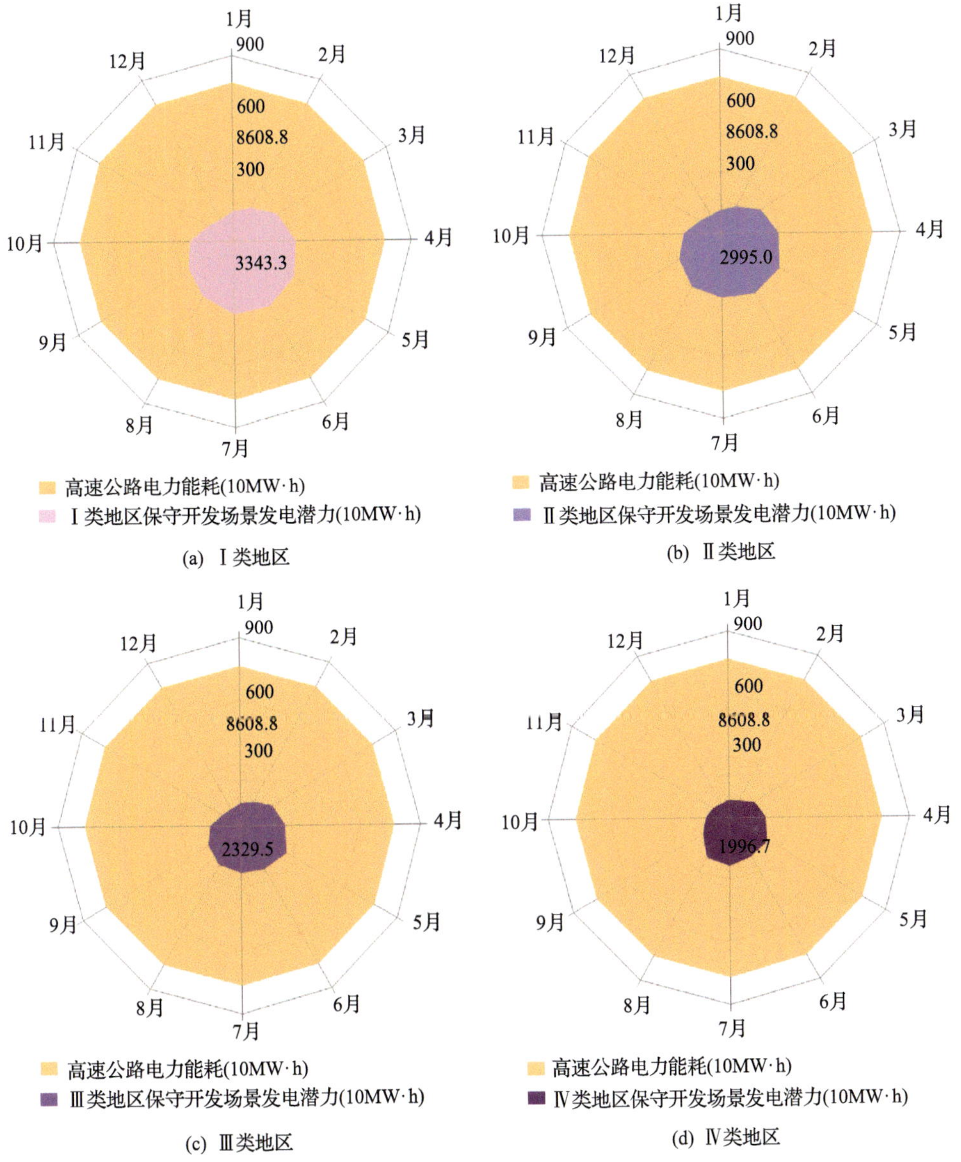

图 4-57　2035 年保守开发场景下百公里高速公路交通能源系统电力产用图

由表 4-47 可见，百公里高速公路交通能源系统自洽率盈缺情况随太阳辐射变化而变化，但可发现在太阳能辐射量较高的 3 月到 9 月间月用电自洽率高出年平均用电自洽率，在 10 月到次年 2 月间月用电自洽率低于年平均用电自洽率。在 15%的保守开发场景下，百公里高速公路交通能源系统在Ⅰ类、Ⅱ类、Ⅲ类和Ⅳ类地区的平均自洽率分别为 38.8%、34.8%、27.1%和 23.2%。图 4-58 为 2035 年保守开发场景下百公里高速公路交通能源系统用电自洽率。

表 4-47　2035 年保守开发场景下百公里高速公路交通能源系统电力生产表

月份	月用电量/(10MW·h)	保守开发场景(15%)							
		Ⅰ类地区		Ⅱ类地区		Ⅲ类地区		Ⅳ类地区	
		发电量/(10MW·h)	自洽率/%	发电量/(10MW·h)	自洽率/%	发电量/(10MW·h)	自洽率/%	发电量/(10MW·h)	自洽率/%
1	717.4	162.2	22.6	128.3	17.9	114.2	15.9	93.2	13.0
2	717.4	206.9	28.8	166.3	23.2	145.4	20.3	103.4	14.4
3	717.4	286.1	39.9	252.6	35.2	207.9	29.0	161.8	22.6
4	717.4	350.2	48.8	317.9	44.3	248.4	34.6	204.4	28.5
5	717.4	391.4	54.6	373.2	52.0	290.8	40.5	239	33.3
6	717.4	402.3	56.1	369.2	51.5	265.4	37.0	237.2	33.1
7	717.4	387.5	54.0	341.9	47.7	247.6	34.5	250.6	34.9
8	717.4	340.3	47.4	324.3	45.2	234	32.6	240.4	33.5
9	717.4	283.5	39.5	270.9	37.8	201.3	28.1	162	22.6
10	717.4	238.8	33.3	207.2	28.9	163.2	22.7	124.5	17.4
11	717.4	159.4	22.2	133.3	18.6	113.6	15.8	97.2	13.5
12	717.4	134.7	18.8	109.9	15.3	97.7	13.6	83	11.6
合计	8608.8	3343.3	38.8	2995	34.8	2329.5	27.1	1996.7	23.2

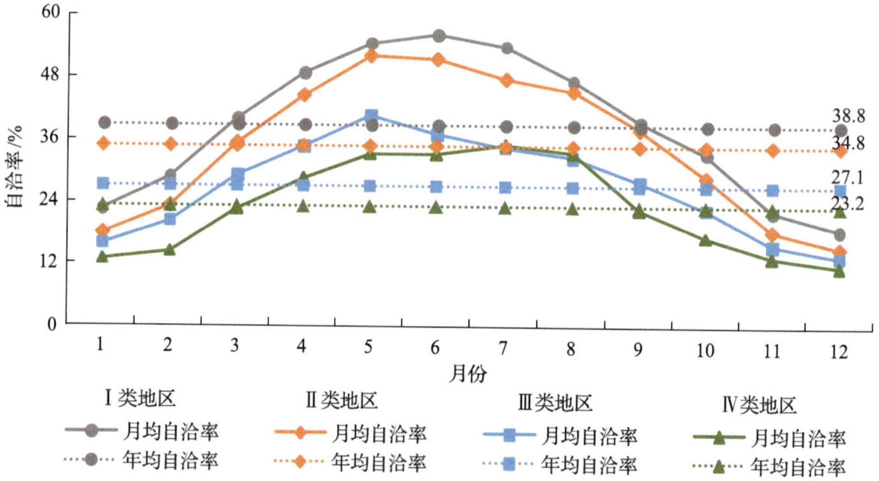

图 4-58　2035 年保守开发场景下百公里高速公路交通能源系统用电自洽率

2）基本开发场景

2035 年高速公路在基本开发场景下，按百公里高速公路较易开发面积的 25%

开发计算，则开发面积为 23.4 万 m^2，分布式光伏发电装机规模约为 37MW。则在太阳能Ⅰ类、Ⅱ类、Ⅲ类和Ⅳ类地区，年发电潜力分别约为 55881MW·h、50059MW·h、38935MW·h 和 33373MW·h。图 4-59 为 2035 年基本开发场景下百公里高速公路交通能源系统电力产用图。

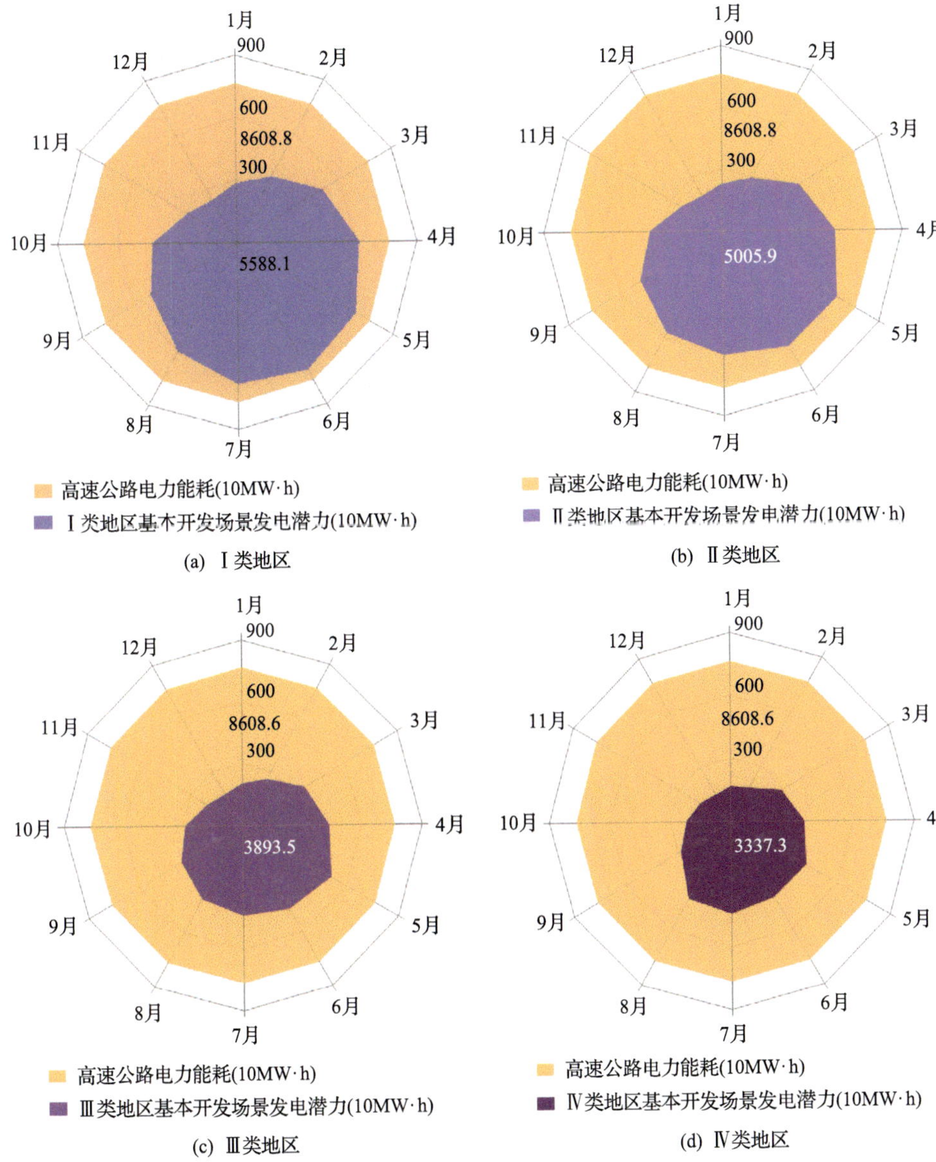

图 4-59　2035 年基本开发场景下百公里高速公路交通能源系统电力产用图

从月用电自洽率来看，在太阳能Ⅰ类地区，6 月交通能源系统发电量最大，为 6725MW·h，用电自洽率最大为 93.7%，而 12 月交通能源系统发电量最小，仅为 2251MW·h，用电自洽率最小为 31.4%；在太阳能Ⅱ类地区，5 月交通能源系统发电量最大，为 6237MW·h，用电自洽率最大为 86.9%，而 12 月交通能源系统发电量最小，仅为 1838MW·h，用电自洽率最小为 25.6%；在太阳能Ⅲ类地区，5 月交通能源系统发电量最大，为 4861MW·h，用电自洽率最大为 67.8%，而 12 月交通能源系统发电量最小，仅为 1634MW·h，用电自洽率最小为 22.8%；在太阳能Ⅳ类地区，7 月交通能源系统发电量最大，为 4189MW·h，用电自洽率最大为 58.4%，而 12 月交通能源系统发电量最小，仅为 1387MW·h，用电自洽率最小为 19.3%。表 4-48 为 2035 年基本开发场景下百公里高速公路交通能源系统电力生产表。

表 4-48　2035 年基本开发场景下百公里高速公路交通能源系统电力生产表

月份	月用电量/(10MW·h)	基本开发场景(25%)							
		Ⅰ类地区		Ⅱ类地区		Ⅲ类地区		Ⅳ类地区	
		发电量/(10MW·h)	自洽率/%	发电量/(10MW·h)	自洽率/%	发电量/(10MW·h)	自洽率/%	发电量/(10MW·h)	自洽率/%
1	717.4	271.1	37.8	214.4	29.9	190.8	26.6	155.9	21.7
2	717.4	345.8	48.2	278.0	38.8	243.0	33.9	172.7	24.1
3	717.4	478.2	66.7	422.2	58.9	347.5	48.4	270.4	37.7
4	717.4	585.4	81.6	531.4	74.1	415.2	57.9	341.7	47.6
5	717.4	654.2	91.2	623.7	86.9	486.1	67.8	399.4	55.7
6	717.4	672.5	93.7	617.2	86.0	443.7	61.8	396.4	55.3
7	717.4	647.7	90.3	571.4	79.6	413.9	57.7	418.9	58.4
8	717.4	568.7	79.3	542.0	75.6	391.2	54.5	401.9	56.0
9	717.4	473.8	66.0	452.7	63.1	336.1	46.8	270.7	37.7
10	717.4	399.2	55.6	346.3	48.3	272.7	38.0	208.1	29.0
11	717.4	266.4	37.1	222.8	31.1	189.9	26.5	162.5	22.7
12	717.4	225.1	31.4	183.8	25.6	163.4	22.8	138.7	19.3
合计	8608.8	5588.1	64.9	5005.9	58.1	3893.5	45.2	3337.3	38.8

由图 4-60 可见，百公里高速公路交通能源系统自洽率盈缺情况随太阳辐射变化而变化，但可发现在太阳能辐射量较高的 3 月到 9 月间月用电自洽率高出年平均用电自洽率，在 10 月到次年 2 月间月用电自洽率低于年平均用电自洽率。在 25%的保守开发场景下，百公里高速公路交通能源系统在Ⅰ类、Ⅱ类、Ⅲ类和Ⅳ

类地区的平均自洽率分别为 64.9%、58.1%、45.2%和 38.8%。

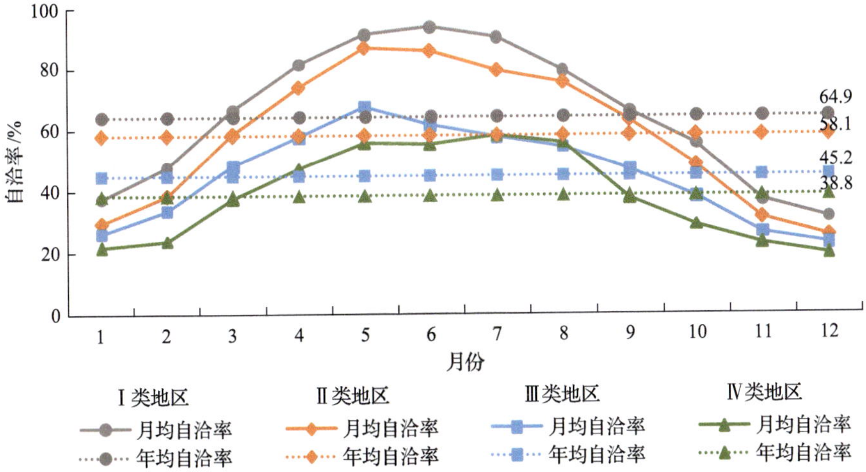

图 4-60 2035 年基本开发场景下百公里高速公路交通能源系统用电自洽率

3) 积极开发场景

2035 年高速公路在积极开发场景下，按百公里高速公路较易开发面积的 35% 开发计算，则开发面积为 32.7 万 m^2，分布式光伏发电装机规模约为 52MW。则在太阳能Ⅰ类、Ⅱ类、Ⅲ类和Ⅳ类地区，年发电潜力分别约为 78089MW·h、69955MW·h、54409MW·h 和 46637MW·h。图 4-61 为 2035 年积极开发场景下百公里高速公路交通能源系统电力产用图。

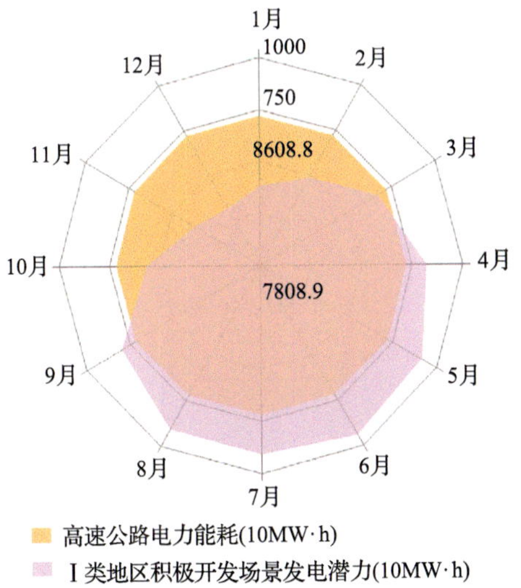

(a) Ⅰ类地区

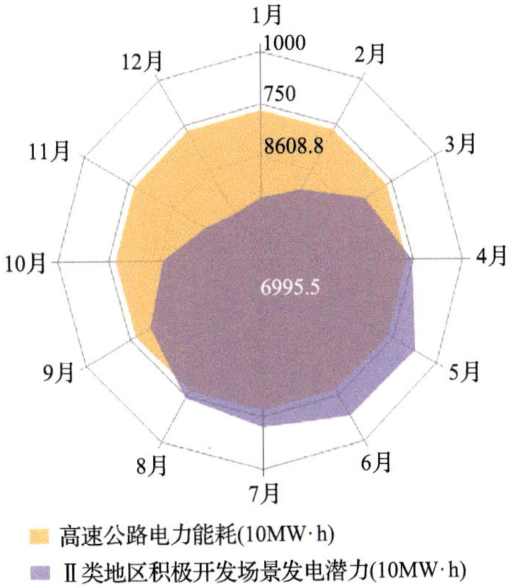

(b) Ⅱ类地区

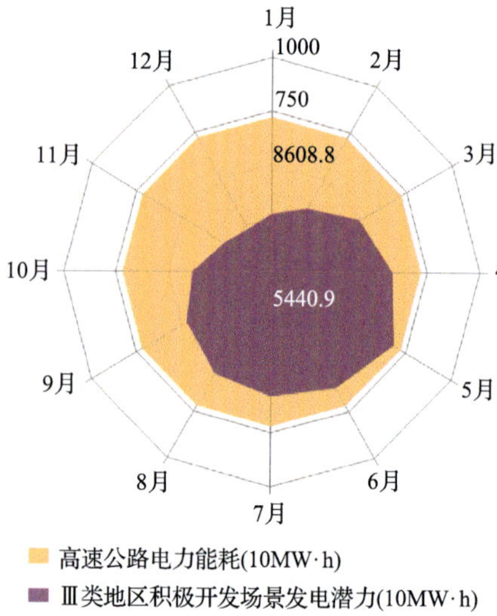

(c) Ⅲ类地区

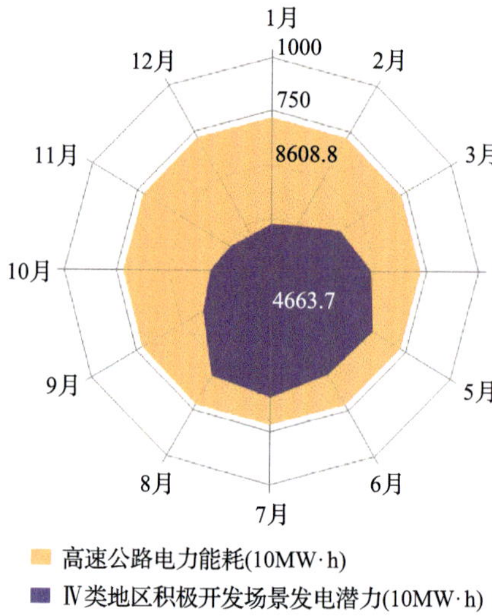

(d) Ⅳ类地区

图 4-61　2035 年积极开发场景下百公里高速公路交通能源系统电力产用图

从月用电自洽率来看，在太阳能Ⅰ类地区，6 月交通能源系统发电量最大，为 9397MW·h，用电自洽率最大为 131.0%，而 12 月交通能源系统发电量最小，仅为 3146MW·h，用电自洽率最小为 43.9%；在太阳能Ⅱ类地区，5 月交通能源系统发电量最大，为 8716MW·h，用电自洽率最大为 121.5%，而 12 月交通能源系统发电量最小，仅为 2568MW·h，用电自洽率最小为 35.8%；在太阳能Ⅲ类地区，5 月交通能源系统发电量最大，为 6793MW·h，用电自洽率最大为 94.7%，而 12 月交通能源系统发电量最小，仅为 2283MW·h，用电自洽率最小为 31.8%；在太阳能Ⅳ类地区，7 月交通能源系统发电量最大，为 5853MW·h，用电自洽率最大为 81.6%，而 12 月交通能源系统发电量最小，仅为 1938MW·h，用电自洽率最小为 27.0%。表 4-49 为 2035 年积极开发场景下百公里高速公路交通能源系统电力生产表。

表 4-49　2035 年积极开发场景下百公里高速公路交通能源系统电力生产表

月份	月用电量/(10MW·h)	积极开发场景(35%)							
		Ⅰ类地区		Ⅱ类地区		Ⅲ类地区		Ⅳ类地区	
		发电量/(10MW·h)	自洽率/%	发电量/(10MW·h)	自洽率/%	发电量/(10MW·h)	自洽率/%	发电量/(10MW·h)	自洽率/%
1	717.4	378.8	52.8	299.6	41.8	266.7	37.2	217.8	30.4
2	717.4	483.3	67.4	388.4	54.1	339.7	47.4	241.4	33.6
3	717.4	668.2	93.1	590	82.2	485.6	67.7	377.9	52.7
4	717.4	818.1	114.0	742.6	103.5	580.2	80.9	477.5	66.6

续表

月份	月用电量/(10MW·h)	积极开发场景(35%)							
		Ⅰ类地区		Ⅱ类地区		Ⅲ类地区		Ⅳ类地区	
		发电量/(10MW·h)	自洽率/%	发电量/(10MW·h)	自洽率/%	发电量/(10MW·h)	自洽率/%	发电量/(10MW·h)	自洽率/%
5	717.4	914.2	127.4	871.6	121.5	679.3	94.7	558.1	77.8
6	717.4	939.7	131.0	862.5	120.2	620	86.4	553.9	77.2
7	717.4	905.1	126.2	798.5	111.3	578.4	80.6	585.3	81.6
8	717.4	794.8	110.8	757.5	105.6	546.6	76.2	561.6	78.3
9	717.4	662.1	92.3	632.7	88.2	469.7	65.5	378.3	52.7
10	717.4	557.8	77.8	483.9	67.5	381.1	53.1	290.8	40.5
11	717.4	372.2	51.9	311.4	43.4	265.3	37.0	227.3	31.7
12	717.4	314.6	43.9	256.8	35.8	228.3	31.8	193.8	27.0
合计	8608.8	7808.9	90.7	6995.5	81.3	5440.9	63.2	4663.7	54.2

由图 4-62 可见，百公里高速公路交通能源系统自洽率盈缺情况随太阳辐射变化而变化，但可发现在太阳能辐射量较高的 3 月到 9 月间月用电自洽率高出年平均用电自洽率，在 10 月到次年 2 月间月用电自洽率低于年平均用电自洽率。在 25%的保守开发场景下，百公里高速公路交通能源系统在Ⅰ类、Ⅱ类、Ⅲ类和Ⅳ类地区的平均自洽率分别为 90.7%、81.3%、63.2%和 54.2%。

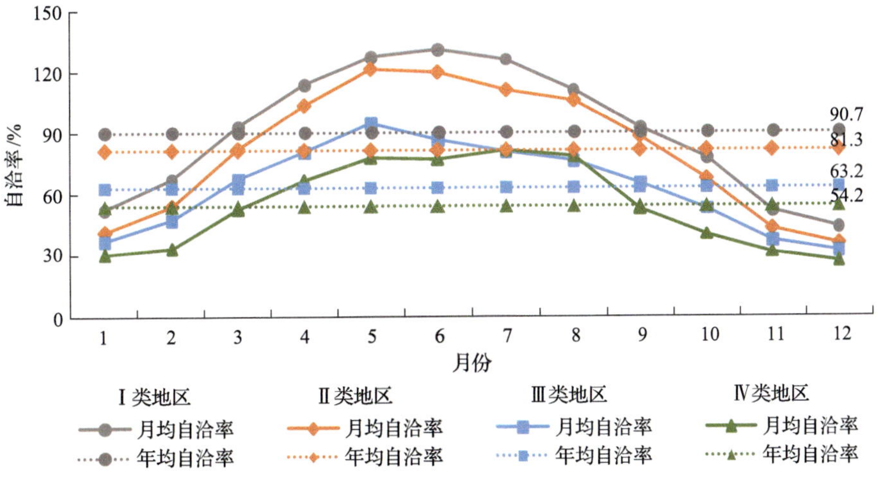

图 4-62　2035 年积极开发场景下百公里高速公路交通能源系统用电自洽率

2. 可再生能源电力渗透率

表 4-50 给出了 2035 年在保守开发场景、基本开发场景、积极开发场景下百

公里高速公路交通能源系统的用电自洽率与渗透率统计表。可见，在太阳能Ⅰ类地区，保守开发场景、基本开发场景、积极开发场景下，百公里高速公路交通能源系统的用电自洽率分别为38.8%、64.9%和90.7%，并且可再生能源电力渗透率分别为54.1%、73.7%和93.0%；在太阳能Ⅱ类地区，保守开发场景、基本开发场景、积极开发场景下，百公里高速公路交通能源系统的用电自洽率分别为34.8%、58.1%和81.3%，并且可再生能源电力渗透率分别为51.1%、68.6%和85.9%；在太阳能Ⅲ类地区，保守开发场景、基本开发场景、积极开发场景下，百公里高速公路交通能源系统的用电自洽率分别为27.1%、45.2%和63.2%，并且可再生能源电力渗透率分别为45.3%、58.9%和72.4%；在太阳能Ⅳ类地区，保守开发场景、基本开发场景、积极开发场景下，百公里高速公路交通能源系统的用电自洽率分别为23.2%、38.8%和54.2%，并且可再生能源电力渗透率分别为42.4%、54.1%和65.6%。图4-63为2035年百公里高速公路交通能源系统的用电自洽率与可再生能源电力渗透率。

表4-50 2035年百公里高速公路用电自洽率与渗透率统计表

地区	保守开发场景		基本开发场景		积极开发场景	
	自洽率/%	渗透率/%	自洽率/%	渗透率/%	自洽率/%	渗透率/%
Ⅰ类地区	38.8	54.1	64.9	73.7	90.7	93.0
Ⅱ类地区	34.8	51.1	58.1	68.6	81.3	85.9
Ⅲ类地区	27.1	45.3	45.2	58.9	63.2	72.4
Ⅳ类地区	23.2	42.4	38.8	54.1	54.2	65.6

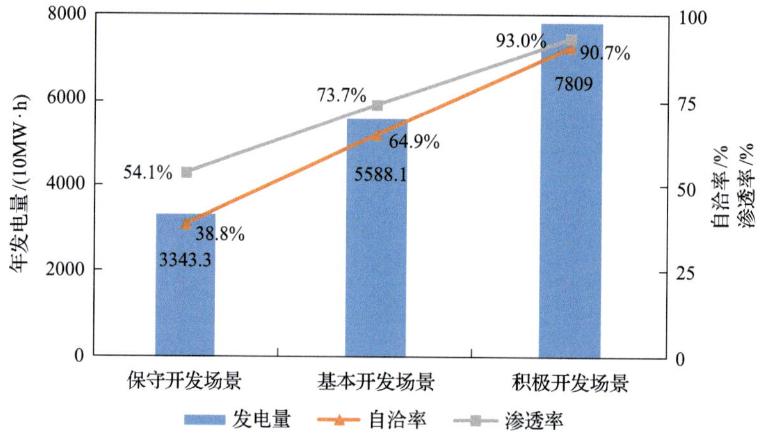

(a) Ⅰ类地区

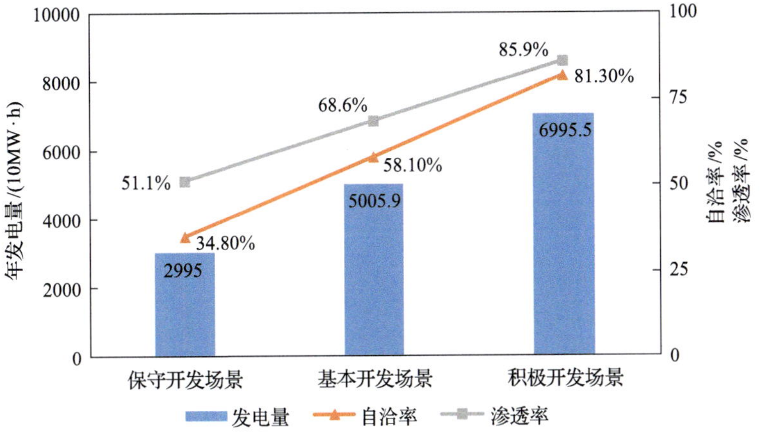

(b) Ⅱ类地区

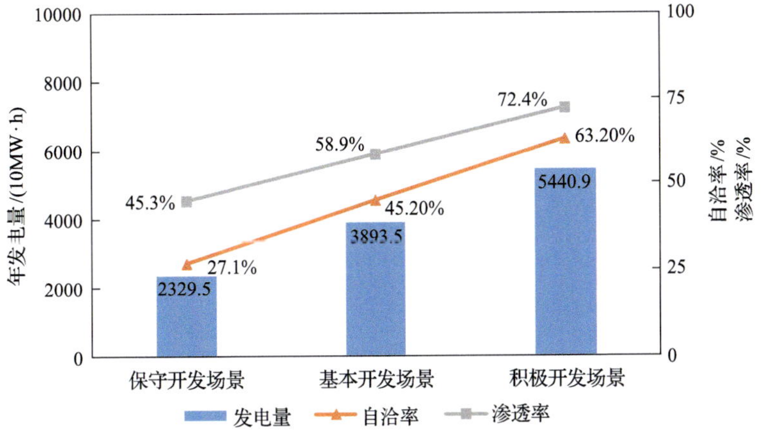

(c) Ⅲ类地区

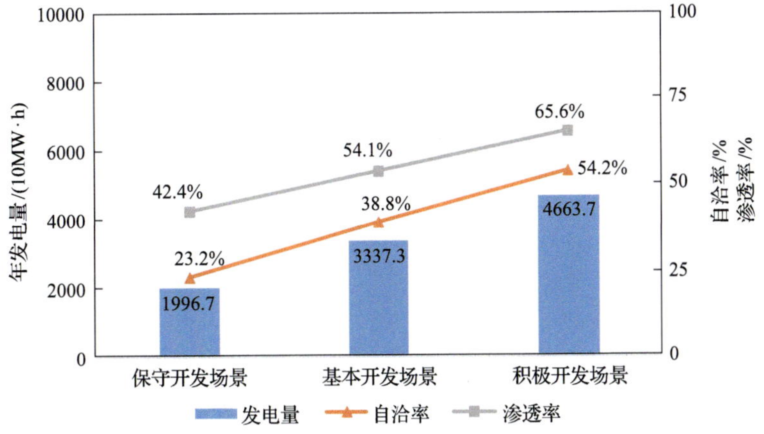

(d) Ⅳ类地区

图 4-63　2035 年百公里高速公路交通能源系统的用电自洽率与可再生能源电力渗透率

3. 用能自洽率

根据上述分析，在考虑公路交通基础设施、载运工具和服务设施电力用能情况后，2035 年百公里高速公路能源消耗预计为 2359781MW·h，

其中，较易开发总面积约为 93.4 万 m^2，在保守开发场景、基本开发场景、积极开发场景下，分布式光伏开发面积分别为 14 万 m^2(15%)、23.4 万 m^2(25%)、32.7 万 m^2(35%)。高速公路分布式光伏发电产能潜力在太阳能Ⅰ类、Ⅱ类、Ⅲ类和Ⅳ类地区保守开发场景、基本开发场景、积极开发场景下的能源自洽率如表 4-51 所示。

表 4-51　2035 年百公里高速公路交通能源系统用能自洽率

月份	Ⅰ类地区			Ⅱ类地区			Ⅲ类地区			Ⅳ类地区		
	保守开发场景/%	基本开发场景/%	积极开发场景/%	保守开发场景/%	基本开发场景/%	积极开发场景/%	保守开发场景/%	基本开发场景/%	积极开发场景/%	保守开发场景/%	基本开发场景/%	积极开发场景/%
1	0.82	1.38	1.93	0.65	1.09	1.52	0.58	0.97	1.36	0.47	0.79	1.11
2	1.05	1.76	2.46	0.85	1.41	1.98	0.74	1.24	1.73	0.53	0.88	1.23
3	1.45	2.43	3.40	1.28	2.15	3.00	1.06	1.77	2.47	0.82	1.38	1.92
4	1.78	2.98	4.16	1.62	2.70	3.78	1.26	2.11	2.95	1.04	1.74	2.43
5	1.99	3.33	4.65	1.90	3.17	4.43	1.48	2.47	3.45	1.22	2.03	2.84
6	2.05	3.42	4.78	1.88	3.14	4.39	1.35	2.26	3.15	1.21	2.02	2.82
7	1.97	3.29	4.60	1.74	2.91	4.06	1.26	2.10	2.94	1.27	2.13	2.98
8	1.73	2.89	4.04	1.65	2.76	3.85	1.19	1.99	2.78	1.22	2.04	2.86
9	1.44	2.41	3.37	1.38	2.30	3.22	1.02	1.71	2.39	0.82	1.38	1.92
10	1.21	2.03	2.84	1.05	1.76	2.46	0.83	1.39	1.94	0.63	1.06	1.48
11	0.81	1.35	1.89	0.68	1.13	1.58	0.58	0.97	1.35	0.49	0.83	1.15
12	0.69	1.14	1.60	0.56	0.93	1.31	0.50	0.83	1.16	0.42	0.71	0.99
年均	1.42	2.37	3.31	1.27	2.12	2.96	0.99	1.65	2.31	0.85	1.41	1.98

从月能源自洽率来看，在太阳能Ⅰ类地区，6 月分布式光伏发电量最大，能源自洽率在保守开发场景、基本开发场景、积极开发场景下最大分别为 2.05%、3.42%、4.78%；而 12 月分布式光伏发电量最小，能源自洽率在保守开发场景、基本开发场景、积极开发场景下最小分别为 0.69%、1.14%、1.60%；在太阳能Ⅱ类地区，5 月分布式光伏发电量最大，能源自洽率在保守开发场景、基本开发场景、积极开发场景下最大分别为 1.90%、3.17%、4.43%；而 12 月分布式光伏发电量最小，能源自洽率在保守开发场景、基本开发场景、积极开发场景下最小分别为 0.56%、0.93%、1.31%；在太阳能Ⅲ类地区，5 月分布式光伏发电量最大，能源自洽率在保守开发场景、基本开发场景、积极开发场景下最大分别为 1.48%、2.47%、3.45%；而 12 月分布式光伏发电量最小，能源自洽率在保守开发场景、

基本开发场景、积极开发场景下最小分别为 0.50%、0.83%、1.16%；在太阳能Ⅳ类地区，7 月分布式光伏发电量最大，能源自洽率在保守开发场景、基本开发场景、积极开发场景下最大分别为 1.27%、2.13%、2.98%；而 12 月分布式光伏发电量最小，能源自洽率在保守开发场景、基本开发场景、积极开发场景下最小分别为 0.42%、0.71%、0.99%。

可知，在太阳能Ⅰ类地区，公路交通能源系统在保守开发场景、基本开发场景、积极开发场景下年平均能源自洽率分别为 1.42%、2.37%、3.31%。在太阳能Ⅱ类地区，公路交通能源系统在保守开发场景、基本开发场景、积极开发场景下年平均能源自洽率分别为 1.27%、2.12%、2.96%。在太阳能Ⅲ类地区，公路交通能源系统在保守开发场景、基本开发场景、积极开发场景下年平均能源自洽率分别为 0.99%、1.65%、2.31%。在太阳能Ⅳ类地区，公路交通能源系统在保守开发场景、基本开发场景、积极开发场景下年平均能源自洽率分别为 0.85%、1.41%、1.98%。

4.4 可再生能源公路交通能源系统发展路线

图 4-64 给出了可再生能源公路交通能源系统发展路线图。按就近开发、就近消纳的原则，新型公路交通能源系统由太阳能Ⅰ类地区逐渐向太阳能Ⅱ类、Ⅲ类地区拓展，依次开发服务区/停车区的屋顶和车棚空间、隧道隔离带空间、公路沿线边坡与匝道空间的易开发空间资源，最后开发承载式公路路面或公路顶棚空间资源。2025 年首先针对太阳能资源Ⅰ类地区开发服务区屋顶、车棚等易开发空间建设新型公路交通能源系统，而后 2030 年启动太阳能Ⅱ类地区服务区的屋顶

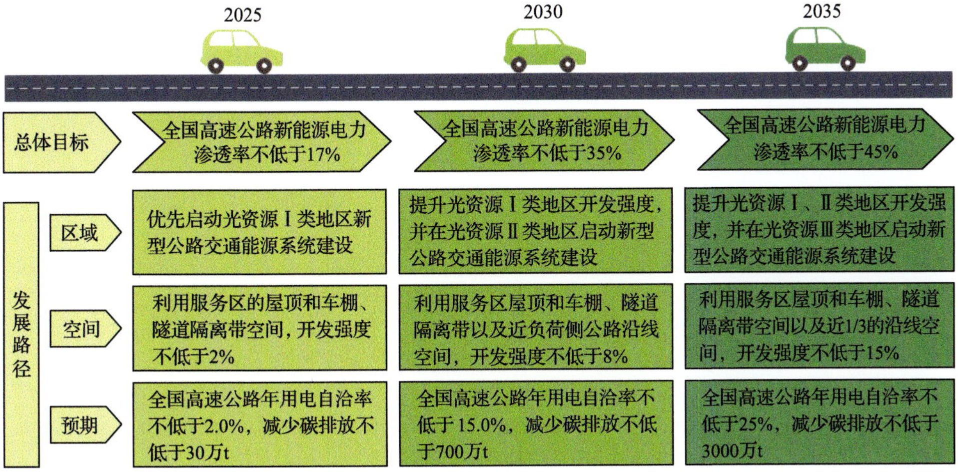

图 4-64 可再生能源公路交通能源系统发展路线图

和车棚空间、隧道隔离带空间以及近负荷的公路沿线边坡和匝道空间的开发，2035年启动太阳能III类地区服务区的屋顶和车棚空间、隧道隔离带空间以及近 1/3 的公路沿线边坡和匝道空间的开发，全面推动新型公路交通能源系统的开发建设。

图 4-65 给出了 2025 年全国高速用电自洽率与可再生能源电力渗透率。在 2025 年，优先启动光资源 I 类地区开发建设。在保守开发场景下，全国高速公路分布式光伏年发电量为 400GW·h，全国高速公路用电自洽率为 2.1%，可再生能源电力渗透率为 17.8%，年减少碳排放 39.8 万 t；在基本开发场景下，全国高速公路分布式光伏年发电量为 780GW·h，全国高速公路用电自洽率为 4.2%，可再生能源电力渗透率为 19.2%，年减少碳排放 77.8 万 t；在积极开发场景下，全国高速公路分布式光伏年发电量为 1180GW·h，全国高速公路用电自洽率为 6.3%，可再生能源电力渗透率为 21.3%，年减少碳排放 117.6 万 t。图 4-66 为 2025 年新型公路交通能源系统的投资盈亏平衡图。

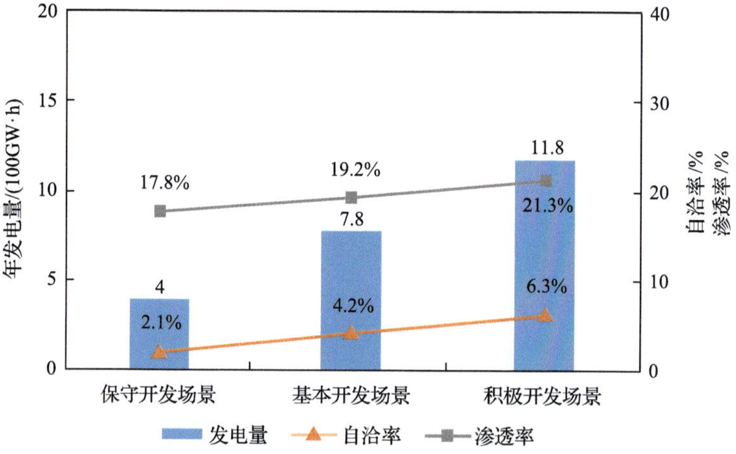

图 4-65　2025 年全国高速用电自洽率与可再生能源电力渗透率

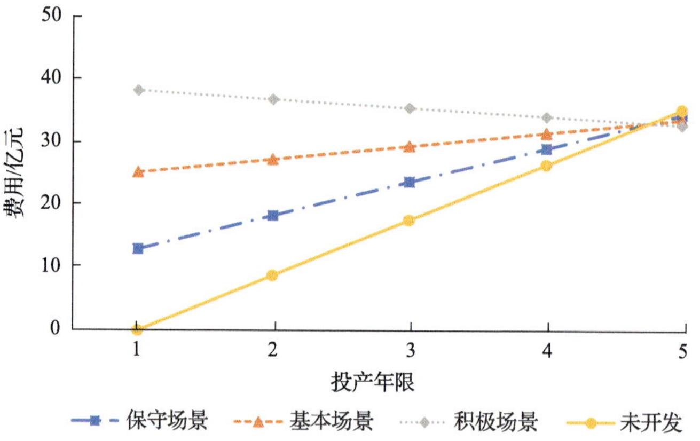

图 4-66　2025 年新型公路交通能源系统的投资盈亏平衡图

根据国网能源研究院发布的《中国可再生能源发电分析报告 2019》，光伏发电投资成本平均为 4.8 元/W。根据国家能源局 2019 年 11 月发布的《2018 年度全国电力价格情况监管通报》，光伏发电平均上网电价为 0.8598 元/(kW·h)。公路交通系统服务区、充电站可按 35kV 以下一般工商业电价计算，假定不执行峰谷电价，全国各省(区、市)工商业平时段电价中位数约为 0.61 元/(kW·h)。预计 2025 年，保守开发场景下，开发区域公路交通系统用电需求为 1221GW·h，分布式光伏年发电量为 400GW·h，剩余 821GW·h 电量按 0.61 元/(kW·h)购入，整体投产后约 4.8 年可实现盈亏平衡；基本开发场景下，开发区域公路交通系统用电需求为 1221GW·h，分布式光伏年发电量为 780GW·h，剩余 441GW·h 电量按 0.61 元/(kW·h)购入，整体投产后约 4.8 年可实现盈亏平衡；积极开发场景下，开发区域公路交通系统用电需求为 1221GW·h，分布式光伏年发电量为 1180GW·h，剩余 41GW·h 电量按 0.61 元/(kW·h)购入，整体投产后约 4.7 年可实现盈亏平衡。

图 4-67 给出了 2030 年全国高速用电自洽率与可再生能源电力渗透率。预计 2030 年，深入推进光资源Ⅰ类、Ⅱ类地区的开发建设。在保守开发场景下，全国高速公路分布式光伏年发电量为 7260GW·h，全国高速公路用电自洽率为 16.0%，可再生能源电力渗透率为 36.2%，年减少碳排放 723.8 万 t；在基本开发场景下，全国高速公路分布式光伏年发电量为 8990GW·h，全国高速公路用电自洽率为 19.9%，可再生能源电力渗透率为 39.1%，年减少碳排放 896.3 万 t；在积极开发场景下，全国高速公路分布式光伏年发电量为 10840GW·h，全国高速公路用电自洽率为 28.4%，可再生能源电力渗透率为 45.6%，年减少碳排放 1080.7 万 t。

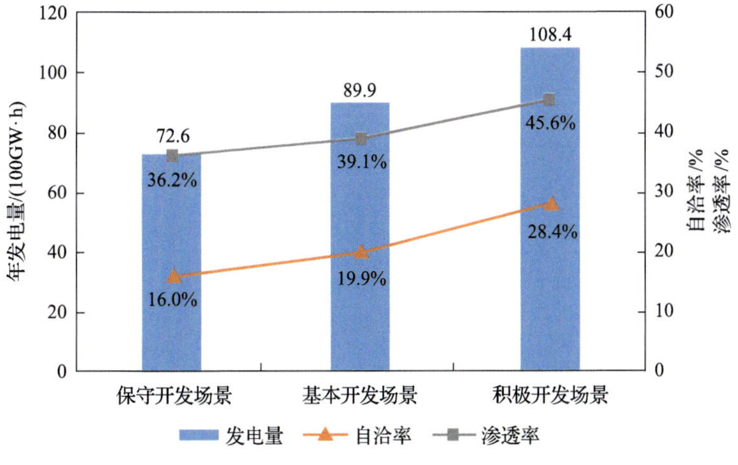

图 4-67　2030 年全国高速用电自洽率与可再生能源电力渗透率

图 4-68 给出了 2030 年新型公路交通能源系统的投资盈亏平衡图。预计 2030 年，保守开发场景下，开发区域公路交通系统用电需求为 14664GW·h，分布式光

伏年发电量为 4855GW·h，剩余 9809GW·h 电量按 0.61 元/(kW·h)购入，整体投产后约 4.8 年可实现盈亏平衡；基本开发场景下，开发区域公路交通系统用电需求为 14664GW·h，分布式光伏年发电量为 6021GW·h，剩余 8643GW·h 电量按 0.61 元/(kW·h)购入，整体投产后约 4.7 年可实现盈亏平衡；积极开发场景下，开发区域公路交通系统用电需求为14664GW·h,分布式光伏年发电量为7251GW·h，剩余 7413GW·h 电量按 0.61 元/(kW·h)购入,整体投产后约 4.6 年可实现盈亏平衡。

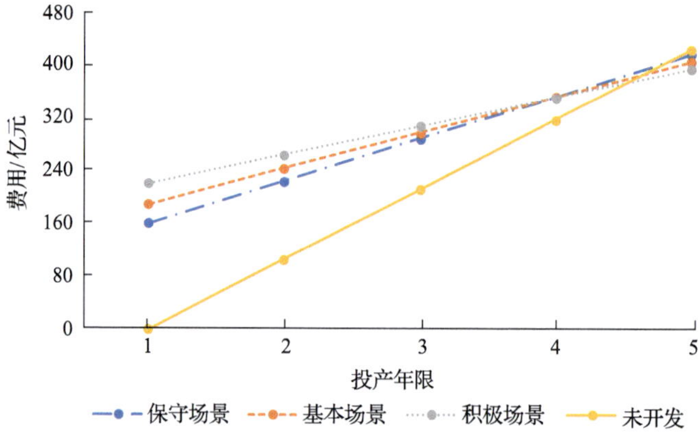

图 4-68　2030 年新型公路交通能源系统的投资盈亏平衡图

图 4-69 给出了 2035 年全国高速用电自洽率与可再生能源电力渗透率。预计 2035 年，逐步向光资源Ⅲ类地区推进，持续提高光资源Ⅰ类、Ⅱ类地区的开发规模。在保守开发场景下，全国高速公路分布式光伏年发电量为 31380GW·h，全国高速公路用电自洽率为 26.7%，可再生能源电力渗透率为 48.7%，年减少碳排放

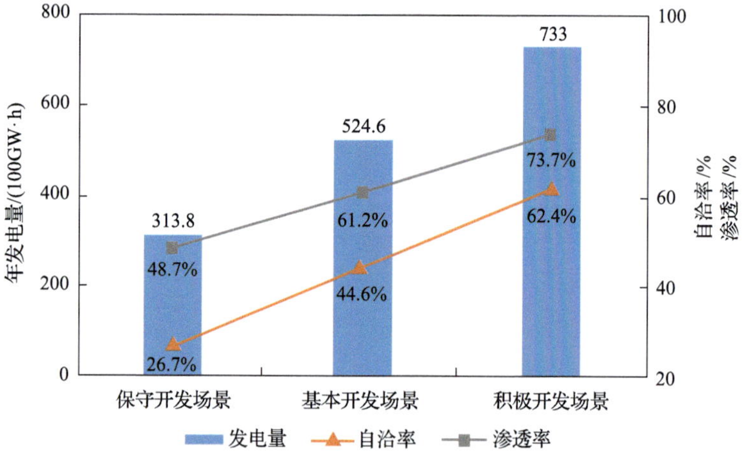

图 4-69　2035 年已开发区域的用电自洽率与可再生能源电力渗透率

3128.6 万 t；在基本开发场景下，全国高速公路分布式光伏年发电量为 52460GW·h，全国高速公路用电自洽率为 44.6%，可再生能源电力渗透率为 61.2%，年减少碳排放 5230.0 万 t；在积极开发场景下，全国高速公路分布式光伏年发电量为 73300GW·h，全国高速公路用电自洽率为 62.4%，可再生能源电力渗透率为 73.7%，年减少碳排放 7308.2 万 t。

图 4-70 给出了 2035 年新型公路交通能源系统的投资盈亏平衡图。预计 2035 年，保守开发场景下，开发区域公路交通系统用电需求为 103980GW·h，分布式光伏年发电量为 14628GW·h，剩余 89352GW·h 电量按 0.61 元/(kW·h)购入，整体投产后约 5.1 年可实现盈亏平衡；基本开发场景下，开发区域公路交通系统用电需求为 103980GW·h，分布式光伏年发电量为 24452GW·h，剩余 79528GW·h 电量按 0.61 元/(kW·h)购入，整体投产后约 5.2 年可实现盈亏平衡；积极开发场景下，开发区域公路交通系统用电需求为 103980GW·h，分布式光伏年发电量为 32302GW·h，剩余 71678GW·h 电量按 0.61 元/(kW·h)购入，整体投产后约 5.3 年可实现盈亏平衡。

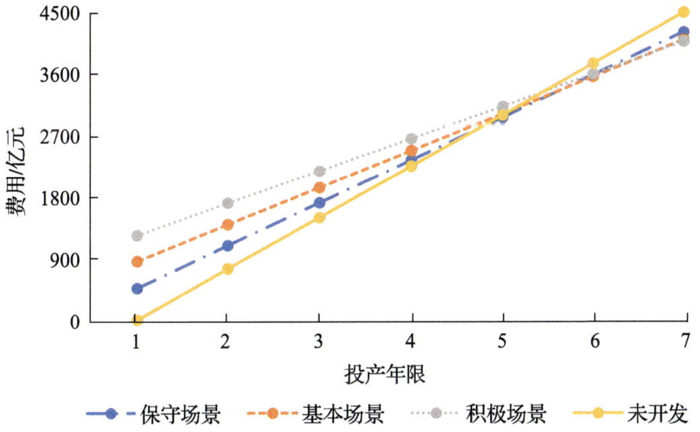

图 4-70　2035 年新型公路交通能源系统的投资盈亏平衡图

上篇参考文献

[1] 朱传征. 高速公路运营管理节能技术研究[D]. 西安: 长安大学, 2015.

[2] 唐珂. 高速公路运营期能耗水平分析与测算方法研究[D]. 西安: 长安大学, 2013.

[3] 储成赞, 刘玉新, 燕凌. 公路隧道节能方式探究[J]. 现代隧道技术, 2016, 53(1): 23-27.

[4] 工业和信息化部. 工业和信息化部系统公共机构能源资源消费统计制度[EB/OL]. [2020-01-15]. http://www.miit.gov.cn/newweb/n1146285/n1146352/n3054355 /n3057853/n3057862/c7590519/content.html.

[5] 公安部. 2018 年全国小汽车保有量首次突破 2 亿辆[EB/OL]. [2019-07-20]. https://www.mps.gov.cn/n2254098/n4904352/c6354939/content.html.

[6] International Renewable Energy Agency. Global Energy Transformation: A roadmap to 2050[EB/OL]. [2019-08-23]. https://www.mps.gov.cn/n2254098/n4904352/c6354939/content.html.

[7] 国务院. 国务院关于印发节能与新能源汽车产业发展规划(2012—2020 年)的通知: 国发〔2012〕22 号[EB/OL]. [2019-08-02]. http://www.gov.cn/xxgk/pub/govpublic/mrlm/201207/t20120709_65317.html.

[8] International Energy Agency. Global EV Outlook 2018 [EB/OL]. [2019-07-06]. https://webstore.iea.org/global-ev-outlook-2018.

[9] International Renewable Energy Agency. Hydrogen: A renewable energy perspective[EB/OL]. [2019-11-13]. https://www.irena.org/publications/2019/Sep/Hydrogen-A-renewable-energy-perspective.

[10] Fuel Cells and Hydrogen Joint Undertaking[EB/OL]. [2019-12-01]. Hydrogen Roadmap Europe: A Sustainable Pathway for The European Energy Transition. https://www.fch.europa.eu/news/hydrogen-roadmap-europe-sustainable-pathway-european-energy-transition.

[11] 中国氢能联盟. 中国氢能源及燃料电池产业白皮书[EB/OL]. [2019-07-25]. http://www.h2cn.org/publicati/215.html.

[12] California Fuel Cell Partnership Headquarters. Road Map to A Us Hydrogen Economy[EB/OL]. [2019-11-21]. https://cafcp.org/blog/us-hydrogen-road-map-released.

[13] Ministry of Economy, Trade and Industry. Basic Strategy for Hydrogen[EB/OL]. [2019-11-25]. https://www.meti.go.jp/press/2017/12/20171226002/20171226002.html.

[14] International Energy Agency. Hydrogen: A renewable energy perspective [EB/OL]. [2019-11-21]. https://webstore.iea.org/the-future-of-hydrogen.

[15] 刘振亚. 全球能源互联网[M]. 北京: 中国电力出版社, 2015.

[16] 周孝信. 构建我国新一代能源系统[R]. 北京: 2015 中国电机工程学会年会, 2015.

[17] 孙宏斌. 能源互联网[M]. 北京: 科学出版社, 2020.

[18] 曹军威, 孙嘉平. 能源互联网与能源系统[M]. 北京: 中国电力出版社, 2016.

[19] 李立涅, 郭剑波, 饶宏. 智能电网与能源网融合技术[M]. 北京: 机械工业出版社, 2018.

[20] 国家能源局. 国家能源局发布 2018 年全国电力工业统计数据[EB/OL]. [2019-09-15]. http://www.nea.gov.cn/2019-01/18/c_137754977.htm.

[21] 国家统计局. 2018 年国民经济和社会发展统计公报[EB/OL]. [2019-09-18]. http://www.stats.gov.cn/tjsj/zxfb/201902/t20190228_1651265.html.

[22] 国家能源局. 我国太阳能资源是如何分布的? [EB/OL]. [2019-07-30]. http://www.nea.gov.cn/2014-08/03/c_133617073.htm.

[23] Zou H, Du H, Brown M A, et al. Large-scale PV power generation in china: A grid parity and techno-economic analysis[J]. Energy, 2017, 134: 256-268.
[24] 中华人民共和国国家质量监督检验检疫总局, 中国国家标准化管理委员会. GB/T 31155 太阳能资源等级 总辐射[S]. 2014: 1.
[25] 张兴, 曹仁贤. 太阳能光伏并网发电及其逆变控制[M]. 2 版. 北京: 机械工业出版社, 2018.
[26] 于立军. 新能源发电技术[M]. 北京: 机械工业出版社, 2018.
[27] 惠晶, 颜文旭. 新能源发电与控制技术[M]. 北京: 机械工业出版社, 2018.
[28] Chanchangi Y, Ghosh A, Sundaram S, et al. Dust and PV performance in Nigeria: A review. Renewable and Sustainable Energy Reviews, 2020, 121: 109704.
[29] 杨金焕. 太阳能光伏发电技术及应用[M]. 北京: 电子工业出版社, 2013.
[30] 孙秋野, 马大中. 能源互联网与能源转换技术[M]. 北京: 机械工业出版社, 2017.
[31] 李海津. 多能源储能系统构建理论与关键技术研究[D]. 杭州: 浙江大学, 2018.
[32] Ralph Z. 能源储存新方法[M]. 赵冬斌, 王革, 巩可欣, 等, 译. 北京: 机械工业出版社, 2017.
[33] Brunet Y. 储能技术及应用[M]. 唐西胜, 徐鲁宁, 周龙, 等, 译. 北京: 机械工业出版社, 2018.
[34] 夏杨红. 多子网型交直流混合微电网协同控制技术研究[D]. 杭州: 浙江大学, 2019.
[35] 郭倩. 面向功率灵活分配的分布式逆变器系统的并联技术研究[D]. 杭州: 浙江大学, 2015.
[36] 王成山, 许洪华. 微电网技术及应用[M]. 北京: 科学出版社, 2018.
[37] 顾伟, 楼冠男, 柳伟. 微电网分布式控制理论与方法[M]. 北京: 科学出版社, 2020.
[38] 曾正, 赵荣祥, 杨欢. 柔性并网逆变器控制技术[M]. 北京: 科学出版社, 2020.
[39] 国家能源局. 我国光伏发电度电成本 10 年下降 90% [EB/OL]. [2019-11-19]. http://www.nea.gov.cn/2018-04/13/c_137108373.htm.
[40] Logan G. A behind the scenes take on lithium-ion battery prices[EB/OL]. [2019-11-24]. https://about.bnef.com/blog/behind-scenes-take-lithium-ion-battery-prices/.
[41] 国家发展和改革委员会. 国家发展改革委关于 2018 年光伏发电项目价格政策的通知: 发改价格规〔2017〕2196 号[EB/OL]. [2019-11-20]. https://www.ndrc.gov.cn/xxgk/zcfb/ghxwj/201712/t20171222_F960932.html.
[42] 国家能源局. 总产值已超过二千亿元 光伏崛起引领绿色转型[EB/OL]. [2019-11-05]. http://www.nea.gov.cn/2015-12/10/c_134902087.htm.
[43] 交通运输部. 2018 年交通运输行业发展统计公报[EB/OL]. [2019-06-09]. http://xxgk.mot.gov.cn/2020/jigou/zhghs/202006/t20200630_3321179.html.
[44] 潘龙. 基于充电选择行为的电动汽车充电设施布局优化研究[D]. 北京: 北京交通大学, 2019.
[45] 节能与新能源汽车技术路线图咨询委员会, 中国汽车工程学会. 节能与新能源汽车技术路线图[M]. 北京: 机械工业出版社, 2018.
[46] 海南省人民政府办公厅. 海南省人民政府办公厅关于印发海南省电动汽车充电基础设施规划（2019-2030）的通知: 琼府办函〔2019〕122 号[EB/OL]. [2019-05-15]. http://www.hainan.gov.cn/hainan/szfbgtwj/201905/1dfbf1dbc5de4c91b0e37fc8850af23c.shtml.
[47] 国家发展和改革委员会. 国家发展改革委关于完善光伏发电上网电价机制有关问题的通知: 发改价格〔2019〕764 号[EB/OL]. [2019-05-30]. https://www.ndrc.gov.cn/xxgk/zcfb/tz/201904/t20190430_962433.html.
[48] 海南省工业和信息化厅. 海南省物价局关于电动汽车用电实行扶持性电价政策有关问题的通知[EB/OL]. [2019-05-25]. http://www.hainan.gov.cn/hainan/ghjh/201712/863f9afac201414999172830bbd65c69.shtml.

[49] 国家发展和改革委员会. 发改委关于印发《电动汽车充电基础设施发展指南(2015-2020 年)》的通知: 发改能源〔2015〕1454 号[EB/OL]. [2019-06-15]. https://www.ndrc.gov.cn/xwdt/ztzl/xxczhjs/ghzc/201605/t20160511_971925.html.

[50] 国家发展和改革委员会. 国家公路网规划(2013 年-2030 年)[EB/OL]. [2019-10-12]. http://zfxxgk.ndrc.gov.cn/web/iteminfo.jsp?id=285.

[51] 国家能源局. 2018 年度全国电力价格情况监管通报[EB/OL]. [2019-12-14]. http://www.nea.gov.cn/2019-11/05/c_138530255.htm.

下篇　铁路交通与可再生能源融合发展的形态、模式与解决方案

第 1 章　铁路交通能源需求的形态和模式

铁路是我国能源消耗的大户，据《2018 年铁道统计公报》统计，2016 年我国铁路运输总能耗约 1700 万 t 标准煤。铁路能耗主要分为三大部分：运输耗能、工业耗能和工程耗能。其中，运输耗能所占比重最大，约占铁路总耗能的 80%，运输耗能中又分为牵引耗能和辅助耗能，其中牵引耗能占总运输耗能的 60%～70%，是铁路耗能的主要部分。

近年来，我国铁路运输的能源消耗变化如图 1-1 所示，我国铁路运输能源消耗由 2000 年的 1859.5 万 t 标准煤减少至 2016 年的 1591.6 万 t 标准煤，年均降低 0.98%；在交通运输业能源消耗总量的比重由 2000 年的 18.75%降至 2016 年的 3.95%，近年来一直处于下降态势。尽管我国铁路运输能源消耗在国家交通能源消耗比重中一直降低，但依然高于美国、英国、加拿大、日本等国家。

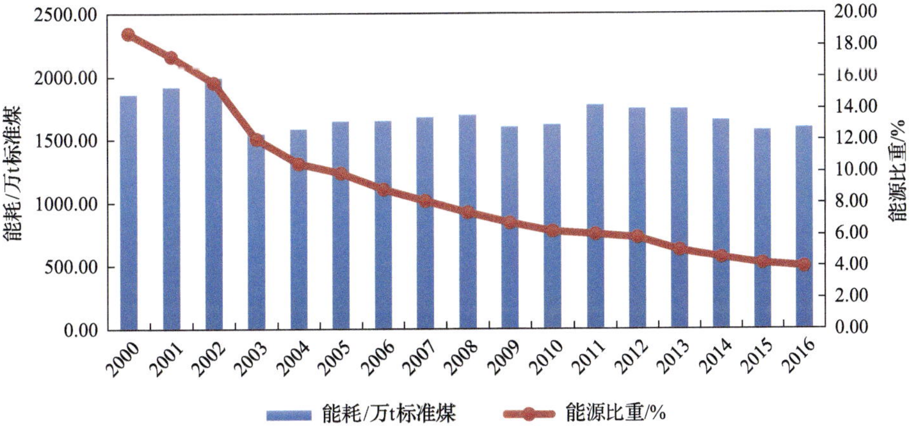

图 1-1　2000～2016 年我国铁路能源消耗变化图

数据来源：国家统计局 http://data.stats.gov.cn

铁路运输能源消耗量与国家交通运输业能源消耗总量的比值称为铁路能源比重。作为交通运输的重要组成部分，2000～2016 年我国铁路能源消耗的结构变化情况如图 1-2 所示。从图 1-2 中可以看出，我国铁路各类能源消耗来源所占的比重处于连续变化的状态。其中，2000～2008 年，燃油消耗比重持续增长，2008 年达到 50.2%的历史最高值，随后缓慢下降至 2016 年的 37.6%；电力比重则在 2008 年后逐年持续增加，在 2016 年达到了 47.6%。铁路运输能源消耗结构的变化是铁路牵引形式变化的重要表现，电力消耗量的不断上升，表明 2008 年后我国铁路电力牵引运输比重逐渐增加，而内燃机车牵引比重则逐渐下降。

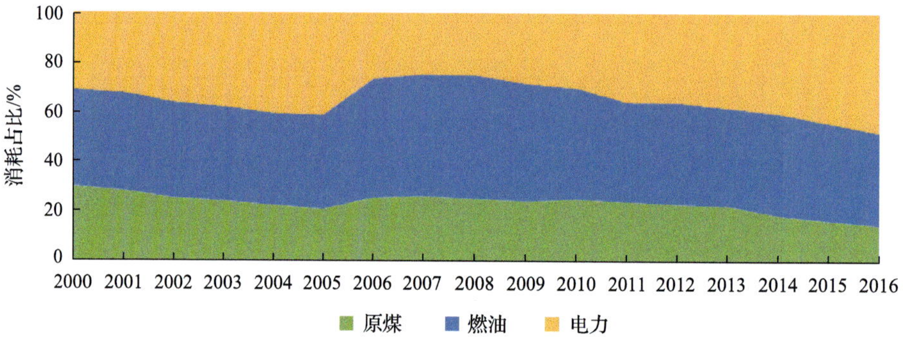

图 1-2 2000～2016 年我国铁路能源消耗结构变化图

数据来源：国家统计局 http://data.stats.gov.cn

铁路能源消耗强度象征铁路能源利用效率，其值越低，表明其能源利用效率越高。2000～2016 年我国铁路能源强度的变化如图 1-3 所示。从图 1-3 中可以看出，2000～2013 年，中国能源强度处于不断下降的过程，降幅达 54.40%，平均年降幅为 3.89%，2003 年能源强度下降幅度最大，达到 24.70%。尽管近几年铁路能源消耗强度降低数值微小，但由于铁路每年巨大的运输生产量，也能引起铁路能源消耗量的巨大变化。2013 年我国铁路能源强度为 4.66t 标准煤/百万换算吨公里，比 2012 年降低 0.08 吨标准煤/百万换算吨公里，在铁路换算周转量不变的情况下，可以节省 29.92 万 t 标准煤[1]。

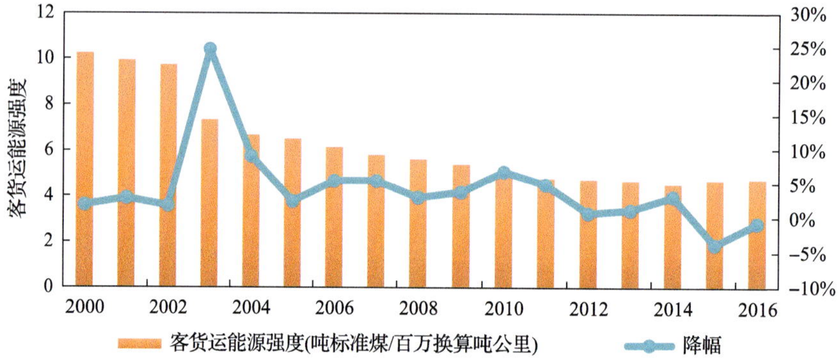

图 1-3 2000～2016 年我国铁路能源强度变化图

1.1 铁路的用能形态

根据铁路系统的组织结构，铁路的用能形态包含三个方面，分别为运载体、基础设施和服务设施，各方面都有其不同的用能形态。

1.1.1 铁路运载体的用能形态

截至2018年底，全国铁路机车拥有量为2.1万台，其中，内燃机车占比为38.5%，比2017年下降1.6个百分点；电力机车占比为61.5%，比2017年提高1.6个百分点。全国铁路客车拥有量为7.2万辆，其中动车组有3256个标准组、26048辆，比2017年增加了321个标准组、2568辆。全国铁路货车拥有量为83.9万辆。2013～2018年铁路机车拥有量变化如图1-4所示。

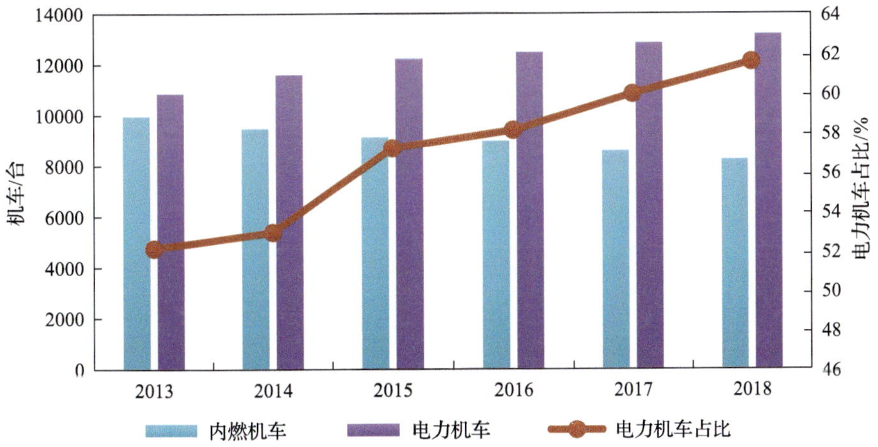

图1-4 2013～2018年我国铁路机车拥有量变化图

数据来源：《2018年铁道统计公报》

对于我国铁路机车而言，主要型号机车对应的运营速度、额定功率以及运行方式如表1-1所示。

表1-1 我国主要型号铁路机车对应的运营速度、额定功率以及运行方式表

型号	运营速度/(km/h)	额定功率/kW	运行方式
HXN3	20.0	4400	内燃
HXN3 高原	16.1	3300	内燃
HXN5	25.0	4400	内燃
DF11A	65.6	3040	内燃
DF11B	57.8	3040	内燃
DF4B	29.3	1985	内燃
DF4C	31.5	2650	内燃
DF4D	39.0	2425	内燃
DF5	10.9	1324	内燃

续表

型号	运营速度/(km/h)	额定功率/kW	运行方式
DF6	22.2	2940	内燃
DF7C	20.0	2200	内燃
DF7G	20.0	2200	内燃
DF7G 高原	20.0	2200	内燃
DF8	30.4	2720	内燃
DF8B	28.2	3100	内燃
DF8CJ	27.5	3650	内燃
DF10F	28.2	2200	内燃
DF11G	83.5	6080	内燃
金轮号	87.3	6620	内燃
NZJ1	73.9	2760	内燃
NDJ3	59.3	2760	内燃
HXD1	120.0	9600	电力
HXD1B	120.0	9600	电力
HXD1C	120.0	7200	电力
HXD1D	160.0	7200	电力
HXD2	120.0	9600	电力
HXD2B	120.0	9600	电力
HXD2C	120.0	7200	电力
HXD3	120.0	7200	电力
HXD3B	120.0	9600	电力
HXD3C	120.0	7200	电力
HXD3D	160.0	7200	电力
中原之星	160.0	6400	电力
中华之星	270.0	9600	电力
CRH1A	200	5500	电力
CRH2A	250	4800	电力
CRH3C	350	8800	电力
CRH5A	250	5300	电力
CRH380A	350	9600	电力
CR400AF	350	10400	电力

以兰新高铁为例说明高速铁路运载体用能的计算方法。兰新铁路东起兰州市，西至乌鲁木齐市，全长1786km，设计速度为250km/h。按照区间可分为4段，分别为兰州—西宁段、西宁—嘉峪关段、嘉峪关—哈密段和哈密—乌鲁木齐段。我国设计的高速列车主要为CRH5A型动车组列车，8编组的牵引功率为5300kW。由于高铁列车编组有8编组和16编组两种方式，16编组的牵引功率为8编组的2倍。假设两种编组方式的列车占比为1∶1，可以得出兰新线上高铁列车的平均牵引功率为7950kW。

高铁列车的车载辅助设施主要有照明、空调、充电机、空调冷凝风机、牵引变流器冷却风机、牵引电机冷却风机等。在稳定运行的情况下，每节高铁列车辅助设施的视在功率不超过100kW，在此以100kW计。按照上述比例假设，兰新高铁各列车辅助设施负荷为1200kW，从而各列车总功率为9150kW。

通过统计网站上的公开信息，可以得出兰新线各区段的部分运营数据，如表1-2所示。兰新高铁全线日车次108次，日所需牵引电量为2815MW·h，年所需牵引电量为103GW·h。

表1-2　兰新线部分运营信息表

区间	双向车次	线路长度/km	运营时间/h	所需电量/(10MW·h)
兰新高铁兰西端	42	201.8	2.2	84.5
兰新高铁西嘉段	32	505.8	3.3	97.5
兰新高铁嘉哈段	12	551.2	3.3	35.7
兰新高铁哈乌段	22	547.4	3.2	63.8
总计	108	1806.2	—	281.5

1.1.2　铁路基础设施的用能形态

铁路基础设施的用能单元包括铁路轨道以及经过的桥梁、隧道等，它们的用能主要包括通信信号、照明、通风设施等，消耗的电能是先经过电力变压器将大电网的电能降压，再经过铁路配电装置等分配电能，为铁路的通信设备、行车信号、桥梁、隧道等设施供电。

1. 隧道

截至2018年底，我国已投入运营的铁路隧道共计15117座，总长16331km。其中高速及城际铁路隧道站共3028座，总长4896km，约占总长的30%；长度大于10km的隧道约142座，总长1930km，约占12%；长度大于20km的隧道约9座，总长219km[2]。中国已投入运营的长度20km以上的特长铁路隧道表，如表1-3所示。

表 1-3　中国已投入运营的长度 20km 以上的特长铁路隧道表

隧道名称	隧道长度/m	线别	单洞/双洞	建成时间	速度目标值/(km/h)	设计单位	施工单位
新关角隧道	32690	西格线	双洞单线	2014-12	160	中铁第一勘察设计院集团有限公司	中铁隧道局集团有限公司、中铁十六局集团有限公司
中天山隧道	22449	南疆线	双洞单线	2014-12	160	中铁第一勘察设计院集团有限公司	中铁隧道局集团有限公司、中铁十八局集团有限公司
乌鞘岭隧道	20050	兰武二线	双洞单线	2006-03	160	中铁第一勘察设计院集团有限公司	中铁一局集团有限公司、中铁二局集团有限公司、中铁五局集团有限公司、中铁十二局集团有限公司、中铁十六局集团有限公司、中铁十七局集团有限公司、中铁十八局集团有限公司、中铁隧道局集团有限公司
西秦岭隧道	28236	兰渝线	2 座单洞	2015-12	200	中铁第一勘察设计院集团有限公司	中铁隧道局集团有限公司、中铁十八局集团有限公司
太行山隧道	27839	石太线	双洞单线	2009-04	250	中国铁路设计集团有限公司	中铁十二局集团有限公司、中铁十六局集团有限公司、中铁十七局集团有限公司、中铁五局集团有限公司、中铁隧道局集团有限公司
吕梁山隧道	20785	太中银	双洞单线	2011-01	200	中国铁路设计集团有限公司	中铁三局集团有限公司、中铁十二局集团有限公司
燕山隧道	21153	张唐线	双洞单线	2015-12	120	中国铁路设计集团有限公司	中铁隧道局集团有限公司
青云山隧道	22175	向莆铁路	双洞单线	2011-09	200	中铁第四勘察设计院集团有限公司	中铁二十三局集团有限公司
南吕梁山隧道	23443	瓦日铁路	双洞单线	2013-04	120	中铁第六勘察设计院集团有限公司	中铁隧道局集团有限公司、中铁十一局集团有限公司

隧道的电力负荷主要包括交通监控设施、紧急呼叫设施、防灾救援设施、中央控制设施、通风及控制设施和照明及控制设施。各类用电负荷的耗能占比如图 1-5 所示，从图 1-5 中可以看出，照明和通风的耗能是隧道的主要耗能单元，其中照明的耗能占比为 91.29%，通风的耗能占 6.7%，其他负荷的耗能不

足 2%。因此，研究隧道的照明及通风的节能技术是设计新型隧道能源供给系统的关键。

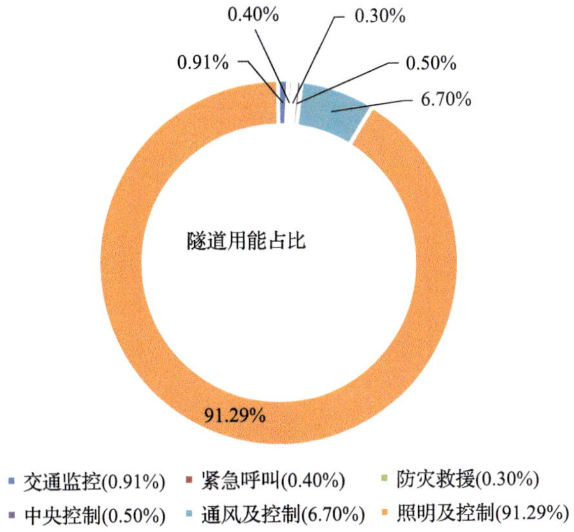

图 1-5　我国铁路隧道中各类负荷用能占比图

目前隧道照明灯实现方式主要为采用高压钠灯和无极灯两种光源灯具间隔安装，双线隧道两排灯具，高压钠灯和无极灯一一对应，每排灯具两灯之间距离为 25m，灯具安装高度为 3.5m。

以成绵乐铁路机场路隧道为例，长 5500m，按照如上隧道照明方案计算，共需安装高压钠灯 220 套，无极荧光灯 220 套。灯具全部工作的总功率约为 34.1kW，按照全部灯具常亮计算，该隧道照明年用电量约为 299MW·h。

按照表 1-4，隧道通风用电量是照明用电量的 1/15，由于成绵乐铁路机场路隧道的通风用电量大约为 20MW·h，因此，成绵乐铁路机场路隧道全年的总用电量约为 320MW·h。

表 1-4　我国铁路隧道常用照明灯具列表

隧道长度	灯具类型	功率/W	备注
500m～5km	高压钠	70	—
5km 以上	高压钠	70	—
	无极荧光灯	85	应急照明

2. 桥梁

我国铁路桥梁包括国家铁路桥梁和合资铁路桥梁。截至 2016 年底，全路有桥梁 78274 座，全长 20129842km，其中，有钢梁桥 1840 座 219.898km，圬工桥 76383 座 19905.776km，临时性桥 51 座 1.842km。其中，桥长超过 500m 的特大桥 6192 座 14305.286km，桥长 100～500m 的大桥 14611 座 3569.776km，中桥 23504 座 1465.89km，小桥 33966 座 786.56km[3]。

公铁两用大桥的电气负荷分散且容量相对较小。以黄冈公铁两用长江大桥为例说明铁路桥梁的用能形态。负荷大致有 3 种类型：①大桥道路照明、景观照明、检修照明、主塔内照明、航空障碍灯、通航桥孔照明；②大桥检修维护动力设备，如空压机、除湿机、电梯等的用电；③大桥道路监控、大桥结构健康检测、大桥收费系统的用电。主要用电负荷等级的划分如表 1-5 所示。

表 1-5　我国铁路桥梁主要用电负荷等级划分表

序号	电力负荷名称	负荷等级	序号	电力负荷名称	负荷等级
1	道路照明	2	7	除湿机	3
2	景观照明	3	8	结构安全监控	1
3	检修照明	2	9	消防设备	1
4	警卫照明	1	10	大桥收费系统	2
5	航空障碍灯、通航桥孔照明	1	11	大桥通信	1
6	电梯、空压机	2	12	道路监控	1

黄冈长江大桥全长 4.01km，其中公铁合建段长 2.567km。设计为双层桥面，下层桥面通行双线高速铁路，上层桥面通行四车道高速公路。主桥为双塔斜拉桥，跨度为 1215m，主跨度为 567m。由于管理体制的原因，大桥的公路、铁路配电各成系统。图 1-6 为黄冈公铁两用长江大桥图。

图 1-6　黄冈公铁两用长江大桥图

铁路电源取自铁路 10kV 贯通线，采取分段配电方式。在 2 号、3 号主塔墩下横梁上各安装 1 台 100A 的埋地式变压器，为桥上检修与道路照明、小型维修动力、航空与内河航运等负荷供电。

1.1.3　铁路服务设施的用能形态

截至 2016 年底，全路有运输站段 836 个，其中直属车站 134 个、车务段 140 个、客运段 38 个、机务段(机车检修段)72 个、车辆段(动车段、动客段)78 个、工务段 155 个、工务机械段(工电大修段、大型养路机械运用检修段)24 个、电务段 64 个、通信段 18 个、供电段 64 个、货运中心 49 个。

我国铁路系统划分为北京、上海、广州等 18 个铁路局，对应着 325 个下属车站城市。其中，上海铁路局下属车站城市最多，为 41 个；下属车站城市最少的铁路局为呼和浩特铁路局和太原铁路局，为 8 个。各铁路局所对应的车站城市数如图 1-7 所示。

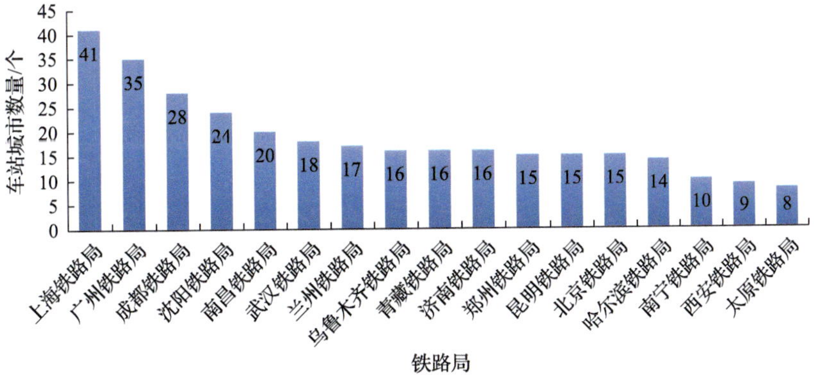

图 1-7　我国各铁路局所对应的车站城市数量对比图

数据来源：《中国铁道年鉴 2017》

我国的铁路车站，按照等级分为特等站、一等站、二等站、三等站、四等站和五等站；其中特等站、一等站通常直属于铁路局，二等站至五等站隶属于车务段或临近的直属大站。按照作业性质分为客运站、货运站、客货运站、工业站、联轨站、港湾站、国境站、换装站、线路所。按技术作业分为编组站、区段站、技术站、中间站、会让站、越行站。

1. 客运站

截至目前，全国共有特等车站 71 个，其中客运站 3 个，货运站 4 个，客货运站 31 个。从地区来看，华北地区有 12 个，东北地区有 10 个，华东地区有 16 个，华中地区有 13 个，华南地区有 8 个，西南地区有 7 个，西北地区有 5 个。此外，全国共有一等车站 205 个[4]。表 1-6 为我国铁路特等客运站表。

表 1-6　我国铁路特等客运站表

地区	我国铁路特等客运站
华北	北京 北京西 北京南 丰台 丰台西 天津 天津西 南仓 石家庄 山海关 太原 大同
东北	沈阳 沈阳北 沈阳南 裕国 苏家屯 长春 哈尔滨 齐齐哈尔 牡丹江 佳木斯
华东	上海 上海虹桥 南翔 北郊 南京南 南京东 无锡 常州 杭州东 合肥南 向塘 鹰潭 济南 济西 济南西 青岛
华中	郑州 郑州东 郑州北 洛阳龙门 汉口 武昌 武汉 武汉北 株洲 株洲北 衡阳 衡阳北 长沙南
华南	广州 广州东 广州南 江村 深圳北 南宁 桂林北 柳州南
西南	成都 成都东 重庆北 贵阳北 贵阳南 昆明南 昆明东
西北	西安 西安北 西安西 兰州西 新丰镇

中型铁路客运站站房建筑面积一般为 1 万～2 万 m^2，大型铁路客运站的站房建筑面积超过 2 万 m^2，特等车站的站顶面积平均约为 4.4 万 m^2，雨棚面积平均为 9.3 万 m^2。

根据上海虹桥铁路客运站能量管理系统（energy management system，EMS）的数据显示，可统计的用电能耗约为 10^5kW·h/天。其中，冷热源、空调、照明、广告、电梯、引导类的电耗排前 6 位，分别为 57%、21%、10%、4%、3%、3%，如图 1-8 所示。

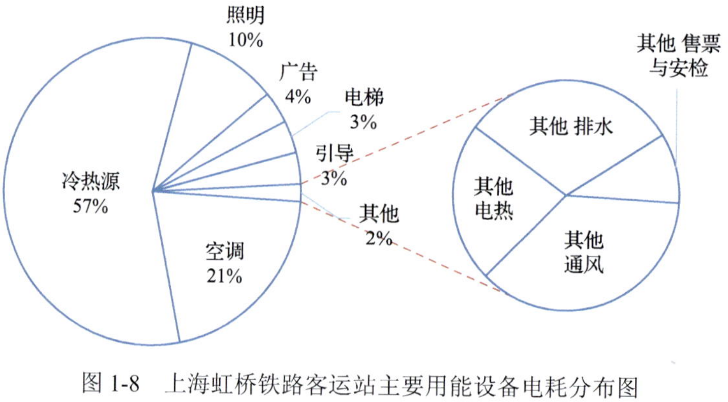

图 1-8　上海虹桥铁路客运站主要用能设备电耗分布图

上海虹桥铁路客运站各层的分时数据如图 1-9～图 1-14 所示。

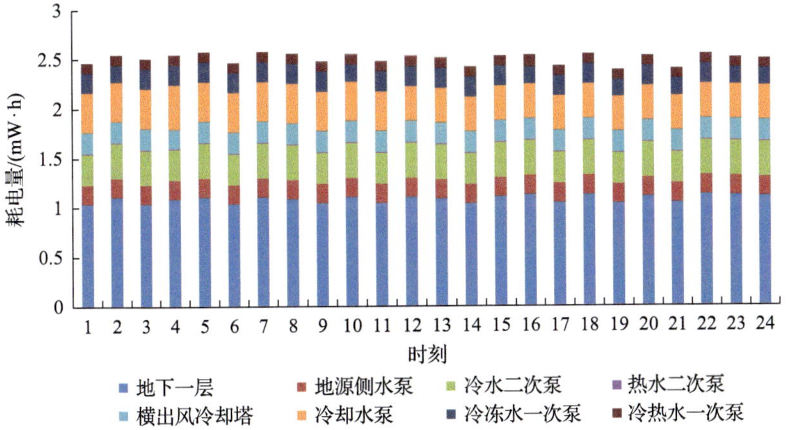

图 1-9 上海虹桥铁路客运站冷热源分时电耗图

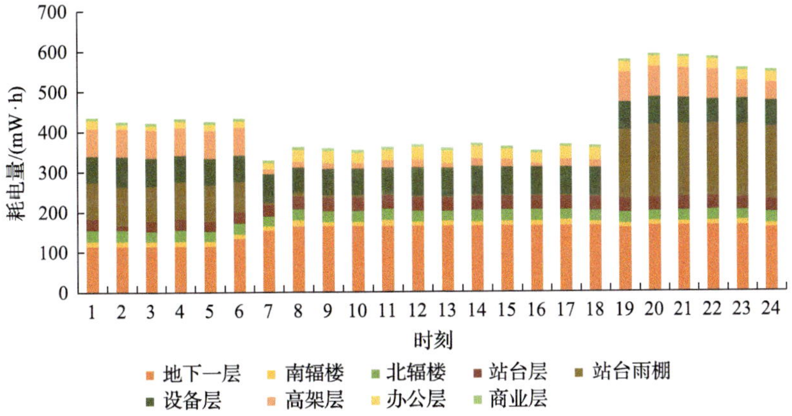

图 1-10 上海虹桥铁路客运站照明分时电耗图

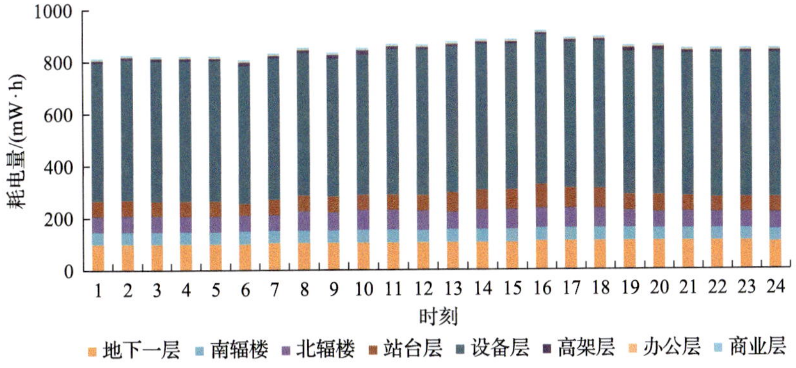

图 1-11 上海虹桥铁路客运站空调分时能耗图

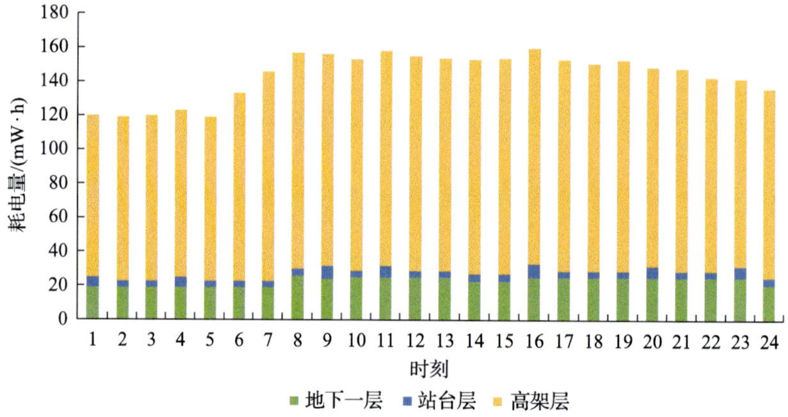

图 1-12　上海虹桥铁路客运站引导显示分时能耗图

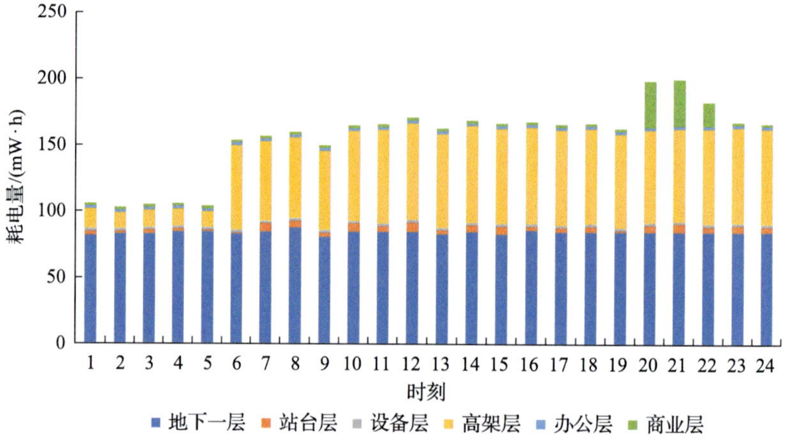

图 1-13　上海虹桥铁路客运站广告分时能耗图

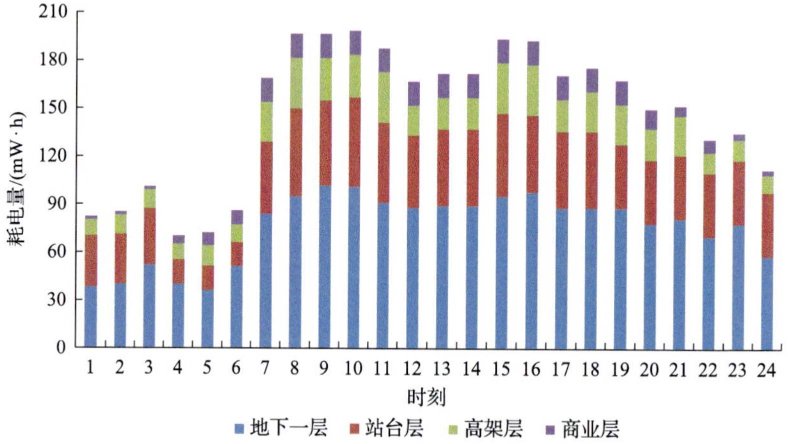

图 1-14　上海虹桥铁路客运站电梯分时能耗图

铁路的服务设施的用能项目包括冬季供暖、夏季空调、照明、电子信息屏、电梯、信息机柜、电热水器等。铁路客运站消耗的能源主要有电、天然气、煤、市政热水等，其中电的消耗量最大。不同地理位置的客运站用电量各不相同，图 1-15 是一些站点全年单位面积电耗指标。

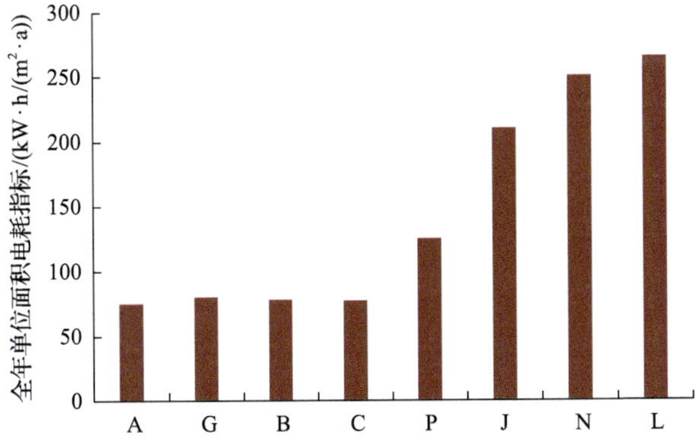

图 1-15　我国不同铁路客站的全年单位面积耗电指标

其中客站 A，G，B，C 全年单位面积电耗指标较小，为 71～81kW·h/(m^2·a)，这 4 个客站地处严寒或寒冷地区，且客站规模较小，旅客活动区域夏季无空调或基本不开空调。J，N，L 这 3 个客站地处夏热冬冷或夏热冬暖地区，旅客活动区域采用全空气集中空调系统，全年单位面积电耗指标较高，为 220～272kW·h/(m^2·a)。P 站地处温和地区，夏季空调开启时间较短，全年单位面积电耗指标为 131kW·h/(m^2·a)[5]。

客站用电又可拆分为空调、照明、电子信息屏、电梯、电热水器、信息机房设备的用电量和其他用电量。其中，空调系统用电项目包括冷源、供冷季输配系统(冷水泵、冷却水泵、空调箱风机等)和供暖季输配系统(供暖泵、空调箱风机等)。除空调系统外，其他用电项目的用电量季节性变化幅度不大。图 1-16 是客站全年用电量的拆分结果。

从图 1-16 可以看出，客站用电空调与照明系统的耗电量的占比较大。

铁路服务设施的站点中的空调系统用电项目包括冷源、供冷季输配系统(冷水泵、冷却水泵、空调箱风机等)和供暖季输配系统(供暖泵、空调箱风机等)。空调各个客站差异很大，客站夏季空调耗电量如图 1-17 所示，可以看出，各个客站差异很大，客站 A，B，C，G 的夏季空调用电量水平很低，为 5～10kW·h/m^2，其中 A，B，C 站的普通候车室不设置空调，软席及贵宾候车室设置分体空调，另外信息机房和售票室等人员长期工作的办公室也设有分体空调；G 站候车室由恒温恒湿机组负责室内温湿度调节，但全年开启时间极短；J，L，N 站夏季均采用全空气集中空调系统，开启时间长，电耗水平高，用电量为 73～152kW·h/m^2，空调系统为全年用电的最大分项。

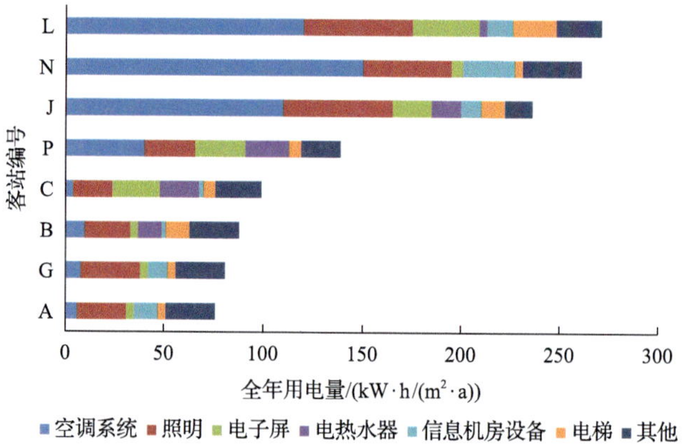

图 1-16　我国不同铁路客站全年用电量拆分结果

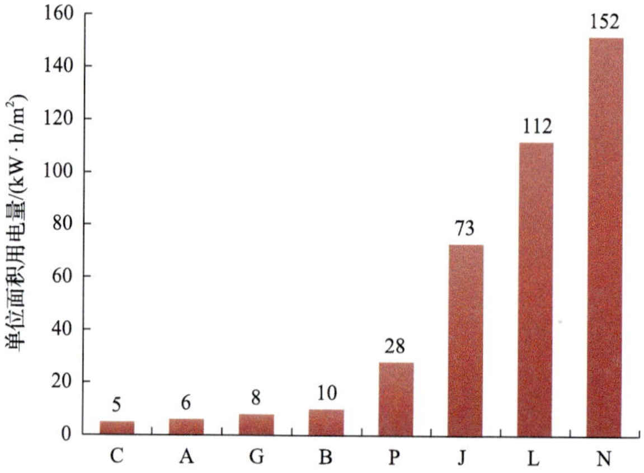

图 1-17　我国不同铁路客站夏季空调单位面积用电量

如图 1-18 所示，客站照明用电量差异较大，变化范围为 22～68kW·h/ $(m^2·a)$，照明用电量与站房夜间是否关闭、照明控制方式、灯具功率密度等相关，如 A，

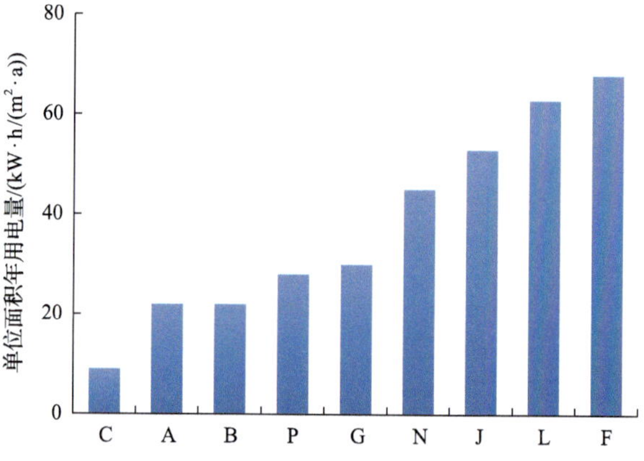

图 1-18　我国不同铁路客站照明全年单位面积用电量对比图

B站夜间全部或部分候车室关闭，其单位面积照明用电量较小。

铁路客站运行能耗的高低既与设计施工相关，也受到客站运行管理水平、服务水平等影响，影响因素众多。从用能分项来看，空调系统、照明、电子信息屏、电梯等是客站用能的主要项目。其中，影响空调系统运行能耗高低的因素主要有空调负荷、设备运行效率、空调时间等，这些又取决于当地的气候条件、建筑围护结构设计、客流密度、运行管理等。而照明能耗高低主要受照明安装功率、照明时间等影响，这些又取决于客站自然采光与人工照明设计、照明系统控制等。此外，不少因素对客站运行能耗的影响往往是多方面的，如增加天窗面积能有效地降低人工照明电耗，但同时会增加夏季进入室内的太阳辐射量，从而导致空调冷负荷增大[6-14]。

2. 货运站

截至2016年底，全国共有货运站3547个。

北京铁路局南仓站地处天津市北辰区，有2个货场，分别为中零货场和西沽货场，总面积为323352m^2；货物仓库2座，面积为1025m^2；货物雨棚4座，面积为28600m^2；货物站台3座，面积为43276m^2；装卸线8条，延展长4666m；装卸有效长3370m。全站年货物到达量500万t，发送量为70万t。

郑州北站占地为5.3km^2，南北长6000余米、东西宽800余米，有898组道岔，信号机828架，228条铁轨，线路总长454km，配线151条，到发线有效长1050m。有冷藏、加水、机械保温、加油等设备，解编能力24000辆每日，总接发能力766列，为全国编组站之首。郑州北站是中国第一个采用双向纵列式三级八场四推双溜机械化驼峰编组站站型，是第一个综合性现代化编组站。

武汉北站投资约24.3亿元，占地4.47km^2，是中国主要路网性编组站之一。负责武汉铁路枢纽长江以北的货物列车编组、调车与检修业务。

1.2 铁路的用能模式

根据铁路系统的组织结构，铁路的用能模式包含三个方面，分别为运载体、基础设施和服务设施，各部分有其不同的用能模式。

1.2.1 铁路运载体的用能模式

铁路运载体可分为电气化机车和内燃机车，其中电气化机车的用能可分为牵引网供电部分和机车用能部分。当前我国铁路列车用能的最终形态均为电能，主要采用交—直—交的传输模式，列车的辅助设施还存在直流供电的情况。

1)电气化铁路列车供能模式

现代电力牵引都以公用电网配电，实质上是取用经变换的单相电。在我国，电气化铁路均采用工频单相制电压，牵引变输出的额定电压为 27.5kV 或 2×27.5kV，电力机车使用的额定电压为 25kV。图 1-19 为我国电气化铁路牵引供电系统示意图。

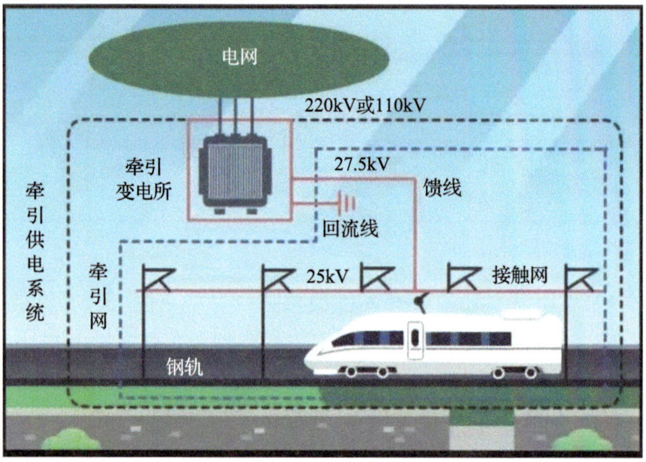

图 1-19　我国电气化铁路列车牵引供电系统示意图

电力系统与输电线为电气化铁路提供高压电源，其电压为 110kV 或 220kV。电气化铁路的牵引负荷是一级负荷，故要求电源有足够的容量和较高的可靠度。

牵引变电所的作用是将电力系统供应的电能转变为适于电力牵引及其供电方式的电能，其中的核心元件是牵引变压器，并设有备用。

牵引网由馈线、接触网、轨道(地)、回流线等组成，完成对电力机车的送电任务。馈线是接在牵引变电所牵引母线和接触网之间的导线，其作用是将电能由牵引变电所引向电气化铁路；接触网是一种特殊的输电线，架设在铁路上方，机车受电弓与其摩擦受电；钢轨既支持列车运行，又支持导线运行，由于轨道和地面都是非绝缘的，故通常轨、地一起接受机车的牵引电流；回流线是指牵引变电所处的横向回流线，它将轨或与轨平行的其他导线与牵引变压器指定端子相连，与馈线一起组成牵引端口的端子线。

牵引网分为架空接触网与第三轨供电网。架空接触网(又称架空电缆)是凭借电杆支撑，架设于电力驱动交通工具行驶轨迹上方半空，在与其接触连接时用于向其直接供电的特殊形式的输电线路。在电气化铁路和城市轨道交通系统中，架空接触网一般只有 1 根接触导线(简称触线)，电力机车或动车通过受电弓取电，再通过金属轮轨回流到电网中；而在无轨电车等使用胶轮的系统中，架空接触网有一正一负2根互相平行的触线，通过2根受电杆取电并形成通路。

架空接触网并非是一条完整的闭合线路，而是人为地划分为很多区段，而每一区段则以分段绝缘器(直流电适用；部分地区俗称“龙虾位”)或中性区(交流电适用)隔开。设置分段绝缘的主要用意是假若某一路段电力供应有故障或因需要进行维修而断电，那么，所影响的范围只是该区域，分段绝缘器后的另一区域则不会受断电影响。

中性区(又称“分相区”)只出现在交流供电的系统中，例如，香港的西铁线、马鞍山线和东铁线。中性区是一段不带电的架空接触网，长度大约是10m。因为电源供应未必只有一个，而是可能由多个馈电网供电。虽然每个电网的供电电压大致相同，但每个电网未必是同相的，它们有可能是异相的。因此，若不设中性区，受电弓会由异相的电源供电而导致车内一些灵敏性较高的电力设备受损。换句话说，中性区就是一段约10m长，不带电的架空接触网，用于隔开由不同馈电网所供应不同相位的电源。

车辆在进入中性区前，必须把列车装在受电弓前的真空断路器打开，以防止列车突然进入0V时产生电弧。真空断路器打开后，列车立即失去外部电力供应，但乘客没有觉得不妥，是因为车内的非动力设备此时由后备电池供电。牵引电动机在真空断路器打开后无电力供应，车辆会以惯性冲过中性区。车辆过了中性区后，真空断路器将会闭合，全车的电力装置恢复由架空接触网供电。

架空接触网的悬挂类型大致为三种：简单悬挂、链式悬挂和刚性悬挂。其中简单悬挂和链式悬挂都是弹性(柔性)悬挂。与此对应，架空接触网也根据悬挂类型分别称为刚性接触网和柔性接触网。

(1)简单悬挂只有导线，没有承力线，优点是结构简单，支柱高度低，支撑点承受的负荷较轻，一般运用于隧道等低净空的场合。在无轨电车和有轨电车中，也广泛地使用简单悬挂。其缺点是跨度小，悬挂点有硬点，且在运行中导线会上下振荡，不适用于高速铁路。图1-20为架空接触网的悬挂类型1-简单悬挂。

图1-20　架空接触网的悬挂类型1-简单悬挂

(2)链式悬挂将导线和承力线之间用悬索连接起来，解决了简单悬挂中跨度小和硬点的问题，因此在城市轨道交通及长距离、高速度、大跨度的电气化铁路中大量使用。链式悬挂是三种悬挂方式里受到隧道净空限制最大的悬挂方式，其电阻为 0.0221Ω/km。图 1-21 为架空接触网的悬挂类型 2-链式悬挂。

图 1-21 架空接触网的悬挂类型 2-链式悬挂

(3)刚性悬挂是以硬质的金属条(通常是铜条)代替软质的导线的新型悬挂方式。随着材料科学和结构力学的发展，刚性悬挂利用了第三轨供电的接触面积大、电阻小(0.0135Ω/km)的优点，而克服了钢轨过重无法悬挂的缺点。城市轨道交通从地下线路开到地上线路时可以直接过渡至链式悬挂，不用更换列车(而部分地面路段也可使用刚性悬挂电缆，例如，港铁屯马线红磡站地面路段)；而在一条路线当中，也可兼容现存链式悬挂及刚性悬挂(例如，港铁港岛线西延、观塘线延线、屯马线(显径站至红磡站)及东铁线(红磡站至金钟站)，新建隧道路段使用刚性悬挂电缆，而现存地面及隧道路段仍能使用链式悬挂电缆)。同时，由于刚性悬挂使用集电弓，没有使用集电靴的第三轨容易脱落的缺点，稳定性更高。但缺点是由于金属条与受电弓炭条的接触面积较大，受电弓炭条的损耗也较大。图 1-22 为架

图 1-22 架空接触网的悬挂类型 3-刚性悬挂

空接触网的悬挂类型 3-刚性悬挂。

第三轨供电系统是一种铁路供电方法。顾名思义，第三轨供电的概念就是在列车行走的两条路轨以外，再加上 1～2 条导电轨，导电轨通常设于两轨之间或外侧；同时在动车组或机车上装设集电装置，以接触导电轨并滑行。这种集电装置因为类似靴子形状，因此被称为 shoe，本报告中译为“集电靴”。图 1-23 为第三轨供电系统图的受流器。

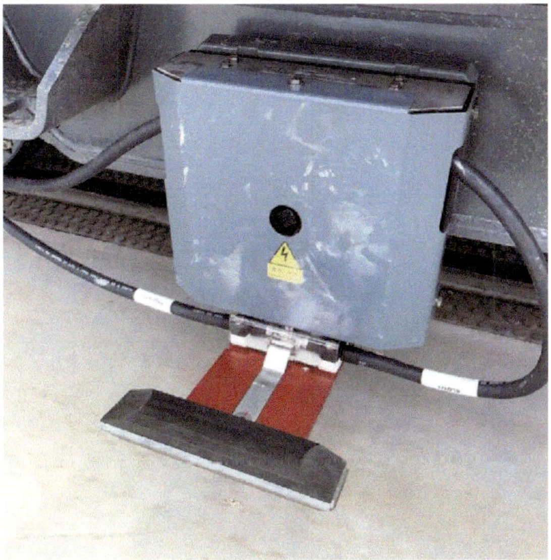

图 1-23　第三轨供电系统图的受流器

由于电力系统需同时具备送电与回流才能完成回路，因此必须有回流轨的设置。在钢轨系统中，可以利用路轨送回电流，而无须另外设置另一回流轨；但在单轨铁路或胶轮路轨系统，由于电流无法透过路轨回流，只能另外增设轨道作为回流轨。但独立设置回流轨的方式，意外地提高系统可靠性，降低对信号系统的干扰，让某些纯钢轨系统也建置独立的回流轨(如伦敦地铁)。图 1-24 为第三轨供电系统的供电轨。图 1-25 为第三轨供电系统中供电轨与受流器接触图。

德国的西门子公司于 1879 年的柏林博览会展示了一列从第三轨取电的概念车。此后许多铁路和轨道系统均装设导电轨，提供铁路电力。位于伦敦的第一条电气化地铁在 1890 年开通时采用第三轨供电方式。

总体来看，架空接触网受到隧道净空的限制比较大，在城市地铁的运用当中会受到土建成本的压力。因此目前已有的城市轨道交通当中，第三轨供电仍然占有较大的比例。另外，架空电缆可能会使部分人产生视觉上的心理障碍，也会对景观造成一定的负面影响。而当遭遇风灾时，也容易因为架空电缆被风吹倒毁坏而使列车班次发生严重误点或取消，必须花费大量时间进行维修。例如，香港地铁近年的多宗车务延误个案均是由架空接触网导致的。因此自港岛线西延起，近年的新建地底线路架空接触网改以刚性悬挂，提高供电稳定度。

图 1-24　第三轨供电系统的供电轨

图 1-25　第三轨供电系统中供电轨与受流器接触图

第三轨有触电的风险，只能用于封闭线路，因此不适合用于与其他交通路线相交的铁路运输系统中。另外，高速铁路为了高速客运和货运重载的需要，会使用更高的电压，如 25kV 的供电系统，如果使用轨道供电会形成电弧，受电弓在列车高速运行时也能更妥善地与架空接触网接触，受电靴则有比较高的机会导致脱离供电轨道。

外部电源的供电方式可分为环形(双侧)单回路供电方式、环形(双侧)双回路供电方式、单电源(单侧)双回路供电方式和放射供电等四种方式。其中，环形(双侧)供电方式比较经济，也可较好地满足供电可靠性要求；环形(双侧)双回路供电方式的电源来自电力系统的两个地区变电所，供电可靠性更为突出；单电源（单侧）双回供电方式的可靠性较低，当其不负担其他用户时，常称其为铁路专用线；放射供电方式要求几个牵引变电所距离电源较近，此方式的优势在于比单边供电方式更为经济[15]。上述四种供电方式的示意图如图 1-26～图 1-29 所示。

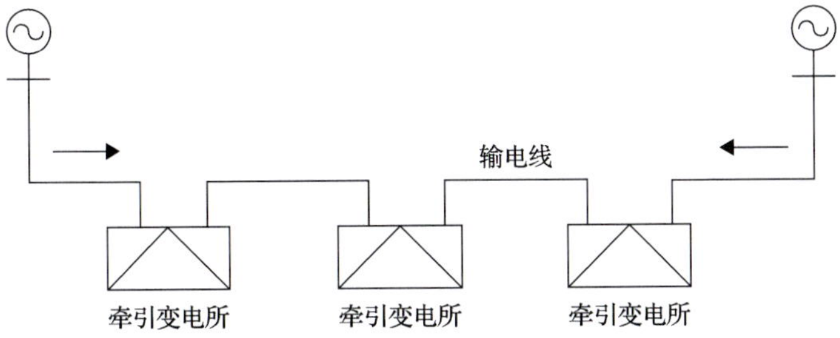

图 1-26　外部电源的环形（双侧）单回路供电方式

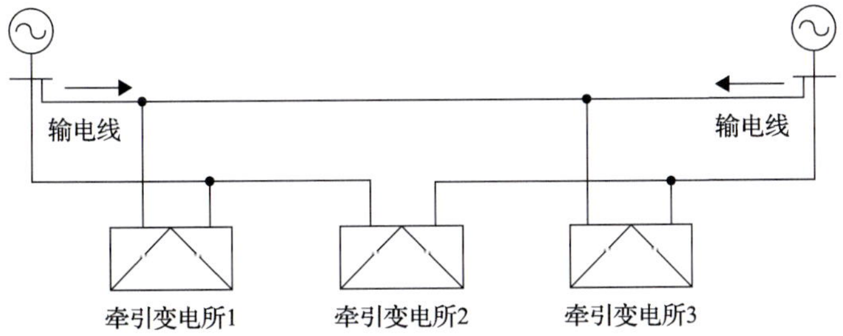

图 1-27　外部电源的环形（双侧）双回路供电方式

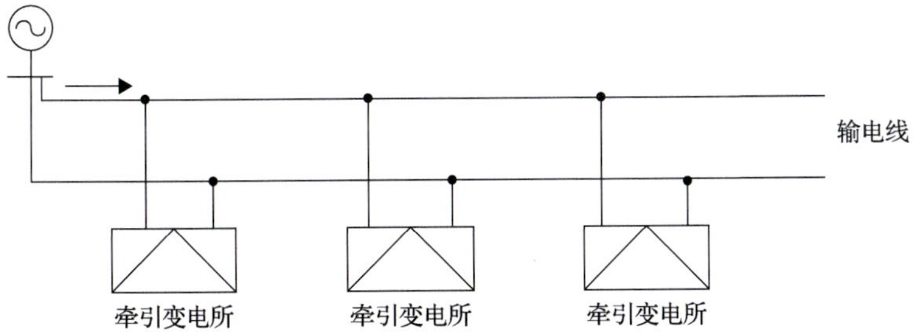

图 1-28　外部电源的单电源（单侧）双回路供电方式

对于牵引网的供电方式，按照分区所的运行状态，可以分为单边供电和双边供电；按牵引网设备类型，可分为直接供电、BT 供电、AT 供电和 CC 供电方式。

单边供电不进行越区供电时，可以大大简化分区所设备，甚至取消分区所，双边供电必须设置分区所。由于我国电网的管理现状，我国电气化铁路没有采用双边供电模式。

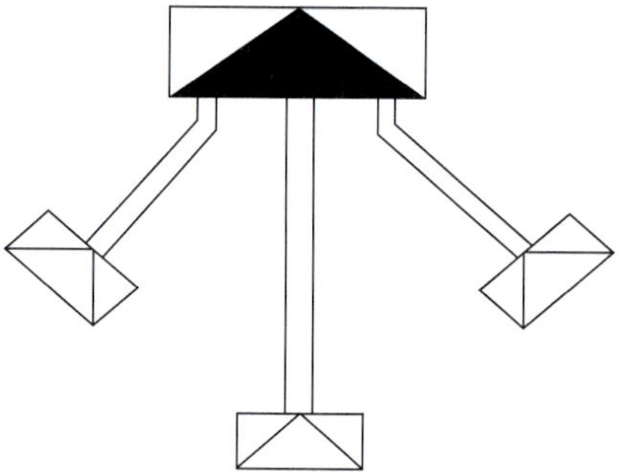

图 1-29　外部电源的放射供电方式

直接供电方式的结构最为简单，投资最小，但钢轨电位较高，对通信线的感应干扰最大，主要适用于通信线路较少的场合；BT 供电方式可减少通信干扰，但供电臂长度减小为直接供电的 3/4，并且存在 BT 分段，不利于高速、重载等大电流运行；AT 供电方式不仅克服了 BT 分段的缺陷，还使供电电压成倍提高，牵引网阻抗小，供电距离长，为直接供电形式的 1.7～2 倍，适于高速、重载等大电流运行；CC 供电方式较为新颖，其优势为对通信线路几乎无干扰，接触网结构较为简单，对净空要求低，宜于高速、重载等大电流运行，但同时其造价太高，限制了其应用[16]。各牵引网的供电方式示意图如图 1-30～图 1-35 所示。

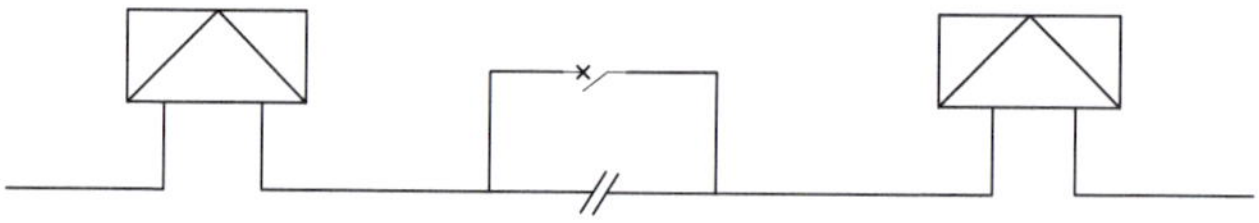

图 1-30　牵引网的单线区段的单边供电

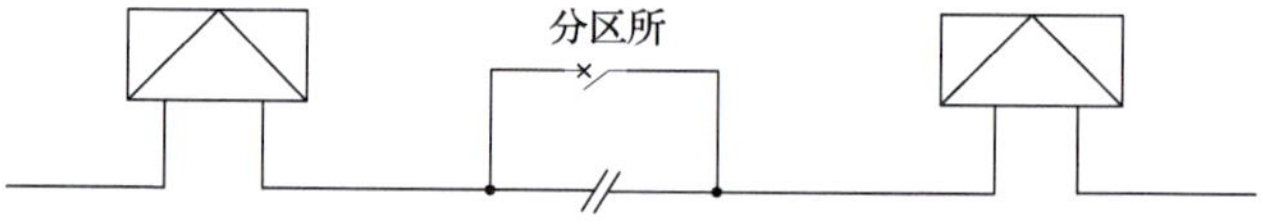

图 1-31　牵引网的单线区段的双边供电

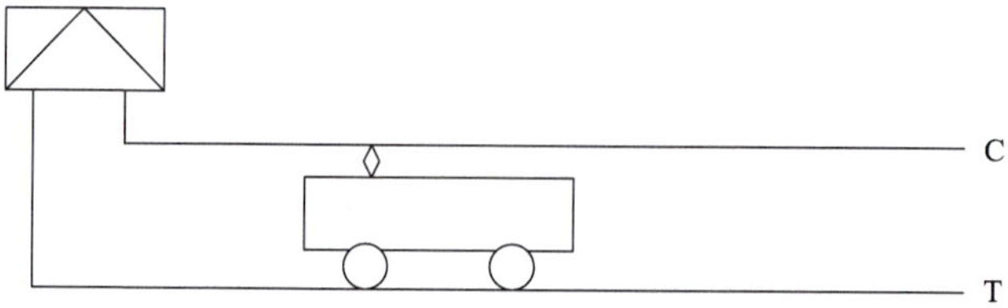

图 1-32　牵引网的直接供电方式

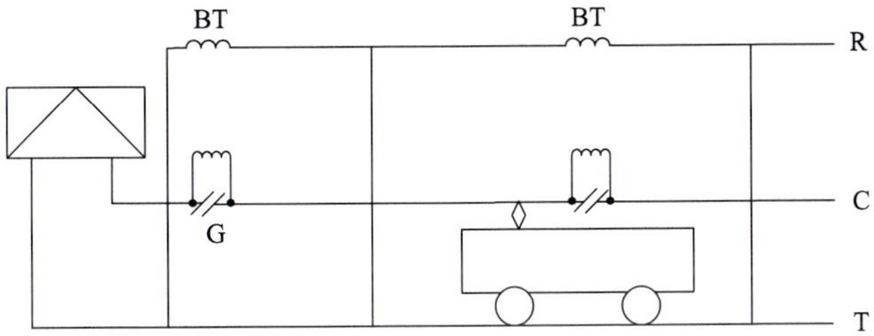

图 1-33　牵引网的 BT 供电方式

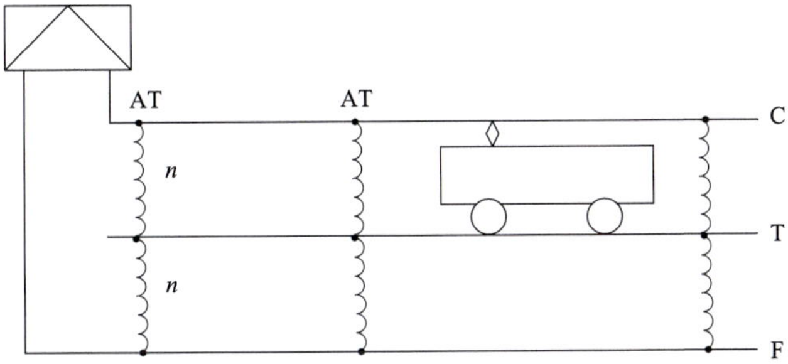

图 1-34　牵引网的 AT 供电方式

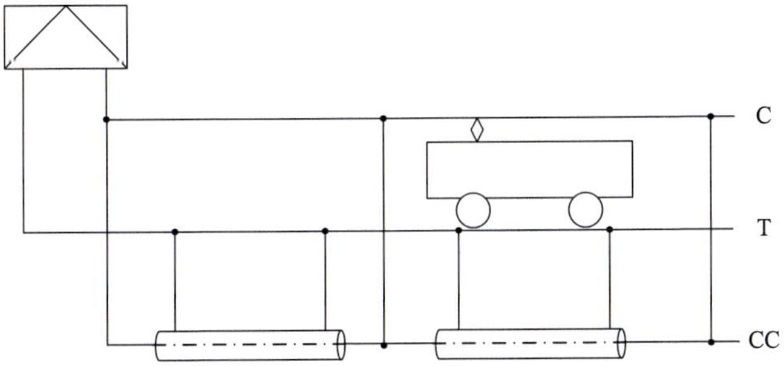

图 1-35　牵引网的 CC 供电方式

2) 电气化铁路列车用能模式

我国电气化铁路包括传统的电力机车和动车组列车。

(1) 传统电力机车的用能模式。

当前我国的传统电力机车主要为“和谐”系列机车，型号有 HXD1、HXD1B、HXD2、HXD3 等，其主变流器形式大体相似。

“和谐”型电力机车的技术参数见表 1-7。从表 1-7 中可以看出，“和谐”型电力机车都采用二电平 PWM 整流器+VVVF 逆变器形式。各型机车最大的不同点在于中间直流环节上的差异。HXD1、HXD1B 和 HXD1C 采用中间直流环节并联，共用中间直流环节和二次谐振电路；HXD2、HXD3 型变流器主电路中间直流环节完全独立，HXD3 则取消了二次谐振电路，通过控制策略来消除二次纹波电压的影响，相对于其他车型的主电路则显得更加整洁。

表 1-7 "和谐"型电力机车技术参数

项目	公司及机车型号				
	西门子		东芝	阿尔斯通	时代电气
	HXD1	HXD1B	HXD3	HXD2	HXD1C
用户	中国	中国	中国	中国	中国
机车功率/kW	2×4800	9600	7200	2×5000	7200
单轴功率/kW	1200	1600	1200	1250	1200
主变流器中间直流环节电压/V	DC1800	DC3600	DC2800	DC1800	DC1800
开关器件	IGBT 3.3kV	IGBT 6.5kV	IGBT 4.5kV	IGBT 3.3kV	IGBT 3.3kV
二次滤波环节	有	有	无	有	有
主辅一体化	是	是	否	是	否
中间直流环节	两重四象限共用中间直流环节	两重四象限共用中间直流环节	中间直流环节完全独立	中间直流环节完全独立	三重四象限共用中间直流环节
控制方式	架控	轴控	轴控	轴控	轴控

HXD1 是由 2 节完全相同的 4 轴电力机车通过固定重连方式构成的 8 轴重载货运电力机车，机车功率为 2×4800kW。其主变流器主电路如图 1-36 所示，通过 2 个四象限并联向中间直流环节供电，1 个 VVVF 逆变器向 1 个转向架的 2 台异步电机供电(架控)。辅助逆变器集成在主变流器中，与主变流器共用中间直流环节。每个辅助逆变器通过一台变压器和滤波电容对输出电压进行变压和滤波后，提供正弦三相交流电源[17,18]。

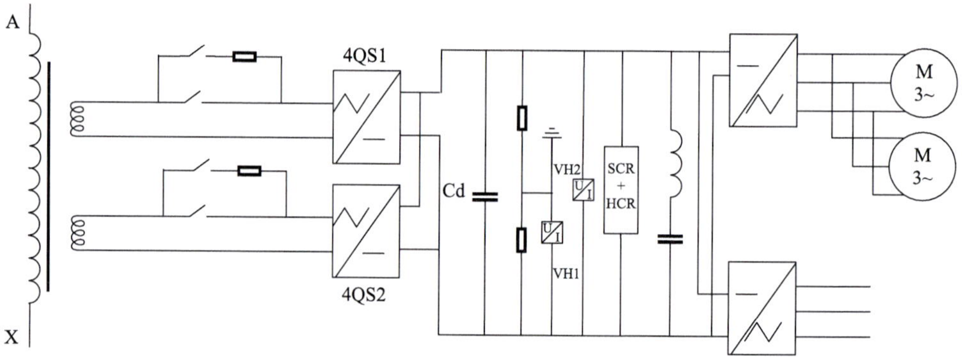

图 1-36 HXD1 型电力机车主变流器主电路图

HXD1B 型电力机车轴式为 C_0-C_0，单轴功率为 1600kW。主变流器主电路如

图 1-37 所示，通过 2 个四象限并联向中间直流环节供电，3 个 VVVF 逆变器向 1 个转向架的 3 台异步电机供电(轴控)。当任意一个主电路单元出现故障时，可以通过电动隔离开关将其隔离，从而将故障造成的影响降到最低。辅助逆变器与主变流器共用中间直流环节，每个辅助逆变器通过 1 台变压器和滤波电容对输出电压进行变压和滤波后，提供正弦三相交流电源。

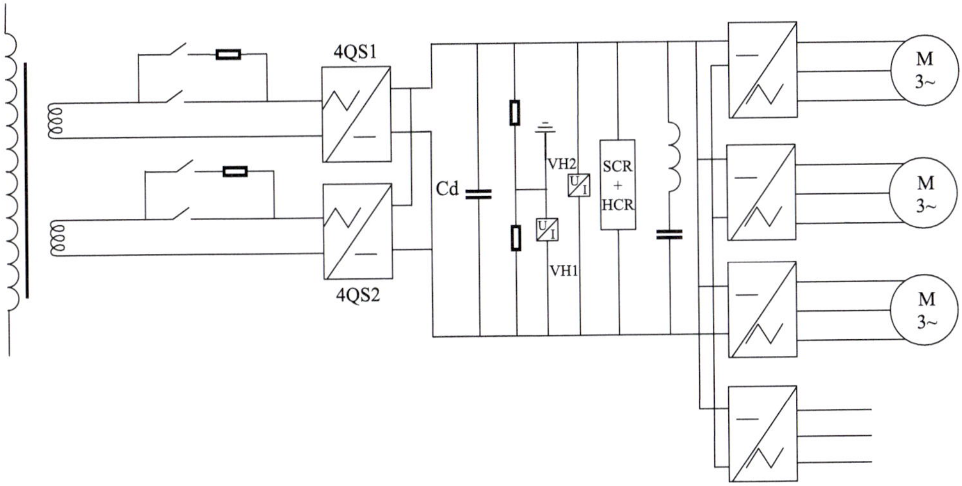

图 1-37 HXD1B 型电力机车主变流器主电路图

HXD2 型电力机车为 8 轴大功率交流传动货运机车，机车功率为 10000kW。主变流器主电路如图 1-38 所示，每节机车配置 4 套功能和结构完全相同的变流器装置，分别放置在 2 台主变流器柜内。每套装置由 1 个四象限整流器、中间直流

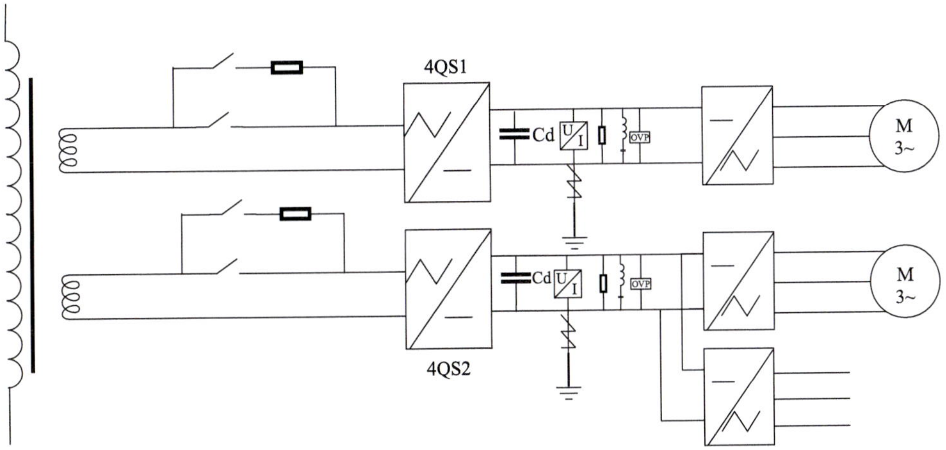

图 1-38 HXD2 型电力机车主变流器主电路图

环节和 1 个三相 VVVF 逆变器组成，驱动 1 台异步电机(轴控)。辅助变流器从主变流器的第 2 轴(或第 4 轴)中间直流环节取电，单节机车有 2 组辅助变流器装置(冗余设计)，一组为变压变频输出，另一组为恒压恒频输出。当其中任意一组故障时，另一组为所有的辅助负载提供电源，确保不影响机车的正常运行。

HXD3 型机车是 6 轴大功率交流传动电力机车系列化产品，机车功率是 7200kW。主变流器主电路如图 1-39 所示，机车配置 6 套功能和结构完全相同的主变流器装置，分别放置在 2 台主变流器柜内，每组电路由 1 个二点式 VVVF 逆变器组成，使用 6 台 1200kW 交流牵引电动机。

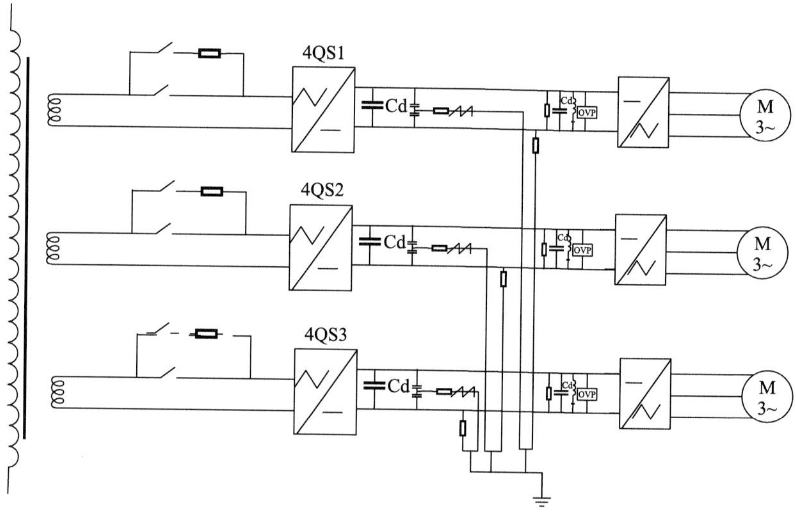

图 1-39　HXD3 型电力机车主变流器主电路图

HXD1C 型电力机车为大功率交流传动 6 轴货运电力机车，机车功率为 7200kW。主变流器主电路图如图 1-40 所示，每台机车配置 2 个主变流器，每个主变流器向 1 个转向架的 3 台牵引电机供电。每个主变流器通过三重四象限变流器向 1 个独立的中间直流环节供电。3 个 VVVF 逆变器向每个转向架的 3 台异步电机供电。3 个主电路单元的直流环节通过隔离开关并在一起，正常工作时隔离开关闭合。3 个单元共用直流环节和二次谐振电路，当其中任意一个主电路单元发生故障时，断开相应的隔离开关，将该故障单元切除，其余 2 个单元正常工作，整台机车只损失 1/6 的动力，从而将故障造成的影响降至最低。

(2)动车组列车的用能模式。

我国现行的动车组列车主要有 CRH1、CRH2、CRH380 等型号，同样采用交—直—交的能量转换形式，主变流器结构与传统电力机车十分相似，区别在于辅助供电模块分布于每节动力车厢当中。

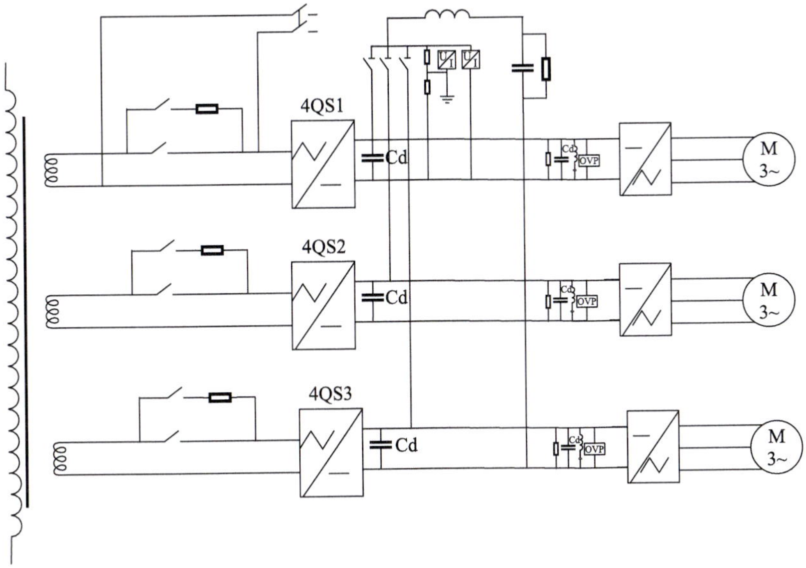

图 1-40　HXD1C 型电力机车主变流器主电路图

CRH1 型动车组牵引变流器主电路沿用庞巴迪的设计方案，主电路如图 1-41 所示，其特点如下。

①采用成熟的两电平结构；采用二重四象限+二重逆变器的结构，单个逆变器

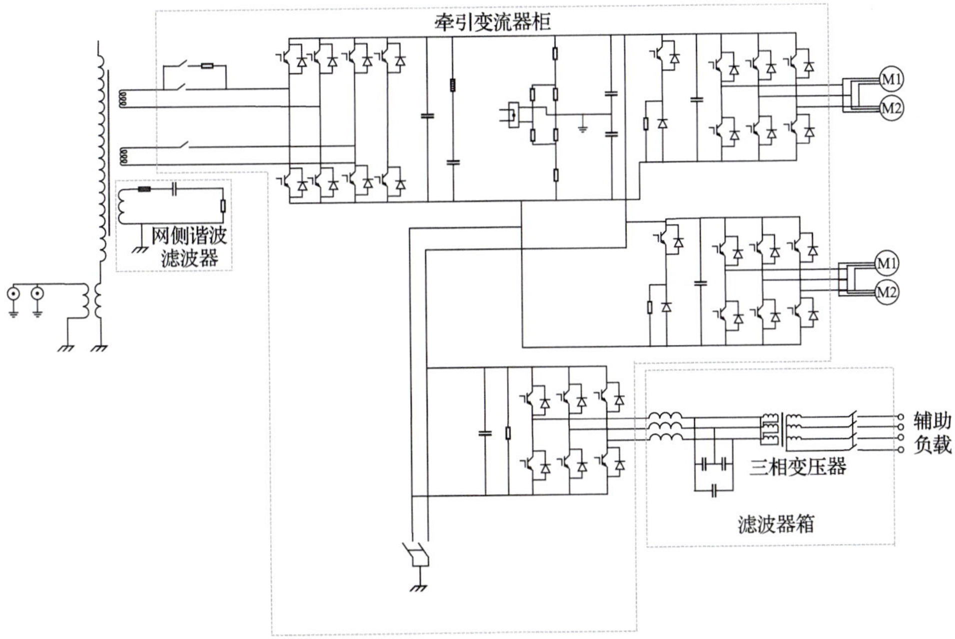

图 1-41　CRH1 型动车组主变流器电路图

模块驱动一个转向架上的 2 台牵引电机。

②中间直流回路设置二次谐振回路(滤除中间直流回路的 100Hz 谐波)、固定放电回路和快速放电回路，充电回路采用单重充电接触器+充电电阻的方案。

③主电路结构既可实现车控也可实现架控。

④接地检测电路由两个串联电阻和多点电流检测装置组成，两个电阻的中点构成一个电气中点，当该点与中点地之间的电压达到一定值时则表明发生接地故障，故障通过节电器出点送给传动控制单元。

⑤主电路采用主辅一体化设计，且在结构上将辅助逆变器模块集成在牵引变流器里面，与四象限脉冲整流器模块、牵引逆变器模块集中布置，共用中间直流汇流，共用水冷系统；中间直流回路采用低感母排把各模块连接在一起。

⑥辅助逆变器直接从牵引变流器的中间直流回路取电，逆变输出通过 *LC* 滤波器滤波以及三相变压器降压后输出稳定的三相 AC400V，给动车组上所有辅助负载供电；采用主辅一体化设计，不仅提高了牵引变流器的集成度，还可实现动车组在过分相区时，牵引逆变器采用轻微制动技术时中间直流电压能够继续维持，以确保辅助系统不断电继续工作，从而提高动车组的舒适度，辅助逆变器输出的 *LC* 滤波器、降压变压器以及接触器单独安装在滤波器箱里。

⑦牵引变压器单独设置一个滤波器绕组，与 *RC* 滤波箱(1 个熔断器、1 个电阻和 1 个电容)组成网侧谐波滤波器，用于滤除网侧电流中的谐波成分，同时减小断路器工作时产生的瞬变电压和电磁干扰。图 1-41 为 CRH1 型动车组主变流器电路图。

CRH2 型动车组和 CRH380 型动车组牵引变流器主电路一样，沿用三菱电机的设计方案，牵引变流器主电路采用两开关功率器件串联与中点带钳位二极管的三电平方案，主电路图如图 1-42 所示，其特点如下所示。

①牵引和辅助完全独立，过分相时不能实现发电功能，辅助系统需断电，影响整车舒适度。

②由于采用三电平结构，二次谐波分量较小，中间直流回路取消二次谐振回路，减轻牵引变流器的质量和成本，但须增大中间直流回路的支撑电容值。

③采用升压变压器和单相全波整流桥的方式作为充电回路，经济性高，但需增加整流桥、变压器等部件。

④采用单重四象限结构，网侧谐波性能较差。

⑤牵引逆变器部分采用相模块(U、V、W 三个相模块)结构，只能采用车控的模式。

⑥接地检测通过电流传感器检测接地电流来判断是否发生接地故障。

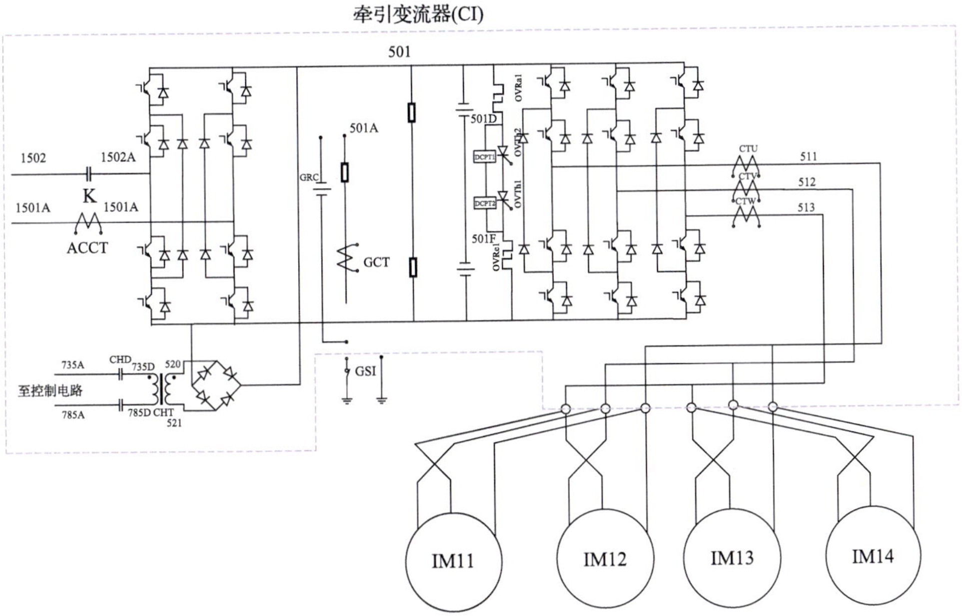

图 1-42　CRH2/CRH380 型动车组主变流器主电路图

CRH3 型动车组和 CRH380B 型动车组牵引变流器主电路一样，沿用西门子的设计方案，主电路图如图 1-43 所示，其主要特点如下所示。

①牵引变流器主电路采用成熟的两电平结构，中间直流回路设置二次谐振回路(滤除中间直流回路的 100Hz 谐波)、固定放电回路和快速放回路。

②牵引变流器主电路采用二重四象限的结构，网侧谐波性能较好。

③四象限和逆变器都采用相模块结构，只能采用车控模式。

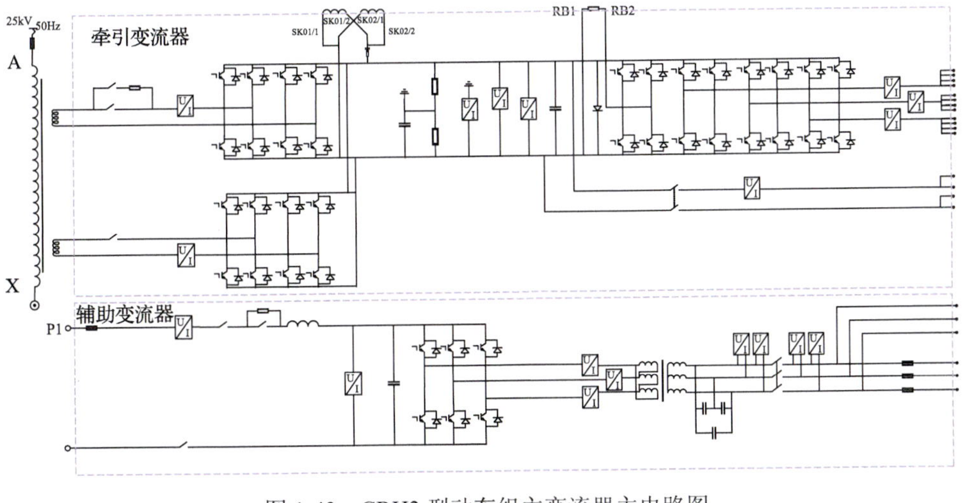

图 1-43　CRH3 型动车组主变流器主电路图

④主电路采用主辅一体化设计，辅助逆变器直接从牵引变流器的中间直流回路取电，可实现过分相区辅助系统不断电功能，舒适度好。

⑤结构采用主辅分离的方式，即牵引变流器和辅助变流器为两个柜体，安装在不同的车上，辅助逆变器模块与中间直流回路通过电缆连接，增设隔离接触器进行辅助逆变器的故障隔离，同时还增设直流电抗器用于抑制辅助变流器的支撑电容器与牵引变流器支撑电容之间的环流。

⑥牵引变流器中四象限脉冲整流器模块和牵引逆变器模块采用强迫水循环冷却，辅助变流器中的辅助逆变器模块采用强迫风冷。

⑦中间直流回路设置了撬棒回路，用于牵引变流器停止运行后的快速放电，提高安全性。

⑧充电回路采用单重充电接触器+充电电阻的方案，简单可靠。

⑨接地检测通过电压传感器检测 1/4 中间直流电压来进行判断是否发生接地故障。

CRH5 型动车组牵引变流器主电路沿用阿尔斯通的设计方案，主电路图如图 1-44 所示，其主要特点如下所示。

①牵引变流器主电路采用成熟的两电平结构，中间直流回路取消二次谐振回路，减轻牵引变流器的重量和成本，但须增大中间直流回路的支撑电容值。

②牵引变流器主电路采用二重四象限的结构，网侧谐波性能较好。

③主电路采用主辅一体化设计，辅助逆变器直接从牵引变流器的中间直流回路取电，可实现过分相区辅助系统不断电功能，舒适度好。

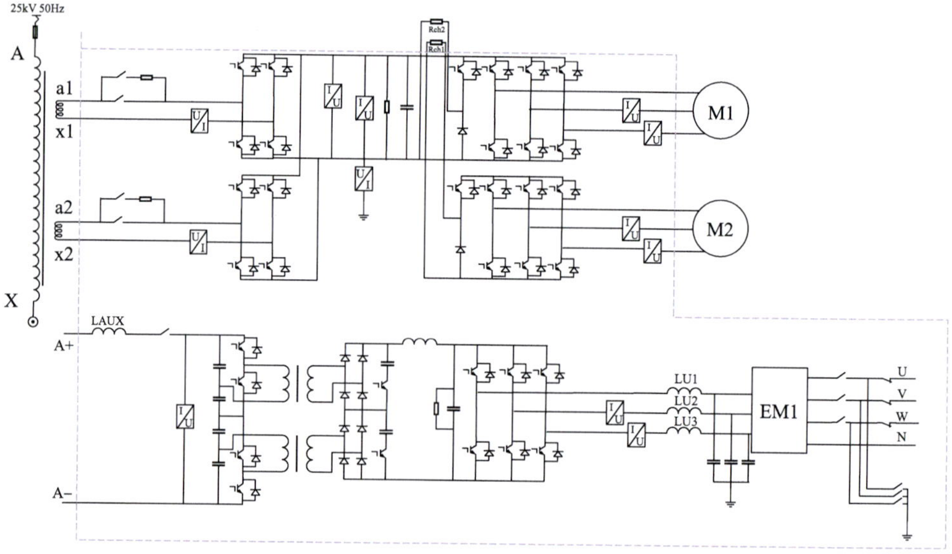

图 1-44　CRH5 型动车组主变流器主电路图

④辅助逆变器模块与四象限脉冲整流器模块、牵引逆变器模块分开布置，辅助逆变器模块与中间直流回路通过电缆和铜排连接，增设隔离接触器进行辅助逆变器的故障隔离，同时还增设直流电抗器用于抑制辅助变流器的支撑电容器与牵引变流器支撑电容之间的环流。

⑤辅助逆变器部分采用半桥逆变串联、高频隔离和不控整流串联的方案，高频辅助逆变器的体积小，质量轻，但增加了很多开关器件，对控制水平、可靠性要求比较高。

⑥充电回路采用二重充电接触器和充电电阻的方案，简单可靠，同时提高了系统的冗余度。

3) 非电气化铁路的用能模式

内燃机车与上述两种列车的主要区别在于，上述两种机车的一次侧能源均为电能，而内燃机车的一次侧能源为燃油。二次侧能源则均为电能，同样通过交—直—交的能量转换形式供列车使用。内燃机车的用能方式如下所示[19,20]。

(1) 供电参数。供电电压：DC600(1±0.05)V。供电功率：400kW。供电电压纹波系数：小于5%。

(2) 工作原理。内燃动车主发电机与供电(辅)发电机制成一体，主发电机与供电发电机同轴串联布置。主发电机输出整流后电力供给牵引电动机，供电发电机输出整流后电力供拖(客)车用电。

供电主电路主要由一台供电发电机和给其励磁的感应子发电机、整流装置、恒压励磁调节器、用于接通或切断向拖(客)车供电的供电接触器、供电连接器和一些保护电路组成。内燃动车供电主电路原理图见图1-45。

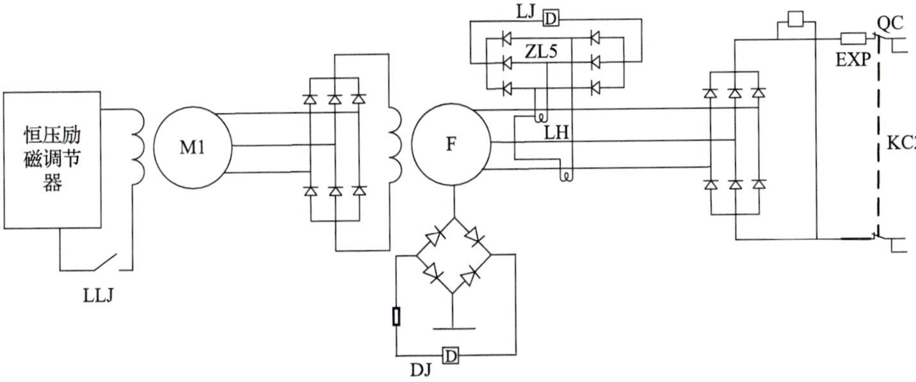

图1-45　内燃动车供电主电路原理图

如图1-45所示，恒压励磁调节器取整流输出电压作为反馈信号，调节与供电发电机配套的感应子励磁机的励磁，控制供电发电机恒压输出；通过直流侧电流(EXP)、电压(SCM)互感器检测信号实现输出过流、过压保护功能。供电发电机输出侧电流互感器 LH、整流装置 ZL5 和过流继电器 LJ 组成过流保护装置。主电路的接地采用传统的无源保护电路，接地继电器通过整流电路与供电发电机中性点相接。

4)非电气化铁路的客车用能模式

传统客车的电能由牵引车或发电车集中供给，客车本身没有发电装置，且不与牵引网接触。客车用电的电压等级主要有 DC600V、AC380V、AC220V 等。此外，客车还装设有储能设施，用于紧急情况下的临时供电。

客车供电装置由车端连接器、列车供电干线、配电柜、变流器、蓄电池组、充电器、空调控制柜、照明控制柜等部件组成。

机(动)车提供的 2 路 DC600V 电源通过车端连接器引入配电柜，配电柜将其中一路输入变流器及充电器。变流器将 DC600V 变换成三相 380V、50Hz 交流电，通过配电柜向电开水炉、温水箱、废排风机等用电负载供电，并通过空调控制柜向空调机组供电。

充电器将 600V 直流电变换成 110V 直流电，向蓄电池充电的同时通过照明控制柜向车内照明及供电装置控制系统等负载供电。每辆车设蓄电池组，蓄电池组与 110V 干线间采用二极管隔离。车内采用日光灯照明，照明变换器将 110V 直流电变换成 220V 交流电。

空调控制柜、变流器、充电器的控制电源均受配电柜控制。配电柜控制电源受机(动)车控制。

1.2.2 铁路基础设施的用能模式

铁路基础设施的用能模式主要是铁路隧道的用电模式。

根据《铁路隧道照明设施与供电技术条件》(TB/T 2275—1991)，铁路隧道的供电模式如图 1-46 所示，即当隧道附近有可靠地方电源时，应优先采用地方电源进行供电；凡有电力贯通线路的隧道，在有供电能力和技术经济条件允许时，应有贯通线路供电；电气化区段在条件允许时，可再用电力牵引电源供电；隧道附近无电源可利用时，应设置发电机组。图 1-46 为我国铁路隧道电源选择流程图。

我国铁路隧道的供电方式为高压采用 10kV 三相三线制供电，低压采用三相四线制供电，照明用电电压为 220V，动力用电电压为 380V。其中，低压单相负荷宜均匀地分配在三相线路中，对连接组为 Yyn0 的三相变压器，中性线电流不

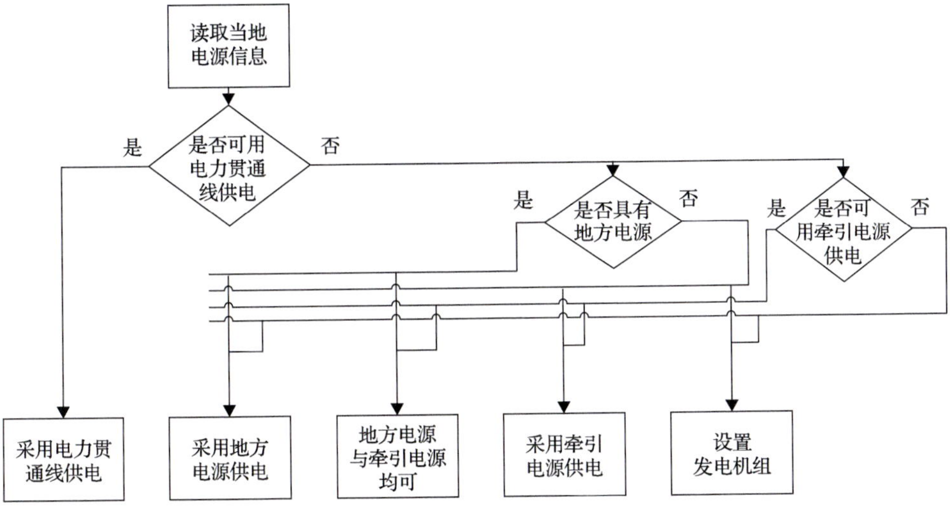

图 1-46　我国铁路隧道电源选择流程图

得大于低压绕组额定电流的 25%，且其任一相的电流在满载时不得大于额定电流值；低压供电半径不宜大于 1.5km，越区供电仅对固定照明供电，并考虑越区一个相邻供电臂供电的条件；一端供电或两端供电以及分段供电，应根据隧道长度、负荷容量、电源情况经比选后确定，参考方式见表 1-8。

对于铁路隧道的配线方式，单线隧道为一侧配线，双线隧道为两侧配线。配电干线与控制线应采用明配的方式。电缆和导线固定支架间的距离不应大于表 1-9 的规定。

表 1-8　我国铁路隧道变压器位置、容量及供电方式

隧道长度/m	变压器容量/(kV·A)		供电方式	
	洞口	洞内	单线隧道	双线隧道
50～1500	20	—	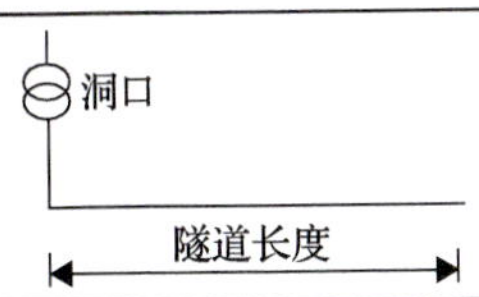	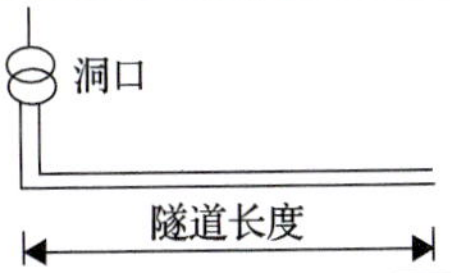
1501～3000	20	—	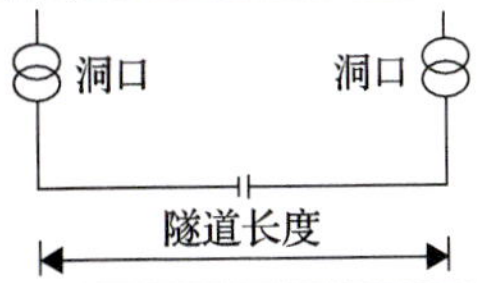	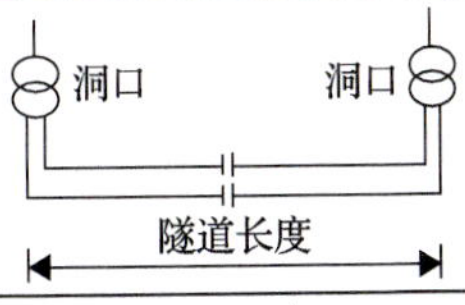
3001～4500	20	30	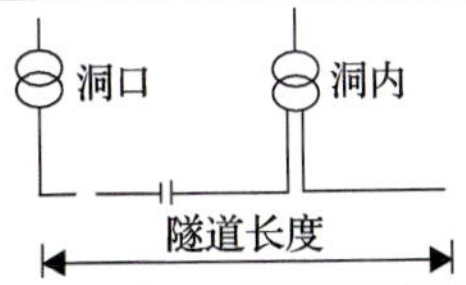	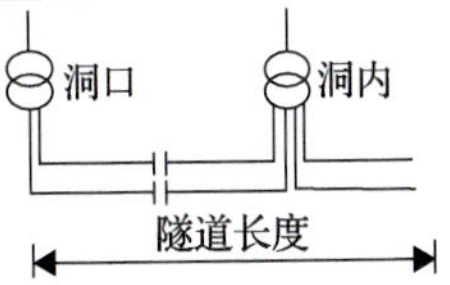

续表

隧道长度/m	变压器容量/(kV·A)		供电方式	
	洞口	洞内	单线隧道	双线隧道
4501～6000	20	30	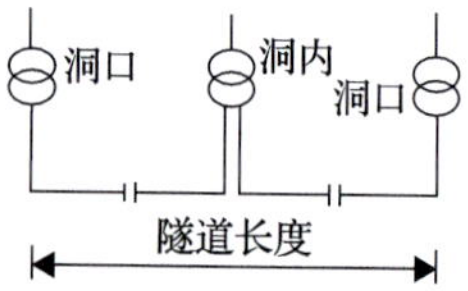	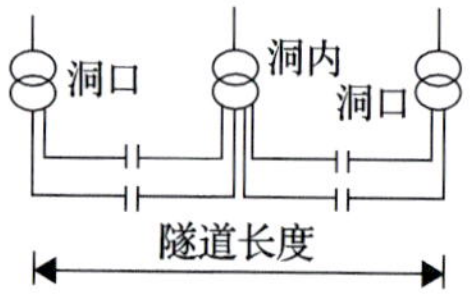

表 1-9　电缆和导线固定支架距离

种类	铺设方式	距离/m
绝缘导线	水平	6.0
	垂直	1.0
电力电缆	水平	1.0
	垂直	1.5
控制电缆	水平	0.8
	垂直	1.0

高、低压电缆及绝缘导线对导线、接触线、隧道壁的净距离，应符合表 1-10 规定。

表 1-10　配电干线与其他电线、隧道壁的最小净距

配电干线 其他电线	10kV 电力电缆/m	低压电力电缆/m	绝缘导线/m
隧道壁	0.10	0.05	0.05
10kV 电力电缆	0.15	0.30	0.30
低压电力电缆	0.30	0.10	0.10
绝缘导线	0.30	0.10	0.10
接触线	2.0	2.0	2.0

1.2.3　铁路服务设施的用能模式

铁路车站的用能模式，一般设置双电源 10kV 配电所为贯通线和站房 10kV/0.4kV 变电所供电，两路独立 10kV 电源接引地方电源。当车站无配电所时，可单独接引一路或两路 10kV 电源为站房供电。大型客站及站区，一般均设置双电源 10kV 配电所为贯通线和站房 10kV/0.4kV 变电所供电。两路独立 10kV 电源接引地方电源。特大型客站及站区，铁路用电负荷较大(如 10 万 m^2 站房

10kV/0.4kV 变压器安装容量约为 10000kV·A)，通常至少有两个及以上的大容量 10kV/0.4kV 站房变电所。对于特大型客站一般采用与牵引变电所合建动力变、铁路自建高等级变电站、铁路与地方合建高等级变电站和铁路就近接引经济可靠的 10kV 地方电源等方案[21]。

第 2 章　铁路能源需求的演化趋势

铁路未来发展趋势将会进一步地改变目前铁路系统的能源结构，最终完全形成电力和燃油(其中以耗电为主)的能源消费结构。可以预测，适应这一能源结构的节能降耗战略可以定位为“节油代油”技术，即机车推广节油技术和以电代油技术。在机车的使用和发展上，做到合理使用内燃机车，大力发展电力机车，逐步淘汰蒸汽机车。

2.1　铁路能源系统的演化趋势

2.1.1　铁路运输结构演化趋势

铁路运输是当今客货运活动的重要组成部分，目前主要国家关于铁路的规划如表 2-1 所示[22]。

表 2-1　主要国家关于铁路运输的规划

地区	描述
欧洲	①到 2030 年建成欧洲运输网络核心以及欧洲铁路交通管理系统 ②2010～2050 年，城际铁路年增长 1.4% ③2010～2050 年，高速铁路年增长 2.5% ④2010～2050 年，货运铁路年增长 1.2%
中国	①到 2020 年，全国铁路营业里程达 15 万 km，其中高速铁路 3 万 km ②到 2025 年，全国铁路营业里程达 17.5 万 km，其中高速铁路 3.8 万 km
俄罗斯	①2017～2025 年，铁路客运年增长 3.0% ②2017～2025 年，铁路货运年增长 4.5%
印度	2017～2025 年，铁路客货运年增长 7.0%

根据国际能源署的测算，到 2050 年，全球铁路网将达到 210 万轨道公里，较 2016 年增长 26%，其中高速铁路增长最快，规模将达到 11.3 万轨道公里，较 2016 年增长 65%。图 2-1 为预计到 2050 年世界各地区铁路规模分布情况。

由于世界各国的铁路电气化政策的实施，铁路的大部分能源需求以电力为主，消费量从 2017 年的近 300TW·h 将增加到 2050 年的近 700TW·h；而柴油在铁路中的消耗量增长较少，从 2017 年的 560 万桶/天增加至 580 万桶/天，仅增加 3.6%。据 IEA 估计，到 2050 年，我国铁路规模将达到约 20 万 km，占世界总里程的 9%

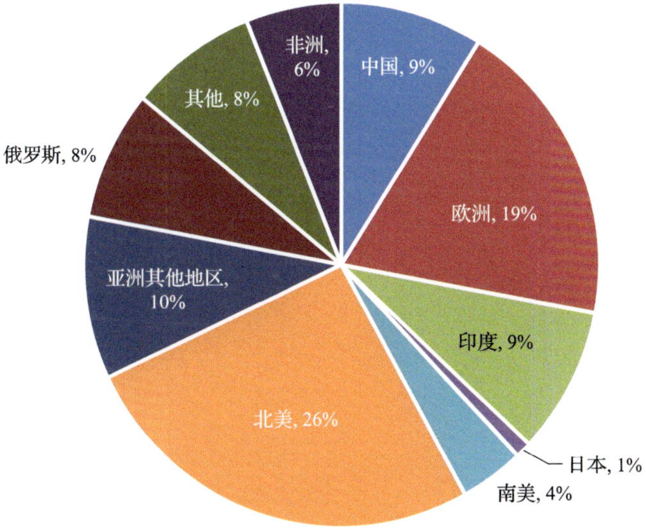

图 2-1　预计到 2050 年世界各地区铁路规模分布情况

数据来源：IEA2018

左右，其中，高速铁路规模将达到 5.1 万 km，占世界总里程的 56%，较 2018 年的 2.9 万 km 增长 76%。我国铁路运输规模增长也极为迅速。2013 年，我国的铁路营业里程为 10.3 万 km，2018 年达到 13.1 万 km，增长 2.10 倍，年均增长率为 9.1%；电气化铁路从 2013 年的 0.97 万 km 增长至 2018 年的 9.2 万 km，电气化率从 54.37%增长至 70.23%。到 2020 年，全国铁路网规模预计达到 15 万 km，其中高速铁路超过 3 万 km，覆盖 80%以上的大城市。可以说，我国的铁路建设正在以中国速度领跑全世界！图 2-2 为预计到 2050 年世界各地区高速铁路规模分布情况。

按照世界经济发展与人口增长预测，到 2050 年，我国交通客运量将达到 19.58 万亿人公里，相较于 2017 年增长 85.94%，占世界总客运规模的 18.7%。其中，我国铁路客运量将达到 3.98 万亿人公里，相较于 2017 年增长 113%，占全国总客运量的 20.3%[23]。

随着电气化进程的加快，铁路运输结构也在悄然发生着变化。如图 2-3 所示，2005 年，我国传统铁路的客运量为 6000 亿客运公里，占各类轨道交通客运量的 93.6%；随着近年来高速铁路的蓬勃建设，到 2016 年，高速铁路承担的客运量为 3700 亿客运公里，占比为 27.4%；传统铁路承担的客运量为 8600 亿客运公里，占比为 63.7%。据 IEA 的预计，到 2030 年，我国传统铁路的客运量将低于高铁的客运量，但是在目前，我国轨道交通的客运活动仍主要由传统铁路承担。因

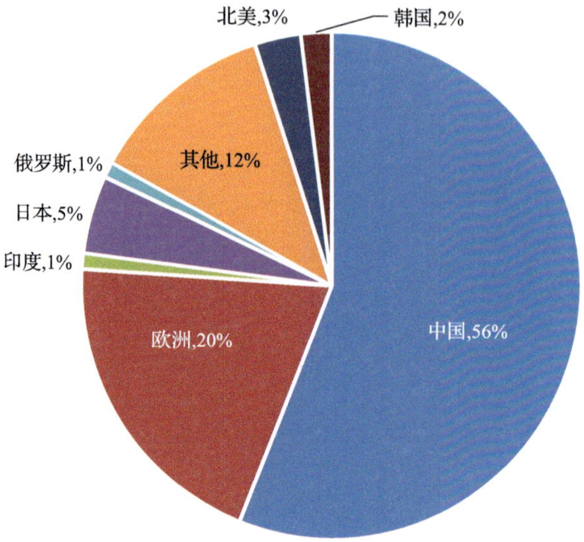

图 2-2　预计到 2050 年世界各地区高速铁路规模分布情况

数据来源：IEA2018

此，对于我国当前轨道交通的能源演化趋势分析，必须同时考虑传统铁路和高速铁路。图 2-3 为近年来我国各类轨道交通长度。图 2-4 为 IEA 对我国铁路客运量发展预测。

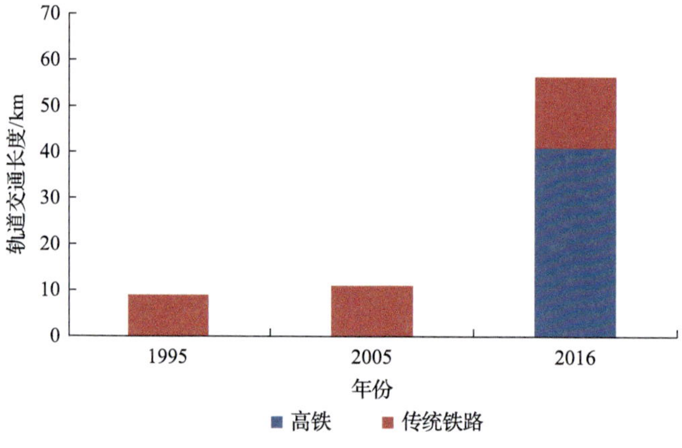

图 2-3　近年来我国各类轨道交通长度

数据来源：IEA2018A

2.1.2　铁路能源系统的演化趋势

作为交通运输的重要组成部分，我国铁路运输的能源消耗状况关系着我国能源消耗的格局。中国铁路运输 2000～2014 年年均消耗能源 1829.9 万 t 标准煤，远

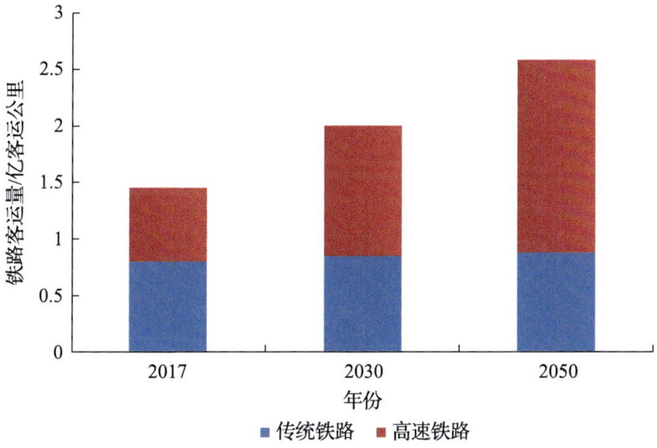

图 2-4　IEA 对我国铁路客运量发展预测

数据来源：IEA2018A

远超出同一时期英国、加拿大、日本等国，仅次于美国。中国铁路运输能源消耗由2000年的1859.5万t标准煤减少至2016年的1591.6万t标准煤，年均降低0.98%，在交通运输业能耗消耗总量的比重由2000年的18.75%降至2016年的3.95%，近年来一直处于下降态势。尽管中国铁路运输能耗消耗在国家交通运输能源消耗比重中一直降低，但依然高于美国、英国、加拿大、日本等国家。在交通运输业铁路能耗比重上，美国、加拿大、日本保持相对稳定，2000～2016年均值分别为2.26%，2.26%，3.41%，英国从2004～2008年处于下降过程，随后在1.7%～1.9%的比重范围内波动[24]。

各国的铁路能耗和比重间接反映了世界各国交通运输结构。在欧美国家和日本，道路交通运输和航空运输占据其运输业的绝大部分市场份额，铁路运输只占很少一部分，因而铁路运输能源消耗所占的能耗比重非常有限。以美国为例，由于其高度发达的公路网和航空网，居民出行和货物运输主要依靠公路和航空。虽然铁路在美国货运市场占据主导地位(以货物周转量计算，铁路占美国货运市场41%的市场份额，高于其他运输方式)，但由于铁路具有较强的社会公益性，在与公路、航空的激烈竞争中，城际客运铁路不具备竞争优势。以旅客周转量计算，10年来Amtrak城际客运铁路市场份额保持在0.1%，远远落后于其他运输方式(公路客运市场份额一直保持在87%左右，航空在10%左右，城市交通份额为1%左右)。同时，铁路能源消耗和比重的变化，也成为各国铁路发展的重要标志与象征。以中国为例，其铁路运输能源消耗总量及能耗比重处于连续下降态势，在下降数据的背后，则是中国高速铁路的快速发展和铁路电气化的巨大提升。根据国际能源署的预测，预计到2050年，我国的铁路将全部电气化，图2-5是我国近年来各种铁路类型的耗能预测，从图2-5中可以看出，在未来的30年里，铁路运输结构将逐步从目前的非电气化和电气化并存的格局向完全电气化转变，铁路的能耗来源将完全来自于电力。

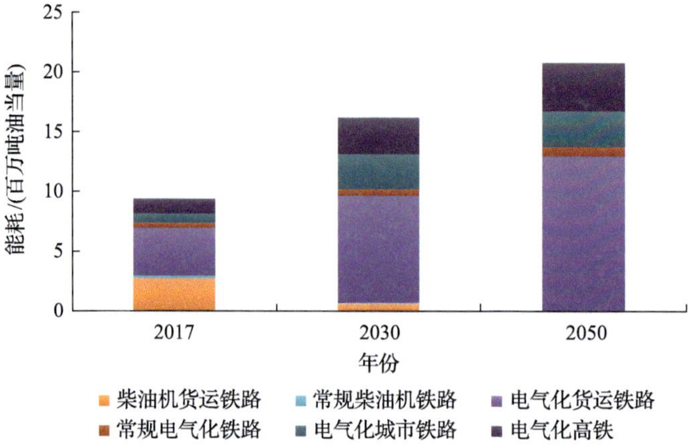

图2-5　中国铁路能耗预测

数据来源：IEA2018A

为了支持铁路运输结构逐渐从目前的非电气化和电气化并存的格局向完全电气化转变，铁路的能源系统必须做出积极的适应性变革。根据我国铁路中长期规划，我国铁路未来十五年能源系统的演化趋势[25]，如图2-6所示。

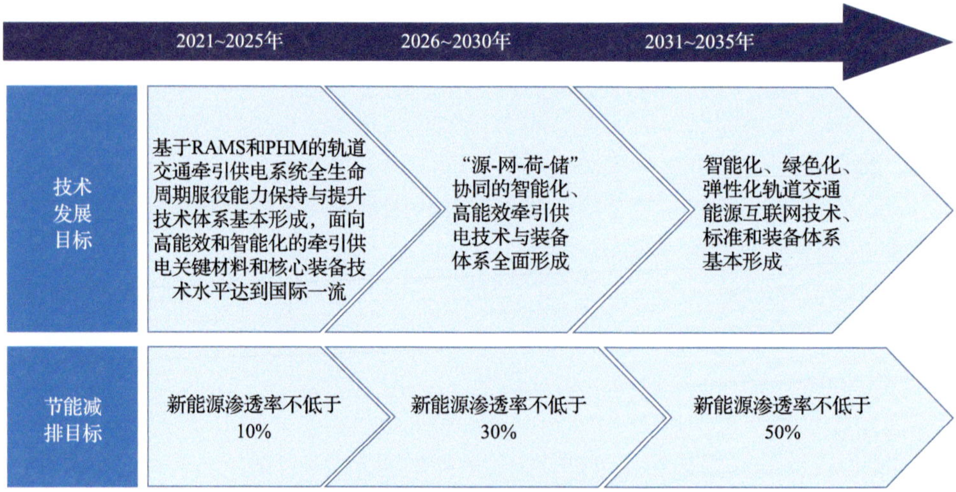

图2-6　我国铁路未来十五年能源系统的演化趋势

数据来源：《铁路科技创新中长期发展纲要(2021～2035年)》

1)2021～2025 年铁路能源系统演化趋势

到 2025 年，铁路网络覆盖进一步扩大，路网结构更加优化，骨干作用更加显著，能源系统综合损耗水平降低 10%，可再生能源利用率不低于 10%；具备适应国际主流标准的牵引供电系统研发、设计、制造、交付和运维支持的技术能力。

2)2026～2030 铁路能源系统演化趋势

到 2030 年，铁路系统基本实现内外互联互通、区际多路畅通、省会高铁连通、地市快速通达、县域基本覆盖，形成完善的广覆盖全国铁路网。“源-网-荷-储”协同的智能化、高能效牵引供电技术与装备体系全面形成，既有牵引供电系统的智能化升级关键技术得到普遍采用；非接触连续供电技术得到工程化应用；基于信息、材料和能源领域新兴颠覆性技术的新一代轨道交通能源供给技术在新线建设和既有线改造中得到规模化应用；能源系统综合损耗水平较 2025 年再降低 10%，可再生能源利用率不低于 30%；具备新型、超高速、多栖化导向运输系统能源供给技术和装备配套能力。

3)2031～2035 铁路能源系统演化趋势

到 2035 年，建成高标准“安全、便捷、高效、绿色、智能”的现代化轨道交通运输体系，进入轨道交通强国前列，基本形成智能化、绿色化、弹性化轨道交通能源互联网技术、标准和装备体系，载运装备的非接触供电技术、基于高比能量储能的非接触间歇供电技术取得系统性突破，可再生能源利用率不低于 50%，新型、超高速、多栖化导向运输系统能源供给技术和装备配套能力达到世界先进水平[26]。

2.2　铁路电能用能形态的发展模式

2.2.1　实现全生命周期的节能减排

WTW(well-to-wheel)碳排放指的是从矿井到车轮的全生命周期的碳排放，是生产、储存和运输燃料到油箱的碳排放(矿井到油箱，well-to-tank)，及燃料在燃烧过程中转化为用于车辆推进的动能(油箱到车轮，tank-to-wheel)的碳排放的总和。

当前，我国电力的一次侧能源主要来自于煤炭，如图 2-7 所示，煤炭占电力一次侧能源的 67%，水电占 18%，而其他可再生能源占比仅为 5.5%。当前铁路的 WTW 中电能的用能形态主要是煤炭—电力—机车。

在未来铁路电能利用形态的发展方向必将围绕全生命周期的节能减排开展研究和实施。

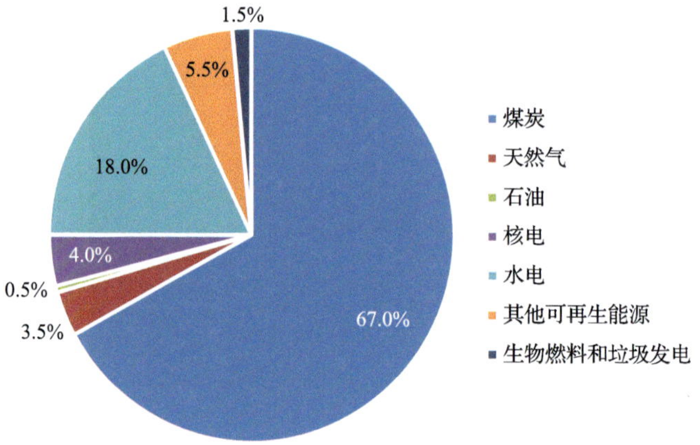

图 2-7　我国电力的一次侧能源占比

数据来源：IEA2018A

2.2.2　积极为可再生能源提供消纳场景和传输路径

为了推动能源转型和能源改革，习近平总书记提出了“四个革命、一个合作”的能源安全新战略，为推进我国能源清洁低碳转型发展指明了方向。同时，为了建设清洁低碳、安全高效的现代能源体系，促进人与自然和谐共生，全面建设节约型社会，我国正式向世界郑重承诺到 2030 年单位国内生产总值二氧化碳排放比 2005 年下降 60%～65%，非化石能源占一次能源消费比重达到 20%左右，节能减排责任重大。

为了实现这一目标，近年来，我国积极推动可再生能源发展，可再生能源并网装机和消纳总量均实现了高速增长。截至 2018 年底，我国太阳能发电装机容量为 180GW，太阳能发电量达到 89.45TW·h，如图 2-8 和图 2-9 所示，太阳能发电

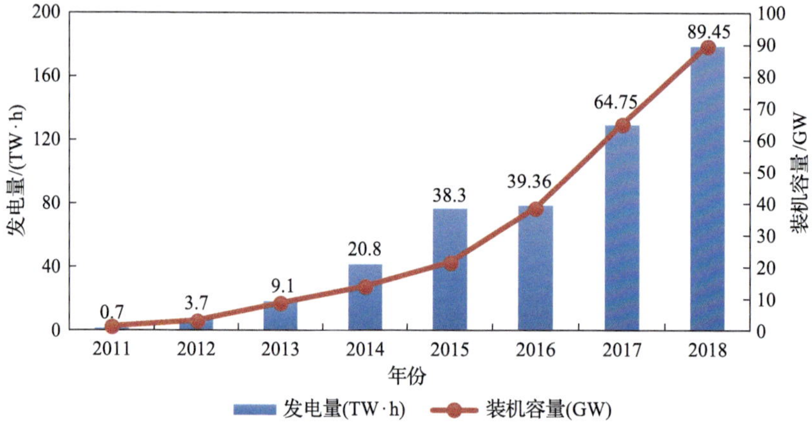

图 2-8　我国太阳能逐年装机容量

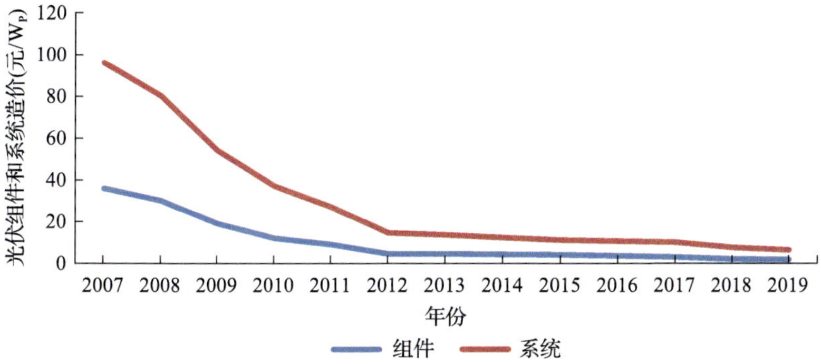

图 2-9　我国光伏组件和系统造价变化图

数据来源：中国光伏行业协会

量增速比同期全国发电量增速高出 28.7 个百分点，太阳能发电量占全部发电量的比例由 0.003%提高到 0.688%[27]。

从可再生能源装机容量来看，我国可再生能源发展取得了举世瞩目的成绩，装机总量已居世界第一，消纳总量也实现了快速增长。

随着光伏发电技术进步和市场规模的不断扩大，我国光伏发电的成本持续下降。“531 新政”之后，光伏行业关注的焦点就是“平价上网”的进程以及系统成本的下降。在过去的十年里，光伏组件、光伏系统的成本分别从 3 万元/kW 和 5 万元/kW 下降至目前的 1800 元/kW 和 4500 元/kW，均下降 90%以上，开展大规模光伏建设的机遇期已经到来。

图 2-10 比较了各种一侧能源产生电力的 WTW(矿井到车轮)碳强度。图 2-10 表明与其他一次侧动力列车相比，可再生能源供给的电动列车的碳密集程度明显

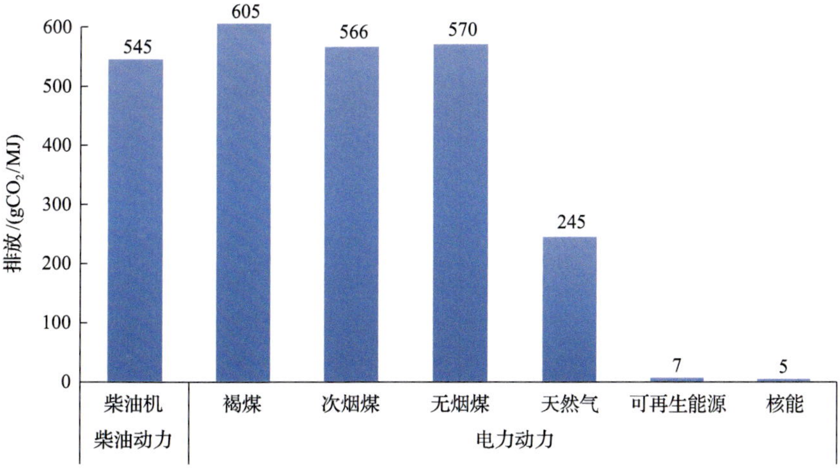

图 2-10　各种动力系统 WTW 碳排放比较

数据来源：IEA2018

低于其他一次侧能源供给的电动列车，可以有效地减少碳排放。

电气化的过程，从最常用的路线开始，并且逐渐转向越来越多地采用自动列车驾驶，越来越多地使用基于通信的列车控制。如今铁路已经是最具电气化的运输方式，虽然我国的电气化轨道份额仍在扩大，但由于电气化铁路的成本与架设电力线路的成本高昂，会导致铁路网络的电气化进程投资回报减少。因此，部分地区的铁路用电量增加可以通过其他技术来满足，如可再生能源微网的形式，不仅可以降低温室气体和当地污染物排放，而且是一种具有较高成本效益的手段。

随着国家大力倡导节能降耗理念，绿色、节能、环保的轨道客车将拥有广阔的市场。无接触网时可通过太阳能发电和储能电池、动力电池组吸收利用制动能量等实现节能、环保，与《国家中长期科学和技术发展规划纲要》中“高速轨道交通系统、低能耗与可再生能源汽车”优先主题的规划相吻合。还可实现在电气化线路故障时自救和救援其他车组。

到 2050 年，铁路能源使用量将增加 75%以上，铁路电力需求将增长 140%左右。由于城市轨道交通和高速铁路都在扩张并且完全是电气轨道，客运铁路运输对电力的依赖程度尤为强劲。如果没有电气化的铁路客运和货运活动，2050 年的石油需求将比当年的运输需求总量高出 16%。

与大多数其他运输方式相比，铁路的碳强度(每乘客或吨公里)要低得多，这意味着铁路部门已经在遏制全球温室气体排放方面发挥了关键作用。如果铁路目前满足的所有客运和货运需求均由飞机和公路车辆(汽车和卡车)提供服务，那么全球温室气体排放量将增加 1.2 亿 t 二氧化碳当量(比运输总排放量高 13%)。展望未来，越来越多的可再生能源注入可以使铁路从全生命周期(WTW)的角度为实现零排放的机动性做出重大贡献。

2.3 铁路非电能用能形态的发展模式

未来，我国铁路化石燃料用能需求将大幅降低，铁路能源需求增长的主要形式是电力。铁路的非电能用能形态主要指的是氢能。氢气长期以来一直被认为是一种潜在的交通燃料，它被视为提供了一种低碳的石油和天然气替代品，随着技术的更迭、成本的降低和系统性能的提升，氢燃料动力的电力机车将会具有竞争力。

2.3.1 铁路化石燃料能用能形态的发展模式

柴油占铁路能源使用量的 53%，大致相当于 60 万桶每天。铁路运输大部分柴油(85%)用于货运服务。中国以柴油形式占所有铁路能源使用的 35%～55%，1/4 的客运铁路运输活动由燃烧柴油的火车进行。在其他条件相同的情况下，电动列车比柴油列车能耗更低，因为电动机的热力学效率比内燃机高得多。电动机也可以更好地实现再生制动，最大限度地减少惯性损失(特别是在频繁停止的情况下)。因此，拥有大量电力列车的国家往往对类似规模的列车每列车公里的能源需求较低。图 2-11 为 2016 年世界主要国家列车能耗与列车大小、活动份额的关系。

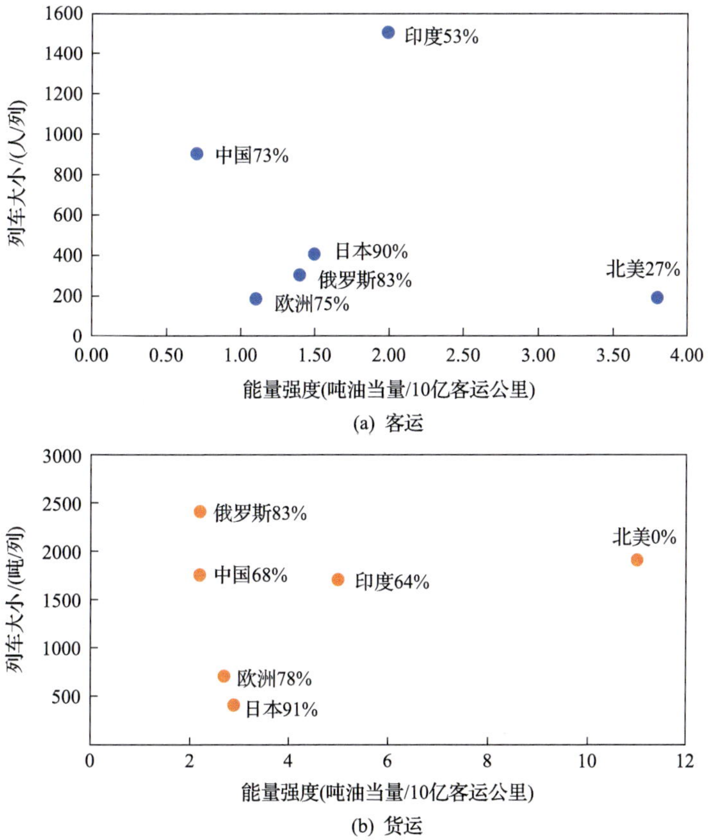

图 2-11　2016 年世界主要国家列车能耗与列车大小、活动份额的关系

数据来源：IEA2018A

另外，全球铁路客运和货运正逐渐转向运用电力供电方式，作为电气化的中间步骤，近几十年来，火车制造商已开始生产双模式柴油电动和电力机车(OLE)。这有助于改善没有电气化轨道的地区的区域常规客运铁路覆盖范围。除了双模式柴油-电动选项，因为大多数地区的电力供应继续脱碳，还有几种技术在非电气化轨道上提供零尾气排放，并且在未来几十年内将向零(WTW)排放发展。电池电动列车设计用于在 OLE 电动和全电池操作阶段之间切换。一些制造商还为货运轨道

引入了混合动力柴油-电池技术。

由图 2-12 可知，到 2017 年，柴油货运列车能源消耗依然占比较大，约占铁路能源消耗的一半。

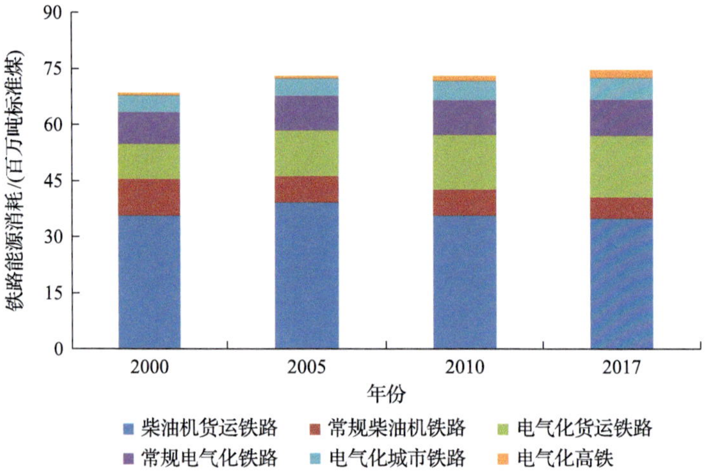

图 2-12　世界各类铁路的能耗对比

数据来源：IEA2018A

由图 2-13 可知，近年来我国铁路总能源不断在加，但化石燃料用能需求大幅降低，电力占铁路能源消耗的 67%，而柴油机占 33%。铁路运输中约 55%的电力用于客运服务，而大部分柴油(85%)用于货运服务。

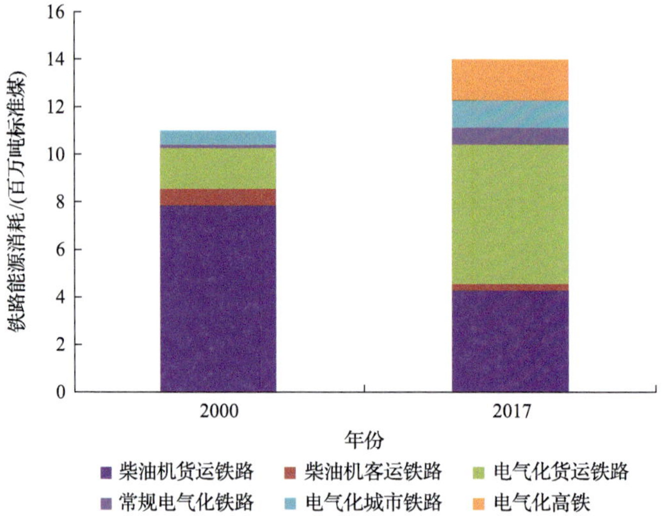

图 2-13　中国各类铁路的能耗对比

数据来源：IEA2018A

铁路货运的能源使用也显示出对火车装载能力的强依赖性。俄罗斯有最节能的铁路货运系统，这要归功于其较高的电力牵引份额和高装载力。美国的货物装载量最高，每公里每吨使用柴油（基本上是美国货运铁路使用的唯一燃料）的火车的能源效率最高。中国、巴西、印度和南非在具体能源使用和火车载重量方面具有类似的特点。

无论是传统铁路或是高铁都计划增加铁路电气化率，从图 2-14 可知，到 2050 年将有一半的货运列车的能源来源从柴油转换为电力。

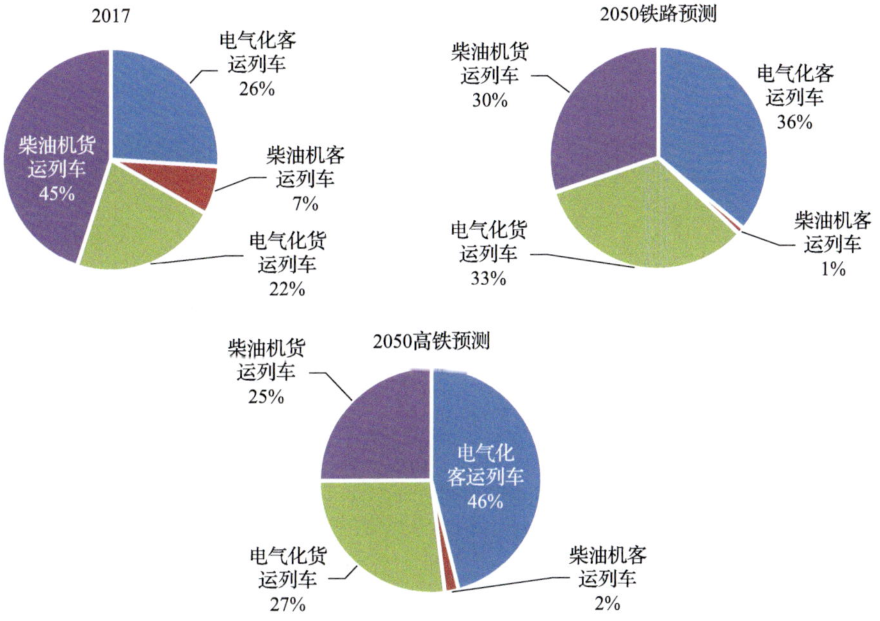

图 2-14　到 2050 年传统铁路及高铁能源消耗对比预测

数据来源：IEA2018A

从图 2-15 可知，我国铁路能源需求增长的主要形式是电力，电力消费预计从 2017 年的近 640 万 t 油当量增加到 2050 年的近 2080 万 t 标准煤。从图 2-15 也可知，预计到 2050 年，我国铁路将全面实现电气化。

2.3.2　铁路氢能用能形态的发展模式

经过多年的工业积累，中国已是世界上最大的制氢国，初步评估现有工业制氢产能为 2500 万 t/年，可为氢能及燃料电池产业化发展初期阶段提供低成本的氢源。富集的煤炭资源辅之以二氧化碳捕捉与封存技术（CCS）可提供稳定、大规模、低成本的氢源供给。同时，中国是全球第一大可再生能源发电国，每年仅风电、光伏、水电等可再生能源弃电约 100000GW·h，可用于电解水制氢约 200 万 t，未

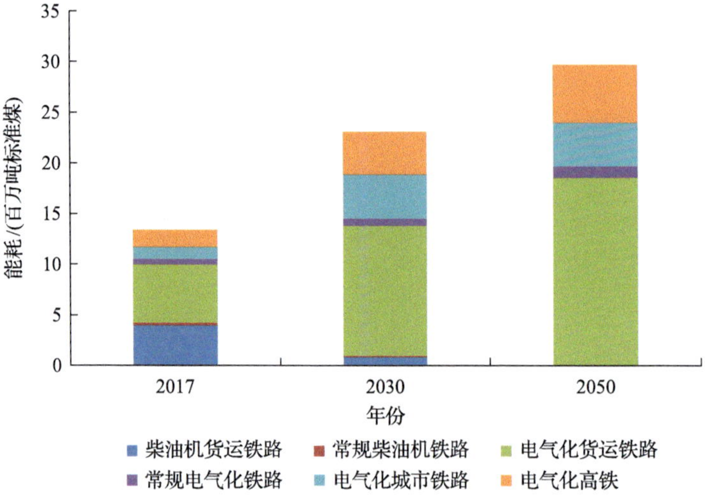

图 2-15 中国各铁路形式能耗预测

数据来源：IEA2018A

来随着可再生能源规模的不断壮大，可再生能源制氢有望成为中国氢源供给的主要来源。

交通领域将是氢能消费的重要突破口，实现从辅助能源到主力能源的过渡。在商用车领域，燃料电池商用车销量在 2030 年将达到 36 万辆，占商用车总销量的 7%(乐观情景将达到 72 万辆，占商用车总销量 13%)；到 2050 年销量有望达到 160 万辆，市场占比达到 37%(乐观情景将达到 300 万辆，占商用车总销量 70%以上)。在乘用车领域，2030 年燃料电池乘用车销量在全部乘用车销量中的比重有望达到 3%；到 2050 年交通领域氢能消费达到 2458 万 t/年，折合 1.2 亿 t 标准煤/年，占交通领域整体用能的 19%(乐观情景将达到 4178 万 t/年，占交通领域整体用能的 28%)。其中货运领域氢能消费占交通领域氢能消费的比重高达 70%，是交通领域氢能消费增长的主要驱动力。图 2-16 为 2016～2050 年交通领域能源消费结构。

铁路已经是最电气化的交通方式了，虽然在大多数国家，电气化铁轨的比例仍在扩大，但铁路网的进一步电气化很可能会使投资收益下降。除了双模式柴油电力的选择，一些其他的技术在非电气化轨道上也能提供零排气管排放，其中最具创新性的技术是电池电动列车和氢燃料电池列车。带有较小电池的电动火车也可以在部分电气化线路上使用，因为它忽略了轨道上最难电气化的部分(如桥梁或隧道)，使得电气化成本大幅降低。氢气长期以来一直被认为是一种潜在的交通燃料。它被视为提供了一种低碳的石油和天然气替代品，就像电力和先进生物燃料

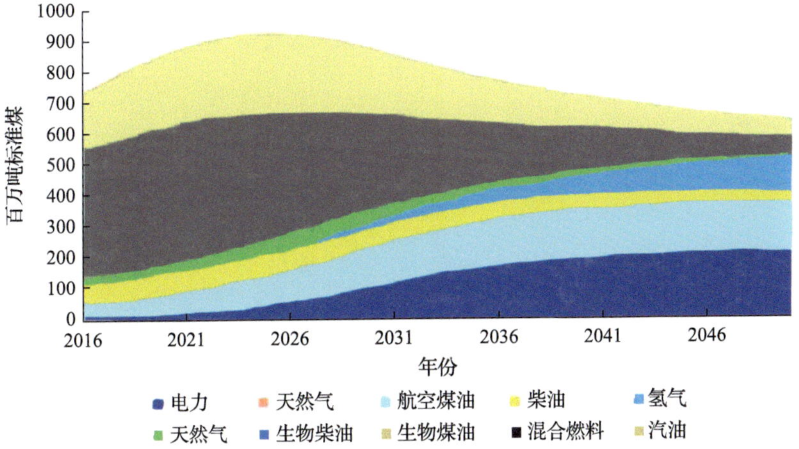

图 2-16　2016～2050 年交通领域能源消费结构

数据来源：《中国氢能源及燃料电池产业白皮书》

等其他替代品。像电池电动汽车（BEV）一样，氢燃料电池电动汽车（FCEV）没有尾气排放，将减少当地的空气污染。氢可以转化为氢基燃料，包括合成甲烷、甲醇和氨，以及合成液体燃料，这些燃料具有一系列潜在的运输用途。由电解氢生产的合成液体燃料通常被称为“液体能量”。

为了评估它们的经济可行性，国际能源署对这些创新技术与柴油机、柴油-电力混合动力车、纯电池驱动以及氢燃料驱动的客运与货运列车等进行了对比评估，如图 2-17 和图 2-18 所示。

电动列车较柴油-电动列车在成本上更有竞争力。与传统电池相比，电动火车在成本上已经具有竞争力。如果降低成本的前景乐观，氢动力列车也将具有竞争力。

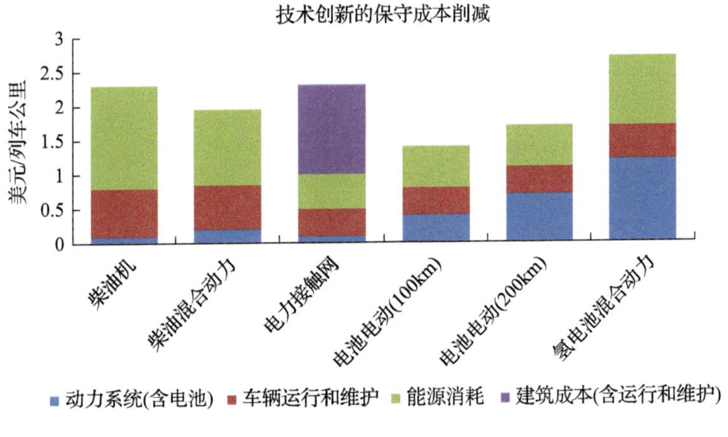

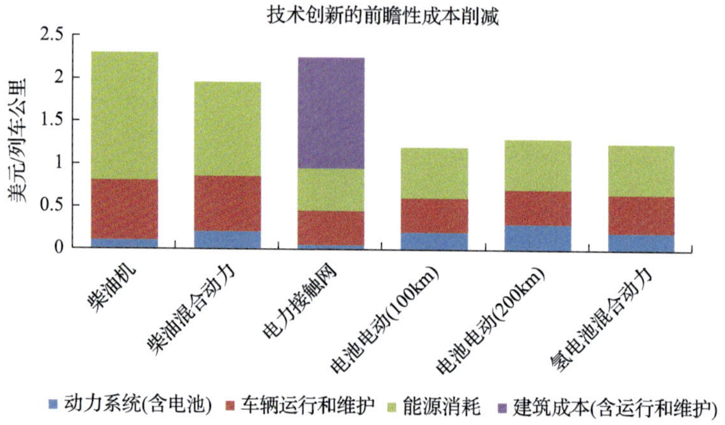

图 2-17　不同动力客运列车经济性对比

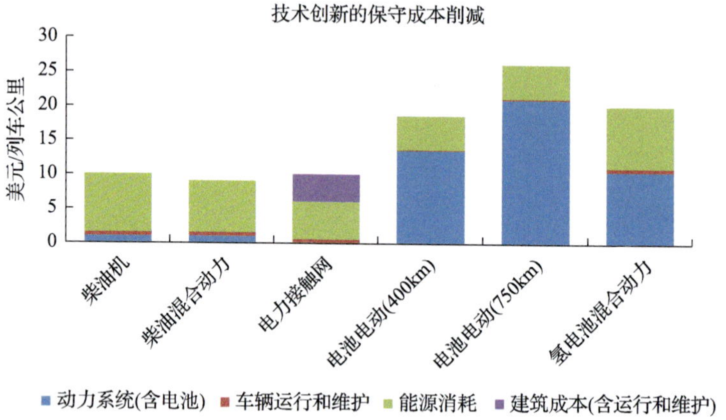

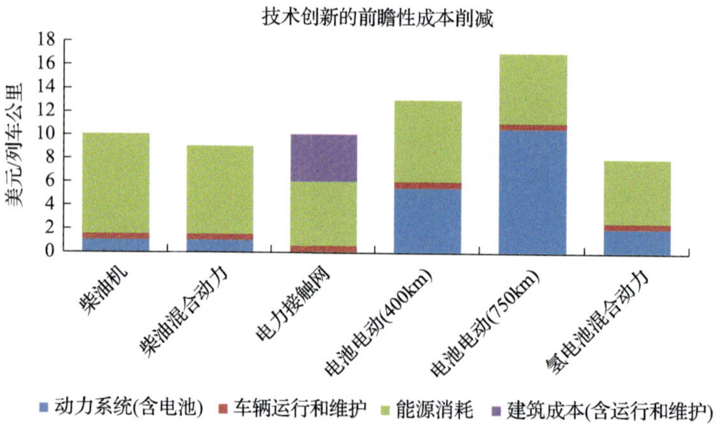

图 2-18　不同动力货运列车经济性对比

数据来源：IEA2018

随着能源转型、生态环境改善需求的日趋紧迫，氢能在全球范围内的能源地位也越来越清晰。广泛使用氢能不仅有助于减少碳排放，同时有助于能源安全和可持续利用。近年来，世界各国政府及铁路部门都致力于研究氢能及燃料电池技术，从而实现雄心勃勃的减排目标。负责英国与列车相关事宜的政府机构已经表示，从 2020 年起，氢动力列车将成为该国火车轨道上的新标准运输方式。这将与 2040 年彻底摆脱柴油动力火车的举措共同完成。很多国家制定了氢气火车的计划，其中，德国已有两辆氢气火车且每天可行驶近 800km，并计划在 2021 年前将氢气火车数量扩大到 14 辆；奥地利的齐勒塔尔巴恩计划到 2022 年部署五列氢气火车，总投资近 1.75 亿美元；英、法、日等国家也都在计划投产第一批氢气火车。加拿大研究由于氢气技术的进步，安大略省交通部于 2017 年 6 月宣布，决定使用燃料电池作为常规电气化的替代方案，并计划从 2025 年起在大多伦多地区的路线上提供全天候双程旅客服务。日本自 2007 年以来也有类似的项目，美国 2012 年在德克萨斯州业已推出了第一辆混合动力机车，荷兰北部也已部署了氢枢纽，计划用于列车供给。

英国伯明翰大学研究发现列车推进系统所需的组件都可以安装在原有的柴油动力 150 级列车的可用空间内。设备的安装不会影响乘客的容量和重量，与原来的 150 级列车类似。实验表明，氢动力列车的能耗减少了 44%，氢混合动力列车的能耗减少了 60%。且使用氢动力列车的二氧化碳排放量减少了 59%，使用氢混合列车的排放量减少了 77%。图 2-19 为世界首辆氢动力列车图(德国)。

图 2-19　世界首辆氢动力列车图(德国)

2015 年，法国火车制造商阿尔斯通与加拿大氢发电、燃料电池等类似技术的生产商 hydroics 建立了伙伴关系，共同开发氢动力火车。2018 年，氢燃料电池概念测试成功，两列氢动力列车沿着德国下萨克森州约 100km 区域的常规客运列车轨道运行。该项目计划到 2021 年将列车数量扩大到 14 辆。已经确定的还有丰田公司与日本铁路局签署了一项合作协议，在日本开发氢动力列车。

我国在氢动力列车方面也已经进行了试验部署，目前正在进一步发展。2017年初，中国中车四方股份公司与佛山签订供货合同，为佛山市高明区现代有轨电车示范线提供8列氢能源有轨电车作为运营车辆，这是国内首个氢能源有轨电车订单，标志着我国氢能源有轨电车实现了批量化生产的新突破。佛山市高明区现代有轨电车示范线，是我国首个以氢能源为动力的有轨电车示范项目，线路长约6.5km，设车站10座，加氢站1座。加氢一次可持续行驶100km，污染物“零排放”，全程“无接触网”。图2-20为我国佛山氢能源有轨电车图。

图 2-20　我国佛山氢能源有轨电车图

在燃料电池成本降低的乐观假设下，氢燃料电池技术可能会与其他低使用率的客运服务选择形成竞争关系。氢燃料电池技术在需要使用低利用率的大型列车进行长途运输的服务中最有竞争力，而低使用率是铁路货运的常见条件。氢在铁路上的使用可以与它在叉车、卡车和其他铁路堆场和物流枢纽机械上的使用相结合，以降低成本和提高灵活性。然后，由于目前氢动力列车的技术成本高、列车运行效率低、安全性能差，增加续航里程与速度是缩短燃料电池列车与既有列车的差距的主要矛盾。因此，氢动力列车的应用时机还未到来，相信随着技术的更迭、成本的降低和系统性能的提升，氢燃料动力的电力机车将会具有竞争力。

2.4　铁路现有用能形态的未来发展方向

铁路现有的用能形态完全依赖于电网，除非电气化线路外，铁路用能几乎全部需要电网进行供应。这种方式不仅基建投资大，而且还广泛存在谐波、负序以及易引起安全事故等问题，寻求新的能量供给方式和能源管理方案，以逐步减少铁路能源系统的单一供给问题，是铁路现有用能形态的必然发展方向。

交通可再生能源化是不可逆转的时代潮流，是关系到国家未来发展的战略布局。小型风力发电系统虽然满足清洁化需求，但其出力十分不稳定，通常情况下夜间出力较白天出力更高，与铁路负荷不匹配，且风力发电系统的设备体积较大，无法利用铁路线路进行布置。而太阳能光伏资源具有元器件体积小、布局灵活、技术成熟、供能相对稳定，而且光伏发电属于清洁能源、无碳排放，而且光伏出力集中于白天时段，与铁路负荷相匹配，因此适于将光伏发电将其引入铁路的能源供给系统中。

我国光伏发电领域的现状在于，一方面我国太阳能资源优势区位于西北部地区地广人稀，本地负荷较少，电能就地消纳的能力有限。电力机车线路的建设不仅要投入大量的资源，同时后期保养维护也是巨大的挑战。太阳能功能技术的探索不仅在该地区拥有良好的运用前景，同时还为一带一路沿线国家提供示范作用；另一方面集中耗能地区土地资源紧张，严重影响着发电成本。合理利用既有空间，为光伏利用寻找合理的应用场景，是挖掘光伏发电技术潜力的重要方向。在铁路交通当中，专用的铁路线路占用了较大的地理空间，同时运行列车长期奔走于户外，具有较长的光照时间，这显然为光伏发电技术的运用提供了有利场景。因此在太阳能资源丰富的地区探讨光伏供电列车，同时结合沿途车站的光伏供电设施，可以为未来的太阳能轨道交通线路提供一种可能，同时铁路系统可以通过引入光伏发电系统以减轻对于电网的依赖，不仅可以促进光伏产业的发展，并且可以减轻电网的负荷，降低铁路供电系统的建设难度，创造一个铁路、电网、光伏产业三赢的局面！

2.4.1　形态演化 SWOT 战略态势分析

根据前面所述的我国不同类型的铁路在四类光伏区域的分布状况、我国铁路能源系统的演化趋势，以及我国铁路能源系统目前的模式和未来模式的演化趋势，可得我国铁路可再生能源融合的 SWOT 分析矩阵，如表 2-2 所示。

2.4.2　铁路用能形态的未来发展方向

根据以上可再生能源铁路融合发展的 SWOT 战略分析可知，铁路能源系统将围绕高效能、高弹性和绿色化三大历史使命进行演进。铁路用能形态将向三大创新方向发展：铁路资产向绿色能源化方向发展，主要是光伏供能技术运用于铁路系统；能源供给向自洽多元化方向发展，指的是通过光伏出力的接入，采用混合储能装置作为中间单元，为铁路系统提供多元化的能源供给；用能管理向协同弹性化方向发展，即通过铁路资产的绿色能源化和能源供给的弹性多元化的发展，运营管理逐渐向高度协同的弹性化方向发展。

表 2-2　我国铁路可再生能源融合的 SWOT 分析矩阵

优势与劣势 机遇与挑战	优势(S)	劣势(W)
	①电气化轨道交通用能需求巨大； ②交通线路占用较大的资源空间，运行车辆奔走于户外，具有较大的车外空间，为光伏的生产和消纳提供了有利条件； ③路网规模大，铁路沿线和站用的可再生能源资源潜力巨大； ④我国幅员辽阔，光照资源充足，且光伏成本低廉； ⑤国际可再生能源列车的成功经验(印度的光伏列车、德国的燃料电池列车)； ⑥储能与信息网发展迅速	①强随机波动的交通用能需求； ②强随机波动的分布式光伏发电； ③铁路负荷较大，尤其是线路繁忙路段，电网末端区域的上网容量小导致可再生能源消纳能力弱； ④勘察、测绘、施工及监测等仪器、装备研发、制造能力弱； ⑤车流不均衡； ⑥电网建设不均衡，东部电网发达，西部地区电网相对薄弱
机遇(O)	SO 战略(优势-机遇)	WO 战略(劣势-机遇)
①国家能源战略规划要求促进交通运输“以电代油”； ②国家交通战略规划要求推进交通空间综合利用和可再生能源运输工具规模化应用； ③国家大力开展西部建设，规划中的铁路包括川藏铁路、滇藏铁路等； ④一带一路建设的战略机遇； ⑤国网大力展开能源互联网建设； ⑥国家积极推进供给侧改革； ⑦牵引供电系统节能、降耗、降低维护成本是铁路提质增效要求； ⑧低碳绿色铁路发展的需求； ⑨国家社会经济发展对铁路发展的需求	①以智能电网、能源微网、可再生能源列车和混合储能等技术为支撑，大力发展能源交通网络； ②把握一带一路、西部建设的战略机遇，推动可再生能源轨道交通的融合发展； ③把握铁路安全、低碳绿色、信息化发展的需求和机遇，对新技术、新材料、新方法、新工艺、新仪器、新设备等进行研究； ④把握国家对铁路建设及路网完善的需求，特别是复杂艰险铁路的机会，加强特殊工况能源系统与交通融合的专业技术研究，提升核心竞争力； ⑤把握安全、便捷、高效、绿色、智能发展的需求和机遇，对能源系统品质提升进行研究； ⑥借鉴国际可再生能源列车的成功经验，推进适宜我国的能源轨道交通融合发展进程	①通过一次能源可储、二次能源可控，实现强随机波动的交通用能需求与分布式光伏发电之间能量的供需平衡与灵活响应； ②借助混合储能实现能源的时间位移，平衡电力供需； ③把握国内外铁路发展机遇，加强专业技术基础研究，对标国际，推进技术创新； ④借鉴电力系统成熟经验，推进电力电子、信息技术、人工智能在轨道交通能源系统专业技术发展； ⑤大力发展可配置列车自洽用能控制系统技术，降低稀疏路网的运行成本
挑战(T)	ST 战略(优势-挑战)	WT 战略(劣势-挑战)
①基建投资高，投资收益低，回收年限长； ②维护成本高； ③生产运营的安全威胁； ④复杂地质环境、恶劣气候以及设备故障条件下的施工面临挑战，如川藏线； ⑤关键基础技术受到国外技术封锁； ⑥不可控的环境因素。如自然灾害，暴雪等； ⑦大功率无线传输技术研究、设备研制进展缓慢	①能源、交通共同做适应性调整的交通能源系统； ②加强管理消除人为因素安全威胁，重点发展基础设施和环境安全检测、监测技术和研制相关仪器、设备； ③研究复杂自然环境下的列车供能新技术，在降低成本的同时，能够抵御自然灾害； ④加快建设高水平人才队伍，统一规划高水平实验室、研究基地的建设，形成合力	①通过铁路系统载运体、基础设施、服务设施的光伏发电，削弱铁路对电网的依赖性，尽量实现铁路能源的自给自足甚至余电上网； ②加快铁路移动装备绿色低碳、信息化研究和建设进度，降低建设和管理成本； ③加强基础材料、基础部件、基础零件的自主化技术的提升，实现行业补短板，解决“卡脖子”难题； ④合理选择新材料技术应用，加大工程技术应用合理性； ⑤加强对与电力系统信息、智能化等方面交流推进在轨道交通能源系统应用； ⑥研究复杂环境下的灾害预警技术，充分利用空天地一体化的信息基础设施； ⑦产学研一体化，探索创新人才培养，扩大国际交往

铁路资产向绿色化转变，使得铁路能源系统对于外界供给的减少，降低并减轻了电网的压力和负担，提高了铁路资产的效能；通过自洽式供能的逐渐推进，将逐渐地减少铁路能源系统与高压电网的接触电压，可以有效地减少电弧、电晕等铁路接触网高压放电危险的发生，对于保障电气化铁路的安全稳定运行极为关键；能源管理的弹性化发展，使得我国丰富的交通可再生资源得以充分利用和调度，铁路系统的充分绿色化将是建设绿色中国、完成《巴黎协定》规定的碳减排目标和任务的有力支撑。图 2-21 为我国铁路可再生能源融合发展的三大历史使命与三大创新方向。

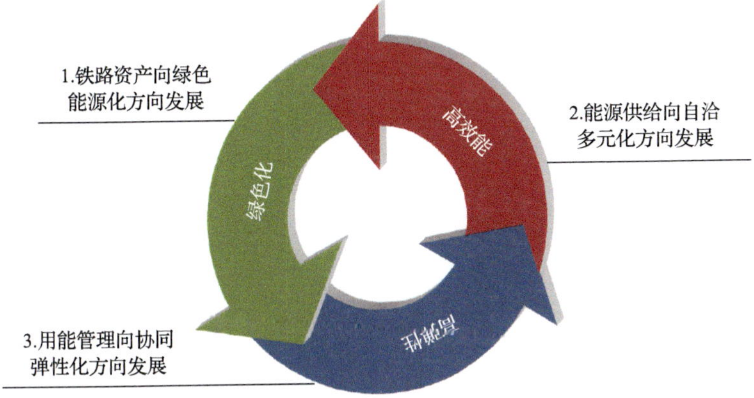

图 2-21　我国铁路可再生能源融合发展的三大历史使命与三大创新方向

1. 方向一：能源供给向多元可持续化方向发展

目前电网作为电气化铁路的唯一能量来源，其供电质量要求非常高，且十分要求供电可靠性，一旦断电将产生极为严重的后果。当牵引侧任一端口单独运行时会产生负序电流，其会造成接入电网的发电机转子中局部过热、机械损坏等问题；谐波注入电力系统将影响全网，波及用户，产生发电机跳闸、大面积停电或系统解列、电动机和电容器大量烧坏、小火电厂不能就近并网等一系列严重后果；无功则会导致功率因数降低，且牵引负荷变化极大，出现最大和最小运行方式的频率高，在最大运行方式下出现比较多的欠补偿，最小运行方式下无功补偿会返送电网，严重影响电网的电能质量及铁路用电的安全性。

此外，将光伏发电系统引入牵引供电系统后，由于光伏出力受到自然环境的影响较大，其波动性十分明显，若直接将其接入牵引网，则会对电网调度与控制提出更高的要求，进一步加重了电网的负担。

因此，探讨多元且可持续供给的铁路能源系统十分必要。为了提高铁路能源系统的稳定、可靠和鲁棒性，积极吸纳可持续供给的铁路自身资产能源化所产生的光伏资源作为铁路能源系统的能源供给来源是铁路能源供给系统的未来发展方向之一。

2. 方向二：交通用能向分布自洽化方向发展

随着铁路资产向能源化方向演进，且铁路能源系统积极消纳和疏导自身产生的光伏资源，铁路用能的自洽率将得到显著提升，铁路用能对于电网的依赖性会逐渐降低。由于光伏出力、铁路运营等情况均呈现与地理位置有关的分布特性，因此，铁路的自洽率分布也呈现与地理位置有关的分布特性。整体上来讲，分布自洽化发展是铁路用能形态的发展方向之二。

3. 方向三：能源管理向协同弹性化方向发展

通过铁路可再生能源系统的能源供给向多元可持续化发展、铁路用能向分布自洽化发展，铁路可再生能源系统将呈现与电网、光伏资源网以及铁路建设网等三网融合的“源-网-荷-储”协同运行状态。此外，传统的电力系统对电源及负荷的随机性，尤其是日内出力随机性考虑不足，导致光伏资源消纳率低，提高日内调度计划调整的频度和准确性是保障含高比例可再生能源电力系统的灵活性是未来亟需解决的问题。通过日内调度增强型“源-网-荷-储”协同调度的建设，可大大提高铁路光伏资源的消纳能力，并大大增强铁路能源系统的弹性与韧性。因此，能源管理向协同弹性化发展是铁路用能形态的未来发展方向之三。

第 3 章　铁路交通能源系统的新模式

将可再生能源作为高份额能源提供方，增加可再生能源的能源效率，实现能源转型，把大规模集成太阳能和风力发电作为电力系统提供能源的重要支柱，可以实现交通系统的高效脱碳。实现能源转型的时间越短，适应气候变化的成本就越低，对社会经济的破坏就越小。金融体系应符合更广泛的可持续性和能源转型要求，更多地参与到能源转型中来。可再生能源的发展离不开未来的技术创新，创新必须涵盖技术的全部生命周期，包括示范、部署和商业化。不仅如此，创新还包括运作能源体系和市场的新方法，并包含新的商业模式。交通系统、能源系统分别或同时做适应性调整将会实现不同的铁路能源系统的新模式。

3.1　考虑交通做适应性调整的铁路能源系统演化新模式

铁路可再生能源系统的建设将使铁路系统根据战略目标的需求做适应性调整，在调整过程中，我国的铁路可再生能源系统将呈现“源-网-荷”三重属性。铁路资产能源化使得铁路系统具有了“源”属性，三合一牵引变的建设使得铁路系统具有了“网”属性，在铁路系统向源属性和网属性转变的过程中，铁路可再生能源系统作为电网的荷属性也相应地做了适应性调整，将呈现与现有的“荷”特性不同的新特性。

3.1.1　考虑交通“源属性”的交通能源系统演化新模式

从“源属性”来考虑交通能源系统的演化，将通过铁路系统的运载体、基础设施和服务设施三个角度均可以铺设太阳能光伏板及部署储能装置来进行演化。

(1) 对于铁路系统的运载体而言，电气化机车与非电气化机车具有不同的源属性演化模式。

对于非电气化机车而言，可在顶部铺设光伏组件，考虑到列车运行时速度较高，若采用倾斜布置方法，光伏组件会承受较大风压，且会破坏列车整体的气动性能，反而会使能耗上升，因而采用平铺的布置方式。由于机车顶部面积有限，且布设角度受到车体外形的限制，车载光伏电源仅能供给列车很小部分的能量，所以目前国内外的研究均针对光伏满足辅助装置用能所需。如印度曾提出在车顶铺设光伏组件为列车灯光、风扇、空调等设施供电，经测算得出光伏出力高于负荷所需，项目的成本回收年限为2.47年，可减少CO_2排放239.12t/(车次·年)。

对于电气化机车而言，于机车上方铺设有牵引网，在车顶布置光伏组件对于绝缘性能的影响尚不明确，因而暂不考虑此情况下的利用模式。

(2)对于铁路系统的服务设施而言，其占地更为集中，且面积较大，周围建筑物对其光照条件影响很小，因而十分有利于建设集中式光伏电站。车站的太阳能光伏主要以并网方式加以利用，组成部分可分为光伏电池组件、并网逆变器、电源汇流箱柜、电源并接装置、防雷接地系统、建通系统以及其辅材等。此项技术较为成熟，且国内已有许多示范性工程实例。例如，上海虹桥客站、武汉火车站、广州南站、青岛火车站和杭州火车站等均铺设了不同程度的光伏电池。目前我国光伏装机容量最大的车站为南京南站，装机功率为10.67MW，年总产能为9.23GW·h。车站光伏发出的电能一般采用“自发自用、余电上网”的原则，剩余电量经汇流后升压至配网电压与电网相连。

(3)对于铁路系统的基础设施而言，铁路线路很长，导致铁路系统的主要占地是基础设施用地。其铺设面积很大，且有净空区，铺设角度十分自由，具有很高的供给大负荷的潜力。对于铁路系统的基础设施而言，有两部分基础设施可以进行光伏铺设，分别是在电气化铁路的轨道上方搭建支撑架和在铁路线路安全保护区内铺设光伏组件。

在电气化铁路的轨道上方搭建光伏隧道，指的是在电气化铁路的轨道上方依据线路走向及当地纬度布置光伏组件。根据现行《铁路技术管理规程》(TG/01—2014)，单线铁路的基本路基宽度为8.6m，双线铁路的基本路基宽度为13.6m，且跨越电气化铁路的各种建筑物与带电部分的最小距离，不小于0.5m。因此支架宽度选择为13.6m，高度设置为7m。

对于不同走向的铁路线路，光伏组件有不同的布置方式：完全东西走向的铁路线，由于太阳辐射的偏角，朝北的区域有一部分在一天内一直无法照射到阳光，而朝南的区域太阳辐射会相对比较充足，因此在设计布置太阳能板布置区域时可以考虑不对称的形状布置；完全南北走向的铁路线，由于太阳东升西落，整个光伏棚顶的每个角度在一天中都有机会受到太阳辐射，而正午应该是太阳辐射最大的时刻，因此可以从中间开始向两侧对称布置弧形；对于走向不完全为东西向或南北向的线路，同样由于太阳的东升西落，整个光伏棚顶的每个角度在一天中都有机会受到太阳辐射，但是偏南的那一侧太阳辐射会比较大，所以可以根据线路的具体角度决定不对称布置还是对称布置。

在铁路线路安全保护区内铺设光伏组件，指的是在各类铁路线两边的安全保护区内铺设光伏组件。根据《铁路运输安全保护条例》第二十七条的规定：铁路线路两侧应当设立铁路线路安全保护区。铁路线路安全保护区的范围，从铁路线路路堤坡脚、路堑坡顶或者铁路桥梁外侧起向外的距离分别为①城市市区高速铁路为 10m，其他铁路为 8m；②城市郊区居民居住区高速铁路为 12m，其他铁路为 10m；③村镇居民居住区高速铁路为 15m，其他铁路为 12m；④其他地区高速铁路为 20m，其他铁路为 15m。实际的铺设长度可根据当地的地理环境来确定，铺设角度仍按照当地最佳倾角布置。图 3-1 为铁路做适应性调整所体现的源属性示意图。

图 3-1　铁路做适应性调整所体现的源属性示意图

3.1.2　考虑交通“网属性”的交通能源系统演化新模式

由于铁路可再生能源系统通过铁路资产的能源化演化具有了源属性，如何传输和高效利用铁路可再生能源是铁路可再生能源系统调整的重要内容。随着智能和信息化基础设施的建设、交通行驶控制信息系统的完善，数据融合与协同管理将是交通能源系统“网属性”演化新模式的关键所在，如图 3-2 所示。

由于电网为了保障自身运行安全，要求小型光伏电站接入电网的总装机容量不能大于上级变压器容量的 15%～30%，因此分布式光伏无法大量接入电网，这对于铁路分布式光伏系统的发展而言极其不利；此外，铁路需要的电能都是由各地发电厂，经过高压电网后传输到负荷侧，再经过输配电站的降压及分配，最后提供给负荷的。对于许多边远及农村、海岛或高原地区，远离大电网，或处于电

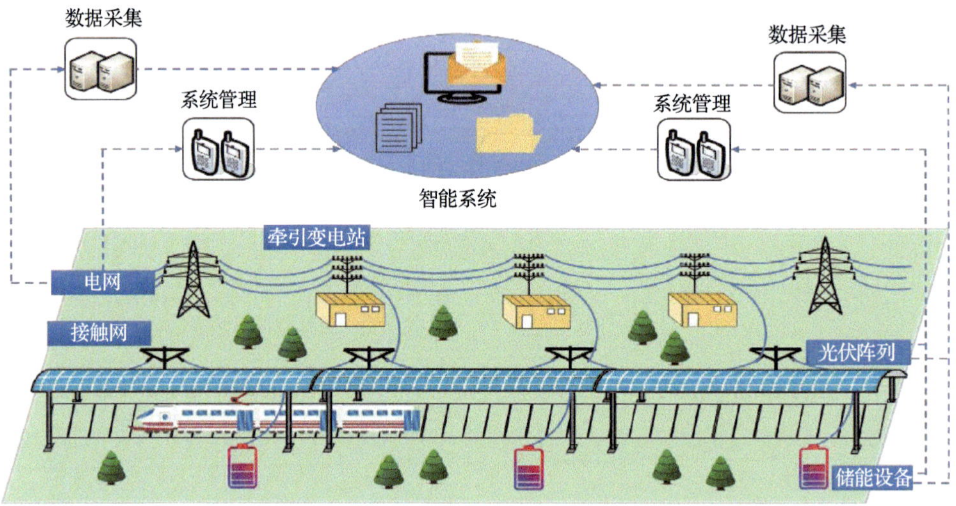

图 3-2　铁路可再生能源系统数据融合与协同管理示意图

网稀疏地区，高压输电线的布置非常不经济或者根本难以从大电网获得电能。因此，铁路可再生能源网络的演化模式向可再生能源微电网方式发展，其模式呈现为以牵引变电站、储能站和信息站合一的三合一型牵引变微网；同时，铁路系统具有的牵引网络，使得铁路可再生能源系统形成独特的沿轨道分布的线性微网群(图 3-3)，即每一个三合一牵引变微网与相邻两侧的微网之间通过信息流的互动实现能量流的互动，这样的模式不仅免去了长距离的输电线路网损，并且可以为实现消纳铁路可再生能源提供合理的负荷与顺畅的输送通道，更为实现铁路用能的自治化发展提供合理的实施途径。

根据我国铁路的建设模式，铁路可再生能源分布式微网有两种运行模式。

(1) 对于电气化铁路，其分布式微网将在直接向负荷供电的同时与电网相连。当分布式微网供电不足时，由电网向负荷供电；当分布式微网发电有富余时，将富余电量输入大电网。此外，大电网同时还可以起到电压支撑的作用，帮助维持微网稳定性。

(2) 对于非电气化铁路，其分布式微网将采用“孤岛”运行模式，即形成一个独立的供电系统，专门为铁路负荷供电。

3.1.3　考虑交通“荷属性”的交通能源系统演化新模式

铁路作为大功率、非线性和强波动的负荷，对电力系统电能质量带来了不可忽略的影响。电力系统的负荷随着铁路的电力负荷而波动，铁路的电力负荷呈现冲击性时，电力系统的负荷也呈现出冲击特性，而铁路的负荷趋于平缓时，电力系统的负荷也趋于平缓。随着铁路作为源属性和网属性的迁移和演化，铁路的负

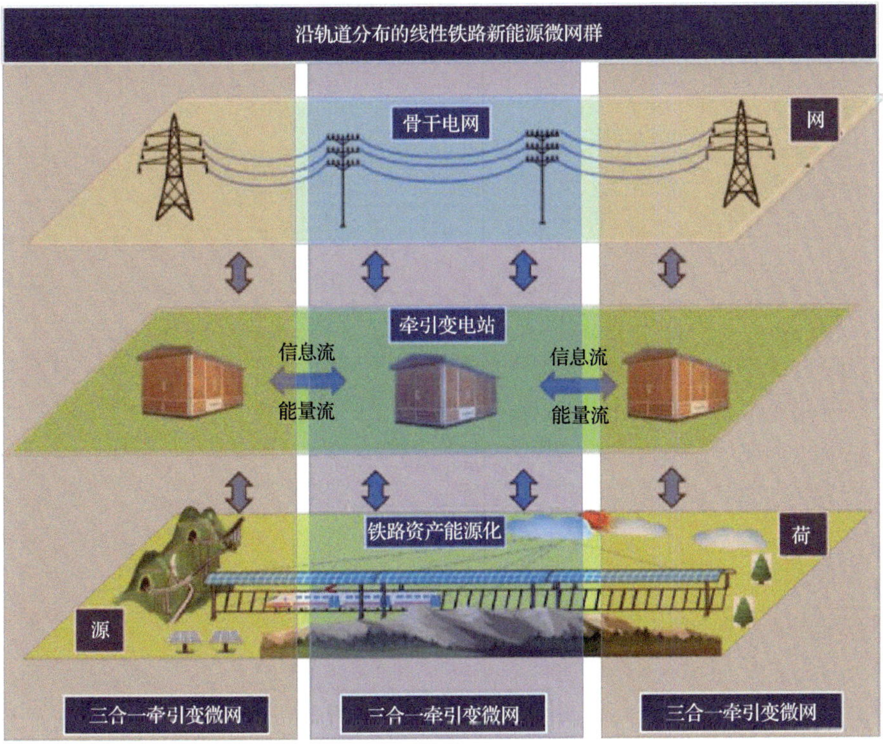

图 3-3　铁路做适应性调整所体现的网属性示意图-沿轨道分布的线性微网群

荷属性将逐渐减小对电网的冲击，具有新型的季节耦合性、空间分布性及时间空间不平稳等特性。

交通能源系统演化新模式在“荷属性”方面将呈现出季节的耦合性。在传统模式下，铁路系统用电仅由电网提供，对于电网来说铁路负荷四季基本相同。而在新模式下，光伏发电具有季节性。在春夏两季光伏发电量很高，可以满足铁路系统负荷用能需求甚至实现余电上网；而在秋冬季节光伏发电量较少，从而需要从电网获取较多的电能。因此对于电网来说，铁路系统负荷四季不再相同，呈现出季节特性。

交通能源系统演化新模式在“荷属性”方面将呈现出空间的分布性。传统模式下，铁路需要的电能都是由各地发电厂，经过互联大电网后传输到负荷侧，再经过输配电站的降压及分配，最后提供给负荷的。而在新模式下，铁路负荷不再由互联大电网供电，而是分配到大量的分布式微网中，呈现出分散特性。

交通能源系统演化新模式在“荷属性”方面将呈现出时间和空间的不平稳性。传统模式下，铁路的间歇冲击性负荷将直接作用于电网，危害电力系统的稳定性，影响电能质量。而在新模式下，铁路的间歇冲击性负荷将转移到各储能装置，避免了对电网产生直接影响，并对负荷的冲击性进行了有效缓冲。

3.2 考虑能源做适应性调整的交通能源系统演化新模式

铁路现有的用能形态完全依赖于电网，除非电气化线路外，铁路用能几乎全部需要电网进行供应。随着电气化铁路的建设速度加快，铁路负荷对电力系统造成的影响有①冲击性负荷增大，对电力系统稳定性带来新的挑战，影响电力系统容量规划，调峰投资增多。②电力系统的峰值负荷增大，致使电力系统的容量增加，用电低谷与容量相差过大，浪费一部分容量。③在电气化铁路运行过程中，在启动、爬坡、制动等工况时会有较大的谐波分量出现。由于谐波分量相应的电流进入电器设备，产生过负荷、过热等危害，并根据运行的速度等因素可能会造成谐波共振的影响，且谐波分量大会使相关仪表产生测量误差。采用单一的能源供给对铁路系统带来的问题包括：①投资成本高，铁路线路分布往往在边远、地理位置特殊的区域，且在铁路沿线的地理区域内的负荷较小，使得当地电网的建设难度大成本较高，阻碍了电气化铁路的发展和普及。②安全性难以保障，铁路负荷的增加对电网带来的大功率强冲击性影响，使得铁路用电安全性指数大大降低。

因此，寻求多元化的能量供给方式和可持续性的能源使用模式，对于逐步减少铁路系统对电网的依赖性，提升铁路系统和电网系统的安全性均大有裨益。

能源做适应性调整的演化模式可以由传统大电网集中式供电转为以共享储能为中间件的微电网群互联供电，共享储能将作为蓄水池和缓冲池。

储能站由储能装置和放电装置组成，储存一定区域内的所有发电量，由于能源的分散化，每隔一定距离就应安装一个储能站。储能装置主要由电容式储能和蓄电池组成，电容式储能元件占地小，放电时间短但容量小，造价高，适合供给列车的冲击性负荷；蓄电池容量大，放电平稳，造价低但占地面积大，适合供给列车的基础负荷。因此储能站的储能容量应根据不同类型的电池特性、不同线路的列车运行特点及不同地域的铁路可再生能源出力特性按比例进行搭配。

由于电气化铁路具有的牵引变电站和接触网可以为可再生能源微网群的建设和能量流的输送提供最佳的路径，因此将储能站放入牵引变电站，同时与信息站形成三合一型牵引变储能站，如图 3-4 所示。

储能电站(系统)在铁路能源系统中的应用目的主要考虑“配合光伏接入、能量储存、功率时移、提高电能质量、孤网运行”等几大功能应用。例如，功率时移，提高供电可靠性，储能电站就像一个蓄水池和缓冲池，可以把光伏发电高峰期富余的水储存起来，在铁路负荷用电高峰的时候再拿出来用，这样就大大提高了光伏供电的可靠性，减少了能源的浪费。

图 3-4 能源做适应性调整所体现的“三合一”型牵引变储能站示意图

在一定区域内的光伏转化装置将太阳能转化为电能输送到储能站进行电能储存，储能站通过牵引网给列车提供电能，这就构成了源-储-荷的微网系统，减少了电能传输过程中的损耗。但由于光能受天气影响导致部分储能站电能不足或者储能站出现故障的情况将影响储能站对列车的正常供电，为了避免这种情况，需要进行储能站互联，即相邻的多个储能站相互连接，具有多余电量的储能站向需要电量的储能站供电以维持列车运行，如果向相邻的储能站提供剩余电量后依然有剩余电量，则采用余电上网的模式输送给电网，获得一定的收益。即共享储能的调度策略是“先就地，再最近，后上网”，如图 3-5 所示。

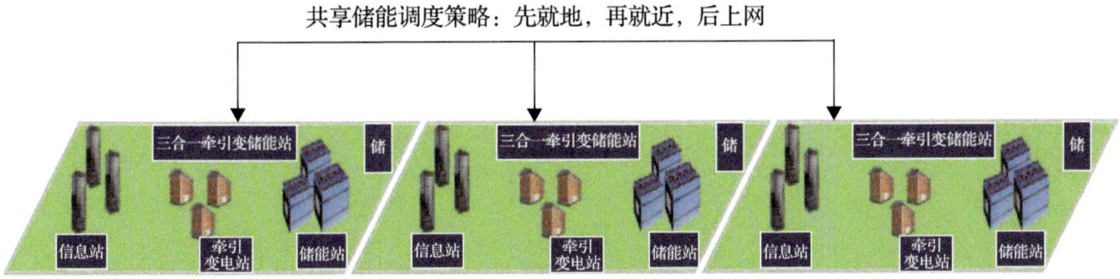

图 3-5 能源做适应性调整所体现的共享储能调度模式

3.3 考虑交通、能源共同做适应性调整的交通能源系统演化新模式

通过以上两节关于交通做适应性调整模式和能源做适应性调整的演化模式的阐述，可知铁路与能源共同做适应性调整的交通能源系统将兼具创能、送能、储能与用能四重属性，新型的铁路可再生能源系统的运营管理模式将在新一代信息、通信和控制技术的支撑下朝向“源-网-荷-储”协同调度的方向逐步演进，如图 3-6 所示。

新型铁路可再生能源系统的建设和优化调度需要综合铁路系统光伏资源的出力特性、我国骨干电网的建设特性以及铁路负荷的分布特性三个方面，建设因地制宜、因网制宜以及因荷制宜的三网合一型铁路可再生能源融合网(图 3-7)。

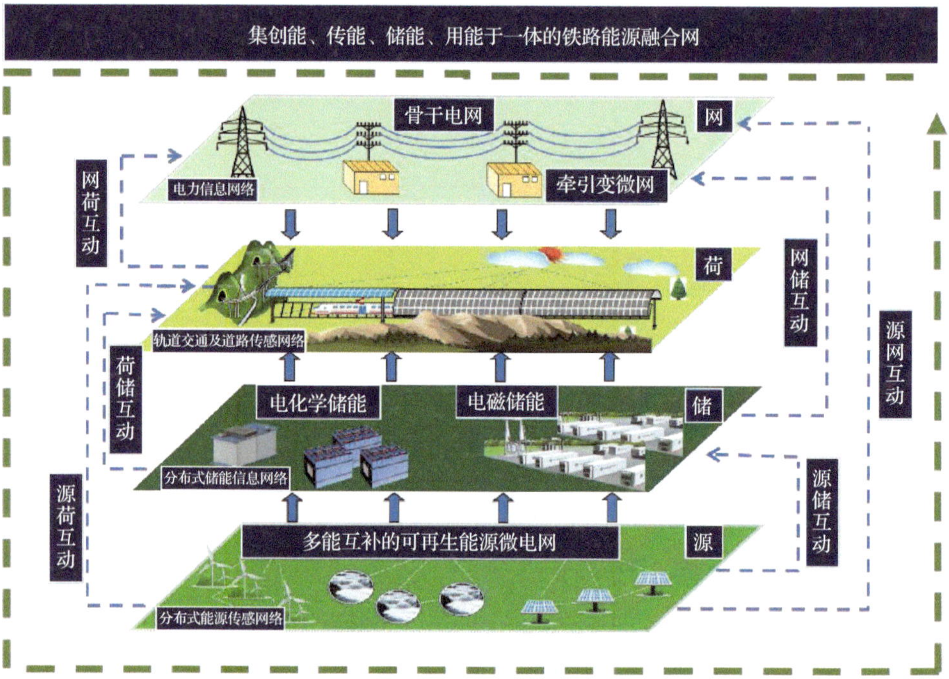

图 3-6 交通、能源共同做适应性调整所体现的“源-网-荷-储”四重属性示意图

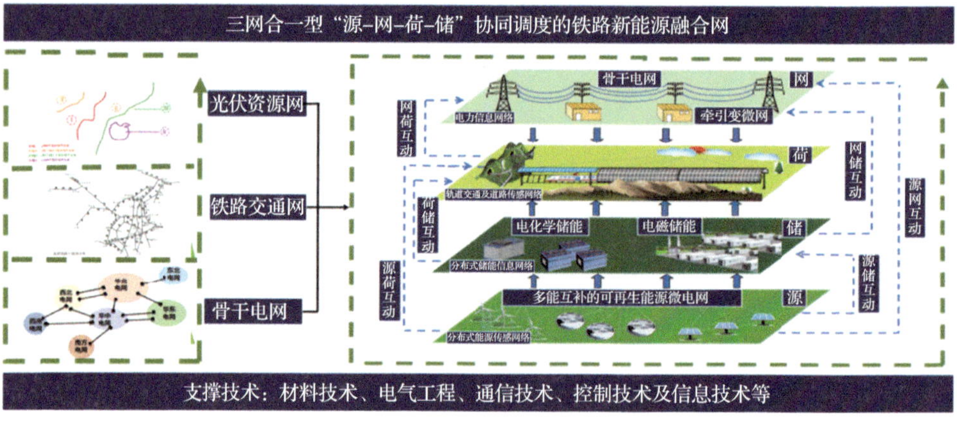

图 3-7 因地制宜、因网制宜以及因荷制宜的三网合一型铁路可再生能源融合网示意图

根据我国的电网建设、铁路负荷及光伏资源特性，“因网制宜”把电网的形态分为强电、无电和末端三类；“因荷制宜”把负荷的形态分为多负荷与少负荷两类；“因地制宜”把光伏资源分为多光与少光两类。因此，三网合一下的铁路可再生能源融合网可以将我国地域分为以下 8 种融合网类型，每种融合网类型对应一种“源网荷储”融合模式，如图 3-8 和表 3-1 所示。

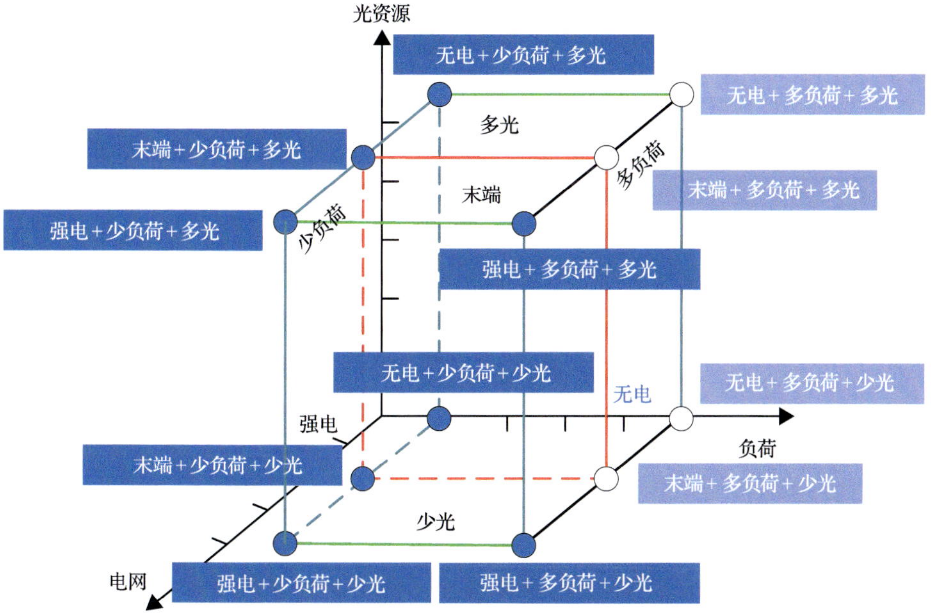

图 3-8　铁路可再生能源融合网的 8 种建设新模式示意图

表 3-1　针对我国不同区域的新模式

编号	场景特点(三网融合特性)	演化新模式(源网荷储协同调度特性)
1	无电+少负荷+多光	内燃机+可再生+微网+自给自足
2	末端+少负荷+多光	可再生+储能+微网为主+余电上网
3	强电+少负荷+多光	可再生+储能+微网+余电上网
4	强电+多负荷+多光	可再生+储能+微网/电网+自给自足
5	无电+少负荷+少光	内燃机+可再生+微网+自给自足
6	末端+少负荷+少光	可再生+储能+微网/电网+自给自足
7	强电+少负荷+少光	可再生+储能+微网/电网+余电上网
8	强电+多负荷+少光	可再生+储能+电网为主+网上购电

根据光伏出力特性、电网布局特性以及负荷特性，以“三网合一型铁路可再生能源网”为总目标，根据交通与能源间需要互动联系的演化新模式和交通与能源分别占主导地位的演化新模式两个视角；根据铁路运输与能源系统之间的关系又可以分为交通专用的能源系统、交通适用的能源系统、交通适配的能源系统以及能源支持的交通系统四个维度，以下从两个视角和四个维度两个层次分别介绍以上八种模式，如图 3-9 所示。

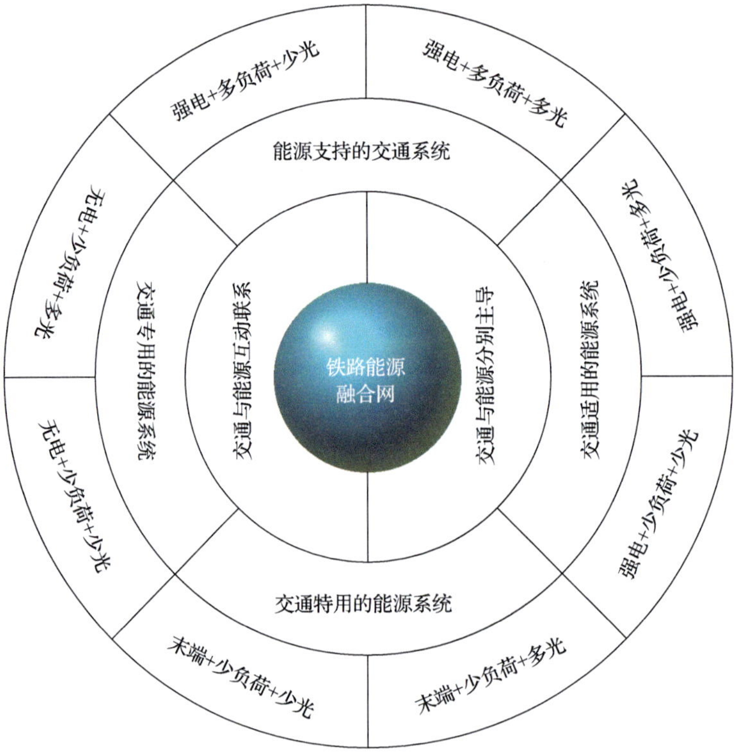

图 3-9　铁路能源融合网架构图(一个目标-两个视角-四个维度-八种模式)

3.3.1　基于交通与能源间互动联系的交通能源系统演化新模式

交通与能源间需要互动的演化新模式包括以下四个场景：强电+多负荷+多光场景、强电+少负荷+多光场景、强电+少负荷+少光场景和末端+少负荷+多光场景。

1. 强电+多负荷+多光场景的演化新模式

强电+多负荷+多光场景下，多光意味着有大量的可再生资源可以利用，列车正是良好的光伏转换载体和光伏消纳的负荷，可以通过储能装置保存能量；同时强电意味着该地区接入电网端容量充足，可根据具体情况采取微网或并网；因此这种场景下采用的演化新模式是可再生+储能+微网/电网+自给自足；同时，此种场景下，负荷较大，需要电网、微网或电网/微网的同时出力，因此属于能源支持的交通系统。图 3-10 为强电+多负荷+多光地区的演化模式。

2. 强电+少负荷+多光场景的演化新模式

强电+少负荷+多光场景下，同样，多光意味着有大量的可再生资源利用，列车作为良好的光伏转换载体和光伏消纳的负荷，同时通过储能装置保存所产生的

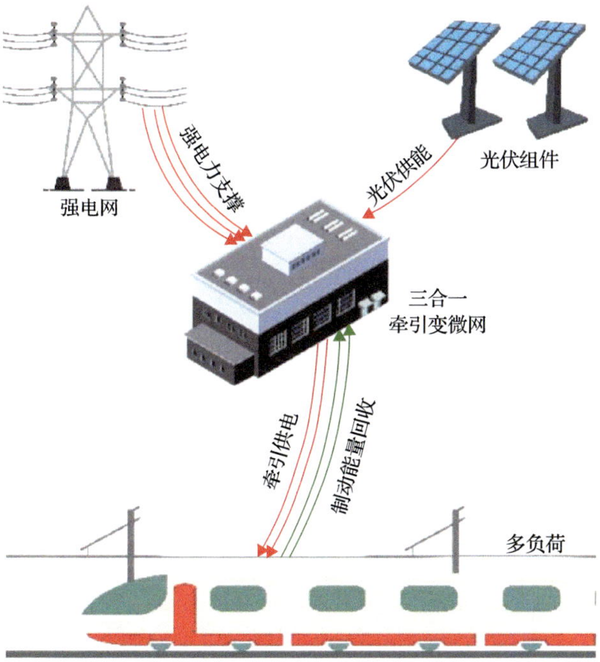

图 3-10 强电+多负荷+多光地区的演化模式

电能；强电意味着接入该地区的电网端电力充足，可以满足列车的冲击性负荷，不需要混合储能，根据具体情况可以采取微网或并网；少负荷意味着该地区出现余电的可能性大，除自给自足外剩下的余电接入电网系统。因此，该场景下采取的演化模式是可再生+储能+微网+余电上网；同时，此种场景下，负荷较小，而光伏资源和电力资源都很充足，因此该场景属于交通适用的能源系统。图 3-11 为强电+少负荷+多光地区的演化模式。

3. 强电+少负荷+少光场景的演化新模式

强电+少负荷+少光地场景下，少光使得光伏出力较小，但是也可以满足少负荷的需求，如果有多余的光伏，则在转化后通过储能装置储存，根据具体情况采取微网或与电网连结，自给自足外剩下的余电接入系统，因此，此种场景下的演化新模式是可再生+储能+微网/电网+余电上网；同时，由于处于强电和少负荷区，此种模式属于交通适用的能源系统。图 3-12 为强电+少负荷+少光地区的演化模式。

4. 末端+少负荷+多光场景的演化新模式

末端+少负荷+多光场景下，多光意味着有大量的可再生资源利用，由于负荷较少，因此，此种场景下会产生余电，虽然位于电力系统末端，但多余的电

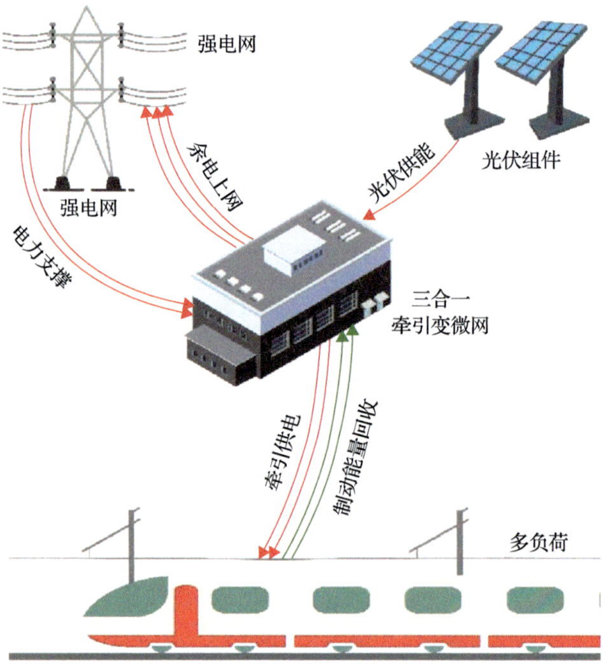

图 3-11　强电+少负荷+多光地区的演化模式

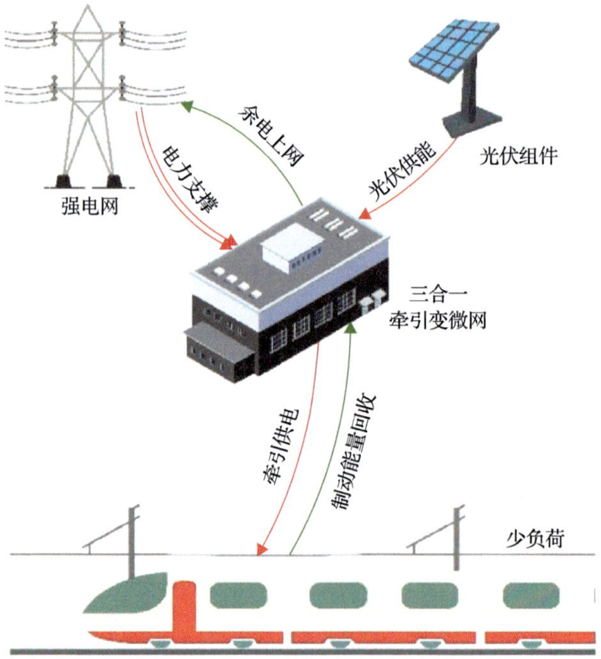

图 3-12　强电+少负荷+少光地区的演化模式

力也可以接入电力系统，因此，此种场景下的演化新模式是可再生+储能+微网为主+余电上网；此外，此场景下，列车的负荷较小，同时地处电网的末端，余量上网的容量不大，因此，多光产生的电力主要供给于列车用能，因此，此种场景的演化模式属于交通特用的能源系统。图 3-13 为末端+少负荷+多光地区的演化模式。

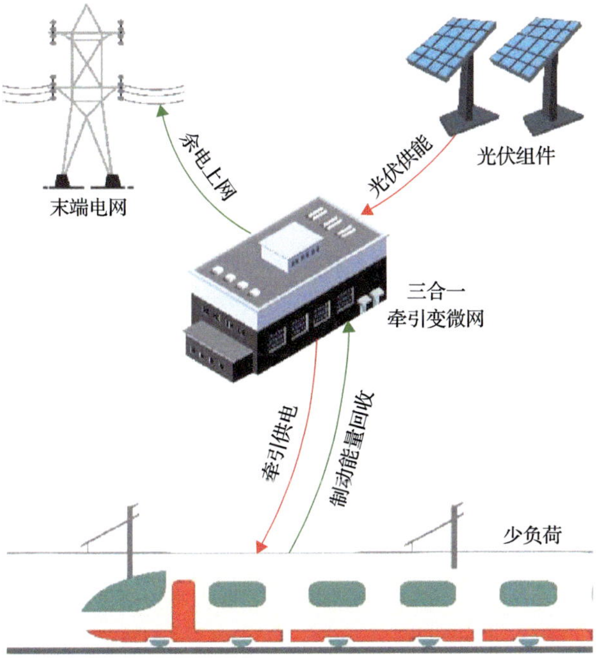

图 3-13　末端+少负荷+多光地区的演化模式

3.3.2　考虑交通与能源不同主导地位的交通能源系统演化新模式

交通与能源占不同主导地位的演化新模式包括无电+少负荷+多光场景、强电+多负荷+少光场景、末端+少负荷+少光场景和无电+少负荷+少光场景。

1. 无电+少负荷+多光场景的演化新模式

无电+少负荷+多光场景下，多光意味着有大量的可再生资源利用，同时负荷少，因此，此种场景下的光伏资源可以做到与负荷匹配，而且由于没有电气化铁路网，此场景的演化模式将以微网为主进行自给自足，用内燃机作为保障避免出现失去动力的情况以及满足列车运行的负荷要求，即此种场景的演化新模式是内燃机+可再生+微网+自给自足；同时，由于没有向电网输送电力，此种场景的演化模式属于交通专用的能源系统。图 3-14 为无电+少负荷+多光地区的演化模式。

图 3-14 无电+少负荷+多光地区的演化模式

2. 强电+多负荷+少光场景的演化新模式

强电+多负荷+少光场景下，少光意味着光伏资源不充足，多负荷意味着需要主要依靠电网的供电来满足列车的负荷，可以在车站和列车上加装光伏转化元件，储存电能供小负荷如照明负荷使用，即此场景的演化新模式是可再生+储能+电网为主+网上购电；同时由于此场景下的列车用电需要电网的强力支撑，因此此场景的演化新模式属于能源支持的交通系统。图 3-15 为强电+多负荷+少光地区的演化模式。

3. 末端+少负荷+少光场景的演化新模式

末端+少负荷+少光场景下，负荷较少，光伏资源也少，因此以自给自足为主，在自给自足后如有多余的电力则通过储能装置储存，根据具体情况采取微网或与电网连结，即此种场景的演化新模式是可再生+储能+微网/电网+自给自足；同时，此场景下，列车的负荷较小，且具有一定的光伏资源，因此，此场景的演化新模式属于交通特用的能源系统。图 3-16 为末端+少负荷+少光地区的演化模式。

4. 无电+少负荷+少光场景的演化新模式

无电+少负荷+少光场景下，负荷较少，光伏资源也少，因此，光伏供电以自给自足为主，同时由于没有电气化铁路网，此种场景由内燃机作为保障避免出现

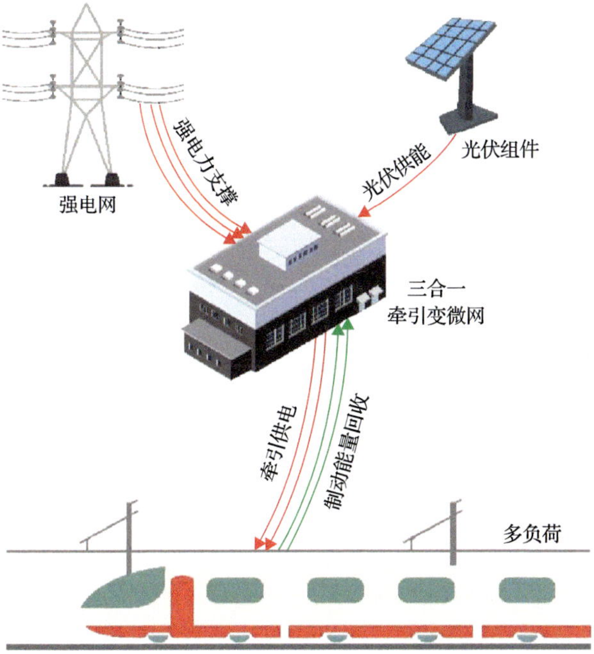

图 3-15　强电+多负荷+少光地区的演化模式

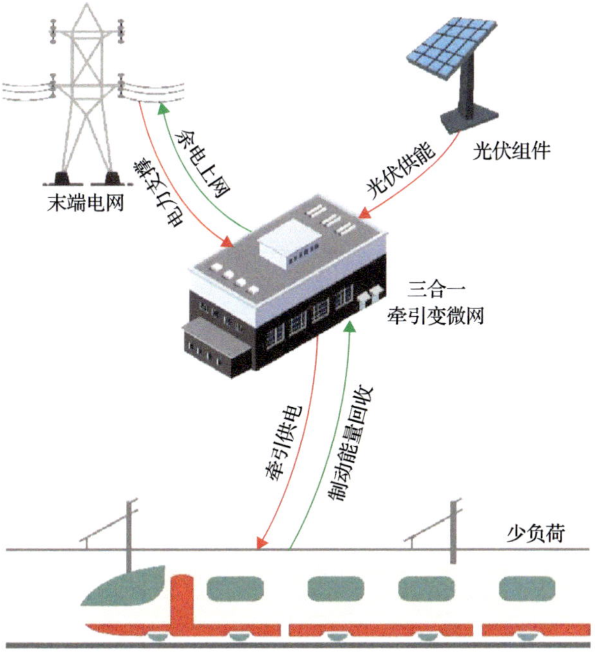

图 3-16　末端+少负荷+少光地区的演化模式

失去动力的情况以及满足列车运行的负荷要求，因此，此种场景的演化新模式是内燃机+可再生+微网+自给自足；同时，由于此种场景光伏所产生的电力没有向电网输送，专门供给于列车负荷，因此，此种场景的演化新模式属于交通专用的能源系统。图 3-17 为无电+少负荷+少光地区的演化模式。

图 3-17　无电+少负荷+少光地区的演化模式

第4章　铁路新模式的技术解决方案

根据上面得到的铁路可再生能源系统的八种不同的创新新模式，本章进行具体的数据测算，并针对铁路能源系统未来15年的规划目标，给出采用新模式下铁路可再生能源的演进步骤和解决方案。

4.1　支持不同可再生能源利用模式的共性技术

解决方案的测算既有共性的配置技术和测算方法，也有特定模式的专门技术。其中共性配置技术包括光伏的铺设方法、储能的配置策略和计算方法、微网的拓扑结构和运行策略等；共性测算方法包括光伏利用率、自洽率和经济性测算方法。

4.1.1　不同利用模式的共性定义和测算说明

1. 开发场景定义

开发场景是指光伏总开发量与光伏总开发潜力的比值。本报告中定义开发强度10%为保守场景，开发强度20%为基本场景，开发强度30%为积极场景。

2. 利用率定义

光伏利用率是在不同开发场景下，光伏总出力中可以用于铁路负荷的部分与光伏总出力的比值。

3. 自洽率定义

自洽率包含两个方面的自洽率，一个是用能自洽率，另一个是用电自洽率。

用能自洽率是指年总光伏出力与负荷年总耗能量的比值，计算方法如下式所示：

$$\mathrm{SCR}_S = \frac{P_{\mathrm{PV}}}{E_{\mathrm{need}}}$$

式中，SCR_S为用能自洽率；P_{PV}为铁路系统年光伏出力；E_{need}为铁路系统的负荷年总耗能量。

用电自洽率是指年总光伏出力与负荷年总耗电量的比值，其计算方法如下式所示：

$$\mathrm{SCR}_E = \frac{P_{\mathrm{PV}}}{P_{\mathrm{need}}}$$

式中，SCR_E 为用电自洽率；P_{need} 为铁路系统的负荷年总耗电量。

4. 渗透率定义

铁路系统可再生能源渗透率为铁路供电系统中可再生能源发电量占总用电量的比例，其中铁路供电系统中可再生能源发电量包括铁路系统自身光伏出力与电网所供电能中可再生能源电力部分。其计算方法如下式所示：

$$\mathrm{NEPR} = \frac{P_{\mathrm{PV}} + (P_{\mathrm{need}} - P_{\mathrm{PV}}) \times \gamma}{P_{\mathrm{need}}}$$

式中，NEPR 为铁路系统可再生能源渗透率；γ为电力系统中可再生能源在电力一次侧能源中所占的比重，取 8.9%。

5. 经济性相关指标测算说明

对于不同模式的经济测算，首先获取全年以分钟为时间间隔的光伏出力数据 $P_{\mathrm{PV}}(i)$ 及负荷需求数据 $P_{\mathrm{need}}(i)$，设蓄电池组的荷电状态 SOC(i) 的初始值 SOC(1) 为蓄电池组的总容量 E_B，i 为时刻，可进行如下计算：

$$\mathrm{SOC}(i+1) = \mathrm{SOC}(i) + p_{\mathrm{PV}}(i) - p_{\mathrm{need}}(i), \quad i = 1, 2, \cdots, 525600$$

式中，$p_{\mathrm{PV}}(i)$ 均为 i 时刻的光伏出力；$p_{\mathrm{need}}(i)$ 为 i 时刻的负荷需求。

当

$$\mathrm{SOC}(i+1) > E_B$$

时，令

$$e_{\mathrm{sold}}(i) = \mathrm{SOC}(i+1) - E_B$$

之后令

$$\mathrm{SOC}(i+1) = E_B$$

除此情况外，

$$e_{\mathrm{sold}}(i) = 0$$

当

$$\mathrm{SOC}(i+1) < 0$$

令

$$e_{\text{bought}}(i) = -\text{SOC}(i+1)$$

之后令

$$\text{SOC}(i+1) = 0$$

除此情况外，

$$e_{\text{bought}}(i) = 0$$

最终，将售电量 $e_{\text{sold}}(i)$ 与购电量 $e_{\text{bought}}(i)$ 进行求和，分别得到该区间全年售电量 E_{sold} 与全年购电量 E_{bought}：

$$E_{\text{sold}} = \sum_{i=1}^{525600} e_{\text{sold}}(i)$$

$$E_{\text{bought}} = \sum_{i=1}^{525600} e_{\text{bought}}(i)$$

节省购电量的计算方法：

$$E_{\text{save}} = P_{\text{need}} - E_{\text{bought}}$$

上网电量即售电量 E_{sold}。

光伏组件投资额计算方法：

$$I_{\text{PV}} = S_{\text{PV}} \cdot U_{\text{PV}}$$

式中，I_{PV} 为光伏组件投资额；S_{PV} 为光伏组件面积；U_{PV} 为光伏组件单价，取 8000 元/m^2。

蓄电池储能投资额计算方法：

$$I_B = E_B \cdot U_B$$

式中，I_B 为蓄电池储能投资；U_B 为蓄电池储能单价，取 2083.33 元/(kW·h)。

超级电容器投资额计算方法：

$$I_C = E_C \cdot U_C$$

式中，I_C 为超级电容器投资；E_C 为超级电容器容量；U_C 为超级电容器单价，取 1.15 万元/(kW·h)。

总投资额计算方法：

$$I_{\text{sum}} = I_{\text{PV}} + I_B + I_C$$

式中，I_{sum} 为总投资；I_B 为蓄电池储能投资；I_C 为超级电容投资。

总收益计算方法：

$$R_{sum} = R_{PV} + R_{sold} + R_{save} = U_{PVS}P_{PV} + U_{sold}E_{sold} + U_{save}E_{save}$$

式中，R_{sum} 为总收益；R_{PV} 为光伏补贴收入；R_{sold} 为上网售电收入；R_{save} 为节省购电量收益；U_{PVS} 为光伏补贴单价，取 0.1 元/(kW·h)；U_{sold} 为上网售电单价，取 0.45 元/(kW·h)，E_{sold} 为上网售电量；U_{save} 为节省购电单价，取 1.0 元/(kW·h)，E_{save} 为节省购电总量。

投资收益比的计算方法：

$$\mathrm{ROI} = \frac{R_{sum}}{I_{sum}} \times 100\%$$

式中，ROI 为投资收益比；R_{sum} 为总收益；I_{sum} 为总投资。

投资回收年限的计算方法：

$$\mathrm{PBY} = \frac{I_{sum}}{R_{sum}}$$

式中，PBY 为回收年限；I_{sum} 为总投资；R_{sum} 为总收益。

6. 光伏系统转化率取值

不同类型的光伏组件其转化率并不相同，并且受到厂家能力的影响，同一类型光伏组件的转化率可能同样存在差异。国内主要光伏板厂家的部分产品参数如表 4-1 所示。

表 4-1 国产主要光伏组件技术参数

厂家	组件型号	类型	版型	长度/mm	宽度/mm	厚度/mm	平均功率/W	平均转化效率/%
天合光能	TSM-DE05H(Ⅱ)	单晶	60	1675	947	35	307	18.6
隆基绿能	LR6-60PE	单晶	60	1650	991	35	312	19.2
隆基绿能	LR6-72	单晶	72	1956	991	45	340	17.5
天合光能	TSM-PE06H	多晶	60	1698	1004	35	293	17.2
天合光能	TSM-DE15M(Ⅱ)	单晶	72	2024	1004	35	403	19.8
天合光能	TSM-PE14H	多晶	72	2000	992	35	338	17
中环股份	HOGJ-60C	单晶	60	1640	992	40	285	17.5
中环股份	HOGJ-72C	单晶	72	1965	992	40	343	17.6

从转化率方面来看，目前单晶硅组件的转化率较高，为 17.5%～20%，平均

值约为 18.4%；多晶硅转化率稍低，在 17%左右，单晶硅组件的转化率比多晶硅组件高出 8.2%左右。组件体积则受厂商影响较大，对于 60 版型的组件而言，单晶硅组件的体积与多晶硅组件没有明显差异；对于 72 版型的组件而言，多晶硅组件具有优势，较单晶硅平均体积减小 12%左右。

综上所述，对于铁路系统运载工具的光伏组件，选择转化率较高的单晶硅光伏组件；对于铁路基础设施的光伏组件，选择成本较低的单晶硅光伏组件。由于组件的转化率受生产厂商的影响较大，因而在后续测算中，保守起见，两种光伏组件的转化率均取 16%。

7. 储能电池相关取值

本报告测算以 12V、100A 的锂离子电池为例进行相关的数据测算。锂离子单体电池的尺寸大约为 342mm×211mm×173mm，售价为 2500 元。锂电池蓄电池组的占地面积按照 0.06019m^2/(kW·h)计算，超级电容器的体积很小，可忽略不计。锂电池价格按照 2083.33 元/(kW·h)计算，超级电容价格按照 1.15 万元/(kW·h)计算。锂电池的使用年限以 5 年计，超级电容使用年限以 20 年计。

4.1.2 不同利用模式的共性配置技术

1. 因地制宜的太阳能资源利用

根据上面所述，铁路系统的组成可以分为载运工具、基础设施和服务设施 3 个部分，这 3 个部分各自拥有不同的太阳能资源利用方法，即光伏铺设的方法。

1) 铁路运载体的光伏铺设方法

对于铁路系统的载运工具而言，光伏系统可选择安装于非电气化铁路客车车厢的顶部，考虑到列车顶部的空间有限，因而组件类型选择为转化率相对更高的单晶硅组件。由于列车运行时速度很快，若选择带有倾角的布置方式，虽然会提高一部分光资源利用率，但会对光伏系统的结构强度以及运行稳定性提出更高的要求，因而采取平铺的方式。电气化铁路和货运列车不进行此种方案的布置，原因在于电气化铁路的车厢上方有高压牵引网，布置光伏板对于车厢绝缘性能的影响尚不明确；货运列车的车厢大多没有顶棚，不具有铺设光伏组件的空间，且大多数货运车厢自身没有能源消耗，因而没有铺设光伏组件的必要性。

2) 铁路基础设施的光伏铺设方法

对于铁路系统的基础设施而言，有两部分基础设施可以进行光伏铺设，分别是①在电气化铁路的轨道上方搭建支撑架；②在铁路线路安全保护区内铺设光伏组件。

(1) 在电气化铁路的轨道上方搭建支撑架。指的是在电气化铁路的轨道上方依据线路走向及当地纬度布置光伏组件。根据现行《铁路技术管理规程》，单线铁路的基本路基宽度为 8.6m，双线铁路的基本路基宽度为 13.6m，且跨越电气化铁路的各种建筑物与带电部分的最小距离，不小于 500mm。因此支架宽度可选择为 13.6m，高度设置为 7000mm。

对于不同走向的铁路线路，光伏组件有不同的布置方式：完全东西走向的铁路线，由于太阳辐射的偏角，朝北的区域有一部分在一天内一直无法照射到阳光，而朝南的区域太阳辐射会相对比较充足，因此在设计布置太阳能板布置区域时可以考虑不对称的形状布置(图 4-1)；完全南北走向的铁路线，由于太阳东升西落，整个光伏棚顶的每个角度在一天中都有机会受到太阳辐射，而正午应该是太阳辐射最大的时刻，因此可以从中间开始向两侧对称布置弧形(图 4-2)；对于走向不完

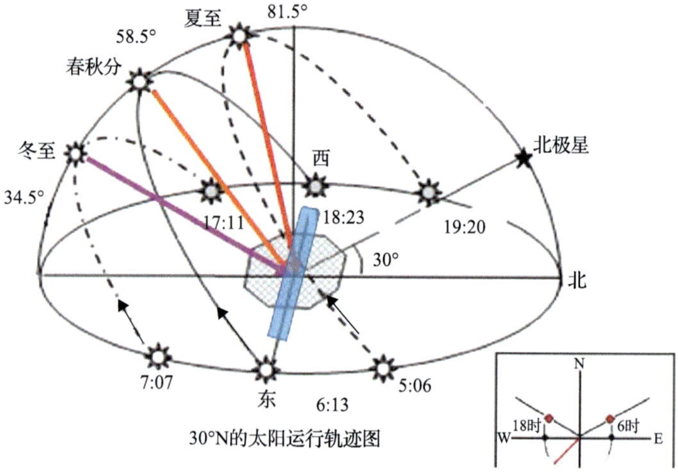

图 4-1　太阳运行轨迹及东西走向铁路线示意图

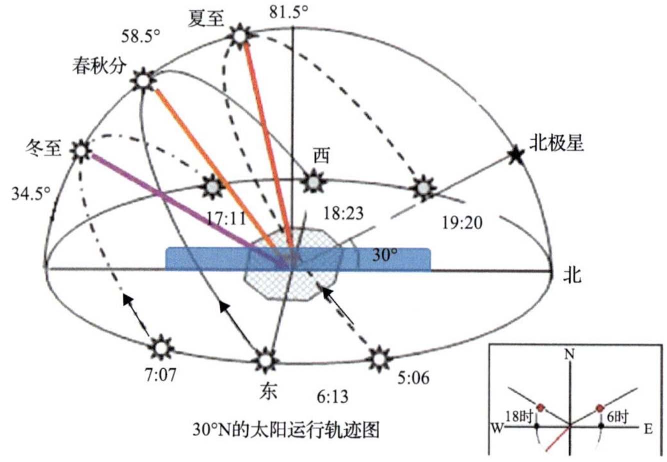

图 4-2　太阳运行轨迹及南北走向铁路线示意图

全为东西向或南北向的线路，同样由于太阳的东升西落，整个光伏棚顶的每个角度在一天中都有机会受到太阳辐射，但是偏南的那一侧太阳辐射会比较大，所以可以根据线路的具体角度决定不对称布置还是对称布置(图 4-3)。

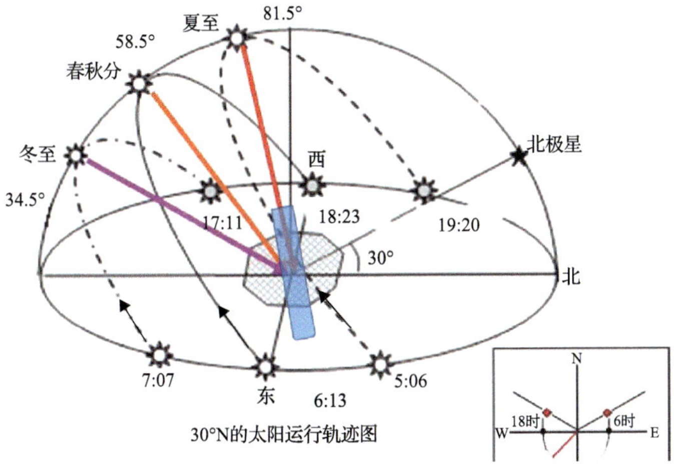

图 4-3　太阳运行轨迹及有偏角的轨道线示意图

根据线路的走向，支架顶层可分为两种不同的布置方式：若线路主要为南北走向，在一天的时间范围内，线路的东西两侧均可被阳光直射，因而可以选择顶层为弧形的布置方式，如图 4-4(a)所示；若线路主要为东西走向，由于我国位于北半球，太阳一直处于南方，线路北侧没有被阳光直射的机会，所以可以选择支架顶层为平面的布置方式，光伏组件布置为当地的最佳倾角，如图 4-4(b)所示。

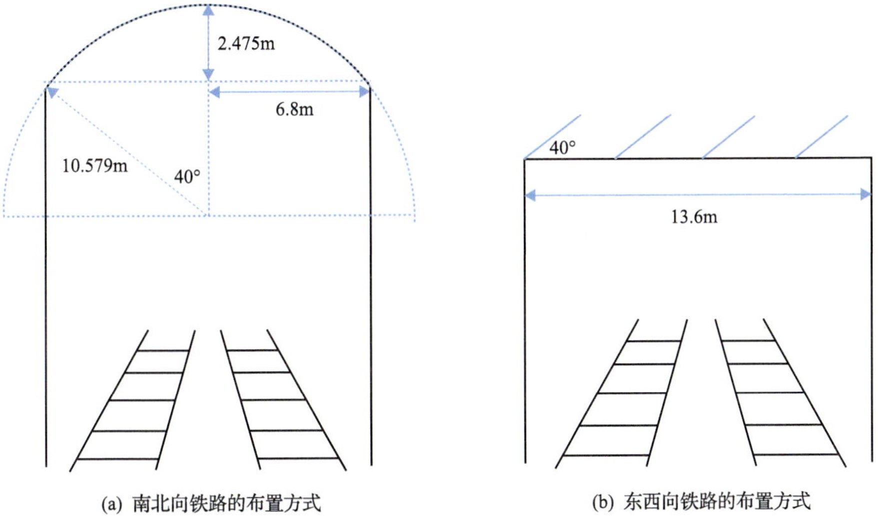

图 4-4　铁路基础设施的两种光伏板布置方式示意图

根据《太阳能光伏发电应用技术》(第 3 版)，我国主要城市的光伏板最佳倾角如表 4-2 所示。

表 4-2　特定城市光伏板布置最佳倾角表

城市	纬度ϕ/(°)	最佳倾角/(°)
哈尔滨	45.68	ϕ+3
长春	43.90	ϕ+1
沈阳	41.77	ϕ+1
北京	39.80	ϕ+4
天津	39.10	ϕ+5
呼和浩特	40.78	ϕ+3
太原	37.78	ϕ+5
乌鲁木齐	43.78	ϕ+12
西宁	36.75	ϕ+1
兰州	36.05	ϕ+8
银川	38.48	ϕ+2
西安	34.30	ϕ+14
上海	31.17	ϕ+3
南京	32.00	ϕ+5
合肥	31.85	ϕ+9
杭州	30.23	ϕ+3
南昌	28.67	ϕ+2
福州	26.08	ϕ+4
济州	36.68	ϕ+6
郑州	34.72	ϕ+7
武汉	3.63	ϕ+7
长沙	28.20	ϕ+6
广州	23.13	ϕ−7
海口	20.03	ϕ+12
南宁	22.82	ϕ+5
成都	30.67	ϕ+2
贵阳	26.58	ϕ+8
昆明	25.02	ϕ−8
拉萨	29.70	ϕ−8

以下以兰新线为例进行说明。首先，由于微网的接线最终都要经过牵引变电站后再为负荷供电，因此对于兰新线光资源比较充足只需布置小段路程的线路，优先选择在牵引变电站前后布置光伏板。根据计算，兰新线平均只需在牵引变电站前后布置 500m 的光伏就能够满足需求，因此选出路线上牵引变电站的坐标(共 36 个点)，并测出在地图上那一点前后 500m 左右路段的走向。根据线路走向以及当地纬度确定光伏板的具体布置方案，图 4-5 是布置结果。其中，序号是指兰州—乌鲁木齐方向上的牵引变编号；走向是指线路的方向，以正北方向为 0°，正西方向为 90°，依次类推。对于隧道的供能可以同样的方式布置光伏组件，将光伏产生的电能引入隧道内的汇流箱即可。

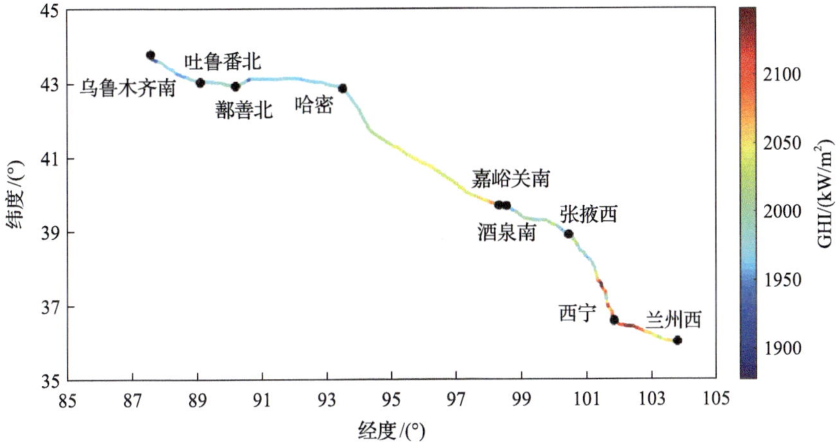

图 4-5　兰新线牵引变配置序号示意图

(2) 在铁路线路安全保护区内铺设光伏组件。根据《铁路运输安全保护条例》的相关规定，铁路线路两侧设立了铁路线路安全保护区，在铁路线路安全保护区铺设光伏组件指的是在各类铁路线两边的安全保护区内铺设光伏组件。为了不影响线路安全保护特性，拟在轨道两侧各布置宽度为 1m 的光伏组件，光伏组件铺设的长度则应与当地负荷相适应，以避免功率不足或资源浪费，还应该考虑当地的地理环境来确定，铺设角度仍按照当地最佳倾角布置。

3) 铁路服务设施的光伏铺设方法

对于铁路系统的服务设施而言，可选择在车站屋顶及雨棚上方布置光伏组件。光伏组件的倾角以贴合建筑物轮廓较为适宜，且光伏组件的颜色也应符合建筑的整体规划。与此同时，光伏板的布置还应考虑到车站本身的采光需要。目前国内已有大量服务设施铺设光伏组件的实例，如上海虹桥、杭州东站、青岛站等，可自行参考。表 4-3 为兰新线光伏板布置方案(部分)。

表 4-3　兰新线光伏板布置方案(部分)

序号	纬度/(°)	经度/(°)	走向/(°)	最佳倾角/(°)	形状
1	36.07	103.74	98.23	44	朝南单面，锯齿状布置，倾角为 44°
2	36.17	103.20	122.14	44	0°～两侧 40°范围内安装
3	36.36	102.69	115.98	40	0°～两侧 40°范围内安装/朝南单面，锯齿状布置，倾角为 40°
4	36.49	102.16	115.80	40	0°～两侧 40°范围内安装/朝南单面，锯齿状布置，倾角为 40°
5	36.77	101.78	183.02	40	0°～两侧 40°范围内安装
6	37.04	101.63	—	40	0°～两侧 40°范围内安装
7	42.93	93.21	110.31	52	0°～两侧 50°范围内安装
8	43.04	92.60	100.61	52	朝南单面，锯齿状布置，倾角为 52°
9	43.12	91.97	90.00	53	朝南单面，锯齿状布置，倾角为 53°
10	43.11	91.34	91.05	53	朝南单面，锯齿状布置，倾角为 53°
11	43.11	90.70	90.92	54	朝南单面，锯齿状布置，倾角为 54°
12	42.92	90.14	93.95	54	朝南单面，锯齿状布置，倾角为 54°
13	43.03	89.53	97.43	55	朝南单面，锯齿状布置，倾角为 55°
14	43.08	88.92	104.07	55	0°～两侧 50°范围内安装/朝南单面，锯齿状布置，倾角为 55°
15	43.29	88.36	124.50	55	0°～两侧 50°范围内安装
16	43.14	88.78	124.67	55	0°～两侧 50°范围内安装

2. 高效可靠的储能系统配置

1) 储能系统构成的配置策略

储能即通过物理或者化学过程，实现能量的高效转换与存储。储能系统可将不可再生或可再生自然资源产生的间歇性能源进行存储与释放接入电网，使用户端得到稳定、安全、高效的清洁能源。同时，储能系统还能平衡各类能量应用需求，提升社会整体能源的使用效率。

储能系统中的储能元件种类很多，大致可分为机械储能、热储能、化学储能、电化学储能等。电化学储能方式是一种最常见的储能方式，包括了传统的铅酸蓄电池、锂离子电池、钠硫电池以及超级电容等。铅酸蓄电池广泛地应用在不间断电源系统，其主要优点是价格相对较低、安全性高。但是，其能量密度低、重量重，此外，重金属铅还会造成环境的污染，这些缺点使得它应用受到限制。锂离子电池能量密度高、重量轻，是一种非常具有潜力的储能元件，锂电池已经广泛地应用于电子设备中，近年来又被应用于电动汽车领域。超级电容功率密度大，能够快速充放很大的功率，通常在系统中作为瞬时功率输出的缓冲单元。化学储能主要包括储氢和合成天然气储能。其中储氢技术被广泛地应用于燃料电池发电系统中，由于其具有无污染、能量大、噪声小等特性，是一种非常有前途的可再生能源储能技术。

图 4-6 给出了储能单元常见的额定功率放电时间和容量的对比。超级电容的额定功率放电时间最短，通常在秒级到分钟级。氢气储能和合成天然气储能具有较长的额定功率放电时间，通常在数小时到数月之间。综上所述，单一的储能单元很难满足复杂应用场景的需求。根据应用需求，选择多种储能单元，并利用不同储能单元的性能互补，可以实现储能系统的最优化设计。同时，多种储能单元互补运行，提高了储能系统的经济性、可靠性和灵活性，有利于储能系统的规模化发展。

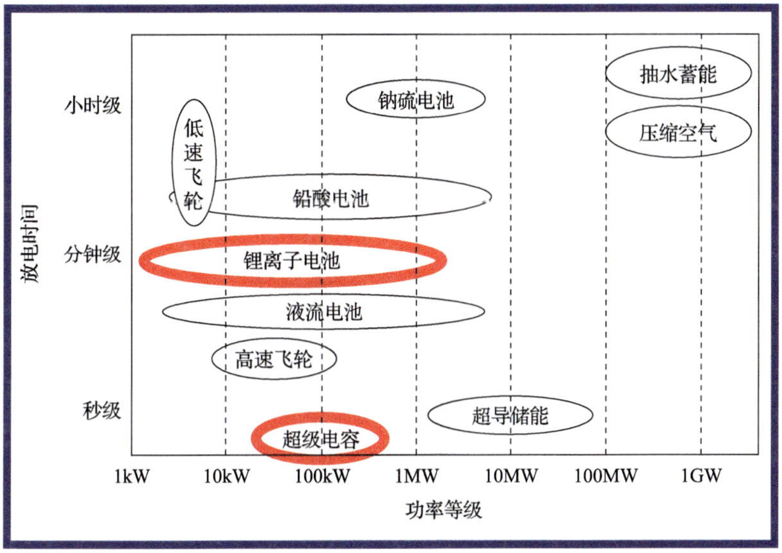

图 4-6　不同储能方式的容量及功率特性对比图

目前，混合储能系统主要包括多种电池混合储能、电池-电容混合储能等。由于多种储能单元互补运行具有显著的优势，未来混合储能系统的应用将具有广阔的前景。据统计，2017 年全球混合储能的系统装机容量为 78.6MW，预计到 2026 年混合储能系统装机容量将达到 2.1GW。其中，多种电池混合储能系统装机容量将达到 600MW，电池-电容混合储能系统将超过 1GW。

对于一个牵引变电站而言，电气化铁路的负荷往往具有间歇冲击性且功率很大。牵引变电站的供电区段划分清晰，两站之间、站内不同相之间均设有分段，从而当列车进入某一供电区间时，其功率要求瞬时上升，因而具有冲击性；并且机车牵引用电的功率很大，通常在 3000kW 以上，高铁列车的牵引功率甚至超过 20MW，对于供电系统的要求很高。

由于上述两方面的原因，作为提供能量的储能系统，其特性必须满足这两方面的要求。一方面，负荷具有冲击性，储能系统必须能够在短时间内将输出功率升至所需值，因而要配置功率型储能装置；另一方面，负荷的功率很大，持续时间较长，能量消耗很大，从而储能系统的容量也要相应提升，需要配置相应的能量型储能装置。

在不同种类的储能方式中，合成天然气、储氢、抽水储能、储热、液态空气储能等储能方式，由于能源类型、设备体积、自然资源要求等方面的原因，不适合作为光储系统的储能设备。可用的储能方式一般包括超级电容、飞轮储能和蓄电池 3 种方式。其中，飞轮储能具有能量密度不够高、自放电率高等缺点，只适合于一些细分市场，如高品质不间断电源等。因此，储能系统的配置应为超级电容与蓄电池的组合，超级电容的充放电速度很快，作为功率型原件满足供电前期的负荷冲击；蓄电池的功率上升稍慢，但价格便宜、容量较大，可以作为能量型原件满足负荷的后续用电。

常见的蓄电池种类有铅蓄电池、镍镉电池、镍氢电池、锂离子电池和锂离子聚合物电池等。表 4-4 给出了不同类型蓄电池的参数。

表 4-4　各类型蓄电池参数对比

电池类型	电压/V	能量密度/(W·h/L)	功率/(W/kg)	效率/%	能量/(W·h)	自放电率/(%/月)	可充放电次数	寿命/年
铅酸电池	2.1	60～75	180	70～92	5～8	3～4	500～800	5～8
镍镉电池	1.2	50～150	150	70～90	1.25～2.5	0.2	1500	—
镍氢电池	1.2	140～300	250～1000	66	2.75	0.3	500～2000	—
镍锌电池	1.7	170	900	—	2～3.3	—	100～500	—
锂离子电池	3.6	250～360	1800	99+	2.8～5	5～10	1200～10000	2～6
锂离子聚合物电池	3.7	300	3000+	99.8	2.8～5	0.05	500～1000	2～3
磷酸锂铁电池	3.25	170	1400	94	0.7～3	—	2000+	>10

从表 4-4 中可以看出，磷酸铁锂电池虽然价格优势明显，但能量密度、功率密度均较低，不符合上述要求；锂离子聚合物电池虽然在上述两方面满足要求，但寿命很短，仅有 2～3 年，在使用过程中需要频繁更换电池，而铁路线路又很长，更换电池极不便利；铅酸电池虽然寿命很长，但同样地，能量密度及功率密度不满足上述要求，且铅酸电池的环境问题较为突出，不适合进行大规模的布置，而锂离子电池的能量密度和功率密度都很高，在大规模的布置中十分节省空间，并

且能量转化效率高，超过 99%，节能效果明显；其可充放电次数是所列电池类型中最多，支持长时间高负荷运行，寿命也可达到 5 年以上；此外，锂离子电池带来的环境问题相对而言小得多，更加符合铁路绿色化的目标；且占地小、寿命长。所以综合来看，锂离子电池是本方案中蓄电池的最佳选择。

2) 储能系统的容量计算方法

储能容量的配置可分为两部分，即功率型储能容量配置以及能量型储能容量配置，两者针对的是在实际铁路运行过程中的不同阶段，具有不同的功率需求和能量需求。

能量型储能容量的配置与光伏出力和负荷特性密切相关，对于这部分的计算，首先要确定光伏组件的配置方式，根据实际光照计算出全年每天以小时为单位的光伏出力情况，然后根据铁路每天的负荷数据，将二者进行比对以确定储能容量的计算方法。

比较每天的光伏日出力和铁路负荷用电，将所配置区段分为三种资源区：若在排除夏季后，光伏出力大于负荷所需的天数仍超过 50%，则称其为资源丰富区；若在排除冬季后，光伏出力小于负荷所需的天数仍超过 50%，则称其为资源匮乏区；其他地区则为一般资源区。

对于资源丰富区，储能容量的配置方法是将每天负荷瞬时功率所需超过光伏出力的累计能量的最大值，作为整个系统的储能容量。图 4-7 为资源丰富区的储能容量计算方法图。

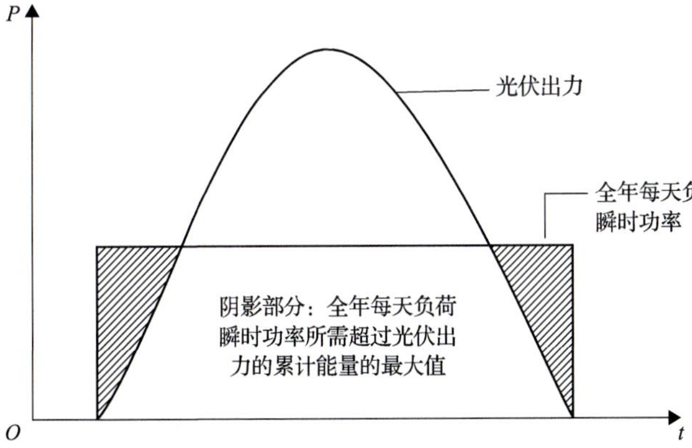

图 4-7　资源丰富区的储能容量计算方法图

对于一般资源区，储能容量的配置方法为，将每天负荷瞬时功率所需超过光伏出力的累计能量的最大值，与全年每天光伏瞬时功率超过负荷所需的累计能量的最大值，两者之间的最大值作为储能系统的容量。图 4-8 为一般资源区的储能容量计算方法图。

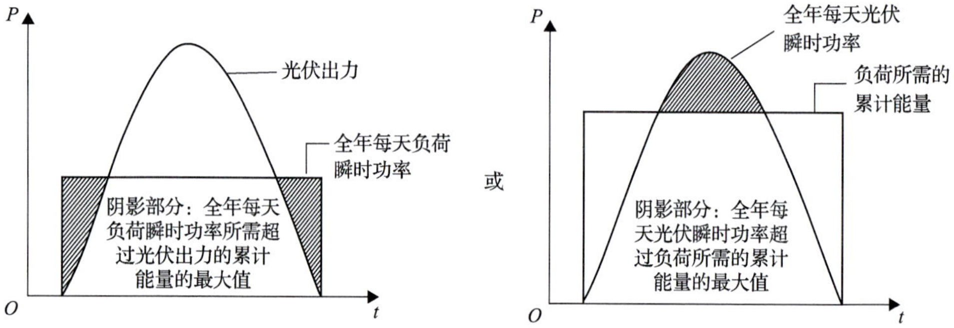

图 4-8　一般资源区的储能容量计算方法图

对于资源匮乏区，储能容量则按照按全年每天光伏瞬时功率超过负荷所需的累计能量的最大值，作为储能系统的容量，如图 4-9 所示。

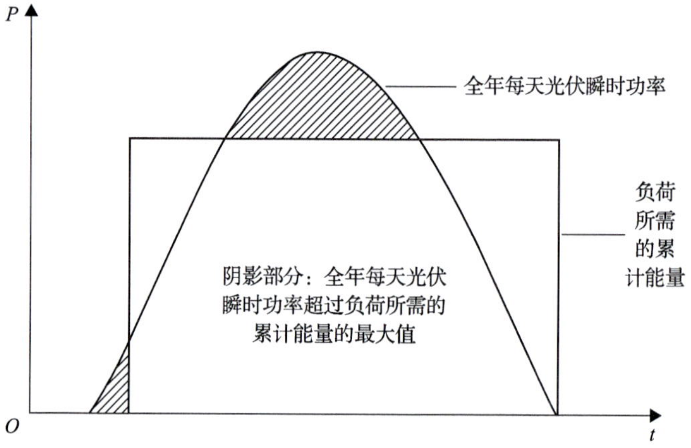

图 4-9　资源匮乏区储能容量的配置方法图

功率型储能容量的配置则与铁路负荷的瞬间特性密切相关。储能系统的最大可输出功率必须超过铁路牵引负荷所需，否则储能系统的配置将毫无意义。首先要估算在本级牵引变区段上最多同时存在多少量列车，同时估算每辆列车的额定功率。将其累加后，还要乘上一个可靠系数 $k(k>1)$，以确保储能装置的功率满足要求。

$$P_{B_{\min}} = k \cdot \sum_{i=1}^{n} P_{\text{train}}(i)$$

能量型储能容量的配置还要兼顾平抑功率波动的作用，其容量应该满足逐时电量缺额的累加值 E_1 以及连续充电或放电过程中的电量变化量 E_2。

$$E_b = \max(E_1, E_2)$$

$$E_1 = \max\left(\left|\Delta P_1 \Delta t\right|, \left|\Delta P_1 \Delta t + \Delta P_2 \Delta t\right|, \cdots, \left|\Delta P_1 \Delta t + \Delta P_2 \Delta t + \cdots + \Delta P_n \Delta t\right|\right)$$

$$E_2 = \max\left(\left|\sum_{i=1}^{m_1} \Delta P_i \Delta t\right|, \left|\sum_{i=m_2}^{m_3} \Delta P_i \Delta t\right|, \cdots, \left|\sum_{i=m_j}^{m_n} \Delta P_i \Delta t\right|\right)$$

式中，E_b 为储能设备的额定容量；ΔP_i 为每个时刻储能系统出力需求；Δt 为时间间隔，取 1h，$1\sim m_1$、$m_2\sim m_3$、$m_j\sim m_n$ 为需要连续充电或者连续放电的时段。

超级电容的配置则与负荷跳变量以及电池组的性能有关。负荷跳变量一般为一列列车的额定负荷，虽然存在两列列车同时进入供电区段的可能性，但概率极小，因而不考虑这种情况。电池组为锂电池，其功率上升时间一般为 1s，从而超级电容所储存的电量要支撑负荷 1s 所需。

$$E_C = \Delta P \cdot \Delta t$$

3. 灵活鲁棒的能量管理策略

1) 光伏铁路微电网的拓扑结构

结合高铁供电方式，光伏铁路的拓扑结构。首先，由于高铁的功率较大，靠蓄电池供电时蓄电池功率无法在短时间内上升到所需功率，因此需要利用超级电容器实现快速充放电，所以储能结构是蓄电池与超级电容器结合的形式。其次，光伏产生的电先要经过最大功率控制后逆变升压，再接入接触网。最后，光伏电池、蓄电池以及超级电容器都在经过各自的 DC/DC 变流器后汇合，光伏与储能系统之间的能量交换在经过逆变器之前进行。综上，得到的高铁光伏+储能的微网结构如图 4-10 所示。

微网可以在两种模式下运行。在并网模式下，变流器可能充当逆变器，也可能充当整流器。若光伏阵列出力大于负荷所需，则变流器充当逆变器，从直流侧向交流侧传输功率，同时光伏出力优先为储能系统充能，剩余电量返送电网；若光伏阵列出力小于负荷所需，且蓄电池组的荷电状态不满足继续输出足够功率的条件，则变流器充当整流器，从交流侧向直流侧输送电能，光伏出力与电网同时为储能设施充电。

在孤岛模式下，电池对电源平衡和电压稳定起着非常重要的作用，各变换器的控制目标由能源管理系统调度。直流母线电压通过蓄电池变换器根据不同的运行条件保持稳定，主变流器则被控制以提供稳定、高质量的交流母线电压。根据系统的运行要求，光伏阵列可以灵活地采取控制方式。

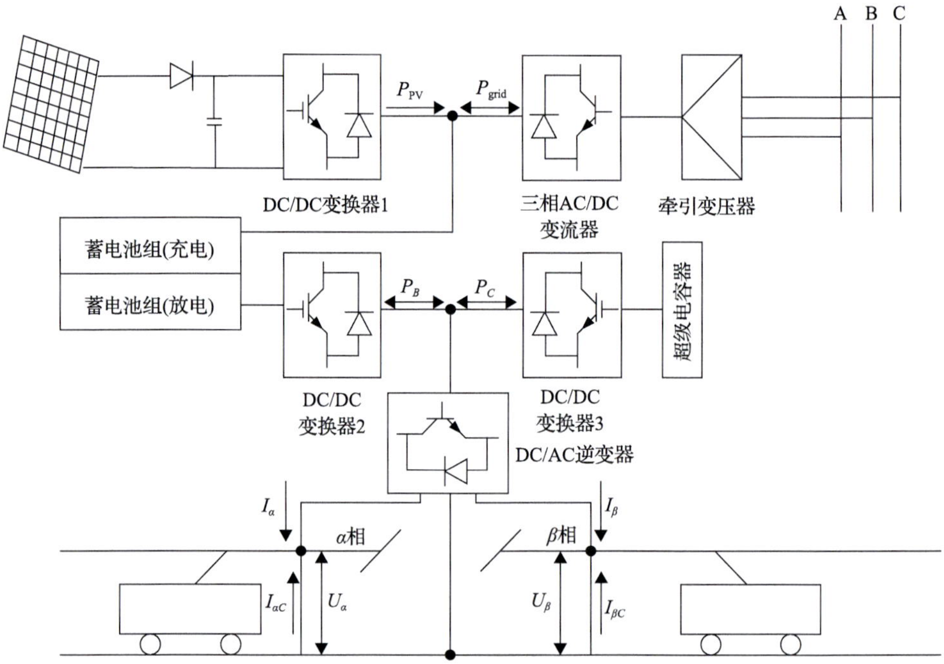

图 4-10　适用于牵引供电的光储系统微网结构图

2) 光伏铁路微电网的运行策略

光伏阵列的模型可由下式描述:

$$\begin{cases} i_{\mathrm{pv}} = n_p I_{\mathrm{ph}} - n_p I_{\mathrm{sat}} \times \left\{ \exp\left[\left(\dfrac{q}{AkT} \right) \left(\dfrac{V_{\mathrm{pv}}}{n_s} + I_{\mathrm{pv}} R_s \right) \right] - 1 \right\} \\ I_{\mathrm{ph}} = \left[I_{\mathrm{sso}} + k_i (T - T_r) \right] \cdot \dfrac{S}{1000} \\ I_{\mathrm{sat}} = I_{rr} \left(\dfrac{T}{T_r} \right)^3 \exp\left[\left(\dfrac{qE_{\mathrm{gap}}}{kA} \right) \cdot \left(\dfrac{1}{T_r} - \dfrac{1}{T} \right) \right] \end{cases}$$

各参数的意义如表 4-5 所示。

表 4-5　光伏组件参数

符号	意义
i_{pv}	光伏组件电流
n_p	并联单元数
n_s	串联单元数
I_{ph}	光电流

续表

符号	意义
I_{sat}	模块反向饱和电流
q	电子电荷，其值为 1.602×10^{-19}C
A	理想系数取 1.5
k	玻尔兹曼常量，其值为 1.38×10^{-23}J/K
T	光伏组件表面温度，取 350K
V_{pv}	光伏组件电压
R_s	光伏电池的串联电阻
I_{sso}	短路电流，其值为 3.27A
k_i	短路电流温度系数，其值为 1.7×10^{-3}
T_r	参考温度，其值为 301.18K
S	太阳辐射水平
I_{rr}	T_r 温度下的反向饱和电流，其值为 2.0793×10^{-6}A
E_{gap}	硅的带隙能，1.1eV

蓄电池的模型中有两个十分重要的变量：终端电压 V_b 及电池的荷电状态 SOC。模型可由下式描述：

$$\begin{cases} V_b = V_o + R_b \cdot i_b - K\dfrac{Q_{BE}}{Q_{BE}+\int i_b \mathrm{d}t} + A\cdot\exp\left(B\int i_b \mathrm{d}t\right) \\ \mathrm{SOC} = 100\left(1+\dfrac{\int i_b \mathrm{d}t}{Q_{BE}}\right) \end{cases}$$

式中，R_b 为蓄电池的内阻抗；V_o 为蓄电池的开路电压；i_b 为电池的充电电流；K 是极化电压；Q_{BE} 为蓄电池的容量；A 为电压常数；B 为容量常数。

微网的光伏逆变器采用最大功率点跟踪(maximum power point tracking，MPPT)的控制方式，以保持光伏组件的出力为可能的最大值；超级电容的 DC/DC 变换器采用双向控制，以在负荷跳变时为电池提供短时的功率支撑，同时在负荷平稳时充能为下次跳变做准备；蓄电池 DC/DC 变换器同样采用双向控制，在光伏出力不足时为负荷提供能量，在光伏出力剩余时储存能量。DC/AC 变换器则与微网的运行方式有关，微网并网运行时，DC/AC 变换器采用双向控制，当光伏出力不足且电池 SOC 低时，功率由交流侧流向直流侧，电网为储能装置充能，当直流侧有功率剩余时，功率由直流侧流向交流侧，剩余功率返送电网；当微网孤岛运行时，主变换器采用单向控制，此时其为单向 DC/AC 逆变器，功率由直流侧流向交流侧，通过控制逆变端电压为负荷提供功率。光伏铁路微网的能量调度逻辑图如图 4-11 所示。

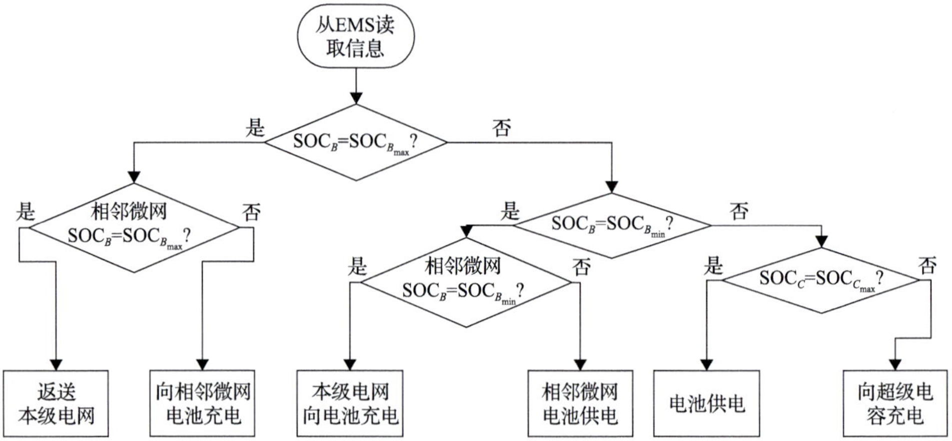

图 4-11　光伏铁路微网的能量调度逻辑图

首先从微网的 EMS 读取本级蓄电池荷电状态信息，判断其是否达到最大值，若达到最大值，则判断相邻微网蓄电池荷电状态是否达到最大值，若达到最大值，则将剩余能量返送本级电网；若未达最大值，则向相邻微网输送能量。若本级蓄电池荷电状态未达最大值，则判断其是否为最小值，若达到最小值，读取相邻微网蓄电池荷电状态并判断其是否为最小值，若同样为最小值，则需由电网提供能量支撑；若不为最小值，则由相邻微网向本级微网输送能量。若本级蓄电池荷电状态未达最小值，则判断本级超级电容是否满电，若满电，则蓄电池向负荷供电；反之，则由蓄电池向超级电容供电。

4.2　特定模式的专门技术解决方案

本节将上面所述的我国可再生能源与铁路融合的八种不同模式，按照地域属性、电网属性以及铁路负荷属性的不同进行耦合，划分为四种特定模式的铁路可再生能源系统建设方案，并对每种方案进行详细的介绍和数据测算。四种特定模式分别为交通专用的能源系统、交通特用的能源系统、交通适用的能源系统以及能源系统支持的交通能源系统。四种特定模式与 3.3 节所介绍的交通能源系统演化新模式之间的对应关系如下所示。

(1) 交通专用的能源系统供给方案，对应无电区域的铁路可再生能源系统建设方案，具体对应无电+少负荷+多光场景和无电+少负荷+少光两个场景，相应的解决方案分别是内燃机+可再生+微网为主+自给自足和内燃机为主+可再生+微网+

自给自足。

(2)交通特用的能源系统供给方案,对应处于电网末端的铁路可再生能源系统建设方案,具体对应末端+少负荷+多光和末端+少负荷+少光两个场景,相应的解决方案分别是可再生+储能+微网为主+余电上网和可再生能源+储能+微网/电网+自给自足。

(3)交通适用的能源系统供给方案,对应处于强电网但是铁路负荷较小区域的铁路可再生能源系统建设方案,具体对应强电网+少负荷+多光和强电网+少负荷+少光两个场景,相应的解决方案分别是可再生能源+储能+微网+余电上网和可再生+储能+微网/电网+余电上网。

(4)能源系统支持的交通系统解决方案,对应处于强电网但是铁路负荷较多区域的铁路可再生能源系统建设方案,对应强电网+多负荷+多光和强电网+多负荷+少光两个场景,相应的解决方案分别是可再生+储能+微网/电网+自给自足和可再生+储能+电网为主+网上购电。

4.2.1 交通专用的能源系统技术解决方案

1. 适用场景及方案介绍

交通专用的能源系统供给方案,是针对无电区域的铁路能源系统而言的新型建设方案。在该模式下,地区所处的位置无电网接入,铁路为非电气化铁路,采用以柴油为动力的内燃机列车,因而可再生能源系统并不能够为地区线路上的主要能源消耗——机车牵引——提供能源支持,仅能够为耗能较少的车载设备提供能源。

本方案适用的地区为西藏自治区以及青海西部地区。下面以青藏铁路格拉段作为本方案的算例,以“无电+少负荷+多光”模式的系统解决方案进行测算说明。由于负荷较小,且地区的光资源十分丰富,铺设少量面积的光伏组件即可满足负荷所需。

本方案的具体实施方法如下所示。

(1)在车厢顶部布置光伏组件。光伏组件的布置方法与前述相同,采取平铺的方式,密布与车体上方。以25T型客车为例,由于列车一端位顶部装设有空调组件,二端位顶部装设有水箱用活盖,在这些位置不铺设光伏组件,从而可铺设长度从25.5m缩短至20.8m。列车宽度为3.1m,同时,列车顶部为一弧形结构。设列车为16编组,通过下式可计算得出列车顶部的可铺设面积为1266m^2。其中,S_{train}为面积;l_{train}为单节列车的长度,取20.8m;c_{train}为列车宽度,取3.1m;n_{train}为列车编组数量,在本例中取16;c_{rad}为弧线转化系数,取1.227。图4-12为Z165次列车侧面示意图。图4-13为Z165次列车截面示意图。

$$S_{\text{train}} = l_{\text{train}} \times c_{\text{train}} \times n_{\text{train}} \times c_{\text{rad}}$$

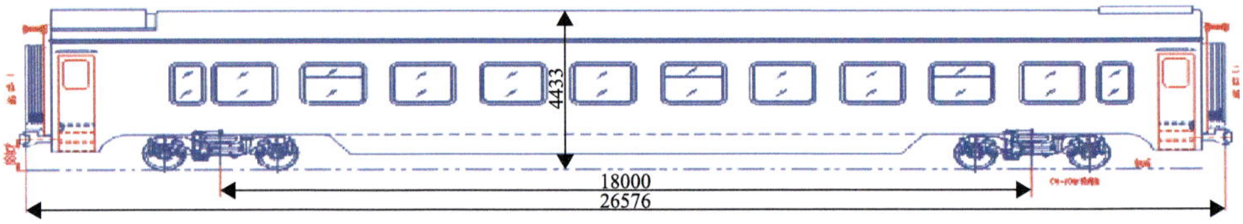

图 4-12　Z165 次列车侧面示意图(单位：mm)

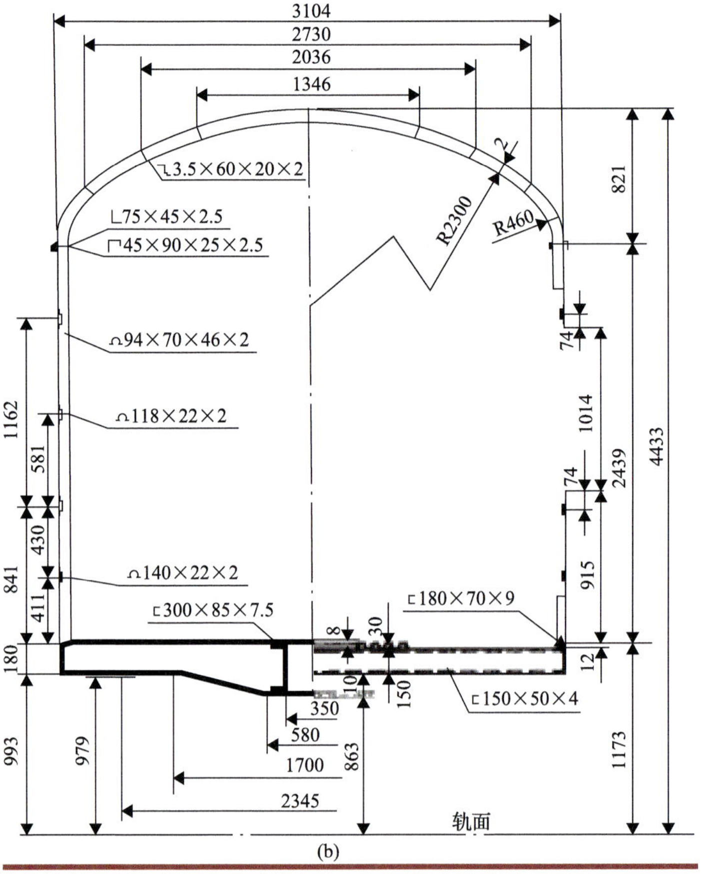

图 4-13　Z165 次列车截面示意图(单位：mm)

图片来源：维基百科 https://zh.wikipedia.org/wiki

(2)在车厢内部布置储能设备。储能设备是组成可再生能源微网的核心设备之一，是平抑光伏出力波动的重要元件。储能设备容量的确定可以根据当地光照强度、列车辅助设备的功率需求以及列车的运行时刻综合考虑。储能设备的配置原则为将光伏组件功率超过列车负荷功率时的能量储存，以提高光伏利用率。

(3)各列车光储系统组成独立微网，全列列车之间组成线性微网群。每节列车均有其各自的光储系统，通过控制模块在本节列车组成微网，形成“可再生能源+列车供能”的能源利用模式。每节列车两端设汇流箱，相邻两节列车之间通过汇流箱形成微网群，实现光储系统能源在全车的灵活调度。微网能源的调度原则与前述保持一致，即光伏出力流动的优先级为本节负荷、本节储能设备、相邻车厢负荷、相邻车厢储能设备；负荷能量来源的优先级为本节光伏出力、本节储能设备、相邻车厢光伏、相邻车厢储能设备、发电车。

青藏铁路格拉段北起青海省格尔木，南至西藏自治区拉萨市，途经当雄、那曲、安多站，全长 1142km，运营速度为 100km/h，每天有 14 班列车运行于格拉段上。格拉段铁路沿线年光照强度在 2000kW·h/m^2 以上，是我国光资源最为丰富的地区之一。此外，铁路沿线仅有 1 条 110kV 输电线，属于电网强度极为薄弱的地区。因此，青藏铁路格拉段满足上述的“无电+少负荷+多光”模式，解决方案为“内燃机+可再生+微网+自给自足”的能源利用模式。图 4-14 为青藏铁路沿线示意图。

由于目前格拉段为非电气化铁路，采用以柴油为动力的内燃机列车，因而可再生能源系统并不能够为该线路上的主要能源消耗——机车牵引——提供能源支持，仅能够为耗能较少车载设备以及车站用能负荷提供能源。因此青藏铁路的改造方案为在列车的车顶位置布置光伏组件，并在车内配置相应的储能设备，通过光储系统形成以列车为单位的微网系统，为车载辅助设备供能，在线路上方搭建光伏篷，通过储能装置为临近车站供能。

以 Z165 次列车为例，该次列车采取 16 节车厢编组，包括 8 节卧车、4 节硬座、2 节软卧车、1 节餐车以及 1 节空调发电车，4:40 由格尔木发车，当日 19:35 到达拉萨，运行时间约 15h。由上述可知，该列车车顶面积约为 1266m^2，辅助设施的功率为 740kW 左右。在保守场景、基本场景及积极场景下，在车顶分别铺设光伏组件的面积分别是 126.6m^2、253.2m^2 和 379.8m^2。

青藏铁路为Ⅱ级单线铁路，全线桥隧总长约占线路总长的 8%。以南北走向为主的线路，支架顶层选择为圆弧形，单位长度光伏板铺设面积为 9.34m^2；以东西走向为主的线路，支架顶层选择为平顶，光伏板倾斜角度以当地最佳倾角布置，控制单位长度光伏板的铺设面积为 9.5m^2。光伏篷的面积如下式所示。

$$S_{\text{rail}} = c_{\text{rail}} L_{\text{rail}} p_n$$

式中，S_{rail} 为光伏篷的面积；c_{rail} 为光伏篷的等效宽度，取 9.5m；L_{rail} 为排除桥隧线路全长，p_n 为铺设比例。以铺设比例为 10%、20%、30%作为阶梯，分析该区段的初始需求以及未来的发展空间。在保守场景、基本场景及积极场景下，光伏组件的面积分别为 126.03 万 m^2、252.06 万 m^2、378.09 万 m^2。图 4-15 为青藏铁路格拉段铺设面积测算结果。

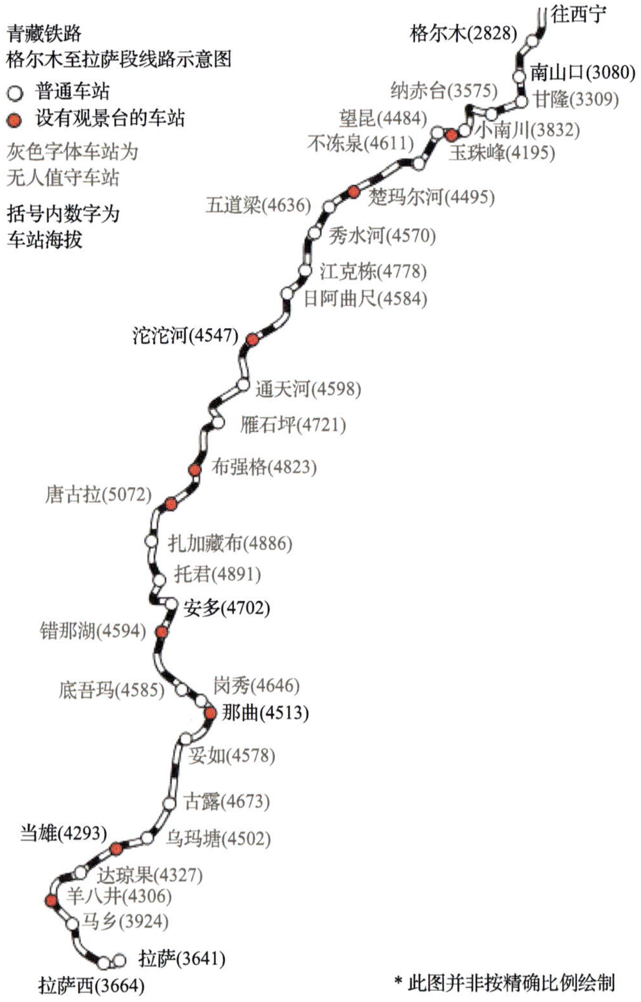

图 4-14　青藏铁路沿线示意图

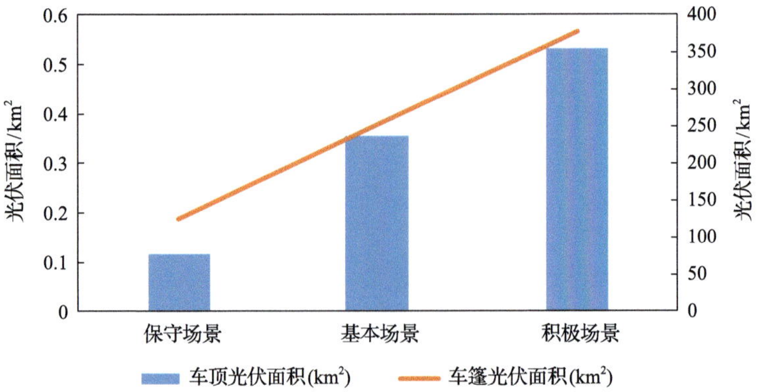

图 4-15　青藏铁路格拉段光伏铺设面积测算结果

青藏铁路格拉段的光照情况如图 4-16 所示。

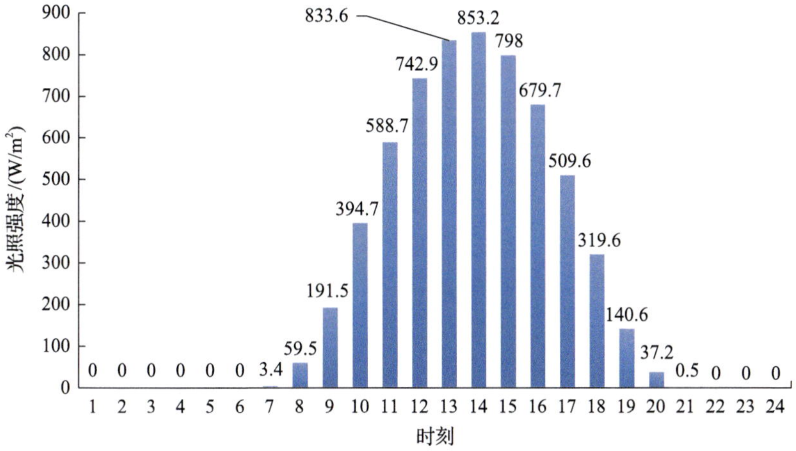

图 4-16　青藏铁路格拉段所处地区各时刻光照平均强度图

通过计算可以得出，列车运行时辅助设备所需的能量为 740kW×15h=11.1MW·h，列车的光伏出力最大潜力如下式所示。

$$\sum_{i=1}^{24}\text{GHI}(i)\cdot S_{\text{train}}=7789.32\text{kW}\cdot\text{h}$$

式中，GHI(i)为 i 时刻辐射量；S_{train}为列车车厢光伏板面积。

光伏篷光伏出力潜力如下式所示。

$$\sum_{i=1}^{24}\text{GHI}(i)\cdot S_{\text{rail}}$$

在保守场景、基本场景及积极场景下，光伏篷出力分别为 1240.7MW·h/天，2481.4MW·h/天，3722.1MW·h/天。

2. 降耗提效及减排测算

根据上述布置和计算方法，可计算得，在不同开发场景下，每列车每天可以减少柴油机发电量 1110kW·h、2220kW·h 和 3330kW·h，则每列车年减少发电量为 401.5MW·h、803.0MW·h、1204.5MW·h；而在保守场景下，光伏出力就已经满足线路上 5 个车站每日 100MW·h 的负荷，每个车站年减少发电量为 36500MW·h。

大型柴油发电机的油耗约为 C_D=0.24kg/kW·h，柴油密度为 ρ_D=0.84kg/L，根据下式可以得出每列年节油量为 11.5 万 L、23 万 L、34.4 万 L；每个车站年节油量为 1042.857 万 L，柴油的排放因子为 C_C=2.6765kg/L，根据下式可以计算得出，每列年减少二氧化碳排放 319.5t、639.1t、955.6t；车站年减少二氧化碳排放 139560.4t。

$$V_d = C_D \div \rho_D \times E_{\text{save}}$$

$$E_{\text{re}} = C_C \cdot V_d$$

式中，V_d为节油量；E_{save}为节省购电量；E_{re}为二氧化碳减排量。

图 4-17 为青藏铁路格拉段分阶段节能减排测算结果。

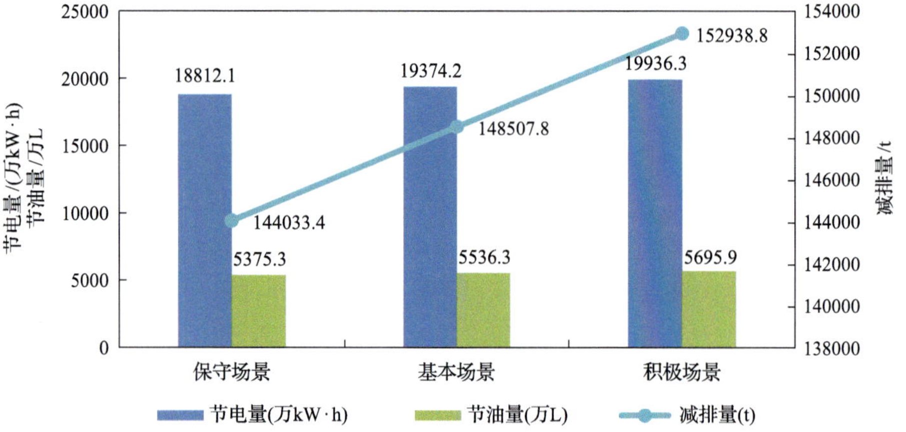

图 4-17　青藏铁路格拉段分阶段节能减排测算结果

根据中国中车官方网站的介绍，HXN3 高原型内燃机车的额定功率为 3300kW，百公里耗油量约为 350L。设列车的平均速度为 90km/h，则列车运行的单位时间耗油量约为 388.9L/h，以热值折算为耗电量约为 3965.0kW。列车运行时间为 15h，以此计算得出单次列车的总牵引耗能约为 5.95×10^4kW·h，总耗能为 7.06×10^4kW·h。则在保守场景、基本场景及积极场景下，Z165 次列车的光伏用能自洽率分别为 1.56%、3.12%、4.67%。

3. 投资收益情况测算

根据上海虹桥铁路客运站 EMS 的数据显示，可统计的用电能根据上海虹桥铁路客运站 EMS 的数据显示，可统计的用电能耗约为 105kW·h/天。以 105kW·h/天作为车站的能耗，则在保守场景、基本场景及积极场景下，铁路系统总光伏自洽率为 83.4%、166.7%、250.1%。测算光伏组件投资额的计算方法为

$$I_{\text{PV}} = S_{\text{PV}} \cdot U_{\text{PV}}$$

蓄电池储能投资额的计算方法为

$$I_B = E_B \cdot U_B$$

总投资的计算方法为

$$I_{\text{sum}} = I_{\text{PV}} + I_B$$

由于青藏铁路格拉段没有电网铺设，所以项目总收益为节省的燃油量，即

$$R_{\text{sum}} = R_D = V_d U_d$$

式中，R_{sum} 为总收益；R_D 为节省燃油收益；V_d 为节省燃油体积；U_d 为柴油单价，取 6.84 元/L。

在保守开发场景下，需要一次性投资 161646.85 万元，年节省油费 89601.8 万元，收益投资比为 0.55；在一般开发场景下，需要追加投资 155608.75 万元，年节省油费 106327.1 万元，收益投资比为 0.68；在积极开发场景下，需要追加投资 155632.95 万元，年节省油费 106405 万元，收益投资比为 0.68。图 4-18 为青藏铁路格拉段投资、收益情况测算结果。图 4-19 为青藏铁路格拉段不同铺设比下的投资收益测算结果。

4. 自洽率测算

对于交通专用的能源利用模式，如上面所述，选取青藏铁路格尔木—拉萨段 Z165 次列车。图 4-20 为青藏铁路格拉段不同开发强度下按月度用能自洽率测算结果。青藏铁路格拉段按照月度的测算数据如表 4-6 所示。

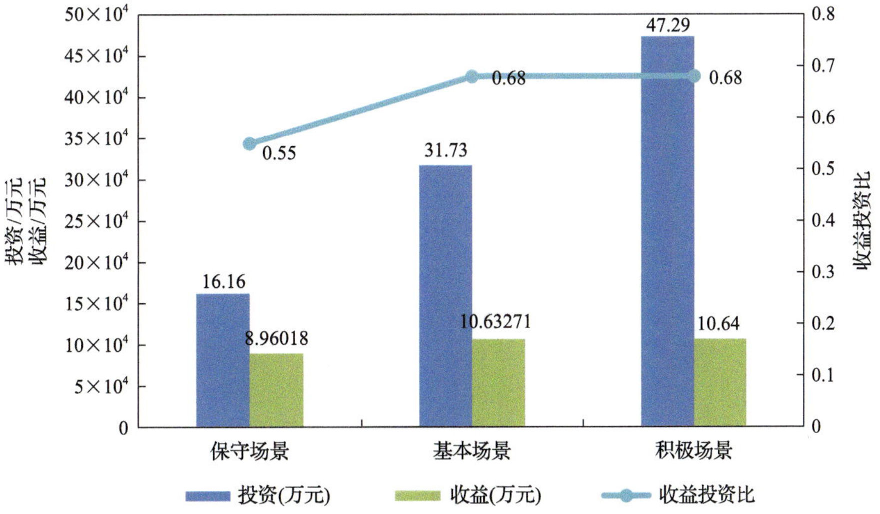

图 4-18　青藏铁路格拉段投资、收益情况测算结果

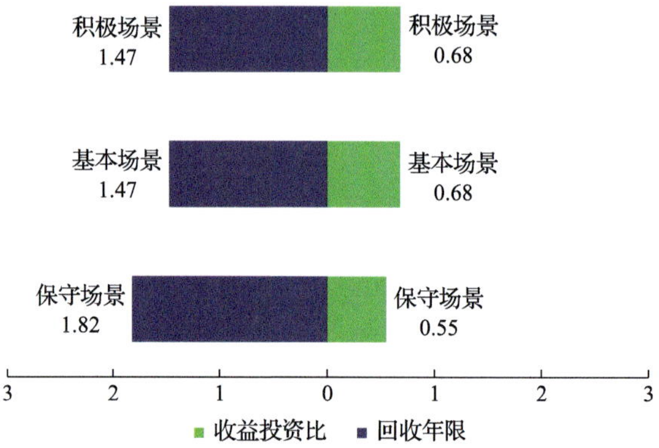

图 4-19　青藏铁路格拉段不同铺设比下的投资收益测算结果

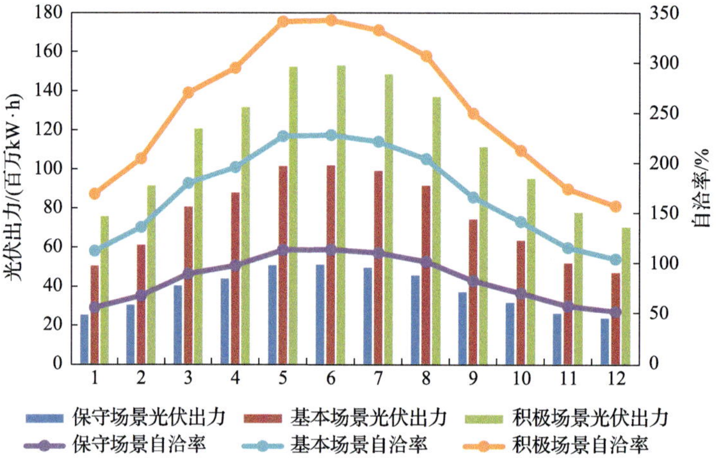

图 4-20　青藏铁路格拉段不同开发强度下按月度用能自洽率测算结果

表 4-6　青藏铁路格拉段不同利用率下按月度用能自洽率测算结果

月份	光照强度/(kW·h/m^2)	负荷用能/(kW·h)	保守场景光伏出力/(kW·h)	保守场景用能自洽率/%	基本场景光伏出力/(kW·h)	基本场景用能自洽率/%	积极场景光伏出力/(kW·h)	积极场景用能自洽率/%
1	124.8	44652000	25201221.43	56.44	50402442.85	112.88	75603664.28	169.32
2	150.8	44652000	30451475.89	68.20	60902951.78	136.39	91354427.67	204.59
3	199.0	44652000	40184639.94	90.00	80369279.87	179.99	120553919.8	269.99
4	217.0	44652000	43819431.49	98.14	87638862.98	196.27	131458294.5	294.41
5	251.1	44652000	50705342.15	113.56	101410684.3	227.11	152116026.5	340.67
6	252.4	44652000	50967854.87	114.14	101935709.7	228.29	152903564.6	342.43
7	245.1	44652000	49493744.97	110.84	98987489.93	221.69	148481234.9	332.53
8	226.1	44652000	45657020.55	102.25	91314041.1	204.50	136971061.7	306.75
9	184.0	44652000	37155646.98	83.21	74311293.95	166.42	111466940.9	249.63
10	156.9	44652000	31683266.36	70.96	63366532.72	141.91	95049799.08	212.87
11	128.4	44652000	25928179.74	58.07	51856359.48	116.13	77784539.21	174.20
12	116.1	44652000	23444405.51	52.50	46888811.02	105.01	70333216.53	157.51

图 4-21 为青藏铁路格拉段在不同开发场景下按季节用能自洽率测算结果。青藏铁路格拉段按照季节的测算数据如表 4-7 所示。

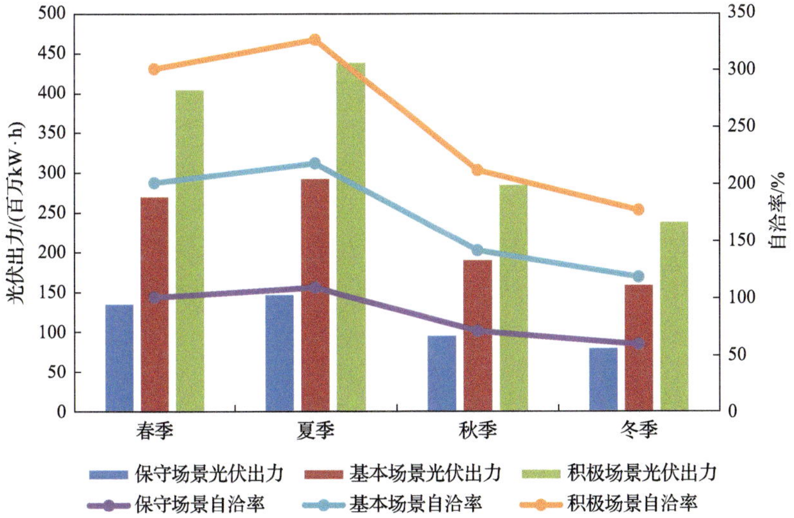

图 4-21　青藏铁路格拉段在不同开发场景下按季节用能自洽率测算结果

表 4-7　青藏铁路格拉段在不同开发场景下按季节用能自洽率测算结果

季度	光照强度 /(kW·h/m²)	负荷用能 /(kW·h)	保守场景光伏出力 /(kW·h)	保守场景用能自洽率/%	基本场景光伏出力 /(kW·h)	基本场景用能自洽率/%	积极场景光伏出力 /(kW·h)	积极场景用能自洽率/%
春季	667.1	133956000	134709413.6	100.56	269418827.1	201.12	404128240.7	301.69
夏季	723.6	133956000	146118620.4	109.08	292237240.8	218.16	438355861.2	327.24
秋季	469.4	133956000	94787286.36	70.76	189574572.7	141.52	284361859.1	212.28
冬季	391.7	133956000	79097102.83	59.05	158194205.7	118.09	237291308.5	177.14

4.2.2　交通特用的能源系统技术解决方案

1. 适用场景及方案介绍

交通特用的能源系统供给方案，是针对处于电网末端的铁路可再生能源系统的特定解决方案。在该模式下，地区所处位置的电网较为薄弱，电气化铁路对电网造成的影响很大，亟需寻求新的供能方式以减轻电网的负担。铁路为电气化铁路，可再生能源系统可为机车所有负荷提供电能，并且由于牵引网的存在，无法使用在列车顶部布置光伏组件的方式。

本报告以“末端+少负荷+多光”模式的系统解决方案，以兰新铁路的乌鲁木齐段为典型案例进行测算说明。由于负荷较少，光伏资源充足，光储系统容易满足负荷所需。因此方案的整体规划为可再生+储能+微网为主+余电上网。

本方案的具体实施方法如下所示。

(1)在轨道上方建设支架以及轨道线路保护区布置光伏组件。根据线路走向，确定支架顶层的形状：以南北走向为主的线路，支架顶层选择为圆弧形，单位长度光伏板铺设面积为 14.77m^2；以东西走向为主的线路，支架顶层选择为平顶，光伏板倾斜角度以当地最佳倾角布置，控制单位长度光伏板的铺设面积为 15m^2。在线路保护区内则按照上述布置方法，在轨道两侧各布置宽度为1m的光伏组件，单位长度光伏板铺设面积为2m^2。因此，整体单位长度光伏组件铺设面积为17m^2。光伏组件铺设的长度应与当地负荷相适应，以避免功率不足或资源浪费。

(2)集中布置储能设施。在此种供给方案下，光伏板面积很大，随之而来的功率波动以及源荷不匹配问题十分凸显，因而需要容量相对较大的储能设施以平抑功率波动和提高光伏利用率。整体而言，光伏出力是高于负荷所需的，故采用上述“资源丰富区”的储能容量计算方法配置储能。储能设施采用集中布置的方式，放置于相应供电区段的牵引变电站内。

(3)在牵引变内布置超级电容设备。由于列车的牵引功率很大，且功率上升很快，接近于冲击负荷，而蓄电池的放电功率受到现有结构限制，无法满足如此激烈的功率响应。因此，各区间要布置相应的超级电容设备，以短时间支持系统的强升功率需求。超级电容器容量的确定应参考负荷功率跳变最大值，以及蓄电池组的功率上升时间。

(4)各牵引变电站区段构成微网，线路全线组成线性微网群。在每一牵引变区段内，光伏组件经额外布置的汇流线、汇流箱等设备引入对应的牵引变中。光伏阵列、超级电容器组和蓄电池组分别经 DC/DC 变换后接入直流母线；直流母线通过逆变器、升压变压器变换至 AC27.5kV 后，接入牵引网，与电网共同为列车供电。微网系统的结构图如图 4-22 所示。相邻区间的微网构成一个微网群，通过电力牵引线完成电能分配。图 4-23 为兰新线主要站点示意图。

以兰新高铁乌鲁木齐—哈密段第一个牵引变区间作为本方案的算例。乌鲁木齐市是我国新疆维吾尔自治区的首府，乌鲁木齐—哈密段位于新疆东部，年平均光照强度约为 1600kW·h/m^2，属于我国二类地区。乌鲁木齐电网通过乌北变 750kV 线路与我国东部地区相连，属于电网末端地区，电网强度较为脆弱。兰新高铁乌哈段每天仅有 22 次列车运行，运营时间为 3.2h，运营速度为 160km/h，列车平均牵引功率为 7200kW。因此，乌鲁木齐市符合上述“末端+少负荷+多光”模式，解决方案为“可再生+混合储能+微网为主+余电上网”的能源利用模式。

列车在此变电站区间上的年所需电量 P_{needs} 可由下式计算得出：

$$P_{\text{needs}} = m_{\text{train}} t_{\text{run}} P_{\text{train}} \times 365$$

式中，计算可得 P_{needs} 值为 18820MW·h；m_{train} 为该区间的日班次数；t_{run} 为运营时间；P_{train} 为每辆列车的牵引功率；最后乘以每年 365 天。

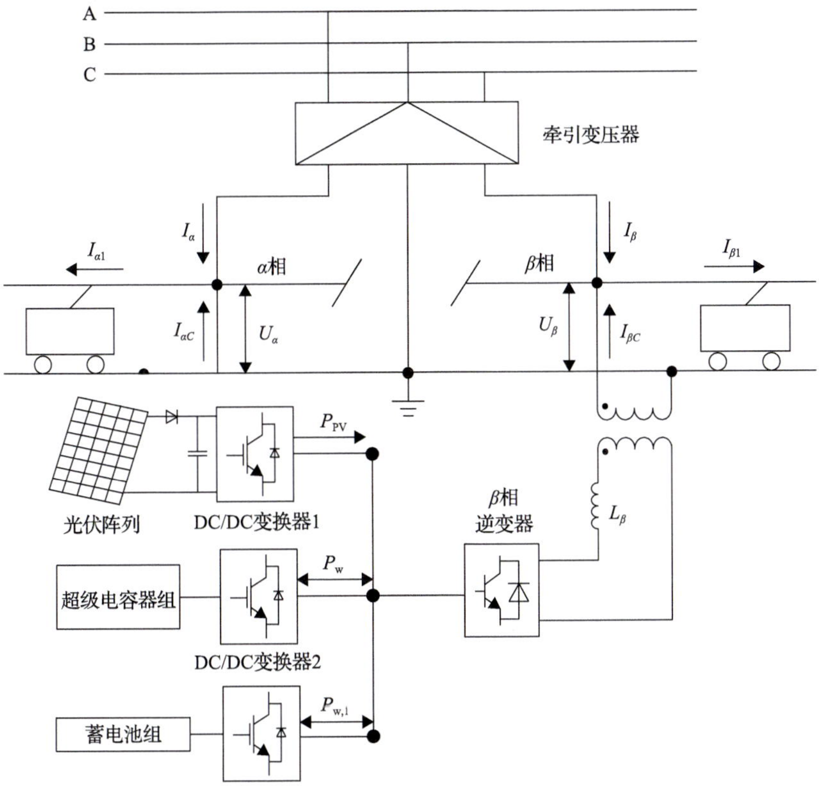

图 4-22　交通特用的能源系统微网结构图

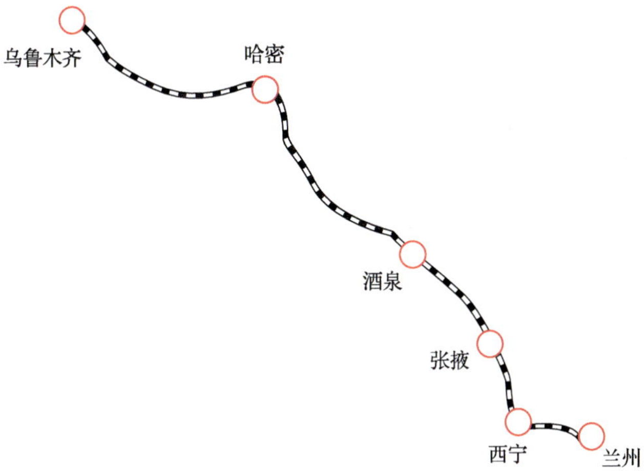

图 4-23　兰新线主要站点示意图

光伏组件铺设面积的计算方法如下式所示：

$$S_{PV} = c_{PV} L_{PV} p_n$$

式中，S_{PV}为光伏组件的面积；c_{PV}为光伏组件的等效宽度，取15m；L_{PV}为光伏组件的等效长度；p_n为铺设比例。计算得出，为实现“微网为主、余电上网”的能源解决方案，至少应铺设4.3万m^2的光伏组件，约占区间全长的10%。因此，本节以铺设比例为10%、20%、30%作为阶梯，分析该区段的初始需求以及未来的发展空间。当铺设比例为10%、20%、30%时，光伏组件的面积分别为4.3万m^2、8.5万m^2、12.8万m^2。

当铺设比例为10%时，本区段全年光伏出力小于负荷所需，因而属于资源匮乏区，按照将每日光伏瞬时功率高于负荷所需累计能量的最大值作为蓄电池组的容量，经计算得应配置16.08MW·h的蓄电池组；当铺设比例为20%时，在排除冬季后，光伏出力大于负荷所需的天数有160天，出力不足天数有114天，有功率剩余的天数占比为58.39%，超过50%，属于资源丰富区，因而储能容量按照每日光伏瞬时功率低于负荷所需累计能量的最大值作为蓄电池组的容量，经计算得应配置21.07MW·h的蓄电池组；当铺设比例为30%时，在排除夏季后，光伏出力大于负荷所需的天数有237天，出力不足天数仅有37天，有功率剩余的天数占比为86.50%，超过50%，属于资源丰富区，因而储能容量按照每日光伏瞬时功率低于负荷所需累计能量的最大值作为蓄电池组的容量，经计算得应配置22.58MW·h的蓄电池组。由下式可计算得出，在铺设比例为10%、20%、30%时，蓄电池储能的占地面积为968m^2、1270m^2、1361m^2。其中，S_B为蓄电池储能总占地面积；S_b为单个蓄电池占地面积，取0.030373m^2/个；E_b为单个蓄电池容量，取1.2kW·h/个；E_B为蓄电池组的总容量。

$$S_B = \frac{S_b}{E_b} E_B$$

将本区段的列车车次进行平均化处理，可得本区段的负荷最大跳变量为4800kW，为支持蓄电池1s内的功率上升需求，超级电容器应配置：

$$4800\text{kW} \cdot \frac{1}{3600}\text{h} = 1.33\text{kW} \cdot \text{h}$$

表4-8为乌鲁木齐分阶段配置方案。

表4-8　乌鲁木齐站分阶段配置方案

铺设比例/%	光伏组件面积/万m^2	蓄电池组容量/(10MW·h)	蓄电池组占地面积/m^2	超级电容器容量/(kW·h)
10	4.3	1.61	968	1.33
20	8.5	2.11	1270	1.33
30	12.8	2.26	1361	1.33

图4-24为乌鲁木齐站光伏、储能占地测算结果。

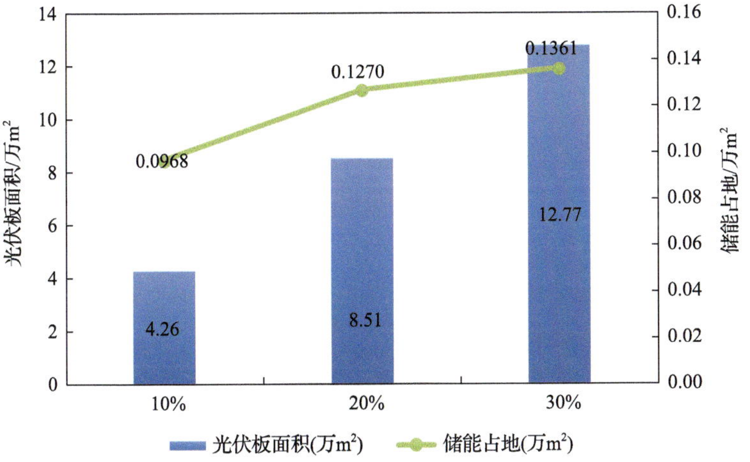

图 4-24 乌鲁木齐站光伏、储能占地测算结果

2. 投资收益情况测算

根据上述的计算方法及布置方式，在 10%、20%、30%的铺设比例下，该牵引变区段每年可节省购电量 14.93GW·h、18.17GW·h、18.74GW·h，在铺设比例为 10%的情况下，需要光伏组件投资 5242.1 万元，蓄电池储能投资 4022.4 万元，超级电容器投资 1.5 万元，合计 9266.0 万元；年总收益为 1781.6 万元，其中上网售电收益为 114.5 万元，光伏补贴收益为 174.5 万元；收益投资比为 19.2%，回收年限为 5.2 年。

在铺设比例为 20%的情况下，需要追加光伏组件投资 5242.1 万元，追加蓄电池储能投资 1250.7 万元，合计追加投资 6492.8 万元，累计投资 1.58 亿元；年总收益为 2920.4 万元，其中上网售电收益为 754.0 万元，光伏补贴收益为 349.1 万元；收益投资比为 45.0%，回收年限为 2.2 年。

在铺设比例为 30%的情况下，需要追加投资 5620.1 万元，其中追加光伏组件投资 5242.1 万元，追加蓄电池储能 378.0 万元，累计投资 2.14 亿元；年总收益为 3910.9 万元，其中上网售电收益为 1513.7 万元，光伏补贴收益为 523.6 万元；收益投资比为 69.6%，回收年限为 1.4 年。表 4-9 为乌鲁木齐站经济测算结果。图 4-25 为乌鲁木齐站投资收益测算结果。图 4-26 为乌鲁木齐站收益投资比、回收年限测算结果。

3. 年总自洽率测算

根据上述的计算方法及布置方式，可计算得，在 10%、20%、30%的铺设比例下，该牵引变区段每年可节省购电量 14.93GW·h、18.17GW·h、18.74GW·h，

表 4-9 乌鲁木齐站经济测算结果

经济测算指标	保守场景	基本场景	积极场景	合计
光伏组件追加投资/万元	5242.1	5242.1	5242.1	15726.3
蓄电池储能追加投资/万元	4022.4	1250.7	378	5651.1
超级电容追加投资/万元	1.5	0.0	0.0	1.5
年上网售电收益/万元	114.5	754	1513.7	—
年光伏补贴收益/万元	174.5	349.1	523.6	—
节省购电量收益/万元	1492.5	1817.3	1873.5	—
总追加投资/万元	9266	6492.8	5620.1	21378.9
年总收益/万元	1781.6	2920.4	3910.9	—
收益投资比/%	19.2	45	69.6	—
回收年限/年	5.2	2.2	1.4	—

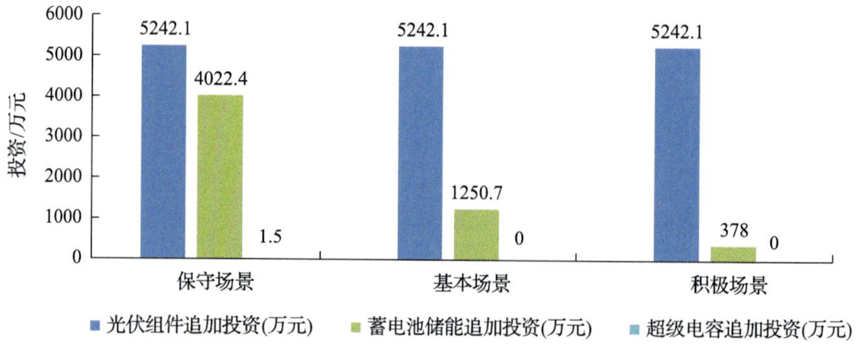

图 4-25 乌鲁木齐站投资收益测算结果

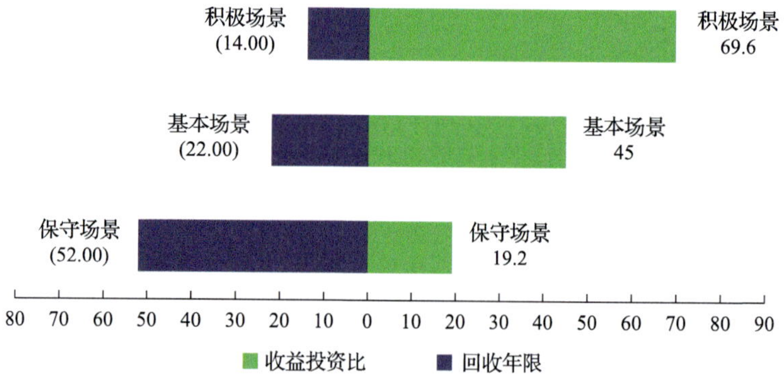

图 4-26 乌鲁木齐站收益投资比、回收年限测算结果

光伏利用率分别为79.30%、96.56%、99.54%，自洽率分别为92.7%、185.5%、278.2%，每年可提供上网电量 2.55GW·h、16.8GW·h、33.6GW·h。表 4-10 为乌鲁木齐站光伏利用率与自洽率对比表。

表 4-10　乌鲁木齐站光伏利用率与自洽率对比表

铺设比例/%	光伏利用率/%	光伏自洽率/%
10	79.30	92.7
20	96.56	185.5
30	99.54	278.2

CO_2减排量可按下式计算。其中，C_{CE}为减排量换算常数，取0.997kg/(kW·h)；P_{PV}为年光伏出力。

$$E_{re} = C_{CE} \cdot P_{PV}$$

经计算可得，在保守场景、一般场景和积极场景下，该区段每年可减少二氧化碳排放 1.74 万 t、3.48 万 t、5.22 万 t。表 4-11 为乌鲁木齐站分阶段降耗提效及减排情况测算结果。图 4-27 为乌鲁木齐站节能减排测算结果。

表 4-11　乌鲁木齐站分阶段降耗提效及减排情况测算结果

铺设比例/%	节省购电量/(GW·h)	减排量/万 t
10	2.55	1.74
20	16.8	3.48
30	33.6	5.22

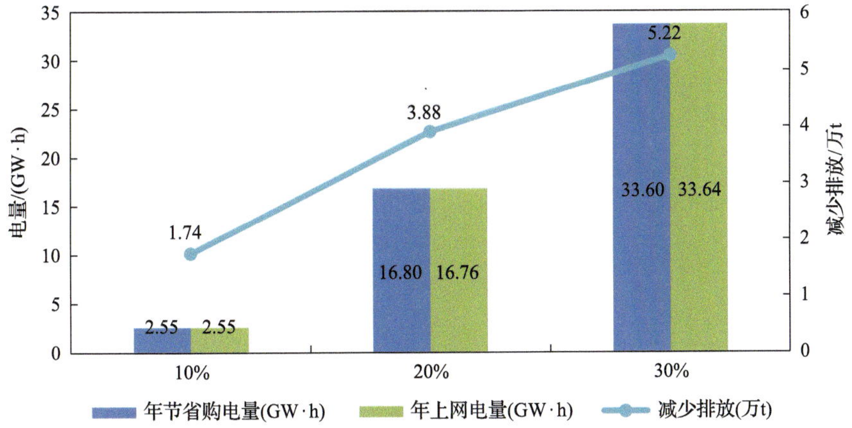

图 4-27　乌鲁木齐站节能减排测算结果

4. 月/季度自洽率测算

对于交通专用的能源利用模式，如上面所述，选取兰新高铁乌鲁木齐—哈密方向第一个牵引站为例进行测算(图 4-28)。

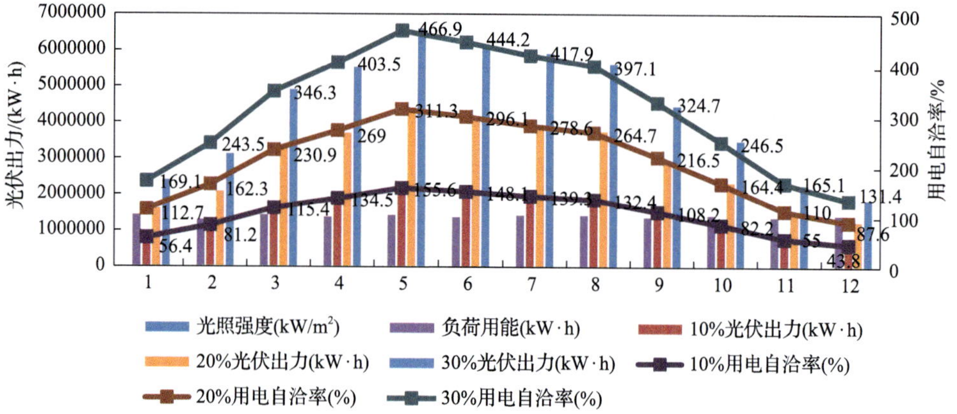

图 4-28　兰新高铁乌哈段不同开发场景下按月度用能自洽率测算结果

兰新高铁乌哈段按照月度的测算数据如表 4-12 所示。

表 4-12　兰新高铁乌哈段不同开发场景下按月度用能自洽率测算结果

月份	GHI /(kW/m²)	负荷用能 /(kW·h)	10%光伏出力 /(kW·h)	10%用电自洽率/%	20%光伏出力 /(kW·h)	20%用电自洽率/%	30%光伏出力 /(kW·h)	30%用电自洽率/%
1	79.8	1414195.2	797114.1	56.4	1594228.2	112.7	2391342.3	169.1
2	103.8	1277337.6	1036625.4	81.2	2073250.8	162.3	3109876.2	243.5
3	163.5	1414195.2	1632533.3	115.4	3265066.6	230.9	4897599.9	346.3
4	184.4	1368576.0	1840812.2	134.5	3681624.4	269.0	5522436.5	403.5
5	220.4	1414195.2	2200980.3	155.6	4401960.6	311.3	6602940.9	466.9
6	202.9	1368576.0	2026208.5	148.1	4052417.0	296.1	6078625.4	444.2
7	197.3	1414195.2	1970067.5	139.3	3940134.9	278.6	5910202.4	417.9
8	187.5	1414195.2	1871767.0	132.4	3743534.0	264.7	5615301.0	397.1
9	148.4	1368576.0	1481475.9	108.2	2962951.7	216.5	4444427.6	324.7
10	116.4	1414195.2	1162192.1	82.2	2324384.1	164.4	3486576.2	246.5
11	75.4	1368576.0	752983.5	55.0	1505967.1	110.0	2258950.6	165.1
12	62.0	1414195.2	619456.5	43.8	1238913.0	87.6	1858369.5	131.4

图 4-29 为兰新高铁乌哈段不同开发场景下按季节用能自洽率测算结果。兰新高铁乌哈段按照季节的测算数据如表 4-13 所示。

4.2.3　交通适用的能源系统技术解决方案

1. 适用场景及方案介绍

交通适用的能源系统供给方案，是针对处于强电网但是铁路负荷较小区域的场景下的解决方案。在该模式下，地区铁路为电气化铁路，地区电网的分布密集，系统结构合理，能够轻松承担铁路负荷对电网带来的负面影响，减轻电网负担的必要性不明显。

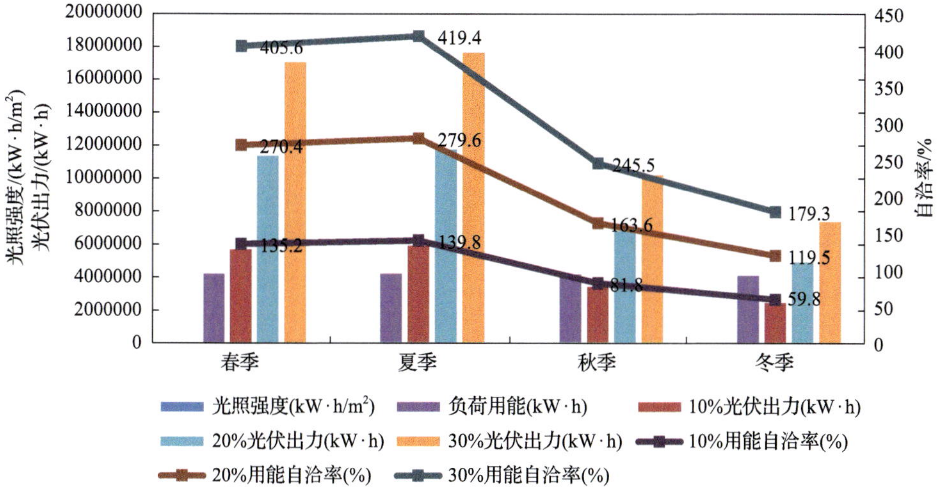

图 4-29　兰新高铁乌哈段不同开发场景下按季节用能自洽率测算结果

表 4-13　兰新高铁乌哈段不同开发场景下按季节用能自洽率测算结果

季度	光照强度/(kW·h/m²)	负荷用能/(kW·h)	10%光伏出力/(kW·h)	10%用能自洽率/%	20%光伏出力/(kW·h)	20%用能自洽率/%	30%光伏出力/(kW·h)	30%用能自洽率/%
春季	568.3	4196966.4	5674325.8	135.2	11348651.5	270.4	17022977.3	405.6
夏季	587.7	4196966.4	5868042.9	139.8	11736085.8	279.6	17604128.8	419.4
秋季	340.2	4151347.2	3396651.5	81.8	6793302.9	163.6	10189954.4	245.5
冬季	245.7	4105728.0	2453196.0	59.8	4906392.0	119.5	7359588.1	179.3

本报告以“强电网、少负荷、多光”模式下的系统能源解决方案为例进行测算说明。由于地区负荷较少，且光资源十分充足，因而光伏组件的效率很高，铺设面积大大减小，有利于节约投资。因此本方案的整体规划为可再生能源+混合储能+微网/电网+自给自足。

本方案的具体实施方法如下所示。

(1)在轨道上方建设支架以及轨道线路保护区布置光伏组件。光伏组件的布置方法与前述类似，布置长度按照光伏利用率进行设计即可。

(2)集中布置储能设施。同样地，储能设施集中布置在相应区段的牵引变电站内。储能容量的计算方法按照“资源匮乏区”的方法进行，即将一年内每天光伏出力大于负荷功率的累计能量的最大值作为储能设备的容量。

(3) 在牵引变布置超级电容设备。与前述保持一致，电容器容量的确定应参考负荷功率跳变最大值，以及蓄电池组的功率上升时间。

(4) 各牵引变电站区段构成微网，微网之间不组成微网群。由于本方案的整体规划为自给自足，光伏出力大部分均可被本级负荷利用，光伏利用率已经很高；并且负荷本身较小，光伏的配置规模更小，即使存在剩余功率，其值也微乎其微，对其进行调度反而会导致设备冗余、控制系统复杂的后果，得不偿失。综上所述，本方案没有对剩余功率进行微网间调度的必要性。微网的构成方式与前述保持一致，光伏阵列、超级电容器组与蓄电池组分别经 DC/DC 变换器后汇流，至逆变器、升压变压器变换为 AC27.5kV 接入牵引网，与经牵引变降压后的电网共同向牵引网供电。

以兰新高铁哈密——嘉峪关段第一个牵引变区间作为本方案的算例。哈密市地处新疆东北部，临近甘肃省，年平均光照强度为 1677kW·h/m^2，属于我国二类地区。哈密地区的电网密度较大，有 750kV 交流、±1000kV 直流线路与新疆西部和我国东部相连，电网强度很高。兰新高铁哈嘉段每天仅有 22 次列车双向运行，运营时间为 3.3h，运营速度为 160km/h，列车平均牵引功率为 7200kW。因此，哈密市负荷上述“强电网、少负荷、多光”模式，解决方案为“可再生能源+混合储能+微网/电网+自给自足”的能源利用模式。

根据 4.2.2 节列车负荷测算与光伏组件铺设面积测算方法，列车在此变电站区间上的年所需电量为 18820MW·h。

在保守、一般和积极三种开发场景下，光伏组件的面积分别为 4.3 万 m^2、8.6 万 m^2、12.8 万 m^2。

在保守开发场景下，排除夏季后，光伏出力大于负荷所需的天数有 156 天，出力不足天数仅有 118 天，有功率剩余的天数占比为 56.93%，超过 50%，属于资源丰富区，因而储能容量按照每日光伏瞬时功率低于负荷所需累计能量的最大值作为蓄电池组的容量，经计算得应配置 1.93×10^4kW·h；当铺设比例为 20%时，在排除夏季后，光伏出力大于负荷所需的天数有 268 天，出力不足天数仅有 6 天，有功率剩余的天数占比为 97.81%，超过 50%，属于资源丰富区，因而储能容量按照每日光伏瞬时功率低于负荷所需累计能量的最大值作为蓄电池组的容量，经计算得应配置 1.88×10^4kW·h 的蓄电池组；当铺设比例为 30%时，在排除夏季后，光伏出力大于负荷所需的天数有 273 天，出力不足天数仅有 1 天，有功率剩余的天数占比为 99.64%，超过 50%，属于资源丰富区，因而储能容量按照每日光伏瞬时功率低于负荷所需累计能量的最大值作为蓄电池组的容量，经计算得应配置 1.68×10^4kW·h 蓄电池组。

根据 4.2.2 节储能占地面积计算方法，可计算得出在保守、一般和积极三种开发场景下，蓄电池储能的占地面积分别为 998.3m²、1045m²、948.8m²。

将本区段的列车车次进行平均化处理，可得本区段的负荷最大跳变量为 4800kW，为支持蓄电池 1s 内的功率上升需求，超级电容器应配置：

$$4800\text{kW}\cdot\frac{1}{3600}\text{h}=1.33\text{kW}\cdot\text{h}$$

表 4-14 为哈密站分阶段配置方案。图 4-30 为哈密站光伏、蓄电池占地面积测算结果。

表 4-14 哈密站分阶段配置方案

铺设比例/%	光伏组件面积/万 m²	蓄电池组容量/(10MW·h)	蓄电池组占地面积/m²	超级电容器容量/(kW·h)
10	4.3	1.93	1163.8	1.33
20	8.6	1.88	1133.6	1.33
30	12.8	1.68	1009.3	1.33

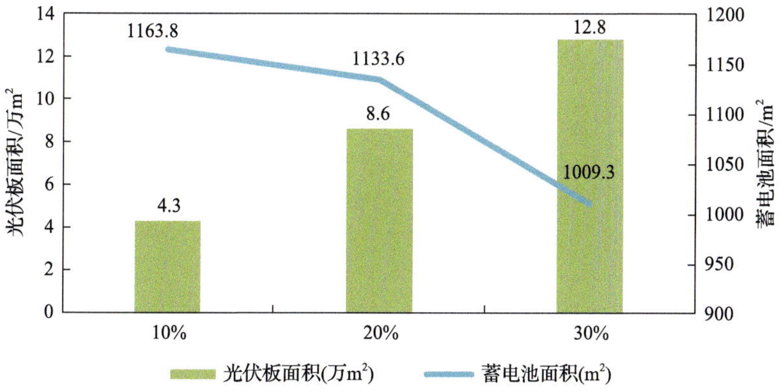

图 4-30 哈密站光伏、蓄电池占地面积测算结果

2. 降耗提效及减排情况测算

根据上述的计算方法和布置方式，在保守、一般和积极三种开发场景下，该牵引变区段每年可节省购电量 9896MW·h、10266MW·h 和 10266MW·h，光伏利用率分别为 96.39%、100%、100%，光伏自洽率分别为 176.4%、352.7%、529.1%，每年可提供上网电量 8225MW·h、25953MW·h 和 44055MW·h。

CO_2 减排量可根据 4.2.2 节减排量测算方法计算，经计算可得，在保守、一般和积极三种开发场景下，该区段每年可减少二氧化碳排放 1.39 万 t、2.79 万 t、

4.18 万 t。表 4-15 为哈密站分阶段降耗提效及减排情况测算结果。图 4-31 为哈密站节能减排测算结果。

表 4-15　哈密站分阶段降耗提效及减排情况测算结果

铺设比例/%	节省购电量/(10MW·h)	减排量/万 t
10	989.6	1.81
20	1026.6	3.61
30	1026.6	5.42

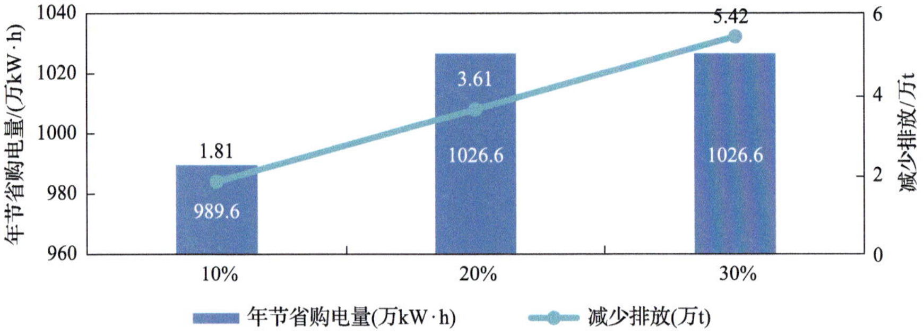

图 4-31　哈密站节能减排测算结果

3. 投资收益情况测算

根据上述的计算方法，可计算得，在铺设比例为 10%的情况下，需要光伏组件投资 5273.6 万元，蓄电池储能投资 4833.6 万元，超级电容器投资 1.5 万元，合计 1.01 亿元；年总收益为 1540.8 万元，其中上网售电收益为 370.1 万元，光伏补贴收益为 181.1 万元；收益投资比为 15.2%，回收年限为 6.6 年。

在铺设比例为 20%的情况下，需要追加光伏组件投资 5273.6 万元，累计投资 1.52 亿元；年总收益为 2556.6 万元，其中上网售电收益为 1167.9 万元，光伏补贴收益为 362.1 万元；收益投资比为 48.5%，回收年限为 2.1 年。

在铺设比例为 30%的情况下，需要追加光伏组件投资 5273.6 万元，累计投资 2.00 亿元；年总收益为 3552.3 万元，其中上网售电收益为 1982.5 万元，光伏补贴收益为 543.2 万元；收益投资比为 67.4%，回收年限为 1.5 年。表 4-16 为哈密站经济测算结果。

图 4-32 为哈密站不同开发场景下的投资收益测算结果。图 4-33 为哈密站不同开发场景下的收益投资比、回收年限测算结果。

表 4-16 哈密站经济测算结果

经济测算指标	保守场景	基本场景	积极场景	合计
光伏组件追加投资/万元	5273.6	5273.6	5273.6	15820.8
蓄电池储能追加投资/万元	4833.6	0	0	4833.6
超级电容追加投资/万元	1.5	0	0	1.5
年上网售电收益/万元	370.1	1167.9	1982.5	—
年光伏补贴收益/万元	181.1	362.1	543.2	—
节省购电量收益/万元	989.6	1026.6	1026.6	—
总追加投资/万元	10108.8	5273.6	5273.6	20656
年总收益/万元	1540.8	2556.6	3552.3	—
收益投资比/%	15.2	48.5	67.4	—
回收年限/年	6.6	2.1	1.5	—

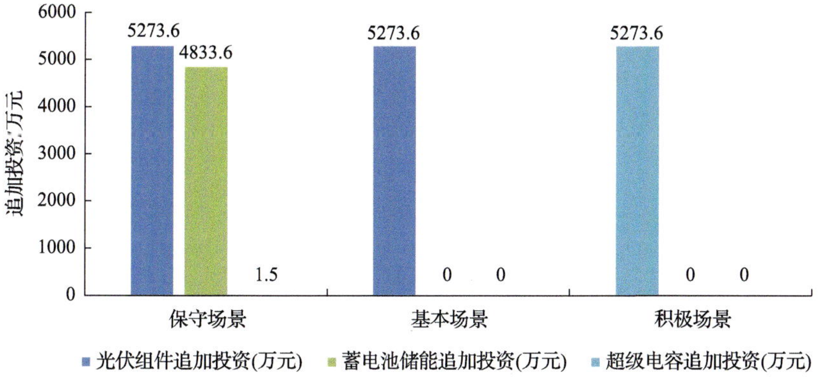

图 4-32 哈密站不同开发场景下的投资收益测算结果

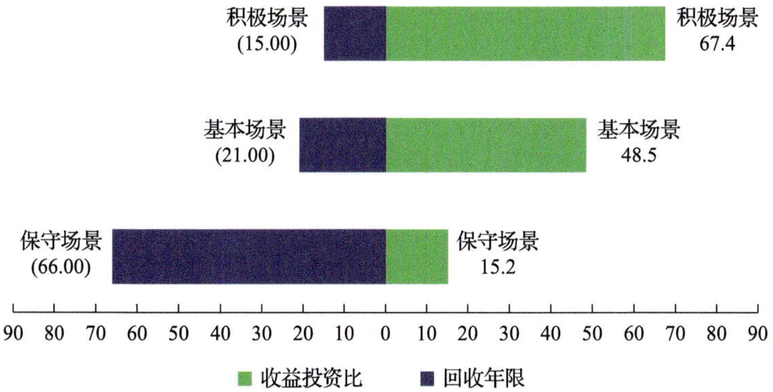

图 4-33 哈密站不同开发场景下的收益投资比、回收年限测算结果

4. 自洽率测算

对于交通适用的能源利用模式，如上面所述，选取兰新高铁哈密嘉峪关方向第一个牵引站为例进行测算。图 4-34 为兰新高铁哈嘉段不同开发场景下按月度用能自洽率测算结果。

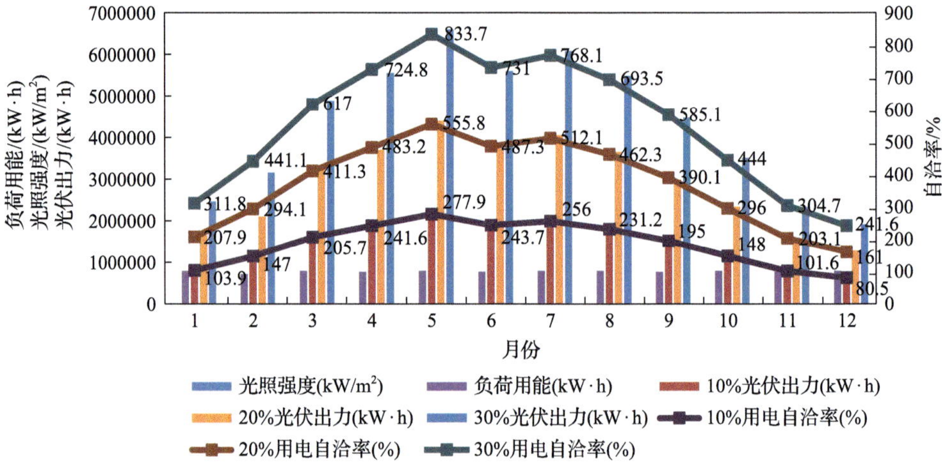

图 4-34 兰新高铁哈嘉段不同开发场景下按月度用能自洽率测算结果

兰新高铁哈嘉段按照月度的测算数据如表 4-17 所示。

表 4-17 兰新高铁哈嘉段不同开发场景下按月度用能自洽率测算结果

月份	GHI /(kW/m^2)	负荷用能 /(kW·h)	10%光伏出力 /(kW·h)	10%用电自洽率/%	20%光伏出力 /(kW·h)	20%用电自洽率/%	30%光伏出力 /(kW·h)	30%用电自洽率/%
1	81.9	791467.2	822649.1	103.9	1645298.1	207.9	2467947.2	311.8
2	104.6	714873.6	1051213.0	147.0	2102426.0	294.1	3153638.9	441.1
3	162.0	791467.2	1627662.1	205.7	3255324.2	411.3	4882986.4	617.0
4	184.2	765936.0	1850562.3	241.6	3701124.7	483.2	5551687.0	724.8
5	218.9	791467.2	2199394.9	277.9	4398789.7	555.8	6598184.6	833.7
6	185.8	765936.0	1866272.6	243.7	3732545.2	487.3	5598817.8	731.0
7	201.7	791467.2	2026415.1	256.0	4052830.2	512.1	6079245.4	768.1
8	182.1	791467.2	1829521.9	231.2	3659043.8	462.3	5488565.7	693.5
9	148.7	765936.0	1493916.4	195.0	2987832.7	390.1	4481749.1	585.1
10	116.6	791467.2	1171481.6	148.0	2342963.2	296.0	3514444.8	444.0
11	77.4	765936.0	777834.8	101.6	1555669.5	203.1	2333504.3	304.7
12	63.4	791467.2	637308.2	80.5	1274616.5	161.0	1911924.7	241.6

兰新高铁哈嘉段按照季节的测算数据如图 4-35 和表 4-18 所示。

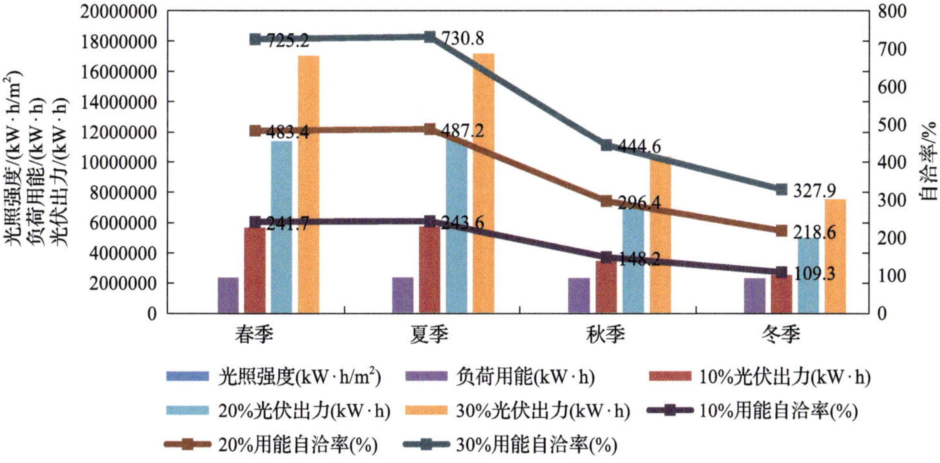

图 4-35　兰新高铁哈嘉段不同开发场景下按季节用能自洽率测算结果

表 4-18　兰新高铁哈嘉段不同开发场景下按季节用能自洽率测算结果

季度	光照强度/(kW·h/m²)	负荷用能/(kW·h)	10%光伏出力/(kW·h)	10%用能自洽率/%	20%光伏出力/(kW·h)	20%用能自洽率/%	30%光伏出力/(kW·h)	30%用能自洽率/%
春季	565.2	2348870.4	5677619.3	241.7	11355238.6	483.4	17032858.0	725.2
夏季	569.6	2348870.4	5722209.6	243.6	11444419.2	487.2	17166628.8	730.8
秋季	342.8	2323339.2	3443232.7	148.2	6886465.4	296.4	10329698.1	444.6
冬季	250.0	2297808.0	2511170.3	109.3	5022340.6	218.6	7533510.8	327.9

4.2.4　能源系统支持的交通技术解决方案

1. 适用场景及方案介绍

能源系统支持的交通系统解决方案，是针对处于强电网但是铁路负荷较多区域的解决方案。在该模式下，地区铁路为电气化铁路，负荷较重；地区电网分布密集，系统强度较高，可以承担铁路大负荷对电网的负面影响。但同时，电网的密集意味着节点十分重要，其可靠性为运行的关键因素，而大负载十分影响其可靠性，所以寻求新供能方式的必要性仍存在。

本报告以“强电网、多负荷、多光”模式下的系统能源解决方案为例进行测算说明。由于该地区负荷很重，光伏出力难以全部覆盖全部负荷，因而可再生能源只能承担一部分负荷，其余负荷仍要电网承担。因此，本方案的整体规划为可再生能源+混合储能+电网为主+网上购电。

本方案的具体实施方法如下所示。

(1)在轨道上方建设支架以及轨道线路保护区布置光伏组件。光伏组件的布置方法与前述类似，布置长度按照光伏利用率进行设计即可。

(2)集中布置储能设施。同样地，储能设施集中布置于相应区段的牵引变电站内。储能容量的计算方法按照“资源匮乏区”的方法进行，即将一年内每天光伏出力大于负荷功率的累计能量的最大值作为储能设备的容量。

(3)在牵引变布置超级电容设备。与前述保持一致，电容器容量的确定应参考负荷功率跳变最大值，以及蓄电池组的功率上升时间。

(4)各牵引变电站区段构成微网，相邻微网之间沿线路构成线性微网群。由于本方案针对地区的负荷很大，尽管光伏出力总体而言不能满足负荷所需，但若瞬间的光伏出力大于负荷所需，其值将会很大，不得不考虑其利用模式。微网群的组成方式与前述类似，通过电力牵引线完成相邻微网之间的电能分配。

以兰新高铁兰州——西宁段第一个牵引变区间作为本方案的算例。兰州市是我国西部主要城市之一，其年光照强度约为 1600kW·h/m^2，属于我国 I 类地区。兰州市处于我国电网西部走廊位置，属于强电网地区。兰新高铁是连接甘肃省兰州市与新疆维吾尔自治区乌鲁木齐市的高速铁路，全长 1786km，其中兰州—西宁段每天有 42 班车次运行，运营时间为 2.2h，运营速度为 160km/h，列车平均牵引功率为 7200kW。因此，兰州地区属于上述“末端+少负荷+多光”模式，解决方案为“可再生+混合储能+微网为主+余电上网”的能源利用模式。

根据 4.2.2 节列车年负荷测算与光伏组件测算方法，列车在此变电站区间上的年所需电量为 18820MW·h。

在保守、一般和积极三种开发场景下，光伏组件的面积分别为 4.3 万 m^2、8.6 万 m^2、12.9 万 m^2。

当铺设比例为 10%时，在排除冬季后，光伏出力仍完全小于负荷所需，属于资源匮乏区，按照将每日光伏瞬时功率高于负荷所需累计能量的最大值作为蓄电池组的容量，经计算得应配置 999.8kW·h 的蓄电池组；当铺设比例为 20%时，在排除冬季后，光伏出力仍完全小于负荷所需，属于资源匮乏区，按照将每日光伏瞬时功率高于负荷所需累计能量的最大值作为蓄电池组的容量，经计算得应配置 11.9MW·h 的蓄电池组；当铺设比例为 30%时，在排除冬季后，光伏出力大于负荷所需的天数有 76 天，出力不足天数有 199 天，无功率剩余的天数占比为 72.36%，超过 50%，属于资源匮乏区，按照将每日光伏瞬时功率高于负荷所需累计能量的最大值作为蓄电池组的容量，经计算应配置 21.5MW·h 的蓄电池组。

根据 4.2.2 节减排量测算方法可计算得出，在铺设比例为 10%、20%、30%时，蓄电池储能的占地面积为 60.2m^2、715.1m^2、1516.8m^2。

将本区段的列车车次进行平均化处理，可得本区段的负荷最大跳变量为 4800W，为支持蓄电池 1s 内的功率上升需求，超级电容器应配置：

$$4800\text{kW} \cdot \frac{1}{3600}\text{h} = 1.33\text{kW} \cdot \text{h}$$

表 4-19 为兰州站分阶段配置方案。图 4-36 为兰州站光伏、储能占地面积测算结果。

表 4-19　兰州站分阶段配置方案

铺设比例/%	光伏组件面积/万 m^2	蓄电池组容量/(10MW・h)	蓄电池组占地面积/m^2	超级电容器容量/(kW・h)
10	4.3	0.10	60.2	1.33
20	8.6	1.19	715.1	1.33
30	12.9	2.52	1516.8	1.33

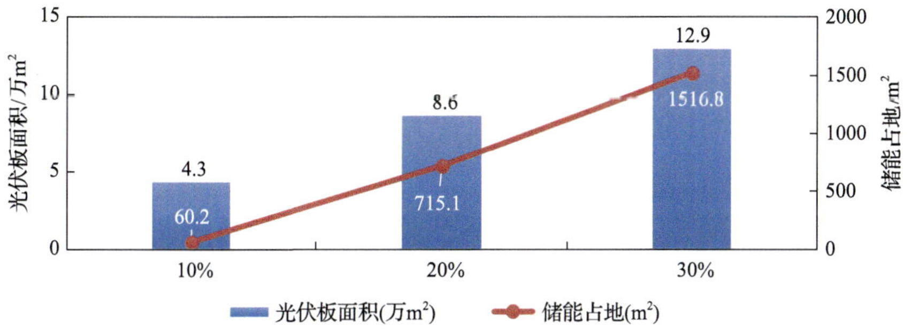

图 4-36　兰州站光伏、储能占地面积测算结果

2. 降耗提效及减排情况测算

根据上述的计算方法和布置方式，在保守、一般和积极三种开发场景下，该牵引变区段每年可节省购电量 21643MW·h、42058MW·h、55065MW·h，光伏利用率分别为 31.03%、60.30%、78.95%，光伏自洽率分别为 31.15%、62.30%、93.45%，每年可提供上网电量 84.9MW·h、1407.1MW·h、10140.1MW·h。

二氧化碳减排量可根据 4.2.2 节减排量测算方法计算。

经计算可得，在保守、一般和积极三种开发场景下，该区段每年可减少二氧化碳排放 2.17 万 t、4.33 万 t、6.50 万 t。表 4-20 为兰州站分阶段降耗提效及减排情况测算结果。图 4-37 为兰州站节能减排测算结果。

表 4-20　兰州站分阶段降耗提效及减排情况测算结果

铺设比例/%	节省购电量/(10MW·h)	减排量/万 t
10	2164.2	2.17
20	4205.8	4.33
30	5506.5	6.50

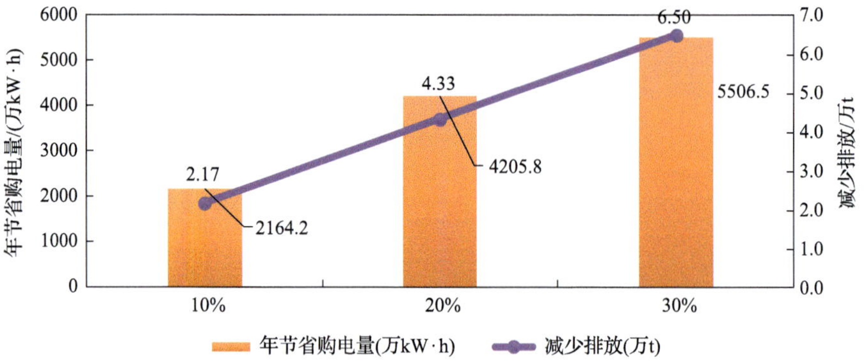

图 4-37　兰州站节能减排测算结果

3. 投资收益情况测算

根据 4.4.1 节的计算方法，在铺设比例为 10%的情况下，需要光伏组件投资 5315.7 万元，蓄电池储能投资 250.2 万元，超级电容器投资 1.5 万元，合计 5567.5 万元；年总收益为 2385.4 万元，其中上网售电收益为 3.8 万元，光伏补贴收益为 217.3 万元；收益投资比为 42.8%，回收年限为 2.3 年。

在铺设比例为 20%的情况下，需要追加光伏组件投资 5315.7 万元，追加锂电池投资 2719.8 万元，总追加投资 8035.5 万元，累计投资 1.36 亿元；年总收益为 4703.6 万元，其中上网售电收益为 63.3 万元，光伏补贴收益为 434.5 万元；收益投资比为 58.5%，回收年限为 1.7 年。

在铺设比例为 30%的情况下，需要追加光伏组件投资 5315.7 万元，追加锂电池投资 3330.0 万元，总追加投资 8645.7 万元，累计投资 2.22 亿元；年总收益为 6614.6 万元，其中上网售电收益为 456.3 万元，光伏补贴收益为 651.8 万元；收益投资比为 76.5%，回收年限为 1.3 年。

表 4-21 为兰州站经济测算结果。图 4-38 为兰州站投资收益测算结果。图 4-39 为兰州站收益投资比、回收年限测算结果。

表 4-21　兰州站经济测算结果

经济测算结果	保守场景	基本场景	积极场景	合计
光伏组件追加投资/万元	5315.7	5315.7	5315.7	15947.1
蓄电池储能追加投资/万元	250.2	2719.8	3330	6300
超级电容追加投资/万元	1.5	0	0	1.5
年上网售电收益/万元	3.8	63.3	456.3	—
年光伏补贴收益/万元	217.3	434.5	651.8	—
节省购电量收益/万元	2164.3	4205.8	5506.5	—
总追加投资/万元	5567.5	8035.5	8645.7	22248.7
年总收益/万元	2385.4	4703.6	6614.6	—
收益投资比/%	42.8	58.5	76.5	—
回收年限/年	2.3	1.7	1.3	—

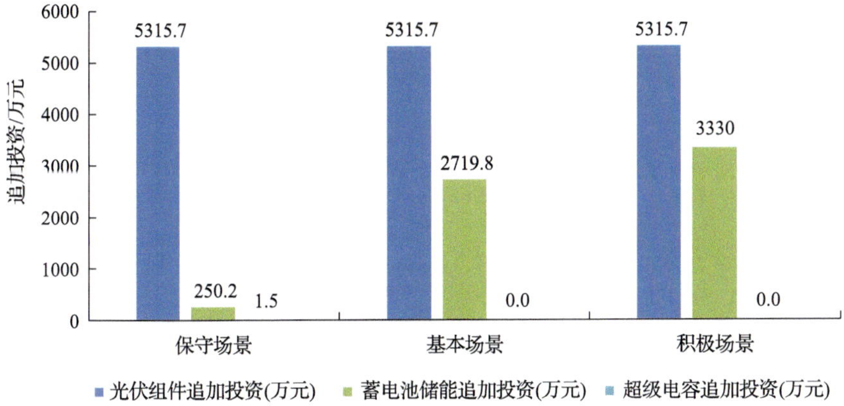

图 4-38　兰州站投资收益测算结果

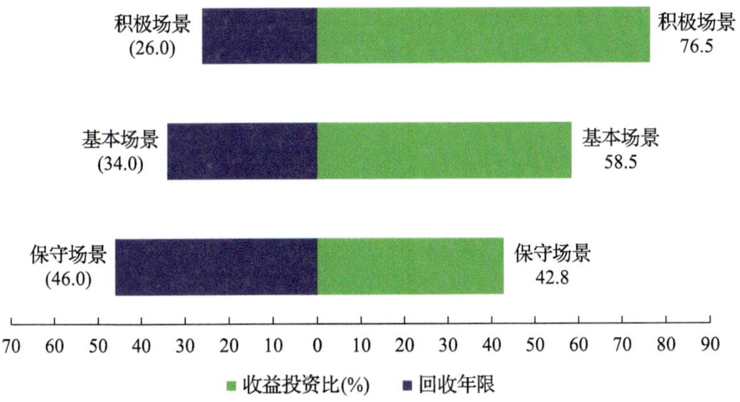

图 4-39　兰州站收益投资比、回收年限测算结果

4. 自洽率测算

对于能源系统支持的能源利用模式，如上面所述，选取兰新高铁兰州—西宁方向第一个牵引站为例进行测算。

兰新高铁兰西段按照月度的测算数据如图 4-40 和表 4-22 所示。

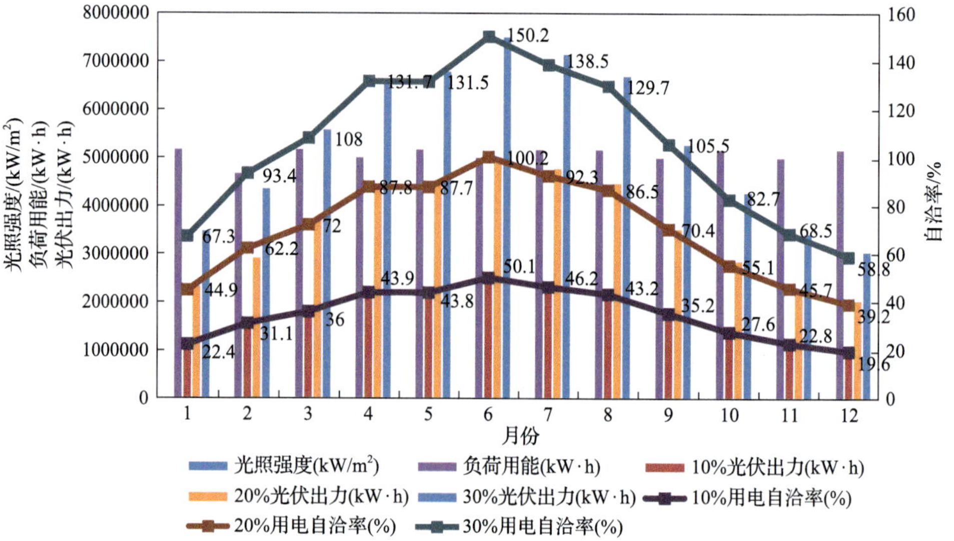

图 4-40　兰州高铁兰西段不同开发场景下按月度用能自洽率测算结果

表 4-22　兰州高铁兰西段不同开发场景下按月度用能自洽率测算结果

月份	GHI /(kW/m²)	负荷用能 /(kW·h)	10%光伏出力 /(kW·h)	10%用电自洽率/%	20%光伏出力 /(kW·h)	20%用电自洽率/%	30%光伏出力 /(kW·h)	30%用电自洽率/%
1	114.3	5155920.0	1157489.8	22.4	2314979.5	44.9	3472469.3	67.3
2	143.1	4656960.0	1449130.4	31.1	2898260.7	62.2	4347391.1	93.4
3	183.3	5155920.0	1855643.9	36.0	3711287.8	72.0	5566931.6	108.0
4	216.3	4989600.0	2190388.9	43.9	4380777.8	87.8	6571166.7	131.7
5	223.3	5155920.0	2260625.4	43.8	4521250.7	87.7	6781876.1	131.5
6	246.8	4989600.0	2498796.8	50.1	4997593.6	100.2	7496390.4	150.2
7	235.1	5155920.0	2380163.2	46.2	4760326.4	92.3	7140489.6	138.5
8	220.2	5155920.0	2229503.8	43.2	4459007.6	86.5	6688511.3	129.7
9	173.3	4989600.0	1755091.9	35.2	3510183.7	70.4	5265275.6	105.5
10	140.3	5155920.0	1420542.3	27.6	2841084.5	55.1	4261626.8	82.7
11	112.5	4989600.0	1139500.3	22.8	2279000.6	45.7	3418500.9	68.5
12	99.8	5155920.0	1010802.7	19.6	2021605.4	39.2	3032408.1	58.8

兰新高铁兰西段按照季节的测算数据如图 4-41 和表 4-23 所示。

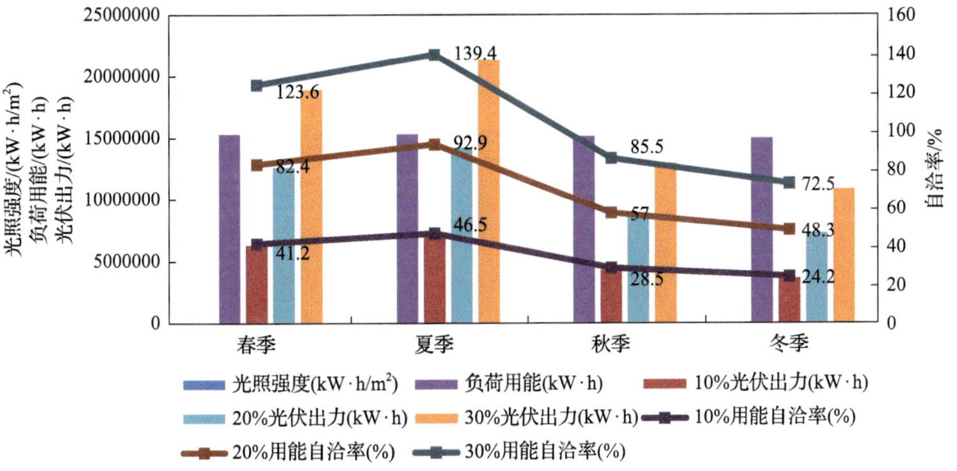

图 4-41　兰新高铁兰西段不同开发场景下按季节用能自洽率测算结果

表 4-23　兰新高铁兰西段不同开发场景下按季节用能自洽率测算结果

季度	光照强度/(kW·h/m²)	负荷用能/(kW·h)	10%光伏出力/(kW·h)	10%用能自洽率/%	20%光伏出力/(kW·h)	20%用能自洽率/%	30%光伏出力/(kW·h)	30%用能自洽率/%
春季	622.8	15301440.0	6306658.1	41.2	12613316.3	82.4	18919974.4	123.6
夏季	702.0	15301440.0	7108463.8	46.5	14216927.6	92.9	21325391.3	139.4
秋季	426.2	15135120.0	4315134.4	28.5	8630268.9	57.0	12945403.3	85.5
冬季	357.2	14968800.0	3617422.8	24.2	7234845.6	48.3	10852268.4	72.5

4.3　系统技术解决方案：利用新模式的铁路可再生能源融合网

如 2.4.2 节所述，我国铁路可再生能源融合网铁路与可再生能源的融合发展将在高效能、高弹性和绿色化三大历史使命的指引下，呈现三大创新方向：①铁路资产向绿色能源化方向发展；②铁路能源供给向自洽多元化方向发展；③铁路用能管理向协同弹性化方向发展。在三大创新方向的指引下，当前的铁路系统、能源系统将从三个调整角度分别或同时做适应性调整以向新型智能化、绿色化、高效化、弹性化与高度环境友好化的铁路能源融合网发展。演化模式和实施步骤如图 4-42 所示，将从现在到 2035 年，每 5 年一个台阶，共三个演进阶段，根据我国光伏出力分布特性、骨干电网分布特性及铁路地域的分布特性，以铁路能源融合网为总目标，从交通与能源互动联系和占不同主导地位两个视角，从交通专用的能源系统、交通特用的能源系统、交通适用的能源系统以及能源支持的交通系统四个维度，从八种因地制宜、因网制宜、因荷制宜的“源-网-荷-储”协同化、智能化、高效化铁路可再生能源系统演化新模式展开。

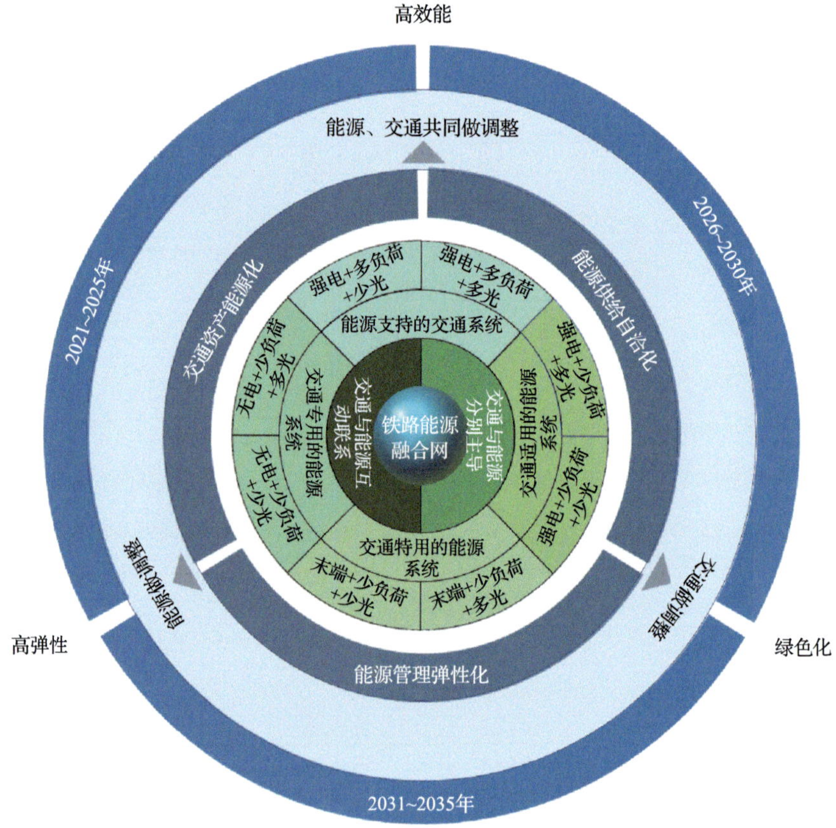

图 4-42　利用新模式的铁路可再生能源融合网演进架构图

4.3.1　目前我国铁路可再生能源融合潜力测算

1. 目前我国铁路资源光伏出力潜力测算

1) 光辐射量取值情况

由于计算难度大数据量多以及区域划分不明显，本报告按照每个区域的年平均辐射量对应该区域的相同辐射量的一点来代替该区域。计算结果为Ⅰ类区域选择(30.72295°N 89.84624°E)，Ⅱ类区域选择(39.44468°N 90.29670°E)，Ⅲ类区域选择(35.25796°N 114.87304°E)，Ⅳ类区域选择(30.21279°N 108.23455°E)。表 4-24 为 2017 年我国水平面各季节辐射量表。图 4-43 为我国四类光照区域各季节辐射量图。表 4-25 为 2017 年我国水平面各月辐射量表。图 4-44 为我国四类光照区域各月辐射量图。

表 4-24 2017 年我国水平面各季节辐射量表 （单位：kW · h/m²）

区域	春季	夏季	秋季	冬季
Ⅰ类地区	556.3	586.5	444.0	393.6
Ⅱ类地区	489.8	535.1	329.3	213.8
Ⅲ类地区	418.0	468.0	259.7	218.0
Ⅳ类地区	312.2	386.5	202.9	184.0

数据来源：大贤 · 风格能源气象平台.

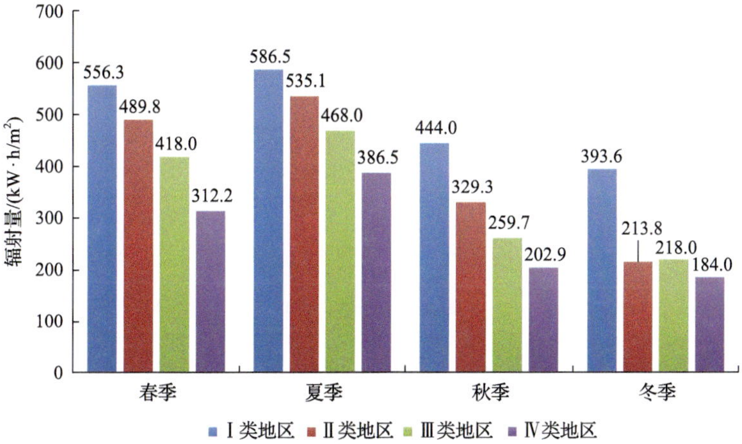

图 4-43 我国四类光照区域各季节辐射量图

表 4-25 2017 年我国水平面各月辐射量表

水平面辐射量 /(kW · h/m²)	1 月	2 月	3 月	4 月	5 月	6 月	7 月	8 月	9 月	10 月	11 月	12 月
Ⅰ类地区	125.7	147.2	167.4	181.5	207.4	193.1	202.1	191.3	150.7	156.2	137.1	120.7
Ⅱ类地区	78.2	88.4	136.1	155.7	198.1	184.0	179.1	172.0	141.9	109.1	78.3	47.2
Ⅲ类地区	76.6	87.4	118.8	133.8	165.4	164.6	163.0	140.5	102.0	79.1	78.6	54.0
Ⅳ类地区	64.5	72.3	88.7	102.1	121.4	104.9	144.5	137.1	70.8	65.9	66.2	47.3

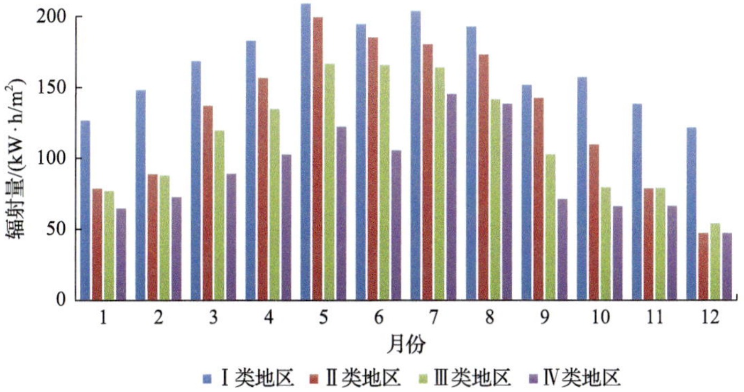

图 4-44 我国四类光照区域各月辐射量图

2）铁路光伏出力测算

（1）铁路运载体与光伏融合的出力测算。

我国干线客运列车按速度等级划分为 120km/h 以下的普速列车，120～160km/h 的中速列车，160～250km/h 的快速列车，200～350km/h 的高速列车，相对应着我国 22 型、25 型、动车组、城际动车组、高速列车等系列客车装备产品。

全国铁路机车拥有量为 2.1 万台，其中，内燃机车为 0.8 万台，电力机车为 1.3 万台。全国铁路客车拥有量为 7.2 万辆，其中，动车共 3256 组，每组 8 节车厢，共 26048 节车厢。全国铁路货车拥有量为 83.0 万辆。

适宜在车厢顶部布置光伏组件的车辆只有非电气化铁路客车车厢。内燃机车 8000 辆，按照一列火车由 2 个内燃机车加 16 编组来算，有 4000×16 辆非电气车厢。全国铁路客车拥有量为 7.2 万辆，货车拥有量为 83.0 万辆，再按这个比例算非电气客车车厢的数量大约为 5109 个。

铁路运载体光伏出力潜力可按下式粗略估计：

$$P_{\text{train}} = n_{\text{train}} \cdot l_{\text{train}} \cdot c_{\text{train}} \cdot c_{\text{rad}} \cdot \text{GHI}_{\text{avg}} \cdot \rho$$

式中，P_{train} 为铁路运载体光伏出力；n_{train} 为非电气化铁路客车的数量；l_{train} 为单节列车的长度；c_{train} 为列车宽度；c_{rad} 为弧线转化系数；GHI_{avg} 为全国平均年辐射量；ρ 为光伏组件转化效率。

根据 4.2.1 节，我们以每节车厢长 20.8m，宽 3.1m，弧线转化系数取 1.227，取平均年辐射量为 $1363.8\text{kW}\cdot\text{h/m}^2$，转化率取 16%，铁路运载体的年光伏出力测算结果为 88GW·h。

（2）铁路基础设施与光伏融合的出力测算。

基础设施是轨道交通运输的基础设备，主要由线路、桥梁和隧道、牵引供电系统和通信信号系统组成。

铁路线路光伏出力潜力可按下式粗略估计：

$$P_{\text{rail}} = (l_{\text{I}} \cdot c \cdot \text{GHI}_{\text{I}} + l_{\text{II}} \cdot c \cdot \text{GHI}_{\text{II}} + l_{\text{III}} \cdot c \cdot \text{GHI}_{\text{III}} + l_{\text{IV}} \cdot c \cdot \text{GHI}_{\text{IV}}) \cdot \rho$$

式中，P_{rail} 为铁路线路光伏出力；l_{I}、l_{II}、l_{III}、l_{IV}分别为四类辐射地区铁路线路长度；c 为铁路线路光伏组件宽度；GHI_{I}、GHI_{II}、GHI_{III}、GHI_{IV}分别为四类地区平均年辐射量；ρ 为光伏组件转化效率。

其中Ⅰ类地区铁路线路长度为 2969km，Ⅱ类、Ⅲ类、Ⅳ类地区铁路线路长度分别为 44303km、77361km 和 14191km；铁路线路等效宽度取 8.55m，根据《铁路运输安全保护条例》，铁路线路两侧的保护区还各有 1m 宽可用于铺设光伏组件；转化率取 16%；铁路系统的基础设施的光伏出力测算结果如图 4-45 所示。

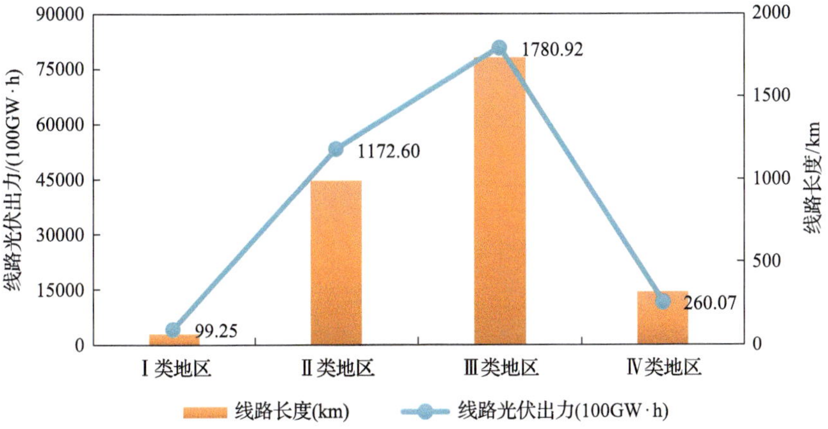

图 4-45 目前我国铁路基础设施光伏出力测算结果

我国铁路基础设施光伏出力占比如图 4-46 所示，其中Ⅰ类、Ⅱ类地区基础设施的年光伏出力达 127294GW·h，占全国铁路基础设施年光伏出力的 38.39%。

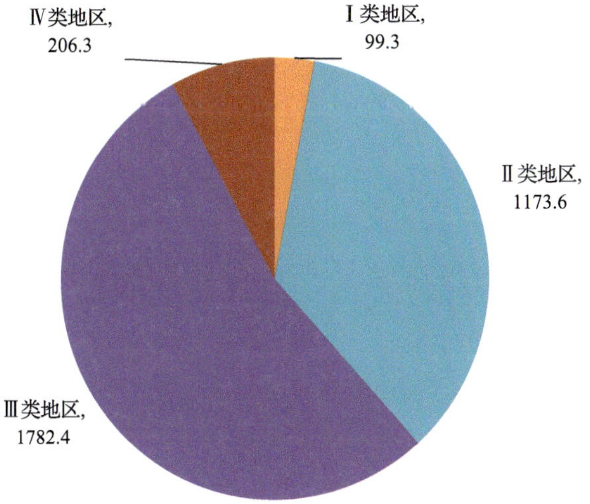

图 4-46 目前四类光照地区我国铁路基础设施光伏出力对比图

(3) 铁路服务设施与光伏融合的出力测算。

铁路牵引变电所光伏出力潜力可按下式粗略估计：

$$P_{\text{trac}} = (n_{\text{tracI}} \cdot \text{GHI}_{\text{I}} + n_{\text{tracII}} \cdot \text{GHI}_{\text{II}} + n_{\text{tracIII}} \cdot \text{GHI}_{\text{III}} + n_{\text{tracIV}} \cdot \text{GHI}_{\text{IV}}) \cdot s_{\text{tracavg}} \cdot \rho$$

式中，P_{trac} 为铁路牵引变电所光伏出力；n_{tracI} 、n_{tracII} 、n_{tracIII} 、n_{tracIV} 分别为四类地区铁路牵引变电所数量；s_{tracavg} 为铁路牵引变电所平均面积；GHI_{I} 、GHI_{II} 、GHI_{III} 、GHI_{IV} 分别为四类地区平均年辐射量；ρ 为光伏组件转化效率。

一条电气化铁路沿线设有多个牵引变电所，相邻变电所间的距离为 40～50km。以每隔 50km 设置一个牵引变电所，以变电所平均有效面积 450m^2 来计算牵引变电所的光伏出力，可得出铁路牵引变电所的年光伏出力为 283GW·h，其中Ⅰ类、Ⅱ类、Ⅲ类和Ⅳ类地区牵引变电所的光伏出力分别为 8GW·h 和 100GW·h、152GW·h 和 22GW·h。图 4-47 为目前四类光照地区我国铁路牵引变电所光伏出力测算。

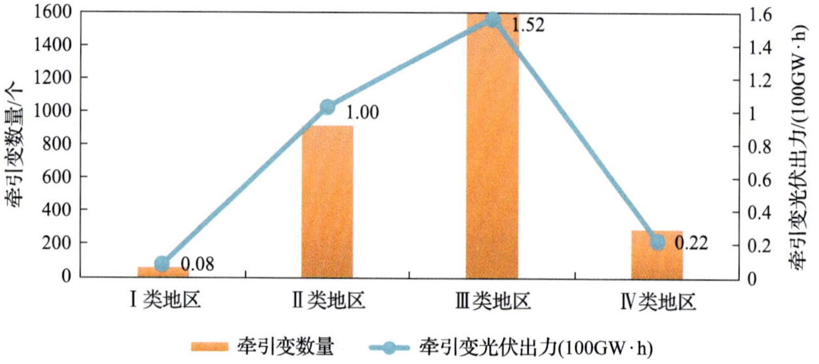

图 4-47　目前四类光照地区我国铁路牵引变电所光伏出力测算

(4) 铁路服务设施与光伏融合的出力测算。

我国的铁路车站按照等级可分为特等站、一等站、二等站、三等站、四等站和五等站；其中特等站、一等站通常直属于铁路局，二等站至五等站隶属于车务段或临近的直属大站。根据 1.1.3 节，全国共有特等车站 71 个，其中客运站 3 个，货运站 4 个，客、货运站 31 个。从地区方面来看，华北地区 12 个，东北地区 10 个，华东地区 16 个，华中地区 13 个，华南地区 8 个，西南地区 7 个，西北地区 5 个。此外，全国共有一等车站 205 个。

铁路服务设施光伏出力潜力可按下式粗略估计：

$$P_{\text{station}} = (n_{\text{sta}\mathrm{I}} \cdot \mathrm{GHI}_{\mathrm{I}} + n_{\text{sta}\mathrm{II}} \cdot \mathrm{GHI}_{\mathrm{II}} + n_{\text{sta}\mathrm{III}} \cdot \mathrm{GHI}_{\mathrm{III}} + n_{\text{sta}\mathrm{IV}} \cdot \mathrm{GHI}_{\mathrm{IV}}) \cdot s_{\text{staavg}} \cdot \rho$$

式中，P_{station} 为铁路服务设施光伏出力；$n_{\text{sta}\mathrm{I}}$、$n_{\text{sta}\mathrm{II}}$、$n_{\text{sta}\mathrm{III}}$、$n_{\text{sta}\mathrm{IV}}$ 分别为四类地区车站数量；s_{staavg} 为铁路车站平均面积；$\mathrm{GHI}_{\mathrm{I}}$、$\mathrm{GHI}_{\mathrm{II}}$、$\mathrm{GHI}_{\mathrm{III}}$、$\mathrm{GHI}_{\mathrm{IV}}$ 分别为四类地区平均年辐射量；ρ 为光伏组件转化效率。

其中Ⅰ类地区没有特等车站，Ⅱ类地区有 19 个特等车站，Ⅲ类、Ⅳ类地区分别有 49 个和 3 个特等车站。通过统计可以得出，特等车站的站顶面积平均约为 4.4 万 m^2，雨棚面积平均为 9.3 万 m^2。转化率取 16%，不考虑光伏板倾角的情况下，特等站的光伏出力测算结果为 2189GW·h。图 4-48 为目前四类光照地区我国特等车站光伏出力测算。

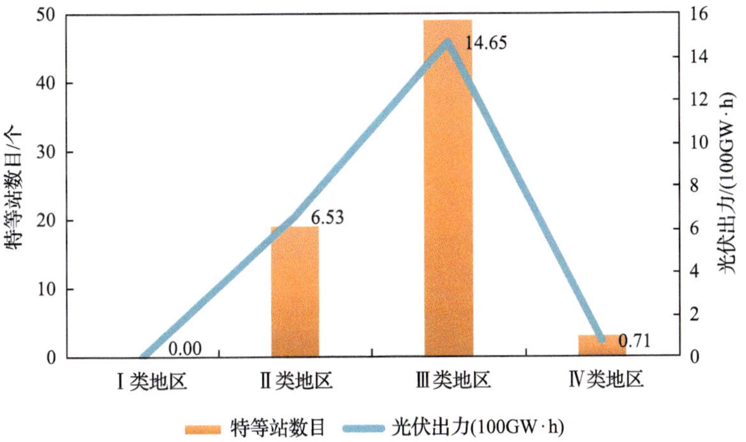

图 4-48　目前四类光照地区我国特等车站光伏出力测算

(5)铁路光伏出力分时情况。

由图 4-49 和表 4-26 可知，铁路的基础设施提供了绝大部分的光伏出力，在夏季Ⅲ类地区基础设施光伏出力最大潜力高达 61169GW·h，而运载体和特等站光伏出力较小。Ⅲ类地区的光伏出力潜力最大，Ⅰ类、Ⅳ类地区光伏出力潜力相对较小。

由图 4-50 和表 4-27 可知，在季节上，铁路的光伏出力更多地集中在春季和夏季，Ⅲ类地区夏季的铁路光伏出力最大潜力有 61683GW·h，秋冬两季光伏出力潜力相对较小。在地区差异上，Ⅱ类、Ⅲ类地区铁路光伏出力潜力较大，Ⅰ类、Ⅳ类地区光伏出力潜力较小。

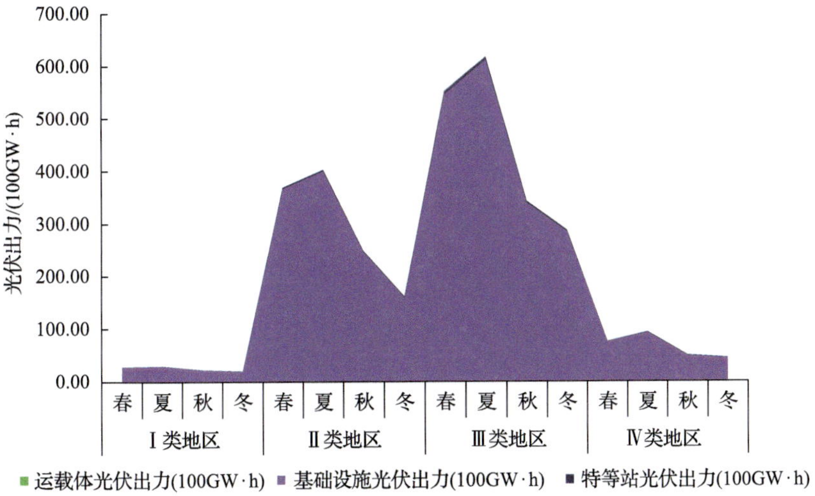

图 4-49　目前四类光照地区我国铁路设施光伏出力测算结果对比(不同季节)

表 4-26　目前四类光照地区我国铁路设施光伏出力测算结果对比（不同季节）

地区	季节	运载体光伏出力/(100GW·h)	基础设施光伏出力/(100GW·h)	特等站光伏出力/(100GW·h)
Ⅰ类地区	春	0.03	27.90	0.00
	夏	0.03	29.42	0.00
	秋	0.02	22.27	0.00
	冬	0.01	19.74	0.00
Ⅱ类地区	春	0.08	366.63	2.04
	夏	0.09	400.52	2.23
	秋	0.05	246.44	1.37
	冬	0.04	160.02	0.89
Ⅲ类地区	春	0.11	546.34	4.49
	夏	0.12	611.69	5.03
	秋	0.07	339.46	2.79
	冬	0.06	284.96	2.34
Ⅳ类地区	春	0.05	74.85	0.21
	夏	0.06	92.67	0.25
	秋	0.03	48.65	0.13
	冬	0.03	44.12	0.12

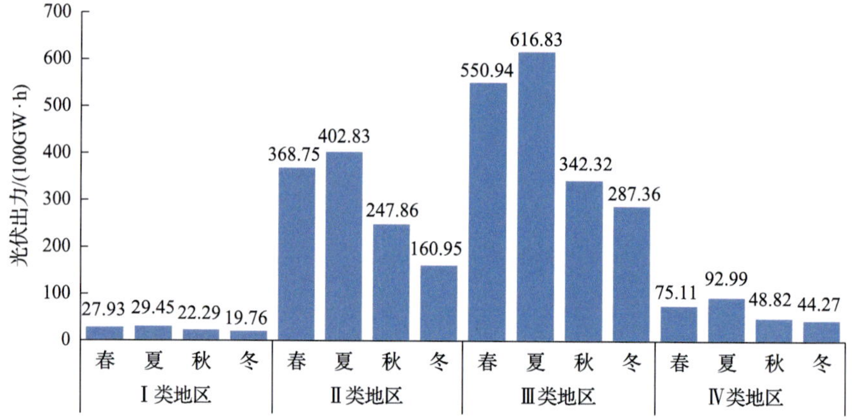

图 4-50　目前四类光照地区我国铁路光伏出力测算结果对比（不同季节）

表 4-27　目前四类光照地区我国铁路光伏出力测算结果对比（不同季节）

地区	季节	运载体光伏出力/(100GW·h)	基础设施光伏出力/(100GW·h)	特等站光伏出力/(100GW·h)	铁路总光伏出力/(100GW·h)
Ⅰ类地区	春	0.03	27.90	0.00	27.93
	夏	0.03	29.42	0.00	29.45
	秋	0.02	22.27	0.00	22.29
	冬	0.01	19.74	0.00	19.76

续表

地区	季节	运载体光伏出力 /(100GW·h)	基础设施光伏出力 /(100GW·h)	特等站光伏出力 /(100GW·h)	铁路总光伏出力 /(100GW·h)
Ⅱ类地区	春	0.08	366.63	2.04	368.75
	夏	0.09	400.52	2.23	402.83
	秋	0.05	246.44	1.37	247.86
	冬	0.04	160.02	0.89	160.95
Ⅲ类地区	春	0.11	546.34	4.49	550.94
	夏	0.12	611.69	5.03	616.83
	秋	0.07	339.46	2.79	342.32
	冬	0.06	284.96	2.34	287.36
Ⅳ类地区	春	0.05	74.85	0.21	75.11
	夏	0.06	92.67	0.25	92.99
	秋	0.03	48.65	0.13	48.82
	冬	0.03	44.12	0.12	44.27

从图 4-51 和表 4-28 可以看出，在 4～8 月份铁路光伏出力潜力较大，光伏出力潜力最大值出现在Ⅲ类地区的 5 月份，单月光伏出力潜力为 21804GW·h。

综上，我国铁路目前光伏出力最大潜力为 333845GW·h。

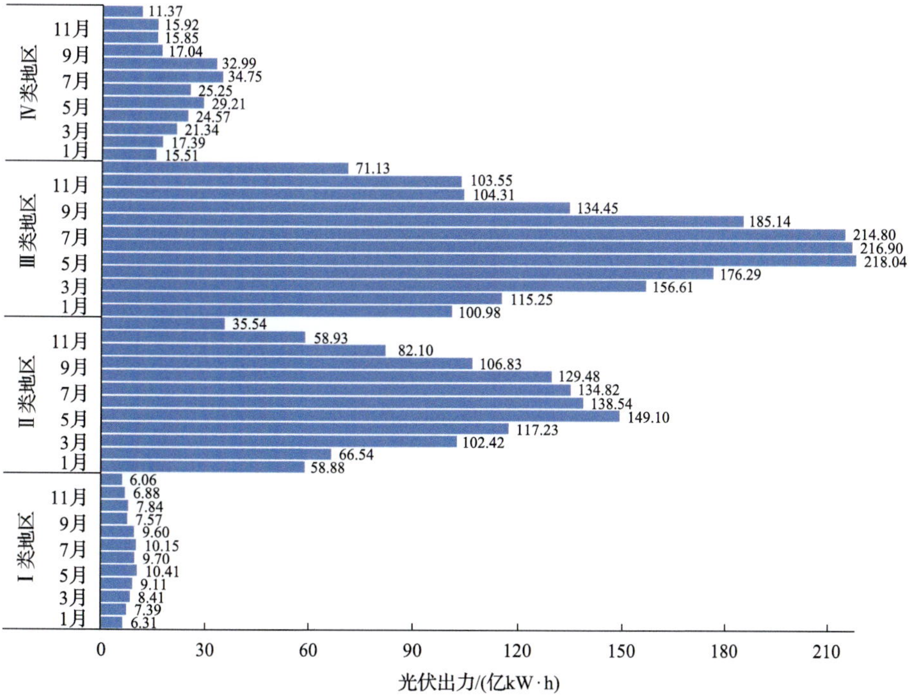

图 4-51　目前四类光照地区我国铁路光伏出力测算结果对比(不同月份)

表 4-28　目前四类光照地区我国铁路光伏出力测算结果对比(不同月份)

地区	月份	运载体光伏出力/(100GW·h)	基础设施光伏出力/(100GW·h)	特等站光伏出力/(100GW·h)	铁路总光伏出力/(100GW·h)
Ⅰ类地区	1 月	0.0050	6.3042	0.0000	6.31
	2 月	0.0057	7.3848	0.0000	7.39
	3 月	0.0077	8.3981	0.0000	8.41
	4 月	0.0087	9.1020	0.0000	9.11
	5 月	0.0107	10.4023	0.0000	10.41
	6 月	0.0106	9.6849	0.0000	9.70
	7 月	0.0105	10.1378	0.0000	10.15
	8 月	0.0091	9.5952	0.0000	9.60
	9 月	0.0066	7.5596	0.0000	7.57
	10 月	0.0051	7.8331	0.0000	7.84
	11 月	0.0051	6.8781	0.0000	6.88
	12 月	0.0035	6.0531	0.0000	6.06
Ⅱ类地区	1 月	0.0149	58.5359	0.3257	58.88
	2 月	0.0170	66.1560	0.3681	66.54
	3 月	0.0231	101.8317	0.5666	102.42
	4 月	0.0260	116.5523	0.6485	117.23
	5 月	0.0321	148.2448	0.8249	149.10
	6 月	0.0319	137.7384	0.7664	138.54
	7 月	0.0316	134.0438	0.7459	134.82
	8 月	0.0273	128.7328	0.7163	129.48
	9 月	0.0198	106.2190	0.5910	106.83
	10 月	0.0154	81.6270	0.4542	82.10
	11 月	0.0152	58.5937	0.3260	58.93
	12 月	0.0105	35.3294	0.1966	35.54
Ⅲ类地区	1 月	0.0198	100.1404	0.8230	100.98
	2 月	0.0226	114.2845	0.9392	115.25
	3 月	0.0307	155.3025	1.2763	156.61
	4 月	0.0346	174.8214	1.4367	176.29
	5 月	0.0428	216.2165	1.7769	218.04
	6 月	0.0426	215.0850	1.7676	216.90
	7 月	0.0422	213.0105	1.7505	214.80
	8 月	0.0363	183.5907	1.5088	185.14
	9 月	0.0264	133.3319	1.0957	134.45
	10 月	0.0205	103.4407	0.8501	104.31
	11 月	0.0203	102.6863	0.8439	103.55
	12 月	0.0140	70.5320	0.5796	71.13

续表

地区	月份	运载体光伏出力/(100GW·h)	基础设施光伏出力/(100GW·h)	特等站光伏出力/(100GW·h)	铁路总光伏出力/(100GW·h)
Ⅳ类地区	1月	0.0099	15.4535	0.0424	15.51
	2月	0.0113	17.3320	0.0475	17.39
	3月	0.0154	21.2624	0.0583	21.34
	4月	0.0173	24.4826	0.0672	24.57
	5月	0.0214	29.1076	0.0798	29.21
	6月	0.0213	25.1613	0.0690	25.25
	7月	0.0211	34.6323	0.0950	34.75
	8月	0.0182	32.8802	0.0902	32.99
	9月	0.0132	16.9847	0.0466	17.04
	10月	0.0102	15.8008	0.0433	15.85
	11月	0.0102	15.8639	0.0435	15.92
	12月	0.0070	11.3336	0.0311	11.37

2. 目前我国铁路负荷测算

当前全国铁路营业里程达到13.1万km，其中，高速铁路营业里程达到2.9万km；复线里程为7.6万km，复线率为58.0%；电气化里程为9.2万km，电化率为70.0%；西部地区铁路营业里程为5.3万km。全国铁路路网密度为136.9km/万km^2。

2018年国家铁路能源消耗折算标准煤为1624.21万t，比上年减少2.57万t，下降0.2%。单位运输工作量综合能耗4.11t标准煤每百万换算吨公里，比上年减少0.23t标准煤每百万换算吨公里，下降5.3%。单位运输工作量主营综合能耗3.90t标准煤每百万换算吨公里，比上年减少0.08t标准煤每百万换算吨公里，下降2.0%。

不同类型的铁路线路有不同的能源结构。对于非电气化铁路而言，其能量来源主要为柴油。图4-52是我国传统铁路用能分布图，可以看出，2000年我国非电气化铁路的总能耗约为8.57百万吨标准煤，占铁路总能耗的77.9%。其中，柴油机货运铁路的能源消耗量为7.86百万吨标准煤，占比71.4%；柴油机客运铁路的能源消耗量为0.71百万吨标准煤，占比6.5%。到2017年，柴油总消耗量降至4.57百万吨标准煤，占当年铁路能源总消耗量的32.7%。其中，柴油机货运铁路的能源消耗量为4.29百万吨标准煤，占比为39.0%；柴油机货运铁路的能源消耗量为0.29百万吨标准煤，占比为2.6%。

对于电气化铁路而言，其能源全部来自电网中的电能。图4-53是我国电气化铁路用能分布图，可以看出，2000年我国铁路电力消耗为2.43百万吨标准煤，占铁路总消耗的22.1%。到2017年，电力总消耗量增加至8.29百万吨标准煤，占当年铁路能源总消耗量的64.44%。其中，常规电气化铁路的能源消耗量为6.57百万吨标准煤，占比为51.11%；电气化高铁的能源消耗量为1.71百万吨标准煤，占比为13.33%。

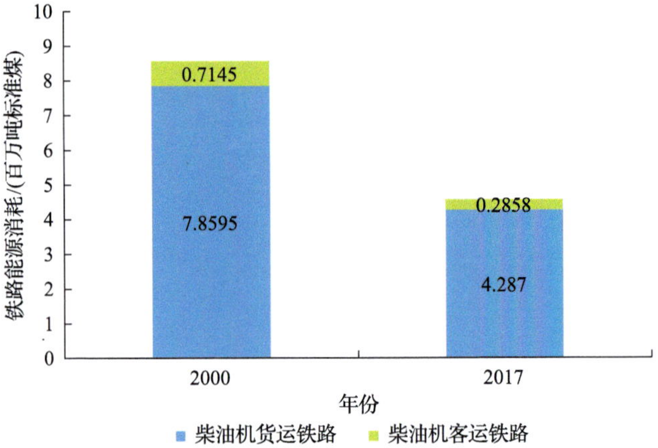

图 4-52　我国传统铁路用能分布图

数据来源：IEA 2018A

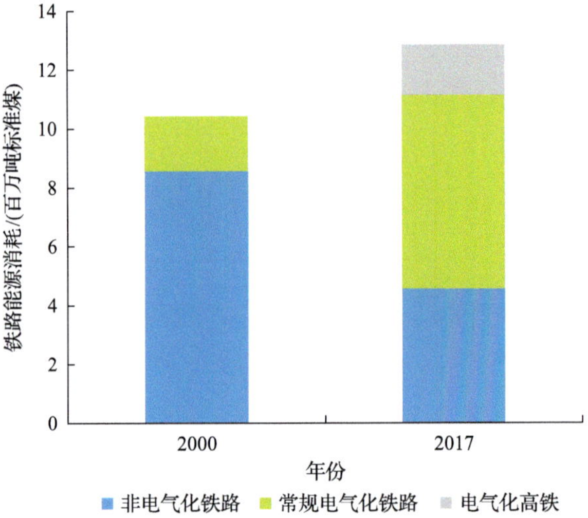

图 4-53　我国电气化铁路用能分布图

数据来源：IEA 2018A

3. 总体融合潜力测算

根据上述对铁路光伏出力和铁路负荷的测算结果，分别计算我国铁路总体光伏自洽率、不同辐射区域自洽率和不同利用模式的自洽率。

图 4-54 和表 4-29 为铁路各季节的光伏出力潜力及自洽率。显然，在春夏两季铁路光伏出力潜力较高，特别是在夏季，铁路的光伏出力最大潜力为 114211GW·h，用能自洽率也相应地达到 346.05%，用电自洽率达到 514.19%；冬季的光伏出力潜力最小，全部利用时为 51233GW·h，用能自洽率为 155.23%，用电自洽率为 230.66%。

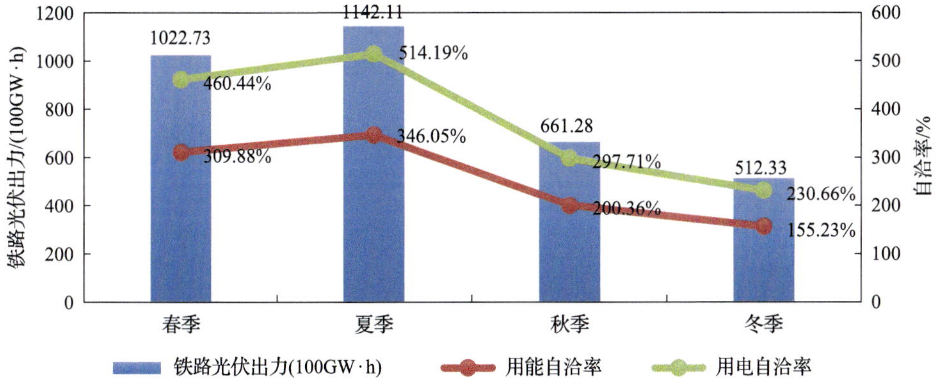

图 4-54　我国铁路系统各季节光伏出力及自洽率

表 4-29　我国铁路系统各季节光伏出力及自洽率对比表

季节	铁路光伏出力/(100GW·h)	用能自洽率/%	用电自洽率/%
春	1022.729777	309.88	460.44
夏	1142.105396	346.05	514.19
秋	661.2813312	200.36	297.71
冬	512.3335855	155.23	230.66

图 4-55 和表 4-30 为各月份铁路光伏出力潜力及自洽率。由图 4-56 易知在 4～8 月铁路光伏出力潜力较高，在 5 月份铁路的光伏出力潜力达到峰值，为 40676GW·h，用能自洽率也相应地达到 369.73%，用电自洽率达到 549.38%；12 月的光伏出力潜力最小，为 12409MW·h，用能自洽率为 112.79%，用电自洽率为 167.60%。不同场景下的光伏出力及自洽率的对比如图 4-56 和表 4-31 所示。

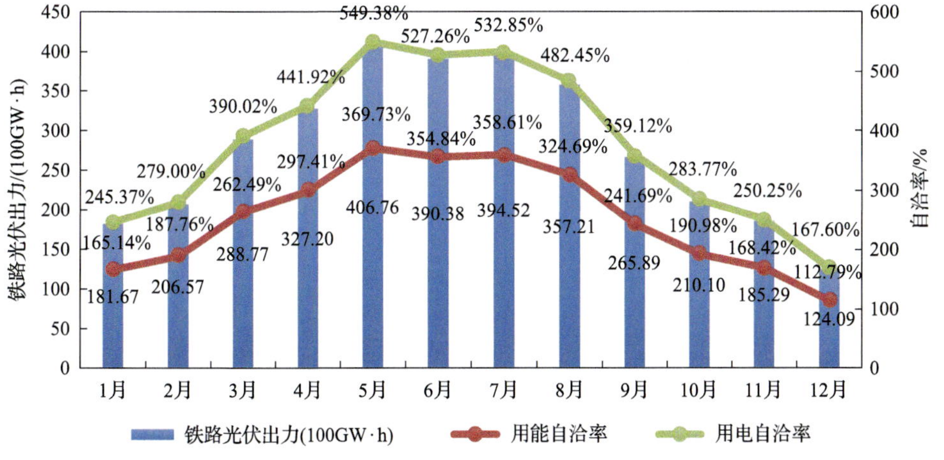

图 4-55　我国铁路系统各月份光伏出力及自洽率对比图

表 4-30　我国铁路系统各月份光伏出力及自洽率对比表

月份	铁路光伏出力/(100GW · h)	用能自洽率/%	用电自洽率/%
1 月	181.6746361	165.14	245.37
2 月	206.5686138	187.76	279.00
3 月	288.7727914	262.49	390.02
4 月	327.1971582	297.41	441.92
5 月	406.7598275	369.73	549.38
6 月	390.3790476	354.84	527.26
7 月	394.5212192	358.61	532.85
8 月	357.2051295	324.69	482.45
9 月	265.8946096	241.69	359.12
10 月	210.1004542	190.98	283.77
11 月	185.2862674	168.42	250.25
12 月	124.0903356	112.79	167.60

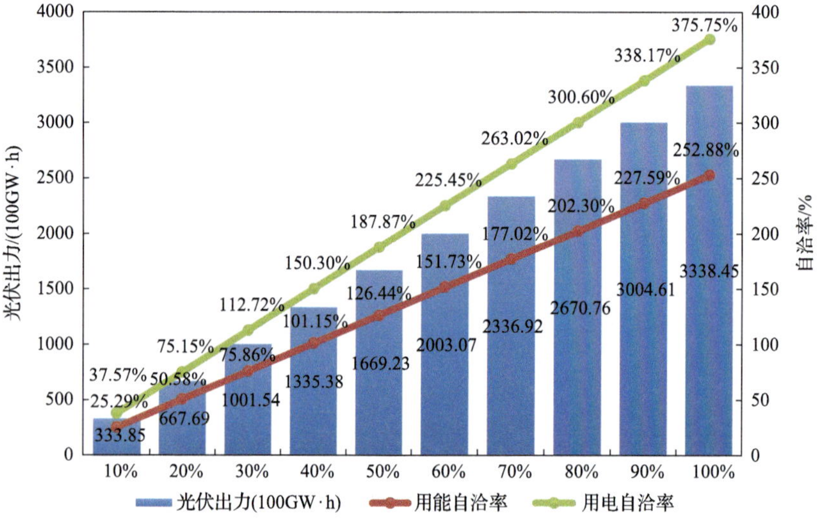

图 4-56　目前在不同开发场景下的我国铁路系统光伏出力及自洽率对比图

表 4-31　目前在不同开发场景下的我国铁路系统光伏出力及自洽率对比表

开发率/%	光伏出力/(100GW · h)	用能自洽率/%	用电自洽率/%
10	333.85	25.29	37.57
20	667.69	50.58	75.15
30	1001.54	75.86	112.72
40	1335.38	101.15	150.30
50	1669.23	126.44	187.87
60	2003.07	151.73	225.45
70	2336.92	177.02	263.02
80	2670.76	202.30	300.60
90	3004.61	227.59	338.17
100	3338.45	252.88	375.75

根据不同利用率下的光伏出力及自洽率情况，我们可以得知在利用率达到39.54%时，铁路自洽率即可达到100%，实现自给自足，此时光伏出力为132017MW·h。

根据上面的测算，可以得知，在四类区域的铁路线长度、光伏出力以及负荷分布如图4-57和表4-32所示。

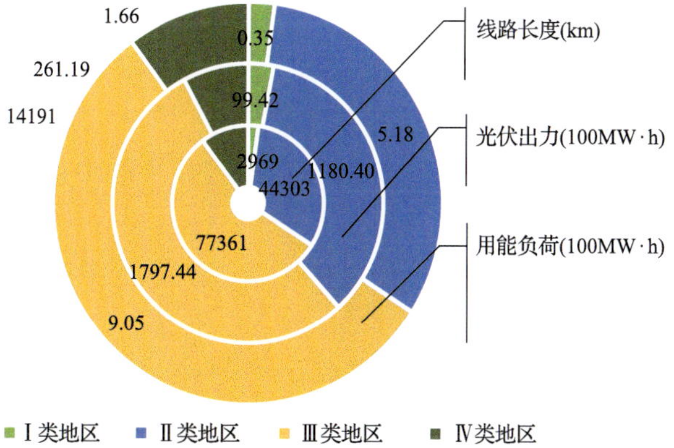

图4-57　目前我国铁路系统在四类光照区域的线路长度、光伏出力和用能负荷对比图

表4-32　目前我国铁路系统在四类光照区域的线路长度、光伏出力和用能负荷对比表

地区	线路长度/km	光伏出力/(100MW·h)	用能负荷/(100MW·h)
Ⅰ类地区	2969	99.42	28.49
Ⅱ类地区	44303	1180.40	421.652
Ⅲ类地区	77361	1797.44	736.67
Ⅳ类地区	14191	261.19	135.124

由此，可计算出四类辐射区域在不同光伏利用率下的年自洽率如图4-58、表4-33、图4-59和表4-34所示。

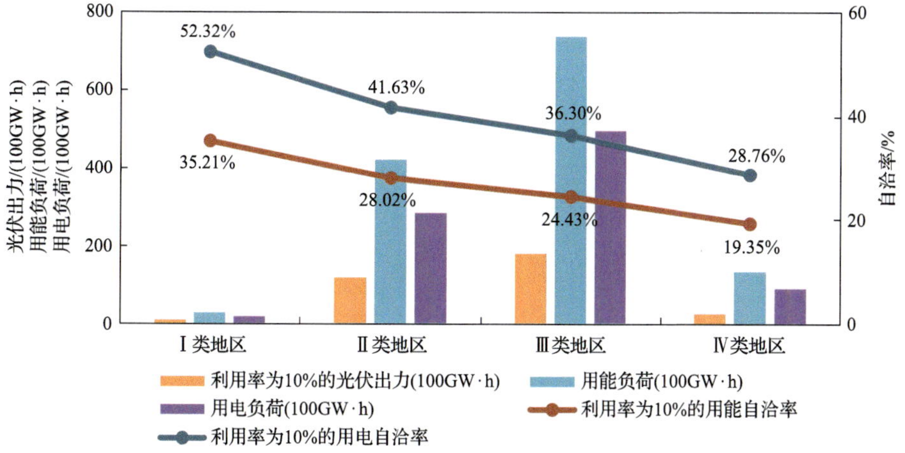

图4-58　保守场景下目前我国铁路系统在四类光照区域的年自洽率对比图

表 4-33 保守场景下目前我国铁路系统在四类光照区域的年自洽率对比表

地区	光伏出力/(100MW·h)	用能负荷/(100MW·h)	用电负荷/(100MW·h)	用能自洽率/%	用电自洽率/%
Ⅰ类地区	9.768	28.49	18.722	35.21	52.32
Ⅱ类地区	118.03	421.652	284.086	28.02	41.63
Ⅲ类地区	179.894	736.67	495.726	24.43	36.30
Ⅳ类地区	26.048	135.124	91.168	19.35	28.76

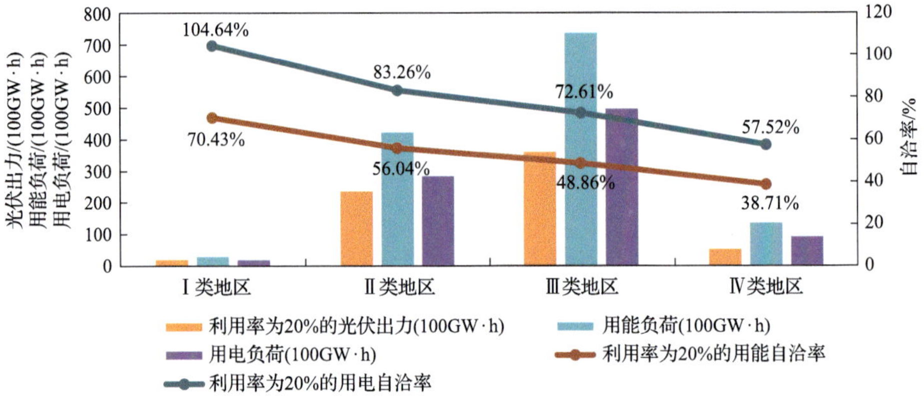

图 4-59 基本场景下目前我国铁路系统在四类光照区域的年自洽率对比图

表 4-34 基本场景下目前我国铁路系统在四类光照区域的年自洽率对比表

地区	光伏出力/(100GW·h)	用能负荷/(100GW·h)	用电负荷/(100GW·h)	用能自洽率/%	用电自洽率/%
Ⅰ类地区	19.536	28.49	18.722	70.43	104.64
Ⅱ类地区	236.06	421.652	284.086	56.04	83.26
Ⅲ类地区	359.788	736.67	495.726	48.86	72.61
Ⅳ类地区	52.096	135.124	91.168	38.71	57.52

从图 4-60 和表 4-35 可看出Ⅰ类地区的自洽率最高，光伏利用率为 10%的时候用能自洽率为 35.21%，用电自洽率为 52.32%；光伏利用率为 30%的时候用能自洽率达到 105.64%，用电自洽率达到 156.97%，即能够实现自给自足。其次为Ⅱ类地区，光伏利用率为 30%时用能自洽率为 84.05%，用电自洽率为 124.89%。Ⅲ类、Ⅳ类地区自洽率相对较低。各个场景下的四类光照区域的季节自洽率如图 4-61～图 4-63 和表 4-36～表 4-38 所示。

图 4-63 和表 4-38 为不同光伏利用率下的四类辐射区域各季节的光伏自洽率。从季节上看，夏季光伏出力大，因此在夏季铁路的光伏自洽率最高，其次为春季，秋冬两季光伏自洽率相对较低。从地区来看，Ⅰ类、Ⅱ类地区铁路的光伏自洽率较高，Ⅲ类、Ⅳ类地区自洽率相对较低。最高自洽率出现在Ⅰ类地区的夏季，光伏利用率为 10%时，用能自洽率为 41.72%，用电自洽率为 61.99%；当光伏利用率为 30%时，用能自洽率达到 125%，用电自洽率也相应达到 186%。

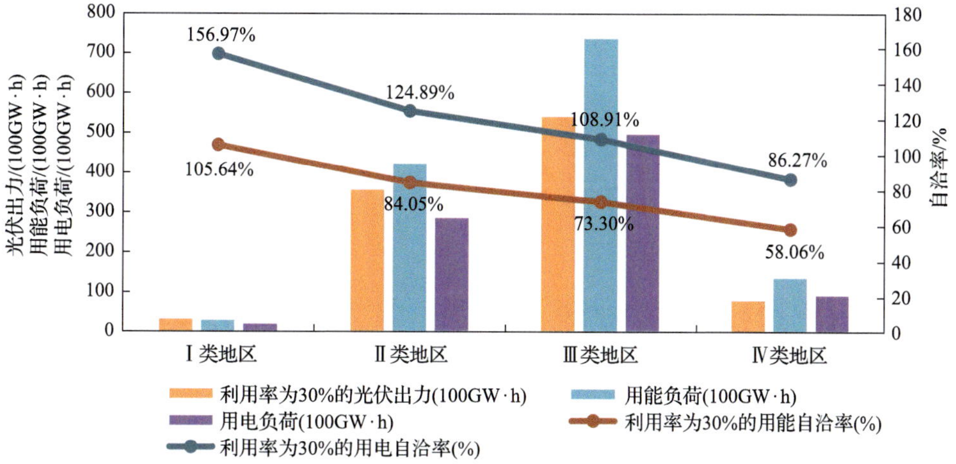

图 4-60　积极场景下目前我国铁路系统在四类光照区域的年自洽率对比图

表 4-35　积极场景下目前我国铁路系统在四类光照区域的年自洽率对比表

地区	光伏出力/(100GW·h)	用能负荷/(100GW·h)	用电负荷/(100GW·h)	用能自洽率/%	用电自洽率/%
Ⅰ类地区	30.118	28.49	18.722	105.64	156.97
Ⅱ类地区	354.904	421.652	284.086	84.05	124.89
Ⅲ类地区	539.682	736.67	495.726	73.30	108.91
Ⅳ类地区	78.144	135.124	91.168	58.06	86.27

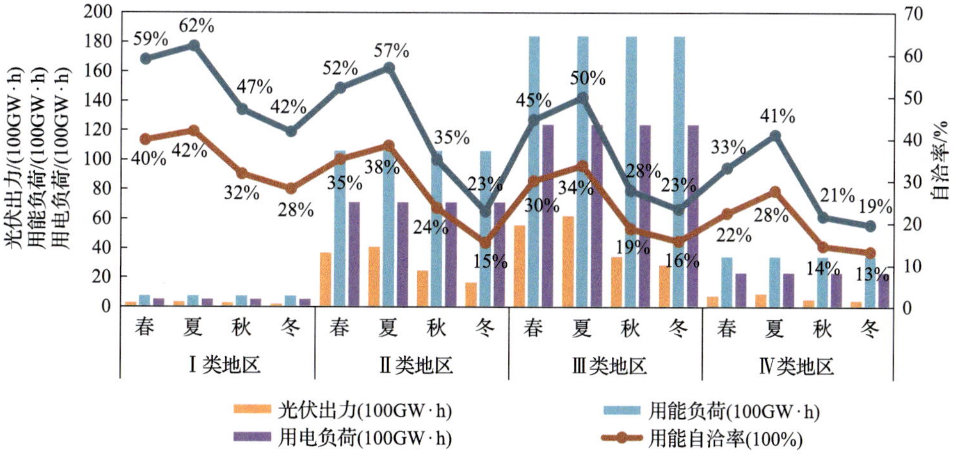

图 4-61　保守场景下目前我国铁路系统在四类光照区域的季节自洽率对比图

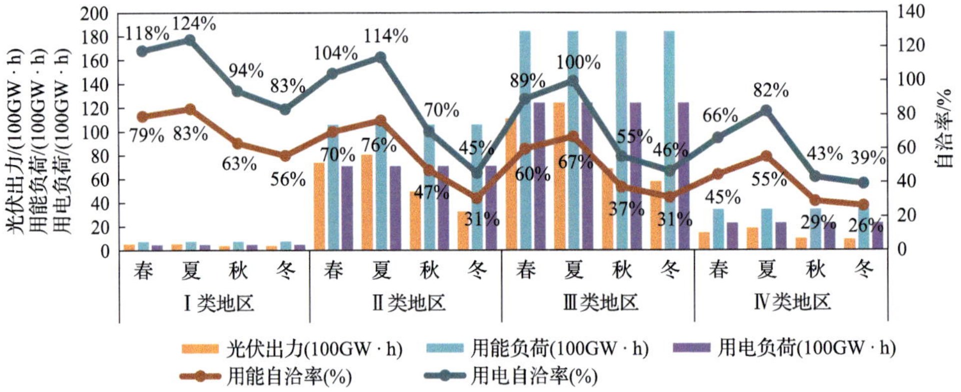

图 4-62　基本场景下目前我国铁路系统在四类光照区域的季节自洽率对比图

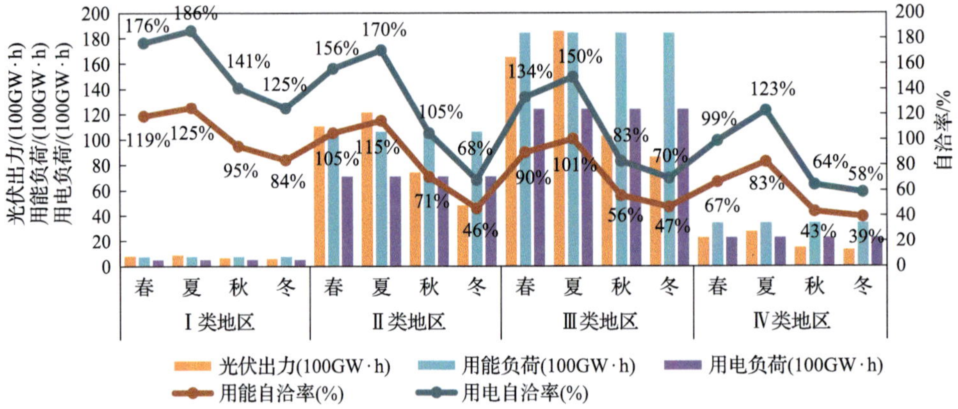

图 4-63　积极场景下目前我国铁路系统在四类光照区域的季节自洽率对比图

表 4-36　保守场景下目前我国铁路系统在四类光照区域的季节自洽率对比表

地区	季节	光伏出力 /(100GW · h)	用能负荷 /(100GW · h)	用电负荷 /(100GW · h)	用能自洽率/%	用电自洽率/%
Ⅰ类地区	春	2.442	7.326	4.884	40	59
	夏	3.256	7.326	4.884	42	62
	秋	2.442	7.326	4.884	32	47
	冬	1.628	7.326	4.884	28	42
Ⅱ类地区	春	36.63	105.82	70.818	35	52
	夏	40.7	105.82	70.818	38	57
	秋	24.42	105.82	70.818	24	35
	冬	16.28	105.82	70.818	15	23

续表

地区	季节	光伏出力/(100GW·h)	用能负荷/(100GW·h)	用电负荷/(100GW·h)	用能自洽率/%	用电自洽率/%
III类地区	春	55.352	183.964	123.728	30	45
	夏	61.864	183.964	123.728	34	50
	秋	34.188	183.964	123.728	19	28
	冬	28.49	183.964	123.728	16	23
IV类地区	春	7.326	34.188	22.792	22	33
	夏	8.954	34.188	22.792	28	41
	秋	4.884	34.188	22.792	14	21
	冬	4.07	34.188	22.792	13	19

表 4-37 基本场景下目前我国铁路系统在四类光照区域的季节自洽率对比表

地区	季节	光伏出力/(100GW·h)	用能负荷/(100GW·h)	用电负荷/(100GW·h)	用能自洽率/%	用电自洽率/%
I 类地区	春	5.698	7.326	4.884	79	118
	夏	5.698	7.326	4.884	83	124
	秋	4.07	7.326	4.884	63	94
	冬	4.07	7.326	4.884	56	83
II 类地区	春	74.074	105.82	70.818	70	104
	夏	80.586	105.82	70.818	76	114
	秋	49.654	105.82	70.818	47	70
	冬	32.56	105.82	70.818	31	45
III类地区	春	110.704	183.964	123.728	60	89
	夏	123.728	183.964	123.728	67	100
	秋	68.376	183.964	123.728	37	55
	冬	57.794	183.964	123.728	31	46
IV类地区	春	14.652	34.188	22.792	45	66
	夏	18.722	34.188	22.792	55	82
	秋	9.768	34.188	22.792	29	43
	冬	8.954	34.188	22.792	26	39

表 4-38 积极场景下目前我国铁路系统在四类光照区域的季节自洽率对比表

地区	季节	光伏出力/(100GW·h)	用能负荷/(100GW·h)	用电负荷/(100GW·h)	用能自洽率/%	用电自洽率/%
I 类地区	春	8.14	7.326	4.884	119	176
	夏	8.954	7.326	4.884	125	186
	秋	6.512	7.326	4.884	95	141
	冬	5.698	7.326	4.884	84	125

续表

地区	季节	光伏出力/(100GW·h)	用能负荷/(100GW·h)	用电负荷/(100GW·h)	用能自洽率/%	用电自洽率/%
Ⅱ类地区	春	110.704	105.82	70.818	105	156
	夏	121.286	105.82	70.818	115	170
	秋	74.074	105.82	70.818	71	105
	冬	48.026	105.82	70.818	46	68
Ⅲ类地区	春	165.242	183.964	123.728	90	134
	夏	185.592	183.964	123.728	101	150
	秋	102.564	183.964	123.728	56	83
	冬	86.284	183.964	123.728	47	70
Ⅳ类地区	春	22.792	34.188	22.792	67	99
	夏	27.676	34.188	22.792	83	123
	秋	14.652	34.188	22.792	43	64
	冬	13.024	34.188	22.792	39	58

图 4-64～图 4-66 和表 4-39～表 4-41 为不同光伏利用率下四类辐射区域各月的光伏自洽率。从月份上看，四类地区均在 5 月份或 7 月份取得最高光伏自洽率，4～8 月份光伏自洽率普遍较高，其他月份光伏自洽率相对较低。从地区来看，Ⅰ类、Ⅱ类地区铁路的光伏自洽率较高，Ⅲ类、Ⅳ类地区自洽率相对较低。最高自洽率出现在Ⅰ类地区的 5 月份，光伏利用率为 10%时，用能自洽率为 44.26%，用电自洽率为 65.76%；当光伏利用率为 30%时，用能自洽率达到 132.77%，用电自洽率也相应地达到 197.28%。

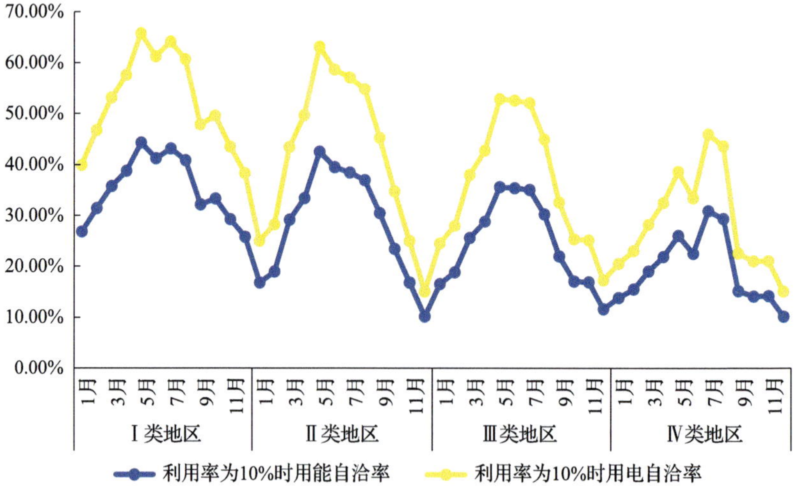

图 4-64　保守场景下目前我国铁路系统在四类光照区域的月度自洽率对比图

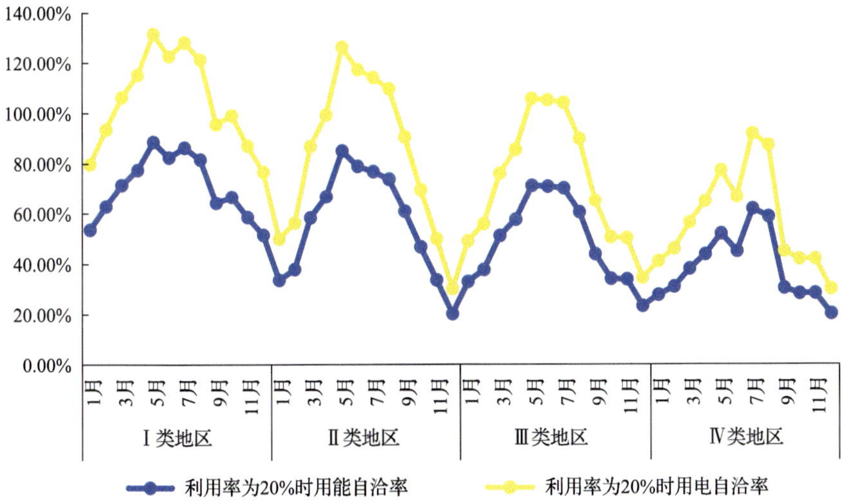

图 4-65　基本场景下目前我国铁路系统在四类光照区域的月度自洽率对比图

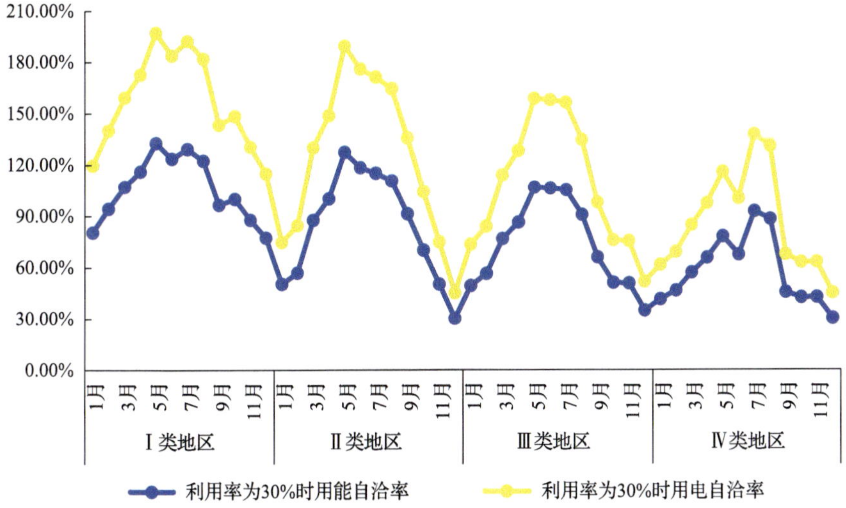

图 4-66　积极场景下目前我国铁路系统在四类光照区域的月度自洽率对比图

表 4-39　保守场景下目前我国铁路系统在四类光照区域的月度自洽率对比表

地区	月份	用能自洽率/%	用电自洽率/%
Ⅰ类地区	1 月	26.81	39.84
	2 月	31.41	46.67
	3 月	35.73	53.08
	4 月	38.72	57.54
	5 月	44.26	65.76
	6 月	41.21	61.23

续表

地区	月份	用能自洽率/%	用电自洽率/%
Ⅰ类地区	7 月	43.13	64.09
	8 月	40.82	60.65
	9 月	32.16	47.78
	10 月	33.31	49.50
	11 月	29.25	43.47
	12 月	25.74	38.25
Ⅱ类地区	1 月	16.77	24.92
	2 月	18.95	28.16
	3 月	29.17	43.35
	4 月	33.39	49.61
	5 月	42.47	63.10
	6 月	39.46	58.63
	7 月	38.40	57.06
	8 月	36.88	54.80
	9 月	30.43	45.21
	10 月	23.38	34.74
	11 月	16.79	24.94
	12 月	10.12	15.04
Ⅲ类地区	1 月	16.47	24.48
	2 月	18.80	27.93
	3 月	25.55	37.96
	4 月	28.76	42.73
	5 月	35.56	52.85
	6 月	35.38	52.57
	7 月	35.04	52.06
	8 月	30.20	44.87
	9 月	21.93	32.59
	10 月	17.01	25.28
	11 月	16.89	25.10
	12 月	11.60	17.24
Ⅳ类地区	1 月	13.79	20.49
	2 月	15.46	22.98
	3 月	18.97	28.19

续表

地区	月份	用能自洽率/%	用电自洽率/%
Ⅳ类地区	4 月	21.85	32.46
	5 月	25.97	38.59
	6 月	22.45	33.36
	7 月	30.90	45.91
	8 月	29.33	43.59
	9 月	15.16	22.52
	10 月	14.10	20.95
	11 月	14.15	21.03
	12 月	10.11	15.02

表 4-40　基本场景下目前我国铁路系统在四类光照区域的月度自洽率对比表

地区	月份	用能自洽率/%	用电自洽率/%
Ⅰ类地区	1 月	53.63	79.69
	2 月	62.82	93.34
	3 月	71.45	106.17
	4 月	77.44	115.07
	5 月	88.51	131.52
	6 月	82.42	122.46
	7 月	86.26	128.18
	8 月	81.64	121.31
	9 月	64.32	95.56
	10 月	66.63	99.00
	11 月	58.51	86.94
	12 月	51.48	76.50
Ⅱ类地区	1 月	33.54	49.84
	2 月	37.91	56.32
	3 月	58.34	86.69
	4 月	66.78	99.23
	5 月	84.94	126.21
	6 月	78.92	117.26
	7 月	76.80	114.12
	8 月	73.76	109.59
	9 月	60.86	90.43
	10 月	46.77	69.49

续表

地区	月份	用能自洽率/%	用电自洽率/%
II类地区	11 月	33.57	49.88
	12 月	20.24	30.08
III类地区	1 月	32.94	48.95
	2 月	37.60	55.86
	3 月	51.09	75.91
	4 月	57.51	85.46
	5 月	71.13	105.69
	6 月	70.76	105.14
	7 月	70.08	104.12
	8 月	60.40	89.74
	9 月	43.86	65.18
	10 月	34.03	50.56
	11 月	33.78	50.19
	12 月	23.20	34.48
IV类地区	1 月	27.58	40.97
	2 月	30.93	45.96
	3 月	37.94	56.38
	4 月	43.69	64.92
	5 月	51.95	77.18
	6 月	44.91	66.73
	7 月	61.80	91.82
	8 月	58.67	87.17
	9 月	30.31	45.04
	10 月	28.20	41.90
	11 月	28.31	42.06
	12 月	20.22	30.05

表 4-41　积极场景下目前我国铁路系统在四类光照区域的月度自洽率对比表

地区	月份	用能自洽率/%	用电自洽率/%
I 类地区	1 月	80.44	119.53
	2 月	94.23	140.02
	3 月	107.18	159.25
	4 月	116.17	172.61
	5 月	132.77	197.28

续表

地区	月份	用能自洽率/%	用电自洽率/%
Ⅰ类地区	6 月	123.62	183.69
	7 月	129.40	192.27
	8 月	122.46	181.96
	9 月	96.47	143.35
	10 月	99.94	148.50
	11 月	87.76	130.41
	12 月	77.22	114.75
Ⅱ类地区	1 月	50.31	74.75
	2 月	56.86	84.48
	3 月	87.52	130.04
	4 月	100.17	148.84
	5 月	127.40	189.31
	6 月	118.38	175.89
	7 月	115.20	171.18
	8 月	110.64	164.39
	9 月	91.28	135.64
	10 月	70.15	104.23
	11 月	50.36	74.83
	12 月	30.37	45.12
Ⅲ类地区	1 月	49.42	73.43
	2 月	56.40	83.80
	3 月	76.64	113.87
	4 月	86.27	128.18
	5 月	106.69	158.54
	6 月	106.14	157.71
	7 月	105.11	156.19
	8 月	90.60	134.61
	9 月	65.79	97.76
	10 月	51.04	75.85
	11 月	50.67	75.29
	12 月	34.80	51.72
Ⅳ类地区	1 月	41.36	61.46
	2 月	46.39	68.93

续表

地区	月份	用能自洽率/%	用电自洽率/%
Ⅳ类地区	3 月	56.92	84.57
	4 月	65.54	97.38
	5 月	77.92	115.78
	6 月	67.36	100.09
	7 月	92.70	137.73
	8 月	88.00	130.76
	9 月	45.47	67.56
	10 月	42.29	62.84
	11 月	42.46	63.09
	12 月	30.34	45.07

4. 不同场景下的融合潜力测算

根据 3.2 节，我国交通能源系统的演化可分为 8 种新模式。在本节中，将其编为 1～8 号，如表 4-42 所示。

表 4-42　交通能源系统的 8 种融合模式编号、场景特点和演化模式的对应关系

区域	编号	场景特点(三网融合特性)	演化新模式(源网荷储协同调度特性)
无电区	1	无电+少负荷+多光	内燃机+可再生+微网+自给自足
	5	无电+少负荷+少光	内燃机+可再生+微网+自给自足
有电区	2	末端+少负荷+多光	可再生+储能+微网为主+余电上网
	3	强电+少负荷+多光	可再生+储能+微网+余电上网
	4	强电+多负荷+多光	可再生+储能+微网/电网+自给自足
	6	末端+少负荷+少光	可再生+储能+微网/电网+自给自足
	7	强电+少负荷+少光	可再生+储能+微网/电网+余电上网
	8	强电+多负荷+少光	可再生+储能+电网为主+网上购电

其中，1 号、5 号区域均为无电区域，采用柴油机作为铁路列车的牵引动力来源，因而在后续的渗透率测算中，不考虑上述两区域；2、3、4、6、7、8 等 6 个区域内绝大部分为电气化铁路，在此将这 6 个区域统称为有电区。

2017 年，我国电气化铁路总耗电量为 829 万 t 标准煤，折合电量 67382GW·h。通过地理信息系统进行测算，得出有电区内各模式区域的线路长度、用能占比、年耗电量等信息，如表 4-43 所示。图 4-67 为我国有电区域铁路长度、用能占比和能耗数据图。

表 4-43 我国有电区域铁路长度、用能占比和能耗数据表

编号	电气化线路长度/km	用能占比/%	区域耗能/(100GW·h)
2	3483.5	2.4	16.2
3	8343.8	8.1	54.8
4	20732.4	10.2	68.7
6	7898.6	7.7	51.9
7	12331.8	6.5	43.8
8	49777.6	65.1	438.4

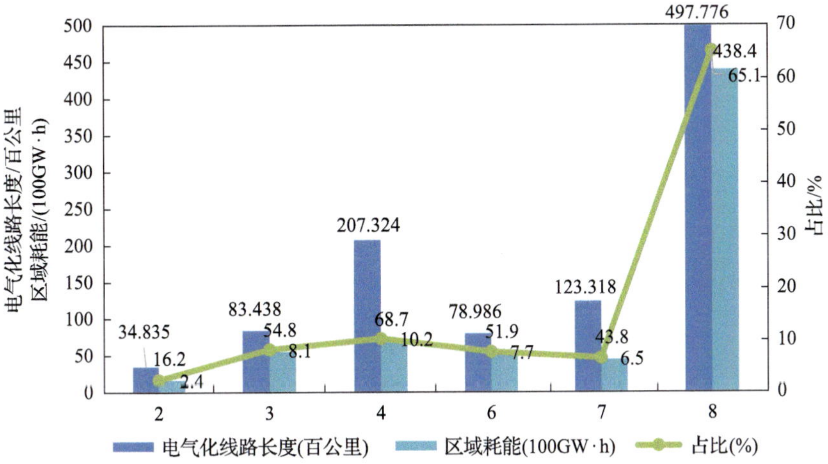

图 4-67 我国有电区铁路长度、用能占比和能耗数据图

有电区内各模式区域的平均年水平辐射总量数据如表 4-44 所示。

表 4-44 我国有电区域的平均年光照水平辐射总量（单位：kW·h/m^2）

月份	2 区	3 区	4 区	6 区	7 区	8 区
1	86.6	111.5	96.4	79.1	63.1	116.1
2	109.9	115.7	121.9	105.0	90.4	92.2
3	162.1	180.9	181.0	158.7	125.9	119.5
4	199.4	195.5	198.8	176.5	116.2	130.0
5	225.6	215.9	240.5	196.7	144.8	120.1
6	196.5	188.7	234.7	211.5	144.3	118.5
7	131.8	201.0	216.4	214.0	140.9	88.6
8	137.9	178.8	211.9	195.9	129.7	85.4
9	111.6	148.0	156.3	126.2	65.7	84.9
10	129.4	131.6	119.7	102.7	44.6	141.9
11	81.9	99.3	86.8	70.2	28.7	86.0
12	63.4	94.9	78.0	60.4	21.5	102.1

图 4-68 为我国有电区域的平均年光照水平辐射总量。

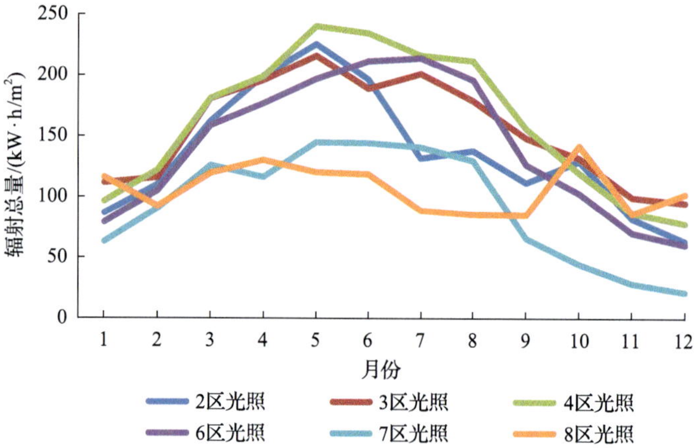

图 4-68　我国有电区域的平均年光照水平辐射总量

按照 4.4.1 节中的共性配置技术以及共性测算方法，可以计算得出有电区内各模式区域的光伏发电潜力，如表 4-45 所示。图 4-69 为我国有电区域的铁路系统光伏发电潜力。

表 4-45　我国有电区域的铁路系统光伏发电潜力（单位：100GW·h）

月份	2 区	3 区	4 区	6 区	7 区	8 区
1	4.1	12.7	27.3	8.5	10.6	79.1
2	5.2	13.2	34.6	11.3	15.2	62.8
3	7.7	20.6	51.3	17.2	21.2	81.4
4	9.5	22.3	56.4	19.1	19.6	88.5
5	10.8	24.6	68.2	21.3	24.4	81.8
6	9.4	21.5	66.6	22.9	24.3	80.7
7	6.3	22.9	61.4	23.1	23.8	60.3
8	6.6	20.4	60.1	21.2	21.9	58.2
9	5.3	16.9	44.3	13.6	11.1	57.8
10	6.2	15.0	34.0	11.1	7.5	96.6
11	3.9	11.3	24.6	7.6	4.8	58.6
12	3.0	10.8	22.1	6.5	3.6	69.5

考虑到政策调整、区域经济发展差异及光伏技术发展等不确定因素，以及在相同开发强度下，某一模式区域内的线路越长，开发难度越大等原因，设计三种场景，分别为保守开发场景，即开发强度为 10%；基本开发场景，即开发强度为 20%；积极开发场景，即开发强度为 30%。根据 4.4.2 节中的计算结果，可以得出各模式区域在不同开发强度下的光伏使用率，即铁路系统直接使用的光伏出力占光伏发电总量的比例，计算结果如表 4-46 所示。图 4-70 为有电区域内不同融合模式及不同开发强度下光伏使用率对比图。

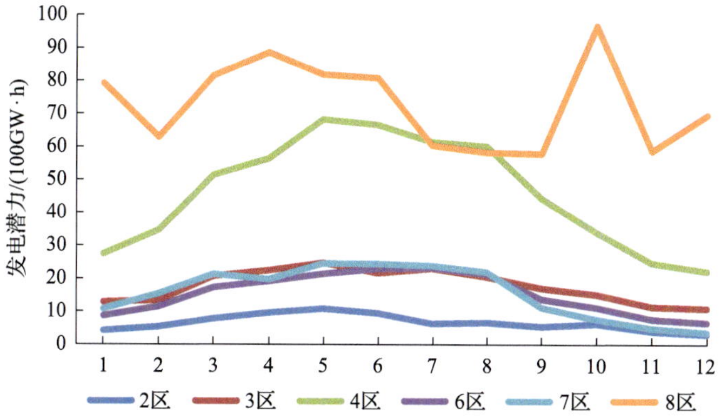

图 4-69 我国有电区域的铁路系统光伏发电潜力

表 4-46 我国有电区域光伏使用率 （单位：%）

区域	保守场景	基本场景	积极场景
2	91.6	57.5	40.3
3	56.8	29.3	19.5
4	99.6	98.5	91.8
6	94.0	60.0	44.0
7	60.0	35.0	24.0
8	99.8	99.1	92.0

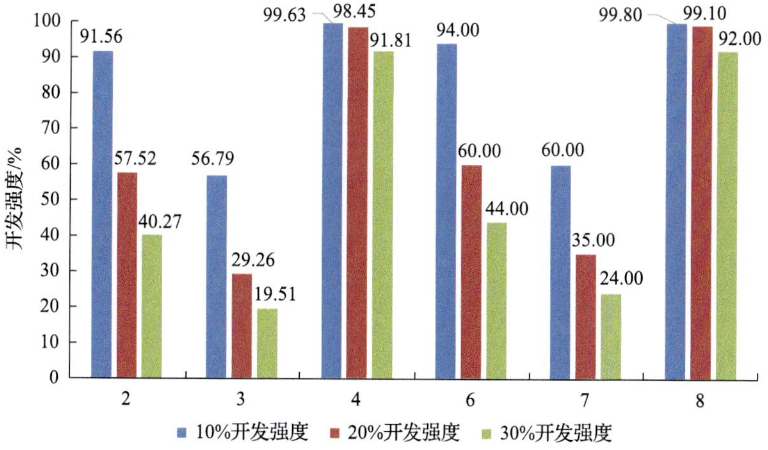

图 4-70 有电区域内不同融合模式及不同开发强度下光伏使用率对比图

针对以上三种场景设计，分别计算在不同开发强度下，全国有电区内 6 种模式区域的可再生能源渗透率。有电区内各模式区域在不同场景下的年渗透率如表 4-47 所示。需要指出的是，在相同开发场景下，模式区域内的线路长度越长，则开发成本越高。图 4-71 为不同开发强度下各模式区域年度渗透率。

表 4-47　不同场景下各模式区域年度渗透率

场景	2 区	3 区	4 区	6 区	7 区	8 区
保守场景	1.1	2.2	7.9	2.9	2.0	16.1
基本场景	1.4	2.2	9.8	3.5	2.2	28.1
积极场景	1.5	2.2	10.2	3.8	2.3	37.6

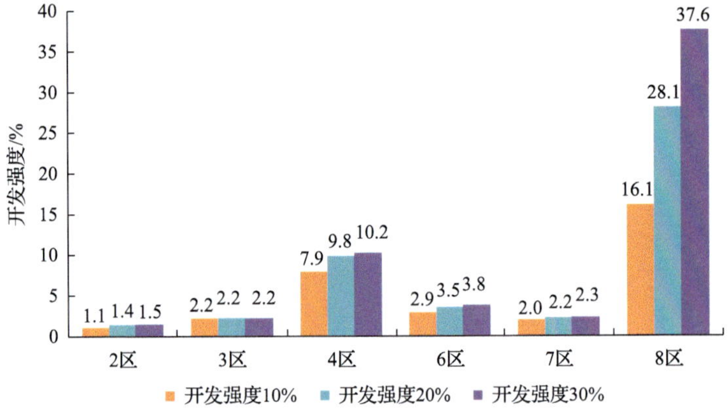

图 4-71　不同开发强度下各模式区域年度渗透率

1)保守场景

在保守场景下,各模式区域月度用电自洽率和用能自洽率测算结果如图 4-72、图 4-73、表 4-48、表 4-49 所示。

在保守场景下，各模式区域月度渗透率测算结果如表 4-50 和图 4-74 所示。可以看出，在 10%开发强度下全国铁路可再生能源渗透率可达 32.2%。

在保守场景下，当前我国铁路系统减排情况如表 4-51 和图 4-75 所示。从表 4-51 中可以看出,开发 10%的潜力,全国铁路年二氧化碳减排量可达 1867.9 万 t,减排效果十分明显。

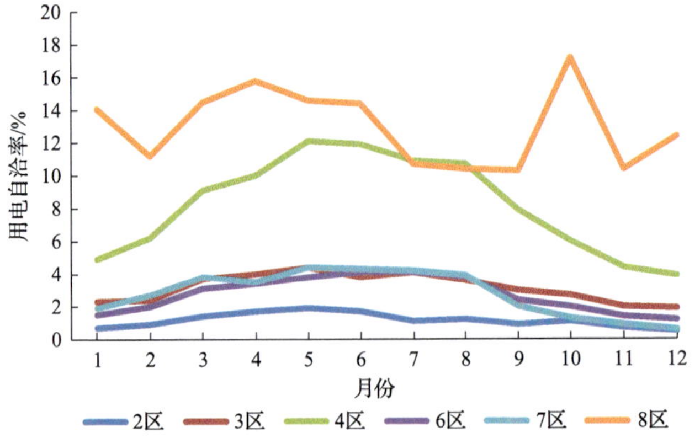

图 4-72　保守场景下目前我国铁路系统各模式区域月度用电自洽率

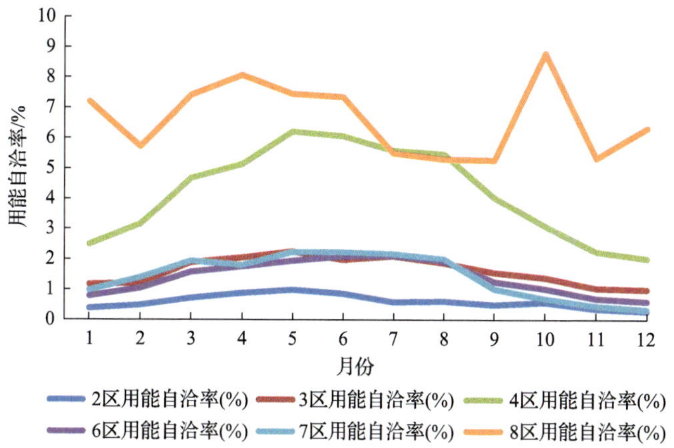

图 4-73 保守场景下目前我国铁路系统各模式区域月度用能自洽率

表 4-48 保守场景下目前我国铁路系统各模式区域月度用电自洽率（单位：%）

月份	2 区	3 区	4 区	6 区	7 区	8 区
1	0.7	2.3	4.9	1.5	1.9	14.1
2	0.9	2.4	6.2	2.0	2.7	11.2
3	1.4	3.7	9.1	3.1	3.8	14.5
4	1.7	4.0	10.0	3.4	3.5	15.8
5	1.9	4.4	12.1	3.8	4.4	14.6
6	1.7	3.8	11.9	4.1	4.3	14.4
7	1.1	4.1	10.9	4.1	4.2	10.7
8	1.2	3.6	10.7	3.8	3.9	10.4
9	0.9	3.0	7.9	2.4	2.0	10.3
10	1.1	2.7	6.0	2.0	1.3	17.2
11	0.7	2.0	4.4	1.4	0.9	10.4
12	0.5	1.9	3.9	1.2	0.6	12.4
全年平均	1.2	3.2	8.2	2.7	2.8	13.0

表 4-49 保守场景下目前我国铁路系统各模式区域月度用能自洽率（单位：%）

月份	2 区	3 区	4 区	6 区	7 区	8 区
1	0.4	1.2	2.5	0.8	1.0	7.2
2	0.5	1.2	3.1	1.0	1.4	5.7
3	0.7	1.9	4.7	1.6	1.9	7.4
4	0.9	2.0	5.1	1.7	1.8	8.0
5	1.0	2.2	6.2	1.9	2.2	7.4
6	0.9	2.0	6.1	2.1	2.2	7.3
7	0.6	2.1	5.6	2.1	2.2	5.5
8	0.6	1.9	5.5	1.9	2.0	5.3
9	0.5	1.5	4.0	1.2	1.0	5.3
10	0.6	1.4	3.1	1.0	0.7	8.8
11	0.4	1.0	2.2	0.7	0.4	5.3
12	0.3	1.0	2.0	0.6	0.3	6.3
全年平均	0.6	1.6	4.2	1.4	1.4	6.6

表 4-50 保守场景下目前我国铁路系统各模式区域月度渗透率（单位：%）

月份	2 区	3 区	4 区	6 区	7 区	8 区	总计
1	0.8	1.7	5.2	1.8	1.5	17.1	28.1
2	0.9	1.7	6.4	2.2	1.9	14.4	27.7
3	1.3	2.5	9.2	3.2	2.5	17.5	36.2
4	1.6	2.6	10.0	3.5	2.4	18.7	38.8
5	1.8	2.8	10.2	3.8	2.8	17.6	39.1
6	1.6	2.5	10.2	4.1	2.8	17.4	38.6
7	1.1	2.7	10.2	4.1	2.8	14.0	34.9
8	1.2	2.4	10.2	3.8	2.6	13.6	33.8
9	1.0	2.1	8.0	2.6	1.5	13.6	28.7
10	1.1	1.9	6.3	2.2	1.1	20.1	32.7
11	0.7	1.6	4.7	1.7	0.9	13.7	23.3
12	0.6	1.5	4.3	1.5	0.8	15.5	24.2
全年平均	1.1	2.2	7.9	2.9	2.0	16.1	32.2

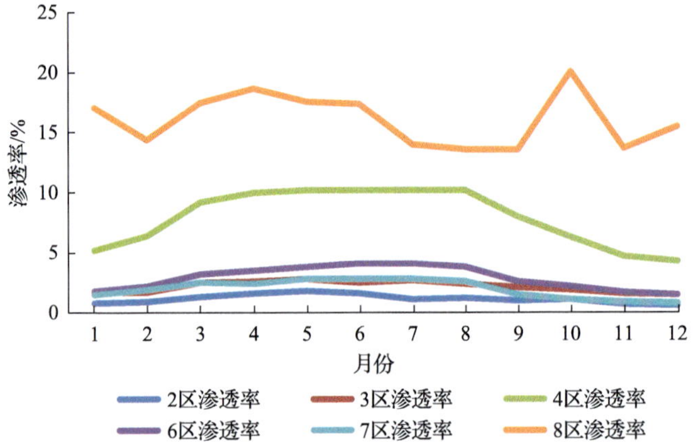

图 4-74 保守场景下目前我国铁路系统各模式区域月度渗透率

表 4-51 保守场景下目前我国铁路系统减排量情况 （单位：万 t）

月份	2 区	3 区	4 区	6 区	7 区	8 区	总计
1	3.77	7.20	27.14	8.01	6.37	78.67	131.16
2	4.78	7.48	34.35	10.63	9.12	62.50	128.86
3	7.05	11.69	50.99	16.07	12.70	80.99	179.50
4	8.67	12.63	56.00	17.88	11.73	88.10	195.01
5	9.82	13.95	57.10	19.92	14.62	81.38	196.79
6	8.55	12.20	57.10	21.42	14.56	80.26	194.09
7	5.73	12.99	57.10	21.67	14.22	60.04	171.75
8	6.00	11.55	57.10	19.83	13.09	57.88	165.45
9	4.85	9.56	44.03	12.78	6.63	57.49	135.35
10	5.63	8.51	33.72	10.40	4.50	96.15	158.90
11	3.56	6.42	24.46	7.11	2.90	58.27	102.72
12	2.76	6.13	21.98	6.11	2.17	69.15	108.30
总计	71.17	120.31	521.09	171.83	112.59	870.89	1867.90

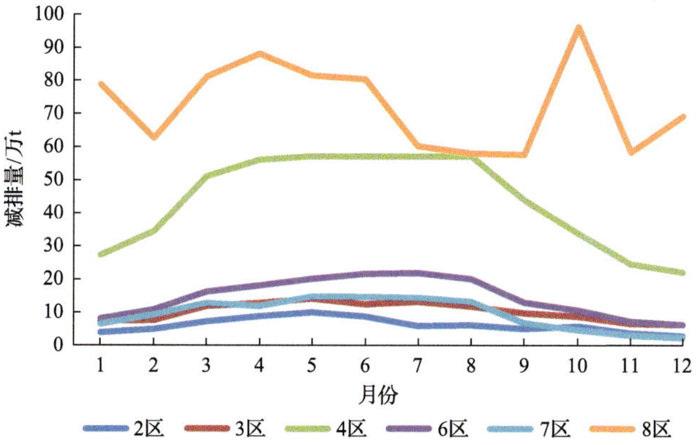

图 4-75　保守场景下目前我国铁路系统减排量情况

2) 基本场景

在基本场景下，各模式区域月度用电自洽率和用能自洽率测算结果如图 4-76、图 4-77、表 4-52 和表 4-53 所示。

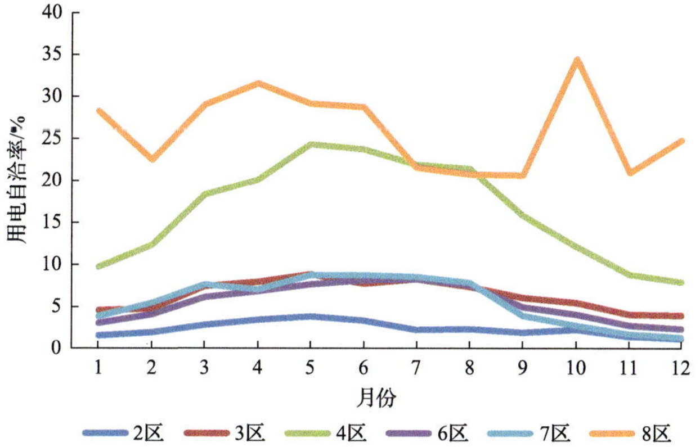

图 4-76　基本场景下目前我国铁路系统各模式区域月度用电自洽率

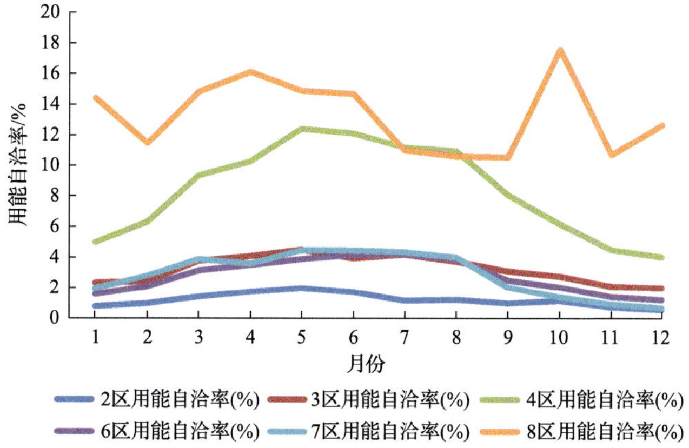

图 4-77　基本场景下目前我国铁路系统各模式区域月度用能自洽率

表 4-52　基本场景下目前我国铁路系统各模式区域月度用电自洽率（单位：%）

月份	2 区	3 区	4 区	6 区	7 区	8 区
1	1.5	4.5	9.7	3.0	3.8	28.2
2	1.9	4.7	12.3	4.0	5.4	22.4
3	2.8	7.4	18.3	6.1	7.6	29.0
4	3.4	7.9	20.1	6.8	7.0	31.5
5	3.8	8.8	24.3	7.6	8.7	29.1
6	3.3	7.7	23.7	8.1	8.7	28.7
7	2.2	8.2	21.9	8.2	8.5	21.5
8	2.3	7.3	21.4	7.5	7.8	20.7
9	1.9	6.0	15.8	4.9	3.9	20.6
10	2.2	5.4	12.1	4.0	2.7	34.4
11	1.4	4.0	8.8	2.7	1.7	20.9
12	1.1	3.9	7.9	2.3	1.3	24.8
全年平均	2.3	6.3	16.4	5.4	5.6	26.0

表 4-53　基本场景下目前我国铁路系统各模式区域月度用能自洽率（单位：%）

月份	2 区	3 区	4 区	6 区	7 区	8 区
1	0.8	2.3	5.0	1.6	1.9	14.4
2	1.0	2.4	6.3	2.1	2.8	11.4
3	1.4	3.8	9.3	3.1	3.9	14.8
4	1.7	4.1	10.2	3.5	3.6	16.1
5	2.0	4.5	12.4	3.9	4.4	14.9
6	1.7	3.9	12.1	4.2	4.4	14.7
7	1.1	4.2	11.2	4.2	4.3	11.0
8	1.2	3.7	10.9	3.8	4.0	10.6
9	1.0	3.1	8.1	2.5	2.0	10.5
10	1.1	2.7	6.2	2.0	1.4	17.6
11	0.7	2.1	4.5	1.4	0.9	10.6
12	0.5	2.0	4.0	1.2	0.7	12.6
全年平均	1.2	3.2	8.3	2.8	2.9	13.3

在基本场景下，各模式区域月度渗透率测算结果如图 4-78 和表 4-54 所示。可以看出，在 20%开发强度下全国铁路可再生能源渗透率可达 47.3%。

在基本场景下，当前我国铁路系统减排情况如表 4-55 所示。从表 4-55 和图 4-79 中可以看出，开发 20%的潜力，全国铁路年二氧化碳减排量可达 2953.05 万 t，减排效果显著。

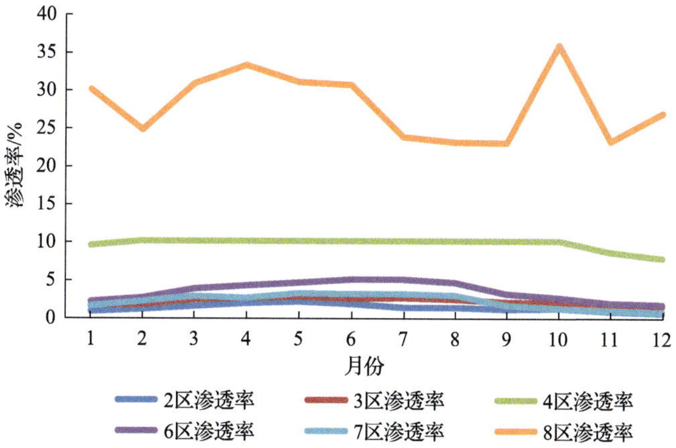

图 4-78　基本场景下目前我国铁路系统各模式区域月度可再生能源渗透率

表 4-54　基本场景下目前我国铁路系统各模式区域月度渗透率（单位：%）

月份	2 区	3 区	4 区	6 区	7 区	8 区	总计
1	0.9	1.7	9.6	2.2	1.6	30.1	46.3
2	1.2	1.8	10.2	2.7	2.2	24.8	42.8
3	1.6	2.5	10.2	3.9	2.9	30.9	52.1
4	2.0	2.7	10.2	4.3	2.7	33.3	55.1
5	2.2	2.9	10.2	4.7	3.3	31.1	54.4
6	1.9	2.6	10.2	5.1	3.2	30.7	53.7
7	1.4	2.7	10.2	5.1	3.2	23.9	46.5
8	1.4	2.5	10.2	4.7	3.0	23.2	45.0
9	1.2	2.1	10.2	3.2	1.7	23.1	41.5
10	1.3	2.0	10.2	2.7	1.3	36.0	53.4
11	0.9	1.6	8.7	2.0	1.0	23.3	37.5
12	0.7	1.6	7.9	1.8	0.8	27.0	39.8
全年平均	1.4	2.2	9.8	3.5	2.2	28.1	47.3

表 4-55　基本场景下目前我国铁路系统减排量情况　　（单位：万 t）

月份	2 区	3 区	4 区	6 区	7 区	8 区	总计
1	4.73	7.42	53.65	10.22	7.43	156.24	239.69
2	6.00	7.71	57.10	13.57	10.64	124.12	219.14
3	8.86	12.05	57.10	20.52	14.82	160.85	274.20
4	10.90	13.02	57.10	22.82	13.68	174.96	292.48
5	12.33	14.38	57.10	25.43	17.05	161.63	287.92
6	10.74	12.57	57.10	27.35	16.99	159.39	284.14
7	7.20	13.38	57.10	27.67	16.58	119.24	241.17
8	7.54	11.91	57.10	25.32	15.27	114.94	232.08
9	6.10	9.86	57.10	16.32	7.74	114.18	211.30
10	7.07	8.77	57.10	13.27	5.25	190.95	282.41
11	4.47	6.61	48.34	9.07	3.38	115.72	187.59
12	3.46	6.32	43.45	7.80	2.53	137.34	200.90
总计	89.40	124.0	659.36	219.36	131.36	1729.56	2953.05

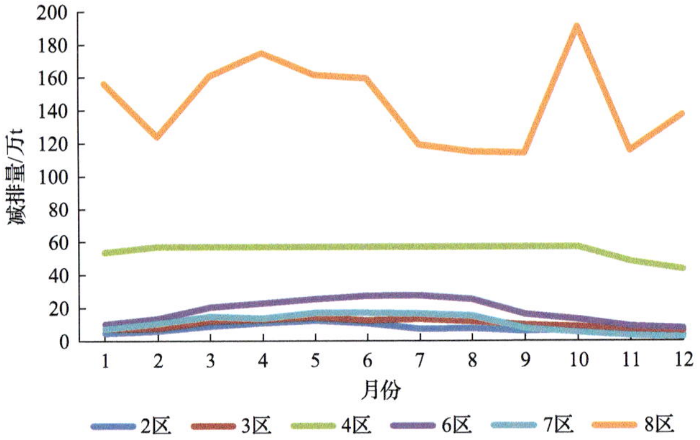

图 4-79　基本场景下目前我国铁路系统减排量情况

3) 积极场景

在积极场景下，各模式区域月度用电自洽率和用能自洽率测算结果如图 4-80、图 4-81、表 4-56 和表 4-57 所示。

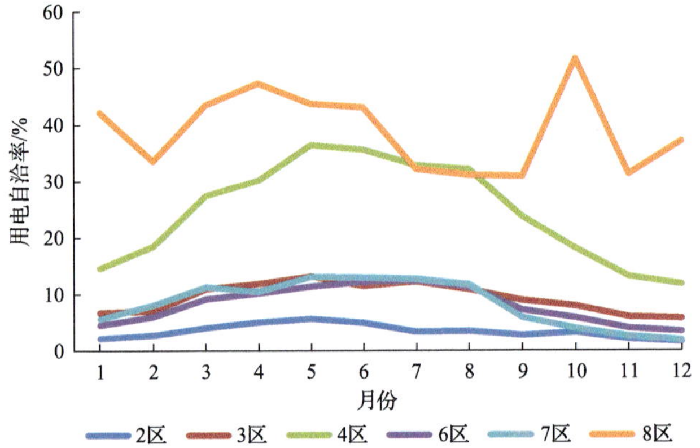

图 4-80　积极场景下目前我国铁路系统各模式区域月度用电自洽率

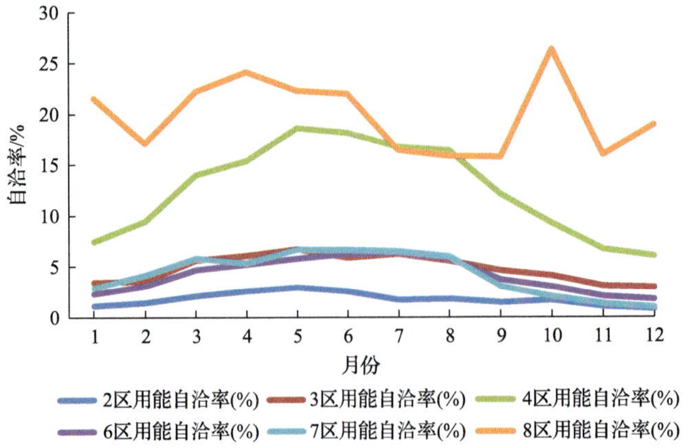

图 4-81　积极场景下目前我国铁路系统各模式区域月度用能自洽率

表 4-56 积极场景下目前我国铁路系统各模式区域月度用电自洽率（单位：%）

月份	2 区	3 区	4 区	6 区	7 区	8 区
1	2.2	6.8	14.6	4.6	5.7	42.2
2	2.8	7.1	18.5	6.1	8.1	33.6
3	4.1	11.0	27.4	9.2	11.3	43.5
4	5.1	11.9	30.1	10.2	10.5	47.3
5	5.7	13.2	36.4	11.4	13.1	43.7
6	5.0	11.5	35.6	12.2	13.0	43.1
7	3.4	12.3	32.8	12.4	12.7	32.2
8	3.5	10.9	32.1	11.3	11.7	31.1
9	2.8	9.0	23.7	7.3	5.9	30.9
10	3.3	8.0	18.1	5.9	4.0	51.6
11	2.1	6.1	13.2	4.1	2.6	31.3
12	1.6	5.8	11.8	3.5	1.9	37.1
全年平均	3.5	9.5	24.5	8.2	8.4	39.0

表 4-57 积极场景下目前我国铁路系统各模式区域月度用能自洽率（单位：%）

月份	2 区	3 区	4 区	6 区	7 区	8 区
1	1.1	3.5	7.5	2.3	2.9	21.6
2	1.4	3.6	9.4	3.1	4.2	17.1
3	2.1	5.6	14.0	4.7	5.8	22.2
4	2.6	6.1	15.4	5.2	5.3	24.1
5	2.9	6.7	18.6	5.8	6.7	22.3
6	2.6	5.9	18.2	6.2	6.6	22.0
7	1.7	6.3	16.7	6.3	6.5	16.5
8	1.8	5.6	16.4	5.8	6.0	15.9
9	1.4	4.6	12.1	3.7	3.0	15.8
10	1.7	4.1	9.3	3.0	2.1	26.4
11	1.1	3.1	6.7	2.1	1.3	16.0
12	0.8	3.0	6.0	1.8	1.0	19.0
全年平均	1.8	4.8	12.5	4.2	4.3	19.9

在积极场景下，各模式区域月度渗透率测算结果如表 4-58 所示。可以看出，在 30%开发强度下全国铁路可再生能源渗透率可达 57.6%。图 4-82 为基本场景下目前我国铁路系统各模式区域月度可再生能源渗透率。

在积极场景下，当前我国铁路系统减排情况如表 4-59 所示。从表 4-59 中可以看出，开发 30%的潜力，全国铁路年二氧化碳减排量可达 3688.02 万 t。图 4-83 为积极场景下目前我国铁路系统减排量情况。

表 4-58　积极场景下目前我国铁路系统各模式区域月度渗透率　（单位：%）

月份	2 区	3 区	4 区	6 区	7 区	8 区	总计
1	1.0	1.7	10.2	2.4	1.7	40.4	57.4
2	1.2	1.8	10.2	3.0	2.2	32.9	51.3
3	1.7	2.5	10.2	4.3	3.0	41.5	63.1
4	2.1	2.7	10.2	4.7	2.8	44.8	67.2
5	2.3	2.9	10.2	5.2	3.3	41.7	65.6
6	2.0	2.6	10.2	5.5	3.3	41.2	64.9
7	1.4	2.7	10.2	5.6	3.3	31.8	55.0
8	1.5	2.5	10.2	5.1	3.0	30.8	53.1
9	1.2	2.1	10.2	3.5	1.7	30.6	49.4
10	1.4	2.0	10.2	2.9	1.3	48.6	66.3
11	0.9	1.6	10.2	2.1	1.0	31.0	46.8
12	0.8	1.6	10.2	1.9	0.8	36.0	51.3
全年平均	1.5	2.2	10.2	3.8	2.3	37.6	57.6

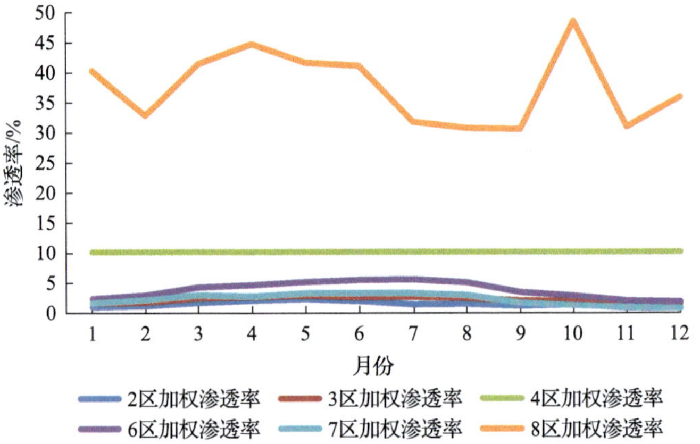

图 4-82　基本场景下目前我国铁路系统各模式区域月度可再生能源渗透率

表 4-59　积极场景下目前我国铁路系统减排量情况　（单位：万 t）

月份	2 区	3 区	4 区	6 区	7 区	8 区	总计
1	4.97	7.42	57.10	11.24	7.64	217.57	305.95
2	6.31	7.71	57.10	14.93	10.95	172.84	269.83
3	9.31	12.05	57.10	22.57	15.24	223.99	340.26
4	11.44	13.02	57.10	25.10	14.07	243.63	364.37
5	12.95	14.38	57.10	27.97	17.54	225.07	355.02
6	11.28	12.57	57.10	30.08	17.47	221.96	350.47
7	7.56	13.39	57.10	30.43	17.06	166.05	291.59
8	7.91	11.91	57.10	27.85	15.70	160.06	280.54
9	6.40	9.86	57.10	17.95	7.96	159.00	258.27
10	7.43	8.77	57.10	14.60	5.40	265.90	359.20
11	4.70	6.62	57.10	9.98	3.48	161.14	243.02
12	3.64	6.32	57.10	8.58	2.60	191.25	269.49
总计	93.90	124.01	685.23	241.30	135.11	2408.46	3688.02

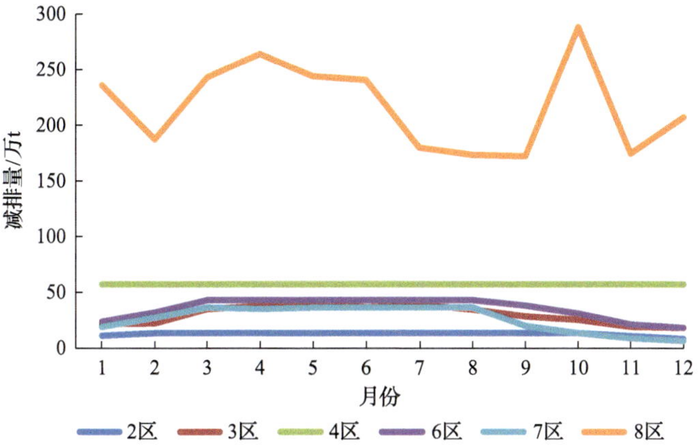

图 4-83 积极场景下目前我国铁路系统减排量情况

4）投资收益估算

根据国网能源研究院发布的《2019 中国可再生能源发电分析报告》的数据显示：光伏电站投资成本为 4.8 元/W。结合市场上光伏组件功率参数，按每平方米可加装光伏组件 160W 计算。同时，根据彭博可再生能源财经 2019 年全球锂离子电池价格调研发现，锂离子电池组的平均价格为 156 美元/(kW·h)。因此，在后续进行投资收益预测时，每千瓦时储能需投资 1079.69 元。

根据国家发展和改革委员会《关于完善光伏发电上网电价机制有关问题的通知》（发改价格〔2019〕761 号），纳入国家财政补贴范围的Ⅰ～Ⅲ类地区新增集中式光伏电站指导价分别确定为每千瓦时 0.40 元(含税，下同)、0.45 元、0.55 元。同时，对工商业分布式光伏发电项目给予 0.10 元/(kW·h)的补贴。

无电区没有电网铺设，所以项目总收益为节省的燃油量，柴油单价取 6.84 元/L。有电区铁路系统平均用电价格取 1.0 元/(kW·h)。

根据 4.1.1 节的计算方法，各区域各场景下的投资收益情况如表 4-60 所示。

4.3.2 未来我国铁路可再生能源融合潜力测算

国家能源局数据显示，2018 年，我国可再生能源发电量达 1.87×10^6GW·h，可再生能源发电量占全部发电量比重的 26.7%，其中水电为 1.2×10^6GW·h，光伏发电 1.775×10^5GW·h。据此计算，2018 年我国光伏发电比例为 2.54%，风电发电比例为 5.23%。

根据国际能源署在最新版的世界能源展望中的情景分析，到 2022 年，我国间歇性可再生能源(风电、光伏)的发电比例将达到 11%，其中光伏的发电比例达到 4%，风电的发电比例将达到 7%。

表 4-60 各场景各区投资收益情况

场景分类	指标	1 区	2 区	3 区	4 区	5 区	6 区	7 区	8 区	全国总计
保守场景	总投资/亿元	26.81	43.06	110.28	173.41	65.91	97.65	162.99	416.36	923.76
	总收益/亿元	9.51	8.21	18.33	29.17	11.72	19.56	17.32	78.14	170.22
	收益投资比	0.35	0.19	0.17	0.17	0.18	0.20	0.11	0.19	0.18
	回收年限/年	2.82	5.24	6.02	5.94	5.63	4.99	9.41	5.33	5.43
	减排量/万 t	16.21	88.72	150.00	649.59	39.83	214.20	140.36	1085.66	2384.57
基本场景	总投资/亿元	46.92	76.13	177.88	401.14	115.34	172.62	262.90	963.13	1824.35
	总收益/亿元	23.81	15.63	36.65	94.88	50.22	41.97	34.63	229.00	417.58
	收益投资比	0.51	0.21	0.21	0.24	0.44	0.24	0.13	0.24	0.23
	回收年限/年	1.97	4.87	4.85	4.23	2.30	4.11	7.59	4.21	4.37
	减排量/万 t	27.81	146.89	203.68	1083.12	68.35	360.34	215.78	2841.13	4947.11
积极场景	总投资/亿元	67.03	105.67	245.49	622.26	164.77	239.61	362.82	1494.02	2724.94
	总收益/亿元	45.58	26.53	70.84	205.82	92.19	69.10	65.46	470.29	810.02
	收益投资比	0.68	0.25	0.29	0.33	0.56	0.29	0.18	0.31	0.30
	回收年限/年	1.47	3.98	3.47	3.02	1.79	3.47	5.54	3.18	3.36
	减排量/万 t	32.41	174.58	230.57	1274.01	79.67	448.64	251.66	4477.92	6969.46

若按照上述两组数据的增速进行估算，到 2025 年，我国间歇性可再生能源的发电比例将达到 13.1%，其中光伏发电比例为 5.1%，风电发电比例为 8%；到 2030 年，我国间歇性可再生能源的发电比例将达到 16.9%，其中光伏发电比例为 6.9%，风电发电比例为 10%；到 2035 年，我国间歇性可再生能源的发电比例将达到 20.7%，其中光伏发电比例为 8.7%，风电发电比例为 12%。

1. 2021～2025 年我国铁路可再生能源融合潜力测算

1) 光伏出力潜力测算

到 2025 年，铁路网络覆盖进一步扩大，路网结构更加优化，骨干作用更加显著，实现以轨道交通为骨干的 100km 范围的通勤化交通、300km 范围的同城化交通、500km 范围的城际化交通、1000km 范围的走廊化交通、2000km 范围的大容量交通，更好地发挥轨道交通对经济社会发展的保障作用，其中铁路网规模达到 17.5 万 km 左右，其中高速铁路 3.8 万 km 左右，能源系统综合损耗水平降低 10%，可再生能源渗透率不低于 10%；具备适应国际主流标准的牵引供电系统研发、设计、制造、交付和运维支持的技术能力。

假设 2021～2025 年列车数量的增长速率与铁路网规模保持一致，列车光伏利用率达到 10%，其他条件保持不变，那么 2025 年我国铁路运载体的光伏出力可达到 11GW·h。

假设铁路网规模在四类光辐射区域的增长情况一致，线路光伏利用率达到 10%，牵引变电所分布规律不变，其他条件保持不变，则 2025 年我国铁路基础设施光伏出力可达到 41797GW·h。其中 Ⅰ 类、Ⅱ 类地区基础设施的年光伏出力达 16047GW·h，占全国铁路基础设施年光伏出力的 38.39%。图 4-84 为 2025 年我国基础设施光伏出力。

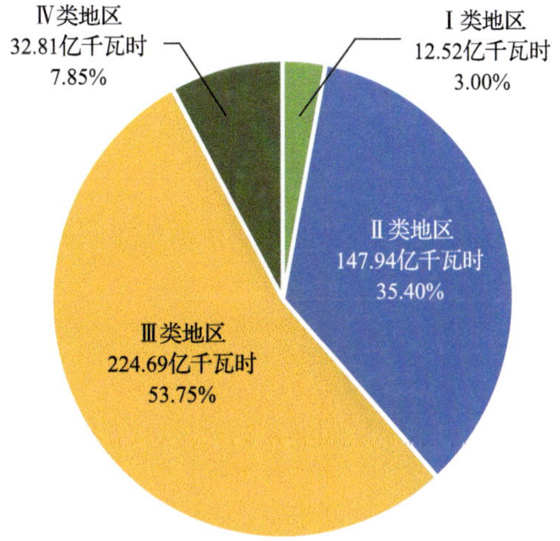

图 4-84　2025 年我国基础设施光伏出力

假设特等站数量在四类光辐射区域的增长情况与铁路规模的增长情况一致，可再生能源利用率达 10%，其他条件保持不变，则 2025 年我国铁路特等站光伏出力可达到 277GW·h。图 4-85 为 2025 年我国特等站光伏出力。

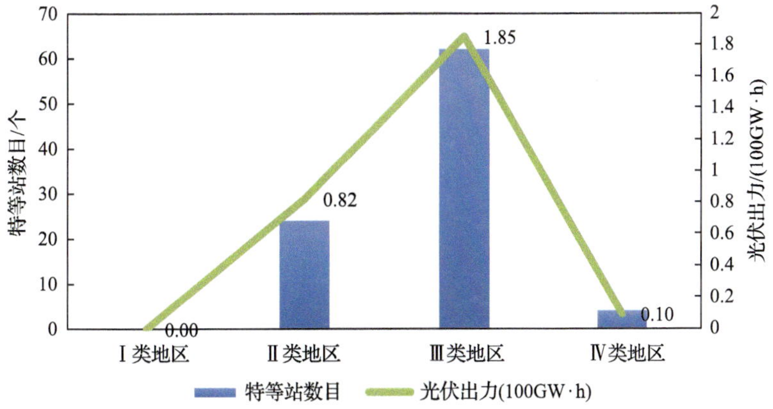

图 4-85　2025 年我国特等站光伏出力

综上，到 2025 年我国铁路光伏出力为 42086GW·h。

2) 铁路负荷测算

作为一种比公路和航空更节能的交通方式，铁路可以节约重要的能源，特别是减少石油需求。根据国际能源署的数据统计，2017 年我国铁路能源需求为 15.719 百万吨标准煤，到 2030 年需要 25.008 百万吨标准煤，到 2050 年则需要 32.867 百万吨标准煤。图 4-86 为 2030 年和 2050 年我国铁路能源需求预测。

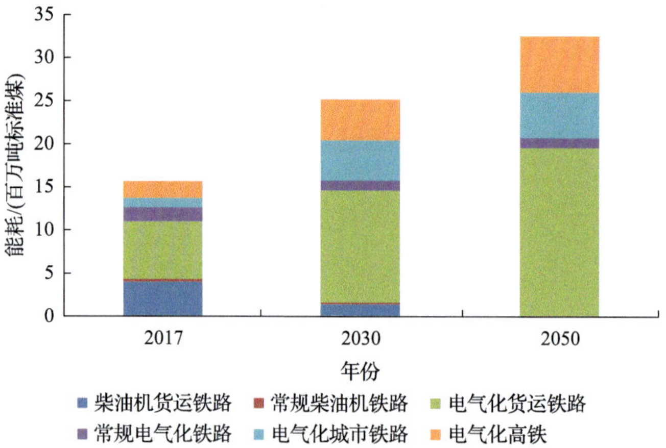

图 4-86　2030 年和 2050 年我国铁路能源需求预测

数据来源：IEA2018A

大多数地区铁路用电的增加可以通过各种技术来满足，包括但不限于架空线路电气化(OLE)，并可提供降低温室气体和当地污染物排放的成本效益手段。电气化程度的逐步提高，据此估计，到 2025 年，我国铁路用电负荷将达 1657.5 万 t，约合 134720GW·h。

3) 总体融合潜力测算

(1)保守场景。

在保守场景下，可再生能源开发强度为 10%，各模式区域月度用电自洽率和用能自洽率测算结果如图 4-87、图 4-88、表 4-61、表 4-62 所示。

保守场景下，到 2025 年，我国整体铁路可再生能源渗透率将达 28.5%(图 4-89 和表 4-63)。

保守场景下，2025 年我国铁路减排量达 2384.57 万 t，具体各月的减排情况如图 4-90 和表 4-64 所示。

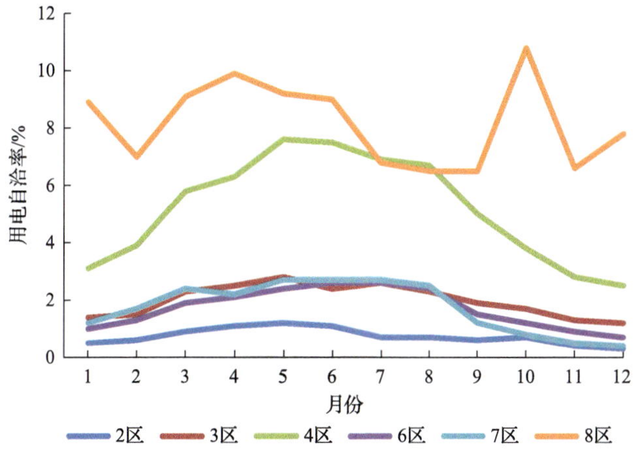

图 4-87　保守场景下 2025 年有电区内各模式区域用电自洽率

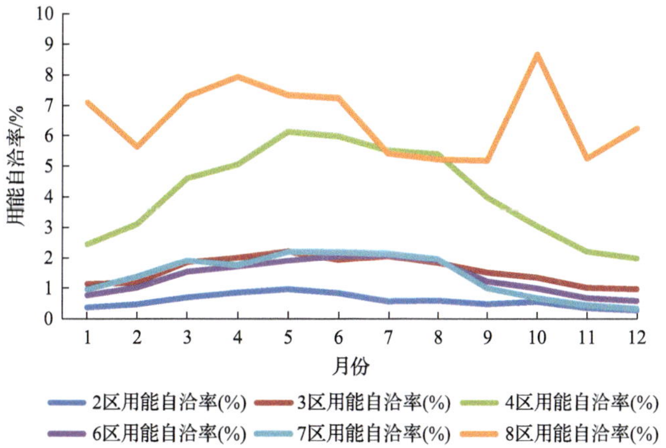

图 4-88　保守场景下 2025 年有电区内各模式区域用能自洽率

表 4-61　保守场景下 2025 年有电区内各模式区域用电自洽率（单位：%）

月份	2 区	3 区	4 区	6 区	7 区	8 区
1	0.5	1.4	3.1	1.0	1.2	8.9
2	0.6	1.5	3.9	1.3	1.7	7.0
3	0.9	2.3	5.8	1.9	2.4	9.1
4	1.1	2.5	6.3	2.1	2.2	9.9
5	1.2	2.8	7.6	2.4	2.7	9.2
6	1.1	2.4	7.5	2.6	2.7	9.0
7	0.7	2.6	6.9	2.6	2.7	6.8
8	0.7	2.3	6.7	2.4	2.5	6.5
9	0.6	1.9	5.0	1.5	1.2	6.5
10	0.7	1.7	3.8	1.2	0.8	10.8
11	0.4	1.3	2.8	0.9	0.5	6.6
12	0.3	1.2	2.5	0.7	0.4	7.8
全年平均	0.7	2.0	5.1	1.7	1.8	8.2

表 4-62　保守场景下 2025 年有电区内各模式区域用能自洽率（单位：%）

月份	2 区	3 区	4 区	6 区	7 区	8 区
1	0.4	1.1	2.5	0.8	1.0	7.1
2	0.5	1.2	3.1	1.0	1.4	5.6
3	0.7	1.9	4.6	1.5	1.9	7.3
4	0.9	2.0	5.1	1.7	1.8	7.9
5	1.0	2.2	6.1	1.9	2.2	7.3
6	0.8	1.9	6.0	2.1	2.2	7.2
7	0.6	2.1	5.5	2.1	2.1	5.4
8	0.6	1.8	5.4	1.9	2.0	5.2
9	0.5	1.5	4.0	1.2	1.0	5.2
10	0.6	1.3	3.0	1.0	0.7	8.7
11	0.4	1.0	2.2	0.7	0.4	5.3
12	0.3	1.0	2.0	0.6	0.3	6.2
全年平均	0.6	1.6	4.1	1.4	1.4	6.5

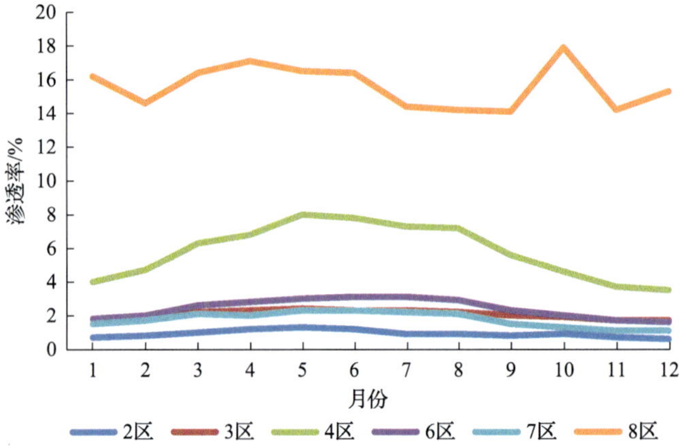

图 4-89　保守场景下 2025 年有电区内各模式区域可再生能源渗透率

表 4-63　保守场景下 2025 年有电区内各模式区域可再生能源渗透率（单位：%）

月份	2 区	3 区	4 区	6 区	7 区	8 区	总计
1	0.7	1.8	4.0	1.8	1.5	16.2	25.9
2	0.8	1.8	4.7	2.0	1.7	14.6	25.7
3	1.0	2.2	6.3	2.6	2.1	16.4	30.6
4	1.2	2.3	6.8	2.8	2.0	17.1	32.2
5	1.3	2.4	8.0	3.0	2.3	16.5	33.4
6	1.2	2.3	7.8	3.1	2.3	16.4	33.0
7	0.9	2.3	7.3	3.1	2.2	14.4	30.3
8	0.9	2.2	7.2	2.9	2.1	14.2	29.5
9	0.8	2.0	5.6	2.3	1.5	14.1	26.3
10	0.9	1.9	4.6	2.0	1.3	17.9	28.6
11	0.7	1.7	3.7	1.7	1.1	14.2	23.1
12	0.6	1.7	3.5	1.6	1.1	15.3	23.7
全年平均	0.9	2.0	5.8	2.4	1.8	15.6	28.5

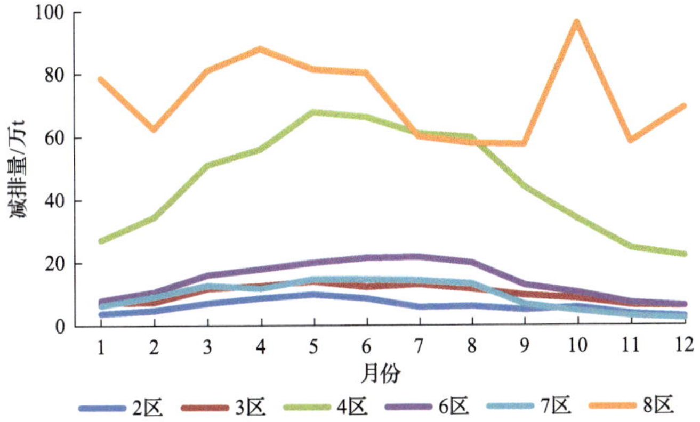

图 4-90 保守场景下 2025 年我国铁路减排情况

表 4-64 保守场景下 2025 年我国铁路减排情况 (单位：万 t)

月份	2 区	3 区	4 区	6 区	7 区	8 区	总计
1	4.74	9.07	34.18	10.08	8.01	99.05	165.13
2	6.02	9.42	43.24	13.39	11.48	78.68	162.23
3	8.88	14.72	64.19	20.24	15.99	101.97	225.99
4	10.92	15.91	70.51	22.51	14.76	110.91	245.52
5	12.36	17.57	85.30	25.08	18.40	102.46	261.16
6	10.76	15.36	83.24	26.97	18.33	101.05	255.71
7	7.22	16.35	76.77	27.29	17.90	75.59	221.11
8	7.55	14.55	75.16	24.97	16.48	72.87	211.58
9	6.11	12.04	55.43	16.09	8.35	72.39	170.41
10	7.09	10.71	42.46	13.09	5.66	121.05	200.06
11	4.48	8.08	30.79	8.95	3.65	73.36	129.32
12	3.47	7.72	27.68	7.69	2.73	87.06	136.36
全年平均	89.60	151.49	688.95	216.34	141.75	1096.44	2384.57

(2)基本场景。

在基本场景下，可再生能源开发强度为 20%，各模式区域月度用电自洽率和用能自洽率测算结果如图 4-91、图 4-92、表 4-65 和表 4-66 所示。

基本场景下，到 2025 年，我国整体铁路可再生能源渗透率将达 39.2%(图 4-93 和表 4-67)。

基本场景下，2025 年我国铁路减排量达 4034.77 万 t，具体各月的减排情况如图 4-94 和表 4-68 所示。

(3)积极场景。

在积极场景下，可再生能源开发强度为 30%，各模式区域月度用电自洽率和用能自洽率测算结果如图 4-95、图 4-96、表 4-69 和表 4-70 所示。

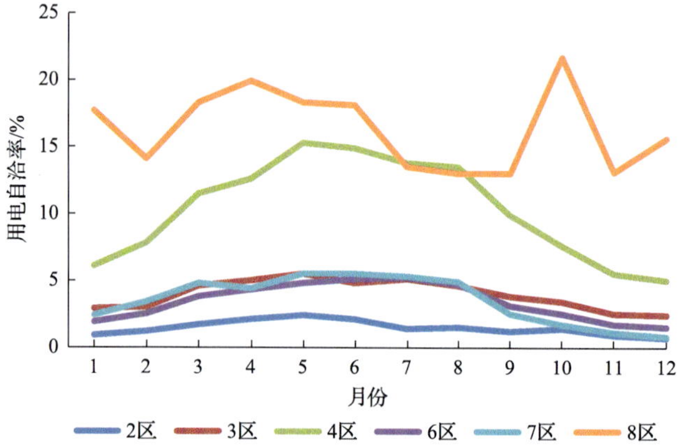

图 4-91　基本场景下 2025 年有电区内各模式区域用电自洽率

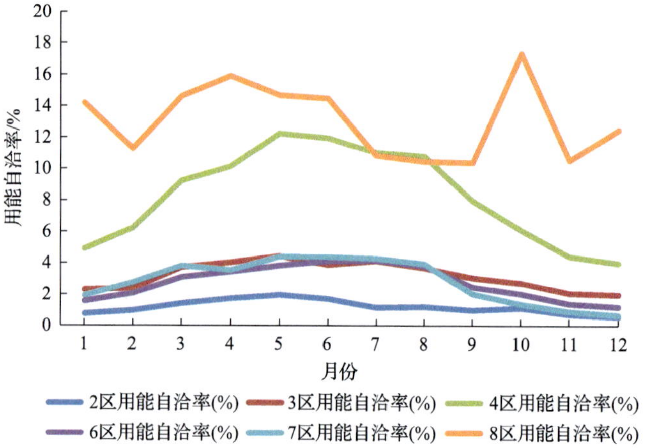

图 4-92　基本场景下 2025 年有电区内各模式区域用能自洽率

表 4-65　基本场景下 2025 年有电区内各模式区域用电自洽率（单位：%）

月份	2 区	3 区	4 区	6 区	7 区	8 区
1	0.9	2.9	6.1	1.9	2.4	17.7
2	1.2	3.0	7.8	2.5	3.4	14.1
3	1.7	4.6	11.5	3.8	4.8	18.3
4	2.1	5.0	12.6	4.3	4.4	19.9
5	2.4	5.5	15.3	4.8	5.5	18.3
6	2.1	4.8	14.9	5.1	5.5	18.1
7	1.4	5.1	13.8	5.2	5.3	13.5
8	1.5	4.6	13.5	4.7	4.9	13.0
9	1.2	3.8	9.9	3.1	2.5	13.0
10	1.4	3.4	7.6	2.5	1.7	21.7
11	0.9	2.5	5.5	1.7	1.1	13.1
12	0.7	2.4	5.0	1.5	0.8	15.6
全年平均	1.5	4.0	10.3	3.4	3.5	16.4

表 4-66　基本场景下 2025 年有电区内各模式区域用能自洽率（单位：%）

月份	2 区	3 区	4 区	6 区	7 区	8 区
1	0.7	2.3	4.9	1.5	1.9	14.2
2	0.9	2.4	6.2	2.0	2.7	11.3
3	1.4	3.7	9.2	3.1	3.8	14.6
4	1.7	4.0	10.1	3.4	3.5	15.9
5	1.9	4.4	12.2	3.8	4.4	14.7
6	1.7	3.9	11.9	4.1	4.4	14.5
7	1.1	4.1	11.0	4.1	4.3	10.8
8	1.2	3.7	10.8	3.8	3.9	10.4
9	1.0	3.0	8.0	2.4	2.0	10.4
10	1.1	2.7	6.1	2.0	1.3	17.3
11	0.7	2.0	4.4	1.4	0.9	10.5
12	0.5	1.9	4.0	1.2	0.7	12.5
全年平均	1.2	3.2	8.2	2.7	2.8	13.1

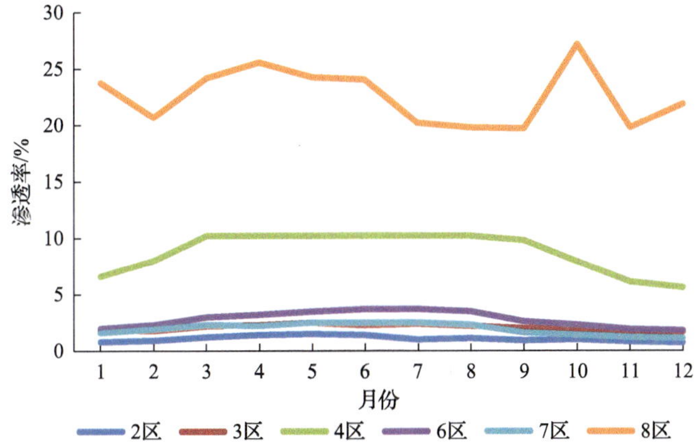

图 4-93　基本场景下 2025 年有电区内各模式区域可再生能源渗透率

表 4-67　基本场景下 2025 年有电区内各模式区域可再生能源渗透率（单位：%）

月份	2 区	3 区	4 区	6 区	7 区	8 区	总计
1	0.8	1.8	6.6	2.0	1.6	23.8	36.5
2	0.9	1.8	8.0	2.3	1.9	20.7	35.6
3	1.2	2.2	10.2	3.0	2.3	24.2	43.2
4	1.4	2.3	10.2	3.2	2.2	25.6	45.0
5	1.5	2.5	10.2	3.5	2.5	24.3	44.5
6	1.4	2.3	10.2	3.7	2.5	24.1	44.2
7	1.0	2.4	10.2	3.7	2.5	20.2	40.0
8	1.1	2.2	10.2	3.5	2.3	19.8	39.1
9	0.9	2.0	9.8	2.6	1.6	19.7	36.7
10	1.0	1.9	7.9	2.3	1.4	27.2	41.6
11	0.8	1.7	6.1	1.9	1.2	19.8	31.4
12	0.7	1.7	5.6	1.8	1.1	21.9	32.7
全年平均	1.0	2.1	8.8	2.8	1.9	22.6	39.2

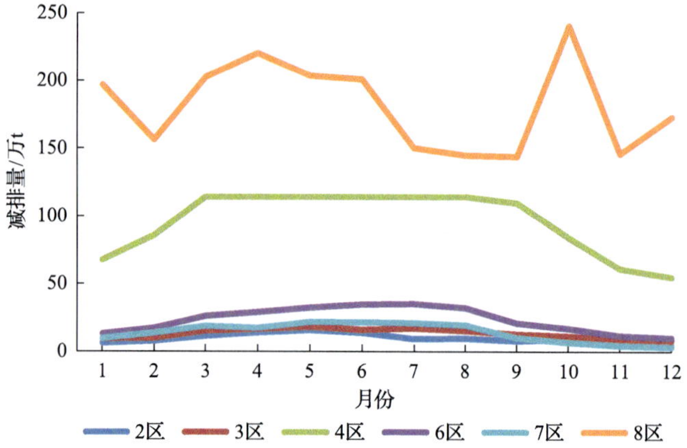

图 4-94　基本场景下 2025 年我国铁路减排情况

表 4-68　基本场景下 2025 年我国铁路减排情况　　（单位：万 t）

月份	2 区	3 区	4 区	6 区	7 区	8 区	总计
1	5.96	9.34	67.54	12.87	9.35	196.71	301.77
2	7.56	9.70	85.46	17.09	13.40	156.26	289.48
3	11.16	15.17	114.17	25.83	18.66	202.51	387.49
4	13.72	16.39	114.17	28.73	17.22	220.27	410.50
5	15.53	18.10	114.17	32.02	21.47	203.49	404.77
6	13.52	15.82	114.17	34.43	21.39	200.68	400.01
7	9.07	16.85	114.17	34.83	20.88	150.12	345.92
8	9.49	14.99	114.17	31.88	19.22	144.71	334.46
9	7.68	12.41	109.55	20.54	9.74	143.75	303.67
10	8.90	11.04	83.91	16.71	6.61	240.40	367.57
11	5.63	8.33	60.86	11.42	4.26	145.69	236.20
12	4.36	7.96	54.70	9.82	3.18	172.91	252.93
总计	112.57	156.10	1147.03	276.18	165.38	2177.50	4034.77

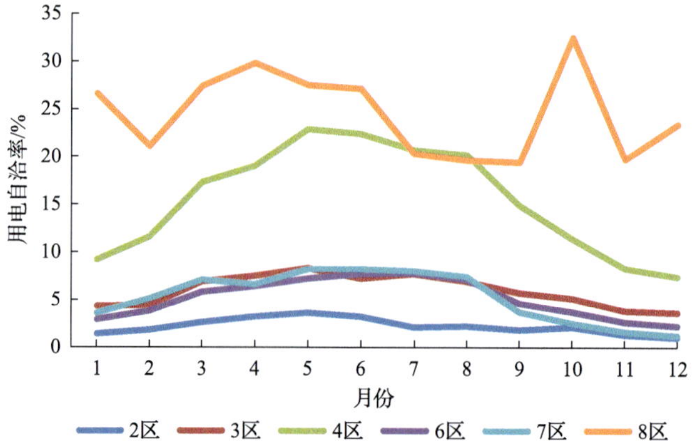

图 4-95　积极场景下 2025 年有电区内各模式区域用电自洽率

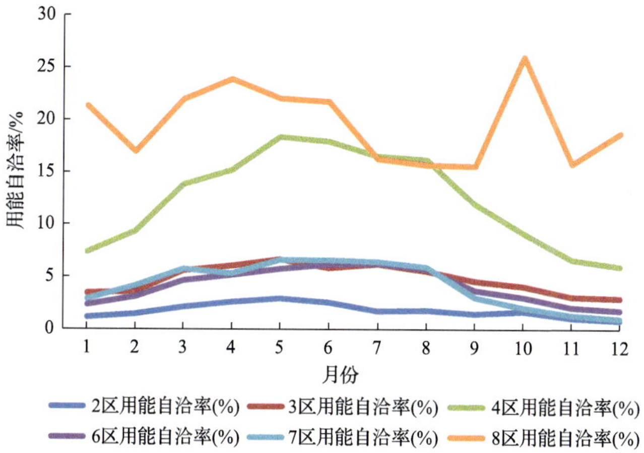

图 4-96 积极场景下 2025 年有电区内各模式区域用能自洽率

表 4-69 积极场景下 2025 年有电区内各模式区域用电自洽率（单位：%）

月份	2 区	3 区	4 区	6 区	7 区	8 区
1	1.4	4.3	9.2	2.9	3.6	26.6
2	1.8	4.4	11.6	3.8	5.1	21.1
3	2.6	6.9	17.3	5.8	7.1	27.4
4	3.2	7.5	19.0	6.4	6.6	29.8
5	3.6	8.3	22.9	7.2	8.2	27.5
6	3.2	7.2	22.4	7.7	8.2	27.1
7	2.1	7.7	20.7	7.8	8.0	20.3
8	2.2	6.9	20.2	7.1	7.4	19.6
9	1.8	5.7	14.9	4.6	3.7	19.4
10	2.1	5.1	11.4	3.7	2.5	32.5
11	1.3	3.8	8.3	2.6	1.6	19.7
12	1.0	3.6	7.4	2.2	1.2	23.4
全年平均	2.2	6.0	15.4	5.1	5.3	24.5

表 4-70 积极场景下 2025 年有电区内各模式区域用能自洽率（单位：%）

月份	2 区	3 区	4 区	6 区	7 区	8 区
1	1.1	3.4	7.4	2.3	2.9	21.3
2	1.4	3.6	9.3	3.1	4.1	16.9
3	2.1	5.6	13.8	4.6	5.7	21.9
4	2.6	6.0	15.2	5.1	5.3	23.8
5	2.9	6.6	18.4	5.7	6.6	22.0
6	2.5	5.8	17.9	6.2	6.6	21.7
7	1.7	6.2	16.5	6.2	6.4	16.2
8	1.8	5.5	16.2	5.7	5.9	15.7
9	1.4	4.5	11.9	3.7	3.0	15.6
10	1.7	4.0	9.1	3.0	2.0	26.0
11	1.1	3.1	6.6	2.0	1.3	15.8
12	0.8	2.9	6.0	1.8	1.0	18.7
全年平均	1.7	4.8	12.4	4.1	4.2	19.6

积极场景下，到 2025 年，我国整体铁路可再生能源渗透率将达 45.9%(图 4-97 和表 4-71)。

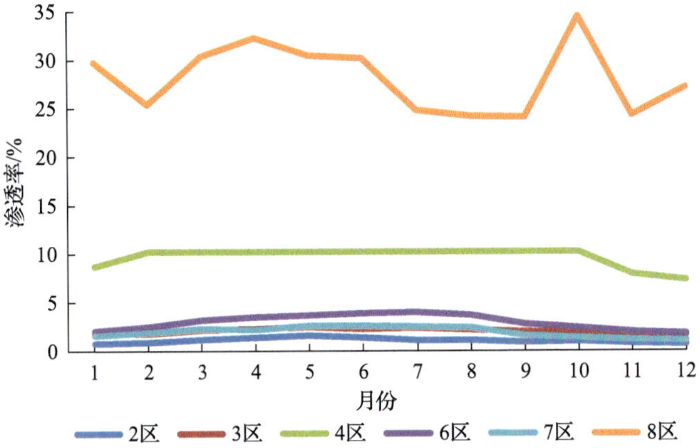

图 4-97　积极场景下 2025 年有电区内各模式区域可再生能源渗透率

表 4-71　积极场景下 2025 年有电区内各模式区域可再生能源渗透率（单位：%）

月份	2 区	3 区	4 区	6 区	7 区	8 区	总计
1	0.8	1.8	8.7	2.1	1.6	29.8	44.8
2	0.9	1.8	10.2	2.5	1.9	25.4	42.8
3	1.2	2.2	10.2	3.2	2.3	30.4	49.6
4	1.4	2.3	10.2	3.5	2.2	32.3	52.0
5	1.6	2.5	10.2	3.7	2.6	30.5	51.1
6	1.4	2.3	10.2	3.9	2.6	30.2	50.6
7	1.1	2.4	10.2	4.0	2.5	24.8	44.9
8	1.1	2.2	10.2	3.7	2.4	24.2	43.8
9	0.9	2.0	10.2	2.8	1.6	24.1	41.6
10	1.0	1.9	10.2	2.4	1.4	34.5	51.5
11	0.8	1.7	7.9	2.0	1.2	24.3	37.9
12	0.7	1.7	7.3	1.8	1.1	27.2	39.8
全年平均	1.1	2.1	9.6	3.0	2.0	28.1	45.9

积极场景下，2025 年我国铁路减排量达 5064.13 万 t，具体各月的减排情况如图 4-98 和表 4-72 所示。

2. 2026～2030 年我国铁路可再生能源融合潜力测算

1) 光伏出力潜力测算

到 2030 年，铁路系统基本实现内外互联互通、区际多路畅通、省会高铁连通、地市快速通达、县域基本覆盖，形成完善的广覆盖全国铁路网。“源-网-荷-储” 协

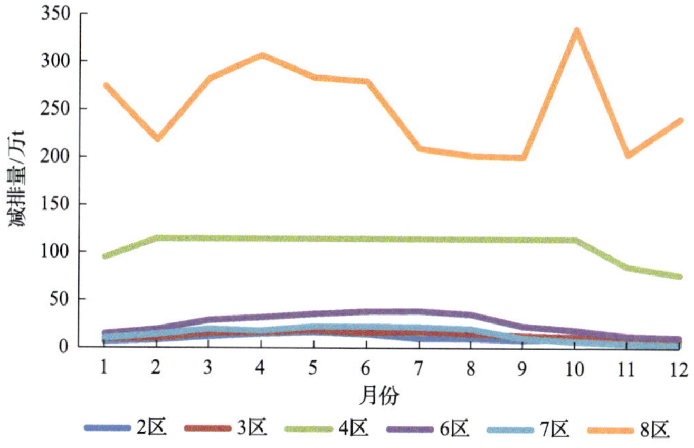

图 4-98 积极场景下 2025 年我国铁路减排情况

表 4-72 积极场景下 2025 年我国铁路减排情况 (单位：万 t)

月份	2 区	3 区	4 区	6 区	7 区	8 区	总计
1	6.26	9.35	94.48	14.15	9.62	273.92	407.77
2	7.94	9.71	114.17	18.80	13.78	217.60	382.00
3	11.72	15.17	114.17	28.42	19.19	282.00	470.66
4	14.41	16.39	114.17	31.61	17.71	306.73	501.02
5	16.31	18.11	114.17	35.22	22.08	283.36	489.24
6	14.20	15.83	114.17	37.87	22.00	279.45	483.52
7	9.52	16.85	114.17	38.32	21.48	209.05	409.39
8	9.96	14.99	114.17	35.06	19.77	201.52	395.48
9	8.06	12.41	114.17	22.59	10.02	200.18	367.44
10	9.35	11.04	114.17	18.38	6.80	334.77	494.51
11	5.92	8.33	85.13	12.57	4.38	202.88	319.20
12	4.58	7.96	76.52	10.81	3.28	240.78	343.92
总计	118.22	156.13	1283.64	303.79	170.11	3032.24	5064.13

同的智能化、高能效牵引供电技术与装备体系全面形成，既有牵引供电系统的智能化升级关键技术得到普遍采用；非接触连续供电技术得到工程化应用；基于信息、材料和能源领域新兴颠覆性技术的新一代轨道交通能源供给技术在新线建设和既有线改造中得到规模化应用；能源系统综合损耗水平较 2025 年再降低 10%，可再生能源渗透率不低于 30%；具备新型、超高速、多栖化导向运输系统能源供给技术和装备配套能力。

假设到 2030 年铁路网规模达到 21 万 km 左右，光伏利用率达到 20%，那么在其他条件保持不变的情况下，我国铁路运载体的光伏出力将达到 27GW·h，基础设施的光伏出力将达到 100313GW·h，特等站的光伏出力将达到 662GW·h。

综上，到 2030 年我国铁路光伏出力为 101002GW·h。

2) 铁路负荷测算

根据国际能源署的数据统计，到 2030 年我国铁路能源需求为 25.008 百万吨标准煤。根据客、货运量预测，并结合我国电气化进程、减排提效等要求，预计到 2030 年，我国铁路运输的电力需求将达到 2250.7 万 t 标准煤，约合 182940GW·h。

3) 总体融合潜力测算

(1) 保守场景。

在保守场景下，可再生能源开发强度为 10%，各模式区域月度用电自洽率和用能自洽率测算结果如图 4-99、图 4-100、表 4-73 和表 4-74 所示。

保守场景下，到 2030 年，我国整体铁路可再生能源渗透率将达 29.9%(图 4-101 和表 4-75)。

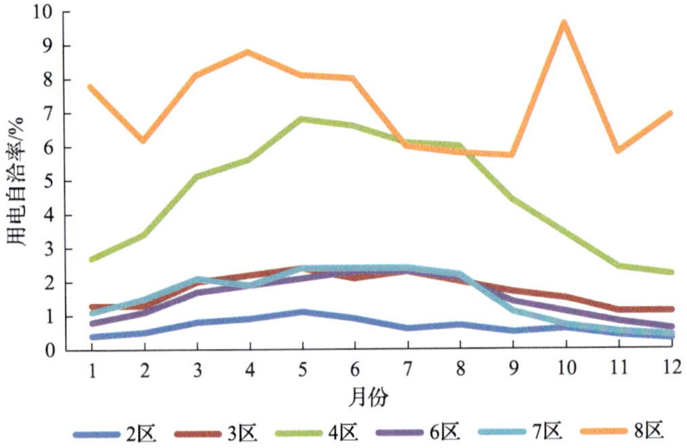

图 4-99　保守场景下 2030 年有电区内各模式区域用电自洽率

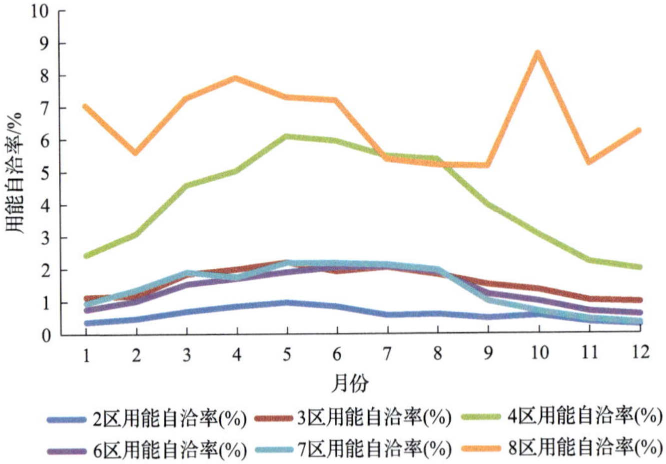

图 4-100　保守场景下 2030 年有电区内各模式区域用能自洽率

表 4-73 保守场景下 2030 年有电区内各模式区域用电自洽率（单位：%）

月份	2 区	3 区	4 区	6 区	7 区	8 区
1	0.4	1.3	2.7	0.8	1.1	7.8
2	0.5	1.3	3.4	1.1	1.5	6.2
3	0.8	2.0	5.1	1.7	2.1	8.1
4	0.9	2.2	5.6	1.9	1.9	8.8
5	1.1	2.4	6.8	2.1	2.4	8.1
6	0.9	2.1	6.6	2.3	2.4	8.0
7	0.6	2.3	6.1	2.3	2.4	6.0
8	0.7	2.0	6.0	2.1	2.2	5.8
9	0.5	1.7	4.4	1.4	1.1	5.7
10	0.6	1.5	3.4	1.1	0.7	9.6
11	0.4	1.1	2.4	0.8	0.5	5.8
12	0.3	1.1	2.2	0.6	0.4	6.9
全年平均	0.6	1.8	4.5	1.5	1.6	7.2

表 4-74 保守场景下 2030 年有电区内各模式区域用能自洽率（单位：%）

月份	2 区	3 区	4 区	6 区	7 区	8 区
1	0.4	1.1	2.4	0.8	0.9	7.1
2	0.5	1.2	3.1	1.0	1.4	5.6
3	0.7	1.8	4.6	1.5	1.9	7.3
4	0.8	2.0	5.0	1.7	1.7	7.9
5	1.0	2.2	6.1	1.9	2.2	7.3
6	0.8	1.9	5.9	2.0	2.2	7.2
7	0.6	2.0	5.5	2.1	2.1	5.4
8	0.6	1.8	5.4	1.9	2.0	5.2
9	0.5	1.5	4.0	1.2	1.0	5.2
10	0.5	1.3	3.0	1.0	0.7	8.6
11	0.3	1.0	2.2	0.7	0.4	5.2
12	0.3	1.0	2.0	0.6	0.3	6.2
全年平均	0.6	1.6	4.1	1.4	1.4	6.5

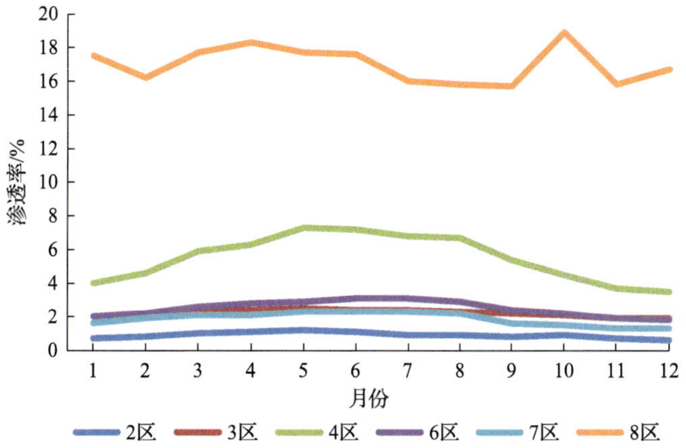

图 4-101 保守场景下 2030 年有电区内各模式区域可再生能源渗透率

表 4-75　保守场景下 2030 年有电区内各模式区域可再生能源渗透率（单位：%）

月份	2 区	3 区	4 区	6 区	7 区	8 区	总计
1	0.7	2.0	4.0	2.0	1.6	17.5	27.7
2	0.8	2.0	4.6	2.2	1.9	16.2	27.5
3	1.0	2.3	5.9	2.6	2.1	17.7	31.7
4	1.1	2.4	6.3	2.8	2.1	18.3	33.0
5	1.2	2.5	7.3	2.9	2.3	17.7	34.0
6	1.1	2.4	7.2	3.1	2.3	17.6	33.7
7	0.9	2.4	6.8	3.1	2.3	16.0	31.4
8	0.9	2.3	6.7	2.9	2.2	15.8	30.8
9	0.8	2.2	5.4	2.4	1.6	15.7	28.1
10	0.9	2.1	4.5	2.2	1.5	18.9	30.0
11	0.7	1.9	3.7	1.9	1.3	15.8	25.4
12	0.6	1.9	3.5	1.8	1.3	16.7	25.8
全年平均	0.9	2.2	5.5	2.5	1.9	17.0	29.9

保守场景下，2030 年我国铁路减排量达 2861.48 万 t，具体各月的减排情况如图 4-102 和表 4-76 所示。

(2) 基本场景。

在基本场景下，可再生能源开发强度为 20%，各模式区域月度用电自洽率和用能自洽率测算结果如图 4-103、图 4-104、表 4-77 和表 4-78 所示。

基本场景下，到 2030 年，我国整体铁路可再生能源渗透率将达 39.4%（图 4-104 和表 4-79）。

基本场景下，2030 年我国铁路减排量达 4947.11 万 t，具体各月的减排情况如图 4-105 和表 4-80 所示。

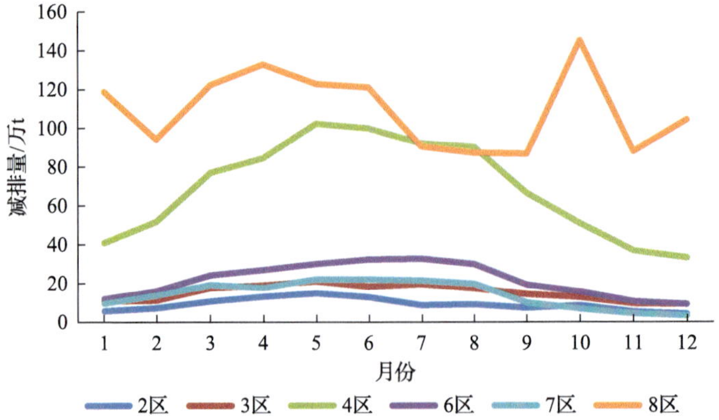

图 4-102　保守场景下 2030 年我国铁路减排情况（单位：万 t）

表 4-76　保守场景下 2030 年我国铁路减排情况　　(单位：万 t)

月份	2 区	3 区	4 区	6 区	7 区	8 区	总计
1	5.69	10.88	41.01	12.10	9.62	118.86	198.15
2	7.22	11.30	51.89	16.06	13.78	94.42	194.68
3	10.66	17.66	77.03	24.28	19.19	122.36	271.19
4	13.10	19.09	84.61	27.01	17.71	133.09	294.62
5	14.83	21.08	102.36	30.10	22.08	122.95	313.40
6	12.92	18.43	99.89	32.36	22.00	121.26	306.85
7	8.66	19.62	92.12	32.74	21.48	90.71	265.33
8	9.06	17.46	90.20	29.96	19.77	87.44	253.89
9	7.33	14.45	66.52	19.31	10.02	86.86	204.49
10	8.50	12.85	50.95	15.71	6.80	145.26	240.07
11	5.38	9.70	36.95	10.74	4.38	88.03	155.18
12	4.17	9.27	33.21	9.23	3.28	104.48	163.63
总计	107.52	181.79	826.74	259.61	170.11	1315.73	2861.48

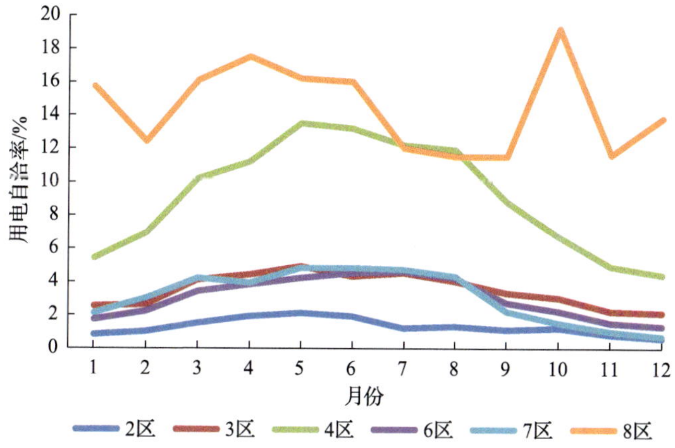

图 4-103　基本场景下 2030 年有电区内各模式区域用电自洽率

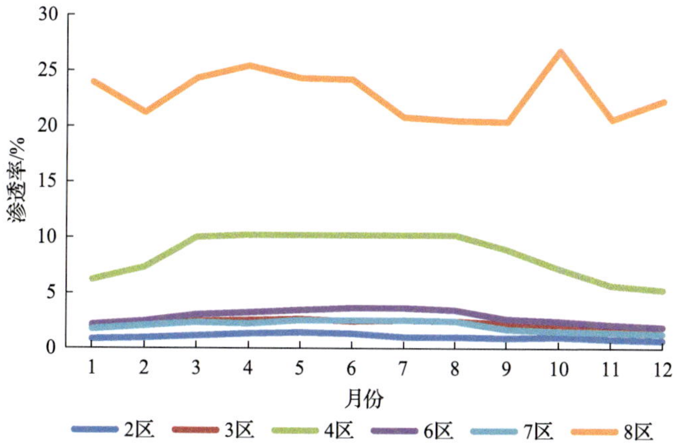

图 4-104　基本场景下 2030 年有电区内各模式区域可再生能源渗透率

表 4-77　基本场景下 2030 年有电区内各模式区域用电自洽率（单位：%）

月份	2 区	3 区	4 区	6 区	7 区	8 区
1	0.8	2.5	5.4	1.7	2.1	15.7
2	1.0	2.6	6.9	2.2	3.0	12.4
3	1.5	4.1	10.2	3.4	4.2	16.1
4	1.9	4.4	11.2	3.8	3.9	17.5
5	2.1	4.9	13.5	4.2	4.8	16.2
6	1.9	4.3	13.2	4.5	4.8	16.0
7	1.2	4.5	12.2	4.6	4.7	12.0
8	1.3	4.0	11.9	4.2	4.3	11.5
9	1.1	3.3	8.8	2.7	2.2	11.5
10	1.2	3.0	6.7	2.2	1.5	19.2
11	0.8	2.2	4.9	1.5	1.0	11.6
12	0.6	2.1	4.4	1.3	0.7	13.8
全年平均	1.3	3.5	9.1	3.0	3.1	14.5

表 4-78　基本场景下 2030 年有电区内各模式区域用能自洽率　（单位：%）

月份	2 区	3 区	4 区	6 区	7 区	8 区
1	0.7	2.3	4.9	1.5	1.9	14.1
2	0.9	2.4	6.2	2.0	2.7	11.2
3	1.4	3.7	9.2	3.1	3.8	14.5
4	1.7	4.0	10.1	3.4	3.5	15.8
5	1.9	4.4	12.2	3.8	4.4	14.6
6	1.7	3.8	11.9	4.1	4.3	14.4
7	1.1	4.1	10.9	4.1	4.2	10.8
8	1.2	3.6	10.7	3.8	3.9	10.4
9	0.9	3.0	7.9	2.4	2.0	10.3
10	1.1	2.7	6.1	2.0	1.3	17.2
11	0.7	2.0	4.4	1.4	0.9	10.4
12	0.5	1.9	3.9	1.2	0.6	12.4
全年平均	1.2	3.2	8.2	2.7	2.8	13.0

表 4-79 基本场景下 2030 年有电区内各模式区域可再生能源渗透率（单位：%）

月份	2 区	3 区	4 区	6 区	7 区	8 区	总计
1	0.8	2.0	6.2	2.1	1.7	23.9	36.7
2	0.9	2.0	7.3	2.4	2.0	21.2	35.9
3	1.1	2.4	10.0	3.0	2.3	24.3	43.2
4	1.3	2.5	10.2	3.2	2.2	25.4	44.8
5	1.4	2.6	10.2	3.4	2.5	24.3	44.4
6	1.3	2.4	10.2	3.6	2.5	24.2	44.1
7	1.0	2.5	10.2	3.6	2.5	20.8	40.6
8	1.0	2.4	10.2	3.4	2.4	20.5	39.8
9	0.9	2.2	8.9	2.6	1.7	20.4	36.8
10	1.0	2.1	7.2	2.4	1.5	26.8	41.0
11	0.8	1.9	5.7	2.1	1.4	20.6	32.4
12	0.7	1.9	5.3	1.9	1.3	22.3	33.5
全年平均	1.0	2.2	8.5	2.8	2.0	22.9	39.4

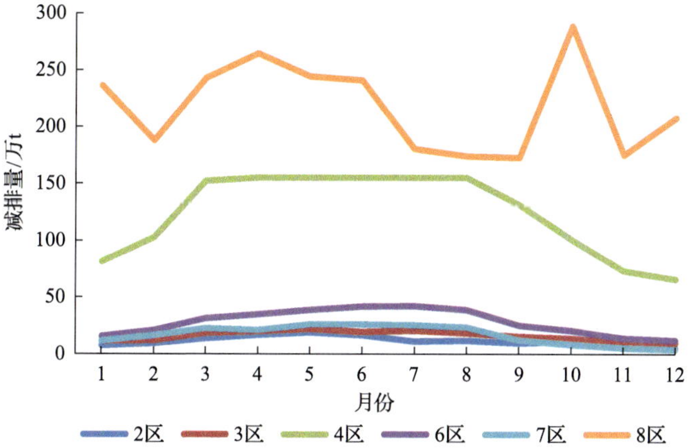

图 4-105 基本场景下 2030 年我国铁路减排情况

表 4-80 基本场景下 2030 年我国铁路减排情况 （单位：万 t）

月份	2 区	3 区	4 区	6 区	7 区	8 区	总计
1	7.15	11.21	81.05	15.44	11.22	236.05	362.12
2	9.07	11.65	102.56	20.51	16.08	187.52	347.38
3	13.39	18.20	152.24	31.00	22.39	243.01	480.23
4	16.46	19.67	155.03	34.48	20.67	264.32	510.63
5	18.63	21.72	155.03	38.42	25.76	244.18	503.75
6	16.23	18.99	155.03	41.32	25.67	240.81	498.04
7	10.88	20.22	155.03	41.80	25.06	180.15	433.14
8	11.38	17.99	155.03	38.25	23.07	173.66	419.38
9	9.21	14.89	131.46	24.65	11.69	172.51	364.41
10	10.68	13.24	100.69	20.05	7.93	288.48	441.09
11	6.76	9.99	73.03	13.71	5.11	174.83	283.43
12	5.23	9.55	65.64	11.79	3.82	207.49	303.52
总计	135.09	187.33	1481.83	331.41	198.46	2613.00	4947.11

(3) 积极场景。

在积极场景下，可再生能源开发强度为30%，各模式区域月度用电自洽率和用能自洽率测算结果如图4-106、图4-107、表4-81和表4-82所示。

积极场景下，到2030年，我国整体铁路可再生能源渗透率将达45.2%(图4-108和表4-83)。

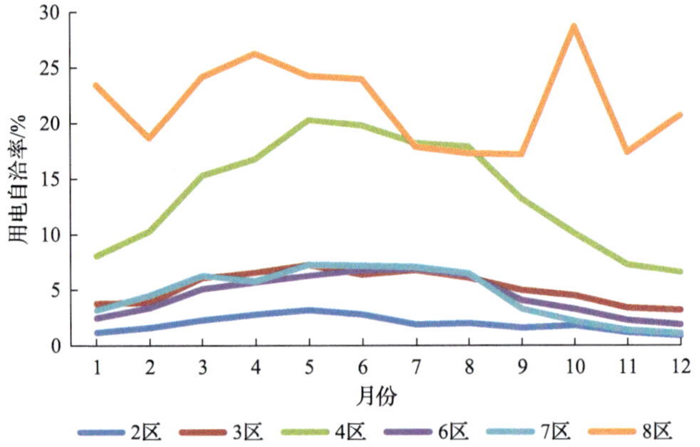

图4-106　积极场景下2030年有电区内各模式区域用电自洽率(单位：%)

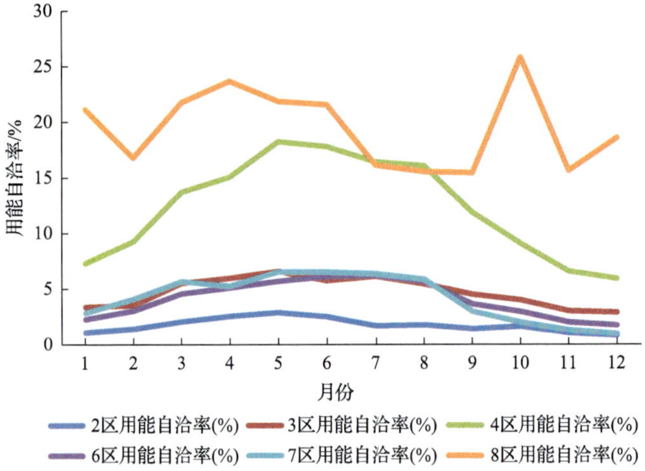

图4-107　积极场景下2030年有电区内各模式区域用能自洽率(单位：%)

表4-81　积极场景下2030年有电区内各模式区域用电自洽率（单位：%）

月份	2区	3区	4区	6区	7区	8区
1	1.2	3.8	8.1	2.5	3.2	23.5
2	1.6	3.9	10.3	3.4	4.5	18.7
3	2.3	6.1	15.3	5.1	6.3	24.2
4	2.8	6.6	16.8	5.7	5.8	26.3

续表

月份	2 区	3 区	4 区	6 区	7 区	8 区
5	3.2	7.3	20.3	6.3	7.3	24.3
6	2.8	6.4	19.8	6.8	7.2	24.0
7	1.9	6.8	18.2	6.9	7.1	17.9
8	2.0	6.1	17.9	6.3	6.5	17.3
9	1.6	5.0	13.2	4.1	3.3	17.2
10	1.8	4.5	10.1	3.3	2.2	28.7
11	1.2	3.4	7.3	2.3	1.4	17.4
12	0.9	3.2	6.6	1.9	1.1	20.7
全年平均	1.9	5.3	13.6	4.5	4.7	21.7

表 4-82 积极场景下 2030 年有电区内各模式区域用能自洽率 （单位：%）

月份	2 区	3 区	4 区	6 区	7 区	8 区
1	1.1	3.4	7.3	2.3	2.8	21.2
2	1.4	3.5	9.3	3.0	4.1	16.8
3	2.1	5.5	13.7	4.6	5.7	21.8
4	2.5	6.0	15.1	5.1	5.2	23.7
5	2.9	6.6	18.3	5.7	6.5	21.9
6	2.5	5.8	17.8	6.1	6.5	21.6
7	1.7	6.1	16.4	6.2	6.4	16.1
8	1.8	5.5	16.1	5.7	5.9	15.6
9	1.4	4.5	11.9	3.6	3.0	15.5
10	1.6	4.0	9.1	3.0	2.0	25.9
11	1.0	3.0	6.6	2.0	1.3	15.7
12	0.8	2.9	5.9	1.7	1.0	18.6
全年平均	1.7	4.7	12.3	4.1	4.2	19.5

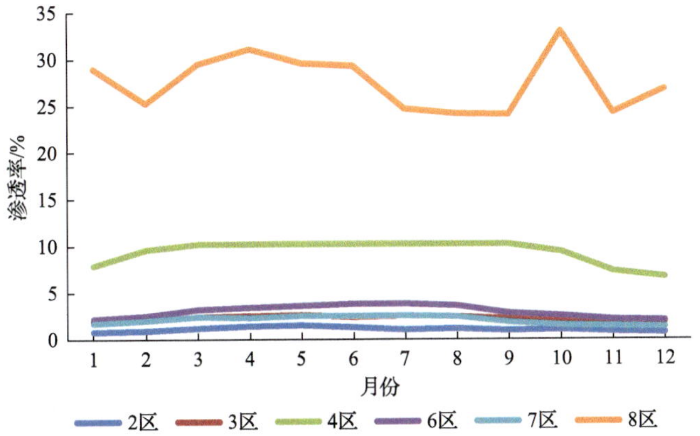

图 4-108 积极场景下 2030 年有电区内各模式区域可再生能源渗透率

表 4-83 积极场景下 2030 年有电区内各模式区域可再生能源渗透率（单位：%）

月份	2 区	3 区	4 区	6 区	7 区	8 区	总计
1	0.8	2.0	7.9	2.2	1.7	29.0	43.7
2	0.9	2.0	9.6	2.5	2.0	25.3	42.3
3	1.2	2.4	10.2	3.2	2.4	29.5	48.8
4	1.4	2.5	10.2	3.4	2.3	31.1	50.8
5	1.5	2.6	10.2	3.6	2.5	29.6	50.0
6	1.3	2.4	10.2	3.8	2.5	29.3	49.6
7	1.0	2.5	10.2	3.8	2.5	24.7	44.7
8	1.1	2.4	10.2	3.6	2.4	24.2	43.8
9	0.9	2.2	10.2	2.8	1.8	24.1	42.0
10	1.0	2.1	9.4	2.5	1.5	33.0	49.6
11	0.8	1.9	7.3	2.1	1.4	24.3	37.8
12	0.7	1.9	6.7	2.0	1.3	26.8	39.5
全年平均	1.1	2.2	9.4	3.0	2.0	27.6	45.2

积极场景下，2030 年我国铁路减排量达 6213.48 万 t，具体各月的减排情况如图 4-109 和表 4-84 所示。

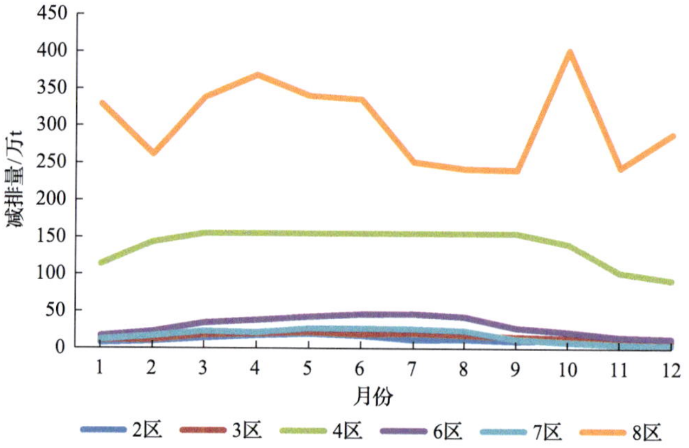

图 4-109 积极场景下 2030 年我国铁路减排情况

3. 2031～2035 年我国铁路可再生能源融合潜力测算

1) 光伏出力潜力测算

到 2035 年，建成高标准“安全、便捷、高效、绿色、智能”的现代化轨道交通运输体系，进入轨道交通强国前列，基本形成智能化、绿色化、弹性化轨道交通能源互联网技术、标准和装备体系，载运装备的非接触供电技术、基于高比能量储能的非接触间歇供电技术取得系统性突破，可再生能源渗透率不低于 50%，新型、超高速、多栖化导向运输系统能源供给技术和装备配套能力达到世界先进水平。

表 4-84 积极场景下 2030 年我国铁路减排情况 (单位：万 t)

月份	2 区	3 区	4 区	6 区	7 区	8 区	总计
1	7.51	11.22	113.37	16.98	11.54	328.70	489.32
2	9.53	11.65	143.46	22.56	16.54	261.12	464.85
3	14.06	18.20	155.03	34.10	23.03	338.40	582.82
4	17.29	19.67	155.03	37.93	21.26	368.08	619.25
5	19.57	21.73	155.03	42.26	26.50	340.03	605.12
6	17.04	18.99	155.03	45.45	26.40	335.34	598.25
7	11.43	20.22	155.03	45.98	25.77	250.86	509.29
8	11.96	17.99	155.03	42.08	23.73	241.82	492.61
9	9.68	14.89	155.03	27.11	12.02	240.22	458.96
10	11.22	13.25	140.85	22.06	8.16	401.72	597.25
11	7.10	10.00	102.16	15.08	5.26	243.45	383.04
12	5.50	9.55	91.82	12.97	3.93	288.94	412.70
总计	141.86	187.36	1676.89	364.55	204.13	3638.69	6213.48

假设到 2035 年铁路网规模达到 23.1 万 km 左右，光伏利用率达到 30%，那么在其他条件保持不变的情况下，我国铁路运载体的光伏出力将达到 44GW·h，基础设施的光伏出力将达到 165516GW·h，特等站的光伏出力将达到 1092GW·h。

综上，到 2035 年我国铁路光伏出力为 166653GW·h。

2) 铁路负荷测算

根据国际能源署的数据统计，到 2030 年我国铁路能源需求为 25.008 百万吨标准煤，到 2050 年则需要 32.867 百万吨标准煤。根据有关统计计算，当前我国的铁路能耗中，运输能耗约占全部能耗的 80%。按照目前的发展规划，由于电气化程度的逐步提高，铁路的运输能源强度将大大降低，预计到 2050 年，铁路客运装备系统能效将提升 30%～50%。与此同时，铁路基础设施的能源效率也将得到相应的提升，到 2050 年将提升 20%左右。依此进行估计，到 2050 年，我国铁路系统中，运输能耗占比应有所下降，约为 75%。根据上述铁路运输系统的能源消耗量预测进行计算，预计 2050 年我国铁路系统的能源消耗量约为 2.29 亿 t 石油当量，即 34.3TW·h。

据此估计，到 2035 年，我国铁路能源需求为 29.0 百万吨标准煤，我国铁路用电负荷将达 2755.0 万 t 标准煤，约合 223930GW·h。

3) 总体融合潜力测算

(1) 保守场景。

在保守场景下，可再生能源开发强度为 10%，各模式区域月度用电自洽率和用能自洽率测算结果如图 4-110、图 4-111、表 4-85 和表 4-86 所示。

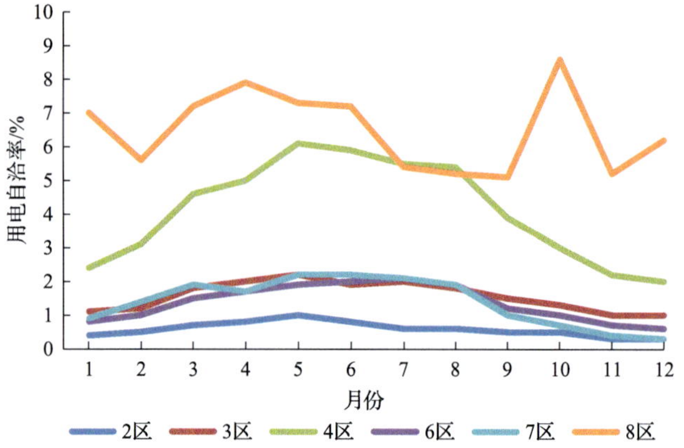

图 4-110　保守场景下 2035 年有电区内各模式区域用电自洽率

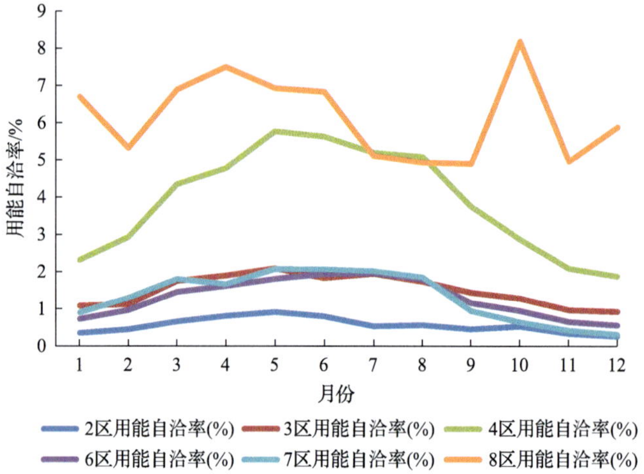

图 4-111　保守场景下 2035 年有电区内各模式区域用能自洽率

表 4-85　保守场景下 2035 年有电区内各模式区域用电自洽率（单位：%）

月份	2 区	3 区	4 区	6 区	7 区	8 区
1	0.4	1.1	2.4	0.8	0.9	7.0
2	0.5	1.2	3.1	1.0	1.4	5.6
3	0.7	1.8	4.6	1.5	1.9	7.2
4	0.8	2.0	5.0	1.7	1.7	7.9
5	1.0	2.2	6.1	1.9	2.2	7.3
6	0.8	1.9	5.9	2.0	2.2	7.2
7	0.6	2.0	5.5	2.1	2.1	5.4
8	0.6	1.8	5.4	1.9	1.9	5.2
9	0.5	1.5	3.9	1.2	1.0	5.1
10	0.5	1.3	3.0	1.0	0.7	8.6
11	0.3	1.0	2.2	0.7	0.4	5.2
12	0.3	1.0	2.0	0.6	0.3	6.2
全年平均	0.6	1.6	4.1	1.4	1.4	6.5

表 4-86　保守场景下 2035 年有电区内各模式区域用能自洽率　（单位：%）

月份	2 区	3 区	4 区	6 区	7 区	8 区
1	0.3	1.1	2.3	0.7	0.9	6.7
2	0.4	1.1	2.9	1.0	1.3	5.3
3	0.7	1.7	4.3	1.5	1.8	6.9
4	0.8	1.9	4.8	1.6	1.7	7.5
5	0.9	2.1	5.8	1.8	2.1	6.9
6	0.8	1.8	5.6	1.9	2.1	6.8
7	0.5	1.9	5.2	2.0	2.0	5.1
8	0.6	1.7	5.1	1.8	1.9	4.9
9	0.4	1.4	3.8	1.2	0.9	4.9
10	0.5	1.3	2.9	0.9	0.6	8.2
11	0.3	1.0	2.1	0.6	0.4	5.0
12	0.3	0.9	1.9	0.6	0.3	5.9
全年平均	0.5	1.5	3.9	1.3	1.3	6.2

保守场景下，到 2035 年，我国整体铁路可再生能源渗透率将达 31.9%（表 4-87 和图 4-112）。

保守场景下，2035 年我国铁路减排量达 3147.63 万 t，具体各月的减排情况如图 4-113 和表 4-88 所示。

(2) 基本场景。

在基本场景下，可再生能源开发强度为 20%，各模式区域月度用电自洽率和用能自洽率测算结果如图 4-114、图 4-115、表 4-89 和表 4-90 所示。

表 4-87　保守场景下 2035 年有电区内各模式区域可再生能源渗透率　（单位：%）

月份	2 区	3 区	4 区	6 区	7 区	8 区	总计
1	0.8	2.2	4.0	2.2	1.8	19.0	30.0
2	0.8	2.2	4.5	2.3	2.0	17.9	29.8
3	1.0	2.5	5.7	2.7	2.2	19.2	33.4
4	1.1	2.6	6.1	2.9	2.2	19.7	34.5
5	1.2	2.7	6.9	3.0	2.4	19.2	35.4
6	1.1	2.5	6.8	3.1	2.4	19.2	35.1
7	0.9	2.6	6.4	3.1	2.4	17.7	33.1
8	0.9	2.5	6.3	3.0	2.3	17.6	32.6
9	0.8	2.4	5.2	2.5	1.8	17.5	30.3
10	0.9	2.3	4.5	2.3	1.7	20.3	32.0
11	0.7	2.1	3.8	2.1	1.6	17.6	28.0
12	0.7	2.1	3.7	2.0	1.5	18.4	28.4
全年平均	0.9	2.4	5.3	2.6	2.0	18.6	31.9

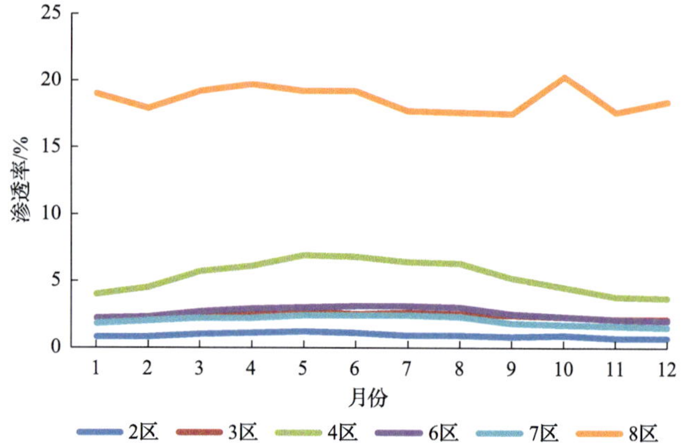

图 4-112 保守场景下 2035 年有电区内各模式区域可再生能源渗透率

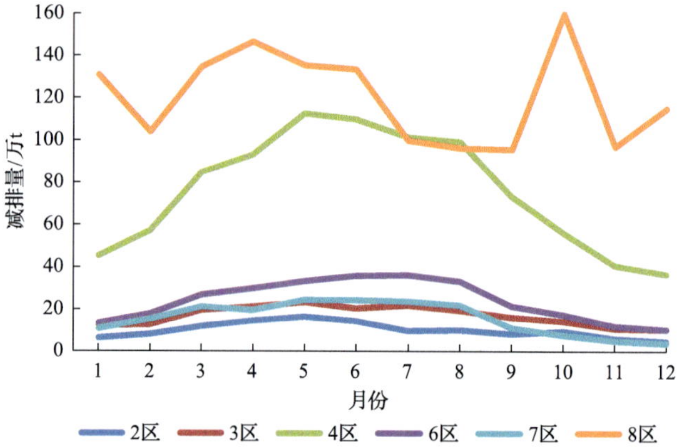

图 4-113 保守场景下 2035 年我国铁路减排情况

表 4-88 保守场景下 2035 年我国铁路减排情况 （单位：万 t）

月份	2 区	3 区	4 区	6 区	7 区	8 区	总计
1	6.26	11.97	45.11	13.30	10.58	130.74	217.97
2	7.94	12.43	57.08	17.67	15.16	103.86	214.15
3	11.72	19.43	84.74	26.71	21.11	134.60	298.31
4	14.41	21.00	93.07	29.71	19.49	146.40	324.08
5	16.31	23.19	112.59	33.10	24.29	135.25	344.74
6	14.21	20.27	109.88	35.60	24.20	133.38	337.54
7	9.53	21.58	101.33	36.02	23.62	99.78	291.86
8	9.97	19.20	99.22	32.96	21.75	96.19	279.28
9	8.07	15.89	73.17	21.24	11.02	95.55	224.94
10	9.35	14.14	56.04	17.28	7.48	159.79	264.08
11	5.92	10.67	40.65	11.81	4.82	96.83	170.70
12	4.58	10.19	36.53	10.16	3.60	114.93	180.00
总计	118.27	199.97	909.42	285.57	187.12	1447.30	3147.63

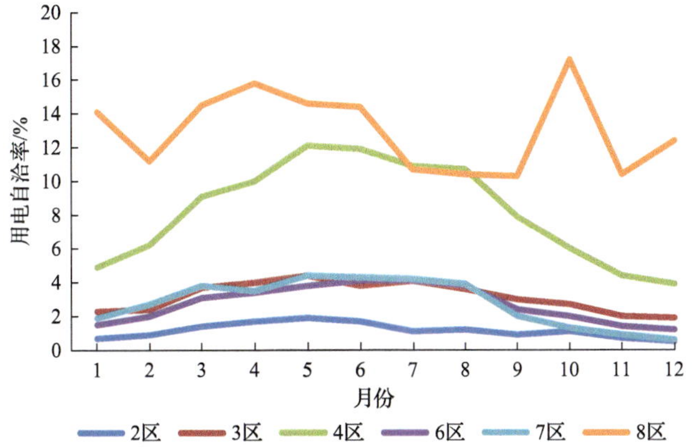

图 4-114 基本场景下 2035 年有电区内各模式区域用电自治率

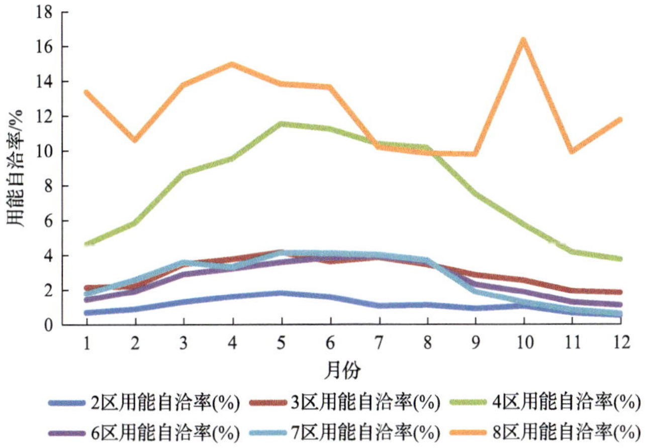

图 4-115 基本场景下 2035 年有电区内各模式区域用能自治率

表 4-89 基本场景下 2035 年有电区内各模式区域用电自治率（单位：%）

月份	2 区	3 区	4 区	6 区	7 区	8 区
1	0.7	2.3	4.9	1.5	1.9	14.1
2	0.9	2.4	6.2	2.0	2.7	11.2
3	1.4	3.7	9.1	3.1	3.8	14.5
4	1.7	4.0	10.0	3.4	3.5	15.8
5	1.9	4.4	12.1	3.8	4.4	14.6
6	1.7	3.8	11.9	4.1	4.3	14.4
7	1.1	4.1	10.9	4.1	4.2	10.7
8	1.2	3.6	10.7	3.8	3.9	10.4
9	0.9	3.0	7.9	2.4	2.0	10.3
10	1.1	2.7	6.0	2.0	1.3	17.2
11	0.7	2.0	4.4	1.4	0.9	10.4
12	0.5	1.9	3.9	1.2	0.6	12.4
全年平均	1.2	3.2	8.2	2.7	2.8	13.0

表 4-90　基本场景下 2035 年有电区内各模式区域用能自洽率　(单位：%)

月份	2 区	3 区	4 区	6 区	7 区	8 区
1	0.7	2.2	4.6	1.4	1.8	13.4
2	0.9	2.2	5.9	1.9	2.6	10.6
3	1.3	3.5	8.7	2.9	3.6	13.8
4	1.6	3.8	9.5	3.2	3.3	15.0
5	1.8	4.2	11.5	3.6	4.1	13.8
6	1.6	3.6	11.3	3.9	4.1	13.6
7	1.1	3.9	10.4	3.9	4.0	10.2
8	1.1	3.5	10.2	3.6	3.7	9.8
9	0.9	2.9	7.5	2.3	1.9	9.8
10	1.0	2.5	5.7	1.9	1.3	16.4
11	0.7	1.9	4.2	1.3	0.8	9.9
12	0.5	1.8	3.7	1.1	0.6	11.8
全年平均	1.1	3.0	7.8	2.6	2.7	12.3

基本场景下，到 2035 年，我国整体铁路可再生能源渗透率将达 40.3%(图 4-116 和表 4-91)。

基本场景下，2035 年我国铁路减排量达 5532.16 万 t，具体各月的减排情况如图 4-117 和表 4-92 所示。

(3) 积极场景。

在积极场景下，可再生能源开发强度为 30%，各模式区域月度用电自洽率和用能自洽率测算结果如图 4-118、图 4-119、表 4-93 和表 4-94 所示。

积极场景下，到 2025 年，我国整体铁路可再生能源渗透率将达 45.5%(图 4-120 和表 4-95)。

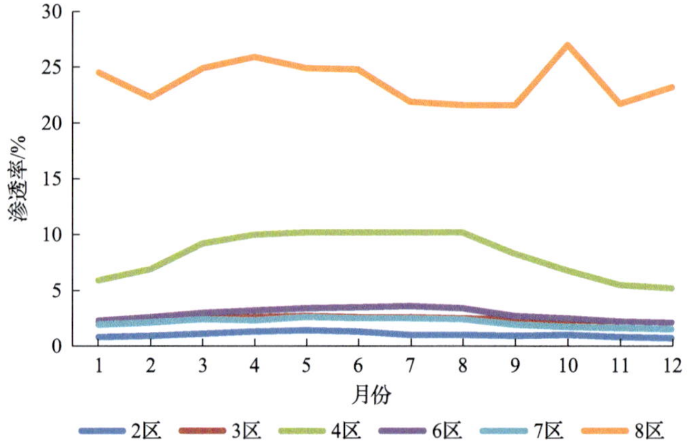

图 4-116　基本场景下 2035 年有电区内各模式区域可再生能源渗透率

表 4-91　基本场景下 2035 年有电区内各模式区域可再生能源渗透率（单位：%）

月份	2 区	3 区	4 区	6 区	7 区	8 区	总计
1	0.8	2.2	5.9	2.3	1.9	24.5	37.7
2	0.9	2.2	6.9	2.6	2.1	22.3	37.0
3	1.1	2.5	9.2	3.0	2.4	24.9	43.2
4	1.3	2.6	10.0	3.2	2.3	25.9	45.2
5	1.4	2.7	10.2	3.4	2.6	24.9	45.1
6	1.3	2.6	10.2	3.5	2.5	24.8	44.9
7	1.0	2.6	10.2	3.6	2.5	21.9	41.8
8	1.0	2.5	10.2	3.4	2.4	21.6	41.2
9	0.9	2.4	8.3	2.7	1.9	21.6	37.8
10	1.0	2.3	6.8	2.5	1.7	27.0	41.4
11	0.8	2.2	5.5	2.2	1.6	21.7	34.0
12	0.7	2.1	5.2	2.1	1.5	23.2	34.9
全年平均	1.0	2.4	8.2	2.9	2.1	23.7	40.3

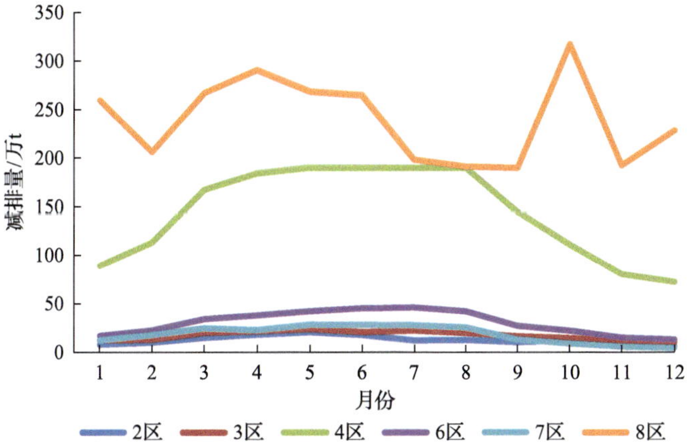

图 4-117　基本场景下 2035 年我国铁路减排情况

表 4-92　基本场景下 2035 年我国铁路减排情况　　（单位：万 t）

月份	2 区	3 区	4 区	6 区	7 区	8 区	总计
1	7.86	12.33	89.15	16.98	12.34	259.65	398.33
2	9.98	12.81	112.81	22.56	17.69	206.27	382.11
3	14.73	20.02	167.47	34.10	24.63	267.31	528.25
4	18.11	21.63	183.94	37.93	22.73	290.75	575.10
5	20.49	23.90	189.77	42.26	28.34	268.60	573.36
6	17.85	20.89	189.77	45.45	28.23	264.89	567.08
7	11.97	22.24	189.77	45.98	27.56	198.16	495.68
8	12.52	19.79	189.77	42.08	25.37	191.02	480.55
9	10.13	16.38	144.60	27.11	12.86	189.76	400.85
10	11.75	14.57	110.76	22.06	8.72	317.33	485.19
11	7.44	10.99	80.34	15.08	5.62	192.31	311.78
12	5.76	10.50	72.20	12.97	4.20	228.24	333.87
总计	148.60	206.06	1720.35	364.55	218.30	2874.30	5532.16

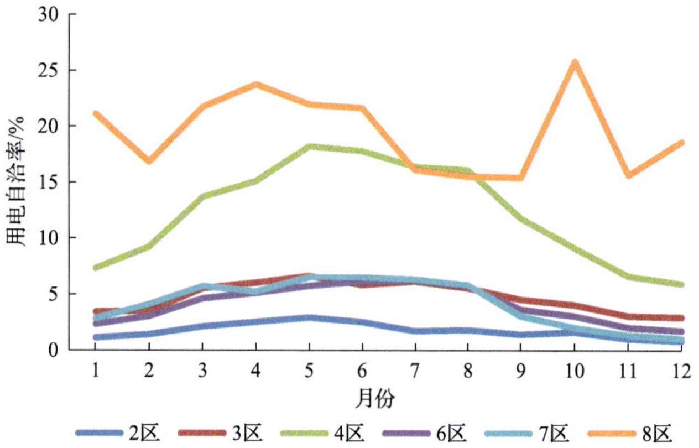

图 4-118　积极场景下 2035 年有电区内各模式区域用电自洽率

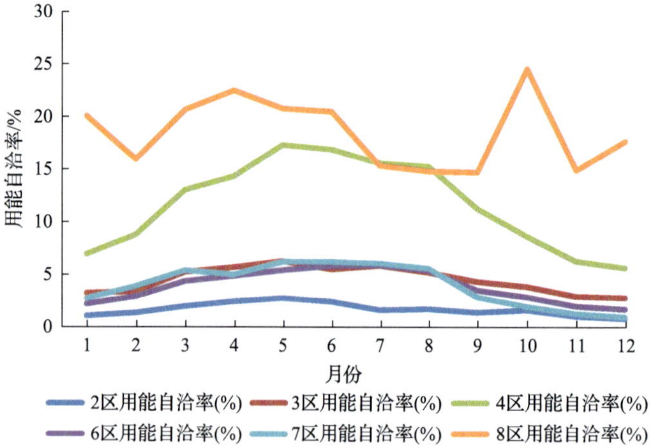

图 4-119　积极场景下 2035 年有电区内各模式区域用能自洽率

表 4-93　积极场景下 2035 年有电区内各模式区域用电自洽率（单位：%）

月份	2 区	3 区	4 区	6 区	7 区	8 区
1	1.1	3.4	7.3	2.3	2.8	21.1
2	1.4	3.5	9.2	3.0	4.1	16.8
3	2.1	5.5	13.7	4.6	5.7	21.7
4	2.5	6.0	15.1	5.1	5.2	23.7
5	2.9	6.6	18.2	5.7	6.5	21.9
6	2.5	5.8	17.8	6.1	6.5	21.6
7	1.7	6.1	16.4	6.2	6.3	16.1
8	1.8	5.5	16.1	5.7	5.8	15.5
9	1.4	4.5	11.8	3.6	3.0	15.4
10	1.6	4.0	9.1	3.0	2.0	25.8
11	1.0	3.0	6.6	2.0	1.3	15.6
12	0.8	2.9	5.9	1.7	1.0	18.6
全年平均	1.7	4.7	12.3	4.1	4.2	19.5

表 4-94 积极场景下 2035 年有电区内各模式区域用能自洽率 （单位：%）

月份	2 区	3 区	4 区	6 区	7 区	8 区
1	1.0	3.2	6.9	2.2	2.7	20.1
2	1.3	3.4	8.8	2.9	3.9	15.9
3	2.0	5.2	13.0	4.4	5.4	20.7
4	2.4	5.7	14.3	4.8	5.0	22.5
5	2.7	6.3	17.3	5.4	6.2	20.8
6	2.4	5.5	16.9	5.8	6.2	20.5
7	1.6	5.8	15.6	5.9	6.0	15.3
8	1.7	5.2	15.3	5.4	5.6	14.8
9	1.3	4.3	11.3	3.5	2.8	14.7
10	1.6	3.8	8.6	2.8	1.9	24.5
11	1.0	2.9	6.3	1.9	1.2	14.9
12	0.8	2.7	5.6	1.7	0.9	17.6
全年平均	1.6	4.5	11.7	3.9	4.0	18.5

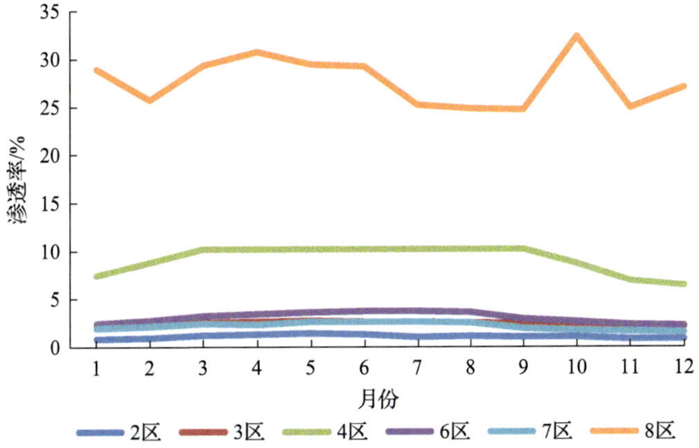

图 4-120 积极场景下 2035 年有电区内各模式区域可再生能源渗透率

表 4-95 积极场景下 2035 年有电区内各模式区域可再生能源渗透率（单位：%）

月份	2 区	3 区	4 区	6 区	7 区	8 区	总计
1	0.8	2.2	7.4	2.4	1.9	28.9	43.6
2	0.9	2.2	8.8	2.7	2.1	25.7	42.5
3	1.2	2.5	10.2	3.2	2.4	29.3	48.8
4	1.3	2.6	10.2	3.4	2.3	30.7	50.6
5	1.4	2.7	10.2	3.6	2.6	29.4	49.9
6	1.3	2.6	10.2	3.7	2.6	29.2	49.6
7	1.0	2.6	10.2	3.7	2.6	25.2	45.4
8	1.1	2.5	10.2	3.6	2.5	24.8	44.6
9	1.0	2.4	10.2	2.9	1.9	24.7	43.0
10	1.0	2.3	8.7	2.6	1.7	32.3	48.7
11	0.8	2.2	6.9	2.3	1.6	24.9	38.7
12	0.8	2.1	6.4	2.2	1.5	27.0	40.0
全年平均	1.1	2.4	9.1	3.0	2.1	27.7	45.5

积极场景下，2035 年我国铁路减排量达 6969.46 万 t，具体各月的减排情况如表 4-96 和图 4-121 所示。

表 4-96　积极场景下 2035 年我国铁路减排情况　（单位：万 t）

月份	2 区	3 区	4 区	6 区	7 区	8 区	总计
1	8.26	12.34	124.71	18.68	12.69	361.57	538.26
2	10.48	12.81	157.81	24.82	18.19	287.23	511.34
3	15.47	20.02	189.77	37.51	25.33	372.24	660.34
4	19.02	21.64	189.77	41.72	23.38	404.88	700.41
5	21.52	23.90	189.77	46.49	29.15	374.04	684.86
6	18.75	20.89	189.77	49.99	29.04	368.87	677.31
7	12.57	22.25	189.77	50.58	28.35	275.95	579.46
8	13.15	19.79	189.77	46.28	26.10	266.01	561.10
9	10.64	16.38	189.77	29.83	13.23	264.24	524.09
10	12.34	14.57	154.93	24.27	8.97	441.90	656.98
11	7.81	10.99	112.38	16.59	5.79	267.80	421.35
12	6.05	10.51	101.00	14.26	4.32	317.83	453.97
总计	156.05	206.09	1979.21	401.01	224.54	4002.55	6969.46

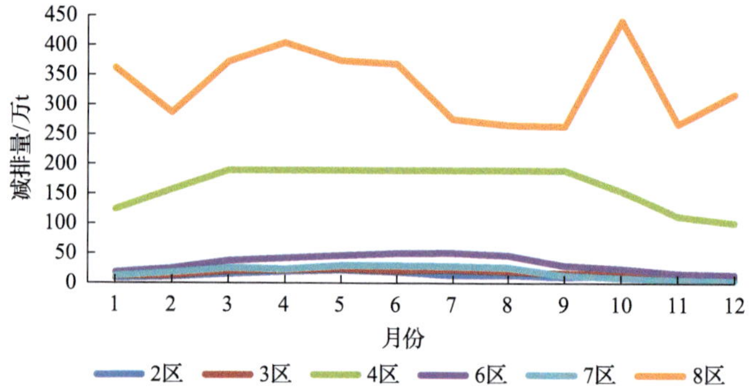

图 4-121　积极场景下 2035 年我国铁路减排情况

4. 总体融合潜力测算

在不同开发场景下，我国铁路可再生能源渗透率测算结果如表 4-97 所示。从表 4-97 中可以看出，我国铁路可再生能源开发可按照开发强度 10%、20%、30%逐步推进，到 2025 年开发 10%，渗透率达 29.3%；到 2030 年开发 20%，渗透率达到 40.9%；到 2035 年开发 30%，渗透率达 47.6%。按照这一建设速度，基本可以满足铁路中长期发展规划的要求。表 4-97 和图 4-122 为不同开发场景下未来我国铁路可再生能源渗透率测算结果。

表 4-97　不同开发场景下未来我国铁路可再生能源渗透率测算结果（单位：%）

开发场景	2025	2030	2035
保守场景	29.3	30.7	32.6
基本场景	40.7	40.9	41.7
积极场景	48.1	47.4	47.6

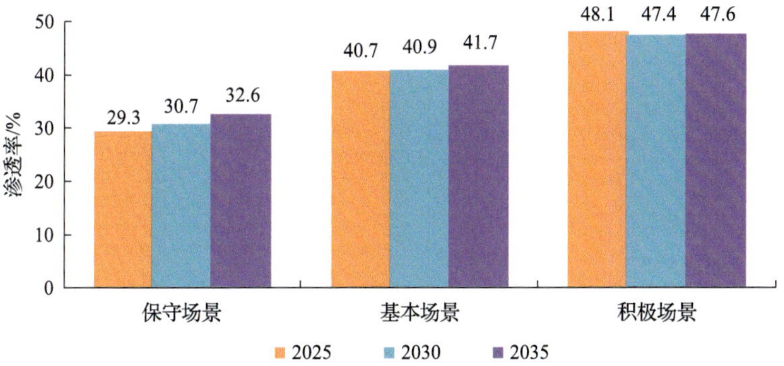

图 4-122　不同开发场景下未来我国铁路可再生能源渗透率测算结果

预计到 2025 年、2030 年、2035 年，光伏开发强度分别可以达到 10%、20%和 30%，则可以计算得到，未来 15 年我国可再生能源铁路系统的融合潜力如下所示。

(1) 到 2025 年，我国可再生能源铁路的用能自洽率为 15.6%，用电自洽率为 19.5%。可再生能源配合混合储能可提供部分有功出力，主要用能仍以电网供电为主。节能减排效果显著，能效逐步提高。

(2) 到 2030 年，我国可再生能源铁路的用能自洽率为 31.0%，用电自洽率为 34.5%。可再生能源配合混合储能可提供的有功出力进一步增多，剩余出力由电网补充。节能减排取得大幅度进展，能效进一步提高。

(3) 到 2035 年，我国可再生能源铁路的用能自洽率可达到 44.2%，用电自洽率达到 46.5%。可再生能源配合混合储能可提供几乎一半的有功出力，剩余出力由电网补充。铁路交通向实现智能化、绿色化、高效化和环境友好性大踏步前进！

4.3.3　我国铁路可再生能源融合系统解决方案

根据上面得到的未来 15 年我国可再生能源铁路融合潜力测算，可以计算得到我国不同开发区域在不同开发场景下，铁路系统到 2025 年、2030 年、2035 年的可再生能源渗透率，如表 4-98 所示。根据《铁路中长期发展规划》中提出的，到 2025 年、2030 年、2035 年，我国铁路可再生能源渗透率要分别达到 10%、20%、30%的具体要求，我国铁路可再生能源融合系统的推进方案，可以根据表 4-98，并在衡量开发的难易程度和经济特性的基础上，选择适宜的开发区域及适宜的开发模式进行协同开发。

表 4-98　不同开发场景下未来我国铁路可再生能源渗透率　（单位：%）

年份	开发场景	1 区	2 区	3 区	4 区	5 区	6 区	7 区	8 区	总计
2025	保守场景	0.1	0.89	2.05	5.79	0.7	2.41	1.77	15.62	29.33
	基本场景	0.2	1.04	2.08	8.76	1.5	2.80	1.92	22.61	40.91
	积极场景	0.3	1.08	2.08	9.64	2.2	2.97	1.95	28.14	48.36
2030	保守场景	0.1	0.90	2.20	5.49	0.7	2.48	1.87	16.99	30.73
	基本场景	0.2	1.02	2.23	8.48	1.5	2.81	2.00	22.90	41.14
	积极场景	0.2	1.05	2.23	9.36	2.2	2.96	2.03	27.57	47.6
2035	保守场景	0.2	0.92	2.39	5.34	1.7	2.61	2.01	18.61	33.78
	基本场景	0.4	1.02	2.42	8.22	2.4	2.89	2.12	23.68	43.15
	积极场景	0.6	1.05	2.42	9.14	4.1	3.02	2.14	27.69	50.16

1. 2021～2025 年：目标与解决方案

铁路中长期规划要求，2025 年我国铁路可再生能源渗透率要达到 10%。以此为目标，可选择在 3 区、4 区开发 20%，其中 3 区可再生能源渗透率贡献为 2.08%，4 区可再生能源渗透率贡献为 8.76%；全国整体可再生能源渗透率达到 10.84%，基本符合中长期规划要求。表 4-99 为不同开发场景下 2025 年我国铁路各模式区域可再生能源渗透率测算结果。

表 4-99　不同开发场景下 2025 年我国铁路各模式区域可再生能源渗透率测算结果

年份	应用场景	1 区	2 区	3 区	4 区	5 区	6 区	7 区	8 区	总计
2025	保守场景	0.1	0.89	2.05	5.79	0.7	2.41	1.77	15.62	29.33
	基本场景	0.2	1.04	2.08	8.76	1.5	2.80	1.92	22.61	40.91
	积极场景	0.3	1.08	2.08	9.64	2.2	2.97	1.95	28.14	48.36

2. 2026～2030 年：目标与解决方案

铁路中长期规划要求，2030 年我国铁路可再生能源渗透率要达到 30%。以此为目标，可选择在 2 区、3 区、4 区开发 30%，其中 2 区可再生能源渗透率贡献为 1.05%，3 区可再生能源渗透率贡献为 2.23%，4 区可再生能源渗透率贡献为 9.36%；8 区开发 20%，可再生能源渗透率贡献为 22.90%；全国整体可再生能源渗透率达到 35.54%，基本符合中长期规划要求。表 4-100 为不同开发场景下 2030 年我国铁路各模式区域可再生能源渗透率测算结果。

3. 2031～2035 年：目标与解决方案

铁路中长期规划要求，2035 年我国铁路可再生能源渗透率要达到 50%。以此为目标，需要所有区域开发 30%，各区域的可再生能源渗透率贡献如表 4-101 所示。全国整体可再生能源渗透率可达 50.16%，满足中长期发展规划的需求。

表 4-100　不同开发场景下 2030 年我国铁路各模式区域可再生能源渗透率测算结果

年份	开发场景	1 区	2 区	3 区	4 区	5 区	6 区	7 区	8 区	总计
2030	保守场景	0.1	0.90	2.20	5.49	0.7	2.48	1.87	16.99	30.73
	基本场景	0.2	1.02	2.23	8.48	1.5	2.81	2.00	22.90	41.14
	积极场景	0.2	1.05	2.23	9.36	2.2	2.96	2.03	27.57	47.6

表 4-101　不同开发场景下 2035 年我国铁路各模式区域可再生能源渗透率测算结果

年份	开发场景	1 区	2 区	3 区	4 区	5 区	6 区	7 区	8 区	总计
2035	保守场景	0.2	0.92	2.39	5.34	1.7	2.61	2.01	18.61	33.78
	基本场景	0.4	1.02	2.42	8.22	2.4	2.89	2.12	23.68	43.15
	积极场景	0.6	1.05	2.42	9.14	4.1	3.02	2.14	27.69	50.16

4. 2021～2035 年系统演进路线图

由于在相同的开发场景下，各模式区域内的地形越复杂，自然环境越恶劣，开发难度越大；区域内的线路长度越长，开发成本越高；区域内的光照越充足，光伏发电潜力越大，经济效益越好。综合考虑多项指标，可得到各模式区域建设难易指数及经济效益指数。表 4-102 为不同开发场景下 2035 年我国铁路各模式区域可再生能源渗透率测算结果。

表 4-102　不同开发场景下 2035 年我国铁路各模式区域可再生能源渗透率测算结果

编号	场景	建设难易指数	经济效益指数
1	无电+少负荷+多光	★	★★★★★
2	末端+少负荷+多光	★★★	★★★★
3	强电+少负荷+多光	★★★	★★★★
4	强电+多负荷+多光	★★★★★	★★★★
5	无电+少负荷+少光	★★	★★★★
6	末端+少负荷+少光	★★★★	★★★
7	强电+少负荷+少光	★★★	★
8	强电+多负荷+少光	★★★	★★★

根据前面所测算得到的各模式下在不同时间阶段内可以达到的自洽率和可再生能源渗透率，根据铁路中长期发展规划中对能源系统的阶段规划目标，可以得到 2021～2035 年铁路可再生能源系统的演进步骤(图 4-123)。

2021～2025 年：优先开发强电且多光区域(第 3、4 区域)，以可再生+储能+微网+余电上网和可再生+储能+微网/电网+自给自足模式为主，用电自洽率为 19.5%，用能自洽率为 15.6%。

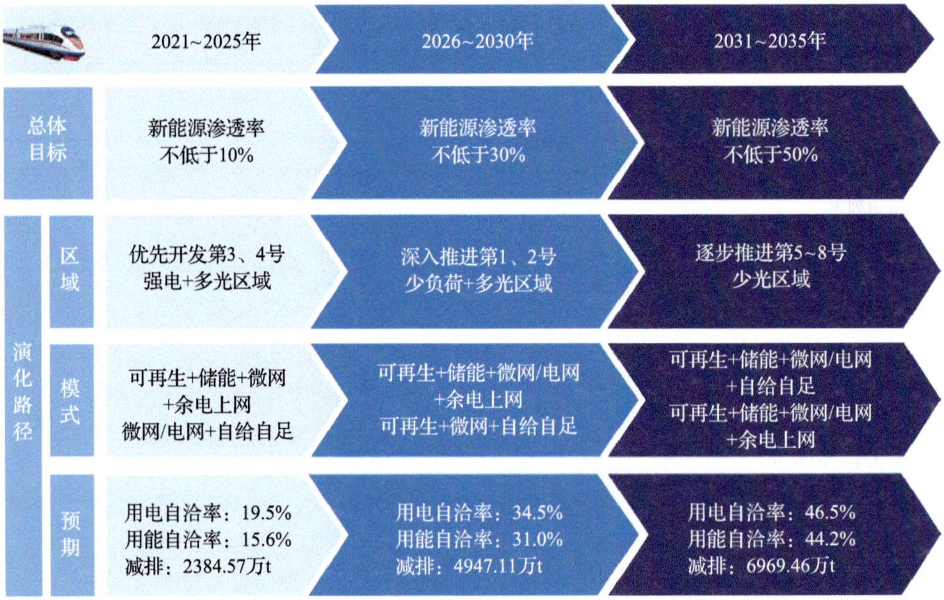

图 4-123　2021～2035 年我国铁路可再生能源融合系统演进路线图

2026～2030 年：持续开发强电且多光区域，逐步推进少负荷且多光区域(第 1、2 区域)，以内燃机+可再生+微网+自给自足和可再生+储能+微网为主+余电上网模式为主，用电自洽率为 34.5%，用能自洽率为 31.0%。

2031～2035 年：持续开发少负荷且多光区域，逐步推进其他区域的开发，逐步推进内燃机+可再生+微网+自给自足、可再生+储能+微网/电网+自给自足等模式，用电自洽率达到 46.5%，用能自洽率达到 44.2%。

下篇参考文献

[1] 国家统计局[DB/OL]. [2019-11-01]. https://data.stats.gov.cn.

[2] 维基百科. 中华人民共和国铁路隧道列表[EB/OL]. [2019-11-14]. https://zh.wikipedia.org/wiki/中华人民共和国铁路隧道列表.

[3] 《中国铁道年鉴》编辑部. 中国铁道年鉴 2017[M]. 北京: 中国铁路总公司. 2018.

[4] 王伟晗, 尹守迁, 王清成. 能源管理系统在大型铁路客运站的应用[J]. 应用技术学报, 2017, 17(1): 67-71, 84.

[5] 宋歌, 刘燕, 朱丹丹, 等. 铁路客站用能现状及其影响因素分析[J]. 暖通空调, 2013, 43(4): 85-90.

[6] 北京铁路局南仓站[J]. 港口经济, 2006(3): 68.

[7] 百度百科. 郑州北站[EB/OL]. [2019-11-14]. https://baike.baidu.com/item/郑州北站/4469846?fr=aladdin.

[8] 大贤・风格能源气象平台[DB/OL]. [2019-11-21]. windgrid.dxwind.com.

[9] 北京大学开放研究数据平台[DB/OL]. [2019-11-21]. https://opendata.pku.edu.cn.

[10] 维基百科. 中华人民共和国高速铁路[EB/OL]. [2019-11-01]. https://zh.wikipedia.org/wiki/中华人民共和国高速铁路.

[11] 中华人民共和国中央人民政府. 发展改革委印发《中长期铁路网规划》[EB/OL]. [2019-11-01]. http://www.gov.cn/xinwen/2016-07/20/content_5093165.htm.

[12] 中华人民共和国中央人民政府. 中共中央 国务院印发《交通强国建设纲要》[EB/OL]. [2019-11-09]. http://www.gov.cn/zhengce/2019-09/19/content_5431432.htm.

[13] 国家铁路局. 国家铁路局关于发布《2018 年铁道统计公报》的公告[EB/OL]. [2019-11-01]. http://www.nra.gov.cn/xwzx/zlzx/hytj/201904/t20190426_77440.shtml.

[14] 《中国电力年鉴》编辑委员会. 2018 中国电力年鉴[M]. 北京: 中国电力出版社. 2019.

[15] 李群湛, 贺建闽. 牵引供电系统分析[M]. 成都: 西南交通大学出版社, 2007.

[16] 中国南方电网. 关于南网[EB/OL]. [2019-11-19]. https://www.csg.cn/m/gynw.

[17] 国家能源局. 我国太阳能资源是如何分布的？[EB/OL]. [2019-11-19]. http://www.nea.gov.cn/2014-08/03/c_133617073.htm.

[18] 徐林云. DC600V 列车供电系统[J]. 铁道车辆, 2001, 39(3): 13-16.

[19] TB/T2275-1991, 铁路隧道照明设施与供电技术条件[S].

[20] International Energy Agency. The future of rail-opportunities for energy and the environment[J/OL]. [2019-12-03]. http://www.uirr.com/en/component/downloads/downloads/1402.html.

[21] 中国氢能联盟. 中国氢能源及燃料电池产业白皮书[M]. 2019.

[22] 搜狐. 国内首个氢能源有轨电车来了！加一次氢可跑 100 公里[EB/OL]. [2019-11-29]. https://www.sohu.com/a/208953482_729676.

[23] 中国铁路总公司, 铁路技术管理规程[M]. 北京: 中国铁道出版社, 2014.

[24] 铁路运输安全保护条例[S]. 国务院第 74 次常务会, 北京, 2004.

[25] 杨金焕. 太阳能光伏发电应用技术[M]. 3 版. 北京: 电子工业出版社, 2017.

[26] 国际能源网[DB/OL]. [2019-11-21]. https://www.in-en.com.

[27] 国家能源院. 2019 中国新能源发电分析报告[R]. 北京, 2019.